Criminal Justice and Law Enforcement Books

of

WEST PUBLISHING COMPANY

St. Paul, Minnesota 55102

November, 1976

CONSTITUTIONAL LAW

Maddex's Cases and Comments on Constitutional Law by James L. Maddex, Professor of Criminal Justice, Georgia State University, 816 pages, 1974.
Maddex's 1976 Supplement.

CORRECTIONS

Burns' Corrections—Organization and Administration by Henry Burns, Jr., Professor of Corrections, The Pennsylvania State University, 578 pages, 1975.

Kerper and Kerper's Legal Rights of the Convicted by Hazel B. Kerper, Late Professor of Sociology and Criminal Law, Sam Houston State University and Janeen Kerper, Attorney, San Diego, Calif., 677 pages, 1974.

Killinger and Cromwell's Selected Readings on Corrections in the Community by George G. Killinger, Director of the Institute of Contemporary Corrections, Sam Houston State University and Paul F. Cromwell, Jr., Member, Texas Board of Pardons and Paroles, 579 pages, 1974.

Killinger and Cromwell's Readings on Penology—The Evolution of Corrections in America by George G. Killinger and Paul F. Cromwell, Jr., 428 pages, 1973.

Killinger, Cromwell and Cromwell's Selected Readings on Issues in Corrections and Administration by George G. Killinger, Paul F. Cromwell, Jr. and Bonnie J. Cromwell, San Antonio College, 644 pages, 1976.

Killinger, Kerper and Cromwell's Probation and Parole in the Criminal Justice System by George G. Killinger, Hazel B. Kerper and Paul F. Cromwell, Jr., 374 pages, 1976.

Krantz' The Law of Corrections and Prisoners' Rights in a Nutshell by Sheldon Krantz, Professor of Law and Director, Center for Criminal Justice, Boston University, 353 pages, 1976.

Model Rules and Regulations on Prisoners' Rights and Responsibilities, 212 pages, 1973.

Rubin's Law of Criminal Correction, 2nd Edition (Student Edition) by Sol Rubin, Counsel Emeritus, Council on Crime and Delinquency, 873 pages, 1973.
Rubin's 1977 Supplement.

CRIMINAL JUSTICE BOOKS

CORRECTIONS—Continued

Smith & Berlin's Introduction to Probation and Parole by Alexander B. Smith, Professor of Sociology, John Jay College of Criminal Justice and Louis Berlin, Chief, Training Branch, New York City Dept. of Probation, 250 pages, 1975.

CRIMINAL JUSTICE SYSTEM

Kerper's Introduction to the Criminal Justice System by Hazel B. Kerper, 558 pages, 1972.

CRIMINAL LAW

Dix and Sharlot's Cases and Materials on Basic Criminal Law by George E. Dix, Professor of Law, University of Texas and M. Michael Sharlot, Professor of Law, University of Texas, 649 pages, 1974.

Ferguson's Readings on Concepts of Criminal Law by Robert W. Ferguson, Administration of Justice Dept. Director, Saddleback College, 560 pages, 1975.

Gardner and Manian's Principles, Cases and Readings on Criminal Law by Thomas J. Gardner, Professor of Criminal Justice, Milwaukee Area Technical College and Victor Manian, Milwaukee County Judge, 782 pages, 1975.

Heymann and Kenety—The Murder Trial of Wilbur Jackson: A Homicide in the Family by Philip Heymann, Professor of Law, Harvard University and William Kenety, Instructor, Catholic University Law School, 340 pages, 1975.

Loewy's Criminal Law in a Nutshell by Arnold H. Loewy, Professor of Law. University of North Carolina, 302 pages, 1975.

CRIMINAL PROCEDURE

Davis' Police Discretion by Kenneth Culp Davis, Professor of Law, University of Chicago, 176 pages, 1975.

Dowling's Teaching Materials on Criminal Procedure by Jerry L. Dowling, Professor of Criminal Justice, Sam Houston State University, 544 pages, 1976.

Ferdico's Criminal Procedure for the Law Enforcement Officer by John N. Ferdico, Assistant Attorney General, State of Maine, 372 pages, 1975.

Israel and LaFave's Criminal Procedure in a Nutshell, 2nd Edition by Jerold H. Israel and Wayne R. LaFave, 372 pages, 1975.

Johnson's Cases, Materials and Text on The Elements of Criminal Due Process by Phillip E. Johnson, Professor of Law, University of California, Berkeley, 324 pages, 1975.

Kamisar, LaFave and Israel's Cases, Comments and Questions on Basic Criminal Procedure, 4th Edition by Yale Kamisar, Professor of Law, University of Michigan, Wayne R. LaFave, Professor of Law, University of Illinois and Jerold H. Israel, Professor of Law, University of Michigan, 790 pages, 1974. Supplement Annually.

Uviller's the Processes of Criminal Justice—Adjudication by H. Richard Uviller, Professor of Law, Columbia University, 991 pages, 1975.

Uviller's the Processes of Criminal Justice-Investigation by H. Richard Uviller, 744 pages, 1974.

CRIMINAL JUSTICE BOOKS

EVIDENCE

Klein's Law of Evidence for Police by Irving J. Klein, Professor of Law and Police Science, John Jay College of Criminal Justice, 416 pages, 1973.

Rothstein's Evidence in a Nutshell by Paul F. Rothstein, Professor of Law, Georgetown Law Center, 406 pages, 1970.

INTRODUCTION TO LAW ENFORCEMENT

More's The American Police—Text and Readings by Harry W. More, Jr., Professor of Administration of Justice, California State University at San Jose, 278 pages, 1976.

Police Tactics in Hazardous Situations by the San Diego, California Police Department, 228 pages, 1976.

Schwartz and Goldstein's Law Enforcement Handbook for Police by Louis B. Schwartz, Professor of Law, University of Pennsylvania and Stephen R. Goldstein, Professor of Law, University of Pennsylvania, 333 pages, 1970.

Sutor's Police Operations—Tactical Approaches to Crimes in Progress by Captain Andrew Sutor, Philadelphia, Pennsylvania Police Department, 329 pages, 1976.

INVESTIGATION

Markle's Criminal Investigation and Presentation of Evidence by Arnold Markle, The State's Attorney, New Haven County, Connecticut, 344 pages, 1976.

JUVENILE JUSTICE

Faust and Brantingham's Juvenile Justice Philosophy: Readings, Cases and Comments by Frederic L. Faust, Professor of Criminology, Florida State University and Paul J. Brantingham, Professor of Criminology, Florida State University, 600 pages, 1974.

Fox's Law of Juvenile Courts in a Nutshell by Sanford J. Fox, Professor of Law, Boston College, 286 pages, 1971.

Johnson's Introduction to the Juvenile Justice System by Thomas A. Johnson, Professor of Criminal Justice, University of Kentucky, 492 pages, 1975.

Senna and Siegel's Cases and Comments on Juvenile Law by Joseph J. Senna, Professor of Criminal Justice, Northeastern University and Larry J. Siegel, Professor of Criminal Justice, Northeastern University, about 600 pages, 1976.

MANAGEMENT AND SUPERVISION

More's Criminal Justice Management: Text and Readings, by Harry W. More, Jr., about 350 pages, 1977.

Wadman, Paxman and Bentley's Law Enforcement Supervision—A Case Study Approach by Robert C. Wadman, Rio Hondo Community College, Monroe J. Paxman, Brigham Young University and Marion T. Bentley, Utah State University, 224 pages, 1975.

POLICE-COMMUNITY RELATIONS

Cromwell and Keefer's Readings on Police-Community Relations by Paul F. Cromwell, Jr., and George Keefer, Former F.B.I. Agent, 368 pages, 1973.

CRIMINAL JUSTICE BOOKS

PSYCHOLOGY

Parker and Meier's Interpersonal Psychology for Law Enforcement and Corrections by L. Craig Parker, Jr., Criminal Justice Dept. Director, University of New Haven and Robert D. Meier, Professor of Criminal Justice, University of New Haven, 290 pages, 1975.

VICE CONTROL

Ferguson's the Nature of Vice Control in the Administration of Justice by Robert W. Ferguson, 509 pages, 1974.

Uelman and Haddox' Cases, Text and Materials on Drug Abuse Law by Gerald F. Uelman, Professor of Law, Loyola University, Los Angeles and Victor G. Haddox, Professor of Criminology, California State University at Long Beach and Clinical Professor of Psychiatry, Law and Behavioral Sciences, University of Southern California School of Medicine, 564 pages, 1974.

BASIC
CRIMINAL LAW
CASES AND MATERIALS

By

GEORGE E. DIX
Professor of Law, University of Texas

M. MICHAEL SHARLOT
Professor of Law, University of Texas

CRIMINAL JUSTICE SERIES

ST. PAUL, MINN.
WEST PUBLISHING CO.
1974

Dix & Sharlot Cs. Crim.Law CrJS
3rd Reprint—1977

PREFACE

The past quarter century has witnessed what has come to be known as the "criminal law revolution." Sweeping judicial pronouncements limiting the authority of the state in the criminalization of conduct and the enforcement of the criminal law have filtered, not always accurately, into the consciousness of most Americans. Simultaneously, although no causal relationship is suggested, our country has seen an apparent upsurge in the incidence of criminal conduct and an expansion in the use of the criminal sanction in efforts to control more and more facets of our increasingly complex society. These phenomena have generated great interest in the processes of the administration of criminal justice, while the area of the substantive criminal law is, in large measure, ignored. Yet the substantive criminal law deserves close attention in every curriculum. First, the increased intrusion of the criminal law into our lives justifies a familiarity with its principles as well as its processes. Second, it is a unique vehicle for examination of the great questions of the relationship of the individual to the state. The goals of the criminal law and the unending debate over how they may best be achieved and at what cost to the values of our society should be part of the intellectual life of every thinking citizen. Thus something more than a vehicle by which the student may be familiarized with the law of crimes is essential to any meaningful criminal law course.

These were the goals of our larger volume, Criminal Law, Cases and Materials, which served as the basis for this book which is basically an abridgment of the former, although some additional items have been inserted. Substantial omissions have been made from the material appearing in the original work, primarily to reduce the depth with which some of the issues are covered. In addition, other portions of the material have been reorganized to provide specific treatment of individual offenses rather than relying heavily upon references to them during an extended treatment of general principles of liability. We hope this modification of format and length will make the material more attractive to teachers who desire to treat various offenses individually and who do not need the more extensive and intensive coverage provided by the original volume.

We also hope, however, we have retained much of the flavor of the original material. This book, as was the original, is designed to facilitate inquiry into the broadest issues involved in the decision to employ the state's ultimate sanction to coerce conduct, as well as into the traditional problems presented by the definition and application of substantive crimes. We have, insofar as possible, attempted to use recent cases, both to demonstrate that the matters are of current significance and to present them in the context of modern criminal justice administration. Extensive selections from statutes have been retained in recognition of the need to refer constantly to legislation as well as judicial decisions in resolving the issues presented by contemporary criminal law.

Part I, the introductory portion, deals with the general framework of the criminal law. It contains coverage of the procedure for processing a criminal case, the basic presumption of innocence, and penalty structures. Part II presents the criminalization issue in the context of the problems posed by alcohol-related activity, especially public drunkenness. Emphasis is placed upon the complexity of both the basic legislative decision as to which, if any, alcohol-related activity is to be criminalized and of the judicial review of this decision in the form of constitutional attacks upon the validity of various legislation. The functioning and effectiveness of a system that makes such conduct criminal is presented with materials that from other disciplines, as well as law, to provide the basis for discussing the nature of criminal liability, the impact of "punishment", and alternative methods of dealing with antisocial behavior.

Sections III through VIII present the substantive criminal law. Section III presents general principles of liability, emphasizing the "act" requirement, the state of mind requirement, and, where applicable, the requirement of a result and attendant problems of causation. Several matters—mistake, ignorance, and intoxication—which conceptually consist of "disproof" of state of mind are presented here. Some teachers may prefer to cover these later during treatment of the "defenses" presented in Section VIII. Since problems of causation arise almost exclusively in connection with homicide offenses, some teachers may prefer to deal with this material following treatment of the homicide offenses. Complicity and vicarious liability are also covered in Section III.

Section IV covers the inchoate crimes of attempt, solicitation, and conspiracy, as well as "defenses" which are unique to these forms of liability. Much of the detailed coverage of various aspects of conspiracy doctrine has been eliminated for this abridgment. Sections V through VII deal with specific offenses. Although we have, often in textual notes, attempted to make clear the traditional "black letter" rules, we have selected cases that illustrate contemporary application of these rules rather than their historical development.

Part VIII deals with "defenses" in the strict sense, i. e., matters that consist not of a challenge to the adequacy of proof of elements of the offense charged but rather of offered justification or excuse. The extensive material dealing with psychological abnormality that appeared in the original volume has been greatly abridged and is presented as a subsection of this section. The Durham-Brawner line of cases from the District of Columbia is retained, however, as an important, albeit ill-fated, effort to deal with this complex problem.

We hope that by abridging the material in this manner we have provided a vehicle that will be attractive to those who wish to offer a treatment of the law of crimes without sacrificing coverage of the broad general issues of substantive criminal law and of criminalization as a societal response to deviance. We express our appreciation to the numerous authors and publishers who have given us permission to reproduce their materials in this volume. A special note of gratitude must go to the American Law Institute which kindly granted permission to reprint extensive portions of the copyrighted Model Penal Code (and the various tentative drafts). In editing the material, we have left out citations and footnotes without any specific indication of such omissions. Footnotes retained from the original material are indicated by numbers. We have chosen not to renumber the footnotes that have been retained. Footnotes indicated by letters are those we have inserted.

Students who wish guidance as to outside reading that may enrich or clarify sections of the book may be well advised to take advantage of the recent hornbook, Handbook on Criminal Law, published in 1972 by Professor Wayne R. LaFave and the late Professor Austin W. Scott, Jr. Also of significant aid are the two volumes of Working Papers of the National Commission on Reform of the Federal Criminal Laws, published in 1970. Somewhat older but more elaborate and by no means outdated is the commentary to the tentative drafts of the American Law Institute's Model Penal Code. Many excerpts from these volumes have been included but, of course, these are but the barest sampling of the thoughtful discussions contained therein. The best single source of information about the actual operation of the criminal justice system and recommendations for its improvement is The Challenge of Crime in a Free Society, A Report by the President's Commission on Law Enforcement and Administration of Justice, published in 1967, and the many Task Force Reports produced by the Commission. Finally, no finer overview of the problems of the criminal law can be recommended than the late Professor Herbert Packer's short volume, The Limits of the Criminal Sanction, published in 1968.

G.E.D.
M.M.S.

Austin, Texas
April, 1974

SUMMARY OF CONTENTS

		Page
PREFACE		IX

I. Introduction _____ 1
   A. Ascertainment of Guilt: The Institutional Framework   1
   B. Ascertainment of Guilt: The Prosecution's Burden
       of Proof Beyond a Reasonable Doubt _____ 10
   C. Penalty Provisions and Grading of Criminal Offenses   13
      1. The task of Assigning Penalties _____ 13
      2. A Proposed Classification Scheme _____ 26

II. The Criminalization Decision _____ 28
   A. Criminalization of Intoxication _____ 29
      1. The Social Problem of Alcohol Abuse _____ 29
      2. The Present Approach: Public Intoxication as a
         Criminal Offense _____ 35
      3. Noncriminal Compelled "Treatment": A Poten-
         tial Alternative to Criminalization _____ 54
   B. Factors Relevant to the Resolution of the Criminaliza-
        tion Issue _____ 68
      1. The Nature of Criminal Liability _____ 68
      2. Justification and Functions of Criminalization _____ 71
        a. Criminalization and Punishment as Retribu-
           tion _____ 72
        b. Criminalization and Punishment as a Reflec-
           tion of Morality _____ 73
        c. Criminalization and Punishment as Satisfying
           A Psychological Urge to Punish _____ 79
        d. Criminalization and Punishment as a Sym-
           bolic Designation of Public Mores _____ 82
        e. Criminalization and Conviction as Preventive
           Measures _____ 84
           (1) Punishment as a Means of Deterring,
               Moralizing and the Like _____ 84
           (2) Criminal Conviction as a Means of Pro-
               viding "Treatment" _____ 90
   C. The Need to be Precise or the Vice of Vagueness _____ 99

III. Principles of Criminal Liability _____ 107
   A. The "Act" _____ 109
      1. General Requirement of an Act _____ 109
      2. Liability Based on Failure to Act _____ 123

SUMMARY OF CONTENTS

Page

III. **Principles of Criminal Liability—Continued**
  B. The State of Mind _____ 128
    1. Types of States of Mind _____ 130
    2. The Standard State of Mind Requirement for Criminal Liability: "General Intent" _____ 133
    3. States of Mind Beyond "General Intent" _____ 141
    4. States of Mind Less Than "General Intent": The "Strict Liability" Offenses _____ 149
    5. "Defenses" Consisting of "Disproof" of State of Mind _____ 162
      a. Ignorance or Mistake of Fact _____ 162
      b. Ignorance or Mistake of Law _____ 167
      c. Intoxication _____ 178
  C. Results and the Requirement of Causation _____ 188
  D. Complicity _____ 207
    1. Liability as an Aider and Abettor or Incitor ____ 208
      a. The Extent of Participation Necessary _____ 210
      b. The State of Mind Necessary _____ 216
      c. Renunciation or Withdrawal _____ 221
    2. Liability for Conduct After the Commission of an Offense _____ 224
  E. Other Aspects of Liability for the Acts of Another __ 230
    1. Vicarious Liability _____ 230
    2. Criminal Liability of Organizations and Their Agents _____ 238

IV. **The Inchoate Crimes** _____ 244
  A. Attempts _____ 245
    1. The Act: Beyond Mere Preparation _____ 247
    2. The State of Mind Required _____ 258
    3. The "Defense" of Impossibility _____ 262
    4. The "Defense" of Abandonment _____ 271
  B. Solicitation _____ 277
  C. Conspiracy _____ 283
    1. Model Statutory Formulations _____ 283
    2. Elements of the Offense _____ 286
      a. Agreement _____ 286
        (1) General Requirement of Agreemcnt ____ 286
        (2) Objective of the Agreement _____ 288
        (3) Defenses Based on the Requirement of an Agreement _____ 293
      b. Overt Act Requirement _____ 300
      c. The State of Mind Required _____ 302
    3. Liability of One Coconspirator for Crimes of Other Conspirators _____ 313
    4. Impossibility _____ 317

SUMMARY OF CONTENTS

IV. The Inchoate Crimes—Continued

    C. Conspiracy—Continued **Page**

        5. The Defense of Abandonment _____ 320

        6. Prosecutorial Advantages in the Use of Conspiracy _____ 323

V. Specific Offenses: Crimes Against Property _____ 331

    A. Larceny _____ 331

    B. Embezzlement _____ 341

    C. False Pretenses _____ 347

    D. Theft _____ 353

    E. Robbery _____ 358

    F. Extortion _____ 365

VI. Specific Offenses: Crimes Against the Habitation _____ 372

    A. Burglary _____ 372

    B. Arson _____ 375

VII. Specific Offenses: Crimes Against the Person _____ 377

    A. Assault and Battery _____ 377

    B. Kidnapping and False Imprisonment _____ 385

    C. Rape _____ 398

    D. Homicide _____ 411

        1. Statutory Formulations _____ 415

        2. The State of Mind Required for Murder: Malice Aforethought _____ 420

            a. Gross Recklessness _____ 426

            b. Intent to do Physical Harm _____ 431

        3. First Degree Murder: Premeditated Killing ____ 433

        4. Felony Murder _____ 447

            a. The Basic Doctrine _____ 447

            b. Limitation of the Doctrine to "Dangerous" Felonies _____ 455

            c. Deaths Caused Directly by Persons Other Than the Felons _____ 463

        5. Voluntary Manslaughter _____ 467

        6. Involuntary Manslaughter _____ 472

            a. Negligent Omission _____ 472

            b. The "Unlawful Act" Doctrine _____ 477

            c. Killings Reduced to Manslaughter by "Imperfect" Defenses _____ 482

VIII. Defenses Not Directly Related to the Basic Requirements for Liability _____ 486

    A. The General Principle of Justification and Duress ___ 486

    B. Entrapment _____ 497

XV

SUMMARY OF CONTENTS

VIII. Defenses Not Directly Related to the Basic Requirements for Liability—Continued

                                                       Page

C. Defense of Persons or Property _____ 514

    1. Defense of Self _____ 518

    2. Defense of Others _____ 527

    3. Defense of Property _____ 533

D. Resistance to Unlawful Arrest _____ 539

E. Prevention of Crime _____ 549

F. Insanity and Related Matters _____ 562

    1. Introduction _____ 564

        a. The Theoretical Legal Framework _____ 564

        b. Incidence of the Issue _____ 567

        c. The Requirement of Mental Illness _____ 570

    2. Formulations of the Insanity Defense _____ 573

        a. The M'Naghten Rules _____ 573

        b. The Irresistable Impulse Test _____ 585

        c. The American Law Institute's "Control" Test 590

        d. The Durham Rule _____ 603

    3. Abandonment of the Insanity Defense _____ 620

    4. Some Practical Aspects of the Insanity Defense 625

    5. The "Partial Defense" of "Diminished Capacity" 630

Table of Cases _____ 639

Index _____ 643

TABLE OF CONTENTS

		Page
PREFACE		IX

I. INTRODUCTION — 1

A. ASCERTAINMENT OF GUILT: THE INSTITUTIONAL FRAMEWORK — 1

President's Commission on Law Enforcement and Administration of Justice, The Challenge of Crime in a Free Society — 1

B. ASCERTAINMENT OF GUILT: THE PROSECUTION'S BURDEN OF PROOF BEYOND A REASONABLE DOUBT — 10

Model Penal Code, § 1.12 (P.O.D.) — 11

Model Penal Code, Comments to § 1.13 (Tent. Draft No. 4) — 12

C. PENALTY PROVISIONS AND GRADING OF CRIMINAL OFFENSES — 13

1. The Task of Assigning Penalties — 13

Wechsler and Michael, A Rationale for the Law of Homicide — 14

American Bar Association Project on Minimum Standards for Criminal Justice, Standards Relating to Sentencing Alternatives and Procedures (Commentary) — 15

The Death Penalty and the Eighth Amendment — 24

2. A Proposed Classification Scheme — 26

Proposed Federal Criminal Code — 26

II. THE CRIMINALIZATION DECISION — 28

A. CRIMINALIZATION OF INTOXICATION — 29

1. The Social Problem of Alcohol Abuse — 29

Blum and Braunstein, Mind-Altering Drugs and Dangerous Behavior, in the President's Commission on Law Enforcement and Administration of Justice, Task Force Report: Drunkenness — 29

2. The Present Approach: Public Intoxication as a Criminal Offense — 35

The Presiednt's Commission on Law Enforcement and and Administration of Justice, Task Force Report: Drunkenness — 35

Powell v. Texas — 38

TABLE OF CONTENTS

II. THE CRIMINALIZATION DECISION—Continued

A. CRIMINALIZATION OF INTOXICATION—Continued   **Page**

  3. Noncriminal Compelled "Treatment": A Potential Alternative to Criminalization 54

    Texas Civil Statutes 54

    Szasz, Alcoholism: A Socio-Ethical Perspective 57

    Kittrie, The Divestment of Criminal Law and the Coming of the Therapeutic State 61

    Ditman, Crawford, Forgy, Moskowitz and MacAndrew, A Controlled Experiment on the Use of Court Probation for Drunk Arrests 65

B. FACTORS RELEVANT TO THE RESOLUTION OF THE CRIMINALIZATION ISSUE 68

  1. The Nature of Criminal Liability 68

    Hart, The Aims of the Criminal Law 68

  2. Justification and Functions of Criminalization 71

    Hart, Murder and the Principles of Punishment: England and the United States 71

    a. Criminalization and Punishment as Retribution 72

      Brett, An Inquiry Into Criminal Guilt 72

    b. Criminalization and Punishment as a Reflection of Morality 73

      Devlin, The Enforcement of Morals 73

      Mill, Utilitarianism: Liberty and Representative Government 73

      Devlin, The Enforcement of Morals 73

      Hart, Social Solidarity and the Enforcement of Morality 75

    c. Criminalization and Punishment as Satisfying A Psychological Urge to Punish 79

      Alexander and Staub, The Criminal, the Judge, and the Public 79

    d. Criminalization and Punishment as a Symbolic Designation of Public Mores 82

      Gussfield, On Legislating Morals: The Symbolic Process of Designating Deviance 82

    e. Criminalization and Conviction as Preventive Measures 84

      (1) Punishment as a Means of Deterring, Moralizing and the Like 84

        Andenaes, The General Preventive Effects of Punishment 84

        Lovald and Stub, The Revolving Door: Reactions of Chronic Drunkenness Offenders to Court Sanctions 88

TABLE OF CONTENTS

II. THE CRIMINALIZATION DECISION—Continued

B. FACTORS RELEVANT TO THE RESOLUTION OF THE CRIMINALIZATION ISSUE—Continued

    2. Justification and Functions of Criminalization—Cont'd

        e. Criminalization and Conviction as Preventive Measures—Continued   **Page**

            (2) Criminal Conviction as a Means of Providing "Treatment" _____ 90

                Menninger, The Crime of Punishment _____ 90

                Ross, Hayes, Friel and Kerper, A Descriptive Study of the Skid Row Alcoholic in Houston, Texas _____ 94

C. THE NEED TO BE PRECISE OR THE VICE OF VAGUENESS _____ 99

    Papachristou v. Jacksonville _____ 99

III. PRINCIPLES OF CRIMINAL LIABILITY _____ 107

    Introductory Note _____ 107

A. THE "ACT" _____ 109

    1. General Requirement of an Act _____ 109

        Proposed Federal Criminal Code _____ 110

        State v. Mercer _____ 110

        Powell v. Texas _____ 114

        Crawford v. United States _____ 117

        State v. Bugger _____ 119

    2. Liability Based on Failure to Act _____ 123

        Jones v. United States _____ 123

B. THE STATE OF MIND _____ 128

    Cowan, Towards an Experimental Definition of Criminal Mind, In Philosophical Essays in Honor of Edgar Arthur Singer, Jr. _____ 128

    1. Types of States of Mind _____ 130

        Proposed Federal Criminal Code _____ 130

        Weinreb, Comment on Basis of Criminal Liability; Culpability; Causation, In Working Papers of the National Commission on Reform of Federal Criminal Laws ____ 131

    2. The Standard State of Mind Requirement for Criminal Liability: "General Intent" _____ 133

        Regina v. Pembliton _____ 133

        United States v. Byrd _____ 134

        Proposed Federal Criminal Code _____ 136

        Weinreb, Comment on Basis of Criminal Liability; Culpability; Causation, In Working Papers of The National Commission on Reform of Federal Criminal Laws ____ 137

    3. States of Mind Beyond "General Intent" _____ 141

        Note: The Distinction Between "Specific" and "General" Intent _____ 141

TABLE OF CONTENTS

III. PRINCIPLES OF CRIMINAL LIABILITY—Continued

B. THE STATE OF MIND—Continued

3. States of Mind Beyond "General Intent"—Continued   **Page**

Lambert v. California _____ 142

United States v. International Minerals & Chemical Corp. 145

4. States of Mind Less Than "General Intent": The "Strict

Liability" Offenses _____ 149

Morissette v. United States _____ 149

5. "Defenses" Consisting of "Disproof" of State of Mind __ 162

  a. Ignorance or Mistake of Fact _____ 162

    People v. Hernandez _____ 162

    United States v. Short _____ 162

    Proposed Federal Criminal Code § 304 _____ 167

  b. Ignorance or Mistake of Law _____ 167

    Proposed Federal Criminal Code §§ 304, 609 _____ 167

    Lambert v. California _____ 169

    Hunter v. State _____ 169

    Model Penal Code, Comment to § 2.02 (Tent. Draft

      No. 4) _____ 170

    Richardson v. United States _____ 171

    Long v. State _____ 173

  c. Intoxication _____ 178

    United States v. Williams _____ 178

    Proposed Federal Criminal Code § 502 and Comment 186

C. RESULTS AND THE REQUREMENT OF CAUSATION _____ 188

Weinreb, Comment on Basis of Criminal Liability; Culpabili-

ty; Causation, In 1 Working Papers of The National Com-

mission on Reform of Federal Criminal Laws _____ 188

People v. Hebert _____ 189

Model Penal Code, § 2.03 and Commentary (Tent. Draft No.

4) _____ 194

Weinreb, Comment on Basis of Criminal Liability; Culpabili-

ty; Causation, In 1 Working Papers of The National Com-

mission on Reform of Federal Criminal Laws _____ 199

Proposed Federal Criminal Code § 305 _____ 201

Commonwealth v. Feinberg _____ 202

D. COMPLICITY _____ 207

1. Liability as an Aider and Abettor or Incitor _____ 208

United States Code, Title 18, § 2 _____ 208

California Penal Code §§ 30, 31 _____ 209

Proposed Federal Criminal Code §§ 401, 1002 _____ 209

  a. The Extent of Participation Necessary _____ 210

    State v. Cobb _____ 210

    State v. Spillman _____ 214

  b. The State of Mind Necessary _____ 216

    Wyatt v. United States _____ 216

    State v. Gladstone _____ 217

TABLE OF CONTENTS

III. PRINCIPLES OF CRIMINAL LIABILITY—Continued

D. COMPLICITY—Continued

    1. Liability as an Aider and Abettor or Incitor—Continued

Page

        c. Renunciation or Withdrawal _____ 221

        Commonwealth v. Huber _____ 221

    2. Liability for Conduct After the Commission of an Offense _____ 224

        United States Code, Title 18, §§ 3, 4 _____ 224

        United States v. Foy _____ 225

E. OTHER ASPECTS OF LIABILITY FOR THE ACTS OF ANOTHER __ 230

    1. Vicarious Liability _____ 230

        Commonwealth v. Koczwara _____ 230

        Commonwealth v. Ali _____ 235

    2. Criminal Liability of Organizations and Their Agents __ 238

        McCollum v. State _____ 239

IV. THE INCHOATE CRIMES _____ 244

    Model Penal Code Comment to Article 5 (Tent. Draft No. 10) 244

A. ATTEMPTS _____ 245

    1. The Act: Beyond Mere Preparation _____ 247

        Model Penal Code, §§ 5.01, 5.05 (P.O.D.) _____ 247

        Model Penal Code, Comment to § 5.01(1) (Tent. Draft No. 10) _____ 249

        Dupuy v. State _____ 255

    2. The State of Mind Required _____ 258

        Model Penal Code, Comment to § 5.01 (Tent. Draft No. 10) _____ 258

        Thacker v. Commonwealth _____ 260

    3. The "Defense" of Impossibility _____ 262

        Booth v. State _____ 262

        Model Penal Code, Comment to § 5.01 (Tent. Draft No. 10) _____ 271

    4. The "Defense" of Abandonment _____ 271

        People v. Staples _____ 271

        Proposed Federal Criminal Code § 1005 _____ 276

B. SOLICITATION _____ 277

    Gervin v. State _____ 277

    Model Penal Code § 5.02 (P.O.D.) _____ 280

    Proposed Federal Criminal Code (Study Draft), § 1003 _____ 281

C. CONSPIRACY _____ 283

    1. Model Statutory Formulations _____ 283

        Model Penal Code §§ 5.03, 5.04 (P.O.D.) _____ 283

        Proposed Federal Criminal Code § 1004 _____ 285

TABLE OF CONTENTS

IV. THE INCHOATE CRIMES—Continued   **Page**

C. CONSPIRACY—Continued

    2. Elements of the Offense ------------------------------------ 286

        a. Agreement --- 286

           (1) General Requirement of Agreement ---------- 286

               Bender v. State --------------------------------- 286

           (2) Objective of the Agreement ------------------ 288

               State v. Bowling -------------------------------- 288

           (3) Defenses Based on the Requirement of an Agreement ------------------------------------- 293

               Regle v. State ----------------------------------- 293

               Model Penal Code, Comment to § 503(1) (Tent. Draft No. 10) ------------------------------ 299

        b. Overt Act Requirement ------------------------------ 300

           People ex rel. Conte v. Flood ------------------------ 300

        c. The State of Mind Required ------------------------- 302

           Cleaver v. United States ---------------------------- 302

           People v. Lauria ----------------------------------- 303

           Model Penal Code, Comment to § 5.03 (Tent. Draft No. 10) -- 311

    3. Liability of One Coconspirator for Crimes of Other Conspirators -- 313

        Pinkerton v. United States ------------------------------ 313

    4. Impossibility --- 317

        State v. Moretti --- 317

    5. The Defense of Abandonment --------------------------- 320

        People v. Brown -- 320

    6. Prosecutorial Advantages in the Use of Conspiracy ----- 323

        Krulewitch v. United States ----------------------------- 323

        Blakey, Aspects of the Evidence Gathering Process in Organized Crime Cases: A Preliminary Analysis, In Task Force Report: Organized Crime ----------------- 327

        Study Draft of a Proposed Federal Criminal Code, § 1005 329

V. SPECIFIC OFFENSES: CRIMES AGAINST PROPERTY -- 331

A. LARCENY -- 331

    Rogers v. State --- 331

    Ray v. United States ------------------------------------- 333

    Virgin Islands v. Williams ------------------------------- 335

    R. v. Cockburn --- 339

B. EMBEZZLEMENT -- 341

    State v. Williams --- 341

    United States v. Powell ---------------------------------- 346

C. FALSE PRETENSES --- 347

    Pollard v. State -- 348

    State v. Mills --- 351

TABLE OF CONTENTS

V. SPECIFIC OFFENSES: CRIMES AGAINST PROPERTY
—Continued

                                                         Page

D. THEFT _____ 353

E. ROBBERY _____ 358
    People v. Heller _____ 358
    Parnell v. State _____ 361

F. EXTORTION _____ 365
    State v. Harrington _____ 366

VI. SPECIFIC OFFENSES: CRIMES AGAINST THE HABITATION _____ 372

A. BURGLARY _____ 372
    Houchin v. State _____ 372

B. ARSON _____ 375
    State v. Nielson _____ 375

VII. SPECIFIC OFFENSES: CRIMES AGAINST THE PERSON _____ 377

A. ASSAULT AND BATTERY _____ 377
    People v. Abrams _____ 377
    Ott v. State _____ 382

B. KIDNAPPING AND FALSE IMPRISONMENT _____ 385
    People v. Adams _____ 385

C. RAPE _____ 398
    State v. Horne _____ 398
    People v. Hernandez _____ 404

D. HOMICIDE _____ 411
    Wolfgang, A Sociological Analysis of Criminal Homicide ____ 411
    1. Statutory Formulations _____ 415
        Penn.Stat.Ann., Title 18, §§ 4701, 4703 _____ 415
        California Penal Code §§ 187–190, 192–193 _____ 416
        Proposed Federal Criminal Code §§ 1601–1603 _____ 418
    2. The State of Mind Required for Murder: Malice Aforethought _____ 420
        People v. Morrin _____ 420
        a. Gross Recklessness _____ 426
            Commonwealth v. Malone _____ 426
            State v. Chalmers _____ 428
        b. Intent to do Physical Harm _____ 431
            People v. Geiger _____ 431
    3. First Degree Murder: The Premeditated Killing _____ 433
        State v. Snowden _____ 433
        People v. Anderson _____ 440
    4. Felony Murder _____ 447
        a. The Basic Doctrine _____ 447
            People v. Phillips _____ 447

TABLE OF CONTENTS

**VII. SPECIFIC OFFENSES: CRIMES AGAINST THE PER-
SON**—Continued

D. HOMICIDE—Continued

    4. Felony Murder—Continued   **Page**

            People v. Stamp _____ 448

            Rex v. Lumley _____ 451

            In re Allen _____ 453

      b. Limitation of the Doctrine to "Dangerous" Felonies 455

            People v. Satchell _____ 455

      c. Deaths Caused Directly by Persons Other Than the
            Felons _____ 463

            Commonwealth ex rel. Smith v. Myers _____ 463

    5. Voluntary Manslaughter _____ 467

            Lang v. State _____ 467

    6. Involuntary Manslaughter _____ 472

      a. Negligent Omission _____ 472

            Commonwealth v. Welansky _____ 472

      b. The "Unlawful Act" Doctrine _____ 477

            State v. Gibson _____ 477

      c. Killings Reduced to Manslaughter by "Imperfect"
            Defenses _____ 482

            Sanchez v. People _____ 482

**VIII. DEFENSES NOT DIRECTLY RELATED TO THE
BASIC REQUIREMENTS FOR LIABILITY** _____ 486

A. THE GENERAL PRINCIPLE OF JUSTIFICATION AND DURESS __ 486

    Proposed Federal Criminal Code (Study Draft), § 608 _____ 486

    People v. Richards _____ 487

    Proposed Federal Criminal Code, § 610 and Comment _____ 496

B. ENTRAPMENT _____ 497

    Sherman v. United States _____ 497

    United States v. Russell _____ 505

C. DEFENSE OF PERSONS OR PROPERTY _____ 514

    Proposed Federal Criminal Code §§ 601, 603–604, 606–608,
      619 _____ 514

    1. Defense of Self _____ 518

        State v. Abbott _____ 518

        Gray v. State _____ 523

    2. Defense of Others _____ 527

        People v. Young _____ 527

        People v. Young _____ 531

    3. Defense of Property _____ 533

        Russell v. State _____ 533

        State v. Dooley _____ 535

D. RESISTANCE TO UNLAWFUL ARREST _____ 539

    State v. Koonce _____ 539

TABLE OF CONTENTS

VIII. DEFENSES NOT DIRECTLY RELATED TO THE BASIC REQUIREMENTS FOR LIABILITY—Cont'd

D. RESISTANCE TO UNLAWFUL ARREST—Continued   **Page**
State v. Mulvihill _____ 543

E. PREVENTION OF CRIME _____ 549
Viliborghi v. State _____ 549
Sauls v. Hutto _____ 554
Proposed Federal Criminal Code § 1619 and Comment _____ 559

F. INSANITY AND RELATED MATTERS _____ 562
  1. Introduction _____ 564
    a. The Theoretical Legal Framework _____ 564
    b. Incidence of the Issue _____ 567
      Lewin, Incompetency to Stand Trial: Legal and Ethical Aspects of an Abused Doctrine, 1969 Law and the Social Order _____ 567
      Matthews, Mental Disability and the Criminal Law __ 568
    c. The Requirement of "Mental Illness" _____ 570
      Szasz, The Myth of Mental Illness _____ 571

  2. Formulations of the Insanity Defense _____ 573
    a. The M'Naghten Rules _____ 573
      Daniel M'Naghten's Case _____ 573
      State v. Harkness _____ 577
    b. The Irresistable Impulse Test _____ 585
      Parsons v. State _____ 585
      State v. Harrison _____ 587
    c. The American Law Institute's "Control" Test _____ 590
      Model Penal Code, § 4.01 and Comment (Tent. Draft No. 4) _____ 590
      Model Penal Code, § 4.01 (P.O.D.) _____ 592
      United States v. Pollard _____ 593
      Pollard v. United States _____ 599
    d. The Durham Rule _____ 603
      Durham v. United States _____ 603
      Washington v. United States _____ 610
      Goldstein, The Insanity Defense _____ 613
      United States v. Brawner _____ 614

  3. Abandonment of the Insanity Defense _____ 620
    Weintraub, Criminal Responsibility: Psychiatry Alone Cannot Determine It _____ 620
    Mental Health Act _____ 620
    Goldstein, The Insanity Defense _____ 621
    President's Version of Revised Federal Criminal Code __ 625

  4. Some Practical Aspects of the Insanity Defense _____ 625
    Matthews, Mental Disability and the Criminal Law ____ 625

TABLE OF CONTENTS

VIII. DEFENSES NOT DIRECTLY RELATED TO THE BASIC REQUIREMENTS FOR LIABILITY—Cont'd

F. INSANITY AND RELATED MATTERS—Continued   **Page**
    5. The "Partial Defense" of "Diminished Capacity" _____ 630
        People v. Wells _____ 630
        Model Penal Code, § 4.02 (P.O.D.) _____ 634
        State v. Sikora _____ 635

Table of Cases _____ 639

Index _____ 643

†

BASIC
CRIMINAL LAW

CASES AND MATERIALS

I.   INTRODUCTION

A.   ASCERTAINMENT OF GUILT: THE INSTITUTIONAL FRAMEWORK

PRESIDENT'S COMMISSION ON LAW ENFORCEMENT AND ADMINISTRATION OF JUSTICE, THE CHALLENGE OF CRIME IN A FREE SOCIETY

7–12 (1967).

AMERICA'S SYSTEM OF CRIMINAL JUSTICE

*   *   *

The criminal justice system has three separately organized parts—the police, the courts, and corrections—and each has distinct tasks. However, these parts are by no means independent of each other. What each one does and how it does it has a direct effect on the work of the others.   The courts must deal, and can only deal, with those whom the police arrest; the business of corrections is with those delivered to it by the courts.   How successfully corrections reforms convicts determines whether they will once again become police business and influences the sentences the judges pass; police activities are subject to court scrutiny and are often determined by court decisions. And so reforming or reorganizing any part or procedure of the system changes other parts or procedures.   Furthermore, the criminal process, the method by which the system deals with individual cases, is not a hodgepodge of random actions.   It is rather a continuum—an orderly progression of events—some of which, like arrest and trial, are highly visible and some of which, though of great importance, occur out of public view.   A study of the system must begin by examining it as a whole.

The chart on the following page sets forth in simplified form the process of criminal administration and shows the many decision

A general view of The Criminal Justice System

This chart seeks to present a simple yet comprehensive view of the movement of cases through the criminal justice system. Procedures in individual jurisdictions may vary from the pattern shown here. The differing weights of line indicate the relative volumes of cases disposed of at various points in the system, but this is only suggestive since no nationwide data of this sort exists.

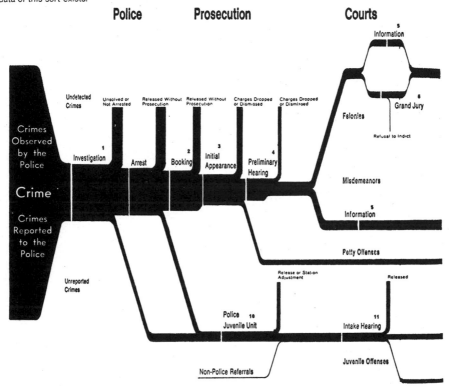

Police **Prosecution** **Courts**

1 May continue until trial.

2 Administrative record of arrest. First step at which temporary release on bail may be available.

3 Before magistrate, commissioner, or justice of peace. Formal notice of charge, advice of rights. Bail set. Summary trials for petty offenses usually conducted here without further processing.

4 Preliminary testing of evidence against defendant. Charge may be reduced. No separate preliminary hearing for misdemeanors in some systems.

5 Charge filed by prosecutor on basis of information submitted by police or citizens. Alternative to grand jury indictment; often used in felonies, almost always in misdemeanors.

6 Reviews whether Government evidence sufficient to justify trial. Some States have no grand jury system; others seldom use it.

[A7374]

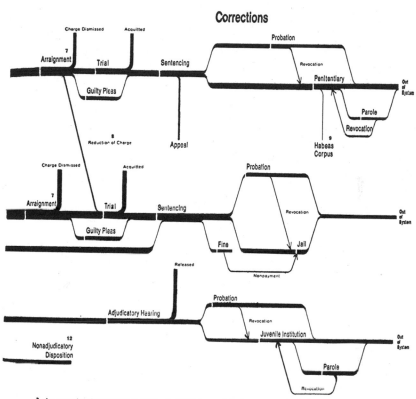

Corrections

7 Appearance for plea; defendant elects trial by judge or jury (if available); counsel for indigent usually appointed here in felonies. Often not at all in other cases.

8 Charge may be reduced at any time prior to trial in return for plea of guilty or for other reasons.

9 Challenge on constitutional grounds to legality of detention. May be sought at any point in process.

10 Police often hold informal hearings, dismiss or adjust many cases without further processing.

11 Probation officer decides desirability of further court action.

12 Welfare agency, social services, counselling, medical care, etc., for cases where adjudicatory handling not needed.

points along its course. Since felonies, misdemeanors, petty offenses, and juvenile cases generally follow quite different paths, they are shown separately.

The popular, or even the lawbook, theory of everyday criminal process oversimplifies in some respects and overcomplicates in others what usually happens. That theory is that when an infraction of the law occurs, a policeman finds, if he can, the probable offender, arrests him and brings him promptly before a magistrate. If the offense is minor, the magistrate disposes of it forthwith; if it is serious, he holds the defendant for further action and admits him to bail. The case then is turned over to a prosecuting attorney, who charges the defendant with a specific statutory crime. This charge is subject to review by a judge at a preliminary hearing of the evidence and in many places if the offense charged is a felony, by a grand jury that can dismiss the charge, or affirm it by delivering it to a judge in the form of an indictment. If the defendant pleads "not guilty" to the charge he comes to trial; the facts of his case are marshaled by prosecuting and defense attorneys and presented, under the supervision of a judge, through witnesses, to a jury. If the jury finds the defendant guilty, he is sentenced by the judge to a term in prison, where a systematic attempt to convert him into a law-abiding citizen is made, or to a term of probation, under which he is permitted to live in the community as long as he behaves himself.

Some cases do proceed much like that, especially those involving offenses that are generally considered "major": serious acts of violence or thefts of large amounts of property. However, not all major cases follow this course, and, in any event, the bulk of the daily business of the criminal justice system consists of offenses that are not major—of breaches of the peace, crimes of vice, petty thefts, assaults arising from domestic or street-corner or barroom disputes. These and most other cases are disposed of in much less formal and much less deliberate ways.

*   *   *

What has evidently happened is that the transformation of America from a relatively relaxed rural society into a tumultuous urban one has presented the criminal justice system in the cities with a volume of cases too large to handle by traditional methods. One result of heavy caseloads is highly visible in city courts, which process many cases with excessive haste and many others with excessive slowness. In the interest both of effectiveness and of fairness to individuals, justice should be swift and certain; too often in city courts today it is, instead, hasty or faltering. Invisibly, the pressure of numbers has effected a series of adventitious changes in the criminal process. Informal shortcuts have been used. The decision making process has often become routinized. Throughout the system the importance of individual judgment and discretion, as distinguished from stated rules and procedures, has increased. In effect, much decision making is being done on an administrative rather than on a judicial basis. Thus, an examination of how the criminal justice system works and a consideration of the changes needed to make it more effective and fair must focus on the extent to which invisible, administrative procedures depart from visible, traditional ones, and on the desirability of that departure.

THE POLICE

At the very beginning of the process—or, more properly, before the process begins at all—something happens that is scarcely discussed in lawbooks and is seldom recognized by the public: law enforcement policy is made by the policeman. For policemen cannot and do not arrest all the offenders they encounter. It is doubtful that they arrest most of them. A criminal code, in practice, is not a set of specific instructions to policemen but a more or less rough map of the territory in which policemen work. How an individual policeman moves around that territory depends largely on his personal discretion.

That a policeman's duties compel him to exercise personal discretion many times every day is evident. Crime does not look the same on the street as it does in a legislative chamber. How much noise or profanity makes conduct "disorderly" within the meaning of the law? When must a quarrel be treated as a criminal assault: at the first threat or at the first shove or at the first blow, or after blood is drawn, or when a serious injury is inflicted? How suspicious must conduct be before there is "probable cause," the constitutional basis for an arrest? Every policeman, however complete or sketchy his education, is an interpreter of the law.

Every policeman, too, is an arbiter of social values, for he meets situation after situation in which invoking criminal sanctions is a questionable line of action. It is obvious that a boy throwing rocks at a school's windows is committing the statutory offense of vandalism, but it is often not at all obvious whether a policeman will better serve the interests of the community and of the boy by taking the boy home to his parents or by arresting him. Who are the boy's parents? Can they control him? Is he a frequent offender who has responded badly to leniency? Is vandalism so epidemic in the neighborhood that he should be made a cautionary example? With juveniles especially, the police exercise great discretion.

Finally, the manner in which a policeman works is influenced by practical matters: the legal strength of the available evidence, the willingness of victims to press charges and of witnesses to testify, the temper of the community, the time and information at the policeman's disposal. Much is at stake in how the policeman exercises this discretion. If he judges conduct not suspicious enough to justify intervention, the chance to prevent a robbery, rape, or murder may be lost.

If he overestimates the seriousness of a situation or his actions are controlled by panic or prejudice, he may hurt or kill someone unnecessarily. His actions may even touch off a riot.

THE MAGISTRATE

In direct contrast to the policeman, the magistrate before whom a suspect is first brought usually exercises less discretion than the law allows him. He is entitled to inquire into the facts of the case, into whether there are grounds for holding the accused. He seldom does. He seldom can. The more promptly an arrested suspect is brought into magistrate's court, the less likelihood there is that much information about the arrest other than the arresting officer's statement will be available to the magistrate. Moreover many magistrates, especially in big cities, have such congested calendars that it is almost impossible for them to subject any case but an extraordinary one to prolonged scrutiny.

In practice the most important things, by far, that a magistrate does are to set the amount of a defendant's bail and in some jurisdictions to appoint counsel. Too seldom does either action get the careful attention it deserves. In many cases the magistrate accepts a waiver of counsel without insuring that the suspect knows the significance of legal representation.

Bail is a device to free an untried defendant and at the same time make sure he appears for trial. That is the sole stated legal purpose in America. The Eighth Amendment to the Constitution declares that it must not be "excessive." Appellate courts have declared that not just the seriousness of the charge against the defendant, but the suspect's personal, family, and employment situation, as they bear on the likelihood of his appearance, must be weighed before the amount of his bail is fixed. Yet more magistrates than not set bail according to standard rates: so and so many dollars for such and such an offense.

The persistence of money bail can best be explained not by its stated purpose but by the belief of police, prosecutors, and courts that the best way to keep a defendant from committing more crimes before trial is to set bail so high that he cannot obtain his release.

THE PROSECUTOR

The key administrative officer in the processing of cases is the prosecutor. Theoretically the examination of the evidence against a defendant by a judge at a preliminary hearing, and its reexamination by a grand jury, are important parts of the process. Practically they seldom are because a prosecutor seldom has any difficulty in making a prima facie case against a defendant. In fact most defendants waive their rights to preliminary hearings and much more often than not grand juries indict precisely as prosecutors ask them to. The prosecutor wields almost undisputed sway over the pretrial progress of most cases. He decides whether to press a case or drop it. He determines the specific charge against a defendant. When the charge is reduced, as it is in as many as two-thirds of all cases in some cities, the prosecutor is usually the official who reduces it.

*   *   *

THE PLEA AND THE SENTENCE

When a prosecutor reduces a charge it is ordinarily because there has been "plea bargaining" between him and a defense attorney. The issue at stake is how much the prosecutor will reduce his original charge or how lenient a sentence he will recommend, in return for a plea of guilty. There is no way of judging how many bargains reflect the prosecutor's belief that a lesser charge or sentence is justified and how many result from the fact that there may be in the system at any one time ten times as many cases as there are prosecutors or judges or courtrooms to handle them, should every one come to trial. In form, a plea bargain can be anything from a series of careful conferences to a hurried consultation in a courthouse corridor. In content it can be anything from a conscientious exploration of the facts and dispositional alternatives available and appropriate to a defendant, to a perfunctory deal. If the interests of a defendant are to be properly protected while his fate is being thus invisibly determined, he obviously needs just as good legal representation as the kind he needs at a public trial. Whether or not plea bargaining is a fair and effective method of disposing of criminal cases depends heavily on whether or not defendants are provided early with competent and conscientious counsel.

Plea bargaining is not only an invisible procedure but, in some jurisdictions, a theoretically unsanctioned one. In order to satisfy the court record, a defendant, his attorney, and the prosecutor will at the time of sentencing often ritually state to a judge that no bargain has been made. Plea bargaining may be a useful procedure, especially in congested urban jurisdictions, but neither the dignity of the law, nor the quality of justice, nor the protection of society from dangerous criminals is enhanced by its being conducted covertly.

*   *   *

An enormously consequential kind of decision is the sentencing decision of a judge. The law recognizes the importance of fitting sentences to individual defendants by giving judges, in most instances, considerable latitude. For example the recently adopted New York Penal Code, which went into effect in autumn of 1967, empowers a judge to impose upon a man convicted of armed robbery any sentence between a 5-year term of probation and a 25-year term in prison. Even when a judge has presided over a trial during which the facts of a case have been carefully set forth and has been given a probation report that carefully discusses a defendant's character, background, and problems, he cannot find it easy to choose a sentence. In perhaps nine-tenths of all cases there is no trial; the defendants are self-confessedly guilty.

In the lower or misdemeanor courts, the courts that process most criminal cases, probation reports are a rarity. Under such circumstances judges have little to go on and many sentences are bound to be based on conjecture or intuition. When a sentence is part of a plea bargain, which an overworked judge ratifies perfunctorily, it may not even be his conjecture or intuition on which the sentence is based, but a prosecutor's or a defense counsel's. But perhaps the greatest lack judges suffer from when they pass sentence is not time or information, but correctional alternatives. Some lower courts do not have any probation officers, and in almost every court the caseloads of probation officers are so heavy that a sentence of probation means, in fact, releasing an offender into the community with almost no supervision. Few States have a sufficient variety of correctional institutions or treatment programs to inspire judges with the confidence that sentences will lead to rehabilitation.

CORRECTIONS

The correctional apparatus to which guilty defendants are delivered is in every respect the most isolated part of the criminal justice system. Much of it is physically isolated; its institutions usually have thick walls and locked doors, and often they are situated in rural areas, remote from the courts where the institutions' inmates were tried and from the communities where they lived. The correctional apparatus is isolated in the sense that its officials do not have everyday working relationships with officials from the system's other branches, like those that commonly exist between policemen and prosecutors, or prosecutors and judges. It is isolated in the sense that what it does with, to, or for the people under its supervision is seldom governed by any but the most broadly written statutes, and is almost never scrutinized by appellate courts. Finally, it is isolated from the public partly by its invisibility and physical remoteness; partly by the inherent lack of drama in most of its activities, but perhaps most importantly by the fact that the correctional apparatus is often used— or misused—by both the criminal justice system and the public as a rug under which disturbing problems and people can be swept.

The most striking fact about the correctional apparatus today is that, although the rehabilitation of criminals is presumably its major purpose, the custody of criminals is actually its major task. On any given day there are well over a million people being "corrected" in America, two-thirds of them on probation or parole and one-third of them in prisons or jails. However, prisons and jails are where four-fifths of correctional money is spent and where nine-tenths of correctional employees work. Furthermore, fewer than one-fifth of the people who work in State prisons and local jails have jobs that are not essentially either custodial or administrative in character. Many jails have nothing but custodial and administrative personnel. Of course many jails are crowded with defendants who have not been able to furnish bail and who are not considered by the law to be appropriate objects of rehabilitation because it has not yet been determined that they are criminals who need it.

What this emphasis on custody means in practice is that the enormous potential of the correctional apparatus for making creative decisions about its treatment of convicts is largely unfulfilled. This is true not only of offenders in custody but of offenders on probation and parole. Most authorities agree that while probationers and parolees need varying degrees and kinds of supervision, an average of no more than 35 cases per officer is necessary for effective attention; 97 percent of all officers handling adults have larger caseloads than that. In the juvenile correctional system the situation is somewhat better. Juvenile institutions, which typically are training schools, have a higher proportion of treatment personnel and juvenile probation and parole officers generally have lighter caseloads. However, these comparatively rich resources are very far from being sufficiently rich.

Except for sentencing, no decision in the criminal process has more impact on the convicted offender than the parole decision, which determines how much of his maximum sentence a prisoner must serve. This again is an invisible administrative decision that is seldom open to attack or subject to review. It is made by parole board members who are often political appointees. Many are skilled and conscientious, but they generally are able to spend no more than a few minutes on a case. Parole decisions that are made in haste and on the basis of insufficient information, in the absence of parole machinery that can provide good supervision, are necessarily imperfect decisions. And since there is virtually no appeal from them, they can be made arbitrarily or discriminatorily. Just as carefully formulated and clearly stated law enforcement policies would help policemen, charge policies would help prosecutors and sentencing policies would help judges, so parole policies would help parole boards perform their delicate and important duties.

B. ASCERTAINMENT OF GUILT: THE PROSECUTION'S BURDEN OF PROOF BEYOND A REASONABLE DOUBT

The burden of proof is a two-part concept in the law: First, the burden of producing evidence or the burden of production; and second, the burden of persuasion. In criminal cases the state bears both burdens with respect to the issue of guilt. That is, the defendant need offer no evidence and the state must offer evidence sufficient to justify a finding of guilt. If it fails a directed verdict of acquittal is proper. If it satisfies its burden of production then the trier of fact —the judge or the jury—is to consider whether the evidence establishes the defendant's guilt *beyond a reasonable doubt*. This very high standard of persuasion—in civil cases the party who bears the burden of persuasion normally need only persuade by a preponderance of the evidence—has been held to be constitutionally required. In re Winship, 397 U.S. 358, 90 S.Ct. 1068, 25 L.Ed. 368 ᵃ (1970)¹.

Although *Winship* stands for the proposition that the state must bear the burden of persuasion of beyond a reasonable doubt with respect to adjudications of guilt or delinquency, other important issues in the administration of criminal justice may be resolved on the basis of a lesser burden. Thus in Lego v. Twomey, 404 U.S. 553, 92 S.Ct. 619, 30 L.Ed.2d 618 (1972), the Supreme Court held that where a criminal defendant claims that his confession is not admissible into evidence because it was made involuntarily it is constitutionally sufficient if, at a preliminary hearing, the prosecution satisfies the judge by a preponderance of the evidence that the confession was voluntary. The Court, with three justices dissenting, distinguished *Winship* on the grounds thta the higher burden was needed there to minimize the danger of convicting the innocent. In contrast, a hearing on the voluntariness of a confession is designed to serve the purposes of the Fifth Amendment's privilege against self-incrimination rather than to improve the reliability of adjudications of guilt. That is, the confession is presumptively reliable evidence so that its admission enhances the search for truth rather than jeopardizes it.

Although the prosecution bears the burden of proof on the issue of guilt, the defendant may bear the burden with respect to some defenses. Thus it is common for the defendant to bear the burden of production with respect to the insanity defense or the defense of self-defense. In addition, some jurisdictions may place the burden of per-

---

a. The citations following the name of the case are in customary legal form. "U.S." stands for "United States Supreme Court Reports", the official reporting system for decision of the United States Supreme Court. The citation here indicates that the decision in the Winship case can be found in volume **397** of the United States Reports at page 358. "S.Ct." stands for "Supreme Court Reporter", and "L.Ed.2d" for Lawyers Edition, United States Supreme Court Reports, Second Series"; both of these are commercial reporting systems for the decisions of the United States Supreme Court.

suasion by a preponderance on the defendant in connection with some defenses. Where the burden of persuasion is put on the defendant the defense is commonly termed an "affirmative defense". In Leland v. Oregon, 343 U.S. 790, 72 S.Ct. 1002, 96 L.Ed. 1302 (1952), the Supreme Court held that placing the burden of persuasion on the defendant with regard to insanity did not violate the constitution. On the other hand, it has been held by an intermediate Federal appellate court that it does violate the constitution for a state law to make alibi an affirmative defense since the defendant's presence at the scene of the crime is an indispensable part of the government's case. In the absence of any showing that evidence of the defense is unavailable to the prosecution—here the defendant was required to give the state the names of his alibi witnesses—the state cannot shift to the defendant the burden of persuasion on an essential element of the crime. Stump v. Bennett, 398 F.2d 711, (8th Cir. 1968), cert. denied 393 U.S. 1001, 89 S.Ct. 483, 21 L.Ed.2d 466 [b]. A model statutory formulation of the distribution of the burden of proof appears below.

MODEL PENAL CODE

(Proposed Official Draft, 1962).

Section 1.12. Proof Beyond a Reasonable Doubt; Affirmative Defenses; Burden of Proving Fact When Not an Element of an Offense; Presumptions.

(1) No person may be convicted of an offense unless each element of such offense is proved beyond a reasonable doubt. In the absence of such proof, the innocence of the defendant is assumed.

(2) Subsection (1) of this Section does not:

(a) require the disproof of an affirmative defense unless and until there is evidence supporting such defense; or

---

[b]. The abbreviation "F.2d" stands for Federal Reporter, Second Series, The Federal Reporter is where the decisions of the ten United States Courts of Appeal are reported. (Decisions of federal trial courts are reported in the Federal Supplement (F.Supp.)). "8th Cir." indicates that the decision in Stump was rendered by the Court of Appeals for the Eighth Circuit. The ten circuits are responsible for appeals from decisions of United States District Courts (trial courts) located within particular geographical areas. The Eighth Circuit, for example, covers the states of Arkansas, Iowa, Minnesota, Missouri, Nebraska, North Dakota and South Dakota. The abbreviation "cert." stands for certiorari, and "cert. denied" means that the party which lost in the Court of Appeals has failed in its efforts to have the Supreme Court review the decision. The decision to grant certiorari is totally within the discretion of the Justices of the Supreme Court —there is no right to have such a case reviewed—and a decision to deny does not mean that the Supreme Court approves or disapproves of the lower court's decision.

(b) apply to any defense which the Code or another statute plainly requires the defendant to prove by a preponderance of evidence.

(3) A ground of defense is affirmative, within the meaning of Subsection (2) (a) of this Section, when:

(a) it arises under a section of the Code which so provides; or

(b) it relates to an offense defined by a statute other than the Code and such statute so provides; or

(c) it involves a matter of excuse or justification peculiarly within the knowledge of the defendant on which he can fairly be required to adduce supporting evidence.

MODEL PENAL CODE, COMMENTS TO § 1.13, 110–11

(Tent. Draft No. 4, 1955).

No single principle can be conscripted to explain when these shifts of burden to defendants are defensible, even if the burden goes no further than to call for the production of some evidence. Neither the logical point that the prosecution would be called upon to prove a negative, nor the grammatical point that the defense rests on an exception or proviso divorced from the definition of the crime is potently persuasive, although both points have been invoked. * * * What is involved seems rather a more subtle balance which acknowledges that a defendant ought not be required to defend until some solid substance is presented to support the accusation but, beyond this, perceives a point where need for narrowing the issues, coupled with the relative accessibility of evidence to the defendant, warrants calling upon him to present his defensive claim. No doubt this point is reached more quickly if, given the facts the prosecution must establish, the normal probabilities are against the defense, but this is hardly an essential factor. Given the mere fact of an intentional homicide, no one can estimate the probability that it was or was not committed in self-defense. The point is rather that purposeful homicide is an event of such gravity to society, and the basis for a claim of self-defense is so specially within the cognizance of the defendant, that it is fair to call on him to offer evidence if the defense is claimed. * * *

C. PENALTY PROVISIONS AND GRADING OF CRIMINAL OFFENSES

___

1. THE TASK OF ASSIGNING PENALTIES

___

TASK FORCE ON ADMINISTRATION OF JUSTICE, THE PRESIDENT'S COMMISSION ON LAW ENFORCEMENT AND ADMINISTRATION OF JUSTICE, TASK FORCE REPORT: THE COURTS

15 (1967).

The penal codes of most jurisdictions are the products of piecemeal construction, as successive legislatures have fixed punishment for new crimes and adjusted penalties for existing offenses through separate sentencing provisions for each offense. As a result the sentencing distinctions among offenses are in excess of those which could rationally be drawn on the basis of relative harmfulness of conduct or the probable dangerousness of the offenders. In Wisconsin, for example, there are 16 variations in the statutory maximum terms of imprisonment for felonies upon a first conviction: 2, 3, 4, 5, 6, 7, 8, 10, 14, 20, 25, 35, and 40 years and life imprisonment. A study of the Oregon penal code revealed that the 1,413 criminal statutes contained a total of 466 different types and lengths of sentences.

The absence of legislative attention to the whole range of penalties may also be demonstrated by comparisons between certain offenses. A recent study of the Colorado statutes disclosed that a person convicted of first degree murder must serve 10 years before becoming eligible for parole, while a person convicted of a lesser degree of the same offense must serve at least 15 years; destruction of a house with fire is punishable by a maximum of 20 years' imprisonment, but destruction of a house with explosives carries a 10-year maximum. In California an offender who breaks into an automobile to steal the contents of the glove compartment is subject to a 15-year maximum sentence, but if he stole the car itself, he would face a maximum 10-year term.

Although each offense must be defined in a separate statutory provision, the number and variety of sentencing distinctions which result when legislatures prescribe a separate penalty for each offense are among "the main causes of the anarchy in sentencing that is so widely deplored."

WECHSLER AND MICHAEL, A RATIONALE FOR
THE LAW OF HOMICIDE

37 Columbia Law Review 701, 1261, 1268–1270 (1937).

[S]ome one, legislator or administrator, must face the problem of ordering the severity of penalties within the limits of popular tolerance so that the welfare of individual offenders shall be sacrificed for the sake of deterrence only in those instances in which the sacrifice is most necessary and serves the most desirable ends. We must, therefore, address ourselves to an analysis of that problem. If we are right in believing that the core of the popular demand is for some gradation of the severity of punitive treatment in accordance with the actual or probable results of crimes of various sorts and the characters of criminals of various sorts, the major criteria for an ordered mitigation of punishment are, it will be observed, inherent in popular sentiment itself.

I.   There are several reasons why the severity of penalties should be correlated with the relative undesirability of the behavior for which they are imposed. The more undesirable any kind of criminal behavior is, the less expedient it is to relax our efforts to prevent it, the more important it is that we make the incentive to avoid it, which the threat of punishment provides, as strong as it can be made. Moreover, such a correlation serves, as we have said, as an inducement to potential offenders to pursue their ends by the least undesirable criminal means; it also serves as an object lesson in relative evil which is not without some value as general moral education.

II.   There are equally valid reasons why the severity of penalties should be correlated with the characters of individual offenders. The more numerous a potential offender's motives to refrain from criminal behavior apart from that of avoiding a threatened penalty, the more he is moved by them habitually, the greater his capacity to guide his conduct by such motives, the less need there is for a vigorous threat to counteract whatever desires to engage in criminal behavior he may have from time to time. Moreover, for the most part, the more severe a penalty, the greater is its incapacitative effect and the more likely it is to harm and the less likely to reform the actual offenders subjected to it. Obviously, the more dangerous men are, the more desirable it is that they be thoroughly incapacitated; the better the lives men can lead, the less desirable it is to debase them; the more likely it is that men are corrigible, the more tragic it is not to attempt to reform them.

Though these are, in our judgment, the major criteria for ordering the severity of punishment, they are not exhaustive. Two subordinate principles merit consideration. They are:

III.   The severity of penalties should be correlated with the strength of the desires which motivate men to engage in criminal behavior of different sorts under different circumstances. The stronger the desire, the more need there is for severity in the threatened penalty in order to counteract it.

IV.   The severity of penalties should also be correlated with the presence or absence of a discernible relation between the criminal act and some injustice done to the actor by another individual or even by society as a whole.   Where such a relationship can be perceived, a mitigation of the penalty on that ground serves, as T. H. Green has pointed out,[25] to direct attention to and strengthen the popular awareness of the original injustice, a result that may be of value in preventing or remedying such injustices in the future.   The greater the injustice, the less vigorous the efforts that are being made to deal with it, the more confidently the criminal act can be attributed to it as a cause, the stronger the case for mitigation for that reason becomes.

To the extent that these principles can be developed and employed, the severity of punishment should be susceptible of a rough ordering which is rationally adapted both to its primary deterrent purpose and to the other ends which even the punitive treatment of offenders should as far as possible serve.

AMERICAN BAR ASSOCIATION PROJECT ON MINIMUM STANDARDS FOR CRIMINAL JUSTICE, STANDARDS RELATING TO SENTENCING ALTERNATIVES AND PROCEDURES (COMMENTARY)

130, 143–54, 133–36, 157–58 (1967).c

There are two basic items of information which must be known about any prison sentence in order adequately to appraise its effect. The first is the date beyond which, at all events, the offender must be released.   This is   *   *   *   the "maximum" term to which he is subject.   The second is the date at which he becomes eligible for discretionary release by parole authorities.   This is   *   *   *   the "minimum" term.

*   *   *

[Minimum Sentences]

The core of the debate between the Model Penal Code and the Model Sentencing Act involves the basic question of whether a minimum sentence should be authorized at all.   The Model Sentencing Act flatly takes the position that there should be immediate parole eligi-

-----

25.   Lectures on the Principles of Political Obligation (1927) 193–4.

c.   Copyright © 1967, by the American Bar Association. Reprinted with permission.   The ABA Standards are printed in individual volumes.   They may be ordered from the American Bar Association Circulation Dept., American Bar Center, 1155 East 60th Street, Chicago, Illinois 60637, telephone (312) 493–0533.   Cost is $2.00 per volume or $1 in lots of 10 or more, whether same or assorted titles.

bility—that there should be no minimum sentences even for the most serious of offenses. The Code is in full agreement with the proposition that the sentencing structure should be dominated by the principle of indeterminacy. But it is not in agreement that the timing of the parole decision should be entirely beyond legislative and judicial control. Judicial control is accomplished by authorizing the sentencing court to fix a minimum term within a range specified for each category of offenses; legislative control is manifested by the requirement that every commitment must be accompanied by a minimum term of at least one year.

It is helpful in assessing the dispute between these two highly respected model provisions to divide the issue into two parts: whether it is sound for the legislature to fix mandatory minimum terms which must be imposed irrespective of the circumstances; and whether the sentencing court should be authorized to impose a minimum term.

It is quite common in this country for legislatures to provide mandatory minimum terms for certain offenses. The most consistent examples are those offenses which carry life imprisonment as the maximum term. Legislatively fixed minimum sentences in such cases range from an apparent low of seven years in Nevada, to thirty years in Maine. More common is the ten year minimum found in Alabama, Colorado, Idaho, Mississippi, North Carolina and Oregon and the fifteen year minimum found in the District of Columbia, Delaware, Iowa, Maryland, Utah and Virginia. * * *

Finally it should be noted that at least four states have adopted across-the-board minima for every prison sentence. In Massachusetts every sentence to the state prison must be for at least a two and one-half year minimum, while in Mississippi and New York all prison sentences must carry at least a one year minimum. In Florida, the term is six months. * * *

The argument most commonly advanced in favor of the imposition of a minimum term is based on community reassurance. The basic purpose of the criminal law is the protection of the public, and the public can only be assured that this purpose will be carried out if dangerous offenders are removed from society for at least a minimum period of time. A second argument is that it is destructive of the effective operation of parole boards to give them total freedom in every case. The parole decision should be a shared responsibility, and the minimum term is the way in which other agencies can participate in the process. A third point is that a minimum period of incarceration is an institutional necessity in order for any valid correctional program to have a meaningful chance to operate. Finally, a related argument is made that if a consensus can be reached on the minimum time needed in order to implement a valid correctional program, legislative specification of that term for every case will serve to emphasize to the sentencing court the nature of the decision being made, and to point up the difference between probation and institutionalization in more meaningful terms.

These four arguments, sometimes supplemented by general references to deterrence and the sureness of punishment, are the ones which are normally suggested in favor of the principle underlying a minimum term. * * *

Support for [the] position [that it is inappropriate for the legislature to prescribe minimum terms which must be imposed by the court without regard to the circumstances] must begin with a consideration of the arguments in favor of a minimum term. The most persuasive argument is the one that relies on the need for community reassurance that the law is performing its task of public protection. Not only is it important that the public in fact be protected, but it is important to develop the confidence in the legal system which is one of its necessary underpinnings.

Thus stated, the argument is ambiguous. Assuming that the minimum term can perform the function of developing this public confidence, the argument does not speak precisely to whether it should be the legislature, the court or some other agency which should determine the instances in which the protection of a minimum term is called for. There are some, however, who would use it for the proposition that the legislature can perform the task by adopting high, across-the-board minima for certain types of offenses. * * *

Public clamor for this position—and the political capitalization on it which feeds its growth—loses sight of the fact that it is at most only some offenders from whom the public needs this protection, and that the legislature is not in a position to identify the precise individuals who pose the feared risk. It is perfectly apparent that *every* robber and *every* mugger, and indeed *every* murderer, does not pose the same type of future danger to the community. The young adult who panics because he cannot find work and who robs to feed his starving family does not pose the same potential danger to the community as the sociopath who robs because his twisted values find that as convenient a way as any to make a living. * * *

The evil of the mandatory term is that it robs the system of the capacity to discriminate between offenders who do and offenders who do not deserve the harsh treatment which the minimum signifies. A far better way to attack the problem would be to arm the system with the funds and the facilities to enable it to identify the particular offenders from whom society legitimately needs protection. * * *

There are several additional reasons why the mandatory minimum is a naive and destructive provision. As noted, the definition of offenses is of necessity in general terms, and the varying circumstances in which an offense can occur will to a certainty lead to cases where all would agree that a long period of confinement is unwarranted. Both judges and prosecuting officials recognize such cases when they arise, and are immediately put in a most awkward position. They may either enforce the letter of the law and perpetrate a clear injustice, or they may ignore the law and defeat the apparent intent of the legislature.   Both results are destructive of the very public confidence in the system which is sought by the mandatory minimum term.

*   *   *

There is one last effect of the mandatory minimum sentence which should be noted.   The choice which is often presented between a plea to a lesser offense and the certainty of a brutal sentence upon conviction of the charged offense has clear coercive effects upon the supposedly consensual process of pleading guilty.   The mandatory minimum can stack the deck, as it were, in favor of inducing pleas to lesser offenses even though there may be a substantial chance of acquittal and even though the defendant may in fact not be guilty of the charged offense.   It can thus compromise the process by which guilt is determined.

It remains to consider the other arguments which have been advanced in favor of a minimum term.   The second argument noted above was that it is destructive of the effective operation of parole boards to give them total freedom, and that it tends to introduce conservatism by the board if it is to shoulder the entire burden in every case.

For reasons similar to those noted above, it would not seem that the objectives sought by this argument would be advanced by legislatively fixed minimum terms.   The parole board is directed to make its judgments in terms of the case presented by each individual offender.   The legislature, on the other hand, must make its judgments before the offender has identified himself by committing a crime.   It would thus seem that to the extent that this argument is valid it is an argument for judicially imposed terms.   The court is the only other agency in the process which is in a position to share in the parole decision by tailoring a minimum term to the particular offender.

There is another aspect of the mandatory minimum term which raises different questions.   As noted above, in at least four states a reasonably short, across-the-board minimum is provided for every prison sentence, ranging from two and one-half years in Massachusetts to six months in Florida.   *   *   *

This type of provision is supported, as the arguments stated above reflect, by the twin aims of assuring a sufficient time for the institution to undertake a meaningful corrections program and of emphasizing to the judge the practical fact that at least such a period of detention will be a necessary result from a sentence to prison.   It is suggested, however, that neither objective justifies the requirement of such a minimum term in every prison sentence.

The danger, of course, is that classification and diagnosis of the individual will disclose that the offender is more likely to respond to probation than he is to a year's incarceration.   The Model Penal Code guards against this possibility by authorizing the institution to return to the sentencing court and request resentencing.   See Model

Penal Code § 7.08(3), Appendix B, * * *. It would seem less cumbersome in such a case to authorize immediate parole eligibility than to require a return to the sentencing court. If the institution in fact needs a one year period or longer during which to implement a satisfactory program for a given offender, there is nothing about such immediate eligibility that would interfere. On the other hand, if the determination is that incarceration itself was a mistake, or that only a very short period of a few months together with parole supervision is a less damaging alternative, then the automatic minimum serves as a hindrance and the requirement of return to the court as an unnecessary clog on crowded dockets.

*   *   *

[T]he second aspect of the problem is whether the sentencing court should be authorized to impose a minimum if suited to the case before it. For while it may be undesirable to force the imposition of such a term, it by no means follows that a minimum term should not be permitted if the court deems it warranted in a particular case. * * *

The most compelling reason advanced in support of authority to impose a minimum sentence is the need to assure the community that a dangerous offender will be removed from society for a minimum period of time. The countervailing consideration is that in the heat of the moment—particularly if the judge is subject to the community pressures of an elected official—an unfair, irrevocable decision will be made. Equally possible, of course, is a decision which is informed at the time it is made, but which—though irrevocably made—is called into question by subsequent events. The vice of the minimum sentence is that it fails to allow for these possibilities.

[Maximum Sentence]

One of the questions which divided the American Law Institute in the formulation of its Model Penal Code was whether, assuming the court has determined to impose a prison sentence, the maximum term should be fixed in advance by the legislature for all offenses within a given class, or the sentencing judge should be authorized to fix the maximum term within a legislatively prescribed range. Present practice is divided between these two approaches, although the federal system and a clear majority of the states allow the sentencing judge a role in determining the maximum to be imposed. * * *

Argument in favor of a maximum term over which the sentencing judge is to have no control proceeds from the premise that the function of the maximum is to express the limit beyond which even the worst risks within a class of offenders should not be detained on the basis of past criminal behavior. Two judgments are therefore involved: the point at which this overall limit should be fixed and the nature of the risk provided by the particular offender. The first judgment is uniformly conceded to be for the legislature. The second

arguably could be divided between judge and parole authority. The
argument advanced by those who would place it exclusively with
the parole authorities is that the decision which is required is one
that can best be made on the basis of the hindsight provided by examination and diagnosis over time: the parole authorities are better
able to determine the risk of release and the character of the offender
at the time when parole is at issue than is the judge at the time of
original sentencing.

In addition, proponents of no judicial control over the maximum
argue that the best device by which to attack the pervasive problem
of sentencing disparities is to reduce the variety of sentences available to the trial judge—and correspondingly to retain variations only
when it is necessary to achieve a specific objective. The judgment
which is thus expressed is that the gains of permitting judicial variation of the maximum are more than offset by the losses which result
from uncontrollable sentencing disparities.

Finally, some critics have suggested that such a system will result in longer sentences. However, since the fixed maximum expresses a legislative judgment about how the worst offender within a given
class should be treated, proponents have argued that less restraint is
exerted on the parole authorities than is the case when the judge has
purportedly tailored the maximum to the particular offender. The
parole authorities would thus be encouraged to grade offenders on
the basis of present condition, rather than intimidated by what can
only be a judicial guess of future condition. In addition, parole authorities would not be limited by a judicially reduced sentence in cases
where present condition did not warrant release. The conclusion is
thus that while the *maximum* sentences imposed will necessarily be
longer, time served may well be shorter, and at the least will be unaf-
fected by a judicial judgment which because of its timing cannot be
made upon optimum information.

On the other hand, those who are of the view that the judge should
exercise control over the maximum sentence actually imposed answer
that a legislatively-fixed maximum deprives the court of a necessary
tool with which to grade the severity of a particular offense. The
legislative grading of offenses is necessarily in broad categories, as
are legislatively fixed ranges within which punishment is authorized.
It ought to be the function of the sentencing judge to particularize
the grading according to the severity of the offense and the character
of the offender—to individualize the sentence, as this process is often
described.

Three further arguments are advanced in favor of judicial control. The first is an attack on the basic premise of the fixed-maximum
proposal. The proposition that parole authorities are in a better position than judges to assess the readiness of the defendant to return to
society needs more support than merely the advantage of more favorable timing. In particular, such a system would seem to call on more
highly developed and more adequately funded correctional and pa-

role facilities than many states have to date provided. In addition, the fact that judicial sentencing occurs in open court following an opportunity to present a case with the assistance of an attorney affords a visibility to the process which is normally absent before parole authorities, as well as greater procedural protection.

The second argument proceeds on the view that sentences in this country are already the longest in the world without any demonstration that such longevity is an aid rather than a hindrance to law enforcement. Permitting judicial control would be one way of reducing the sentences imposed, and also should effect the reduction of actual time served.

The third argument is based on wholly different considerations. The effect sought by the denial of discretion to determine the maximum sentence is a transfer of control to the parole authorities over the actual time to be served. Denying judicial control, the argument goes, will in fact frustrate rather than advance this objective. A great majority of convicted defendants—approaching ninety per cent in many jurisdictions—are convicted after a plea rather than a trial, and a majority of these tender their plea in the hope if not the expectation that sentencing leniency will be the reward. If the judge has no power to be lenient by reducing the otherwise legislatively fixed maximum, then the only concession left for the defendant to seek is charge reduction. Since the plea-bargaining process is so well entrenched, the practical result is a shift of discretion from the court to the prosecutor, rather than from the court to the parole authorities as is desired.

* * *

[Relationship Between Minimum and Maximum Sentences]

[There is also a] need for assurance that the principle of indeterminancy will not be undercut by the imposition of too high a minimum term. The laws of most states accomplish this by denying authority to impose a minimum term which approaches the maximum in severity. The "definite" sentence states, for example—those in which parole eligibility turns on a fixed percentage of the sentence imposed—have built into their system the requirement that there be an adequate spread between minimum and maximum terms. Thus, in the Virginia example given in comment *b*, supra, a twelve year sentence automatically means that the period between three and twelve years is indeterminate. This principle is likewise followed in most jurisdictions where the trial court is given discretion as to the minimum. In Alaska and the District of Columbia, for example, the sentencing court can select a minimum term at any point up to one-third of the maximum actually imposed. * * *

NOTES

1. To what extent is it reasonable to expect that the choice as to the severity of penalty will affect the incidence of the crime? Schwartz, The Effect in Philadelphia of Pennsylvania's Increased Penalties for Rape and

Attempted Rape, 59 J.Crim.L., C. & P.S. 509 (1968) attempted to assess the effect of a change in penalties for rape and attempted rape. After a particularly offensive rape on April 3, 1966, the maximum penalty for rape with bodily injury was increased from fifteen years to life. A minimum of fifteen years was established; none had previously been imposed. For rape without bodily injury, the maximum was raised from fifteen to twenty years. The changes were widely publicized by news media and in Philadelphia were accompanied by an announcement that trials for such offenders would be speeded up. The statutory changes were signed by the governor on May 12, 1966. Schwartz compared the incidence of rapes and attempted rapes in Philadelphia during 1966 with 1965 and the period 1958 to 1965. This showed no significant decrease following the increased penalties. Nor was there any discernable reduction in the seriousness of the offenses following the enactment of heavier penalties for offenses involving bodily injury. What significance, if any, does this study have for the assignment of penalties for offenses? Explain. How might more helpful studies of the effect of penalties be structured? Cf. Ball, The Deterrent Concept in Criminology and Law, 46 J.Crim.L., C. & P.S. 347 (1955).

The classical criminologists argued that severity of penalty was irrelevant to the deterrent effect of criminal punishment and that greater certainty of punishment was more likely than greater severity to produce a deterrent effect. It has been argued that the results of experiments conducted by experimental psychologists confirm this. Jeffery, Criminal Behavior and Learning Theory, 56 J.C.L., C. & P.S. 294 (1965). Singer, Psychological Studies of Punishment, 58 Cal.L.Rev. 405 (1970) questions this. He reports finding no experimental evidence which directly contrasts the results of increased severity with those of increased certainty. The indirect evidence, Singer concludes, suggests that "a sufficiently severe punishment will suppress behavior effectively even if it is only occasional, whereas a mild punishment will permit complete recovery of the punished behavior even if it is administered every time [the behavior is performed]." Id. at 417. The matter is complicated, he asserts, by the fact that delaying punishment has an effect equivalent to reducing its severity. As a result, "a five-year sentence beginning a year after the commission of a crime may not be as effective as a six-month sentence administered without delay." Id. at 421. When, however, society responds to continuing or increasing crime by increasing the severity of penalties, there is a corresponding desire to increase the procedural safeguards used to assure that the penalty is never imposed upon an innocent person. The delay caused by these procedural safeguards is likely to offset any effect the increased severity might have. Is this information helpful? If so, how?

2. Two especially distinguished federal judges have recently addressed themselves to the question of the enormous discretion entrusted to the judiciary with respect to sentencing. Both conclude that it is excessive given the absence of special training. Frankel, Criminal Sentences (1973) and United States v. Miller, 361 F.Supp. 825, 13 Cr.L.Rptr. 2504 (W.D.N.C. 1973) (Craven, J.). Judge Craven suggests that the probation officer is better qualified and that a panel of experts might be preferable. Judge Frankel's thoughtful book strongly attacks indeterminate sentences and proposes the creation of a permanent commission to study sentencing, corrections and parole; to formulate laws and rules to implement the insights gained from such studies; and to enact such laws and rules.

3.   What impact is an increase in the severity of sentences imposed likely to have upon sentences actually served?   Consider the following from U. S. Department of Justice, Federal Bureau of Prisons Statistical Report, Fiscal Years 1969 and 1970 p. 16 (undated):

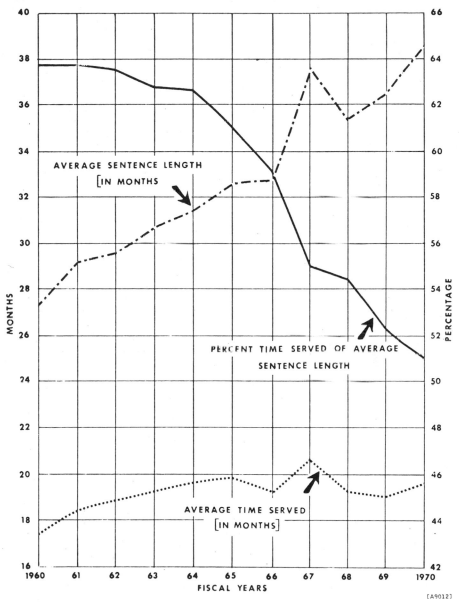

AVERAGE TIME SERVED AND AVERAGE SENTENCE LENGTH OF FIRST RELEASES FROM FEDERAL INSTITUTIONS

Fiscal Years 1960-1970 [Excludes Youth Corrections Act Releases]

How might this be explained?   If it is viewed as undesirable, how might it be changed?

4. Should the imposition of fines be treated differently than the imposition of other penalties? Consider the following provision of the New York Penal Law:

§ 80.00   Fine for felony

1. Criterion for fine. The court may impose a fine for a felony if the defendant has gained money or property through the commission of the crime.

2. Amount of fine. A sentence to pay a fine for a felony shall be a sentence to pay an amount, fixed by the court, not exceeding double the amount of the defendant's gain from the commission of the crime.

3. Determination of amount. As used in this section the term "gain" means the amount of money or the value of property derived from the commission of the crime, less the amount of money or the value of property returned to the victim of the crime or seized by or surrendered to lawful authority prior to the time sentence is imposed.

When the court imposes a fine for a felony the court shall make a finding as to the amount of the defendant's gain from the crime. If the record does not contain sufficient evidence to support such a finding the court may conduct a hearing upon the issue.

If this approach is proper when the offense is a felony, why should it not also be applied to the imposition of a fine for less serious offenses?

THE DEATH PENALTY AND THE EIGHTH AMENDMENT

In 1972, history was made when the Supreme Court by a vote of 5–4 held the death penalty as administered in the cases before it to be unconstitutional as in violation of the prohibition of "cruel and unusual punishments" found in the Eighth Amendment to the Constitution and applied to the states through the Fourteenth Amendment. Furman v. Georgia, 408 U.S. 238, 92 S.Ct. 2726, 33 L.Ed.2d 346. Inasmuch as there were nine separate opinions it is difficult to be certain as to the exact grounds on which the decision rested. One theme which was sounded in each of the opinions of the majority was the arbitrariness of the imposition of the penalty. Some were disturbed that the absence of guidelines by which the relative handful of those who committed capital crimes received a death sentence allowed for discrimination on the basis of wealth or race or sex. For some the infrequency of imposition gave rise to questions as to whether it could be justified for its alleged deterrent effect. Thus, whether a death penalty provision that carefully guides the discretion of the sentencing authority, or even a mandatory death penalty, would pass constitutional muster remains unclear.

In the wake of *Furman* many jurisdictions have adopted, and many others, including the United States, are considering the adoption of, new death penalty statutes which attempt to reduce discretion. In State v. Dixon, Fla., 283 So.2d 1, 13 Cr.L.Rptr. 2495 (1973), the Florida Supreme Court upheld such a new law because of its requirement for a separate punishment hearing; a decision by the judge after the jury's recommendation; specific findings by the judge to support imposition of the penalty; and legislatively drawn criteria of aggravation and mitigation. Compare People v. Fitzpatrick, 32 N.Y.2d 499, 300 N.E.2d 139 (1973) where the highest New York court struck down a death penalty provision despite its requirements for a special proceeding after a finding of guilt at which the death penalty was to be imposed if the jury unanimously agrees and the judge is satisfied that the victim was a peace officer in the course of performing his official duties.

Prior to *Furman* few penalties had been held by the Supreme Court to violate the "cruel and unusual punishment" clause, which was thought to speak largely to torture and unnecessary cruelty. There were only three exceptions. In Weems v. United States, 217 U.S. 349, 30 S.Ct. 544, 54 L.Ed. 793 (1910) the Court found the sentence of 12 years in chains at hard and painful labor for the falsification of an official record to be, as compared with punishments for more serious crimes, unnecessarily severe. In Trop v. Dulles, 356 U.S. 86, 78 S.Ct. 590, 2 L.Ed.2d 630 (1958), expatriation was held to violate the clause. Finally, in Robinson v. California, 370 U.S. 660, 82 S.Ct. 1417, 8 L.Ed.2d 758 (1962), imprisonment for being addicted to narcotics fell beneath the ban. When the issue shifts from the technique of punishment constitutional line drawing become most difficult. It has been common for courts to reject challenges to very long sentences of ordinary imprisonment by asserting that any such sentence that is within legislatively prescribed limits is not subject to judicial review under the Eighth Amendment or its equivalent in state constitutions. In re Lynch, 8 Cal.3d 410, 105 Cal.Rptr. 217, 503 P.2d 921 (1972)[d], represents a recent rejection of this view. There the court overturned a life sentence for a second conviction for indecent exposure on the grounds that the disproportion between the crime and the punishment—as measured by the nature of the offense, the punishments prescribed in California for other offenses, and by punishments prescribed elsewhere for this offense—was so great as to violate the state constitution.

d. The citation indicates that the opinion is by the Supreme Court of California—since it can be found in "Cal. 3d"—and that it can be found in three different law reporter series. For most state court decisions there will be only two reporting systems; one official and designated by an abbreviation of the state's name, the other, an "unofficial" regional reporter which includes the decisions of the higher courts of a number of states. In this case the regional reporter is "Pacific".

2. A PROPOSED CLASSIFICATION SCHEME

PROPOSED FEDERAL CRIMINAL CODE
(1971)

§ 3002. **Classification of Offenses**

(1) Felonies. Felonies are classified for the purpose of sentence into the following three categories:

(a) Class A felonies [including murder, kidnapping and forcible rape];

(b) Class B felonies [including manslaughter, arson, burglary of a dwelling at night, robbery with a deadly weapon, and theft of property exceeding $100,000 value]; and

(c) Class C felonies [including negligent homicide, aggravated assault, reckless endangerment of human life, burglaries not class B felonies, robberies not class B felonies, and theft of property exceeding $500 value but not exceeding $100,000 value].

*   *   *

§ 3102. **Incidents of Probation**

(1) Periods. Unless terminated as provided in subsection (2), the periods during which a sentence to probation shall remain conditional and be subject to revocation are:

(a) for a felony, 5 years;

(b) for a misdemeanor, 2 years;

(c) for an infraction, 1 year.

(2) Early Termination. The court may terminate a period of probation and discharge the defendant at any time earlier than that provided in subsection (1) if warranted by the conduct of the defendant and the ends of justice.

§ 3201. **Sentence of Imprisonment: Incidents**

(1) Authorized Terms. The authorized terms of imprisonment are:

(a) for a Class A felony, no more than 30 years;

(b) for a Class B felony, no more than 15 years;

(c) for a Class C felony, no more than 7 years;

(d) for a Class A misdemeanor, no more than 1 year [6 months];

(e) for a class B misdemeanor, no more than 30 days.

*   *   *

§ 3202.　Upper-Range Imprisonment for Dangerous Felons

(1) Authorization.　The maximum term for a felony shall not be set at more than 20 years for a Class A felony, 10 years for a Class B felony or 5 years for a Class C felony unless, having regard to the nature and circumstances of the offense and the history and character of the defendant as it relates to that offense, the court is of the opinion that a term in excess of these limits is required for the protection of the public from further criminal conduct by the defendant because the defendant is a dangerous special offender.

(2) Definitions.　A defendant is a dangerous special offender for purposes of this section if:

    (a) he has previously been convicted of two or more felonies committed on occasions different from one another and from such felony and for one or more of such convictions he has been imprisoned prior to the commission of such felony, and less than five years have elapsed between the commission of such felony and either his release, on parole or otherwise, from imprisonment for one such conviction or his commission of the last such previous felony;　or

    (b) he committed such felony as part of a pattern of criminal conduct which constituted a substantial source of his income, and in which he manifested special skill or expertise;　or

    (c) his mental condition is abnormal, and makes him a serious danger to the safety of others, and he committed such felony as an instance of aggressive behavior with heedless indifference to the consequences of such behavior.　An offender shall not be found to be a dangerous special offender under this paragraph unless the court has obtained a report from the Bureau of Corrections　*　*　*　which includes the results of a comprehensive psychiatric examination;

    (d) such felony was, or he committed such felony in furtherance of, a conspiracy with three or more other persons to engage in a pattern of criminal conduct and he did, or agreed that he would, initiate, organize, plan, finance, direct, manage, or supervise all or part of such conspiracy or conduct, or give or receive a bribe or use force as all or part of such conduct;　or

    (e) he manifested his special dangerousness by using a firearm or destructive device in the commission of the offense or flight therefrom.

*　　*　　*

II. THE CRIMINALIZATION DECISION

The decision whether or to what extent to use the criminal law to deal with a social problem (whether to "criminalize" some or all aspects of the problem) is obviously an extremely complex one. Considerations as to the existence, definition, and seriousness of the social problem, the effectiveness of criminalization as a means of eliminating or minimizing the problem, alternative means of dealing with the social problem and their effectiveness, and potential adverse effects ("costs") of criminalization must all be considered. Professor Packer has defined the problem as follows:

> What are the criteria that ought to guide the exercise of * * * judgment regarding the appropriate occasions for invoking the criminal sanction? How are we to decide what kinds of conduct should be made criminal?
>
> *   *   *
>
> In a sense, all limiting criteria reduce themselves to a simple prescription: first things first. The criminal sanction is the law's ultimate threat. Being punished for a crime is different from being regulated in the public interest, or being forced to compensate another who has been injured by one's conduct, or being treated for a disease. The sanction is at once uniquely coercive and, in the broadest sense, uniquely expensive. It should be reserved for what really matters.
>
> Considerations of several kinds enter into a determination of what "things" should be considered "first." On the credit side of the ledger are the social gains that will accrue from the successful prevention or reduction of the conduct in question, discounted by the prospects of achieving success (however defined). On the debit side are the moral and practical costs reckoned in terms of values other than the prevention of antisocial conduct. Finally, there is the question of alternatives: what other means of social control are available to achieve the same ends? The question of alternatives is particularly crucial. If there are readily available alternatives that avoid or minimize the formidable battery of objections and obstacles we have been considering, they must be carefully weighed. If there are not, we must face, rather than reject out of hand, the alternative of doing nothing.
> * * *

H. Packer, The Limits of the Criminal Sanction 250 (1968).
Initially, of course, the problem is one of legislative decision-making.

28

But Robinson v. California and Powell v. Texas raise the question of whether a similar analysis can—or should—be avoided when the legislative decision to criminalize is attacked in the courts on constitutional grounds.

It is generally difficult to discuss such matters in the abstract. Therefore, the following material presents, in addition to general considerations, selections discussing in some detail one of the many current social problems raising issues concerning the propriety of criminalization: alcohol intoxication or intoxication-related activity.

A. CRIMINALIZATION OF INTOXICATION

1. THE SOCIAL PROBLEM OF ALCOHOL ABUSE

BLUM AND BRAUNSTEIN, MIND–ALTERING DRUGS AND DANGEROUS BEHAVIOR, IN THE PRESIDENT'S COMMISSION ON LAW ENFORCEMENT AND ADMINISTRATION OF JUSTICE, TASK FORCE REPORT: DRUNKENNESS

29, at 29–30 (1967).

In the case of alcohol use, unlike the situation with other drugs, we are fortunate to have recently completed national survey data on drinking practices which allow excellent estimates of who drinks how much in the United States. * * * 68 percent of all American adults have had at least one drink within the past year. Twenty-two percent of the population report they have never tried an alcoholic beverage. With reference to alcoholism, * * * the number of Americans who are alcoholics probably ranges between 4,500,000 * * * and 6,800,000 escapist heavy drinkers * * *. The "actual" number of alcoholics may be less or greater than the foregoing range, depending on the definition of alcoholism employed and the estimation method.

*   *   *

Among the 12 percent of the total population classified as heavy drinkers, 6 percent were found to be escape-oriented heavy drinkers or problem drinkers. * * * These escapist drinkers were older, of lower socioeconomic status and included more than an expected number of Negroes. They were people not well integrated in society. They were also people who worried about their drinking, who said they had more than their share of problems, who had unhappy childhoods, who claimed poor health, and who were dissatisfied with their achievements in life.

NOTES

1. To what extent, if any, should the law be concerned with the physical health of some drinkers? with their public appearances in an intoxicated condition? with their "disorderly conduct?" with their general life style? To what extent, if any, are other factors proper subjects of concern? Consider the following from Blum and Braunstein, Mind-Altering Drugs and Dangerous Behavior, in The President's Commission on Law Enforcement and Administration of Justice, Task Force Report: Drunkenness 29, at 35–37, 39, 40–43 (1967):

SUICIDE AND ALCOHOL USE: SUMMARY

Alcoholics attempt and also complete suicide at a rate much higher than the nonalcoholic population. Drinking by nonalcoholics also appears to precede much suicidal behavior. Although alcoholism itself may not cause suicide—since the history and life circumstances of the drinker undoubtedly are necessary elements for a suicidal outcome—the presence of alcoholism is a strong warning of suicidal risk. * * *

Alcohol and Traffic Accidents

* * *

Estimates on the percentage of accidents caused by drinking drivers compared to nondrinking drivers vary considerably, the range being from 1 to 50 percent. Unfortunately, sufficient care is not exercised in many studies in separating cause from involvement. In any case, alcohol is only a conditional variable among a number of other possible causative factors. * * *

Results of investigations agree that there is an excess of drivers in accidents with levels of blood alcohol beginning at 0.04 to 0.05 percent as compared with now-accident controls. As alcohol level increases the percentage of such drivers included in accidents increases sharply. Smith and Popham state that drivers with 0.15 percent and over were present eight times more often in the accident than in the control group. On the basis of their findings, it was estimated that accident involvement with blood alcohol levels between 0.05 and 0.10 percent is 1½ times greater than below 0.05 percent and beyond 0.15 percent is approximately 10 times greater. * * *

What are the characteristics of the accident-involved "drinking and driving" population? Although popular belief has it that most alcoholic drivers are but social drinkers (normal, moderate, or heavy) the high levels of blood alcohol concentration present in the fatal car drivers and fatally injured pedestrians might lead one to wonder whether a sizable subgroup are not problem or pathological drinkers. From a statistical standpoint it is unlikely that most drinking drivers are alcoholics—only 1 out of every 14 to 20 citizens (+/−) is an alcoholic. Moreover some alcoholics rapidly become so drunk that they are unable to drive, or knowing themselves, take care not to drive. However, numerous studies analyzing the drinking patterns of accident-involved drivers reveal that a large proportion of them do have alcohol problems. * * *

* * * A study by the State of California Transportation Agency correlated the drunken drivers' alcohol level at the time of the fatal accident with their previous number of drunkenness arrests. The correlation was 0.92. That means that a drinking driver with high blood alcohol levels who kills someone nearly always (over 80 percent of the time) had prior drunk driving arrests. It is noteworthy that studies of the characteristics of problem drinkers involved in accidents show them as would be expected to be heavily drawn from the lower class. The chances are that this group is least likely to carry liability insurance and least able to pay indemnities to accident victims or their families. So it is that problem drinkers not only cause the most suffering and loss but are least likely to be able to make reparations. It would be useful to know what the actual insurance coverage of such drivers is. Such a study recommends itself.

49,000 deaths and 1,800,000 injuries [were caused] during 1965 in motor vehicle accidents. * * *

Alcohol and Crime

The basic question is, is alcohol related to crime? The basic answer is, "yes." When one gets away from the basic question and begins to seek an understanding of the many ways in which alcohol is implicated in criminality, the questions become more complex. * * *

Alcohol Implication by Type of Crime

In addition to the 55 percent of arrests that are for alcohol use offenses per se, a considerable number of other offenses are committed by persons—or suffered by victims—who have been drinking just prior to the commission of the offense. Some crimes show a high frequency of alcohol involvement; others a low one. Homicide for example is an alcohol-related crime; Cleveland in a Cincinnati study found that 44 percent of a sample of homicide victims had blood alcohol levels over 0.15 percent. Bullock in a Texas study found that 28.5 percent of a time sample of homicides took place in public places where liquor was served. Fisher in a Baltimore report states that 69 percent of homicide victims there had been drinking. Bowden and Wilson found 47 percent of homicide victims in Australia had been drinking. Shupe in an Ohio study found 43 percent of the homicide offenders had been drinking. Spain et al. found 87 percent of a small sample of homicide offenders had been drinking. The most comprehensive study of homicides is that by Wolfgang. Among 588 Philadelphia cases alcohol was *absent* from both victim and offender in only 36 percent of the cases. In 9 percent of the cases alcohol was present in the victim only; in 11 percent of the cases it was present in the offender only. In 44 percent of the cases it was present in *both* the victim and offender. Consequently in 64 percent of the homicide cases alcohol was a factor; and in the majority of these alcohol was present in both parties to the crime.

*   *   *

On the basis of the present data one can say that there is a strong link between alcohol and homicide and that the presumption is that alcohol plays a causal role as one of the necessary and precipitating elements for violence. Such a role is in keeping with the most probable effects of alcohol as a depressant of inhibition control centers in the brain—leading to release of impulses. One must keep in mind that even if alcohol is a necessary element for some murders, it is not necessary for all of them and further that alcohol use quite obviously does not necessarily lead to violence. An additional point is that alcohol use is likely to be but one element in a life pattern which increases the risk of being a homicide offender or victim (and it is sometimes chance which says which a person will turn out to be). For example, the Wolfgang study showed that 64 percent of the offenders and 47 percent of the victims had prior arrests. More important, the majority of these arrests were not for crimes against property (the predominant kind of nonalcohol use crime) but for crimes against person.

There is no study of other types of crime which compares with that of Wolfgang for careful and detailed analysis of persons and settings. Shupe examined blood and urine for alcohol in a group of 882 Columbus, Ohio, felons arrested either during or immediately after the offense. Presuming guilt, he found that alcohol was present more often in crimes of violence (e. g., 92 percent of the "cuttings" and concealed weapon arrests) and less often during more skilled offenses against property; e. g., 60 percent in forgery. The curious thing is that the 60 percent forgery figure is the lowest one. Two questions immediately arise. One is, given the criterion for inclusion in the study of immediate arrest during or after the offense, is it only inebriates who get caught right away? Perhaps "yes" since the majority of the alcohol blood levels of the arrested offenders were over 0.20. The second question is, what is the prevalence of alcohol in the blood for nonarrested persons in the same setting or with similar characteristics to the offenders? Quite possibly the arrests occurred among populations most of whom were accustomed to having some liquor inside them.

*   *   *

Criminal Histories of Alcoholics

*   *   *

Pittman and Gordon have done the most careful and detailed study of chronic offenders, in their case a sample of 187 chronic drunkenness offenders whose criminal careers were examined. All were imprisoned recidivists in New York State. The average frequency of arrest was 16.5 with the number of arrests increasingly progressing with age. Nearly one-quarter of all past arrests had been for other than drunkenness; these other crimes had not increased with age. The authors point out that inebriates who have as youths and young men been involved in theft, burglary, etc., change their conduct and show more intoxication offenses as they get older, age 35 to 40 being the critical period. The past histories of the inebriates showed gambling and homicide to be the least frequent but present other type of crimes; with increasing percentages of men involved in burglary (12 percent), larceny (23 percent), disorderly conduct (22 percent), and vagrancy (35 percent). One-third of the sample had been arrested only for alcohol use offenses. Thirty-seven percent had serious arrest records; many of their crimes being committed under the influence of alcohol. Pittman and Gordon remind us that many of their fellow inebriates had not committed such crimes. They suggest a "career" pattern, that many men who become drunkenness offenders started out with purer criminal interests but that they failed as criminals and drifted into alcoholism as an adjustment to criminal career failure. The authors find that the criminal career of the drunkenness offender is divided into two phases; under age 40 it is filled with many arrests unrelated to alcohol; afterwards their offenses are for alcohol use. (The authors are aware that arrest records are but a dim reflection of actual offenses.) Categorizing their men into three groups, approximately one-third with no crimes other than alcohol use, one-third with minor crimes, and one-third with serious crimes, they compared them on background characteristics and found no differences. Their proposal that criminal failures become alcoholics, gravitating to skid row, is limited to the special subgroup of one-third who started their offending career with property acquisition ambitions rather than alcohol interests per se.

*   *   *

The weight of argument on alcohol leading to crime rarely considers alcohol as an inhibitor of crime, yet alcohol does suppress function as well as release inhibition. As a sedative or tranquilizer ("perhaps the best tranquilizer," said Leake and Silverman) it must account for the reduction of action too, some of that action criminal.   *   *   *

On the basis of available information it is plausible to assume that alcohol does play an important and damaging role in the lives of offenders, particularly chronic inebriates and in the production of crime. Yet one cannot be sure on the basis of the work done to date that the alcohol use of offenders exceeds that of nonoffenders with similar social and personal characteristics (if any such match is possible). One cannot be sure that the alcohol use of offenders is any greater at the moments of their offense than during their ordinary noncriminal moments. One cannot be sure that the alcohol-using offenders would not have committed some offense had they not been drinking. One is not sure that the alcohol use of offenders differs from that of the other persons possibly present in the same or like situations which inspired or provoked the criminality of one and not the other. Finally, and this is an important point in view of the fact that all studies have been done on apprehended offenders, one does not know that the relationship now shown between alcohol use and crime is not in fact a relationship between being caught and being a drinker rather than in being a criminal and being a drinker. Given the foregoing questions and given the likelihood that people who do use alcohol to excess—and who explode into violence or sneak into thievery in the process—also have other characteristics which mark them as ones who disregard the welfare of their fellow men (and are equally unable to secure their own well-being), a prudent student of conduct will not hasten to label alcohol a cause and crime a result when it is equally likely that both alcohol excesses and crimes are "results."

2. H. Silving, Essays on Mental Incapacity and Criminal Conduct 251–53 (1967):

No doubt, since alcohol tends to reduce inhibitions, it "contributes" to this extent to crime. As reported by Henderson and Gillespie,[83] more than half of the 9028 persons proceeded against in Glasgow for Breach of the Peace (including Petty Assault) were found to be under the influence of intoxicating liquor at the time of the offense. The same writers point out that while few reliable figures are available to show how much alcohol contributes to other offenses or crimes, "authorities agree that it is an important factor in the genesis particularly of sexual and aggressive crimes (including suicide and murder.)" On the other hand, Banay concluded from results of his investigation of 3135 Sing Sing prisoners that, contrary to common belief, the contribution of alcoholism to crime is not very substantial and that it is greater in the minor than in the major crimes.[84] More significant than mere statistics of the apparent relationship between alcohol and criminality is new insight into the meaning of "contribution." Banay contends that the mere quantitative relationship between alcohol and criminality, even assuming it to be substantial, would not by itself afford a proof that alcohol is the source of a person's dangerousness. Such proof would rather require establishment of a causal nexus between these two phenomena. As regards the causal prob-

83. Henderson & Gillespie, A Textbook of Psychiatry 58–59 (8th ed., Oxford University Press, London 1956).

84. Banay, Alcohol and Aggression, in Alcohol, Science and Society, [Quarterly Journal of Studies on Alcohol [1945]] 143, at 147–149. In this study the incidence of inebriety was shown to be 25 per cent, whereas it was formerly estimated to be 60 per cent. The leading offense in this group of 3,135 prisoners, was among the inebriates, assault, while in the control group this crime took only fifth place. Of the acquisitive crimes, burglary was more common among the inebriate prisoners and grand larceny was more common among the noninebriate ones. The most aggressive of all crimes, homicide, constituted 9 per cent of the crimes committed by the inebriate group and 8 per cent by the noninebriate ones. Of the crimes most prominently associated in the public mind with habitual inebriety and acute intoxication, sex crimes, 7.5 per cent of the inebriates were committed to prison because of such crimes, while the ratio among the noninebriates was 5 per cent, so that the contribution of alcohol to this crime category was apparently substantiated. But, as the investigator remarked, criminal inebriates are generally known to be arrested more often for exhibitionism rather than for rape, while in noninebriate criminals the reverse is true.

lem, "[t]here is now an increasing tendency to consider that both alcohol and criminalism are caused by similar social and psychological factors" and that "[m]ore frequently is the relation of alcohol to crime one of a common cause rather than of cause and effect." [85] It follows that elimination of the practice of drinking would at best afford but a relative reduction of the scope of crime at present connected with alcohol consumption. In individuals disposed toward criminal conduct who are also alcohol consumers it is reasonable to assume that other methods of reducing inhibitions would probably lead to the same criminal results.[86]

2. THE PRESENT APPROACH: PUBLIC INTOXICATION AS A CRIMINAL OFFENSE

THE PRESIDENT'S COMMISSION ON LAW ENFORCEMENT AND ADMINISTRATION OF JUSTICE, TASK FORCE REPORT: DRUNKENNESS

1–3 (1967).

The Existing System

DRUNKENNESS LAWS

Drunkenness is punishable under a variety of laws, generally describing the offense as being "drunk in a public place," often without providing a precise definition of drunkenness itself. Some laws include as a condition that the offender is "unable to care for his own safety."

In some jurisdictions there are no laws prohibiting drunkenness, but any drunkenness that causes a breach of the peace is punishable. In Georgia and Alabama, for example, drunkenness that is manifested by boisterous or indecent conduct, or loud and profane discourse, is a crime. Other jurisdictions apply disorderly conduct statutes to those who are drunk in public. In Chicago, for example, the police, having no drunkenness law to enforce, use a disorderly conduct statute to arrest nondisorderly inebriates. Some jurisdictions permit police to make public drunkenness arrests under both State laws and local ordinances.

The laws provide maximum jail sentences ranging from 5 days to 6 months; the most common maximum sentence is 30 days. In some

---

85. Noyes & Kolb, [Modern Clinical Psychiatry] 167, (6th ed., 1963). For this reason one should not attribute too much importance to statistics, and there is no need to engage in an inquiry into the statistical methodology followed by Banay.

86. On this see Jellinek, [Effects of Small Amounts of Alcohol on Psychological Functions, in Alcohol, Science and Society (Quarterly Journal of Studies on Alcohol [1945])] at 84–86, 91.

States an offender convicted of "habitual drunkenness" may be punished by a 2-year sentence of imprisonment.

THE OFFENDERS

The 2 million arrests for drunkenness each year involve both sporadic and regular drinkers. Among the number are a wide variety of offenders—the rowdy college boy; the weekend inebriate; the homeless, often unemployed single man. How many offenders fall into these and other categories is not known. Neither is it known how many of the offenders are alcoholics in the medical sense of being dependent on alcohol. There is strong evidence, however, that a large number of those who are arrested have a lengthy history of prior drunkenness arrests, and that a disproportionate number involve poor persons who live in slums. In 1964 in the city of Los Angeles about one-fifth of all persons arrested for drunkenness accounted for two-thirds of the total number of arrests for that offense. Some of the repeaters were arrested as many as 18 times in that year.[8]

*   *   *

OPERATION OF THE CRIMINAL SYSTEM AFTER ARREST

Following arrest, the drunk is usually placed in a barren cell called a "tank," where he is detained for at least a few hours. The tanks in some cities can hold as many as 200 people, while others hold only 1 or 2.   *   *   *

The chronic alcoholic offender generally suffers from a variety of ailments and is often in danger of serious medical complications,[18] but medical care is rarely provided in the tank; and it is difficult to detect or to diagnose serious illness since it often resembles intoxica-

8. Statistics gathered by the Los Angeles Police Dep't. During 1964 there were 71,494 drunkenness arrests— 47,401 of which involved 13,048 offenders. In 1955, 45,748 of the drunkenness arrests in Los Angeles involved 6,665 offenders. In 1961, 12,000 individuals accounted for approximately 30,000 of the 49,000 arrests in Atlanta, Ga. Dep't of Psychiatry, Emory Univ. School of Medicine, Alcohol Study Project 5 (unpublished 1963) [hereinafter cited as Emory Dep't of Psychiatry].

18. Univ. of Minn. & Minneapolis Housing and Redevelopment Authority. A General Report on the Problem of Relocating the Population of the Lower Loop Redevelopment Area 170 (unpublished 1958) ("health conditions in this area are catastrophically bad"). The report provided a detailed description of illnesses which exist in skid row areas and states that the "tuberculosis rate in the lower loop is 320 times as high as the rate for the rest of the city." Id. at 170. See also Dep't of Psychiatry, Temple Univ., School of Medicine. The Men of Skid Row, A Study of Philadelphia's Homeless Man Population 88 (unpublished 1960) (57% of the men reported one or more serious conditions). Bogue's study [Bogue, Skid Row in American Cities 222–23 (1963)] depicted the great need for medical care and observed that "among the heavy drinkers, alcoholism is complicated by chronic sickness in a substantial portion of cases."

tion. Occasionally, chronic offenders become ill during pretrial detention and die without having received adequate medical attention.[20]

If the offender can afford bail, he usually obtains release after he sobers up.[21] In many jurisdictions an offender is permitted to forfeit bail routinely by not appearing in court.[22] Thus, if the arrested person has the few dollars required, he can avoid prosecution;[23] if he has no money, as is usually the case, he must appear in court.

Drunkenness offenders are generally brought before a judge the morning after their arrest, sometimes appearing in groups of 15 or 20. Rarely are the normal procedural or due process safeguards applied to these cases. Usually defendants are processed through the court system with haste and either released or sentenced to several days or weeks in jail. In some cities only those offenders who request it are jailed. In others chronic offenders, who are likely to be alcoholics, are generally sent to jail.[27]

When a defendant serves a short sentence, he is fed, sheltered, and given access to available recreational facilities. In most institutions there is such a lack of facilities and financial resources that it is not possible to do more.

*　　*　　*

After serving a brief sentence, the chronic offender is released, more likely than not to return to his former haunts on skid row, with

20. Man, 52, Dies in Court Lockup, Washington Post, Sept. 5, 1965, p. A3; Man Detained as Drunk Dies From Pneumonia, id., Dec. 15, 1965, p. D21, cols. 1–2; Man, 63, Found Dead in Alexandria Jail Cell, id., Nov. 22, 1966, p. B4, cols. 1–2. In the Pres.'s Comm'n on Crime in the District of Columbia, Rep. 476 (1966), it was reported that "16 persons arrested for intoxication died while in police custody in 1964–1965."

21. Stationhouse bail permits the release of defendants pending a subsequent court appearance. See generally Freed & Wald, Bail in the United States (1964). Outright release—with no obligation to return to court—is sometimes permitted by the police. See LaFave, op. cit. supra note 16, at 440–42, for a variety of release systems ranging from outright police discretion to a payment to the city of $4.35. In Detroit the police have a "golden rule" procedure which resulted in 1965 in the release of 2,383 offenders out of a total of 8,715 drunkenness arrests. In Omaha, Neb., the majority of offenders are released after a few hours of detention. The Omaha system includes referral to community agencies following release, in appropriate cases. The police bring some offenders to the agencies where shelter and food are provided.

22. Bail or collateral forfeiture is common in some jurisdictions. The defendant pays $10 to $20, depending upon the stipulated amount in the jurisdiction, and he is not penalized for failing to return to court. See Pres.'s Comm'n on Crime in the District of Columbia, Rep. 477 (1966); Emory Dep't of Psychiatry 11.

23. In Washington, D.C., for example, approximately 20,000 of the 44,218 people arrested during 1965 obtained release by forfeiting $10 collateral. Pres.'s Comm'n on Crime in the District of Columbia, Rep. 475 (1966). In Atlanta, Ga., approximately 20,000 of 49,805 arrests during 1961 resulted in ($15) collateral forfeitures. Emory Dep't of Psychiatry 11. Those who post and forfeit collateral avoid the risk of a jail sentence.

27. See Pittman & Gordon, Revolving Door: A Study of the Chronic Police Case Inebriate 30, 125 (1958) * * *.

no money, no job, and no plans.   Often he is rearrested within a matter of days or hours.

————

The *Powell* case which follows must be read in light of Robinson v. California, 370 U.S. 660, 82 S.Ct. 1417, 8 L.Ed.2d 758, which had been decided six years earlier.   California had made it criminal to "be addicted to the use of narcotics".   Robinson had been convicted under this statute on the basis of evidence of needle marks on his arm and his alleged admission to the arresting officer of prior use. There was no direct evidence that he had possessed narcotics in California.

The Court held that although the state might properly criminalize manufacture, sale, purchase or possession of narcotics, or provide for compulsory treatment of addicts, it could not constitutionally punish the "status" of narcotic addiction.   The decision was predicated on the view that addiction is an illness and that the state could not, consistent with the constitutional prohibition against cruel and unusual punishment, punish one for being ill, e. g., mentally ill, a leper, or having a venereal disease.

————

POWELL v. TEXAS

Supreme Court of the United States, 1968.
392 U.S. 514, 88 S.Ct. 2145, 20 L.Ed.2d 1254.

Mr. Justice MARSHALL announced the judgment of the Court and delivered an opinion in which THE CHIEF JUSTICE, Mr. Justice BLACK, and Mr. Justice HARLAN join.

In late December 1966, appellant was arrested and charged with being found in a state of intoxication in a public place, in violation of Vernon's Ann.Texas Penal Code, Art. 477 (1952), which reads as follows:

"Whoever shall get drunk or be found in a state of intoxication in any public place, or at any private house except his own, shall be fined not exceeding one hundred dollars."

Appellant was tried in the Corporation Court of Austin, Texas, found guilty, and fined $20.   He appealed to the County Court at Law No. 1 of Travis County, Texas, where a trial *de novo* was held.   His counsel urged that appellant was "afflicted with the disease of chronic alcoholism," that "his appearance in public [while drunk was] * * * not of his own volition," and therefore that to punish him criminally for that conduct would be cruel and unusual, in violation of the Eighth and Fourteenth Amendments to the United States Constitution.

The trial judge in the county court, sitting without a jury, made certain findings of fact, * * * but ruled as a matter of law that chronic alcoholism was not a defense to the charge. He found appellant guilty, and fined him $50. There being no further right to appeal within the Texas judicial system, appellant appealed to this Court * * *.

I.

The principal testimony was that of Dr. David Wade, a Fellow of the American Medical Association, duly certificated in psychiatry. His testimony consumed a total of 17 pages in the trial transcript. Five of those pages were taken up with a recitation of Dr. Wade's qualifications. In the next 12 pages Dr. Wade was examined by appellant's counsel, cross-examined by the State, and re-examined by the defense, and those 12 pages contain virtually all the material developed at trial which is relevant to the constitutional issue we face here. Dr. Wade sketched the outlines of the "disease" concept of alcoholism; noted that there is no generally accepted definition of "alcoholism"; alluded to the ongoing debate within the medical profession over whether alcohol is actually physically "addicting" or merely psychologically "habituating"; and concluded that in either case a "chronic alcoholic" is an "involuntary drinker," who is "powerless not to drink," and who "loses his self-control over his drinking." He testified that he had examined appellant, and that appellant is a "chronic alcoholic," who "by the time he has reached [the state of intoxication] * * * is not able to control his behavior, and [who] * * * has reached this point because he has an uncontrollable compulsion to drink." Dr. Wade also responded in the negative to the question whether appellant has "the willpower to resist the constant excessive consumption of alcohol." He added that in his opinion jailing appellant without medical attention would operate neither to rehabilitate him nor to lessen his desire for alcohol.

On cross-examination, Dr. Wade admitted that when appellant was sober he knew the difference betwen right and wrong, and he responded affirmatively to the question whether appellant's act in taking the first drink in any given instance when he was sober was a "voluntary exercise of his will." Qualifying his answer, Dr. Wade stated that "these individuals have a compulsion, and this compulsion, while not completely overpowering, is a very strong influence, an exceedingly strong influence, and this compulsion coupled with the firm belief in their mind that they are going to be able to handle it from now on causes their judgment to be somewhat clouded."

Appellant testified concerning the history of his drinking problem. He reviewed his many arrests for drunkenness; testified that he was unable to stop drinking; stated that when he was intoxicated he had no control over his actions and could not remember them later, but that he did not become violent; and admitted that he did not remember his arrest on the occasion for which he was being tried. On cross-examination, appellant admitted that he had had one drink on the morning of the trial and had been able to discontinue drinking. On redirect examination, appellant's lawyer elicited the following:

> "Q.   Leroy, isn't the real reason why you just had one drink today because you just had enough money to buy one drink?

> "A.   Well, that was just give to me.

*   *   *

Evidence in the case then closed.   The State made no effort to obtain expert psychiatric testimony of its own, or even to explore with appellant's witness the question of appellant's power to control the frequency, timing, and location of his drinking bouts, or the substantial disagreement within the medical profession concerning the nature of the disease, the efficacy of treatment and the prerequisites for effective treatment.   It did nothing to examine or illuminate what Dr. Wade might have meant by his reference to a "compulsion" which was "not completely overpowering," but which was "an exceedingly strong influence," or to inquire into the question of the proper role of such a "compulsion" in constitutional adjudication.   Instead, the State contented itself with a brief argument that appellant had no defense to the charge because he "is legally sane and knows the difference between right and wrong."

Following this abbreviated exposition of the problem before it, the trial court indicated its intention to disallow appellant's claimed defense of "chronic alcoholism."   Thereupon defense counsel submitted, and the trial court entered, the following "findings of fact":

> "(1)   That chronic alcoholism is a disease which destroys the afflicted person's will power to resist the constant, excessive consumption of alcohol.

> "(2)   That a chronic alcoholic does not appear in public by his own volition but under a compulsion symptomatic of the disease of chronic alcoholism.

> "(3)   That Leroy Powell, defendant herein, is a chronic alcoholic who is afflicted with the disease of chronic alcoholism."

Whatever else may be said of them, those are not "findings of fact" in any recognizable, traditional sense in which that term has been used in a court of law; they are the premises of a syllogism transparently designed to bring this case within the scope of this Court's opinion in Robinson v. State of California, 370 U.S. 660, 82 S.Ct. 1417, 8 L.Ed.2d 758 (1962).   Nonetheless, the dissent would have us adopt these "findings" without critical examination; it would use them as the basis for a constitutional holding that "a person may not be punished if the condition essential to constitute the defined crime is part of the pattern of his disease and is occasioned by a compulsion symptomatic of the disease." * * *

The difficulty with that position, as we shall show, is that it goes much too far on the basis of too little knowledge. In the first place, the record in this case is utterly inadequate to permit the sort of informed and responsible adjudication which alone can support the announcement of an important and wide-ranging new constitutional principle. We know very little about the circumstances surrounding the drinking bout which resulted in this conviction, or about Leroy Powell's drinking problem, or indeed about alcoholism itself. The trial hardly reflects the sharp legal and evidentiary clash between fully prepared adversary litigants which is traditionally expected in major constitutional cases. The State put on only one witness, the arresting officer. The defense put on three—a policeman who testified to appellant's long history of arrests for public drunkenness, the psychiatrist, and appellant himself.

Furthermore, the inescapable fact is that there is no agreement among members of the medical profession about what it means to say that "alcoholism" is a "disease." One of the principal works in this field states that the major difficulty in articulating a "disease concept of alcoholism" is that "alcoholism has too many definitions and disease has practically none." [2] This same author concludes that "*a disease is what the medical profession recognizes as such.*" In other words, there is widespread agreement today that "alcoholism" is a "disease," for the simple reason that the medical profession has concluded that it should attempt to treat those who have drinking problems. There the agreement stops. Debate rages within the medical profession as to whether "alcoholism" is a separate "disease" in any meaningful biochemical, physiological or psychological sense, or whether it represents one peculiar manifestation in some individuals of underlying psychiatric disorders.

Nor is there any substantial consensus as to the "manifestations of alcoholism." E. M. Jellinek, one of the outstanding authorities on the subject, identifies five different types of alcoholics which predominate in the United States, and these types display a broad range of different and occasionally inconsistent symptoms. * * *

The trial court's "finding" that Powell "is afflicted with the disease of chronic alcoholism," which "destroys the afflicted person's will power to resist the constant, excessive consumption of alcohol" covers a multitude of sins. Dr. Wade's testimony that appellant suffered from a compulsion which was an "exceedingly strong influence,"

2. E. Jellinek, The Disease Concept of
Alcoholism 11 (1960).

but which was "not completely overpowering" is at least more carefully stated, if no less mystifying. Jellinek insists that conceptual clarity can only be achieved by distinguishing carefully between "loss of control" once an individual has commenced to drink and "inability to abstain" from drinking in the first place. Presumably a person would have to display both characteristics in order to make out a constitutional defense, should one be recognized. Yet the "findings" of the trial court utterly fail to make this crucial distinction, and there is serious question whether the record can be read to support a finding of either loss of control or inability to abstain.

Dr. Wade did testify that once appellant began drinking he appeared to have no control over the amount of alcohol he finally ingested. Appellant's own testimony concerning his drinking on the day of the trial would certainly appear, however, to cast doubt upon the conclusion that he was without control over his consumption of alcohol when he had sufficiently important reasons to exercise such control. However that may be, there are more serious factual and conceptual difficulties with reading this record to show that appellant was unable to abstain from drinking. Dr. Wade testified that when appellant was sober, the act of taking the first drink was a "voluntary exercise of his will," but that this exercise of will was undertaken under the "exceedingly strong influence" of a "compulsion" which was "not completely overpowering." Such concepts, when juxtaposed in this fashion, have little meaning.

Moreover, Jellinek asserts that it cannot accurately be said that a person is truly unable to abstain from drinking unless he is suffering the physical symptoms of withdrawal. There is no testimony in this record that Leroy Powell underwent withdrawal symptoms either before he began the drinking spree which resulted in the conviction under review here, or at any other time.   *   *   *

It is one thing to say that if a man is deprived of alcohol his hands will begin to shake, he will suffer agonizing pains and ultimately he will have hallucinations; it is quite another to say that a man has a "compulsion" to take a drink, but that he also retains a certain amount of "free will" with which to resist. It is simply impossible, in the present state of our knowledge, to ascribe a useful meaning to the latter statement. This definitional confusion reflects, of course, not merely the undeveloped state of the psychiatric art but also the conceptual difficulties inevitably attendant upon the importation of scientific and medical models into a legal system generally predicated upon a different set of assumptions.

II.

Despite the comparatively primitive state of our knowledge on the subject, it cannot be denied that the destructive use of alcoholic beverages is one of our principal social and public health problems.

The lowest current informed estimate places the number of "alcoholics" in America (definitional problems aside) at 4,000,000, and most authorities are inclined to put the figure considerably higher. The problem is compounded by the fact that a very large percentage of the alcoholics in this country are "invisible"—they possess the means to keep their drinking problems secret, and the traditionally uncharitable attitude of our society toward alcoholics causes many of them to refrain from seeking treatment from any source. Nor can it be gainsaid that the legislative response to this enormous problem has in general been inadequate.

There is as yet no known generally effective method for treating the vast number of alcoholics in our society. Some individual alcoholics have responded to particular forms of therapy with remissions of their symptomatic dependence upon the drug. But just as there is no agreement among doctors and social workers with respect to the causes of alcoholism, there is no consensus as to why particular treatments have been effective in particular cases and there is no generally agreed-upon approach to the problem of treatment on a large scale. Most psychiatrists are apparently of the opinion that alcoholism is far more difficult to treat than other forms of behavioral disorders, and some believe it is impossible to cure by means of psychotherapy; indeed, the medical profession as a whole, and psychiatrists in particular, have been severely criticised for the prevailing reluctance to undertake the treatment of drinking problems. Thus it is entirely possible that, even were the manpower and facilities available for a full-scale attack upon chronic alcoholism, we would find ourselves unable to help the vast bulk of our "visible"—let alone our "invisible" —alcoholic population.

However, facilities for the attempted treatment of indigent alcoholics are woefully lacking throughout the country. It would be tragic to return large numbers of helpless, sometimes dangerous and frequently unsanitary inebriates to the streets of our cities without even the opportunity to sober up adequately which a brief jail term provides. Presumably no State or city will tolerate such a state of affairs. Yet the medical profession cannot, and does not, tell us with any assurance that, even if the buildings, equipment and trained personnel were made available, it could provide anything more than slightly higher-class jails for our indigent habitual inebriates. Thus we run the grave risk that nothing will be acomplished beyond the hanging of a new sign—reading "hospital"—over one wing of the jailhouse.

One virtue of the criminal process is, at least, that the duration of penal incarceration typically has some outside statutory limit; this is universally true in the case of petty offenses, such as public drunkenness, where jail terms are quite short on the whole. "Therapeutic civil commitment" lacks this feature; one is typically committed until one is "cured." Thus, to do otherwise than affirm might subject indigent alcoholics to the risk that they may be locked up for an indefinite period of time under the same conditions as before, with no more hope than before of receiving effective treatment and no prospect of periodic "freedom."

Faced with this unpleasant reality, we are unable to assert that the use of the criminal process as a means of dealing with the public aspects of problem drinking can never be defended as rational. The picture of the penniless drunk propelled aimlessly and endlessly through the law's "revolving door" of arrest, incarceration, release and re-arrest is not a pretty one. But before we condemn the present practice across-the-board, perhaps we ought to be able to point to some clear promise of a better world for these unfortunate people. Unfortunately, no such promise has yet been forthcoming. If, in addition to the absence of a coherent approach to the problem of treatment, we consider the almost complete absence of facilities and manpower for the implementation of a rehabilitation program, it is difficult to say in the present context that the criminal process is utterly lacking in social value. This Court has never held that anything in the Constitution requires that penal sanctions be designed solely to achieve therapeutic or rehabilitative effects, and it can hardly be said with assurance that incarceration serves such purposes any better for the general run of criminals than it does for public drunks.

Ignorance likewise impedes our assessment of the deterrent effect of criminal sanctions for public drunkenness. The fact that a high percentage of American alcoholics conceal their drinking problems, not merely by avoiding public displays of intoxication but also by shunning all forms of treatment, is indicative that some powerful deterrent operates to inhibit the public revelation of the existence of alcoholism. Quite probably this deterrent effect can be largely attributed to the harsh moral attitude which our society has traditionally taken toward intoxication and the shame which we have associated with alcoholism. Criminal conviction represents the degrading public revelation of what Anglo-American society has long condemned as a moral defect, and the existence of criminal sanctions may serve to reinforce this cultural taboo, just as we presume it serves to reinforce other, stronger feelings against murder, rape, theft, and other forms of antisocial conduct.

Obviously, chronic alcoholics have not been deterred from drinking to excess by the existence of criminal sanctions against public drunkenness. But all those who violate penal laws of any kind are by definition undeterred. The long-standing and still raging debate over the validity of the deterrence justification for penal sanctions has not reached any sufficiently clear conclusions to permit it to be said that such sanctions are ineffective in any particular context or for any particular group of people who are able to appreciate the consequences of their acts.   *   *   *

III.

*   *   *

Appellant, however, seeks to come within the application of the Cruel and Unusual Punishment Clause announced in Robinson v. State of California, 370 U.S. 660, 82 S.Ct. 1417, 8 L.Ed.2d 758 (1962), which involved a state statute making it a crime to "be addicted to the use of narcotics." This Court held there that "a state law which imprisons a person thus afflicted [with narcotic addiction] as a criminal, even though he has never touched any narcotic drug within the State or been guilty of any irregular behavior there, inflicts a cruel and unusual punishment   *   *   *." Id., at 667, 82 S.Ct., at 1420–1421.

On its face the present case does not fall within that holding, since appellant was convicted, not for being a chronic alcoholic, but for being in public while drunk on a particular occasion. The State of Texas thus has not sought to punish a mere status, as California did in Robinson; nor has it attempted to regulate appellant's behavior in the privacy of his own home. Rather, it has imposed upon appellant a criminal sanction for public behavior which may create substantial health and safety hazards, both for appellant and for members of the general public, and which offends the moral and esthetic sensibilities of a large segment of the community. This seems a far cry from convicting one for being an addict, being a chronic alcoholic, being "mentally ill, or a leper   *   *   *." Id., at 666, 82 S.Ct., at 1420.

Robinson so viewed brings this Court but a very small way into the substantive criminal law. And unless Robinson is so viewed it is difficult to see any limiting principle that would serve to prevent this Court from becoming, under the aegis of the Cruel and Unusual Punishment Clause, the ultimate arbiter of the standards of criminal responsibility, in diverse areas of the criminal law, throughout the country.

It is suggested in dissent that Robinson stands for the "simple" but "subtle" principle that "[c]riminal penalties may not be inflicted upon a person for being in a condition he is powerless to change." Post, at 2171. In that view, appellant's "condition" of public intoxication was "occasioned by a compulsion symptomatic of the disease" of chronic alcoholism, and thus, apparently, his behavior lacked the critical element of mens rea. Whatever may be the merits of such a doctrine of criminal responsibility, it surely cannot be said to follow from Robinson. The entire thrust of Robinson's interpretation of the Cruel and Unusual Punishment Clause is that criminal penalties may be inflicted only if the accused has committed some act, has engaged in some behavior, which society has an interest in preventing, or perhaps in historical common law terms, has committed some *actus reus*. It thus does not deal with the question of whether certain conduct cannot constitutionally be punished because it is, in some sense, "involuntary" or "occasioned by a compulsion."

Likewise, as the dissent acknowledges, there is a substantial definitional distinction between a "status," as in *Robinson*, and a "condition," which is said to be involved in this case. Whatever may be the merits of an attempt to disinguish between behavior and a condition, it is perfectly clear that the crucial element in this case, so far as the dissent is concerned, is whether or not appellant can legally be held responsible for his appearance in public in a state of intoxication. The only relevance of *Robinson* to this issue is that because the Court interpreted the statute there involved as making a "status" criminal, it was able to suggest that the statute would cover even a situation in which addiction had been acquired involuntarily. 370 U.S., at 667, n. 9, 82 S.Ct., at 1420. That this factor was not determinative in the case is shown by the fact that there was no indication of how Robinson himself had become an addict.

Ultimately, then, the most troubling aspects of this case, were *Robinson* to be extended to meet it, would be the scope and content of what could only be a constitutional doctrine of criminal responsibility. In dissent it is urged that the decision could be limited to conduct which is "a characteristic and involuntary part of the pattern of the disease as it afflicts" the particular individual, and that "[i]t is not foreseeable" that it would be applied "in the case of offenses such as driving a car while intoxicated, assault, theft, or robbery." Post, at 2167, n. 2. That is limitation by fiat. In the first place, nothing in the logic of the dissent would limit its application to chronic alcoholics. If Leroy Powell cannot be convicted of public intoxication, it is difficult to see how a State can convict an individual for murder, if that individual, while exhibiting normal behavior in all other respects, suffers from a "compulsion" to kill, which is an "exceedingly strong influence," but "not completely overpowering." Even if we limit our consideration to chronic alcoholics, it would seem impossible to confine the principle within the arbitrary bounds which the dissent seems to envision.

It is not difficult to imagine a case involving psychiatric testimony to the effect that an individual suffers from some aggressive neurosis which he is able to control when sober; that very little alcohol suffices to remove the inhibitions which normally contain these aggressions, with the result that the individual engages in assaultive behavior without becoming actually intoxicated; and that the individual suffers from a very strong desire to drink, which is an "exceedingly strong influence" but "not completely overpowering." Without being untrue to the rationale of this case, should the principles advanced in dissent be accepted here, the Court could not avoid holding such an individual constitutionally unaccountable for his assaultive behavior.

Traditional common-law concepts of personal accountability and essential considerations of federalism lead us to disagree with appellant. We are unable to conclude, on the state of this record or on the current state of medical knowledge, that chronic alcoholics in general, and Leroy Powell in particular, suffer from such an irresistible compulsion to drink and to get drunk in public that they are utterly unable to control their performance of either or both of these acts and thus cannot be deterred at all from public intoxication. And in any event this Court has never articulated a general constitutional doctrine of *mens rea.*

We cannot cast aside the centuries-long evolution of the collection of interlocking and overlapping concepts which the common law has utilized to assess the moral accountability of an individual for his antisocial deeds. The doctrines of *actus reus, mens rea,* insanity, mistake, justification, and duress have historically provided the tools for a constantly shifting adjustment of the tension between the evolving aims of the criminal law and changing religious, moral, philosophical, and medical views of the nature of man. This process of adjustment has always been thought to be the province of the States.

Nothing could be less fruitful than for this Court to be impelled into defining some sort of insanity test in constitutional terms. Yet, that task would seem to follow inexorably from an extension of *Robinson* to this case. If a person in the "condition" of being a chronic alcoholic cannot be criminally punished as a constitutional matter for being drunk in public, it would seem to follow that a person who contends that, in terms of one test, "his unlawful act was the product of mental disease or mental defect," Durham v. United States, 94 U.S.App.D.C. 228, 241, 214 F.2d 862, 875, 45 A.L.R.2d 1430 (1954), would state an issue of constitutional dimension with regard to his criminal responsibility had he been tried under some different and perhaps lesser standard, e. g., the right-wrong test of *M'Naghten's Case.* The experimentation of one jurisdiction in that field alone indicates the magnitude of the problem. * * * But formulating a constitutional rule would reduce, if not eliminate, that fruitful experimentation, and freeze the developing productive dialogue between law and psychiatry into a rigid constitutional mold. It is simply not yet the time to write the Constitutional formulas cast in terms whose meaning, let alone relevance, is not yet clear either to doctors or to lawyers.

Affirmed.

Mr. Justice BLACK, whom Mr. Justice HARLAN joins, concurring. [a portion of this opinion is reprinted at page 115 infra.]

* * *

Mr. Justice WHITE, concurring in the result.

If it cannot be a crime to have an irresistible compulsion to use narcotics, Robinson v. State of California, 370 U.S. 660, 82 S.Ct. 1417, 8 L.Ed.2d 758, rehearing denied, 371 U.S. 905, 83 S.Ct. 202, 9 L.Ed.2d 166 (1962), I do not see how it can constitutionally be a crime to yield to such a compulsion. Punishing an addict for using drugs convicts for addiction under a different name. Distinguishing between the two crimes is like forbidding criminal conviction for being sick with flu or epilepsy but permitting punishment for running a fever or having a convulsion. Unless *Robinson* is to be abandoned, the use of narcotics by an addict must be beyond the reach of the criminal law. Similarly, the chronic alcoholic with an irresistible urge to consume alcohol should not be punishable for drinking or for being drunk.

Powell's conviction was for the different crime of being drunk in a public place. Thus even if Powell was compelled to drink, and so could not constitutionally be convicted for drinking, his conviction in this case can be invalidated only if there is a constitutional basis for saying that he may not be punished for being in public while drunk. The statute involved here, which aims at keeping drunks off the street for their own welfare and that of others, is not challenged on the ground that it interferes unconstitutionally with the right to frequent public places. No question is raised about applying this statute to the nonchronic drunk, who has no compulsion to drink, who need not drink to excess, and who could have arranged to do his drinking in private or, if he began drinking in public, could have removed himself at an appropriate point on the path toward complete inebriation.

The trial court said that Powell was a chronic alcoholic with a compulsion not only to drink to excess but also to frequent public places when intoxicated. Nothing in the record before the trial court supports the latter conclusion, which is contrary to common sense and to common knowledge.[1] The sober chronic alcoholic has no compulsion to be on the public streets; many chronic alcoholics drink at home and are never seen drunk in public. Before and after taking the first drink, and until he becomes so drunk that he loses the power to know where he is or to direct his movements, the chronic alcoholic with a home or financial resources is as capable as the nonchronic drinker of doing his drinking in private, of removing himself from public places and, since he knows or ought to know that he will become intoxicated, of making plans to avoid his being found drunk in public. For these reasons, I cannot say that the chronic alcoholic

---

1. The trial court gave no reasons for its conclusion that Powell appeared in public due to "a compulsion symptomatic of the disease of chronic alcoholism." No facts in the record support that conclusion. The trial transcript strongly suggests that the trial judge merely adopted proposed findings put before him by Powell's counsel. The fact that those findings were of no legal relevance in the trial judge's view of the case is very significant for appraising the extent to which they represented a well-considered and well-supported judgment. For all these reasons I do not feel impelled to accept this finding, and certainly would not rest a constitutional adjudication upon it.

who proves his disease and a compulsion to drink is shielded from conviction when he has knowingly failed to take feasible precautions against committing a criminal act, here the act of going to or remaining in a public place. On such facts the alcoholic is like a person with smallpox, who could be convicted for being on the street but not for being ill, or, like the epileptic, who would be punished for driving a car but not for his disease.[2]

The fact remains that some chronic alcoholics must drink and hence must drink *somewhere*. Although many chronics have homes, many others do not. For all practical purposes the public streets may be home for these unfortunates, not because their disease compels them to be there, but because, drunk or sober, they have no place else to go and no place else to be when they are drinking. This is more a function of economic station than of disease, although the disease may lead to destitution and perpetuate that condition. For some of these alcoholics I would think a showing could be made that resisting drunkenness is impossible and that avoiding public places when intoxicated is also impossible. As applied to them this statute is in effect a law which bans a single act for which they may not be convicted under the Eighth Amendment—the act of getting drunk.

It is also possible that the chronic alcoholic who begins drinking in private at some point becomes so drunk that he loses the power to control his movements and for that reason appears in public. The Eighth Amendment might also forbid conviction in such circumstances, but only on a record satisfactorily showing that it was not feasible for him to have made arrangements to prevent his being in public when drunk and that his extreme drunkenness sufficiently deprived him of his faculties on the occasion in issue.

2. Analysis of this difficult case is not advanced by preoccupation with the label "condition." In *Robinson* the Court dealt with "a statute which makes the 'status' of narcotic addiction a criminal offense * * *." 370 U.S., at 666, 82 S.Ct., at 1420. By precluding criminal conviction for such a "status" the Court was dealing with a condition brought about by acts remote in time from the application of the criminal sanctions contemplated, a condition which was relatively permanent in duration, and a condition of great magnitude and significance in terms of human behavior and values. Although the same may be said for the "condition" of being a chronic alcoholic, it cannot be said for the mere transitory state of "being drunk in public." "Being" drunk in public is not far removed in time from the acts of "getting" drunk and "going" into public, and it is not necessarily a state of any great duration. And, an isolated instance of "being" drunk in public is of relatively slight importance in the life of an individual as compared with the condition of being a chronic alcoholic. If it were necessary to distinguish between "acts" and "conditions" for purposes of the Eighth Amendment, I would adhere to the concept of "condition" implicit in the opinion in *Robinson*; I would not trivialize that concept by drawing a nonexistent line between the man who appears in public drunk and that same man five minutes later who is then "being" drunk in public. The proper subject of inquiry is whether volitional acts brought about the "condition" and whether those acts are sufficiently proximate to the "condition" for it to be permissible to impose penal sanctions on the "condition."

These prerequisites to the possible invocation of the Eighth Amendment are not satisfied on the record before us.[4] Whether or not Powell established that he could not have resisted becoming drunk on December 19, 1966, nothing in the record indicates that he could not have done his drinking in private or that he was so inebriated at the time that he had lost control of his movements and wandered into the public street. Indeed, the evidence in the record strongly suggests that Powell could have drunk at home and made plans while sober to prevent ending up in a public place. Powell had a home and wife, and if there were reasons why he had to drink in public or be drunk there, they do not appear in the record.

* * *

It is unnecessary to pursue at this point the further definition of the circumstances or the state of intoxication which might bar conviction of a chronic alcoholic for being drunk in a public place. For the purposes of this case, it is necessary to say only that Powell showed nothing more than that he was to some degree compelled to drink and that he was drunk at the time of his arrest. He made no showing that he was unable to stay off the streets on the night in question.[5]

4. A holding that a person establishing the requisite facts could not, because of the Eighth Amendment, be criminally punished for appearing in public while drunk would be a novel construction of that Amendment, but it would hardly have radical consequences. In the first place when as here the crime charged was being drunk in a public place, only the compulsive chronic alcoholic would have a defense to both elements of the crime —for his drunkenness because his disease compelled him to drink and for being in a public place because the force of circumstances or excessive intoxication sufficiently deprived him of his mental and physical powers. The drinker who was not compelled to drink, on the other hand, although he might be as poorly circumstanced, equally intoxicated, and equally without his physical powers and cognitive faculties, could have avoided drinking in the first place, could have avoided drinking to excess, and need not have lost the power to manage his movements. Perhaps the heavily intoxicated, compulsive alcoholic who could not have arranged to avoid being in public places may not, consistent with the Eighth Amendment, be convicted for being drunk in a public place. However, it does not necessarily follow that it would be unconstitutional to convict him for committing crimes involving much greater risk to society.

Outside the area of alcoholism such a holding would not have a wide impact. Concerning drugs, such a construction of the Eighth Amendment would bar conviction only where the drug is addictive and then only for acts which are a necessary part of addiction, such as simple use. Beyond that it would preclude punishment only when the addiction to or the use of drugs caused sufficient loss of physical and mental faculties. This doctrine would not bar conviction of a heroin addict for being under the influence of heroin in a public place (although other constitutional concepts might be relevant to such a conviction), or for committing other criminal acts.

5. I do not question the power of the State to remove a helplessly intoxicated person from a public street, although against his will, and to hold him until he has regained his powers. The person's own safety and the public interest require this much. A statute such as the one challenged in this case is constitutional insofar as it authorizes a police officer to arrest any seriously intoxicated person when he is encountered in a public place. Whether such a person may be charged and convicted for violating the statute will depend upon whether he is entitled to the protection of the Eighth Amendment.

Because Powell did not show that his conviction offended the Constitution, I concur in the judgment affirming the Travis County court.

Mr. Justice FORTAS, with whom Mr. Justice DOUGLAS, Mr. Justice BRENNAN, and Mr. Justice STEWART join, dissenting.

*   *   *

I.

The issue posed in this case is a narrow one. There is no challenge here to the validity of public intoxication statutes in general or to the Texas public intoxication statute in particular. This case does not concern the infliction of punishment upon the "social" drinker—or upon anyone other than a "chronic alcoholic" who, as the trier of fact here found, cannot "resist the constant, excessive consumption of alcohol." Nor does it relate to any offense other than the crime of public intoxication.

The sole question presented is whether a criminal penalty may be imposed upon a person suffering the disease of "chronic alcoholism" for a condition—being "in a state of intoxication" in public—which is a characteristic part of the pattern of his disease and which, the trial court found, was not the consequence of appellant's volition but of "a compulsion symptomatic of the disease of chronic alcoholism." We must consider whether the Eighth Amendment, made applicable to the States through the Fourteenth Amendment, prohibits the imposition of this penalty in these rather special circumstances as "cruel and unusual punishment." This case does not raise any question as to the right of the police to stop and detain those who are intoxicated in public, whether as a result of the disease or otherwise; or as to the State's power to commit chronic alcoholics for treatment. Nor does it concern the responsibility of an alcoholic for criminal *acts*. We deal here with the mere *condition* of being intoxicated in public.

*   *   *

Robinson stands upon a principle which, despite its subtlety, must be simply stated and respectfully applied because it is the foundation of individual liberty and the cornerstone of the relations between a civilized state and its citizens: Criminal penalties may not be inflicted upon a person for being in a condition he is powerless to change. In all probability, Robinson at some time before his conviction elected to take narcotics. But the crime as defined did not punish this conduct. The statute imposed a penalty for the offense of "addiction"—a condition which Robinson could not control. Once Robinson had become an addict, he was utterly powerless to avoid criminal guilt. He was powerless to choose not to violate the law.

In the present case, appellant is charged with a crime composed of two elements—being intoxicated and being found in a public place while in that condition. The crime, so defined, differs from that in *Robinson*. The statute covers more than a mere status. But the essential constitutional defect here is the same as in *Robinson*, for in both cases the particular defendant was accused of being in a condition which he had no capacity to change or avoid. The trial judge sitting as trier of fact found upon the medical and other relevant testimony, that Powell is a "chronic alcoholic." He defined appellant's "chronic alcoholism" as "a disease which destroys the afflicted person's will power to resist the constant, excessive consumption of alcohol." He also found that "a chronic alcoholic does not appear in public by his own volition but under a compulsion symptomatic of the disease of chronic alcoholism." I read these findings to mean that appellant was powerless to avoid drinking; that having taken his first drink, he had "an uncontrollable compulsion to drink" to the point of intoxication; and that, once intoxicated, he could not prevent himself from appearing in public places.

Article 477 of the Texas Penal Code is specifically directed to the accused's presence while in a state of intoxication, "in any public place, or at any private house except his own." This is the essence of the crime. Ordinarily when the State proves such presence in a state of intoxication, this will be sufficient for conviction, and the punishment prescribed by the State may, of course, be validly imposed. But here the findings of the trial judge call into play the principle that a person may not be punished if the condition essential to constitute the defined crime is part of the pattern of his disease and is occasioned by a compulsion symptomatic of the disease. This principle, narrow in scope and applicability, is implemented by the Eighth Amendment's prohibition of "cruel and unusual punishment," as we construed that command in *Robinson*. It is true that the command of the Eighth Amendment and its antecedent provision in the Bill of Rights of 1689 were initially directed to the type and degree of punishment inflicted. But in *Robinson* we recognized that "the principle that would deny power to exact capital punishment for a petty crime would also deny power to punish a person by fine or imprisonment for being sick." 370 U.S., at 676, 82 S.Ct., at 1425 (Mr. Justice DOUGLAS, concurring).

*   *   *

I would reverse the judgment below.

NOTES

1. Prior to the Supreme Court's decision in Powell, two United States Courts of Appeal had held that chronic alcoholics could not be convicted under public drunkenness statutes. Driver v. Hinnant, 356 F.2d 761 (4th Cir. 1966) was decided on Eighth Amendment cruel and unusual punishment grounds. Easter v. District of Columbia, 124 U.S.App.D.C. 33, 361 F.2d 50 (1966) rested upon the ground that legislative intent (evidenced

by an extensive noncriminal program dealing with alcoholism) directed this result. Following Powell, a number of other courts rejected such arguments, often on reasoning that includes an evaluation of the evidence as inadequate to establish true involuntariness of the intoxication or appearance in public. See Budd v. Madigan, 418 F.2d 1032 (9th Cir. 1969), certiorari denied 397 U.S. 1053, 90 S.Ct. 1394, 25 L.Ed.2d 669 (1970); Vick v. State, 453 P.2d 342 (Alaska, 1969); People v. Hoy, 380 Mich. 597, 158 N.W.2d 436 (1968); Portland v. Juntunen, 488 P.2d 806 (Or.App.1971); Seattle v. Hill, 72 Wash.2d 786, 435 P.2d 692 (1967), certiorari denied 393 U.S. 872, 89 S.Ct. 163, 21 L.Ed.2d 142 (1968). The Minnesota Supreme Court, however, held in State v. Fearon, 283 Minn. 90, 166 N.W.2d 720 (1969) that legislative intent precluded the conviction of a chronic alcoholic under a statute declaring that "every person who becomes intoxicated by voluntarily drinking intoxicating liquor is guilty of the crime of drunkenness. . . . "

2. Biglow, Cohen, Liebson and Faillace, Abstinence or Moderation? Choice by Alcoholics, 10 Journal of Behavior Research and Therapy 209 (1972) reports on a study involving nineteen male "chronic alcoholics" referred from a hospital emergency room. During the period of the study, one ounce drinks of 95 proof liquor were available to the subjects upon their request. Upper limits upon consumption were enforced, but the subjects could consume up to six ounces of liquor in a two-hour period and up to ten or 24 ounces per day. On certain days each subject was given access to an "enriched environment" if he did not consume more than five ounces of liquor. The "enriched environment" included a recreational room, opportunity to socialize with staff members and other patients in the facility, the right to have visitors, a bedside chair and reading materials, a job that paid $1.00 per hour, and a regular diet. On those days when abstinence or moderation in drinking were rewarded by access to the enriched environment, the subjects tended to drink but not to exceed the five ounce limit that determined their access to the "enriched environment." The nineteen subjects spent a total of 278 "subject days" under conditions offering such a choice. Only 27 subject days (9.7 percent) involved consumption of over five ounces of liquor. On the other hand, only 38 subject days (13.7 percent) involved total abstinence. The remaining 213 subject days (76.6 percent) involved moderate drinking. Those subjects that drank moderately tended to drink up to—but not beyond—the limit. 92.5 percent of the subject days involving moderate drinking were characterized by consumption of the five ounce limit. How helpful is this study in resolving the issues posed by Powell?

3.   NONCRIMINAL COMPELLED "TREATMENT": A POTENTIAL ALTERNATIVE TO CRIMINALIZATION

TEXAS CIVIL STATUTES

(1970 Supp.)

Art. 5561c.   Alcoholism

Purpose

Section 1.   The purpose of this Act is to prevent broken homes and the loss of lives by creating the Texas Commission on Alcoholism, which shall co-ordinate the efforts of all interested and affected State and local agencies; develop educational and preventive programs; and promote the establishment of constructive programs for treatment aimed at the reclamation, rehabilitation and successful re-establishment in society of alcoholics.   Alcoholism is hereby recognized as an illness and a public health problem affecting the general welfare and the economy of the State.   Alcoholism is further recognized as an illness subject to treatment and abatement and the sufferer of alcoholism is recognized as one worthy of treatment and rehabilitation.   The need for proper and sufficient facilities, programs and procedures within the State for the control and treatment of alcoholism is hereby recognized.   It is hereby declared that the procedure for commitment of alcoholics as hereinafter provided for is not punitive but is a committal for treatment of an illness affecting not only the individual involved but the public welfare as well.

*   *   *

Definitions

Sec. 3.   As used in this Act, (a) "Commission" means the Texas Commission on Alcoholism.

*   *   *

(c) An "alcoholic" means any person who chronically and habitually uses alcoholic beverages to the extent that he has lost the power of self control with respect to the use of such beverages, or while chronically and habitually under the influence of alcoholic beverages endangers public morals, health, safety or welfare.

(d) "Alcoholism," as used herein, has reference to any condition of abnormal behavior or illness leading directly or indirectly to the chronic and habitual use of alcoholic beverages.

Texas Commission on Alcoholism

Sec. 4. Commission established. (a) There is hereby created a Commission to be known as the Texas Commission on Alcoholism, hereinafter called the Commission. The Commission shall consist of six (6) members to be appointed by the Governor * * *[.]

Admission and Certification of Alcoholics

Sec. 9. (a) The county judge of the county where an alleged alcoholic resides may certify or remand him or her to the custody of the Commission or its authorized representative for the treatment and rehabilitation of such alcoholic, upon proper proof as hereinafter provided, and with the consent in writing of the Commission or its authorized representative.

(b) The Court may remand an alcoholic to the Commission or its authorized representative for treatment when it is properly shown to the court upon petition or application filed by the alleged alcoholic's husband, wife, child, mother, father, next of kin, next friend, or the county health officer, that such a person is an alcoholic, is a resident of the county, is over eighteen years of age, and is not capable of, or is unfit properly to conduct himself or herself, or to conduct and look after his or her affairs or is dangerous to himself, or others, or has lost the power of self-control because of use of alcohol. Such a petition or application must show that the alleged alcoholic is in actual need of care and treatment and that his or her detention, care and treatment would improve his health.

(c) Upon filing of a petition or application, the court shall set a day for the hearing, which hearing must be held not less than five (5) days and no more than fourteen (14) days from the filing of the petition. * * *

(d) If the alleged alcoholic admits the allegations of the application, or if the court finds that the material allegations of the application have been proven, it shall issue the proper certificate for his or her commitment or remand to the Commission or its authorized representative for such confinement and treatment as the Commission shall direct. Upon such a finding, the court shall order that he or she be remanded to the Commission or its authorized representative for a period of not less than fifteen (15) days nor more than three (3) months as the necessity of the case may require, subject, however, to earlier discharge at the discretion of the Commission.

NOTES

1. If some persons who abuse alcohol should be compelled to submit to treatment, does the Texas statute adequately define those who should and distinguish them from those who should not? Consider the following from

Hutt, Modern Trends in Handling the Chronic Offender: The Challenge of the Courts, 19 S.Carolina L.Rev. 305, 320 (1967):

> I am wholly opposed to any form of involuntary treatment except in two limited areas. I do believe that, in a situation where a person is not mentally competent to make a rational choice as to whether he wishes to undergo treatment, a court has a right and a duty to make that choice for him. Thus, if a person is mentally incompetent and also is an alcoholic, involuntary treatment may be appropriate. But this is the very rare case. The vast majority of chronic alcoholics do not suffer from severe mental illness. For these people, involuntary treatment is not appropriate.
>
> Some would argue that any person who fails voluntarily to accept treatment for his alcoholism must ipso facto be considered mentally incompetent to make a rational choice. This is obviously fallacious. A person who chooses not to undergo surgery for heart disease is not considered mentally incompetent to make that choice. Nor is a person who chooses not to undergo a simple vaccination against disease or any other form of medical treatment that might be considered by the majority of our population to be an obviously intelligent step. In our democratic society, we respect the free choice of the individual to accept treatment or to reject it.
>
> When a derelict alcoholic becomes so debilitated that he is virtually dying in the street, however, he is obviously not in a position to make a rational choice about treatment.
>
> A court should have the power, under those limited circumstances, to commit him for treatment until he once again is capable of making a rational choice. But this does not mean an indeterminate sentence, or indeed any commitment longer than about thirty days. The unfortunate plight of the derelict inebriate cannot lead us to deprive him of his liberty on humanitarian grounds any more than it should lead us to deprive him of his liberty on criminal grounds.

2. To what extent is coercion necessary? Consider the experience of the Vera Institute's Bowery program in New York City as described in R. Nimmer, Two Million Unnecessary Arrests 128–141 (1971). The Project maintains a detoxification center where individuals may be detoxified under medical supervision and a social service staff that refers detoxified individauls to other programs. In addition to accepting "walk in" cases, the Project sends two-man rescue teams into the Bowery streets. These teams *offer* assistance only to persons so obviously intoxicated or debilitated that they are unable to take care of themselves on the street. No coercion is used, in fact as well as in theory. Despite frequent refusals of admission to walk in cases, about 25 percent of the total patient load consists of such walk ins. Approximately sixty percent of the persons approached by the rescue teams accept the offer to take them to the detoxification center. Approximately sixty to seventy percent of patients accept post-detoxification referrals to other programs. After it became clear that the Project was removing too few persons from the street to satisfy community pressure, an out-patient medical clinic was established to provide medical care to Bowery inhabitants whether or not intoxicated.

During the clinic's first year of operation, the rescue teams approached 4,717 men on the street who appeared to be in need of medical attention; only 689 (14 percent) refused the offer of help from the clinic.

To what extent does such a program adequately meet the demands responsible for public intoxication laws and their enforcement? To what extent does it meet the problems with which the law ought to be concerned? What effect does this experience with a noncoercive program have upon the arguments for replacing criminal liability with a program of compulsory "treatment"?

SZASZ, ALCOHOLISM: A SOCIO-ETHICAL PERSPECTIVE

6 Washburn L.J. 255, 258–63, 266–67 (1967).

The demand that alcoholism be considered an illness constitutes a late stage in a moral revolution that has swept the Western world during the past century. [I]t has manifested itself in the redefining of diverse types of behavior—from homosexuality to political "extremism"—as expressions of mental illness. No doubt those who strive to medicalize human problems are usually well-intentioned. The consequences of their actions are none the less morally and socially disastrous. Their posture is essentially one of medical prohibitionism: they combat drinking (or smoking, or certain types of sexual practices) not as a sin or a crime, but as a disease. The upshot is deprivation of personal liberties in the name of medical help.

I believe that before we accept or reject the disease concept of alcoholism, we ought to understand exactly what is meant by it.

First, the view that alcoholism is a disease may be held on the ground that the excessive use of alcohol causes specific illnesses, such as chronic gastritis and cirrhosis of the liver. Properly understood, this view is unobjectionable. It is misleading, however, because it confuses the *cause of an illness* with the *illness itself*. Excessive drinking may cause cirrhosis, but does this suffice to define the act of chronic imbibing as a disease? If we say yes, we shall have to label every other activity that predisposes to or causes illness as an illness. This would render not only excessive drinking as an illness, but also excessive eating and smoking. Furthermore, since many occupations are hazardous to health and life, these too would have to be classified as diseases.

Second, the view that alcoholism is a disease may be held on the ground that the alcoholic undergoes periodic episodes of acute intoxication, during which he is physically ill and may even die. Properly understood, this view also is unobjectionable. Acute alcoholism is a state of poisoning. As such, it is a disease. The difficulty with this view (as with the previous one) is that the poisoning is self-induced. To be sure, from a patho-physiological point of view, it is immaterial how a person becomes poisoned. But from a socio-ethical point of view, this "how" is very significant. In other words, the alcoholic both resembles and differs from the diabetic—just as the soldier who shoots himself in the foot (to be evacuated from the front lines) both resembles and differs from his buddy wounded by the enemy. From a surgical point of view, both soldiers are injured. But from the point of view of law, military discipline, and morals, their conditions could not differ more sharply.   *   *   *

Third, the view that alcoholism is a disease may be held on the ground that the alcoholic suffers from a genetic or biochemical dysfunction which interferes with the proper metabolism of alcohol; he thus becomes the victim of the peculiar interaction between alcohol and his particular body chemistry. I am not competent to pass on the validity of this hypothesis. However, even if it proves to be correct, the same socio-ethical considerations apply to it as to the first two views. Even though the alcoholic's physiological makeup might differ from that of other men, his alcoholism still depends on whether and how much he drinks. Assuming the existence of a medical disability such as postulated by this hypothesis, the individual suffering from it may be compared to a person who is allergic to ragweed pollen. The first few times such a person succumbs to the effects of alcohol (or ragweed pollen), his illness resembles ordinary diseases (such as pneumonia or cancer of the stomach). But once he grasps the nature of his "sensitivity," he must be held responsible —not, to be sure, for his sensitivity itself, but for protecting himself (and others) from its forseeable consequences. In this view, the individual predisposed to alcoholism who imbibes is like the man with ragweed allergy who plants ragweed on his lawn and spends his leisure time in late August working in his yard.

Fourth and last, the view that alcoholism is a disease may be held on the ground that the alcoholic suffers from a defect of his personality as a result of which he uses alcohol in an excessive and intemperate fashion. This view differs from those previously listed in that it identifies the excessive drinking itself as a manifestation of illness. According to the first three propositions alcoholism is a bodily (organic) illness; according to this last one, it is a mental (emotional) illness. This view of alcoholism aptly illustrates my contention that mental illness is a myth and a metaphor. What we call "mental illness" is a type of action or conduct: we call a-person "mentally ill" when he behaves in certain "abnormal" ways. Thus the term "mental illness" is but a new name for certain types of social performances or roles.

Students of alcoholism usually emphasize that the alcoholic drinks "compulsively." Marty Mann, for example, defines alcoholism as "a disease which manifests itself chiefly by the uncontrollable drinking of the victim   *   *   *" [10]

10. M. Mann, Primer on Alcoholism 3 (1950).

I, on the other hand, stress the issue of choice and freedom in the use (and abuse) of alcohol. Physicians, someone might object, do not speak of the freedom to suffer from cancer or hypertension. Why, then, do I speak of the freedom to suffer from alcoholism? This question strikes at the heart of the differences between cancer and alcoholism, and more generally, between bodily and mental diseases.

The disease concept of alcoholism, in contrast to, say, the disease concept of cancer, is confused and confusing because it fails to distinguish between the individual's helplessness and hence lack of responsibility for falling ill—and his power and hence responsibility for trying to recover from an illness. The medical profession has been woefully remiss—especially in addressing the lay public—in failing to clarify this difference.

*　　*　　*

When we say that a person is ill, we mean either that he suffers from an anatomical or physiological disorder of his body, or that he assumes the role of patient, or both. The point to remember is that sickness as a physical condition and as a social role are two quite different things and that they may vary independently from one another.

From a socio-ethical point of view, the single most important fact about being a medical patient is that the sick role must be assumed voluntarily. In general, the state does not have the right to cast the adult citizen in the role of patient; nor does it have the right to cast the citizen who defines himself as sick into the role of non-patient. Accordingly, a person may be ill (in the sense of having a disease), but may prefer not to assume the sick role. Most of us have made such a decision when, for example, we have a severe cold but go about our ordinary business and accept our usual responsibilities, rather than go to bed and seek medical help. Conversely, a person may be healthy (in the sense of not having a disease), but may prefer to assume the sick role. We may offer illness as an excuse for avoiding an obligation to go to the office or a party. Let us look at the implications of these concepts for the problem of alcoholism.

The alcoholic, it is claimed, does not choose to be an alcoholic. According to Mann, "He has lost the power of choice in the matter of drinking, and that is precisely the nature of his disease, alcoholism." Although I disagree with this statement, let us for the present discussion assume that it is true. The assertion that the alcoholic has no choice in the matter of drinking can only mean that he does not choose to crave alcohol any more than the cancer patient craves a malignancy; it cannot mean that, given his craving, he cannot choose to take certain steps to alter it (such as joining Alcoholics Anonymous). Whether or not alcoholism is a disease, a crucial and frequent psychological and social characteristic of the person who drinks to excess happens to be that he does not wish to be "treated" for it. In this respect, the alcoholic resembles the Jehovah's Witness suffering from a bleeding peptic ulcer who refuses a blood transfusion for it. The ordinary medical patient, let us remember, has the right to be sick and refuse treatment. When we proclaim the alcoholic as sick, are we prepared to accord him this same right? Or do we intend to view his illness as similar to mental disease—that is, as a condition for which the patient lacks understanding and one, moreover, that threatens the safety of others—and hence prescribe involuntary treatment for it?

Since we have chosen this second course, it is quite clear that the fundamental purpose of defining alcoholism as a disease is to bring it under the umbrella of mental illness and so justify the involuntary hospitalization and treatment of the so-called patient.
* * *

The proposition that alcoholism is a disease disguises and obscures several fundamental moral problems. Do we, as American citizens, have a right to ingest drugs and other substances (e.g., alcohol, amphetamines, barbiturates, nicotine, fatty foods, etc.), if we so choose? Further, if we take certain drugs but act as responsible and law-abiding citizens, do we have the right to be unmolested by the government? Lastly, if we take drugs and break social customs or laws, do we have the right to be treated as undesirable individuals or as persons accused of crime, rather than as involuntary (mental) patients?

*   *   *

[L]et us assume that [a] hypothetical alcoholic disturbs the peace while under the influence of alcohol. How should the law regard his conduct? Two important decisions have already been handed down by * * * courts finding that alcoholics are ill and that, although they may be forcibly retained for treatment, they are not criminals and should be hospitalized rather than imprisoned. These decisions may be due to fuzzy thinking, or a desire to use doctors instead of jailers to control undesirable social behavior, or both. For the alcoholic who comes before the courts must, by definition, be a person who has disturbed *someone*. The man who drinks himself into oblivion in his own bedroom whence he does not emerge until he is sober is not a candidate for imprisonment. The alternative between jailing and hospitalizing "the alcoholic" is thus a spurious one. It applies only to the individual who is *publicly* intoxicated (or who commits some other crime). But in such a case, it is not the drinking itself that is, or ought to be, of interest to the courts, but rather the socially deviant conduct that provoked and justified the man's arrest. Intoxication with alcohol is of course no more a cause of crime than is any other bodily state or illness. The alcoholic *knows* he is an alcoholic and owes society the same responsibility for controlling his behavior, drunk or sober, as any other man. If we were really serious about regarding chronic alcoholism as a disease—and used this assertion not merely as a rhetorical device but as a morally binding proposition—-we would arrive at an attitude toward alcoholic misbehavior diametrically opposite to the currently prevalent view.

Blindness, everyone will admit, is an organic disability of considerable proportions. Does it excuse the blind person from socially deviant or inept behavior? No, it does not, and should not. "In the law's appraisal,"—according to the late Professor Edmond Cahn—"a blind man is not of a different species from one who has the sight of his eyes. A blind man is simply another member of the total society; he must take suitable and reasonable precautions for his and others' safety. So must a man who is too short, or too heavy, or whose reflexes are slowing with the years; so also must every one of us. . . . Persons who are afflicted and disabled must not be categorized even by themselves as an inferior or pitiable species. They are, on the contrary men in all essentials like their neighbors—with the needs, duties, dignities, and singular potentialities of the genus." [16]

Among the needs, duties, dignities, and singular potentialities of the alcoholic I would emphasize his obligation to assume responsibility for his drinking and its consequences. From this point of view, there cannot be such a category as the "alcoholic criminal." Like all classes, this one is created by man and may be abolished by him. In the United States, we do not recognize, as separate categories, the "obese criminal" or the "Jewish criminal" or the "syphilitic criminal." So far as the law is concerned, all these men are individuals "accused of crime," or, if convicted, "criminals." In my opinion, the demonstrable disadvantage of creating a category of "alcoholic offenders" far outweighs its alleged advantages.

KITTRIE, THE DIVESTMENT OF CRIMINAL LAW AND THE COMING OF THE THERAPEUTIC STATE

1 Suffolk U.L.Rev. 43, 43–44, 65–67, 69–76 (1967).

Criminal law in the United States has been undergoing a process of divestment resulting in the relinquishment of its jurisdiction over many of its prior subjects and subject areas. Many classes of criminal offenders are no longer subject to its sanctions. * * *

This divestment, carried out in the name of the new social aims of therapy and rehabilitation * * * as contrasted with criminal law's emphasis upon retribution, incapacitation and deterrence, has produced new types of borderland proceedings, lodged between the civil and criminal law. * * * This process began * * * with the recognition in the early 19th century that the institutionali-

----

16. E. Cahn, The Moral Decision, Right and Wrong in the Light of American Law 220–21 (1956).

zation of the insane should be separated from the incarceration of criminals. * * *

The process of divestment has continued through a similar recognition, at the end of the 19th century, that juveniles, likewise, should not be subject to traditional criminal sanctions and proceedings. * * * Through subsequent legislative and judicial actions [in some jurisdictions], psychopaths * * * drug addicts * * * and alcoholics were similarly outside the boundaries of criminal law.

What are the specific reasons for the divestment of criminal law and what social needs does it fulfill? What are the major reasons for dissatisfaction with criminal law resulting in the divestment procedure?

The first factor to be considered is the influence of canon law which bases punishment upon moral guilt. * * * The growing recognition that certain classes of offenders are incapable of guilt because affected mentally, has resulted in the exemptions of lunatics and idiots from criminal sanctions as early as the beginning of the 14th century. * * * Over the years, [the] standards have been liberalized in various jurisdictions and could now well encompass a broader segment of mentally affected offenders. * * *

The second factor is the humanistic awakening which distinguished the ill and the immature from the evil and considered the punishment of those who require treatment as inhumane and morally objectionable. * * *

Having commenced with religious and humanitarian considerations against the applicability of criminal sanctions, the process of divestment continued under the steam generated by other factors. One of these was the growing disillusionment with the determinate sentence utilized under the criminal law. * * *

The traditional standard of criminal law has been to fit the punishment to the crime, not to the criminal. Society, acting through the modern legislature, continues in setting criminal penalties that respond to the severity of the crime. Yet the severity of the crime provides no meaningful measure for the time or tools required by society to deal with a particular offender. The conduct of an alcoholic charged with disturbing the peace is not extremely offensive and, consequently, the penalties prescribed for him are not severe. Yet, the reformation of an alcoholic may require more time and facilities than the rehabilitation of the passion murderer whose conduct is extremely condemnable and thus traditionally results in more severe criminal sanctions. As long as society's emphasis was upon the punishment of the offender and the deterrence of others, a punishment which fits the crime was perfectly in order. Once the emphasis began shifting to the rehabilitation of the offender and his return to society as an unlikely future delinquent, the traditional system of penalties appeared totally inappropriate. The answer was therefore sought outside criminal law, under a non-criminal "parens patriae" system in which the period of detention and the applicable sanctions are responsive to the therapeutic needs of the delinquent rather than the nature of his offense.

Additionally, the movement for the divestment of criminal justice allows for the replacement of penal facilities with therapeutically oriented institutions. Increasingly, it has been recognized that traditional punitive sanctions are not effective as means of social control. Society has increasingly undertaken, therefore, in the case of selected offenders or others posing a threat to social tranquility, to deemphasize punishment and to emphasize therapy. Divestment thus allows for new experimental programs, in hospitals rather than prisons.

The shift from a penal or punitive orientation to a therapeutic one is also looked upon by behavioral scientists as allowing for a better rehabilitation atmosphere and potential. Relevant in this connection is the concept of "double-expectancy" as described by Psychiatrist George Sturup.[92] According to Sturup, offenders respond according to what they perceive society expects of them. The offender who is tagged as a criminal responds to the negative social expectation that he perceives and recovery is therefore inadequate; the offender who is tagged ill responds to the perception of a much more positive social expectation and recovery is better.

Resort to non-criminal proceedings has the further effect of dispensing with some of the cumbersome formalism and procedural requirements of criminal law: counsel, adversary hearing, jury, non-hearsay evidence, etc. Accordingly, the courts have repeatedly emphasized the civil or non-criminal nature of these new proceedings and the inapplicability of the criminal law standards. * * * The non-criminal process also professes the laudatory desire and policy of removing the criminal stigma from those who are either too young or too lacking medically and mentally to be forever branded.

Finally, the divestment of criminal law and the substitution of civil proceedings permits another drastic departure from the criminal law standards, by allowing the treatment of a general condition or status, considered hazardous to society, instead of waiting until the commission of a prohibited overt act. Traditionally, criminal law is primarily a system designed to deal with criminals after the fact. Thus, while the general public's awareness of criminal sanctions is expected to exert a deterring influence and to curb prohibited conduct, the actual sanctions of criminal law do not, generally, come into use until after a criminal act has indeed been carried out or attempted. The non-criminal procedures, on the other hand, have been utilized as a means of preventive control for prospective offenders:

92. George Sturup, Superintendent of Herstedvester Institution, Denmark, A Situational Approach to Behavior Disorders, reprinted from the Leeds Symposium on Behavior Disorders, 25–27 March (1965).

the mentally ill person likely to become dangerous to himself or others, the mental defective likely to produce defective offspring, the child exposed to dangerous influences. In being directed towards crime prevention, not merely crime management, the non-criminal proceedings have appealed and will undoubtedly demonstrate an ever increasing appeal to those seeking new tools for society's struggle against crime and delinquency.

*   *   *

By emphasizing the therapeutic function of the state and by giving sympathetic consideration to mental and other aberrations, the therapeutic state acts to hasten the divestment of criminal justice. Yet this divestment, which increasingly frees persons from criminal responsibility, is not the final step in the process. The need for social defense does not permit the complete release of the recognized or prospective delinquent. What is resorted to, therefore, as a means of both therapy and social defense is the non-criminal incarceration and treatment—still involuntary or even coercive and quite often resulting in even more objectionable deprivations of liberty than are possible under the criminal process.

* * * These still comparatively new areas of non-criminal treatment raise a host of legal and non-legal questions. Foremost is the question of the basic balance between society's right to protect and improve itself and its members through preventive measures and the individual's right to liberty or, otherwise phrased, to be left alone. How much of a social hazard must one be demonstrated to be before society may step in? And may society involuntarily seek to remedy one's status, absent a dangerous act on his part? This is in essence the question of substantive due process. The traditional approach of our Anglo-American society has been for the state to step in only once an anti-social act has been committed or once "clear and present danger" has been demonstrated. Our society seeks generally not to control a status but an act. * * * Yet in the therapeutic "parens patriae" realm we often ignore the question of whether a particular offense had been committed. Instead we are often triggered to exercise therapeutic sanctions by a finding of the general social undesirability of one's condition or status.

Beyond the substantive questions regarding the exercise of state sanctions, even in the name of the "parens patriae", absent an overt "clear and present" danger, there also looms the question of procedural due process. Assuming that a non-criminal program is being utilized to accomplish a therapeutic social aim, what procedural safeguards must be required in order to protect the rights of the person allegedly requiring treatment? How carefully should the disabling medical or mental status be defined by law? Should there be a requirement of proof of previous anti-social behavior? Should there be a right to a hearing and counsel? Does an administrative confinement or one based on a medical certificate, without prior hearing, suffice if followed by an opportunity for judicial review? Should the state be required to disclose the record upon which it proceeds against a certain person? What should be the term of the therapeutic treatment —determinate or indeterminate? Should the social sanctions depend on the availability of treatment and should the person against whom sanctions are exercised have the right to treatment?

DITMAN, CRAWFORD, FORGY, MOSKOWITZ AND MacANDREW, A CONTROLLED EXPERIMENT ON THE USE OF COURT PROBATION FOR DRUNK ARRESTS

124 Am.J. Psychiatry 160 (1967).[a]

The courts are increasingly coming to view chronic drunk offenders as sick people who deserve treatment rather than punishment, although there is no available body of evidence which clearly indicates the relative effectiveness of these two approaches.

We have been studying this matter for the past four and a half years in the San Diego Municipal Court. During this time, there have been various reports of municipal court programs throughout the country, programs using such approaches as probation, referral to clinic treatment, Alcoholics Anonymous, court-sponsored honor classes, halfway houses, and camps instead of jail sentences. However, for two reasons little if anything can be safely concluded from the reports. First, they do not record and compare the results from different approaches in a systematic fashion, and second, other factors, such as various changes over a period of time, are confounded with the variations in approach so that therapeutic differences cannot properly be attributed to the programs per se. Until such deficiencies as these are corrected in controlled studies, claims for the particular value of any one program over another are of dubious worth.

Our previous work has led us to expect that the use of probation with suspended sentence would be an effective way both of getting the chronic drunk offender into treatment and of decreasing the likelihood of his being rearrested. The first study was a pilot program in which chronic drunk offenders were probated to Alcoholics Anonymous. If this failed, they were probated to clinic treatment, and if clinic treatment also failed, they were sent to an honor camp for six months. A marked decrease in the over-all number of drunk arrests in the city resulted.

We next instituted a controlled study to compare the effectiveness of three different "treatments." In this study a chronic drunk offender was defined as one who has had either two drunk arrests in

a. Reprinted from The American Journal of Psychiatry, volume 124, pages 160–63, 1967. Copyright 1967, the American Psychiatric Association.

the previous three months or three drunk arrests in the previous year. When such individuals came before the court and were found guilty, they were fined $25 and given a 30-day sentence suspended as a condition of a one-year probation. Other conditions of probation were that they complete an 80-item biographical questionnaire and that they abstain from alcoholic beverages for one year.

Each offender was then assigned to one of three treatment conditions: no treatment; alcoholic clinic; or Alcoholics Anonymous. To avoid bias, the judge followed a random assignment schedule. It was also required that each offender report back to the court at the end of six months. Evidence of cooperation in clinic treatment was given to the court by the clinic. In Alcoholics Anonymous such evidence was brought to the court by the offender in the form of signed statements from AA secretaries proving attendance at five meetings within 30 days. If the offender failed to comply, a bench warrant was issued for his arrest. Those unable to pay the $25 fine served one day in jail for each $5 and were then released to probation and one of the three treatments.

Our sample consisted of 301 chronic drunk arrestees who came before the San Diego Municipal Court between July 1964 and January 1965. Ninety percent were men with a median age in the early 40s. They had an average of 12 prior drunk arrests, with one exemplary case having a total of 153. (Not too surprisingly, he became one of our treatment failures.)

*   *   *

Results

*   *   *

Two independent sources of information were used to ascertain whether or not an individual was subsequently rearrested: a local police "rap" sheet and the State of California Criminal Identification and Investigation Report, which purports to list all arrests made in California for any offense and at least some arrests made elsewhere in the U.S.A. All offenders were followed for at least one year after their conviction. On all but seven of the 301 cases at least one of these reports was available, and on 241 cases both reports were obtained.

It was observed that relationships were usually clearer for the 241 complete data cases; thus figures based upon only these offenders will be presented here.   *   *   *

TABLE 1
Number of Rearrests Among 241 Offenders in Three Treatment Groups

TREATMENT GROUP	REARRESTS			
	NONE	ONE	TWO OR MORE	TOTAL
No treatment	32 (44%)	14 (19%)	27 (37%)	73
Alcoholism clinic	26 (32%)	23 (28%)	33 (40%)	82
Alcoholics Anonymous	27 (31%)	19 (22%)	40 (47%)	86
Total	85	56	100	241

TABLE 2
Time Before Rearrest in Three Treatment Groups

TREATMENT GROUP	NO REARRESTS	AFTER FIRST MONTH OF TREATMENT	WITHIN FIRST MONTH OF TREATMENT	TOTAL
No treatment	32 (44%)	25 (34%)	16 (22%)	73
Alcoholism clinic	26 (32%)	39 (47%)	17 (21%)	82
Alcoholics Anonymous	27 (31%)	40 (47%)	19 (22%)	86
Total	85	104	52	241

[A9011]

While Table 1 seems to suggest that the no-treatment condition was more effective than either Alcoholics Anonymous or clinic treatment, the chi-square tests of these frequencies failed to reach statistical significance at the .05 level of confidence. Even when Table 1 was collapsed so that the two treatments were lumped together and one or more arrests were lumped together, chi-square still did not quite achieve the .05 level of significance.

Another way of looking at the effectiveness of these three treatment conditions is to determine the length of time that elapsed before the recidivists became treatment failures. As can be seen in Table 2, the no-treatment condition again comes out on top; and again there is little difference between Alcoholics Anonymous and clinic treatment. Once more, however, the chi-square test failed to indicate that this trend was statistically significant at the .05 level of confidence.

* * *

Discussion

The failure of both Alcoholics Anonymous and the alcoholism clinic to produce fewer recidivists than did no treatment at all ought to be of great concern. Some of the present writers were quite optimistic about the possibilities of enforced referral to treatment, but the early encouraging anecdotal reports are not borne out by present data.

Possible reasons for this are: 1) the 30 days in jail suspended for one year was so powerful that any additional efforts such as treatment had little meaning to the offender; 2) even if the treatment had been initiated by the offender, the number of treatment sessions required as a condition of probation may have been too few to achieve positive results; or 3) the conditions of court-imposed referral confronted the offender with an anxiety-producing situation which may have *increased* the likelihood that he would resume his previous drinking pattern.

Be this as it may, the present data offer no support for a general policy of forced referrals to brief treatment. It is too early to tell whether a policy of *selective referral* would be of benefit. If such differential trends as we have described stand up under cross-validation, they would seem to offer some hope for the future. The data from which to construct such an empirically based referral strategy are still being collected.

NOTE

Selzer and Holloway, A Follow-Up of Alcoholics Committed to a State Hospital, 18 Q.J. Studies of Alcohol 98 (1957) report on a follow-up study of 83 patients committed to a Michigan mental hospital in 1948–49. At the time of the study (1955), 35 percent of the sample were "frequently intoxicated" despite the compelled treatment. 22 percent were completely abstinent, however, and 19 percent were only moderate drinkers with good adjustment to their life situations, causing the authors to conclude that "41 percent of the patients who could be evaluated were essentially rehabilitated." Id. at 118. They further commented:

> These results must be viewed in the light of knowledge that almost every patient was an unwilling participant in the effort to rehabilitate him. Since these patients displayed little or no realistic motivation towards obtaining help for their problem, they are probably representative of alcoholics in the community least likely to recover from their illness if left to their own devices.

Id. at 119.

But consider the significance of these results in light of other studies. LeMere, What Happens to Alcoholics, 109 Am.J.Psychiatry 674 (1953) reported that 21 percent of untreated alcoholics either became abstinent or moderated their drinking. Cowen, A Six Year Follow-up of a Series of Committed Alcoholics, 15 Q.J. Studies Alcohol 413 (1954) reported that of 68 alcoholics given "hardly more than custodial care" in a state mental hospital for 60 days, 37 percent were "substantially improved" six years later.

B. FACTORS RELEVANT TO THE RESOLUTION OF THE CRIMINALIZATION ISSUE

---

1. THE NATURE OF CRIMINAL LIABILITY

HENRY M. HART, JR., THE AIMS OF THE CRIMINAL LAW

23 Law and Contemporary Problems 401, 402–06 (1958).

What do we mean by "crime" and "criminal"?   *   *   *

A great deal of intellectual energy has been misspent in an effort to develop a concept of crime as "a natural and social phenomenon" abstracted from the functioning system of institutions which make use of the concept and give it impact and meaning. But the criminal law, like all law, is concerned with the pursuit of human purposes through the forms and modes of social organization, and it needs always to be thought about in that context as a method or process of doing something.

What then are the characteristics of this method?

1.   The method operates by means of a series of directions, or commands, formulated in general terms, telling people what they must or must not do. Mostly, the commands of the criminal law are "must-nots," or prohibitions, which can be satisfied by inaction. "Do not murder, rape, or rob." But some of them are "musts," or affirmative requirements, which can be satisfied only by taking a specifically, or relatively specifically, described kind of action. "Support your wife and children," and "File your income tax return."

2.   The commands are taken as valid and binding upon all those who fall within their terms when the time comes for complying with them, whether or not they have been formulated in advance in a single authoritative set of words. They speak to members of the community, in other words, in the community's behalf, with all the power and prestige of the community behind them.

3.   The commands are subject to one or more sanctions for disobedience which the community is prepared to enforce.

Thus far, it will be noticed, nothing has been said about the criminal law which is not true also of a large part of the noncriminal, or civil, law. The law of torts, the law of contracts, and almost every other branch of private law that can be mentioned operate, too, with general directions prohibiting or requiring described types of conduct, and the community's tribunals enforce these commands. What, then, is distinctive about the method of the criminal law?

Can crimes be distinguished from civil wrongs on the ground that they constitute injuries to society generally which society is interested in preventing? The difficulty is that society is interested also in the due fulfillment of contracts and the avoidance of traffic accidents and most of the other stuff of civil litigation. The civil law is framed and interpreted and enforced with a constant eye to these social interests. Does the distinction lie in the fact that proceedings to enforce the criminal law are instituted by public officials rather than private complainants? The difficulty is that public officers may also bring many kinds of "civil" enforcement actions—for an injunction, for the recovery of a "civil" penalty, or even for the detention of the defendant by public authority. Is the distinction, then, in the peculiar character of what is done to people who are adjudged to be criminals? The difficulty is that, with the possible exception of death, exactly the same kinds of unpleasant consequences, objectively considered, can be and are visited upon unsuccessful defendants in civil proceedings.

If one were to judge from the notions apparently underlying many judicial opinions, and the overt language even of some of them, the solution of the puzzle is simply that a crime is anything which is *called* a crime, and a criminal penalty is simply the penalty provided for doing anything which has been given that name. So vacant a concept is a betrayal of intellectual bankruptcy. Certainly, it poses no intelligible issue for a constitution-maker concerned to decide whether to make use of "the method of the criminal law." Moreover, it is false to popular understanding, and false also to the understanding embodied in existing constitutions. By implicit assumptions that are more impressive than any explicit assertions, these constitutions proclaim that a conviction for crime is a distinctive and serious matter— a something, and not a nothing. What is that something?

4. What distinguishes a criminal from a civil sanction and all that distinguishes it, it is ventured, is the judgment of community condemnation which accompanies and justifies its imposition. As Professor Gardner wrote not long ago, in a distinct but cognate connection:

> The essence of punishment for moral delinquency lies in the criminal conviction itself. One may lose more money on the stock market than in a court-room; a prisoner of war camp may well provide a harsher environment than a state prison; death on the field of battle has the same physical characteristics as death by sentence of law. It is the expression of the community's hatred, fear, or contempt for the convict which alone characterizes physical hardship as punishment.

If this is what a "criminal" penalty is, then we can say readily enough what a "crime" is. It is not simply anything which a legislature chooses to call a "crime." It is not simply antisocial conduct which public officers are given a responsibility to suppress. It is not simply any conduct to which a legislature chooses to attach a "criminal" penalty. It is conduct which, if duly shown to have taken place, will incur a formal and solemn pronouncement of the moral condemnation of the community.

5. The method of the criminal law, of course, involves something more than the threat (and, on due occasion, the expression) of community condemnation of antisocial conduct. It involves, in addition, the threat (and, on due occasion, the imposition) of unpleasant physical consequences, commonly called punishment. But if Professor Gardner is right, these added consequences take their character as punishment from the condemnation which precedes them and serves as the warrant for their infliction. Indeed, the condemnation plus the added consequences may well be considered, compendiously, as constituting the punishment. Otherwise, it would be necessary to think of a convicted criminal as going unpunished if the imposition or execution of his sentence is suspended.

In traditional thought and speech, the ideas of crime and punishment have been inseparable; the consequences of conviction for crime have been described as a matter of course as "punishment." The Constitution of the United States and its amendments, for example, use this word or its verb form in relation to criminal offenses no less than six times. Today, "treatment" has become a fashionable euphemism for the older, ugly word. This bowdlerizing of the Constitution and of conventional speech may serve a useful purpose in discouraging unduly harsh sentences and emphasizing that punishment is not an end in itself. But to the extent that it dissociates the treatment of criminals from the social condemnation of their conduct which is implicit in their conviction, there is danger that it will confuse thought and do a disservice.

At least under existing law, there is a vital difference between the situation of a patient who has been committed to a mental hospital and the situation of an inmate of a state penitentiary. The core of the difference is precisely that the patient has not incurred the moral condemnation of his community, whereas the convict has.

NOTE

Does it really make any significant difference whether a criminal or civil approach is taken to alcohol-related activity? Is there likely to be any difference between a system in which at least some of those who engage in antisocial alcohol-related activity are compelled on a noncriminal basis to receive treatment and one in which all are convicted of crimes but the disposition is to a program of treatment? Can these questions be answered by examining the language of the statutory frameworks? If not, what else must be considered?

2.   JUSTIFICATION AND FUNCTIONS OF CRIMINALIZATION

H. L. A. HART, MURDER AND THE PRINCIPLES OF PUNISHMENT: ENGLAND AND THE UNITED STATES

52 Nw.U.L.Rev. 433, 448–49 (1957).[b]

[W]e must distinguish two questions commonly confused. They are, first "Why do men in fact punish?" * * * The second question * * * is "What justifies men in punishing? Why is it morally good or morally permissible for them to punish?" It is clear that no demonstration that in fact men have punished or do punish for

b. Reprinted by special permission of the Northwestern University Law Review (Northwestern University School of Law), Copyright © 1958, Vol. 52, No. 4.

certain reasons can amount *per se* to a justification for this practice unless we subscribe to what is itself a most implausible moral position, namely, that whatever is generally done is justified or morally right * * *.

When this simple point is made clear and the two questions * * * are forced apart, very often the objector to the utilitarian position will turn out to be a utilitarian of a wider and perhaps more imaginative sort. He will perhaps say that what justifies punishment is that it satisfies a popular demand (perhaps even for revenge) and explain that it is good that it satisfies this demand because if it did not there would be disorder in society, disrespect for the law, or even lynching. Such a point of view, of course, raises disputable questions of fact * * *. Nevertheless, this objection itself turns out to be a utilitarian position, emphasizing that the good to be secured by punishment must not be narrowly conceived as simply protecting society from the harm represented by the particular type of crime punished but also as a protection from a wider set of injuries to society.

---

a. CRIMINALIZATION AND PUNISHMENT AS RETRIBUTION

P. BRETT, AN INQUIRY INTO CRIMINAL GUILT

51 (1963).

The retributive theory of punishment can be formulated in a number of ways. Its distinguishing feature is that it asks for no further justification of the right to punish than that the offender has committed a wrong. "Judicial punishment * * * can never serve merely as a means to further *another* good, whether for the offender himself or of society, but must always be inflicted on him for the sole reason that he *has committed a crime.* * * * The law of punishment is a categorical imperative, and woe to him who crawls through the serpentine windings of the happiness theory seeking to discover something which in virtue of the benefit it promises will release him from the duty of punishment or even from a fraction of its full severity." Thus Kant expounded the theory, and he based it upon his view that man must always be treated as an end in himself and never as a means of achieving some other end. Kant's position here is an intuitive one, with which one can only either agree or disagree in the light of one's own intuitions. Other formulations of the retributive theory are likewise intuitive, and occasionally they take on a somewhat mystical tinge, as with Hegel's view that crime is a negation and punishment a negation of that negation.

b. CRIMINALIZATION AND PUNISHMENT AS A REFLECTION OF MORALITY

P. DEVLIN, THE ENFORCEMENT OF MORALS

9 (1965).

I think it is clear that the criminal law as we know it is based upon moral principle. In a number of crimes its function is simply to enforce a moral principle and nothing else.

J. MILL, UTILITARIANISM: LIBERTY AND REPRESENTATIVE GOVERNMENT 73 [c]

The sole end for which mankind is warranted, individually or collectively, in interfering with the liberty of action of any of their number is self-protection. That the only purpose for which power can be rightfully exercised over any member of a civilized community, against his will, is to prevent harm to others. His own good, whether physical or moral, is not a sufficient warrant. He cannot rightfully be compelled to do or forbear because it will be better for him to do so, because it will make him happier, because, in the opinion of others, to do so would be wise, or even right. These are good reasons for remonstrating with him, or reasoning with him or persuading him, or entreating him but not for compelling him, or visiting him with any evil in case he do otherwise. To justify that, the conduct from which it is desired to deter him must be calculated to produce evil to some one else. The only part of the conduct of any one, for which he is amenable to society, is that which concerns others. In the part which merely concerns himself, his independence is, of right, absolute.

P. DEVLIN, THE ENFORCEMENT OF MORALS

9–10 (1965).[d]

What makes a society of any sort is community of ideas, not only political ideas but also ideas about the way its members should behave and govern their lives; these latter ideas are its morals. Every society has a moral structure as well as a political one: or rather, since that might suggest two independent systems, I should say that

c. From the book Utilitarianism: Liberty and Representative Government by John Stuart Mill. Everyman's Library Edition. Published by E. P. Dutton & Co., Inc. and used with their permission.

d. From Morals and the Criminal Law included in The Enforcement of Morals by Lord Devlin, published by Oxford University Press.

the structure of every society is made up both of politics and morals. Take, for example, the institution of marriage. Whether a man should be allowed to take more than one wife is something about which every society has to make up its mind one way or the other. In England we believe in the Christian idea of marriage and therefore adopt monogamy as a moral principle. Consequently the Christian institution of marriage has become the basis of family life and so part of the structure of our society. It is there not because it is Christian. It has got there because it is Christian, but it remains there because it is built into the house in which we live and could not be removed without bringing it down. The great majority of those who live in this country accept it because it is the Christian idea of marriage and for them the only true one. But a non-Christian is bound by it, not because it is part of Christianity but because, rightly or wrongly, it has been adopted by the society in which he lives. It would be useless for him to stage a debate designed to prove that polygamy was theologically more correct and socially preferable; if he wants to live in the house, he must accept it as built in the way in which it is.

We see this more clearly if we think of ideas or institutions that are purely political. Society cannot tolerate rebellion; it will not allow argument about the rightness of the cause. Historians a century later may say that the rebels were right and the Government was wrong and a percipient and conscientious subject of the State may think so at the time. But it is not a matter which can be left to individual judgement.

The institution of marriage is a good example for my purpose because it bridges the division, if there is one, between politics and morals. Marriage is part of the structure of our society and it is also the basis of a moral code which condemns fornication and adultery. The institution of marriage would be gravely threatened if individual judgements were permitted about the morality of adultery; on these points there must be a public morality. But public morality is not to be confined to those moral principles which support institutions such as marriage. People do not think of monogamy as something which has to be supported because our society has chosen to organize itself upon it; they think of it as something that is good in itself and offering a good way of life and that it is for that reason that our society has adopted it. I return to the statement that I have already made, that society means a community of ideas; without shared ideas on politics, morals, and ethics no society can exist. Each one of us has ideas about what is good and what is evil; they cannot be kept private from the society in which we live. If men and women try to create a society in which there is no fundamental agreement about good and evil they will fail; if, having based it on common agreement, the agreement goes, the society will disintegrate. For society is not something that is kept together physically; it is held by the invisible bonds of common thought. If the bonds were too far relaxed the members would drift apart. A common morality is part of the bondage. The bondage is part of the price of society; and mankind, which needs society, must pay its price.

Common lawyers used to say that Christianity was part of the law of the land. That was never more than a piece of rhetoric * * * [.] What lay behind it was the notion which I have been seeking to expound, namely that morals—and up till a century or so ago no one thought it worth distinguishing between religion and morals— were necessary to the temporal order.

H. L. A. HART, SOCIAL SOLIDARITY AND THE ENFORCEMENT OF MORALITY

35 U.Chi.L.Rev. 1, 8–13 (1967).

If we ask in relation to theories such as Lord Devlin's * * * precisely what empirical claim they make concerning the connection between the maintenance of a common morality and the existence of society, some further disentangling of knots has to be done.

It seems a very natural objection to such theories that if they are to be taken seriously * * * the justification which they attempt to give for the enforcement of social morality is far too general. It is surely both possible and good sense to discriminate between those parts of a society's moral code (assuming it has a single moral code) which arc essential for the existence of a society and those which are not. Prima facie, at least, the need for such a discrimination seems obvious even if we assume that the moral code is only to be enforced where it is supported by "sentiments which are strong and precise" * * * or by "intolerance, indignation and disgust" * * *. For the decay of all moral restraint or the free use of violence or deception would not only cause individual harm but would jeopardise the existence of a society since it would remove the main conditions which make it possible and worthwhile for men to live together in close proximity to each other. On the other hand the decay of moral restraint on, say, extramarital intercourse, or a general change of sexual morality in a permissive direction seems to be quite another matter and not obviously to entail any such consequences as "disintegration" or "men drifting apart."

It seems, therefore, worthwhile pausing to consider two possible ways of discriminating within a social morality the parts which are to be considered essential.

(i) The first possibility is that the common morality which is essential to society, and which is to be preserved by legal enforcement, is that part of its social morality which contains only those restraints and prohibitions that are essential to the existence of any society of human beings whatever. Hobbes and Hume have supplied us with general characterisations of this moral minimum essential for social life: they include rules restraining the free use of violence and minimal forms of rules regarding honesty, promise keeping, fair dealing, and property. It is, however, quite clear that * * * Devlin * * * [does not mean] that only those elements, which are to be found in common morality, are to be enforced by law * * *. Quite clearly the argument * * * concerns moral rules which may differ from society to society * * *

(ii) The second possibility is this: the morality to be enforced, while not coextensive with every jot and tittle of an existent moral code, includes not only the restraints and prohibitions such as those relating to the use of violence or deception which are necessary to any society whatever, but also what is essential for a particular society. The guiding thought here is that for any society there is to be found, among the provisions of its code of morality, a central core of rules or principles which constitutes its pervasive and distinctive style of life. Lord Devlin frequently speaks in this way of what he calls monogamy adopted "as a moral principle," and of course this does deeply pervade our society in two principal ways. First, marriage is a *legal* institution and the recognition of monogamy as the sole legal form of marriage carries implications for the law related to wide areas of conduct: the custody and education of children, the rules relating to inheritance and distribution of property, etc. Second, the principle of monogamy is also morally pervasive: monogamous marriage is at the heart of our conception of family life, and with the aid of the law has become part of the structure of society. Its disappearance would carry with it vast changes throughout society so that without exaggeration we might say that it had changed its character.

On this view the morality which is necessary to the existence of society is neither the moral minimum required in all societies (Lord Devlin himself says that the polygamous marriage in a polygamous society may be an equally cohesive force as monogamy is in ours), nor is it every jot and tittle of a society's moral code. What is essential and is to be preserved is the central core. On this footing it would be an open and empirical question whether any particular moral rule or veto, *e. g.,* on homosexuality, adultery, or fornication, is so organically connected with the central core that its maintenance and preservation is required as a vital outwork or bastion. There are perhaps traces of some of these ideas in Lord Devlin * * *. But even if we take this to be the position, we are still not really confronted with an empirical claim concerning the connection of the maintenance of a common morality and the prevention of disintegration or "drifting apart." Apart from the point about whether a particular rule is a vital outwork or bastion of the central core, we may still be confronted only with the unexciting tautology depending now on the identification of society, not with the whole of its morality but only with its central core or "character" and this is not the disintegration thesis.

* * *

What is required to convert the last mentioned position into the disintegration thesis?   It must be the theory that the maintenance of the core elements in a particular society's moral life is in fact necessary to prevent disintegration, because the withering or malignant decay of the central morality is a disintegrating factor.   But even if we have got thus far in identifying an empirical claim, there would of course be very many questions to be settled before anything empirically testable could be formulated.   What are the criteria in a complex society for determining the existence of a single recognised morality or its central core?   What is "disintegration" and "drifting apart" under modern conditions?   I shall not investigate these difficulties but I shall attempt to describe in outline the types of evidence that might conceivably be relevant to the issue if and when these difficulties are settled.   They seem to be the following:

(a) Crude historical evidence in which societies—not individuals —are the units.   The suggestion is that we should examine societies which have disintegrated and enquire whether their disintegration was preceded by a malignant change in their common morality.   This done, we should then have to address ourselves to the possibility of a causal connection between decay of a common morality and disintegration.   But of course all the familiar difficulties involved in macroscopic generalisations about society would meet us at this point, and anyone who has attempted to extract generalisations from what is called the decline and fall of the Roman Empire would know that they are formidable.   To take only one such difficulty: suppose that all our evidence was drawn from simple tribal societies or closely knit agrarian societies   * * *   We should not, I take it, have much confidence in applying any conclusions drawn from these to modern industrial societies.   Or, if we had, it would be because we had some well developed and well evidenced theory to show us that the differences between simple societies and our own were irrelevant to these issues as the differences in the size of a laboratory can safely be ignored as irrelevant to the scope of the generalisations tested by laboratory experiments.
* * *

(b) The alternative type of evidence must be drawn presumably from social psychology and must break down into at least two subforms according to the way in which we conceive the alternatives to the maintenance of a common morality.   One alternative is general uniform *permissiveness* in the area of conduct previously covered by the common morality.   The lapse, for example, of the conception that the choices between two wives or one, heterosexuality or homosexuality, are more than matters of personal taste.   This (the alternative of permissiveness) is what Lord Devlin seems to envisage or to fear when he says: "The enemy of society is not error but indifference," and "Whether the new belief is better or worse than the old, it is the interregnum of disbelief that is perilous." On the other hand the alternative may not be permissivenes but *moral pluralism* involving divergent submoralities in relation to the same area of conduct.

To get off the ground with the investigation of the questions that either of these two alternatives opens up, it would be reasonable to abandon any general criteria for the disintegration of society in favour of something sufficiently close to satisfy the general spirit of the disintegration thesis. It would be no doubt sufficient if our evidence were to show that malignant change in a common morality led to a general increase in such forms of antisocial behavior as would infringe what seem the minimum essentials: the prohibitions and restraints of violence, disrespect for property, and dishonesty. We should then require some account of the conceivable psychological mechanisms supposed to connect the malignant decay of a social morality with the increase in such forms of behavior. Here there would no doubt be signal differences between the alternatives of permissiveness and moral pluralism. On the permissiveness alternative, the theory to be tested would presumably be that in the "interregnum conditions," without the discipline involved in the submission of one area of life, *e. g.,* the sexual, to the requirements of a common morality, there would necessarily be a weakening of the general capacity of individuals for self control. So, with permissiveness in the area formally covered by restrictive sexual morality, there would come increases in violence and dishonesty and a general lapse of those restraints which are essential for any form of social life. This is the view that the morality of the individual constitutes a seamless web. There is a hint that this, in the last resort, is Lord Devlin's view of the way in which the "interregnum" constitutes a danger to the existence of society: for he replied to my charge that he had assumed without evidence that morality was a seamless web by saying that though "[s]eamlessness presses the simile rather hard," "most men take their morality as a whole." But surely this assumption cannot be regarded as obviously true. The contrary view seems at least equally plausible: permissiveness in certain areas of life (even if it has come about through the disregard of a previously firmly established social morality) might make it easier for men to submit to restraints on violence which are essential for social life.

If we conceive the successor to the "common morality" to be not permissiveness but moral pluralism in some area of conduct once covered by a sexual morality which has decayed through the flouting of its restrictions, the thesis to be tested would presumably be that where moral pluralism develops in this way quarrels over the differences generated by divergent moralities must eventually destroy the minimal forms of restraints necessary for social cohesion. The counter-thesis would be that plural moralities in the conditions of modern large scale societies might perfectly well be mutually tolerant. To many indeed it might seem that the counter-thesis is the more cogent of the two, and that over wide areas of modern life, sometimes hiding behind lip service to an older common morality, there actually are divergent moralities living in peace.

---

c. CRIMINALIZATION AND PUNISHMENT AS SATISFYING A PSYCHOLOGICAL URGE TO PUNISH

F. ALEXANDER AND H. STAUB, THE CRIMINAL, THE JUDGE, AND THE PUBLIC

5–9, 13, 9, 213–15 (1931).

In general, any restriction of an impulse is undertaken or accepted as a result of two factors: fear of pain and expectation of pleasure. Such restrictions are expressions of the adjustment which our subjective instinctive drives make to the objective demands of reality. One renounces the satisfaction of certain impulses either because such gratification is impossible, or because such gratification would cause more pain than the renunciation. In order to avoid the pain of immediate gratification of an impulse, it is not infrequently sufficient to defer such a gratification to the future and in the meantime bear a certain amount of tension; such a postponement may also serve as an insurance of gratification with which external circumstances might otherwise interfere for the present. Freud called this process the evolution of the individual from the pleasure principle to the reality principle. The reality principle thus represents nothing else but the pleasure principle which adjusted itself to the demands of reality.

Human instinctual drives demand expression, gratification. Reality puts obstacles in the way of expression; the reality principle consists of a purposive adjustment of the instinctual demands to the available possibilities of gratification. It is quite natural that renunciation goes just as far as it is possible, not further. Thus an equilibrium is established between renunciation and gratification of the demands of one's impulses. If an added renunciation is demanded, the equilibrium becomes disturbed.

The whole process of education is based on this principle. Education presents a systematic guidance in the direction of adjustment of the instinctual originally asocial, impulses of the child to the demands of the educator. The adjustment to society, like the adjustment to reality, is based on the evolutionary transition from the pleasure principle to the reality principle. The unpleasant or painful sensations, which we experience when our actions do not honor the demands of nature, correspond in the field of education and in the domain of social life in general to *punishment*.

* * * Fear of punishment and hope of being loved thus represent the two social regulators of human instinctive life. Freud came to these simple formulations in his last two works on instinctual life. ("The Ego and the Id," and "Inhibition, Symptom and Anxiety.")

* * *

Thus, fear of punishment and of not being loved (this, too, is a special form of punishment) are the two factors of education; later, throughout the life of the adult, these two factors remain the chief regulators of the instinctual life of man. Our analytical experience shows us that the conscious self-restraint of one's instinctual life plays but a very modest role as compared with the above-mentioned emotional factors. The fundamental principle of all adjustment is that of obtaining pleasure and of avoiding pain.

These considerations contain a silent recognition of the following fact: in the case of each restriction of our instinctual life, we deal with an outer world whose power to restrict this instinctual life happens to be stronger than our instinctual demands; it does not matter particularly who or what happens to be the representative of this restricting outer world; it may be Nature, educator, public leader, or the stronger social class. This process of restriction of our instinctual expressions, i. e., the adjustment to a stronger, restricting force brings about a state of equilibrium; in this state our psychic apparatus renounces just the minimal necessary amount of its wishes in order to obtain the greatest possible security in the matter of gratifying the remaining instinctual demands. What is called social order means just the equilibrium between the renunciation of instinctual demands and the assured gratification; it is a sort of a contract between the powers which restrict our instinctual expression and the instinctual demands of the individual. The very sensitive, emotional regulator of this equilibrium is the *sense of justice*. * * * whenever the accepted instinctual gratifications, which were acquired through such bitter restrictions of one's instinctual life, are threatened the sense of justice feels injured.

* * *

The sense of justice must be recognized as one of the foundations of social life. It may be considered as a sort of an inner psychic regulator, which automatically guarantees certain self-imposed restrictions in the interest of the community. * * * [A]ny injury to this sense of justice brings about an embitterment and rebellion, and the individual finds himself, as a result, unwilling to continue the renunciation which he observed heretofore. Under the latter circumstances, the continuation of law and order becomes possible only through the increase of the external power of the law. We must remember that within every law-abiding citizen there must live a police officer, for it is practically impossible to keep law and order only by means of external compulsion; the psycho-economic significance of the citizens' voluntary readiness to support the law becomes self-evident; this readiness, as we have seen is based upon the common sense of justice remaining uninjured. When the public shows undisturbed confidence in the legal institutions and their official representatives, then we may say that the common sense of justice is in harmony with the demands of the powers that be.

*   *   *

If, however, * * * an individual is treated unjustly, his fellow members of the same community, to whom the same might happen, perceive it as a betrayal, for it appears then that one gained nothing by renunciation. Thus, one rebels; there appears a spiteful determination to live out fully and unrestrainedly all those instinctual drives which one held heretofore in check.

This is the reason why one feels so stirred and provoked when a miscarriage of justice occurs and either an innocent man is convicted by mistake and thus treated like a criminal, or when it comes to light that too harsh a sentence has been imposed as a result of arbitrary judgment of those in power.

* * * [I]n the case of escape from justice, however, every member of the community feels that he was wronged, for a man who violated the law escaped punishment; he was forgiven, as it were, for a transgression which is forbidden the righteous member of the community. We deal in both cases with the struggle for the individual freedom of one's instinctual drives; it is a protest against the restriction of these drives. It is as if the individual member of the community said to himself: "If other people are punished unjustly, then *my* personal freedom is also in danger, or if *another* escapes the punishment he deserves, why should *I* continue to conform?"

These simple psychological considerations lead to the understanding of one of the fundamental motives which prompts the public demand for the expiation of offenses. To put it in psychoanalytical language, the failure to punish an offender means to us a threat to our own repressive trends. * * *

The demand that every crime should be expiated represents, then, a defense reaction on the part of the Ego against one's own instinctual drives; the Ego puts itself at the service of the inner repressing forces, in order to retain the state of equilibrium, which must always exist between the repressed and the repressing forces of the personality. The demand that the lawbreaker be punished is thus a demonstration against one's own inner drives, a demonstration which tends to keep these drives amenable to control: "I forbid the lawbreaker what I forbid myself."

NOTE

Is the Alexander and Staub argument based upon a retributive theory of criminal liability and punishment? Should it be entitled to any weight in the decision whether—or to what extent—to criminalize intoxication-related conditions or activities? In the *Powell* decision? Can these questions be answered without first having more information? If not, what additional information is necessary?

———

d. CRIMINALIZATION AND PUNISHMENT AS A SYMBOLIC DESIGNATION OF PUBLIC MORES

GUSSFIELD, ON LEGISLATING MORALS: THE SYMBOLIC PROCESS OF DESIGNATING DEVIANCE

56 Cal.L.Rev. 54, 57–59 (1968).c

Analysis of the designation of public norms begins with a distinction between instrumental and symbolic functions of governmental acts. Acts of officials, legislative enactments, and court decisions clearly affect behavior in an instrumental manner; they directly influence the actions of people. The National Labor Relations Act and the Taft-Hartley Act, for example, have deeply affected the conditions of collective bargaining in the United States. Tariff legislation directly affects the prices of import commodities. The instrumental function of such law lies in its enforcement; unenforced it has little instrumental effect.

Symbolic aspects of law and government, however, do not depend for their effect on enforcement. They are symbolic in a sense close to that used in literary analysis. The symbolic act "invites consideration rather than overt action." Symbolic behavior has meaning beyond its immediate significance in its connotation for the audience that views it. The symbol "has acquired a meaning which is added to its immediate intrinsic significance." The use of the wine and wafer in the Mass or the importance of the national flag cannot be appreciated without knowing their symbolic meaning for the users. In analyzing law as symbolic we are oriented less to its behavioral consequences than to its meaning as an act or gesture important in itself, as a symbol.

A governmental agent's act may have symbolic import because it affects the designation of public norms. The courtroom decision or the legislative act often glorifies the values of one group and demeans those of another. Government actions can be seen as ceremonial and ritual performances, designating the content of public morality. Law is not only a means of social control but also symbolizes the public affirmation of social ideals and norms. The statement, promulgation, or announcement of law has a symbolic dimension unrelated to its function of influencing behavior through enforcement.

Students of government and law recognize that these two functions, instrumental and symbolic, may often be separated in more than the analytical sense. Many laws are honored as much in the breach as in the performance. Proscribed behavior which nevertheless regularly occurs in a socially organized manner and is unpunished has been described as a "patterned evasion of norms." The kinds of crimes discussed here quite clearly fall into this category. Gambling, prostitution, abortion and public drunkenness are all common modes of behavior although prohibited by law. Such systematic evasion may mediate conflict between cultures; the law can proclaim one set of norms as public morality and use another set of norms in actually controlling behavior.

Even where patterned evasion of norms exists, however, the passage of legislation, the acts of officials, and decisions of judges do have significance as gestures of public affirmation. First, the affirmation of a norm as the public norm prevents recognition of the norm violator's existence by the public. The existence of law quiets and comforts those whose interests and sentiments it embodies. Second, public affirmation of a moral norm directs the major institutions of the society to its support. Despite the fact of a patterned practice of abortion in the United States, obtaining abortions does require access to subterranean social structure and is not as easy as obtaining an appendectomy. Law has instrumental functions even where there is patterned evasion.

The third impact of public affirmation is the one that most interests us here. Affirmation through law and governmental acts expresses the public worth of one subculture's norms relative to those of others, demonstrating which cultures have legitimacy and public domination. Accordingly it enhances the social status of groups carrying the affirmed culture and degrades groups carrying that which is condemned as deviant. We have argued elsewhere, for example, that the significance of Prohibition in the United States lay less in its enforcement than in the fact that it occurred. Enforcement of Prohibition law apparently was often limited by the unwillingness of "Dry" forces to utilize all their political strength for fear of creating intensive opposition. The "Dry" forces gained great satisfaction from the passage and maintenance of the legislation itself.

Whatever its instrumental effects, public designation of morality itself generates deep conflict. The designating gesture is a dramatic event, "since it invites one to consider the matter of motives in a perspective that, being developed in the analysis of drama, treats language and thought primarily as modes of action." Therefore, designation of behavior as violating public norms confers status and honor on those groups with conventional cultures and derogates those whose cultures are considered deviant.　My analysis of the American temperance movement has shown how the issue of drinking and abstinence became a politically significant focus for the conflicts between Protestant and Catholic, rural and urban, native and immigrant, middle class and lower class in American society, as an abstinent Protestant middle class attempted to control the public affirmation of morality in drinking.　Victory or defeat thus symbolized the status and power of the opposing cultures, indicating that legal affirmation or rejection can have symbolic as well as instrumental importance.

NOTES

1.　Assuming that Gussfield is correct, is his statement merely an interesting observation or does it have some relevance for legal issues? Specifically, if he is correct, what results might flow from a decision to criminalize all intoxication-related activity?　Would these results be significantly different if the law did not formally brand them as "criminal" but made clear that they were disapproved and if committed rendered the person committing them subject to "treatment" until it was likely that he would not repeat them?　Would they be different if the formal law was silent as to intoxication but prohibited any unreasonably disturbing behavior, whether related to intoxication or not?

2.　Would the results Gussfield predicts flow from a formal passage of a statute, without regard to the manner or extent of its enforcement? Once a statute was passed, would its enforcement have any affect upon the results that he discusses?　Suppose, for example, that despite Furman v. Georgia, 408 U.S. 238, 92 S.Ct. 2726, 33 L.Ed.2d 346 (1972) (discussed at page 24) a state legislature enacts a broad death penalty provision.　Because of *Furman*, however, the death penalty is never imposed upon a defendant or executed if imposed.

---

e.　CRIMINALIZATION AND CONVICTION AS PREVENTIVE MEASURES

(1)　PUNISHMENT AS A MEANS OF DETERRING, MORALIZING AND THE LIKE

ANDENAES, THE GENERAL PREVENTIVE EFFECTS OF PUNISHMENT

114 U.Pa.L.Rev. 949–51 (1966).[f]

In continental theories of criminal law, a basic distinction is made between the effects of punishment on the man being punished—individual prevention or special prevention—and the effects of punishment upon the members of society in general—general prevention. The characteristics of special prevention are termed "deterrence," "reformation" and "incapacitation," and these terms have meanings similar to their meanings in the English speaking world. General prevention, on the other hand, may be described as the *restraining influences emanating from the criminal law and the legal machinery*.

By means of the criminal law, and by means of specific applications of this law, "messages" are sent to members of a society. The criminal law lists those actions which are liable to prosecution, and it specifies the penalties involved. The decisions of the courts and actions by the police and prison officials transmit knowledge about the law, underlining the fact that criminal laws are not mere empty threats, and providing detailed information as to what kind of penalty might be expected for violations of specific laws. To the extent that these stimuli restrain citizens from socially undesired actions which they might otherwise have committed, a general preventive effect is secured. While the effects of special prevention depend upon how the law is implemented in each individual case, general prevention occurs as a result of an interplay between the provisions of the law and its enforcement in specific cases. In former times, emphasis was often placed on the physical exhibition of punishment as a deterrent influence, for example, by performing executions in public. Today it is customary to emphasize the *threat* of punishment as such. From this point of view the significance of the individual sentence and the execution of it lies in the support that these actions give to the law. It may be that some people are not particularly sensitive to an abstract threat of penalty, and that these persons can be motivated toward conformity only if the penalties can be demonstrated in concrete sentences which they feel relevant to their own life situations.

The effect of the criminal law and its enforcement may be *mere deterrence*. Because of the hazards involved, a person who contemplates a punishable offense might not act. But it is not correct to regard general prevention and deterrence as one and the same thing. The concept of general prevention also includes the *moral* or *socio-pedagogical* influence of punishment. The "messages" sent by law and the legal processes contain factual information about what would be risked by disobedience, but they also contain proclamations specifying that it is *wrong* to disobey. * * *

*   *   *

Making a distinction between special prevention and general prevention is a useful way of calling attention to the importance of legal punishment in the lives of members of the general public, but the distinction is also to some extent an artificial one. The distinction is simple when one discusses the reformative and incapacitative effects of punishment on the individual criminal. But when one discusses the deterrent effects of punishment the distinction becomes less clear.

Suppose a driver is fined ten dollars for disregarding the speed limit. He may be neither reformed or incapacitated but he might, perhaps, drive more slowly in the future. His motivation in subsequent situations in which he is tempted to drive too rapidly will not differ fundamentally from that of a driver who has not been fined; in other words a general preventive effect will operate. But for the driver who has been fined, this motive has, perhaps, been strengthened by the recollection of his former unpleasant experience. We may say that a general preventive feature and special preventive feature here act together.

NOTES

1. Which of the potential preventive effects of punishment should be relied upon in evaluating the propriety of criminalizing intoxication-related offenses? How should this choice be made?

2. Which, if any, persons who commit intoxication-related acts does the material suggest are most likely to be specially prevented (in Andenaes' terminology) from reoffending? Why? Which persons who might commit such acts are most likely to be "generally deterred"? Why? Do we know enough about the actual or potential effects of punishing any category of offenders to rely upon such considerations in making the criminalization decisions? In making the *Powell* decision?

3. Can the law justifiably rely upon an expectation that criminal punishment will have a general preventive effect? Consider the following from Lukas, A Criminologist Looks at Criminal Guilt in Social Meaning of Legal Concepts: Criminal Guilt 121–22 (1950):

> [T]he Roman Empire devised a criminal code under which, though crime was a hurt to the community which must be revenged, it was provided that the revenge would be proportionate to the injury inflicted on the victim. However, penal codes and the manner in which they are popularly interpreted are often poles apart—then, as now. The record plainly shows that despite the avowed purpose of the Roman code, punishments were totally disproportionate, and their infliction at times brought a touch of carnival to the occasions. During the Emperor Constantine's reign (early fourth century), Christianity having become the Empire's official religion, the Church arrogated to itself some of the power to prosecute those who offended against moral sanctions as well as ecclesiastic edicts. Criminal courts were distinct from civil courts, and were separated from the administration of government. Their status was unchallenged as the final arbiter of guilt. Evil wills were sinful; hence the Church exhorted the evildoer to seek penitence. From that to atonement was but a short step, and from atonement to harsh punishment was shorter still.
>
> This was held to be expiation of sin, reminiscent of the primitive posture toward crime. But it also gave impetus to the new doctrine of "deterrence." Because the presumably enlightened Church could not appear to descend to the level of primitive revenge, it engaged in the derived rationalization that severe pun-

ishment would serve to deter unknown others from committing similar offenses. That pseudo-scientific apology for punishment, artlessly distinguished from punishment for its own sake, has survived and flowered—like a hardy perennial—into the present. It is probably superfluous to remark that there was no convincing proof then—just as there is none now—that punishment in any form acts as an effective deterrent.

The deterrence doctrine now, just as it was in Constantine's day, is one of the many disingenuous excuses for criminal justice, and is woven inextricably into the more ancient tragic pattern of man's unremitting effort to shift to a substitute his own unexpressed criminal impulses.

Andenaes, The Morality of Deterrence, 37 U.Chi.L.Rev. 649, 663–64 (1970):

[I]t is often asserted that there is no scientific proof for the general preventive effects of punishment, and it may be argued that it is morally unjustifiable to inflict punishment on the basis of a belief which is not corroborated by scientific evidence. The burden of proof, it is sometimes said, is on those who would invoke punishment. Others may answer that the burden of proof is on those who would experiment at the risk of society by removing or weakening the protection which the criminal law now provides.

Two points should be made. First, our lack of knowledge of general prevention may be exaggerated. In some areas of criminal law we have experiences which come as close to scientific proof as could be expected in human affairs. In many other areas it seems reasonably safe to evaluate the general preventive effects of punishment on a common sense basis. Modern psychology has shown that the pleasure-pain principle is not as universally valid as is assumed, for instance, in Bentham's penal philosophy. Nevertheless, it is still a fundamental fact of social life that the risk of unpleasant consequences is a very strong motivational factor for most people in most situations.

Second, even in questions of social and economic policy we rarely are able to base our decisions on anything which comes close to strict scientific proof. Generally we must act on the basis of our best judgment. In this respect, the problems of penal policy are the same as problems of education, housing, foreign trade policy, and so on. The development of social science gradually provides a better factual foundation for decisions of social policy, but there is a long way to go. Besides, research always lags behind the rapid change of social conditions.

However, it is undeniable that punishment—the intentional infliction of suffering—is a special category among social policies. It contrasts sharply with the social welfare measures which characterize our modern state. This calls for caution and moderation in its application. I do not think the legal concept of "burden of proof" is very useful in this context. The balance that should be struck between defense of society and humaneness towards the offender can hardly be expressed in a simple formula. The solution of the conflict will depend on individual attitudes. Some people identify more with the values threatened by criminal behavior; others identify more with the lawbreaker. But certainly punishment should not be imposed precipitously. History provides a multitude of examples of shocking cruelty based on ideas of deterrence, often in combination with ideas of just retribution.

Morris and Zimring, Deterrence and Corrections, 381 Annals 137, 138–39 (1969):

> Our dedication to corrections must not lead us to repudiate deterrence. Our criminal-law system has deterrence as its primary and essential postulate. And there are many examples of the threat of punishment under the criminal law clearly influencing human behavior. Honest reader, consider your income tax return, and what it would be like were you assured that it could not be checked. If we have misjudged you, consider the impact on your neighbor's tax return! On the other hand, there are many areas where variations in the severity of the penal sanction seem to be irrelevant to the incidence of the behavior threatened—capital punishment as distinguished from protracted imprisonment for homicide; the gross increase in sanctions for narcotics offenses; and, generally, variations in minima and maxima of terms of imprisonment for a wise diversity of criminal offenses. Here, as elsewhere, the compelling lesson is that it is foolish in the extreme to offer general propositions about crime and criminals. We must address ourselves [to] the diversity of our purposes and the varieties of human behavior we seek to influence.

LOVALD AND STUB, THE REVOLVING DOOR: REACTIONS OF CHRONIC DRUNKENNESS OFFENDERS TO COURT SANCTIONS

59 J.Crim.L., C. & P.S. 525, 525–27, 529 (1968).[g]

In 1957 there were 11,031 arrests for public intoxication in Minneapolis, Minnesota. As a result of police surveillance and action, a total of 5,763 persons appeared in Municipal Court to answer charges of drunkenness or such related charges as drunk and disorderly conduct. In a manner typical of most lower courts in the United States, the cases were disposed of either by committing the individual to the workhouse, imposing a fine, or suspending the charge. Although a majority of these individuals were not arrested and punished again for

g. Reprinted by special permission of the Journal of Criminal Law, Criminology & Police Science (Northwestern University School of Law), Copyright ©, 1968, Vol. 59, No. 4.

their drinking behavior (even a suspended sentence may entail a tongue-lashing from the presiding judge), a total of 1,649 did reappear in Municipal Court on a drunkenness charge at least once more during that year. These individuals contributed to what has been called the "revolving door" phenomenon of our lower courts.

*   *   *

Although we may hypothesize that in general punishment does not deter acts of drunkenness, individuals caught in the process of the revolving door may, in fact, react differentially to the type of sanction imposed by the court. It is generally thought that the lower courts tend to incarcerate recidivists; therefore, the possibility that a fine or even a suspended sentence may account for variability in the reactions of recidivists to court actions may be overlooked. The purpose of the present paper is to investigate the reactions to various "degrees" of punishment meted out to the 1649 Minneapolis recidivists.

*   *   *

Discussion

*   *   *

We may hypothesize that variations in frequency of drunkenness arrests are partly a function of the ability to absorb financial sacrifice resulting from indulgence in drinking. Our findings show that financial loss apparently deters future drunkenness episodes more effectively than does incarceration. In addition to difficulty in raising money for fines, the use of "the drinking money" for this purpose may act as a further deterrent. Thus, the economic status of the Skid Row resident may provide one reason why the workhouse sentence is less of a deterrent than a fine to future drunkenness behavior. Many of the men living on Skid Row rely solely on monthly OASI or public assistance checks. During a period of imprisonment, an offender is unable to spend any money, and he may find an extra check waiting for him at his place of residence upon his release. The individual who is fined for his drinking offense must spend money that might otherwise be used to buy liquor. A court fine is a luxury few can afford. Our data indicate no difference in length of time between arrests for the workhouse sentence and the suspended sentence. Neither of these two types of court sanctions involve a financial loss.

Another aspect of Skid Row life may be linked to the revolving door. Skid Row residents attach no particular stigma to serving time in jail. This does not mean that Skid Row lacks a normative structure, but rather that middle class norms do not operate there. Knowledge that a man has served a jail sentence has little if any effect upon his status in the community, since Skid Row residents regard a month in jail (especially during the winter) as a good way to recuperate from the effects of cheap liquor, poor food, and haphazard sleeping arrangements.

(2) CRIMINAL CONVICTION AS A MEANS OF PROVIDING "TREATMENT"

K. MENNINGER, THE CRIME OF PUNISHMENT

253, 257–61 (1968).[h]

The medical use of the word *treatment* implies a program of presumably beneficial action prescribed for and administered to one who seeks it. The purpose of treatment is to relieve pain, correct disability, or combat an illness. Treatment may be painful or disagreeable but, if so, these qualities are incidental, not purposive.

* * *

When the community begins to look upon the expression of aggressive violence as the symptom of an illness or as indicative of illness, it will be because it believes doctors can do something to correct such a condition. At present, some better-informed individuals do believe and expect this. However angry at or sorry for the offender, they want him "treated" in an effective way so that he will cease to be a danger to them. And they know that the traditional punishment, "treatment-punishment," will not effect this.

What *will*? What effective treatment is there for such violence? It will surely have to begin with motivating or stimulating or arousing in a cornered individual the wish and hope and intention to change his methods of dealing with the realities of life. Can this be done by education, medication, counseling, training? I would answer *yes*. It can be done successfully in a majority of cases, if undertaken in time.

The present penal system and the existing legal philosophy do not stimulate or even expect such a change to take place in the criminal. Yet change is what medical science always aims for. The prisoner, like the doctor's other patients, should emerge from his treatment experience a different person, differently equipped, differently functioning, and headed in a different direction from when he began the treatment.

It is natural for the public to doubt that this can be accomplished with criminals. But remember that the public used to doubt that change could be effected in the mentally ill. * * * The average length of time required for restoring a mentally ill patient to health in [one particular] hospital has been reduced from years, to months, to weeks. Four-fifths of the patients living there today will be back in their homes by the end of the year. There are many empty beds, and the daily census is continually dropping.

What Is This Effective Treatment?

If these "incurable" patients are now being returned to their homes and their work in such numbers and with such celerity, why not something similar for offenders?   Just what are the treatments used to effect these rapid changes?   Are they available for use with offenders?

The forms and techniques of psychiatric treatment used today number in the hundreds.   Psychoanalysis;   electroshock therapy; psychotherapy;   occupational and industrial therapy;   family group therapy;   milieu therapy;   the use of music, art, and horticultural activities;   and various drug therapies—these are some of the techniques and modalities of treatment used to stimulate or assist the restoration of a vital balance of impulse control and life satisfaction. No one patient requires or receives all forms, but each patient is studied with respect to his particular needs, his basic assets, his interests, and his special difficulties.   In addition to the treatment modalities mentioned, there are many facilitations and events which contribute to total treatment effect: a new job opportunity (perhaps located by a social worker) or a vacation trip, a course of reducing exercises, a cosmetic surgical operation or a herniotomy, some night school courses, a wedding in the family (even one for the patient!), an inspiring sermon.   Some of these require merely prescription or suggestion;   others require guidance, tutelage, or assistance by trained therapists or by willing volunteers.   A therapeutic team may embrace a dozen workers—as in a hospital setting—or it may narrow down to the doctor and the spouse.   Clergymen, teachers, relatives, friends, and even fellow patients often participate informally but helpfully in the process of readaptation.

All of the participants in this effort to bring about a favorable change in the patient, i. e., in his vital balance and life program, are imbued with what we may call a *therapeutic attitude*.   This is one in direct antithesis to attitudes of avoidance, ridicule, scorn, or punitiveness.   Hostile feelings toward the subject, however justified by his unpleasant and even destructive behavior, are not in the curriculum of therapy or in the therapist.   This does not mean that therapists approve of the offensive and obnoxious behavior of the patient;   they distinctly disapprove of it.   But they recognize it as symptomatic of continued imbalance and disorganization, which is what they are seeking to change.   *   *   *   A patient may cough in the doctor's face or may vomit on the office rug;   a patient may curse or scream or even struggle in the extremity of his pain.   But these acts are not "punished."   Doctors and nurses have no time or thought for inflicting unnecessary pain even upon patients who may be difficult, disagreeable, provocative, and even dangerous.   It is their duty to care for them, to try to make them well, and to prevent them from doing themselves or others harm.   This requires love, not hate.

This is the deepest meaning of the therapeutic attitude. Every doctor knows this; every worker in a hospital or clinic knows it (or should). * * *

"But you were talking about the mentally ill," readers may interject, "those poor, confused, bereft, frightened individuals who yearn for help from you doctors and nurses. Do you mean to imply that willfully perverse individuals, our criminals, can be similarly reached and rehabilitated? Do you really believe that effective treatment of the sort you visualize can be applied to people *who do not want any help,* who are so willfully vicious, so well aware of the wrongs they are doing, so lacking in penitence or even common decency that punishment seems to be the only thing left?"

Do I believe there is effective treatment for offenders, and that they *can* be changed? *Most certainly and definitely I do.* Not all cases, to be sure; there are also some physical afflictions which we cannot cure at the moment. Some provision has to be made for incurables—pending new knowledge—and these will include some offenders. But I believe the majority of them would prove to be curable. The willfulness and the viciousness of offenders are part of the thing for which they have to be treated. These must not thwart the therapeutic attitude.

NOTES

1. Is it reasonable or realistic to expect correctional programs to seek to change behavior by use of methods patterned upon techniques used in treating the "mentally ill?" Compare P. Tappan, Crime, Justice and Correction 523–24 (1960):

The Role of Clinical Methods in Prevention and Treatment

In the light of the extremely exiguous facilities available for clinical treatment and the wide prevalence of relatively serious disorders in the general population, it appears desirable to employ measures of individual or intensive psychiatric therapy with prisoners only when there is reasonable ground to believe that their criminality was directly related to a psychiatric deviation and that treatment may significantly reduce the danger of criminal conduct. It is not a specific objective of the criminal law or the correctional system to alleviate the mental or emotional distress of offenders. The effort to accomplish this can be justified only in so far as it may result in increased public protection through diminishing criminality. At the present level of knowledge and technique, we cannot be exact in making the decisions called for here, but there is no sound reason to believe that psychiatric ministration to offenders displaying ordinary emotional difficulties will curtail their crimes more effectively than present measures of correctional treatment do. A large proportion of offenders who have drawn their attitudes and behavior from the criminal norms of antisocial minorities display no more and possibly less psychological distress than does the ordinary man in the street.

The primary legal and correctional objective is to protect the public against criminal recidivism with reasonable economy and humanity. This means using effective measures of control and correctional treatment of many sorts, derived from the various behavioral and social disciplines. The increasingly prevalent emphasis today upon psychotherapy and the removal of emotional problems as *the* means of prevention and reformation is an illusory diversion. The ends of deterrence, incapacitation, and rehabilitation must be sought through widely varied methods and in some instances, at least, the result should be to increase the frustrations and guilt feelings of those who are criminally inclined. Psychiatry, psychology, and casework, all important phases of correctional treatment, will fulfill their potential roles in that field best by adapting their specialized techniques to the essential objectives of correction rather than by attempting to alleviate neurosis or other discomforts on a wholesale basis. As psychiatrists and clinical psychologists incorporate a criminological orientation, they should contribute more fully to the prevention and treatment of crime. This will involve not only a refinement of their diagnostic skills but also instructing nonclinical workers in the treatment approaches that are most effective in reorienting the antisocial toward authority and reality. It is quite apparent that clinical specialists will not be able themselves to carry on individual psychotherapy with offenders to any considerable extent, either in institutions or in the community.

2. Robison and Smith, Effectiveness of Correctional Programs, 17 Crime and Delinquency 67 (1971) examined the results of research done in the California correctional system in an effort to determine the extent to which research results supported theoretical assertions that recidivism could be reduced by use of institutional programs rather than probation, longer periods of institutionalization, group counseling during incarceration, smaller caseloads during postsentence parole supervision, or parole supervision upon completion of sentence rather than immediate and complete discharge. The findings, Robison and Smith report, "strongly suggest" that "there is no evidence to support any program's claim of superior rehabilitative efficacy." Id. at 80. In evaluating the effectiveness of "treatment" during imprisonment, Robison and Smith reported an unpublished study comparing the recidivism rate or the rate of return to prison, either for violation of parole or upon a new conviction, of prison inmates who voluntarily choose to participate in group counseling, inmates compelled to participate in such counseling, inmates who voluntarily choose not to participate in group counseling, and a control group not offered the opportunity to participate in group counseling. The rates of recidivism after three years were as follows:

compelled treatment	51% recidivated
voluntary treatment	49
voluntary nonparticipants	55
control group	48

The differences among the groups were not statistically significant.

3.   If the object of the law is to compel persons to submit to treatment, why not make them liable for a crime and "treat" them after they have been convicted?

ROSS, HAYES, FRIEL AND KERPER, A DESCRIPTIVE STUDY OF THE SKID ROW ALCOHOLIC IN HOUSTON, TEXAS

42–44 (1970) (Criminal Justice Monograph, Vol. II, No. 2, Institute of
Contemporary Corrections and the Behavioral Sciences,
Sam Houston State University).

Houston Police Department statistics show that of the 61,985 arrests made by the Houston Police Department in 1966, 26,453 were for public intoxication.   Police officials estimate that of the 26,543 arrests, approximately two thirds (65%) to three fourths (75%) were made among the bottom ten per cent of the alcoholic community.   This "bottom ten per cent" includes the "skid row bum," the "wino," and the "sociopathic-hobohemian" who inhabit the "Avenue" or skid row section in Houston.   From interviews with Houston police patrolmen who work the skid row area the problems that arise most often invoke the police practice called "keeping the peace" rather than "law enforcement" which demands more stringent control.   The procedures employed in keeping the peace are not determined by legal mandates so much as they are responses to certain demand conditions.   Major among these conditions is the concentration of certain types mentioned above, such as the "skid row bum," the "wino," et cetera.   As Bittner points out, the lives of the inhabitants of skid row are in most instances lacking in prospective coherence.[1]   The consequent reduction of predictability constitutes the main problem of keeping the peace on skid row.   One of the major complaints made by the subjects in the research sample was: "I was just standing there, minding my own business, and they picked me up and charged me with being drunk."   This type of arrest is most often the result of a police practice known as "sweeping the street."   Answering a disturbance call to a point within the "Avenue" section the Police will arrest, not only those involved in the "disturbance," but all others in sight who have the appearance of being a "skid row bum," a "wino," et cetera.   This tendency to proceed against persons mainly on the basis of perceived risk rather than on the basis of culpability, springs from the desire of the patrolmen to reduce the aggregate total of troubles in the area.   It is easier to eliminate all sources of "trouble" by mass arrest than painstakingly evaluate individual cases of "trouble," on merit.

1.   Egon Bittner, "The Police on Skid-
Row, American Sociological Review,
Vol. 32, No. 5 (October 1967), 712–715.

NOTES

1. To what extent may the situations described here be regarded as a "cost" of some alcohol-related offenses? Consider the possibility that insofar as the existence of an offense of public intoxication constitutes a demand upon law enforcement agencies for its enforcement, enforcement may be too difficult or impossible unless "short cuts" are taken which infringe or endanger other rights. This argument is often made in the context of marijuana regulation: the existence of a prohibition against possession of marijuana for personal use creates too costly an incentive for improper police enforcement activities. See Note, Possession of Marijuana in San Mateo County: Some Social Costs of Criminalization, 22 Stan.L.Rev. 101, 115 (1969), stating that of 80 marijuana prosecutions studied, one-fifth raised "serious questions for the critical observer as to whether the officer had probable cause either to search or to arrest." Need such a situation—if it exists—be a "cost" of criminalization? Why not simply restrict enforcement to those situations in which enforcement can be had without infringement of other rights? Is this practical? How might it be done? By excluding evidence obtained by improper methods from a subsequent prosecution, thereby removing the incentive for such enforcement techniques? For an exhaustive examination of the effectiveness of such an exclusionary rule, see Oaks, Studying the Exclusionary Rule in Search and Seizure, 37 U.Chi.L.Rev. 665 (1970). What practical problems would you anticipate in the enforcement of a right to exclusion by the subjects of the procedures of the Houston, Texas police described above?

2. To what extent would "decriminalization" prevent the costs described above? Arrests and detentions without any intent to bring formal charges have been documented in the drunkenness area. See W. LaFave, Arrest 439–49 (1965). If community pressure to "keep the streets clean" remained after repeal or invalidation of public intoxication crimes, to what extent would the lot of present subjects of improper enforcement techniques be improved? If criminal penalties were replaced by authorizations for involuntary treatment, would it be likely that the means used to "collect" individuals for such treatment would be less offensive than those presently used? Why?

3. President's Commission on Law Enforcement and Administration of Justice, Task Force Report; Drunkenness 1–2 (1967):

> Two million arrests in 1965—one of every three arrests in America—were for the offense of public drunkenness.[1] The great volume of these arrests places an extremely heavy load on

1. 1965 FBI Uniform Crime Reports 117 (table 25). In 1965, 1,516,548 drunkenness arrests were reported by 4,043 agencies, embracing a total population of 125,139,000. Projections based upon these figures indicate that there were over 2 million arrests in the entire country during 1965. An undetermined number of additional arrests for drunkenness are made under disorderly conduct, vagrancy, loitering, and related statutes. See, e. g., Foote, Vagrancy-Type Law and Its Administration, 104 U.Pa.L.Rev. 603 (1956) (discussion of interchanging of statutes for like purposes); Murtagh, Arrests for Public Intoxication, 35 Fordham L. Rev. 1–7 (1966) (description of the prior New York City practice of using a disorderly conduct statute to arrest nondisorderly inebriates).

the operations of the criminal justice system. It burdens police, clogs lower criminal courts, and crowds penal institutions throughout the United States.

*   *   *

The police do not arrest everyone who is under the influence of alcohol.[12] Sometimes they will help an inebriate home. It is when he appears to have no home or family ties that he is most likely to be arrested and taken to the local jail.[13]

One policeman assigned to a skid row precinct in a large eastern city recently described how he decided whom to arrest:

> I see a guy who's been hanging around; a guy who's been picked up before or been making trouble. I stop him. Sometimes he can convince me he's got a job today or got something to do. He'll show me a slip showing he's supposed to go to the blood bank, or to work. I let him go. But if it seems to me that he's got nothing to do but drink, then I bring him in.[14]

Drunkenness arrest practices vary from place to place. Some police departments strictly enforce drunkenness statutes, while other departments are known to be more tolerant. In fact, the number of arrests in a city may be related less to the amount of public drunkenness than to police policy. Some of the wide variations in police practices can be seen in the table below that compares drunkenness arrests by two police departments known to be guided by policies of strict enforcement (Atlanta, Ga., and Washington, D. C.) to arrests by a department that is considered more tolerant (St. Louis, Mo.).

In some large and medium-size cities, police departments have "bum squads" that cruise skid rows and border areas to apprehend inebriates who appear unable to care for their own safety, or who are likely to annoy others.[15] Such wholesale arrests sometimes include homeless people who are not intoxicated.[16]

*   *   *

12. It is often the express policy of a police department to refrain from arresting a person for drunkenness in cases in which he may be placed in a taxicab or he is with friends who are able to escort him home. See, e. g., 1 Columbus, Ohio, Police Dep't Training Bull., rev. Aug. 1958, unit 6, p. 2; Pres.'s Comm'n on Crime in the District of Columbia, Rep. 475 (1966), citing letter from District of Columbia Police Chief John B. Layton to Pres.'s Comm'n on Crime in the District of Columbia, Apr. 1, 1966.

13. The police make this determination by observing, *inter alia*, the apparent affluence of the inebriate. Moreover, the lack of funds for transportation will influence the determination to arrest. The result is that the poor are more likely to be arrested than the well-to-do. See Pres.'s Comm'n on Crime in the District of Columbia, Rep. 475 (1966). See also Washington Daily News, Dec. 21, 1965, p. 5, at p. 35 (interview with precinct commanding officer: "We do tend to enforce the laws more rigidly on 14th Street than in, say, Crestwood, a better part of the precinct.").

14. Interview with a police officer assigned to a large-city skid row by a staff member of the Vera Institute of Justice.

15. LaFave, Arrest: The Decision to Take a Suspect Into Custody 441 n. 13 (1965).

16. The Atlanta Alcohol Study Project found that there are a "significant

Comparison of Drunkenness Arrests in Three Cities

	Popu-lations 1965 estimates	Number of arrests (1965)			(Percentage of all arrests) accounted for by:	
		Drunken-ness arrests	Disorderly conduct and vagrancy arrests	All arrests	Drunk arrests	Drunk, disorderly, and vagrancy arrests
Washington, D.C.	802, 000	44, 792	21, 338	86, 464	51. 8	76. 5
St. Louis, Mo.	699, 000	2, 445	5, 994	44, 701	5. 5	18. 9
Atlanta, Ga.	522, 000	48, 835	22, 379	92, 965	52. 5	76. 6

[A9014]

4.   A criminal conviction may not, of course, be based upon activity that is constitutionally protected, such as the exercise of free speech of freedom of religion.   Recent United States Supreme Court cases have developed a general "right of privacy" that has to some extent limited the conduct which can be criminalized.

In Griswold v. Connecticut, 381 U.S. 479, 85 S.Ct. 1678, 14 L.Ed.2d 510 (1965) the Court held that use of a contraceptive device by a married couple was protected by the right of marital privacy.   Without deciding whether the distribution of such devices could be prohibited, the statute penalizing use was struck down and the conviction, as an accessory, of the physician who prescribed the device was overturned.   Then, in Eisenstadt v. Baird, 405 U.S. 438, 92 S.Ct. 1029, 31 L.Ed.2d 349 (1972), the Court, again without deciding whether the distribution of contraceptives might constitutionally be prohibited, held that a statute which distinguished married from single persons for purposes of determining the availability of contraceptives could not stand.   The Court said that if *Griswold* barred such a prohibition it extended to single persons since the right of privacy is a right of the individual "to be free from unwarranted governmental intrusion into matters so fundamentally affecting a person as the decision whether to bear or beget a child".   If *Griswold* permitted such a prohibition it was unreasonable to distinguish single from married persons and such invidious discrimination violated the Equal Protection Clause of the Constitution.

This right of the individual to be free of unwarranted governmental intrusion was supported in *Eisenstadt* by the citation of Stanley v. Georgia, 394 U.S. 557, 89 S.Ct. 1243, 22 L.Ed.2d 542 (1969).   There the Court held that private possession of obscene material in one's home could not be made a criminal offense.   It should be noted that efforts to extend this "right" of private possession to the distribution of such material have been rejected. United States v. Orito, 413 U.S. 139, 93 S.Ct. 2674, 37 L.Ed.2d 513, 13 Cr. L.Rptr. 3192 (1973) (transportation of obscene matter in interstate com-

number of individuals who are arrested for public intoxication and who are not drunk at the time of arrest." Emory Dep't of Psychiatry 18.   Similar findings were reported in other cities; see, for example, reports by Klein, The Criminal Law Process vs. the Public Drunkenness Offender in San Francisco, 1964 (unpublished, on file at Stanford Univ. Institute for the Study of Human Problems), and by Nash, Habitats of Homeless Men in Manhattan, Nov. 1964 (unpublished, on file at Columbia Univ. Bureau of Applied Social Research).

merce by a common carrier may be criminalized) and United States v. 12 200-Ft. Reels of Film, 413 U.S. 123, 93 S.Ct. 2665, 37 L.Ed.2d 500, 13 Cr.L. Rptr. 3197 (1973) (importation of obscene matter may be prohibited even if for the importer's private, personal use).

The most recent "privacy" case is Roe v. Wade, 410 U.S. 113, 93 S.Ct. 705, 35 L.Ed.2d 147 (1973) which held that the performance of an abortion by a physician during the first three months of pregnancy could not be criminalized. After the first trimester, said the Court, the state might regulate the procedure in a manner reasonably designed to protect the woman from abortions dangerous to her health. In the final trimester the woman's right of privacy was held to give way, if the state so desired, to the interest in preserving potential life so that abortions during that period might be prescribed except when necessary to preserve the woman's life or health.

In terms of the substantive criminal law's effect on the behavior of individuals, the *Roe* decision is the most significant "privacy" case to date. Although anti-abortion statutes resulted in relatively few convictions there is strong evidence that by deterring physicians they did frustrate the desire of many women to have abortions and caused most abortions which were obtained to be performed, due to their illegality, by inadequate personnel and/or under undesirable circumstances. See Callahan, Abortion: Law, Choice and Morality (1970); Tietze, "Two Years' Experience With a Liberal Abortion Law", 5 Family Planning Perspectives 36 (1973); and Zimring, "Of Doctors, Deterrence and the Dark Figure of Crime: A Note on Abortion in Hawaii", 39 U.Chi.L.Rev. 699 (1972).

The direct effect of these decisions upon the decision to criminalize alcohol-related conduct is not great. It is arguable however, that possession of alcoholic beverages (and perhaps some other substances) in the privacy of a home is constitutionally protected and that unusual or even bizzare lifestyles are similarly within the right of privacy so that a person may not be forcibly "treated" so as to change that lifestyle. The most likely expansion, if any, of the privacy decisions is in the area of the criminalization of certain sexual conduct. For example, in most jurisdictions sodomy is proscribed without regard to whether it is heterosexual or homosexual, whether between married or single persons, or whether or not engaged in privately. Attacks on such laws as well as those proscribing prostitution, fornication and adultery are likely to increase in the future. In addition to the privacy argument, some such statutes may be vulnerable on the grounds of vagueness, and with respect to homosexual conduct on the *Robinson/Powell* theory that the state cannot criminalize a condition which the individual is powerless to change.

The indirect implications of the legal right to privacy are more pervasive. Criminalizing certain conduct may infringe upon some person's interest in "privacy", but not to the extent that the criminal statute in unconstitution-Nevertheless, the fact that criminalization infringes this interest must be regarded as a "cost" of this criminalization. For example, criminalizing public intoxication may prevent a person from consuming given amounts of certain substances at a social occasion. This is a "cost" of such criminalization, even if the person has no legally-enforceable right of privacy that permits him to consume that amount of the substance.

There are other "personal" costs of criminalization that cannot be ignored. Those persons actually apprehended pay costs in terms of the inconvenience and expense of being arrested, charged, and tried. If convicted, they may pay further costs in terms of fines or time spent in incarceration. (This may also involve indirect costs such as loss of earnings while in custody and perhaps loss of future earnings because conviction and incarceration reduces employability.) Those who engage in the prohibited activity but are not apprehended may also pay a cost in terms of experiencing anxiety and concern over the possibility of apprehension.

Whether there are countervailing considerations that justify paying these costs is another matter. To the extent that these conditions exist, it is clear that they are "costs" of criminalization.

C. THE NEED TO BE PRECISE OR THE VICE OF VAGUENESS

The material above and Powell v. Texas deal with the basic policy decision of what to make criminal. But the task of the law is not only to make such a decision but to embody it in a "rule." As with the decision to make given activity criminal, the decision as to how to express the result can best be initially approached by examining constitutional limitations upon possible solutions. In the case of expressing the result, the basic constitutional limitation is the due process requirement of precision or, in negative terms, the defect of vagueness. Consider, in light of the material in this chapter, the extent to which the statute involved in Powell v. Texas might be subject to attack on vagueness grounds. Consider the same matter in regard to the various other statutes presented in this chapter as embodying various approaches—both criminal and noncriminal—towards alcohol-related activity.

PAPACHRISTOU v. JACKSONVILLE

Supreme Court of the United States, 1972.
405 U.S. 156, 92 S.Ct. 839, 31 L.Ed.2d 110.

Mr. Justice DOUGLAS delivered the opinion of the Court.

This case involves eight defendants who were convicted in a Florida municipal court of violating a Jacksonville, Florida, vagrancy ordinance.[1] * * * For reasons which will appear, we reverse.

---

1. Jacksonville Ordinance Code § 26–57 provided at the time of these arrests and convictions as follows:

"Rogues and vagabonds, or dissolute persons who go about begging, common gamblers, persons who use juggling or unlawful games or plays, common drunkards, common night walkers, thieves, pilferers or pickpockets, traders in stolen property, lewd, wanton and lascivious persons, keepers of gambling places, common railers and brawlers, persons wandering or strolling around from place to place without any lawful

At issue are five consolidated cases. Margaret Papachristou, Betty Calloway, Eugene Eddie Melton, and Leonard Johnson were all arrested early on a Sunday morning, and charged with vagrancy— "prowling by auto."

*   *   *

The facts are stipulated. Papachristou and Calloway are white females. Melton and Johnson are black males. Papachristou was enrolled in a job-training program sponsored by the State Employment Service at Florida Junior College in Jacksonville. Calloway was a typing and shorthand teacher at a state mental institution located near Jacksonville. She was the owner of the automobile in which the four defendants were arrested. Melton was a Vietnam war veteran who had been released from the Navy after nine months in a veterans' hospital. On the date of his arrest he was a part-time computer helper while attending college as a full-time student in Jacksonville. Johnson was a tow-motor operator in a grocery chain warehouse and was a lifelong resident of Jacksonville.

At the time of their arrest the four of them were riding in Calloway's car on the main thoroughfare in Jacksonville. They had left a restaurant owned by Johnson's uncle where they had eaten and were on their way to a night club. The arresting officers denied that the racial mixture in the car played any part in the decision to make the arrest. The arrest, they said, was made because the defendants had stopped near a used-car lot which had been broken into several times. There was, however, no evidence of any breaking and entering on the night in question.

Of these four charged with "prowling by auto" none had been previously arrested except Papachristou who had once been convicted of a municipal offense.

[The details of the arrests in the other cases are omitted.]

Jacksonville's ordinance and Florida's statute were "derived from early English law," * * * and employ "archaic language" in their definitions of vagrants. The history is an often-told tale. The break-up of feudal estates in England led to labor shortages which in turn resulted in the Statutes of Laborers, designed to stabilize the labor

purpose or object, habitual loafers, disorderly persons, persons neglecting all lawful business and habitually spending their time by frequenting houses of ill fame, gaming houses, or places where alcoholic beverages are sold or served, persons able to work but habitually living upon the earnings of their wives or minor children shall be deemed vagrants and, upon conviction in the Municipal Court shall be punished as provided for Class D offenses."

Class D offenses at the time of these arrests and convictions were punishable by 90 days imprisonment, $500 fine, or both. Jacksonville Ordinance Code § 1–8 (1965). The maximum punishment has since been reduced to 75 days or $450. § 304.101 (1971). We are advised that that downward revision was made to avoid federal right-to-counsel decisions. The Fifth Circuit case extending right to counsel in misdemeanors where a fine of $500 or 90-days imprisonment could be imposed is Harvey v. Mississippi, 340 F.2d 263 (CA 5 1965).

force by prohibiting increases in wages and prohibiting the movement of workers from their home areas in search of improved conditions. Later vagrancy laws became criminal aspects of the poor laws. The series of laws passed in England on the subject became increasingly severe. But "the theory of the Elizabethan poor laws no longer fits the facts," Edwards v. California, 314 U.S. 160, 174, 62 S.Ct. 164, 167, 86 L.Ed. 119. The conditions which spawned these laws may be gone, but the archaic classifications remain.

This ordinance is void-for-vagueness, both in the sense that it "fails to give a person of ordinary intelligence fair notice that his contemplated conduct is forbidden by the statute," United States v. Harriss, 347 U.S. 612, 617, 74 S.Ct. 808, 812, 98 L.Ed. 989, and because it encourages arbitrary and erratic arrests and convictions. * * *

Living under a rule of law entails various suppositions, one of which is that "All [persons] are entitled to be informed as to what the State commands or forbids." Lanzetta v. New Jersey, 306 U.S. 451, 453, 59 S.Ct. 618, 619, 83 L.Ed. 888.

Lanzetta is one of a well-recognized group of cases insisting that the law give fair notice of the offending conduct. * * * In the field of regulatory statutes governing business activities, where the acts limited are in a narrow category, greater leeway is allowed. * * *

The poor among us, the minorities, the average householder are not in business and not alerted to the regulatory schemes of vagrancy laws; and we assume they would have no understanding of their meaning and impact if they read them. Nor are they protected from being caught in the vagrancy net by the necessity of having a specific intent to commit an unlawful act. * * *

The Jacksonville ordinance makes criminal activities which by modern standards are normally innocent. "Nightwalking" is one. Florida construes the ordinance not to make criminal one night's wandering, Johnson v. State, [Fla., 202 So.2d 852, 855,] only the "habitual" wanderer or as the ordinance describes it "common night walkers." We know, however, from experience that sleepless people often walk at night, perhaps hopeful that sleep-inducing relaxation will result.

"Persons able to work but habitually living on the earnings of their wives or minor children"—like habitually living "without visible means of support"—might implicate unemployed pillars of the community who have married rich wives.

"Persons able to work but habitually living on the earnings of their wives or minor children" may also embrace unemployed people out of the labor market, by reason of a recession or disemployed by reason of technological or so-called structural displacements.

Dix & Sharlot Cs. Crim. Law CrJS.—5

Persons "wandering or strolling" from place to place have been extolled by Walt Whitman and Vachel Lindsay. The qualification "without any lawful purpose or object" may be a trap for innocent acts. Persons "neglecting all lawful business and habitually spending their time by frequenting * * * places where alcoholic beverages are sold or served" would literally embrace many members of golf clubs and city clubs.

Walkers and strollers and wanderers may be going to or coming from a burglary. Loafers or loiterers may be "casing" a place for a holdup. Letting one's wife support him is an intra-family matter, and normally of no concern to the police. Yet it may, of course, be the setting for numerous crimes.

The difficulty is that these activities are historically part of the amenities of life as we have known it. They are not mentioned in the Constitution or in the Bill of Rights. These unwritten amenities have been in part responsible for giving our people the feeling of independence and self-confidence, the feeling of creativity. These amenities have dignified the right of dissent and have honored the right to be nonconformists and the right to defy submissiveness. They have encouraged lives of high spirits rather than hushed, suffocating silence.

This aspect of the vagrancy ordinance before us is suggested by what this Court said in 1875 about a broad criminal statute enacted by Congress: "It would certainly be dangerous if the legislature could set a net large enough to catch all possible offenders, and leave it to the courts to step inside and say who could be rightfully detained, and who should be set at large." United States v. Reese, 92 U.S. 214, 221, 23 L.Ed. 563.

While that was a federal case, the due process implications are equally applicable to the States and to this vagrancy ordinance. Here the net cast is large, not to give the courts the power to pick and choose but to increase the arsenal of the police. * * *

Where the list of crimes is so all-inclusive and generalized as that one in this ordinance, those convicted may be punished for no more than vindicating affronts to police authority:

"The common ground which brings such a motley assortment of human troubles before the magistrates in vagrancy-type proceedings is the procedural laxity which permits 'conviction' for almost any kind of conduct and the existence of the House of Correction as an easy and convenient dumping-ground for problems that appear to have no other immediate solution." Foote, Vagrancy Type Law and Its Administration, 104 U.Pa.L.Rev. 603, 631.

Another aspect of the ordinance's vagueness appears when we focus, not on the lack of notice given a potential offender, but on the effect of the unfettered discretion it places in the hands of the Jacksonville police. Caleb Foote, an early student of this subject, has called the vagrancy-type law as offering "punishment by analogy." Id., at 609. Such crimes, though long common in Russia, are not compatible with our constitutional system. We allow our police to make arrests only on "probable cause," a Fourth and Fourteenth Amendment standard applicable to the States as well as to the Federal Government. Arresting a person on suspicion, like arresting a person for investigation, is foreign to our system, even when the arrest is for past criminality. Future criminality, however, is the common justification for the presence of vagrancy statutes. See Foote, op. cit. supra, at 625. Florida has indeed construed her vagrancy statute "as necessary regulations," *inter alia*, "to deter vagabondage and prevent crimes." Johnson v. State, Fla., 202 So.2d 852; Smith v. State, Fla., 239 So.2d 250, 251.

A direction by a legislature to the police to arrest all "suspicious" persons would not pass constitutional muster. A vagrancy prosecution may be merely the cloak for a conviction which could not be obtained on the real but undisclosed grounds for the arrest. People v. Moss, 309 N.Y. 429, 131 N.E.2d 717. But as Chief Justice Hewart said in Frederick Dean, 18 Cr.App.Rep. 133, 134 (1924):

> "It would be in the highest degree unfortunate if in any part of the country those who are responsible for setting in motion the criminal law should entertain, connive at or coquette with the idea that in a case where there is not enough evidence to charge the prisoner with an attempt to commit a crime, the prosecution may, nevertheless, on such insufficient evidence, succeed in obtaining and upholding a conviction under the Vagrancy Act, 1824."

Those generally implicated by the imprecise terms of the ordinance—poor people, nonconformists, dissenters, idlers—may be required to comport themselves according to the life-style deemed appropriate by the Jacksonville police and the courts. Where, as here, there are no standards governing the exercise of the discretion granted by the ordinance, the scheme permits and encourages an arbitrary and discriminatory enforcement of the law. It furnishes a convenient tool for "harsh and discriminatory enforcement by prosecuting officials, against particular groups deemed to merit their displeasure." Thornhill v. Alabama, 310 U.S. 88, 97–98, 60 S.Ct. 736, 742, 84 L.Ed. 1093. It results in a regime in which the poor and the unpopular are permitted to "stand on a public sidewalk * * * only at the whim of any police officer." * * *

The implicit presumption in these generalized vagrancy standards—that crime is being nipped in the bud—is too extravagant to deserve extended treatment. Of course, vagrancy statutes are useful to the police. Of course they are nets making easy the roundup of so-called undesirables. But the rule of law implies equality and justice in its application. Vagrancy laws of the Jacksonville type teach that the scales of justice are so tipped that that even-handed administration of the law is not possible. The rule of law, evenly applied to minorities as well as majorities, to the poor as well as the rich, is the great mucilage that holds society together.

The Jacksonville ordinance cannot be squared with our constitutional standards and is plainly unconstitutional.

Reversed.

Mr. Justice POWELL and Mr. Justice REHNQUIST took no part in the consideration or decision of this case.

NOTES

1. Consider the following comment by Mr. Justice Frankfurter, dissenting in Winters v. New York, 333 U.S. 507, 68 S.Ct. 665, 92 L.Ed. 840 (1948):

[The] requirement of fair notice that there is a boundary of prohibited conduct not to be overstepped is included in the conception of "due process of law." The legal jargon for such failure to give forewarning is to say that the statute is void for "indefiniteness."

But "indefiniteness" is not a quantitative concept. It is not even a technical concept of definite components. It is itself an indefinite concept. There is no such thing as "indefiniteness" in the abstract, by which the sufficiency of the requirement expressed by the term may be ascertained. The requirement is fair notice that conduct may entail punishment. But whether notice is or is not "fair" depends upon the subject matter to which it relates. Unlike the abstract stuff of mathematics, or the quantitatively ascertainable elements of much of natural science, legislation is greatly concerned with the multiform psychological complexities of individual and social conduct. Accordingly, the demands upon legislation, and its responses, are variable and multiform. That which may appear to be too vague and even meaningless as to one subject matter may be as definite as another subject matter of legislation permits, if the legislative power to deal with such a subject is not to be altogether denied. The statute books of every State are full of instances of what may look like unspecific definitions of crime, of the drawing of wide circles of prohibited conduct.

In these matters legislatures are confronted with a dilemma. If a law is framed with narrow particularity, too easy opportunities are afforded to nullify the purposes of the legislation. If the legislation is drafted in terms so vague that no ascertainable line is drawn in advance between innocent and condemned conduct, the purpose of the legislation cannot be enforced because no purpose is defined. It is not merely in the enactment of tax measures that the task of reconciling these extremes—of avoiding throttling particularity or unfair generality—is one of the most delicate and dif-

ficult confronting legislators. The reconciliation of these two con-
tradictories is necessarily an empiric enterprise largely depending
on the nature of the particular legislative problem.

What risks do the innocent run of being caught in a net not
designed for them? How important is the policy of the legislation,
so that those who really like to pursue innocent conduct are not
likely to be caught unaware? How easy is it to be explicitly particular? How necessary is it to leave a somewhat penumbral margin but sufficiently revealed by what is condemned to those who
do not want to sail close to the shore of questionable conduct?
These and like questions confront legislative draftsmen. Answers
to these questions are not to be found in any legislative manual
nor in the work of great legislative draftsmen. They are not to be
found in the opinions of this Court. These are questions of judgment, peculiarly within the responsibility and the competence of
legislatures. The discharge of that responsibility should not be
set at naught by abstract notions about "indefiniteness."

If "indefiniteness" or "vagueness" is not definable as an abstract matter,
how should the judicial decision as to whether, in a specific context, the
legislature has been "too indefinite" or "too vague" be made? Is the question whether, given the possible justifications for imprecision and the potential costs of such imprecision, the legislative judgment that the imprecision was worth the risks was "unreasonable?" If so, what factors—
in addition to those enumerated by Mr. Justice Frankfurter—might be
considered? See Note, The Void-For-Vagueness Doctrine in the Supreme
Court, 109 U.Penn.L.Rev. 67 (1961).

2. In Giaccio v. Pennsylvania, 382 U.S. 399, 86 S.Ct. 518, 15 L.Ed.
2d 447 (1966) the Court struck down a statute authorizing the imposition
of court costs upon an acquitted defendant in a nonfelony case "whenever
the jury shall [so] determine." Explaining, the Court stated:

> [A] law fails to meet the requirements of Due Process if it is so
> vague and standardless that it * * * leaves judges and jurors
> free to decide, without any legally fixed standards, what is pro-
> hibited and what is not in each particular case. * * * [The
> statute at issue] contains no standards at all, nor does it place any
> conditions of any kind upon the jury's power to impose costs upon
> a defendant who has been found by the jury to be not guilty of a
> crime charged against him. * * * Certainly one of the basic
> purposes of the Due Process Clause has always been to protect a
> person against having the Government impose burdens upon him
> except in accordance with the valid laws of the land. Implicit in
> this constitutional safeguard is the premise that the law must be
> one that carries an understandable meaning with legal standards
> that courts must enforce. This state Act as written does not even
> begin to meet this constitutional requirement.

382 U.S. at 402–03. Is this an indication of another interest that the constitutional requirement of precision is intended to protect? Does not efficient administration of a court system—on both the trial and appellate
levels—require that the participants have laws to work with that are rea-

sonably precise? If so, does the constitutional requirement of precision serve the purpose of furthering the administrative efficiency of the judicial system, either expressly or implicitly? Is it important whether or not it does so?

3. Is the due process requirement of precision in language applicable only to statutes imposing "criminal" liability? In the *Giaccio* case the Supreme Court responded to the argument that the statute did not impose criminal liability:

> Whatever label be given the * * * Act, there is no doubt that it provides the State with a procedure for depriving an acquitted defendant of his liberty and his property. Both liberty and property are specifically protected by the Fourteenth Amendment against any state deprivation which does not meet the standards of due process, and this protection is not to be avoided by the simple label a State chooses to fasten upon its conduct or its statute. So here this state Act whether labeled "penal" or not must meet the challenge that it is unconstitutionally vague.

382 U.S. at 402. But isn't the nature of the liability imposed—whether "criminal" or "civil"—relevant to the degree of precision that will be required of a legislature? In other words, might not certain language that would be unconstitutionally vague in a criminal statute survive attack if it was used in imposing noncriminal liability?

The District of Columbia Code authorizes the hospitalization of a mentally ill person determined to be "likely to injure himself or other persons if allowed to remain at liberty." D.C.Code 1967, § 21–545(b). This has been upheld against attack on due process vagueness grounds. See In re Alexander, 336 F.Supp. 1305 (D.D.C.1972).

III. PRINCIPLES OF CRIMINAL LIABILITY

INTRODUCTORY NOTE

Crimes are generally—and perhaps constitutionally must be—statutory. Nevertheless, it is often difficult or impossible to evaluate the liability of defendants from the face of the offenses with which they are charged. With the possible exception of some of the recently revised statutory criminal codes, most statutory schemes were initially written as codifications of the common law of crimes and have received only piecemeal revision. Thus many statutory definitions of crimes must be read in light of the common law of crimes to determine the elements of the offense, and recourse must often be had to general defenses which may or may not be codified in the statutory scheme.

The material in Parts III–VII makes almost no attempt to deal directly with the definition of particular common law offenses. Rather, it proposes a scheme of analysis which is designed to provide the facility and background necessary to deal with a body of law that is essentially statutory. Basically the task is to define the elements of liability, given the statute and general principles of substantive and constitutional law, and to ascertain the defenses to liability in light of the same factors.

The analysis proposed here is a three-step one. The first step is the ascertainment of the elements of the offense, those matters as to which the prosecution must introduce sufficient evidence to avoid a directed verdict of not guilty. For the sake of convenience and clarity, it is valuable to consider elements of offenses in terms of four categories. A particular crime may not contain an element in each category, although to some extent constitutional considerations may require that a crime require proof of some element in each of the first two categories:

1. The "Act". Although the latin phrase "actus reus" has a much broader meaning, it is valuable to think of the act required for liability in terms of what physical activity must be shown on the part of the accused. The statutory definition may rather specifically describe the type of physical activity, as, for example, requiring that the defendant have been "driving". Or, it may make no attempt to describe the required physical activity, in which case any action or failure to act that meets general requirements will suffice.

2. The State of Mind. For policy reasons, the criminal law is concerned with the accused's conscious state of mind at the time of the offense. Probably all offenses require

that the trier of fact be convinced beyond a reasonable doubt that the accused was, at the time he performed the physical act required for liability, aware of something, but the state of mind required differs drastically among offenses.

3. Circumstances. Some offenses require a showing of the existence of particular circumstances. These differ from results (see the fourth category) in that there is no necessity of a causal relationship between the accused's actions and circumstances, while such a relationship must be shown between his actions and results. Circumstances may serve an important policy purpose, or they may be of relatively minor importance. Federal crimes, for example, often require the showing of circumstances for the purpose of establishing federal jurisdiction over the offense.

4. Results. A number of offenses require that a particular result be shown to have occurred. It is important to differentiate between circumstances and results because the complex problems of causation arise only in regard to the latter.

The second step of the analysis involves the ascertainment of any so-called "defenses" which are really means of disproving one of the elements of the offense. Most often this amounts to disproving the state of mind required for the crime. Proof of a defendant's mistake as to the facts at the time of his acts, for example, may well serve simply to raise in the jury's mind a reasonable doubt as to whether he entertained the requisite state of mind.

The final step involves consideration of defenses in the true sense. These are matters which, if established to the satisfaction of the trier of fact, prevent (or reduce) liability despite proof of all elements of the offense. One who kills to preserve his own life, for example, may have entertained an awareness that his action would cause the death of the victim that suffices (under most statutes) for second degree murder; yet if the elements of self defense are established he is relieved of liability.

While one should not pretend that the substantive criminal law may be analyzed "scientifically" it may be helpful to visualize the basic framework of analysis through the following formula: $\text{Act} + \text{State of Mind} \xrightarrow{\text{Causation}} \text{Results} = \text{Liability}$. In considering the material which follows periodically pause to place it within the framework of the above formula. See whether a reduction in the importance of any particular element in the definition of an offense is accompanied by a compensatory increase in the emphasis given another element on the left of the equation or a reduction to the right of it, and, if so, reflect on why this is the case.

A. THE "ACT"

---

1. GENERAL REQUIREMENT OF AN ACT

Conceptually, it is possible to include within the "act" required for criminal liability not only the physical activity which the accused must be shown to have performed but also the circumstances under which it was performed and the consequences of it. It is more satisfactory, however, to differentiate "circumstances" and "results" from the act required, as this forces a more thorough examination of the proof necessary for liability. As to the constitutional necessity that a crime require proof of some act on the part of the accused, review Mr. Justice Marshall's interpretation of Robinson v. California in Powell v. Texas, infra. Aside from any possible constitutional imperative, the act requirement places an obvious restriction on the authority of the state to employ the criminal sanction. Given that it marks an extreme outer limit on the exercise of governmental power, the student should consider whether the requirement is desirable, and why. Consider also whether it is of any practical importance: For purposes of determining whether the state may employ the criminal sanction; for purposes of determining the severity of the sanction which may be employed?

Several of the most basic questions regarding the requirement of an "act" are raised in this section. What is the significance, if any, of the requirement that the "act" be "willed" or "voluntary"? In particular, after becoming familiar with the "state of mind" requirement, Section III. B, infra, the student should reconsider the *Mercer* case, infra, to decide whether the issues involved there could not have been as effectively analyzed and resolved without any reference whatever to the "act" requirement.

18 U.S.C.A. § 1792 provides, in pertinent part: "Whoever conveys * * * from place to place [within a Federal penal institution] any * * * weapon * * * designed to kill, injure or disable any officer, agent, employee or inmate thereof * * *. Shall be imprisoned not more than ten years." Does a prisoner violate this provision if, while carrying a knife under his clothing, he walks from his cell pursuant to a guard's order? What if he is running a knife across a sander in the prison workshop and, on the approach of his foreman, he drops it to the floor? Which of the following factors would control your interpretation: the meaning of the verb "convey"; the "voluntariness" of the conduct; or the purpose of the statute given the fact that mere possession of a knife by an inmate is not criminal? Compare United States v. Meador, 456 F.2d 197 (10th Cir. 1972) with United States v. Bedwell, 456 F.2d 448 (10th Cir. 1972).

To what extent is a failure to act sufficient for liability? To what extent may a defendant be held liable if the acts relied upon are performed by someone other than himself, i. e., to what extent may "vicarious liability" be imposed?

PROPOSED FEDERAL CRIMINAL CODE (1971)

§ 301. Basis of Liability for Offenses

(1) Conduct. A person commits an offense only if he engages in conduct, including an act, an omission, or possession, in violation of a statute which provides that the conduct is an offense.

(2) Omissions. A person who omits to perform an act does not commit an offense unless he has a legal duty to perform the act.

(3) Publication Required. A person does not commit an offense if he engages in conduct in violation only of a statute or regulation thereunder that has not been published.

Comment

Federal criminal law does not, at present, contain statutes stating basic conditions of liability. Chapter 3 would make the treatment and understanding of these issues clear and uniform.

Subsection (1) states the minimum condition of criminal liability: a person must engage in conduct; that he has a certain status or that certain circumstances exist will not render him criminally liable. Conduct includes omissions and possessions. The issue of the voluntariness of the conduct, i. e., whether or not it is conscious and the result of determination or effort, is not dealt with explicitly in this subsection because, while doing so would have limited utility, it would raise the possibility of evasion of limitations placed on defenses such as intoxication and mental illness through inquiries as to voluntariness.

Subsection (2) restates present federal law: a person is not liable for an omission unless he has a duty to act.

Subsection (3) constitutes the basic prohibition against secret criminal laws.

STATE v. MERCER

Supreme Court of North Carolina, 1969.
275 N.C. 108, 165 S.E.2d 328.

Separate indictments charged defendant with the first degree murder on September 14, 1967, of (1) Myrtle R. Mercer, defendant's wife, (2) Ida Mae Dunn, and (3) Jeffrey Lane Dunn, Ida's five-year-old son. * * *

There was evidence tending to show the facts narrated below.

Defendant, a member of the United States Army for 19½ years, was stationed at Fort Benning, Georgia, at the time of the trial.

Defendant and Myrtle Mercer were married in Fayetteville, N. C., in April, 1965. Thereafter, he was stationed at duty posts in and out of the United States. Myrtle Mercer, Ida Mae Dunn, and Jeffrey Lane Dunn, Ida's five-year-old boy, lived together in Wilson, N. C. Defendant visited Myrtle in Wilson from time to time when on leaves. He was thirty-nine; Myrtle was twenty-three.

Marital difficulties developed. Defendant had heard that Myrtle was having affairs with other men. He thought Myrtle's relationship with Ida involved more than normal affection. As time passed, defendant's strong affection for Myrtle was not reciprocated.

On July 6, 1967, defendant received a letter from Myrtle, referred to in the evidence as a "Dear John" letter, in which she told him she was tired of being tied down and wanted to come and go as she pleased. In a letter mailed August 10th from Kentucky (where he was then stationed), defendant wrote Myrtle: "Please don't make me do something that will send both of us to our graves." Also: "I could never see you with another man, and I would die and go to hell before I would see you with some other man, and take myself with you."

In September, 1967, defendant obtained a ten-day leave "to come home and see if he could get straightened out with his wife. * * * " Defendant told his first sergeant that "if he did not get straightened out he would not be back."

On September 13, 1967, defendant visited the house in Wilson where Myrtle, Ida, and Jeffrey lived. He talked with Myrtle. However, she would not discuss their marital problems and did not want him to stay at that house.

Defendant stayed at the home of his cousin, Mrs. Mable Owens, in Tarboro. He left there on the morning of September 14, 1967, and arrived at Myrtle's around noon. She would not talk with him. (Note: Defendant testified Myrtle at that time gave him some clothes, a camera and a paper bag containing a pistol he had given to her for her protection.) At the conclusion of this visit, he returned to the home of Mrs. Owens. Sometime during the day defendant bought a pint of vodka and had two drinks from it.

About 8:30 p. m., Mrs. Owens, at the request of defendant, drove defendant to Myrtle's house in Wilson. The two children of Mrs. Owens accompanied them. Defendant knocked. There was no response. The house was unlighted and apparently no one was there. They left and visited defendant's brother (in Wilson) for some twenty-five or thirty-five minutes. While there, defendant telephoned Myrtle's house. The line was busy. They went back to Myrtle's house. Defendant asked Mrs. Owens if she and her children would go into the house with him. She replied that they would wait in the car.

Defendant went to the front door and knocked several times. There was no answer. Defendant shot at the door twice, pushed it open with his foot and went inside. At that time, a light came on in the front bedroom. Someone said, "Ervin, don't do that." Defendant fired three or four shots killing Myrtle instantly and fatally wounding Ida and Jeffrey. He then left the house. A neighbor called the police.

*   *   *

Defendant was arrested at the home of his brother in Wilson, a few hours after the fatal shots were fired. He accompanied the officers to a lot behind Myrtle's house where the gun which inflicted the fatal injuries was hidden.

Testimony of defendant, in addition to that referred to above, is set out in the opinion. It tended to show he was completely unconscious of what transpired when Myrtle, Ida and Jeffrey were shot.

In each case, the jury returned a verdict of guilty of murder in the second degree.   *   *   *

BOBBITT, Judge.

*   *   *

The court's final instructions were as follows: "(T)he Court instructs you that the evidence in regard and surrounding the alleged loss of memory by the defendant will be considered by you *on the question of premeditation and deliberation in the charge of murder in the first degree.*   *   *   *   if you find from the evidence, not by the greater weight, nor by the preponderance, but if the defendant has satisfied you—merely satisfied you—that he lost consciousness, sufficient consciousness, to the extent that he did not have sufficient time to *premeditate or deliberate*, that is, if he did not have sufficient time to form in his mind the intent to kill, under the definition of *premeditation* and *deliberation*, then it would be your duty to return a verdict of not guilty of murder in the first degree, because the Court has instructed you if the State has failed to satisfy you of the element of *premeditation* or *deliberation*, or if there arises in your minds a reasonable doubt in regard to those two elements or either one of those two elements, it would be your duty to return a verdict of not guilty. And further in regard, when you come to consider those elements of *premeditation* and *deliberation*, if the defendant has satisfied you, not beyond a reasonable doubt, not by the greater weight of the evidence, but has merely satisfied you that he lost consciousness to such an extent that he was unable to *premeditate*, and was unable to *deliberate*, according to the definition of those terms that the law has given you, then he could not be guilty of murder in the first degree, and it would be your duty to return a verdict of not guilty as to murder in the first degree, under those circumstances. Now, *the Court feels that those are the only two elements in the case in which this evidence in regard to his loss of consciousness applies*, and the Court has ruled that there is no element of legal insanity in the evidence." (Our italics.)

Defendant's assignment of error, based on his exception to the foregoing portion of the charge, must be sustained. Defendant testified he was completely unconscious of what transpired when Myrtle, Ida and Jeffrey were shot. The court instructed the jury that this evidence was for consideration *only* in respect of the elements of premeditation and deliberation in first degree murder. This restriction of the legal significance of the evidence as to defendant's unconsciousness was erroneous.

* * *

"If a person is in fact unconscious at the time he commits an act which would otherwise be criminal, he is not responsible therefor. The absence of consciousness not only precludes the existence of any specific mental state, but also excludes the possibility of a voluntary act without which there can be no criminal liability." 1 Wharton's Criminal Law and Procedure (Anderson), § 50, p. 116.

"Unconsciousness is a complete, not a partial, defense to a criminal charge." 21 Am.Jur.2d, Criminal Law § 29, p. 115.

"Unconsciousness. A person cannot be held criminally responsible for acts committed while he is unconscious. Some statutes broadly exempt from responsibility persons who commit offenses without being conscious thereof. Such statutes, when construed in connection with other statutes relating to criminal capacity of the insane and voluntarily intoxicated, do not include within their protection either insane or voluntarily intoxicated persons, and are restricted in their contemplation to persons of sound mind suffering from some other agency rendering them unconscious of their acts * * *." 22 C.J.S. Criminal Law § 55, p. 194.

Defendant contends he had no knowledge of and did not consciously commit the act charged in the indictments. He does not contend he was insane. Unconsciousness and insanity are separate grounds of exemption from criminal responsibility.

* * *

There was no evidence defendant was a somnambulist or an epileptic. Nor was there evidence he was under the influence of intoxicants or narcotics. Under cross-examination, defendant testified his only previous "blackout" experience, which was of brief duration, occurred when he received and read the "Dear John" letter.

Upon the present record, defendant was entitled to an instruction to the effect the jury should return verdicts of not guilty if in fact defendant was *completely* unconscious of what transpired when Myrtle, Ida and Jeffrey were shot.

* * *

It should be understood that unconsciousness, although always a factor of legal significance, is not a complete defense under all circumstances. Without undertaking to mark the limits of the legal principles applicable to varied factual situations that will arise from time to time, but solely by way of illustration, attention is called to the following: In California, "unconsciousness produced by voluntary intoxication does not render a defendant incapable of committing a crime." People v. Cox, 67 Cal.App.2d 166, 153 P.2d 362, and cases cited. In Colorado, a person who precipitates a fracas and as a result is hit on the head and rendered semi-conscious or unconscious cannot maintain that he is not criminally responsible for any degree of homicide above involuntary manslaughter, or that he is not criminally responsible at all. Watkins v. People, 158 Colo. 485, 408 P.2d 425. In Oklahoma, a motorist is guilty of manslaughter if he drives an automobile with knowledge that he is subject to frequent blackouts, when his continued operation of the automobile is in reckless disregard to the safety of others and constitutes culpable or criminal negligence. Carter v. State, [376 P.2d 351 (Okl.Cr.1962)]; Smith v. Commonwealth, [268 S.W.2d 937 (Ky.1954)]. As to somnambulism, see Fain v. Commonwealth, [78 Ky. 183 (1879)], and Lewis v. State, 196 Ga. 755, 27 S.E.2d 659.

POWELL v. TEXAS

United States Supreme Court, 1968.
392 U.S. 514, 88 S.Ct. 2145, 20 L.Ed.2d 1254.

[The opinion of Mr. Justice MARSHALL for the Court, from which this excerpt is taken, is more fully reprinted at page 138].

Appellant * * * seeks to come within the application of the Cruel and Unusual Punishment Clause announced in Robinson v. California, 370 U.S. 660 (1962), which involved a state statute making it a crime to "be addicted to the use of narcotics." This Court held there that "a state law which imprisons a person thus afflicted [with narcotic addiction] as a criminal, even though he has never touched any narcotic drug within the State or been guilty of any irregular behavior there, inflicts a cruel and unusual punishment * * *." Id., at 667.

On its face the present case does not fall within that holding, since appellant was convicted, not for being a chronic alcoholic, but for being in public while drunk on a particular occasion. The State of Texas thus has not sought to punish a mere status, as California did in Robinson; nor has it attempted to regulate appellant's behavior in the privacy of his own home. Rather, it has imposed upon appellant a criminal sanction for public behavior which may create substantial health and safety hazards, both for appellant and for members of the general public and which offends the moral and esthetic sensibilities of a large segment of the community. This seems a far cry from convicting one for being an addict, being a chronic alcoholic, being "mentally ill, or a leper * * *." Id., at 666.

Robinson so viewed brings this Court but a very small way into the substantive criminal law. And unless Robinson is so viewed it is difficult to see any limiting principle that would serve to prevent this Court from becoming, under the aegis of the Cruel and Unusual Punishment Clause, the ultimate arbiter of the standards of criminal responsibility, in diverse areas of the criminal law, throughout the country.

It is suggested in dissent that *Robinson* stands for the "simple" but "subtle" principle that "[c]riminal penalties may not be inflicted upon a person for being in a condition he is powerless to change." *Post*, at 567. In that view, appellant's "condition" of public intoxication was "occasioned by a compulsion symptomatic of the disease" of chronic alcoholism, and thus, apparently, his behavior lacked the critical element of *mens rea*. Whatever may be the merits of such a doctrine of criminal responsibility, it surely cannot be said to follow from *Robinson*. The entire thrust of *Robinson*'s interpretation of the Cruel and Unusual Punishment Clause is that criminal penalties may be inflicted only if the accused has committed some act, has engaged in some behavior, which society has an interest in preventing or perhaps in historical common law terms, has committed some *actus reus*. It thus does not deal with the question of whether certain conduct cannot constitutionally be punished because it is, in some sense, "involuntary" or "occasioned by a compulsion."

Mr. Justice BLACK, whom Mr. Justice HARLAN joins, concurring.

Punishment for a status is particularly obnoxious, and in many instances can reasonably be called cruel and unusual, because it involves punishment for a mere propensity, a desire to commit an offense; the mental element is not simply one part of the crime but may constitute all of it. This is a situation universally sought to be avoided in our criminal law; the fundamental requirement that some action be proved is solidly established even for offenses most heavily based on propensity, such as attempt, conspiracy, and recidivist crimes.[4] In fact, one eminent authority has found only one isolated instance, in all of Anglo-American jurisprudence, in which criminal responsibility was imposed in the absence of any act at all.[5]

The reasons for this refusal to permit conviction without proof of an act are difficult to spell out, but they are nonetheless perceived and universally expressed in our criminal law. Evidence of propensity can be considered relatively unreliable and more difficult for a defendant to rebut; the requirement of a specific act thus provides some protection against false charges. See 4 Blackstone, Commentaries 21. Perhaps more fundamental is the difficulty of distinguish-

---

4. As Glanville Williams puts it, "[t]hat crime requires an act is *invariably* true if the proposition be read as meaning that a private thought is not sufficient to found responsibility." Williams, Criminal Law—the General Part 1 (1961). (Emphasis added.) For the requirement of some act as an element of conspiracy and attempt, see id., at 631, 663, 668; R. Perkins, Criminal Law 482, 531–532 (1957).

5. Williams, supra, n. 4, at 11.

ing, in the absence of any conduct, between desires of the day-dream variety and fixed intentions that may pose a real threat to society; extending the criminal law to cover both types of desire would be unthinkable, since "[t]here can hardly be anyone who has never thought evil. When a desire is inhibited it may find expression in fantasy; but it would be absurd to condemn this natural psychological mechanism as illegal."

In contrast, crimes that require the State to prove that the defendant actually committed some proscribed act involve none of these special problems. In addition, the question whether an act is "involuntary" is, as I have already indicated, an inherently elusive question, and one which the State may, for good reasons, wish to regard as irrelevant. In light of all these considerations, our limitation of our *Robinson* holding to pure status crimes seems to me entirely proper.

NOTES

1. As Mr. Justice Marshall makes clear there must be "some act * * * some behavior" before criminal penalties may be imposed. The Court in *Robinson* explictly included "possession of narcotics" in its recitation of acts which might properly be criminalized. Is possession an "act" or "behavior"? The Texas Penal Code provides in § 6.01:

> "Possession is a voluntary act if the possessor knowingly obtains or receives the thing possessed or is aware of his control of the thing for a sufficient time to permit him to terminate his control."

The Committee on Revision commented:

> "Although possession is often treated in the criminal law as the equivalent of an act, it is not strictly speaking a bodily movement so this section is necessary to treat it as such.

> "The section does not determine whether an actor must know the nature of the thing possessed or just know that he possesses a thing; this issue is determined by the definition of the specific (possessory) offense involved * * *."

The question of whether it is necessary that the possession be "knowing" is examined later.

2. As is suggested by the definition of possession quoted in note 1 supra, the contraband need not be actually possessed in the sense of being on the person of the possessor. The ambit of possession statutes is significantly broadened by the doctrine of "constructive possession" which extends culpability to situations where the defendant may be found to have been "in a position to exercise dominion or control" over the contraband. United States v. Holland, 445 F.2d 701, 703 (D.C.Cir.1971). See Annotation, 91 A.L.R.2d 810. An especially common problem in this area arises where the alleged possession is not only constructive but joint; as where the contraband is found in a car or room occupied by more than one person. See Folk v. State, 11 Md.App. 508, 275 A.2d 184 (1971).

3. As is indicated by the following case, joint, constructive possession of the prohibited drug has not been the minimum "behavior" on which the use of the criminal sanction has been predicated.

CRAWFORD v. UNITED STATES

District of Columbia Court of Appeals, 1971.
278 A.2d 125.

Before GALLAGHER, REILLY and YEAGLEY, Associate Judges.

GALLAGHER, Associate Judge. Appellant was charged with carrying a pistol without a license and possession of implements of a crime—narcotics paraphernalia. A jury found him not guilty of carrying a pistol without a license and rendered a special verdict finding him guilty of possession of one hypodermic needle and one hypodermic syringe found under the front seat of the car he was driving. He was found not guilty of possession of implements of a crime as to other narcotics paraphernalia found in the rear seat. Appellant was sentenced to serve 180 days in jail.

At the close of the Government's case in chief and again upon final submission of the case, appellant moved for judgment of acquittal contending the Government's evidence was insufficient to support a finding that he was in possession of the narcotics paraphernalia. The trial judge denied the motions and appellant now contends this was reversible error.

The Government's evidence consisted of the following: Officer Richardson testified that he stopped appellant's car for speeding and while waiting for appellant (who had alighted from the car) to produce his license he noticed a syringe at the foot of one of the occupants in the rear seat.[3] Upon the arrival of other officers he had called by radio, the occupants were removed from the car. He then recovered two pieces of tinfoil, a spoon, two syringes and one needle from the rear seat and one syringe and needle protruding from beneath the front seat on the driver's side where appellant had been sitting. A pistol was also recovered from the rear seat. A Detective Dotson testified that he examined appellant at the precinct on the day of the arrest and found ten to twenty "individual needle marks—small punctures on the arm." The Government chemist testified that neither the spoon nor the aluminum foil recovered contained any narcotics. He could not testify each syringe positively contained heroin because the sample he tested was a composite from all three syringes; and consequently, he could not testify specifically that there was heroin in the syringe found under appellant's seat.[a]

---

3. There were three youths in the rear seat and one in the front passenger seat in addition to appellant.

a. Is there any point to requiring that the drug paraphernalia contain at least a trace of the prohibited drugs? In a jurisdiction which permits conviction of possession of less than a usable amount?

"A motion for acquittal must be granted when the evidence, viewed in the light most favorable to the Government, is such that a reasonable juror must have a reasonable doubt as to the existence of any of the essential elements of the crime." * * * If, on the other hand, the evidence is such that a reasonable man might or might not have a reasonable doubt as to the defendant's guilt, the case should go to the jury. We think the motions were properly denied under this standard.

Possession in this instance could have been either actual or constructive, i. e., the exercise of, or right to exercise, dominion and control over the narcotics paraphernalia under appellant's seat. See Hill v. District of Columbia, D.C.App., 264 A.2d 145, 146 (1970); cf. Garza v. United States, 395 F.2d 899, 901 (5th Cir. 1967). There is no question but that appellant did not have actual possession of the needle and syringe at the time of his arrest. But appellant had been present in the automobile immediately before the officer noticed the paraphernalia protruding from under the seat where appellant had just been seated. He had been driving the car immediately prior to the time the articles were recovered in plain view from beneath that seat. He was the owner of the vehicle. The single needle and syringe were certainly within his reach. Additionally, puncture marks were found on his arm which indicated he was a user of drugs. Garza v. United States, supra, 385 F.2d at 900. From these facts it was reasonable to infer that appellant had dominion and control over the needle and syringe under his seat. Viewing the evidence in the light most favorable to the Government, as we must, we conclude it was adequate to support the jury's finding that appellant had possession of that needle and syringe.

Appellant also contends that possession of a single hypodermic needle and syringe alone will not support a conviction under the statute [5] without proof of specific intent to use the instruments to commit a crime since they do not in themselves raise "sinister" implications. See McKoy v. United States, D.C.App., 263 A.2d 649, 651 (1970). He raises this point for the first time on appeal. "[O]ur power to notice errors raised for the first time on appeal is discretionary, and will be exercised only where the error alleged is 'plain error' and clearly prejudicial to the appellant." Bunter v. United States, D.C.App., 245 A.2d 839, 842 (1968). Our review of the record in this case reveals no such plain error. We conclude upon the record before us that there existed sufficient independent circumstantial evidence of appellant's intent above and beyond his mere possession of a single needle

5. D.C.Code 1967, § 22–3601 provides in part:
 No person shall have in his possession in the District any instrument, tool, or other implement for picking locks or pockets, or that is usually employed, or reasonably may be employed in the commission of any crime, if he is unable satisfactorily to account for the possession of the implement. * * *

and syringe to support his conviction of possession of implements of a crime. Therefore, we are not met with the issue posed by appellant that possession of the needle and syringe, standing alone, would not violate the statute.

This court has recognized the use of surrounding circumstances to evidence the requisite criminal intent under the statute. McKoy v. United States, supra. In the present case appellant possessed a hypodermic needle and syringe but, in addition, two other syringes and one other needle, with two pieces of foil and a spoon, were found in the rear seat of the automobile driven by appellant. While it is true that the jury found that appellant did not possess these items in the rear seat, this is not to say that he did not know of their presence. And their presence would indicate an apparent intention to administer narcotics illegally, if this had not already been done. These materials constituted a narcotics "kit" and thus appellant was in the immediate company of others who had this "kit." There was evidence that at least one of the syringes contained heroin, though which one could not be determined due to the nature of the chemist's test. Further, ten to twenty puncture marks were observed on appellant's left forearm by Detective Dotson indicating appellant was a drug user.

We believe that these circumstances taken together, and when viewed in a light most favorable to the Government, were sufficient for the jury to conclude that appellant possessed the hypodermic needle and syringe with the intent to use them for a criminal purpose.

For these reasons, the judgment of the trial court is

Affirmed.

STATE v. BUGGER

Supreme Court of Utah, 1971.
25 Utah 2d 404, 483 P.2d 442.

TUCKETT, Justice. The defendant was found guilty of a violation of Section 41–6–44, U.C.A.1953, and from that conviction he has appealed to this court.

During the night of July 28, 1969, the defendant was asleep in his automobile which was parked upon the shoulder of a road known as Tippet's Lane in Davis County. The automobile was completely off the traveled portion of the highway and the motor was not running. An officer of the Highway Patrol stopped at the scene and discovered the defendant was asleep. With some effort the officer succeeded in awakening the defendant, at which time the officer detected the smell of alcohol and arrested the defendant for being in actual physical control of the vehicle while under the influence of intoxicating liquor.

The complaint charges the defendant with the violation of the statute above referred to which provides as follows:

It is unlawful and punishable as provided in subsection (d) of this section for any person who is under the influence of intoxicating liquor to drive or be in actual physical control of any vehicle within this state.

The defendant is here challenging the validity of the statute on the grounds of vagueness. However, we need not decide the case upon that ground. That part of the statute which states: "be in actual physical control of any vehicle" has been before the courts of other jurisdictions which have statutes with similar wordings. The word "actual" has been defined as meaning "existing in act or reality; * * * in action or existence at the time being; present; * * *." The word "physical" is defined as "bodily," and "control" is defined as "to exercise restraining or directing influence over; to dominate; regulate; hence, to hold from actions; to curb." The term in "actual physical control" in its ordinary sense means "existing" or "present bodily restraint, directing influence, domination or regulation." It is clear that in the record before us the facts do not bring the case with-in the wording of the statute. The defendant at the time of his arrest was *not* controlling the vehicle, nor was he exercising any dominion over it. It is noted that the cases cited by the plaintiff in support of its position in this matter deal with entirely different fact situations, such as the case where the driver was seated in his vehicle on the traveled portion of the highway; or where the motor of the vehicle was operating; or where the driver was attempting to steer the automobile while it was in motion; or where he was attempting to brake the vehicle to arrest its motion.

We are of the opinion that the facts in this case do not make out a violation of the statute and the defendant's conviction is re-versed. We do not consider it necessary to discuss the other claimed errors raised by the defendant.

CALLISTER, C. J., and HENRIOD and CROCKETT, JJ., con-cur.

ELLETT, Justice (dissenting).

I dissent.

The statute formerly made it unlawful for a person under the influence of intoxicating liquor to drive any vehicle upon any high-way within this state. The amendment added a provision making it unlawful to be in actual physical control of a vehicle while under the influence of intoxicating liquor. It removed the need to be upon a highway before the crime was made out and did away with the necessity of driving before a crime was committed.

The reason for the change is obvious. It is better to prevent an intoxicated person in charge of an automobile from getting on the highway than it is to punish him after he gets on it. The amended statute gives officers a right to arrest a drunk person in the control of an automobile and thus prevent him from wreaking havoc a minute later by getting in traffic, or from injuring himself by his erratic driving.

It does not matter whether the motor is running or is idle nor whether the drunk is in the front seat or in the back seat. His potentiality for harm is lessened but not obviated by a silent motor or a backseat position—provided, of course, that he is the one in control of the car. It only takes a flick of the wrist to start the motor or to engage the gears, and it requires only a moment of time to get under the wheel from the back seat. A drunk in control of a motor vehicle has such a propensity to cause harm that the statute intended to make it criminal for him to be in a position to do so.

Restraining the movement of a vehicle is controlling it as much as moving it is. A person finding a drunk in the back seat of a car parked in one's driveway is likely to learn who is in control of that car if he should attempt to move it. A drunk may maliciously block one's exit, and in doing so he is in control of his own vehicle.

I think the defendant in this case was in control of his truck within the meaning of the statute even though he may have been asleep. He had the key and was the only one who could drive it. The fact that he chose to park it is no reason to say he was not in control thereof.

I, therefore, think that we should consider the question which he raises in his brief as to the validity of the statute.

Cases wherein an attack was made on statutes like ours have been decided in a number of jurisdictions. They hold the statute good.

In the case of State v. Webb, 78 Ariz. 8, 274 P.2d 338 (1954), the defendant was intoxicated and asleep in a truck parked next to some barricades in a lane of traffic. An officer passed by and observed no one in the car. Later he returned and found the defendant "passed out." The statute made it a crime to be in actual physical control of a car while under the influence of intoxicating liquor. The defendant contended that the wording of the statute was not meant to apply to a situation where the car was parked and that it was only concerned with the driving of an automobile and other acts and conduct of a positive nature. In holding that the statute was applicable to the conduct of the defendant, the court said:

> An intoxicated person seated behind the steering wheel of a motor vehicle is a threat to the safety and welfare of the public. The danger is less than that involved when the vehicle is actually moving, but it does exist.

In the case of Parker v. State, 424 P.2d 997 (Okl.Cr.App.1967), the appellant challenged the constitutionality of a statute making it unlawful for "any person who is under the influence of intoxicating liquor to drive, operate, or be in actual physical control of any motor vehicle within this state." There the defendant (appellant) claimed that the statute was unconstitutional in that it was so vague and indefinite that a person charged thereunder would be deprived of due process of law. The court held that the statute did not violate any of appellant's constitutional rights.

Under a similar statute the Montana Supreme Court in State v. Ruona, 133 Mont. 243, 321 P.2d 615 (1958), held that the statute was not void for vagueness, and in doing so said:

> * * * Thus one could have "actual physical control" while merely parking or standing still so long as one was keeping the car in restraint or in position to regulate its movements. Preventing a car from moving is as much control and dominion as actually putting the car in motion on the highway. Could one exercise any more regulation over a thing, while bodily present, than prevention of movement or curbing movement. As long as one were physically or bodily able to assert dominion, in the sense of movement, then he has as much control over an object as he would if he were actually driving the vehicle.

> * * * * * * * *

> * * * [I]t is quite evident that the statute in the instant case is neither vague nor uncertain. * * *

The appellant here claims some federally protected rights in that he says he was improperly arrested. It is difficult for me to see where that has anything to do with guilt or innocence. If he were improperly arrested, he would have an action against the officer for false arrest, but surely our courts have not lost contact with reality to the extent that we turn a guilty man free simply "because the constable may have blundered".

From what has been said above, there is absolutely no merit to this claim. By being in control of an automobile while under the influence of intoxicating liquor, the defendant was guilty of a misdemeanor which was in the presence of the officer, and the officer had a right and a duty to arrest him.

The defendant was found guilty in the court below of being in actual physical control of his truck while he was under the influence of intoxicating liquor. He does not dispute that he was drunk. If the statute is good, we should not attempt to overrule the trier of the facts and find that the defendant was not the one actually controlling his truck.

I would affirm the judgment of the trial court.

2. LIABILITY BASED ON FAILURE TO ACT

JONES v. UNITED STATES

United States Court of Appeals for the District of Columbia, 1962.
113 U.S.App.D.C. 352, 308 F.2d 307.

WRIGHT, Circuit Judge. Appellant, together with one Shirley Green, was tried on a three-count indictment charging them jointly with (1) abusing and maltreating Robert Lee Green, (2) abusing and maltreating Anthony Lee Green, and (3) involuntary manslaughter through failure to perform their legal duty of care for Anthony Lee Green, which failure resulted in his death. At the close of evidence, after trial to a jury, the first two counts were dismissed as to both defendants. On the third count, appellant was convicted of involuntary manslaughter. Shirley Green was found not guilty.

Appellant urges several grounds for reversal. We need consider but two. First, appellant argues that there was insufficient evidence as a matter of law to warrant a jury finding of breach of duty in the care she rendered Anthony Lee. Alternatively, appellant argues that the trial court committed plain error in failing to instruct the jury that it must first find that appellant was under a legal obligation to provide food and necessities to Anthony Lee before finding her guilty of manslaughter in failing to provide them. The first argument is without merit. Upon the latter we reverse.

A summary of the evidence, which is in conflict upon almost every significant issue, is necessary for the disposition of both arguments. In late 1957, Shirley Green became pregnant, out of wedlock, with a child, Robert Lee, subsequently born August 17, 1958. Apparently to avoid the embarrassment of the presence of the child in the Green home, it was arranged that appellant, a family friend, would take the child to her home after birth. Appellant did so, and the child remained there continuously until removed by the police on August 5, 1960. Initially appellant made some motions toward the adoption of Robert Lee, but these came to naught, and shortly thereafter it was agreed that Shirley Green was to pay appellant $72 a month for his care. According to appellant, these payments were made for only five months. According to Shirley Green, they were made up to July 1960.

Early in 1959 Shirley Green again became pregnant, this time with the child Anthony Lee, whose death is the basis of appellant's conviction. This child was born October 21, 1959. Soon after birth, Anthony Lee developed a mild jaundice condition, attributed to a blood incompatability with his mother. The jaundice resulted in his retention in the hospital for three days beyond the usual time, or until October 26, 1959, when, on authorization signed by Shirley Green, Anthony Lee was released by the hospital to appellant's custody. Shirley Green, after a two or three day stay in the hospital, also lived with appellant for three weeks, after which she returned to her parents' home, leaving the children with appellant. She testified she did not see them again, except for one visit in March, until August 5, 1960. Consequently, though there does not seem to have been any specific monetary agreement with Shirley Green covering Anthony Lee's support,[5] appellant had complete custody of both children until they were rescued by the police.

With regard to medical care, the evidence is undisputed. In March, 1960, appellant called a Dr. Turner to her home to treat Anthony Lee for a bronchial condition. Appellant also telephoned the doctor at various times to consult with him concerning Anthony Lee's diet and health. In early July, 1960, appellant took Anthony Lee to Dr. Turner's office where he was treated for "simple diarrhea." At this time the doctor noted the "wizened" appearance of the child and told appellant to tell the mother of the child that he should be taken to a hospital. This was not done.

On August 2, 1960, two collectors for the local gas company had occasion to go to the basement of appellant's home, and there saw the two children. Robert Lee and Anthony Lee at this time were age two years and ten months respectively. Robert Lee was in a "crib" consisting of a framework of wood, covered with a fine wire screening, including the top which was hinged. The "crib" was lined with newspaper, which was stained, apparently with feces, and crawling with roaches. Anthony Lee was lying in a bassinet and was described as having the appearance of a "small baby monkey." One collector testified to seeing roaches on Anthony Lee.

On August 5, 1960, the collectors returned to appellant's home in the company of several police officers and personnel of the Women's Bureau. At this time, Anthony Lee was upstairs in the dining room in the bassinet, but Robert Lee was still downstairs in his "crib." The officers removed the children to the D. C. General Hospital where Anthony Lee was diagnosed as suffering from severe malnutrition and lesions over large portions of his body, apparently caused by severe diaper rash. Following admission, he was fed repeatedly, apparently with no difficulty, and was described as being very hungry. His death, 34 hours after admission, was attributed without dispute to malnutrition. At birth, Anthony Lee weighed six pounds, fifteen ounces—at death at age ten months, he weighed seven pounds, thirteen ounces. Normal weight at this age would have been approximately 14 pounds.

Appellant argues that nothing in the evidence establishes that she failed to provide food to Anthony Lee. She cites her own testimony and the testimony of a lodger, Mr. Wills, that she did in fact feed the baby regularly. At trial, the defense made repeated attempts to ex-

5. It was uncontested that during the entire period the children were in appellant's home, appellant had ample means to provide food and medical care.

tract from the medical witnesses opinions that the jaundice, or the condition which caused it, might have prevented the baby from assimilating food. The doctors conceded this was possible but not probable since the autopsy revealed no condition which would support the defense theory. It was also shown by the disinterested medical witnesses that the child had no difficulty in ingesting food immediately after birth, and that Anthony Lee, in the last hours before his death, was able to take several bottles, apparently without difficulty, and seemed very hungry. This evidence, combined with the absence of any physical cause for nonassimilation, taken in the context of the condition in which these children were kept, presents a jury question on the feeding issue.

Moreover, there is substantial evidence from which the jury could have found that appellant failed to obtain proper medical care for the child. Appellant relies upon the evidence showing that on one occasion she summoned a doctor for the child, on another took the child to the doctor's office, and that she telephoned the doctor on several occasions about the baby's formula. However, the last time a doctor saw the child was a month before his death, and appellant admitted that on that occasion the doctor recommended hospitalization. Appellant did not hospitalize the child, nor did she take any other steps to obtain medical care in the last crucial month. Thus there was sufficient evidence to go to the jury on the issue of medical care, as well as failure to feed.

Appellant also takes exception to the failure of the trial court to charge that the jury must find beyond a reasonable doubt, as an element of the crime, that appellant was under a legal duty to supply food and necessities to Anthony Lee. Appellant's attorney did not object to the failure to give this instruction, but urges here the application of Rule 52(b).

The problem of establishing the duty to take action which would preserve the life of another has not often arisen in the case law of this country.[7] The most commonly cited statement of the rule is found in People v. Beardsley, 150 Mich. 206, 113 N.W. 1128, 1129, 13 L.R.A.,N.S., 1020:

> "The law recognizes that under some circumstances the omission of a duty owed by one individual to another, where such omission results in the death of the one to whom the duty is owing, will make the other chargeable with manslaughter. * * * This rule of law is always based upon the proposition that the duty neglected must be a legal duty, and not a mere moral obligation. It must be a duty imposed

---

7. The problem has evoked considerable study. See, e. g., Holmes, The Common Law, p. 278 (1881); Moreland, A Rationale of Criminal Negligence, ch. 10 (1944); Hughes, Criminal Omissions, 67 Yale L.J. 590, 620–626 (1958); Annot., 10 A.L.R. 1137 (1921).

by law or by contract, and the omission to perform the duty must be the immediate and direct cause of death.   *   *   * "

There are at least four situations in which the failure to act may constitute breach of a legal duty. One can be held criminally liable: first, where a statute imposes a duty to care for another; second, where one stands in a certain status relationship to another;[9] third, where one has assumed a contractual duty to care for another; and fourth, where one has voluntarily assumed the care of another and so secluded the helpless person as to prevent others from rendering aid.

It is the contention of the Government that either the third or the fourth ground is applicable here. However, it is obvious that in any of the four situations, there are critical issues of fact which must be passed on by the jury—specifically in this case, whether appellant had entered into a contract with the mother for the care of Anthony Lee or, alternatively, whether she assumed the care of the child and secluded him from the care of his mother, his natural protector. On both of these issues, the evidence is in direct conflict, appellant insisting that the mother was actually living with appellant and Anthony Lee, and hence should have been taking care of the child herself, while Shirley Green testified she was living with her parents and was paying appellant to care for both children.

In spite of this conflict, the instructions given in the case failed even to suggest the necessity for finding a legal duty of care. The only reference to duty in the instructions was the reading of the indictment which charged, inter alia, that the defendants "failed to perform their legal duty." A finding of legal duty is the critical element of the crime charged and failure to instruct the jury concerning it was plain error.

*   *   *

Reversed and remanded.

NOTES

1. The following statute is proposed for your jurisdiction. Would you support it or not? What if any changes would you recommend?

Liability for Omission. A person shall be criminally responsible for a result if he fails to take action to prevent that result, but for his failure to take action the result would not have occurred, and the failure to take action constitutes a substantial deviation from common decency. In determining whether a failure to act constitutes a substantial deviation from common decency the following factors shall be taken into account:

    1. the seriousness of the result,

---

9. A.L.R. Annot., supra, Note 7 (parent to child); Territory v. Manton, 8 Mont. 95, 19 P. 387 (husband to wife); Regina v. Smith, 8 Carr. & P. 153 (Eng. 1837) (master to apprentice); United States v. Knowles, 26 Fed.Cas. 800 (No. 15,540) (ship's master to crew and passengers); cf. State v. Reitze, 86 N. J.L. 407, 92 A. 576 (innkeeper to inebriated customers).

2. the likelihood that the result would occur without action,

3. any burden or risk which taking action would have required the person to assume, and

4. any responsibility of the person for creating the need for action.

Compare this proposal with the Texas Penal Code.

Sec. 6.01(c) A person who omits to perform an act does not commit an offense unless a statute provides that the omission is an offense or otherwise provides that he has a duty to perform the act.

Statutes quite similar to the first proposal are found in European Codes. Feldbrugge, "Good and Bad Samaritans," 14 Am.J.Comp.L. 630 (1966). The Texas proposal is typical of the Anglo-American approach to this issue. Why do you think there is this difference? Which is preferable in dealing with the following problems?

a. A, from the safety of his home, sees a young woman being assaulted by a man on a deserted street in the early hours of the morning. She cries for aid, screaming: "Oh my God, he stabbed me! Please help me!" A shouts at the assailant who stops momentarily but then pursues the victim. A takes no further action and the victim is again struck. The police, responding to a call from B who passes by after the assault has ended, arrive within two minutes after being notified. The victim dies on the way to the hospital.

b. A, a physician who has stopped at a rural restaurant while on vacation, hears a distraught young man announce that his wife is in very painful labor in a car outside. He asks if there is a doctor there or nearby. A does not respond but gets in his car and drives away. For want of proper assistance the woman and child perish.

c. A, a school-crossing guard, leaves her post to obtain a cup of coffee on a bitterly cold winter day. A first-grader, slightly late for school, dashes across the street and is struck and killed by a car.

2. Can one be convicted of a criminal omission in the absence of knowledge of the duty to act? See Lambert v. California, 355 U.S. 225, 78 S.Ct. 240, 2 L.Ed.2d 228 (1957) reprinted at page 442. If it had been established that the defendant in *Jones* had contracted to care for the child would a defense of ignorance as to the scope of her duties been permitted?

3. What relevance, if any, does the law regarding liability for failure to act have to the criminalization of possession?

B. THE STATE OF MIND

COWAN, TOWARDS AN EXPERIMENTAL DEFINITION OF CRIMINAL MIND, IN PHILOSOPHICAL ESSAYS IN HONOR OF EDGAR ARTHUR SINGER, JR.

163 (F. Clarke and M. Nahm eds. 1942).

In the 17th year of the reign of Edward IV, Brian pronounced his celebrated dictum that a man is responsible only for his words and deeds and not for his thoughts, because "the devil himself knoweth not the mind of man." What the learned judge apparently took to be an axiomatic rule of evidence has become a part of the substantive law of contracts in the form of the doctrine of objective intent. Contract law is now taken to be concerned only with intent as outwardly manifested by the conduct of the parties.

Similarly, the law of torts is almost exclusively occupied with the external behavior of the parties. Only in the case of intentional wrongs does it purport to refer to states of mind as qualifying responsibility. The great body of non-intentional torts applies what are called "objective standards." In determining negligence, for instance, the law does not inquire whether the harmful act was accompanied by a culpable state of mind. On the contrary, it merely decides whether the defendant failed to conform to external standards of reasonably expectable conduct. His state of mind is immaterial. Anglo-American *civil* law, therefore, has from the earliest times indicated that, with certain few exceptions, objective intent is the only kind of intent with which it is prepared to deal.

The theory of the *criminal* law is different. Here it is still felt necessary to investigate a man's secret thought, or absence of thought, whenever intention, or malice, or even negligence is an element of the crime in question.

NOTES

1. The so-called subjective theory of criminal liability assumes that state of mind and therefore "mind" itself is ascertainable. This underlying assumption has been called into question on both practical and theoretical grounds.

The practical ground is based upon difficulty of proof. If there is such a "thing" as state of mind, it is nevertheless so subjective and difficult of proof that it is unrealistic to believe that an individual's state of mind at a past time can generally be reliably determined. Thus, it is argued, the criminal law should not attempt to make criminal liability turn on state of mind.

The theoretical ground is more basic. This view holds that "mind" is a mere abstraction and therefore it is artificial to treat states of mind as if they actually existed. Rather than waste time attempting to infer an offender's state of mind from his behavior, this view holds that the law would better serve its purposes if it regarded the so-called mind as the criminal behavior itself rather than using the behavior as evidence from which to infer "mind". See T. Cowan, Towards an Experimental Definition of Criminal Mind, in Philosophical Essays in Honor of Edgar Arthur Singer, Jr. (F. Clarke and M. Nahm eds. 1942); Cowan, A Critique of the Moralistic Conception of Criminal Law, 97 U.Pa.L.Rev. 502, 510 (1949). In fact, Cowan represents, the law in fact does this by procedural devices such as the presumption that a person "intends" the natural consequences of his act. Inserting the concept of "state of mind", he concludes, merely serves to confuse analysis.

2. The historical development of the criminal law's emphasis upon an alleged offender's state of mind (the mens rea requirement) is traced in the following portions of Sayre, Mens Rea, 45 Harv.L.Rev. 974, 981–83, 988–89, 993–94 (1932): [b]

[S]tudy of the early law seems to show that up to the twelfth century the conception of *mens rea* in anything like its present sense was non-existent. In certain cases at least criminal liability might attach irrespective of the actor's state of mind. But because the old records fail to set forth a *mens rea* as a general requisite of criminality one must not reach the conclusion that even in very early times the mental element was entirely disregarded. The very nature of the majority of the early offenses rendered them impossible of commission without a criminal intent. Waylaying and robbery are impossible without it; so is rape; and the same is roughly true of housebreaking. * * *

Furthermore, the intent of the defendant seems to have been a material factor, even from the very earliest times, in determining the extent of punishment.

By the end of the twelfth century two influences were making themselves strongly felt. One was the Roman law[;] * * * the Roman law conceptions of *dolus* and *culpa* required careful consideration of the mental element in crime.

A second influence, even more powerful, was the canon law, whose insistence upon moral guilt emphasized still further the mental element in crime. * * * Henceforth, the criminal law of England, developing in the general direction of moral blameworthiness, begins to insist upon a *mens rea* as an essential element of criminality. * * *

We can trace the changed attitude in the new generalizations concerning the necessity of an evil intent which are found scattered through the Year Books in the remarks of judges and counsel * * *. We sense it in the growing insistence upon more and more sharply defined mental requisites as essentials of the common-law felonies. We find it fermenting in the form of new defenses which show the absence of an evil mind and therefore of criminal liability-defenses such as infancy or insanity or compulsion.

* * *

b. Reprinted from 45 Harvard Law Review 974 (1932).

By the second half of the seventeenth century, it was universally accepted law that an evil intent was as necessary for felony as the act itself. * * *

At the outset when the *mens rea* necessary for criminality was based on general moral blameworthiness, the conception was an exceedingly vague one. As a result of the slow judicial process of discriminating one case from another and "talking of diversities," much sharper and more precise lines gradually came to be drawn as to the exact mental requisites for various crimes. Since each felony involved different social and public interests, the mental requisites for one almost inevitably came to differ from those of another.

---

1. TYPES OF STATES OF MIND

PROPOSED FEDERAL CRIMINAL CODE

(1971).

§ 302   Requirements of Culpability

(1) Kinds of Culpability.   A person engages in conduct:

(a) "intentionally" if, when he engages in the conduct, it is his purpose to do so;

(b) "knowingly" if, when he engages in the conduct, he knows or has a firm belief unaccompanied by substantial doubt that he is doing so, whether or not it is his purpose to do so;

(c) "recklessly" if he engages in the conduct in conscious and clearly unjustifiable disregard of a substantial likelihood of the existence of the relevant facts or risks, such disregard involving a gross deviation from acceptable standards of conduct   *   *   *;

(d) "negligently" if he engages in the conduct in unreasonable disregard of a substantial likelihood of the existence of the relevant facts or risks, such disregard involving a gross deviation from acceptable standards of conduct;   and

(e) "willfully" if he engages in the conduct intentionally, knowingly, or recklessly.

WEINREB, COMMENT ON BASIS OF CRIMINAL LIABILITY; CULPABILITY; CAUSATION, IN WORKING PAPERS OF THE NATIONAL COMMISSION ON REFORM OF FEDERAL CRIMINAL LAWS

106–28 (1970).

2. *Subsection (1). Kinds of Culpability.* * * *

The degrees of culpability, or categories of mental state, are reduced to four; culpable conduct is conduct in which a person engages *intentionally, knowingly, recklessly,* or *negligently.* All other statutory formulations are eliminated. The four degrees of culpability that are retained express the significant distinctions found by the courts, and are adequate for all the distinctions which can and should be made to accomplish the purposes of a Federal Criminal Code.

"Intentionally." The highest degree of culpability is present when a person engages in conduct *intentionally*, that is "when he engages in the conduct, it is his purpose to do so, whether or not there is a further objective toward which the conduct is directed."

The law can properly single out conceptually and functionally the person who engages in prohibited conduct with the very purpose of engaging in it, who adopts as a guide to his conduct the doing of a prohibited act (or failing to do a required act), the possessing of a prohibited article, or the accomplishing of a prohibited objective. A common way to describe conduct intentional in this sense is to say that it is done "on purpose." [51]

*   *   *

"Knowingly." A high, but not the highest, degree of culpability is present when a person engages in conduct *knowingly*, that is "when he engages in the conduct, he knows or has a firm belief unaccompanied by substantial doubt that he is doing so, whether or not it is his purpose to do so."

In many situations, there may be little reason for the criminal law to distinguish between a man who engages in prohibited conduct purposefully and a man who engages in the same conduct not on purpose but knowing that he is doing so. Both are consciously conducting themselves in a way that the law prohibits. In some situations, however, it seems reasonable that the law should distinguish between a man who wills that a particular act or result take place and another who is merely willing that it should take place. The distinction is drawn between the main direction of a man's conduct and the (antici-

51. The choice of the word "intentionally" rather than "purposely" for this category of conduct was made because the former is more familiar to the law. Also, the latter word may too easily suggest a requirement of a particular purpose rather than simply that conduct be purposive. The Model Penal Code makes the latter word primary and provides that the two have the same meaning. The California, Illinois, Michigan, and New York Codes use the word "intentionally."

pated) side effects of his conduct. For example, a man might intentionally blow up the grocery store next to the post office, with knowledge that the post office will be blown up as well. A category of
conduct in which a person engages knowingly is warranted not only
to allow a distinction between purposeful and knowing conduct but
also because in most cases it will be sufficient for liability that a person engaged in prohibited conduct knowingly, whether or not it was
his purpose to do so.

*   *   *

"Recklessly."   A different order of culpability is present when a
person engages in conduct *recklessly*, that is "he engages in the conduct in conscious [,] and [plain and] clearly unjustifiable disregard
of a substantial likelihood of the existence of the relevant facts [, such
disregard involving a gross deviation from acceptable standards of
conduct]."

*   *   *

Addition of the concluding clause, "such disregard involving a
gross deviation from acceptable standards of conduct," would import into the definition of recklessness the distinction between negligence for civil cases and criminal negligence recognized (at least) in
the crime of manslaughter.   *   *   *

[A]lthough the courts have regularly used phrases like "simple"
and "gross" negligence, it is doubtful whether such shades of meaning have substantive significance. If it is established that a person has
consciously disregarded a likelihood that he is engaging in prohibited
conduct, and that his disregard is (plain and) clearly unjustifiable,
that may be all that can meaningfully be said. To ask a jury to determine also whether his conduct violates standards of conduct "grossly" or only "simply" is very likely to entrust to it the power to judge
the conduct at large without standards.

"Negligently."   The lowest degree of culpability is involved when
a person acts *negligently*, that is, "he engages in the conduct in unreasonable disregard of a substantial likelihood of the existence of the
relevant facts [, such disregard involving a gross deviation from acceptable standards of conduct]."

*   *   *

The formulation used distinguishes negligent conduct from reckless conduct by requiring only an "unreasonable" disregard for the
former, in comparison with the requirement of "conscious and [plain
and] clearly unjustifiable" disregard for the latter. The major difference is that the negligent person need not be aware of the likelihood
that he is engaging in the prohibited conduct. Because he may not be
aware, it seems more appropriate to talk of "unreasonable" rather
than "unjustifiable" disregard; the former word more easily encom-
passes a negligent failure to be aware of, as well as a negligent failure
to give sufficient weight to, the danger involved. In addition, the

omission of the word "clearly," which appears in the definition of reckless conduct, emphasizes the difference in degree between the two levels of culpability. Aside from the distinction drawn between recklessness and negligence on the basis of awareness, the formulations allow a jury to conclude that although the defendant was conscious of a risk, the nature and extent of the risk or the manner or degree of the defendant's disregard of it or the reasons for his disregard of it indicate that he was not reckless, but only negligent. Since all of these elements are relevant to the question whether a person was reckless or entirely without fault, it should be possible to reach the middle ground of negligence on the same basis.

Again, the clause "such disregard involving a gross deviation from acceptable standards of conduct" is added in brackets at the end. For the reasons discussed above, its inclusion is not recommended.

* * *

"Willfully." There may be no word in the Federal criminal lexicon which has caused as much confusion as the word "willfully" (or "willful"). In ordinary speech, the word probably connotes something between purpose and malice, and also something of obstinacy. Despite the confusion that the word has engendered, it has an accepted place in Federal criminal law and can be eliminated only with difficulty. The next best thing to eliminating it entirely is to attempt to give it a clear, fixed meaning. This has been done by providing that a person engages in conduct "willfully" if he engages in it "intentionally," "knowingly," or "recklessly." So confined, the word offers a useful means of referring to the more serious degrees of culpability. None of its connotations have significance for the criminal law.

2. THE STANDARD STATE OF MIND REQUIREMENT FOR CRIMINAL LIABILITY: "GENERAL INTENT"

REGINA v. PEMBLITON

Court of Criminal Appeal, 1874.
12 Cox Crim. Cases 607.

LORD COLERIDGE, C. J.—I am of opinion that this conviction must be quashed. The facts of the case are these. The prisoner and some other persons who had been drinking in a public house were turned out of it at about 11 p.m. for being disorderly, and they then began to fight in the street near the prosecutor's window. The prisoner separated himself from the others, and went to the other side of the street, and picked up a stone, and threw it at the persons he had been fighting with. The stone passed over their heads, and broke a large plate glass window in the prosecutor's house, doing damage to an amount exceeding 5*l*. The jury found that the prisoner threw the stone at the people he had been fighting with, intending to strike one or more of them with it, but not intending to break the window. The question is whether under an indictment for unlawfully and maliciously committing an injury to the window in the house of the prosecutor the proof of these facts alone, coupled with the finding of the jury, will do? Now I think that is not enough. The indictment is framed under the 24 & 25 Vict. c. 97, s. 51. The Act is an Act relating to malicious injuries to property, and sect. 51 enacts that whosoever shall unlawfully and maliciously commit any damage, &c., to or upon any real or personal property whatsoever of a public or a private nature, for which the punishment is hereinbefore provided, to an amount exceeding 5l shall be guilty of a misdemeanor. There is also the 58th section which deserves attention. "Every punishment and forfeiture by this Act imposed on any person maliciously committing any offence, whether the same be punishable upon indictment or upon summary conviction, shall equally apply and be enforced whether the offence shall be committed from malice conceived against the owner of the property in respect of which it shall be committed, or otherwise." It seems to me on both these sections that what was intended to be provided against by the Act is the wilfully doing an unlawful Act, and that the Act must be wilfully and intentionally done on the part of the person doing it, to render him liable to be convicted. Without saying that, upon these facts, if the jury had found that the prisoner had been guilty of throwing the stone recklessly, knowing that there was a window near which it might probably hit, I should have been disposed to interfere with the conviction, yet as they have found that he threw the stone at the people he had been fighting with intending to strike them and not intending to break the window, I think the conviction must be quashed. I do not intend to throw any doubt on the cases which have been cited and which show what is sufficient to constitute malice in the case of murder. They rest upon the principles of the common law, and have no application to a statutory offence created by an Act in which the words are carefully studied.

UNITED STATES v. BYRD

United States Court of Appeals for the Second Circuit, 1965.
352 F.2d 570.

ANDERSON, Circuit Judge. [Defendant, an office auditor for the Internal Revenue Service, was convicted of receiving an unauthorized fee in connection with his official tasks.]

On this appeal Byrd claims that the trial court committed plain error in its charge to the jury in failing to include criminal intent as one of the essential elements of the offense alleged in the three counts. There was no exception taken to the court's instructions but the appellant asserts that there were several other mistakes in the charge of sufficient gravity to constitute plain error. We conclude that, in the circumstances of this case, the omission of criminal intent as one of the enumerated essential elements of the offense charged, constituted plain error and that, therefore, the judgment must be reversed and the case remanded for a new trial.

By failing specifically to instruct the jury that criminal intent was an essential element of the offense, the court left what it did say about intent and the act being knowingly committed, unrelated to the other elements of the crime and omitted any instruction that criminal intent was an element which the Government, to convict, was required to prove beyond a reasonable doubt. While it did not define criminal intent as such, it did give one of the generally used definitions of "knowingly"[1] which in the circumstances of the case would have sufficed, because a finding that one acts knowingly presupposes that he was apprised of all of the facts which constitute the offense.

> "Ordinarily one is not guilty of a crime unless he is aware of the existence of all those facts which make his conduct criminal. That awareness is all that is meant by the mens rea, the 'criminal intent', necessary to guilt,   *   *   *."

United States v. Crimmins, 123 F.2d 271, 272 (2d Cir.1941).

Examining the charge as a whole, however, this definition stands entirely unrelated to the other essential elements of the crime. What its significance is in the case and how it should be treated by the jury is left to conjecture.   *   *   *

*   *   *   [T]he court's treatment of the issue might have survived the test of plain error, Rule 52(b) F.R.Crim.P., except for its specific delineation of the essential elements of the offense.

The instructions which bore on intent came in the early part of the charge. Thereafter the court gave fairly full explanations of types of evidence, rulings on evidence, evaluation of testimony, an analysis of Government and defense evidence, the definition of accomplice and the cautionary remarks on dealing with accomplices' testimony, a reading of the applicable statute and comments on the three counts of the indictment. Then toward the end of the charge the court specified the essential elements of each of the offenses charged as follows:

> "1.   That the defendant was an employee of the United States.
>
> 2.   That he was acting in connection with the revenue laws of the United States.

---

1. "Now, the word 'knowingly,' as used in the indictment, means that the act or acts which were committed by the defendant were done voluntarily and purposely, not because of a mistake or inadvertence or in good faith.

Now, the knowledge may be proven by the defendant's conduct and by all the facts and circumstances surrounding the case.

No person can intentionally avoid knowledge by closing his eyes to facts which prompt him to investigate.

*   *   *"

3. That he received a fee not prescribed by law.

4. That he received a fee for the performance of a duty."

It briefly mentioned how the jury should handle the separate counts and then said,

> "Now, if you find, after such examination, that the government has proven all the four elements which I have just described to you beyond a reasonable doubt as to any of these counts, then he should be convicted on that count."

Thus in the very climax of the charge the court in short explicit terms gave the jury what they would naturally regard as the nub of the law of the case and which, coming at the end of the exposition of the law, gave them what they were most likely to hold in their minds and apply to the facts in their deliberations, and which, not only completely omitted criminal intent as an essential element but, specifically told the jury that, if they found the other four elements which were mentioned, they had a duty to convict.

Byrd made no special attack on the element of intent, for he denied accepting any bribes. The jury disbelieved him. But to sustain a conviction the Government had to prove and the jury had to find criminal intent. It was an unavoidable issue in the case.

We conclude that the court's failure to explain the relevance of criminal intent to the other factors in the case and to describe it as one of the essential elements of the offense, requiring, as such, proof beyond a reasonable doubt, was tantamount to no instruction at all on the subject. There was, therefore, plain error which requires reversal even though no exception was taken below to the charge as given.

PROPOSED FEDERAL CRIMINAL CODE

(1971).

§ 302. Requirements of Culpability

*   *   *

(2) Where Culpability Not Specified. If a statute or regulation thereunder defining a crime does not specify any culpability and does not provide explicitly that a person may be guilty without culpability, the culpability that is required is willfully. Except as otherwise expressly provided or unless the context otherwise requires, if a statute provides that conduct is an infraction without including a requirement of culpability, no culpability is required.

(3) Factors to Which Requirement of Culpability Applies.

(a) Except as otherwise expressly provided, where culpability is required, that kind of culpability is required with respect to every element of the conduct and to those attendant circumstances specified in the definition of the offense, except that where the required culpability is "intentionally", the culpability required as to an attendant circumstance is "knowingly."

(b) Except as otherwise expressly provided, if conduct is an offense if it causes a particular result, the required kind of culpability is required with respect to the result.

(c) Except as otherwise expressly provided, culpability is not required with respect to any fact which is solely a basis for federal jurisdiction or for grading.

(d) Except as otherwise expressly provided, culpability is not required with respect to facts which establish that a defense does not exist, if the defense is defined in Part A of this Code [covering all generally applicable defenses] or Chapter 10 [covering attempt, facilitation, solicitation, conspiracy, and regulatory offenses and defenses related to those offenses]; otherwise the least kind of culpability required for the offense is required with respect to such facts.

(e) A factor as to which it is expressly stated that it must "in fact" exist is a factor for which culpability is not required.

(4) Specified Culpability Requirement Satisfied by Higher Culpability. If conduct is an offense if a person engages in it negligently, the conduct is an offense also if a person engages in it intentionally, knowingly, or recklessly. If conduct is an offense if a person engages in it recklessly, the conduct is an offense also if a person engages in it intentionally or knowingly. If conduct is an offense if a person engages in it knowingly, the conduct is an offense also if a person engages in it intentionally.

(5) No Requirement of Awareness that Conduct is Criminal. Culpability is not required as to the fact that conduct is an offense, except as otherwise expressly provided in a provision outside this Code.

WEINREB, COMMENT ON BASIS OF CRIMINAL LIABILITY; CULPABILITY; CAUSATION, IN 1 WORKING PAPERS OF THE NATIONAL COMMISSION ON REFORM OF FEDERAL CRIMINAL LAWS

118–21, 129 (1970).

This section follows the example of the Model Penal Code and other recent codifications in their efforts to restate the general requirement of culpability ("mens rea") in a limited number of relatively specific principles. It defines a group of specific mental states and provides that, unless a law explicitly provides otherwise, one of them must accompany conduct for it to be criminal. In addition, it provides general rules of statutory construction with respect to the requirement of culpability.

* * *

An issue basic to the proposed Federal Code is resolved in this subsection. Insofar as it provides that, in the absence of an explicit provision to the contrary, willfulness is a requirement of all crimes, the subsection states a presumption that conduct is a crime only if a person engages in it intentionally, knowingly, or recklessly. The subsection also, however, does acknowledge that some conduct may be declared criminal even though a person engages in it not culpably.

* * *

NOTES

1. In State v. Hatley, 72 N.M. 377, 384 P.2d 252 (1963), the defendant was charged with mayhem, based upon striking a blow that put out the eye of the victim. Challenging the adequacy of the proof against him, the defendant argued that there was no proof of "intent to maim" and that if the victim had not turned his head at the moment of the blow the injury to the eye would not have resulted. Affirming the conviction, the appellate court stated:

> We think the conduct of appellant falls well within the rule so as to make him liable for the consequences of an unlawful act, even though such consequences may not have been intended. One who, in the commission of a wrongful act, commits another wrong not meant by him, is nevertheless liable for the latter wrong. * * * Here, the appellant deliberately committed the crime of assault and battery, and, in so doing, committed mayhem.

Id. at 382, 384 P.2d at 252.

Note that although the result in Pembliton is different the cases are not contradictory. The law has developed the notion of transferred intent. If A, intending to murder B, kills C by mistake A's intent will be seen as applying to the killing of C making it murder. But where there is not such a concurrence of mind and act this principle does not apply. If A intends to break a window and, missing his target, hits and kills B he would not be guilty of murder unless recklessness with respect to the danger of killing a person would suffice under the applicable statute. To be distinguished from the doctrine of transferred intent is the doctrine of constructive or implied malice under which a defendant who, in the course of attempting to commit a felony, does by mistake or accident another act which if done voluntarily would have been a felony is to be punished as though he had committed that felony. This doctrine, which is rejected by most commentators, represents a negation of the traditional requirement that the actor have had the state of mind required by the statute for the specific crime for which he is prosecuted.

2. The position of the Proposed Federal Criminal Code and of the Model Penal Code—that in the absence of a specific indication to the contrary "willfullness" would be required—was defended by the draftsmen of the Model Penal Code as representing "what is usually regarded as the common law position." Model Penal Code, Comments to § 2.02, 127 (Tent.Draft

No. 4, 1955).   It also, according to the comments, "represents the most convenient norm for drafting purposes, since when purpose or knowledge is to be required, it is normal to so state; and negligence ought to be viewed as an exceptional basis of liability."   Id.   In view of this, can the analysis of the Proposed Federal Criminal Code be satisfactorily applied to criminal statutes in existing codes as a framework for analysis, an aid in construction, or both?

Why should negligence be regarded as "an exceptional basis of liability," to be used only where the legislative intent to impose it is extremely clear? Consider the following:

Since negligence involves no *mens rea*, the question is raised as to the advisability of punishing negligent conduct with criminal sanctions.   Professor Edwin Keedy responded to this question as follows: "If the defendant, being mistaken as to the material facts, is to be punished because his mistake is one an average man would not make, punishment will sometimes be inflicted *when the criminal mind does not exist*.   Such a result is contrary to fundamental principles, and is plainly unjust, for a man should not be held criminal because of lack of intelligence." [10]   This argument is persuasive, especially when considered in conjunction with the traditional concepts and goals of criminal punishment.

The concept of criminal punishment is based on one, or a combination, of four theories: deterrence, retribution, rehabilitation and incapacitation.

The deterrence theory of criminal law is based on the hypotheses that the prospective offender knows that he will be punished for any criminal activity, and, therefore, will adjust his behavior to avoid committing a criminal act.   This theory rests on the idea of "rational utility," i. e., prospective offenders will weigh the evil of the sanction against the gain of the contemplated crime.   However, punishment of a negligent offender in no way implements this theory, since the negligent harm-doer is, by definition, unaware of the risk he imposes on society.   It is questionable whether holding an individual criminally liable for acts the risks of which he has failed to perceive will deter him from failing to perceive in the future.

The often-criticized retributive theory of criminal law presupposes a "moral guilt," which justifies society in seeking its revenge against the offender.   This "moral guilt" is ascribed to those forms of conduct which society deems threatening to its very existence, such as murder and larceny.   However, the negligent harm-doer has not actually committed this type of morally reprehensible act, but has merely made an error in judgment.   This type of error is an everyday occurrence, although it may deviate from a normal standard of care.   Nevertheless, such conduct does not approach the moral turpitude against which the criminal law should seek revenge.   It is difficult to comprehend how retribution requires such mistakes to be criminally punished.

10.   Keedy, Ignorance and Mistake in the Criminal Law, 22 Harv.L.Rev. 75, 84 (1908) (Emphasis added.)

It is also doubtful whether the negligent offender can be re-habilitated in any way by criminal punishment. Rehabilitation pre-supposes a "warped sense of values" which can be corrected. Since inadvertence, and not a deficient sense of values, has caused the "crime," there appears to be nothing to rehabilitate.

The underlying goal of the incapacitation theory is to protect society by isolating an individual so as to prevent him from per-petrating a similar crime in the future. However, this approach is only justifiable if less stringent methods will not further the same goal of protecting society. For example, an insane individual would not be criminally incarcerated, if the less stringent means of medical treatment would afford the same societal protection. Likewise, with a criminally negligent individual, the appropriate remedy is not in-carceration, but "to exclude him from the activity in which he is a danger."

The conclusion drawn from this analysis is that there appears to be no reasonable justification for punishing negligence as a crim-inal act under any of these four theories. It does not further the purposes of deterrence, retribution, rehabilitation or incapacitation; hence, there is no rational basis for the imposition of criminal lia-bility on negligent conduct.

This view, favoring exclusion of negligence from the criminal law, is not without support. The chief exponent of this position is Professor Jerome Hall, who maintains that there are persuasive historical, ethical and scientific reasons to support the exclusionary argument.[16]

Hall's historical ground rests upon a continuing trend toward restricting criminal negligence in many Anglo-American legal sys-tems. In addition, the same trend can be noted in civil law systems, where negligence is not criminally punishable absent a specific pro-vision to that effect. Such provisions are very few. While Hall rec-ognizes that history is often a dubious ground upon which to support a thesis, he argues that a long and sustained movement, such as that limiting the applicability of criminal negligence, places the burden of retention upon the proponents of penalization. This bur-den, Hall maintains, has not been carried.

Professor Hall's ethical argument is based on the premise that, throughout the long history of ethics, the essence of fault has been voluntary harm-doing. He maintains that this requirement of vol-untary action becomes even more persuasive in the penal law, be-cause no one should be criminally punished unless he has clearly acted immorally, by voluntarily harming someone. Negligence, of course, cannot be classified as voluntary harm-doing. Therefore, no fault is involved and accordingly no punishment is justified.

In addition, Hall suggests scientific arguments for the exclu-sion of negligence from penal liability. One contention is that the incorporation of negligence into the penal law imposes an impossible

16. Hall, Negligent Behavior Should be
Excluded from Penal Liability, 63
Colum.L.Rev. 632 (1963).

function on judges, namely, to determine whether a person, about whom very little is known, had the competence and sensitivity to appreciate certain dangers in a particular situation when the facts plainly indicate that he did not exhibit that competence. Also, Hall maintains that "the inclusion of negligence bars the discovery of a scientific theory of penal law, i. e., a system of propositions interrelating variables that have a realistic foundation in fact and values."

Comment, Is Criminal Negligence A Defensible Basis for Penal Liability?, 16 Buffalo L.Rev. 749, 750–52 (1967).[c] See also Fletcher, The Theory of Criminal Negligence: A Comparative Analysis, 119 U.Pa.L.Rev. 401 (1971); Note, Negligence and the General Problem of Criminal Liability, 81 Yale L.J. 949 (1972).

_____

3. STATES OF MIND BEYOND "GENERAL INTENT"

_____

NOTE: THE DISTINCTION BETWEEN "SPECIFIC" AND "GENERAL" INTENT

The case law often speaks of "specific" or "general" intents, but there is wide disagreement concerning the meaning of these terms. Compare the following uses of the terminology:

State v. Daniels, 109 So.2d 896, 899 (La.1958):

> "[S]pecific intent is present when from the circumstances the offender must have subjectively desired the prohibited result; whereas general intent exists when from the circumstances the prohibited result may reasonably be expected to follow from the offender's voluntary act, irrespective of any subjective desire to have accomplished such result."

State v. Binders, 24 Conn.Sup. 214, 216, 189 A.2d 408, 409 (1962):

> "Crimes are either mala in se or mala prohibita, and intent is a necessary element. In crimes which are mala in se, a specific intent, a wrongful intent, to commit the crime must be established, but in crimes that are mala prohibita the only intent requisite to a conviction is the intent or purpose to do the prohibited act."

> "Some crimes require a specified intention in addition to the intentional doing of the *actus reus* itself * * *. The physical part of the crime of larceny, for example, is the trespassory taking and carrying away of the personal goods of another, but this may be done intentionally, deliberately,

and with full knowledge of all the facts and complete understanding of the wrongfulness of the act, without constituting
larceny. If this willful misuse of another's property is done
with the intention of returning it *   *   *   the special
mens-rea requirement of larceny is lacking *   *   *. This
additional requirement is a 'specific intent,' an additional
intent specifically required for guilt of the particular offense."

What difference does it make whether a particular state of mind be
proven is labeled "specific" or "general" intent? Consider the following cases and raise the issue again when the defenses of mistake
of fact and intoxication are considered.

LAMBERT v. CALIFORNIA

Supreme Court of the United States, 1957.
355 U.S. 225, 78 S.Ct. 240, 2 L.Ed.2d 228.

Mr. Justice DOUGLAS delivered the opinion of the Court.

Section 52.38(a) of the Los Angeles Municipal Code defines "convicted person" as follows:

"Any person who, subsequent to January 1, 1921, has
been or hereafter is convicted of an offense punishable as a
felony in the State of California, or who has been or who is
hereafter convicted of any offense in any place other than
the State of California, which offense, if committed in the
State of California, would have been punishable as a felony."

Section 52.39 provides that it shall be unlawful for "any convicted
person" to be or remain in Los Angeles for a period of more than five
days without registering; it requires any person having a place of
abode outside the city to register if he comes into the city on five
occasions or more during a 30-day period; and it prescribes the information to be furnished the Chief of Police on registering.

Section 52.43(b) makes the failure to register a continuing offense, each day's failure constituting a separate offense.

Appellant, arrested on suspicion of another offense, was charged
with a violation of this registration law. The evidence showed that
she had been at the time of her arrest a resident of Los Angeles for
over seven years. Within that period she had been convicted in Los
Angeles of the crime of forgery, an offense which California punishes
as a felony. Though convicted of a crime punishable as a felony, she
had not at the time of her arrest registered under the Municipal Code.
At the trial, appellant asserted that § 52.39 of the Code denies her due
process of law and other rights under the Federal Constitution, unnecessary to enumerate. The trial court denied this objection. The

case was tried to a jury which found appellant guilty. The court fined her $250 and placed her on probation for three years. Appellant, renewing her constitutional objection, moved for arrest of judgment and a new trial. This motion was denied. On appeal the constitutionality of the Code was again challenged. The Appellate Department of the Superior Court affirmed the judgment, holding there was no merit to the claim that the ordinance was unconstitutional. The case is here on appeal. * * * The case having been argued and reargued, we now hold that the registration provisions of the Code as sought to be applied here violate the Due Process requirement of the Fourteenth Amendment.

The registration provision, carrying criminal penalties, applies if a person has been convicted "of an offense punishable as a felony in the State of California" or, in case he has been convicted in another State, if the offense "would have been punishable as a felony" had it been committed in California. No element of willfulness is by terms included in the ordinance nor read into it by the California court as a condition necessary for a conviction.

We must assume that appellant had no actual knowledge of the requirement that she register under this ordinance, as she offered proof of this defense which was refused. The question is whether a registration act of this character violates due process where it is applied to a person who has no actual knowledge of his duty to register, and where no showing is made of the probability of such knowledge.

We do not go with Blackstone in saying that "a vicious will" is necessary to constitute a crime, 4 Bl.Comm. 21, for conduct alone without regard to the intent of the doer is often sufficient. There is wide latitude in the lawmakers to declare an offense and to exclude elements of knowledge and diligence from its definition. * * * But we deal here with conduct that is wholly passive—mere failure to register. It is unlike the commission of acts, or the failure to act under circumstances that should alert the doer to the consequences of his deed. * * * The rule that "ignorance of the law will not excuse" is deep in our law, as is the principle that of all the powers of local government, the police power is "one of the least limitable." District of Columbia v. Brooke, 214 U.S. 138, 149, 29 S.Ct. 560, 563, 53 L.Ed. 941. On the other hand, due process places some limits on its exercise. Engrained in our concept of due process is the requirement of notice. Notice is sometimes essential so that the citizen has the chance to defend charges. Notice is required before property interests are disturbed, before assessments are made, before penalties are assessed. Notice is required in a myriad of situations where a penalty or forfeiture might be suffered for mere failure to act. [citations omitted] These cases involved only property interests in civil litigation. But the principle is equally appropriate where a person, wholly passive and unaware of any wrongdoing, is brought to the bar of justice for condemnation in a criminal case.

Registration laws are common and their range is wide. * * *
Many such laws are akin to licensing statutes in that they pertain to
the regulation of business activities. But the present ordinance is entirely different. Violation of its provisions is unaccompanied by
any activity whatever, mere presence in the city being the test. Moreover, circumstances which might move one to inquire as to the necessity of registration are completely lacking. At most the ordinance is
but a law enforcement technique designed for the convenience of law
enforcement agencies through which a list of the names and addresses
of felons then residing in a given community is compiled. The disclosure is merely a compilation of former convictions already publicly
recorded in the jurisdiction where obtained. Nevertheless, this appellant on first becoming aware of her duty to register was given no opportunity to comply with the law and avoid its penalty, even though
her default was entirely innocent. She could but suffer the consequences of the ordinance, namely, conviction with the imposition of
heavy criminal penalties thereunder. We believe that actual knowledge of the duty to register or proof of the probability of such knowledge and subsequent failure to comply are necessary before a conviction under the ordinance can stand. As Holmes wrote in The Common
Law, "A law which punished conduct which would not be blameworthy
in the average member of the community would be too severe for that
community to bear." Id., at 50. Its severity lies in the absence of an
opportunity either to avoid the consequences of the law or to defend
any prosecution brought under it. Where a person did not know of the
duty to register and where there was no proof of the probability of
such knowledge, he may not be convicted consistently with due process. Were it otherwise, the evil would be as great as it is when the
law is written in print too fine to read or in a language foreign to the
community.

Reversed.

Mr. Justice BURTON, dissents because he believes that, as applied to this appellant, the ordinance does not violate her constitutional rights.

Mr. Justice FRANKFURTER, whom Mr. Justice HARLAN and
Mr. Justice WHITTAKER join, dissenting.

The present laws of the United States and of the forty-eight States
are thick with provisions that command that some things not be done
and others be done, although persons convicted under such provisions
may have had no awareness of what the law required or that what
they did was wrongdoing. The body of decisions sustaining such
legislation, including innumerable registration laws, is almost as
voluminous as the legislation itself. The matter is summarized in
United States v. Balint, 258 U.S. 250, 252, 42 S.Ct. 301, 302, 66 L.Ed.
604: "Many instances of this are to be found in regulatory measures
in the exercise of what is called the police power where the emphasis

of the statute is evidently upon achievement of some social betterment rather than the punishment of the crimes as in cases of *mala in se*."

Surely there can hardly be a difference as a matter of fairness, of hardship, or of justice, if one may invoke it, between the case of a person wholly innocent of wrongdoing, in the sense that he was not remotely conscious of violating any law, who is imprisoned for five years for conduct relating to narcotics, and the case of another person who is placed on probation for three years on condition that she pay $250, for failure, as a local resident, convicted under local law of a felony, to register under a law passed as an exercise of the State's "police power." Considerations of hardship often lead courts, naturally enough, to attribute to a statute the requirement of a certain mental element—some consciousness of wrongdoing and knowledge of the law's command—as a matter of statutory construction. Then, too, a cruelly disproportionate relation between what the law requires and the sanction for its disobedience may constitute a violation of the Eighth Amendment as a cruel and unusual punishment, and, in respect to the States, even offend the Due Process Clause of the Fourteenth Amendment.

But what the Court here does is to draw a constitutional line between a State's requirement of doing and not doing. What is this but a return to Year Book distinctions between feasance and non-feasance—a distinction that may have significance in the evolution of common-law notions of liability, but is inadmissible as a line between constitutionality and unconstitutionality. * * *

If the generalization that underlies, and alone can justify, this decision were to be given its relevant scope, a whole volume of the United States Reports would be required to document in detail the legislation in this country that would fall or be impaired. I abstain from entering upon a consideration of such legislation, and adjudications upon it, because I feel confident that the present decision will turn out to be an isolated deviation from the strong current of precedents—a derelict on the waters of the law. Accordingly, I content myself with dissenting.

UNITED STATES v. INTERNATIONAL MINERALS & CHEMICAL CORP.

Supreme Court of the United States, 1971.
402 U.S. 558, 91 S.Ct. 1697, 29 L.Ed.2d 178.

Mr. Justice DOUGLAS delivered the opinion of the Court.

The information charged that appellee shipped sulfuric acid and hydrofluosilicic acid in interstate commerce and "did knowingly fail to show on the shipping papers the required classification of said property, to wit, Corrosive Liquid, in violation of 49 CFR 173.427."

18 U.S.C.A. § 834(a) gives the Interstate Commerce Commission power to "formulate regulations for the safe transportation" of "corrosive liquids" and 18 U.S.C.A. § 834(f) states that whoever "knowingly violates any such regulation" shall be fined or imprisoned.

Pursuant to the power granted by § 834(a) the regulatory agency promulgated the regulation already cited which reads in part:

> "Each shipper offering for transportation any hazardous material subject to the regulations in this chapter, shall describe that article on the shipping paper by the shipping name prescribed in § 172.5 of this chapter and by the classification prescribed in § 172.4 of this chapter, and may add a further description not inconsistent therewith.   Abbreviations must not be used."   49 CFR § 173.427.

The District Court * * * ruled that the information did not charge a "knowing violation" of the regulation and accordingly dismissed the information, 318 F.Supp. 1335.

Here as in United States v. Freed, 401 U.S. 601, 91 S.Ct. 1112, 28 L.Ed.2d 356, which dealt with the possession of hand grenades, strict or absolute liability is not imposed; knowledge of the shipment of the dangerous materials is required. The sole and narrow question is whether "knowledge" of the regulation is also required. It is in that narrow zone that the issue of *"mens rea"* is raised; and appellee bears down hard on the provision in 18 U.S.C.A. § 834(f) that whoever "knowingly violates any such regulation" shall be fined, etc.

Boyce Motor Lines, Inc. v. United States, 342 U.S. 337, 72 S.Ct. 329, on which the District Court relied is not dispositive of the issue. It involved a regulation governing transporting explosive, inflammable liquid, and the like and required drivers to "avoid, so far as practicable, and, where feasible, by prearrangement of routes, driving into or through congested thoroughfares, places where crowds are assembled, streetcar tracks, tunnels, viaducts, and dangerous crossings."   The statute punished whoever "knowingly" violated the regulation. Id., at 339, 72 S.Ct. at 330. The issue of *"mens rea"* was not raised below, the sole question turning on whether the standard of guilt was unconstitutionally vague. Id., at 340, 72 S.Ct. 330–331.   In holding the statute was not void for vagueness we said:

> "The statute punishes only those who knowingly violate the Regulation. This requirement of the presence of culpable intent as a necessary element of the offense does much to destroy any force in the argument that application of the Regulation would be so unfair that it must be held invalid. That is evident from a consideration of the effect of the requirement in this case. To sustain a conviction, the Government not only must prove that petitioner could have taken another route which was both commercially practicable and

appreciably safer (in its avoidance of crowded thoroughfares, etc.) than the one it did follow. It must also be shown
that petitioner knew that there was such a practicable, safer
route and yet deliberately took the more dangerous route
through the tunnel, or that petitioner willfully neglected to
exercise its duty under the Regulation to inquire into the
availability of such an alternative route.

* * *

"In an effort to give point to its argument, petitioner
asserts that there was no practicable route its trucks might
have followed which did not pass through places they were
required to avoid. If it is true that in the congestion surrounding the lower Hudson there was no practicable way of
crossing the River which would have avoided such points of
danger to a substantially greater extent than the route taken,
then petitioner has not violated the Regulation. But that is
plainly a matter for proof at the trial. We are not so conversant with all the routes in that area that we may, with no
facts in the record before us, assume the allegations of the
indictment to be false. We will not thus distort the judicial
notice concept to strike down a regulation adopted only after
much consultation with those affected and penalizing only
those who knowingly violate its prohibition." Id., at 342–
343, 72 S.Ct. at 331–332.

The *"mens rea"* that emerged in the foregoing discussion was not
knowledge of the regulation but knowledge of the more safe and the
less safe routes within the meaning of the regulation. * * *

We * * * see no reason why the word "regulations" should
not be construed as a shorthand designation for specific acts or omissions which violate the Act. The Act, so viewed, does not signal an
exception to the rule that ignorance of the law is no excuse and is
wholly consistent with the legislative history.

The principle that ignorance of the law is no defense applies
whether the law be a statute or a duly promulgated and published
regulation. In the context of these 1960 amendments we decline to
attribute to Congress the inaccurate view that that Act requires proof
of knowledge of the law, as well as the facts, and intended to endorse
that interpretation by retaining the word "knowingly." We conclude
that the meager legislative history of the 1960 amendments makes unwarranted the conclusion that Congress abandoned the general rule
and required knowledge of both the facts and the pertinent law before
a criminal conviction could be sustained under this Act.

So far as possession, say, of sulfuric acid is concerned the requirement of *"mens rea"* has been made a requirement of the Act as evidenced by the use of the word "knowingly." A person thinking in

good faith that he was shipping distilled water when in fact he was shipping some dangerous acid would not be covered. * * *

There is leeway for the exercise of congressional discretion in applying the reach of *"mens rea."* United States v. Balint, 258 U.S. 250, 42 S.Ct. 301, 66 L.Ed. 604. United States v. Murdock, 290 U.S. 389, 54 S.Ct. 223, 78 L.Ed. 381, closely confined the word "wilfully" in the income tax law to include a purpose to bring about the forbidden result * * *.

In *Balint* the Court was dealing with drugs, in *Freed* with hand grenades, in this case with sulfuric and other dangerous acids. Pencils, dental floss, paper clips may also be regulated. But they may be the type of products which might raise substantial due process questions if Congress did not require, as in *Murdock, "mens rea"* as to each ingredient of the offense. But where, as here and as in *Balint* and *Freed,* dangerous or deleterious devices or products or obnoxious waste materials are involved, the probability of regulation is so great that anyone who is aware that he is in possession of them or dealing with them must be presumed to be aware of the regulation.

Reversed.

Mr. Justice STEWART, with whom Mr. Justice HARLAN and Mr. Justice BRENNAN join, dissenting.

This case stirs large questions—questions that go to the moral foundations of the criminal law. Whether postulated as a problem of *"mens rea,"* of "willfulness," of "criminal responsibility," or of *"scienter,"* the infliction of criminal punishment upon the unaware has long troubled the fair administration of justice. * * * But there is no occasion here for involvement with this root problem of criminal jurisprudence, for it is evident to me that Congress made punishable only knowing violations of the regulation in question. That is what the law quite clearly says, what the federal courts have held, and what the legislative history confirms.

The statutory language is hardly complex. Section 834(a) of Title 18, U.S.C.A., gives the regulatory agency power to "formulate regulations for the safe transportation" of, among other things, "corrosive liquids." Section 834(f) provides that "[w]hoever knowingly violates any such regulation shall be fined not more than $1,000 or imprisoned not more than one year, or both." In dismissing the information in this case because it did not charge the appellee shipper with knowing violation of the applicable labeling regulation, District Judge Porter did no more than give effect to the ordinary meaning of the English language.

* * *

The Court today * * * grants to the Executive Branch what Congress explicitly refused to grant * * *. It effectively deletes the word "knowingly" from the law. I cannot join the Court in this exercise, requiring as it does such a total disregard of plain statutory language, established judicial precedent, and explicit legislative history.

A final word is in order. Today's decision will have little practical impact upon the prosecution of interstate motor carriers or institutional shippers. For interstate motor carriers are members of a regulated industry, and their officers, agents, and employees are required by law to be conversant with the regulations in question. As a practical matter, therefore, they are under a species of absolute liability for violation of the regulations despite the "knowingly" requirement. This, no doubt, is as Congress intended it to be. Cf. United States v. Dotterweich, 320 U.S. 277, 64 S.Ct. 134, 88 L.Ed. 48; United States v. Balint, 258 U.S. 250, 42 S.Ct. 301, 66 L.Ed. 604. Likewise, prosecution of regular shippers for violations of the regulations could hardly be impeded by the "knowingly" requirement, for triers of fact would have no difficulty whatever in inferring knowledge on the part of those whose business it is to know, despite their protestations to the contrary. The only real impact of this decision will be upon the casual shipper, who might be any man, woman, or child in the Nation. A person who had never heard of the regulation might make a single shipment of an article covered by it in the course of a lifetime. It would be wholly natural for him to assume that he could deliver the article to the common carrier and depend upon the carrier to see that it was properly labeled and that the shipping papers were in order. Yet today's decision holds that a person who does just that is guilty of a criminal offense punishable by a year in prison. This seems to me a perversion of the purpose of criminal law.

I respectfully dissent from the opinion and judgment of the Court.

---

4. STATES OF MIND LESS THAN "GENERAL INTENT": THE "STRICT LIABILITY" OFFENSES

MORISSETTE v. UNITED STATES

Supreme Court of the United States, 1952.
342 U.S. 246, 72 S.Ct. 240, 96 L.Ed. 288.

Mr. Justice JACKSON delivered the opinion of the Court.

This would have remained a profoundly insignificant case to all except its immediate parties had it not been so tried and submitted to the jury as to raise questions both fundamental and far-reaching in federal criminal law, for which reason we granted certiorari.

On a large tract of uninhabited and untilled land in a wooded and sparsely populated area of Michigan, the Government established a practice bombing range over which the Air Force dropped simulated bombs at ground targets. These bombs consisted of a metal cylinder about forty inches long and eight inches across, filled with sand and enough black powder to cause a smoke puff by which the strike could be located. At various places about the range sings read "Danger—Keep Out—Bombing Range." Nevertheless, the range was known as good deer country and was extensively hunted.

Spent bomb casings were cleared from the targets and thrown into piles "so that they will be out of the way." They were not stacked or piled in any order but were dumped in heaps, some of which had been accumulating for four years or upwards, were exposed to the weather and rusting away.

Morissette, in December of 1948, went hunting in this area but did not get a deer. He thought to meet expenses of the trip by salvaging some of these casings. He loaded three tons of them on his truck and took them to a nearby farm, where they were flattened by driving a tractor over them. After expending this labor and trucking them to market in Flint, he realized $84.

Morissette, by occupation, is a fruit stand operator in summer and a trucker and scrap iron collector in winter. An honorably discharged veteran of World War II, he enjoys a good name among his neighbors and has had no blemish on his record more disreputable than a conviction for reckless driving.

The loading, crushing and transporting of these casings were all in broad daylight, in full view of passers-by, without the slightest effort at concealment. When an investigation was started, Morissette voluntarily, promptly and candidly told the whole story to the authorities, saying that he had no intention of stealing but thought the property was abandoned, unwanted and considered of no value to the Government. He was indicted, however, on the charge that he "did unlawfully, wilfully and knowingly steal and convert" property of the United States of the value of $84, in violation of 18 U.S.C. § 641, 18 U.S.C.A. § 641, which provides that "whoever embezzles, steals, purloins, or knowingly converts" government property is punishable by fine and imprisonment. Morissette was convicted and sentenced to imprisonment for two months or to pay a fine of $200. The Court of Appeals affirmed, one judge dissenting.

On his trial, Morissette, as he had at all times told investigating officers, testified that from appearances he believed the casings were cast-off and abandoned, that he did not intend to steal the property, and took it with no wrongful or criminal intent. * * * The court stated: "I will not permit you to show this man thought it was abandoned. * * * I hold in this case that there is no question of abandoned property." The court refused to submit or to allow counsel to argue to the jury whether Morissette acted with innocent intention. It charged: " * * * That if this young man took this property (and he says he did), without any permission (he says he did), that was on the property of the United States Government (he says it was), that it was of the value of one cent or more (and evidently it was), that he is guilty of the offense charged here. If you believe the government, he is guilty. * * * The question on intent is whether or not he intended to take the property. He says he did. Therefore, if you believe either side, he is guilty." Petitioner's counsel contended, "But the taking must have been with a felonious intent." The court ruled, however: "That is presumed by his own act."

The Court of Appeals * * * ruled that this particular offense requires no element of criminal intent. This conclusion was thought to be required by the failure of Congress to express such a requisite and this Court's decisions in United States v. Behrman, 258 U.S. 280, 42 S.Ct. 303, 66 L.Ed. 619, and United States v. Balint, 258 U.S. 250, 42 S.Ct. 301, 66 L.Ed. 604.

I.

In those cases this Court did construe mere omission from a criminal enactment of any mention of criminal intent as dispensing with it. If they be deemed precedents for principles of construction generally applicable to federal penal statutes, they authorize this conviction. Indeed, such adoption of the literal reasoning announced in those cases would do this and more—it would sweep out of all federal crimes, except when expressly preserved, the ancient requirement of a culpable state of mind. We think a résumé of their historical background is convincing that an effect has been ascribed to them more comprehensive than was contemplated and one inconsistent with our philosophy of criminal law.

The contention that an injury can amount to a crime only when inflicted by intention is no provincial or transient notion. It is as universal and persistent in mature systems of law as belief in freedom of the human will and a consequent ability and duty of the normal individual to choose between good and evil. A relation between some mental element and punishment for a harmful act is almost as instinctive as the child's familiar exculpatory "But I didn't mean to," and has afforded the rational basis for a tardy and unfinished substitution of deterrence and reformation in place of retaliation and vengeance as the motivation for public prosecution. Unqualified acceptance of this doctrine by English common law in the Eighteenth Century was indicated by Blackstone's sweeping statement that to constitute any crime there must first be a "vicious will." Common-law commentators of the Nineteenth Century early pronounced the same principle, although a few exceptions not relevant to our present problem came to be recognized.

Crime, as a compound concept, generally constituted only from concurrence of an evil-meaning mind with an evil-doing hand, was congenial to an intense individualism and took deep and early root in American soil. As the states codified the common law of crimes, even if their enactments were silent on the subject, their courts assumed that the omission did not signify disapproval of the principle but merely recognized that intent was so inherent in the idea of the offense that it required no statutory affirmation. Courts, with little hesitation or division, found an implication of the requirement as to offenses that were taken over from the common law. The unanimity with which they have adhered to the central thought that wrongdoing must be conscious to be criminal is emphasized by the variety, disparity and confusion of their definitions of the requisite but elusive mental element. However, courts of various jurisdictions, and for the purposes of different offenses, have devised working formulae, if not scientific ones, for the instruction of juries around such terms as "felonious intent," "criminal intent," "malice aforethought," "guilty knowledge," "fraudulent intent," "wilfulness," *"scienter,"* to denote guilty knowledge, or *"mens rea,"* to signify an evil purpose or mental culpability. By use or combination of these various tokens, they have sought to protect those who were not blameworthy in mind from conviction of infamous common-law crimes.

However, the Balint and Behrman offenses belong to a category of another character, with very different antecedents and origins. The crimes there involved depend on no mental element but consist only of forbidden acts or omissions. This, while not expressed by the Court, is made clear from examination of a century-old but accelerating tendency, discernible both here and in England, to call into existence new duties and crimes which disregard any ingredient of intent. The industrial revolution multiplied the number of workmen exposed to injury from increasingly powerful and complex mechanisms, driven by freshly discovered sources of energy, requiring higher precautions by employers. Traffic of velocities, volumes and varieties unheard of came to subject the wayfarer to intolerable casualty risks if owners and drivers were not to observe new cares and uniformities of conduct. Congestion of cities and crowding of quarters called for health and welfare regulations undreamed of in simpler times. Wide distribution of goods became an instrument of wide distribution of harm when those who dispersed food, drink, drugs, and even securities, did not comply with reasonable standards of quality, integrity, disclosure and care. Such dangers have engendered increasingly numerous and detailed regulations which heighten the duties of those in control of particular industries, trades, properties or activities that affect public health, safety or welfare.

While many of these duties are sanctioned by a more strict civil liability,[13] lawmakers, whether wisely or not,[14] have sought to make

13. The development of strict criminal liability regardless of intent has been roughly paralleled by an evolution of a strict civil liability for consequences regardless of fault in certain relationships, as shown by Workmen's Compension Acts, and by vicarious liability for fault of others as evidenced by various Motor Vehicle Acts.

14. Consequences of a general abolition of intent as an ingredient of serious

such regulations more effective by invoking criminal sanctions to be applied by the familiar technique of criminal prosecutions and convictions. This has confronted the courts with a multitude of prosecutions, based on statutes or administrative regulations, for what have been aptly called "public welfare offenses." These cases do not fit neatly into any of such accepted classifications of common-law offenses, such as those against the state, the person, property, or public morals. Many of these offenses are not in the nature of positive aggressions or invasions, with which the common law so often dealt, but are in the nature of neglect where the law requires care, or inaction where it imposes a duty. Many violations of such regulations result in no direct or immediate injury to person or property but merely create the danger or probability of it which the law seeks to minimize. While such offenses do not threaten the security of the state in the manner of treason, they may be regarded as offenses against its authority, for their occurrence impairs the efficiency of controls deemed essential to the social order as presently constituted. In this respect, whatever the intent of the violator, the injury is the same, and the consequences are injurious or not according to fortuity. Hence, legislation applicable to such offenses, as a matter of policy, does not specify intent as a necessary element. The accused, if he does not will the violation, usually is in a position to prevent it with no more care than society might reasonably expect and no more exertion than it might reasonably exact from one who assumed his responsibilities. Also, penalties commonly are relatively small, and conviction does no grave damage to an offender's reputation. Under such considerations, courts have turned to construing statutes and regulations which make no mention of intent as dispensing with it and holding that the guilty act alone makes out the crime. This has not, however, been without expressions of misgiving.

crimes have aroused the concern of responsible and disinterested students of penology. Of course, they would not justify judicial disregard of a clear command to that effect from Congress, but they do admonish us to caution in assuming that Congress, without clear expression, intends in any instance to do so.

Radin, Intent, Criminal, 8 Encyc.Soc.Sci. 126, 130, says, " * * * as long as in popular belief intention and the freedom of the will are taken as axiomatic, no penal system that negates the mental element can find general acceptance. It is vital to retain public support of methods of dealing with crime." * * *

Sayre, Public Welfare Offenses, 33 Col. L.Rev. 55, 56, says: "To inflict sub-

stantial punishment upon one who is morally entirely innocent, who caused injury through reasonable mistake or pure accident, would so outrage the feelings of the community as to nullify its own enforcement."

Hall, Prolegomena to a Science of Criminal Law, 89 U. of Pa.L.Rev. 549, 569, appears somewhat less disturbed by the trend, if properly limited, but, as to so-called public welfare crimes, suggests that "There is no reason to continue to believe that the present mode of dealing with these offenses is the best solution obtainable, or that we must be content with this sacrifice of established principles. *The raising of a presumption of knowledge might be an improvement.*" (Italics added.)

* * *

The pilot of the movement in this country appears to be a holding that a tavernkeeper could be convicted for selling liquor to an habitual drunkard even if he did not know the buyer to be such. Later came Massachusetts holdings that convictions for selling adulterated milk in violation of statutes forbidding such sales require no allegation or proof that defendant knew of the adulteration. * * *

After the turn of the Century, a new use for crimes without intent appeared when New York enacted numerous and novel regulations of tenement houses, sanctioned by money penalties. Landlords contended that a guilty intent was essential to establish a violation. Judge Cardozo wrote the answer: "The defendant asks us to test the meaning of this statute by standards applicable to statutes that govern infamous crimes. The analogy, however, is deceptive. The element of conscious wrongdoing, the guilty mind accompanying the guilty act, is associated with the concept of crimes that are punished as infamous. * * * Even there it is not an invariable element. * * * But in the prosecution of minor offenses there is a wider range of practice and of power. Prosecutions for petty penalties have always constituted in our law a class by themselves. * * * That is true, though the prosecution is criminal in form." Tenement House Department of City of New York v. McDevitt, 1915, 215 N.Y. 160, 168, 109 N.E. 88, 90.

Soon, employers advanced the same contention as to violations of regulations prescribed by a new labor law. Judge Cardozo, again for the court, pointed out, as a basis for penalizing violations whether intentional or not, that they were punishable only by fine "moderate in amount", but cautiously added that in sustaining the power so to fine unintended violations "we are not to be understood as sustaining to a like length the power to imprison. We leave that question open." People ex rel. Price v. Sheffield Farms-Slawson-Decker Co., 1918, 225 N.Y. 25, 32–33, 121 N.E. 474, 476, 477.

Thus, for diverse but reconcilable reasons, state courts converged on the same result, discontinuing inquiry into intent in a limited class of offenses against such statutory regulations.

Before long, similar questions growing out of federal legislation reached this Court. Its judgments were in harmony with this consensus of state judicial opinion, the existence of which may have led the Court to overlook the need for full exposition of their rationale in the context of federal law. In overruling a contention that there can be no conviction on an indictment which makes no charge of criminal intent but alleges only making of a sale of a narcotic forbidden by law, Chief Justice Taft, wrote: "While the general rule at common law was that the *scienter* was a necessary element in the indictment and proof of every crime, and this was followed in regard to statutory crimes even where the statutory definition did not in terms include it * * *, there has been a modification of this view in respect to prosecutions under statutes the purpose of which would be obstructed by such a requirement. It is a question of legislative intent to be construed by the court. * * *" United States v. Balint, supra, 258 U.S. 251–252, 42 S.Ct. 302.

* * *

On the same day, the Court determined that an offense under the Narcotic Drug Act does not require intent, saying, "If the offense be a statutory one, and intent or knowledge is not made an element of it, the indictment need not charge such knowledge or intent." United States v. Behrman, supra, 258 U.S. at page 288, 42 S.Ct. at page 304.

Of course, the purpose of every statute would be "obstructed" by requiring a finding of intent, if we assume that it had a purpose to convict without it. Therefore, the obstruction rationale does not help us to learn the purpose of the omission by Congress. And since no federal crime can exist except by force of statute, the reasoning of the Behrman opinion, if read literally, would work far-reaching changes in the composition of all federal crimes.

* * *

It was not until recently that the Court took occasion more explicitly to relate abandonment of the ingredient of intent, not merely with considerations of expediency in obtaining convictions, nor with the *malum prohibitum* classification of the crime, but with the peculiar nature and quality of the offense. We referred to "* * * a now familiar type of legislation whereby penalties serve as effective means of regulation", and continued, "such legislation dispenses with the conventional requirement for criminal conduct—awareness of some wrongdoing. In the interest of the larger good it puts the burden of acting at hazard upon a person otherwise innocent but standing in responsible relation to a public danger." But we warned: "Hardship there doubtless may be under a statute which thus penalizes the transaction though consciousness of wrongdoing be totally wanting." United States v. Dotterweich, 320 U.S. 277, 280–281, 284, 64 S.Ct. 134, 136, 88 L.Ed. 48.

Neither this Court nor, so far as we are aware, any other has undertaken to delineate a precise line or set forth comprehensive criteria for distinguishing between crimes that require a mental element and crimes that do not. We attempt no closed definition, for the law on the subject is neither settled nor static. The conclusion reached in the Balint and Behrman cases has our approval and adherence for the circumstances to which it was there applied. A quite different question here is whether we will expand the doctrine of crimes without intent to include those charged here.

Stealing, larceny, and its variants and equivalents, were among the earliest offenses known to the law that existed before legislation; they are invasions of rights of property which stir a sense of insecurity in the whole community and arouse public demand for retribution, the penalty is high and, when a sufficient amount is involved, the infamy is that of a felony, which, says Maitland, is " *   *   * as bad a word as you can give to man or thing." State courts of last resort, on whom fall the heaviest burden of interpreting criminal law in this country, have consistently retained the requirement of intent in larceny-type offenses. If any state has deviated, the exception has neither been called to our attention nor disclosed by our research.

Congress, therefore, omitted any express prescription of criminal intent from the enactment before us in the light of an unbroken course of judicial decision in all constituent states of the Union holding intent inherent in this class of offense, even when not expressed in a statute. Congressional silence as to mental elements in an Act merely adopting into federal statutory law a concept of crime already so well defined in common law and statutory interpretation by the states may warrant quite contrary inferences than the same silence in creating an offense new to general law, for whose definition the courts have no guidance except the Act. Because the offenses before this Court in the Balint and Behrman cases were of this latter class, we cannot accept them as authority for eliminating intent from offenses incorporated from the common law. Nor do exhaustive studies of state court cases disclose any well-considered decisions applying the doctrine of crime without intent to such enacted common-law offenses, although a few deviations are notable as illustrative of the danger inherent in the Government's contentions here.

The Government asks us by a feat of construction radically to change the weights and balances in the scales of justice. The purpose and obvious effect of doing away with the requirement of a guilty intent is to ease the prosecution's path to conviction, to strip the defendant of such benefit as he derived at common law from innocence of evil purpose, and to circumscribe the freedom heretofore allowed juries. Such a manifest impairment of the immunities of the individual should not be extended to common-law crimes on judicial initiative.

The spirit of the doctrine which denies to the federal judiciary power to create crimes forthrightly admonishes that we should not enlarge the reach of enacted crimes by constituting them from anything less than the incriminating components contemplated by the words used in the statute. And where Congress borrows terms of art in which are accumulated the legal tradition and meaning of centuries of practice, it presumably knows and adopts the cluster of ideas that were attached to each borrowed word in the body of learning from which it was taken and the meaning its use will convey to the judicial mind unless otherwise instructed. In such case, absence of contrary direction may be taken as satisfaction with widely accepted definitions, not as a departure from them.

We hold that mere omission from § 641 of any mention of intent will not be construed as eliminating that element from the crimes denounced.

* * *

III.

As we read the record, this case was tried on the theory that even if criminal intent were essential its presence (a) should be decided by the court (b) as a presumption of law, apparently conclusive, (c) predicated upon the isolated act of taking rather than upon all of the circumstances. In each of these respects we believe the trial court was in error.

NOTES

1. Is "strict liability" appropriate or defensible in regard to those "regulatory offenses" as to which it has traditionally been imposed? Consider the following comments from Mueller, Mens Rea and the Law Without It, 58 W.Va.L.Rev. 34, 37–38, 50, 59–60 (1955):

> The reasons for * * * [imposing strict liability in regard to such offenses] have been variously stated: If "mens rea" were required, (1) the enforcement of the statute would be impeded; or (2) the courts would be overburdened; or (3) justice would be hampered; or (4) fraudulent defenses could be fabricated, etc. Prima facie such claims can be just as easily made as refuted. The often stated reason here listed under (1), for instance, seems to be nothing more than a woman's "because", and proves no more.

> (2) supra, is a little more specific. It is certainly true that there is hardly any aspect of human activity which has escaped control by the law. When we eat, the (pure food and drug) law eats with us; when we walk, the (traffic) law walks with us; and even the health and soundness of our sleep is regulated by law. To litigate every one of the regulated problems of daily life would surely hamper the administration of justice. But what good will it do to punish indiscriminately, regardless of guilt or innocence, merely to save the time it would take to determine the validity of a defense? And what of the deterrent effect of such a frustrating law? Would it not ease the burden on the court and reduce the length of the court calendar much more if, for instance, in January we would prosecute only blond culprits, in February only bald ones, in March brunettes, etc.? That would at least deter some of the culprits some of the time, whereas absolute criminal liability is totally without deterrent effect. * * *

> Ad (3) it might be answered that absolute criminal liability surely is not the vehicle to unhamper criminal justice. If anything, it does away with justice altogether by distributing penalties indiscriminately. Ad (4) it will suffice to ask: what crime is there which is not subject to the interposition of fraudulent defenses? Surely the temptation for tricking one's way out of

a jam is much greater in crimes threatening serious consequences than it is in petty offenses.

*   *   *

[It has been feared that the enforcement of the regulatory schemes would bog down if strict liability were not imposed.]

Now then, how can a law deter anybody which inflicts punishment for the mere doing of the outward act? Is it not manifest that a law which punishes without caring about the factual and moral blamelessness of a defendant thereby frustrates him and the community at large? Why should the citizen bother to use care if the courts do not bother whether or not he used care, inflicting punishment in any event? Punishment which befalls the innocent and the guilty alike, like hay fever, hail or hurricane, can have no good effect at all, except perhaps for insurance companies, for whom it creates a new insurable interest.

*   *   *

[It has also been argued that unless strict liability were imposed, "many unscrupulous persons would not hesitate to fabricate such facts as would be needful to accomplish" the assertion of a defense of mistake of fact.]

The ease of manufacturing surreptitious or fraudulent defenses is, as any lawyer knows, not confined to such cases. * * Since the temptation to fabricate defenses is even greater in prosecutions in which the stakes are higher, for instance in murder prosecutions, why then not dispense with "mens rea" altogether and make every act, e. g., the killing of a human being, conclusive evidence of a criminal intent to do the act, e. g., killing a human being conclusive evidence of a criminal intent, thus murder?

* * * All other arguments in favor of absolute criminal liability failing, it has sometimes been reasoned that the raising of issues in defense of regulatory violations would require dealing with collateral and irrelevant issues. Hence, too much time, in proportion to the slightness of the offense, would have to be devoted to the matter if the defendant were permitted to present an elaborate defense, or, indeed, any defense. It has been said that courts would never be able to clear their calendars if in this vast mass of petty offenses a judge, or a jury, were to try all defensive facts. Speediness of "justice" is said to be the compelling reason for absolute criminal liability.

If this were truly the only, or major, reason for resort to absolute criminal liability, then it would be sheer folly to dispense with the "mens rea" and nevertheless to consider all defensive arguments for the purpose of possibly mitigating the punishment * * *. Of course, this only goes to show that the "speediness of justice" argument is absurd. The choice does not lie between speedy justice and slow justice, but between speedy injustice and justice of whatever celerity we can achieve by whatever court reform may be necessary. Justice ought to be speedy, but absolute criminal liability is not apt to achieve it.

*   *   *

[It has also been argued in support of strict liability that "as the penalty is slight, no great injustice is perpetrated by enforcing this type of statute regardless of knowledge".]

Are we compelled to prefer small injustice over justice? I do not think that the writer regarded this point as a major reason for the imposition of absolute criminal liability. But even as collateral support it fails miserably. Such reasoning may be appropriate in a country where absolutism and dictatorial utility sacrifice life, liberty and property to the Moloch state, but not here.

2. What, if any, significance upon "strict liability" issues does the following observation concerning the administration of such offenses have?

* * * [B]oth legislature and court have in substantial measure sanctioned the imposition of liability under the food and drug sections containing no express fault requirement upon persons who violate the provisions completely through inadvertence or mistake and without any measure of subjective fault. These sections are not self-executing, however; the enforcement policies of the Wisconsin department of agriculture play an important role in determining the practical working significance of these provisions.

The general policy of the department has been to refrain from prosecuting inadvertent violations of the food and drug sections until a specific warning has been given and the violator has had ample opportunity to cease the offending action or correct the offensive condition. The considerations underlying this policy are many. Some of the more clearly defined factors include: (1) The department believes that the most effective control and the best public relations can be achieved by co-operation with the regulated group and correction of the average offender, coupled with selective prosecution of only the uncooperative recalcitrant minority. (2) The state would incur substantial cost from large numbers of food and drug prosecutions. (3) Administrative officers and field inspectors alike share a natural reluctance to be responsible for the imposition of punishment for a wholly unintended violation by a defendant free from any subjective fault. (4) The department faces the necessity of convincing the appropriate district attorney to institute prosecution, even after the inspector has decided that prosecution is desirable and has prepared a case. Evidence that a warning has been issued to the prospective defendant and has been ignored will often encourage a district attorney, who might otherwise be hesitant to do so, to prosecute. (5) Courts and juries may be reluctant to find an offender guilty even in the face of conclusive evidence of an actual violation, unless this evidence is accompanied by some showing of moral culpability, or subjective fault, such as might be provided by proof of failure to heed an express warning issued by the department.

Standard operating procedure calls for the issuance of a warning notice by the field inspector immediately upon discovery of an inadvertently offensive condition or action. If the offender does not make the required corrections immediately, he may be given several more warnings and opportunities to evince a willingness to co-operate with the department before prosecution is instituted. The final decision to prosecute is usually made by the administrative head of the division concerned, who is kept constantly informed of the progress of each case.   There are several offenses under the cognizance of the department, however, which manifestly demonstrate guilty intent and knowledge on the part of the offender.   When an inspector uncovers a violation of this type he is authorized to institute prosecution through the district attorney immediately without either the issuance of a warning to the offender or notification to the division head.   An example of this type of offense is "watering of milk"   *   *   *.

A case history selected from the correspondence files of the dairy and food division of the department presents a vivid illustration of the department's technique of issuing warning notices before resorting to prosecution.   A field inspector discovered unsanitary conditions in a small town cheese factory, particularly in relation to milk cans and milk trucks.   Warning notices were issued on March 18, 1953, May 13, 1953, July 28, 1953, August 5, 1953, February 3, 1954, and June 21, 1954.   Finally, on July 9, 1954, prosecution was instituted under section 97.32, which provides a penalty for any cheese factory operator who does "maintain his premises and utensils in an insanitary condition."   Defendant was found guilty and fined $100.

Another case from the same file illustrates the department's policy of prosecuting only upon a showing of subjective fault and unwillingness to co-operate on the part of the violator.   Prosecution had been instituted under section 97.32 against a dairy farmer for maintaining his milking machine and equipment in an unsanitary condition.   In court, the defendant argued that this was his first offense, that he had co-operated fully with the department in the past, and that he had hired a contractor who would begin immediate construction of a milkhouse on defendant's farm. Convinced of defendant's sincerity, the department dropped the charge upon payment of costs by the defendant.

To a certain extent the practical effect of these enforcement policies is to nullify the significance of the liability without fault character of the food and drug sections, since prosecution under them takes place only when the defendant has demonstrated subjective fault by showing a conscious intent to violate or, at least, a wilful heedlessness in failing to respond to repeated warnings. However, the liability without fault character of these provisions is still of prime importance to successful regulation of foods and drugs because the necessity of proving guilty knowledge or intent to the satisfaction of the court or jury would in many instances present an insurmountable burden to the department and greatly hinder efforts at control and regulation.   This would be true even in many cases of conscious and advertent violation.

Consider the example of a cheesemaker who insists in spite of repeated warnings upon using only the bare minimum of milk fat permissible under statutory standards, thus producing on the narrowest possible margin of safety. It is inevitable that such methods will result in continued occasional production of below-standard cheese. If the cheesemaker refuses to raise his standards so as to insure the production of only above-minimum cheese, he will, under existing department policy, be prosecuted each time he turns out a substandard batch. His actual subjective intent, however, is to produce only cheese which will meet the statutory standards. It would therefore be impossible for the department to regulate his conduct if proof of subjective fault on his part were essential to conviction under the sections involved.

* * *

In actual effect then the principal functional significance of the liability without fault character of the food and drug sections is not to make possible wholesale conviction of inadvertent offenders untinted by subjective fault; it is rather to provide widened areas of administrative discretion within which the department of agriculture can administer and enforce the regulations with greater flexibility and effectiveness than would be possible if proof of subjective fault were necessary.

Comment, Liability Without Fault in the Food and Drug Statutes, 1956 Wis.L.Rev. 641, 653–55.

3. As a matter of constitutional law, the line between strict liability offenses which are permissible and those which are not remains uncertain. In United States v. Freed, 401 U.S. 601, 91 S.Ct. 1112, 28 L.Ed.2d 356 (1971), the defendants were indicted for possessing and conspiring to possess hand grenades not registered under the National Firearms Act. The trial court dismissed the indictments because they, in accord with the act, failed to allege any specific intent or knowledge by the defendants that the grenades were unregistered. The Supreme Court reversed. It examined a continuum of statutes from that involved in Lambert—page 142 supra—where a mere conviction for failure to register as a convicted felon was held unconstitutional since there were no circumstances to alert the actor to the need to act—and Morrissette—with its insistence on the requirement of mens rea in a crime derived from the common law in the absence of a clear legislative indication to the contrary—to the Food and Drug Act provision challenged in United States v. Dotterweich, 320 U.S. 277, 64 S.Ct. 134, 88 L.Ed. 48 (1943)—where the Court upheld the imposition of a penalty on a corporate officer whose firm had shipped adulterated and misbranded drugs even if consciousness of wrong doing was absent. Freed, the Court held, was closer to Dotterweich in that it involved a regulatory measure in the interest of public safety which might "be premised on the theory that one would hardly be surprised to learn that possession of hand grenades is not an innocent Act. They are highly dangerous offensive weapons, no less dangerous than the narcotics involved in United States v. Balint". Compare Speidel v. State, 460 P.2d 77 (Alaska 1969) where the court held unconstitutional a statute making it a felony (punishable by up to five years imprisonment) for one in possession of a motor vehicle under a written agreement to fail

to return it as required by the agreement, if he does this "without regard for the rights of the owner, or with indifference whether a wrong is done the owner or not." Since the statute permitted the conviction of one who had no intention of depriving the owner of his property, of converting the property to his own use, or of doing any wrong to the owner, the court concluded, it was contrary to the general conditions of penal liability requiring the existence of a guilty mind during the commission of the act. "To convict a person of a felony for such an act, without proving criminal intent, is to deprive such person of due process of law."

4. For discussions of "strict" liability offenses, see Starrs, The Regulatory Offense in Historical Perspective, in Essays in Criminal Science (G. Mueller ed. 1961); Packer, Mens Rea and the Supreme Court, 1962 Sup.Ct.Rev. 107; Borre, Public Welfare Offenses: A New Approach, 52 J.Crim.L.C. & P.S. 418 (1961); Sayre, Public Welfare Offenses, 33 Colum.L.Rev. 55 (1933); Wasserstrom, Strict Liability in the Criminal Law, 12 Stan.L.Rev. 731 (1960); Comment, Liability Without Fault: Logic and Potential of a Developing Concept, 1970 Wis.L.Rev. 1201.

---

5. "DEFENSES" CONSISTING OF "DISPROOF" OF STATE OF MIND

---

a. IGNORANCE OR MISTAKE OF FACT

PEOPLE v. HERNANDEZ

Supreme Court of California, 1964.
61 Cal.2d 529, 39 Cal.Rptr. 361, 393 P.2d 673.

[The opinion in this case is reprinted at page 803]

UNITED STATES v. SHORT

United States Court of Military Appeals, 1954.
4 USCMA 437, 16 CMR 11.

ROBERT E. QUINN, Chief Judge. A general court-martial in Japan convicted the accused of assault with intent to commit rape, and sentenced him to dishonorable discharge, total forfeitures, and confinement at hard labor for ten years. The convening authority modified the sentence by reducing the period of confinement to five years. A board of review affirmed the conviction and the modified sentence. We granted review to consider the correctness of the law officer's general instructions and his denial of certain defense requests for specific instructions.

The events of this case took place on November 28, 1952, in Tokyo. At about 11:30 p. m., two Japanese girls, Yayoi Tomobe and Tokiko Okano, left the shop in which they worked to dispose of some waste paper in a public latrine located across the street. Apparently as the girls were crossing the street, they were approached from behind by the accused and his companion, Private O'Rourke. From their speech, Okano deduced that the "foreigners" were intoxicated. She was frightened. Calling out to Tomobe to run, Okano ran back to the shop. Tomobe, however, tripped over a stone. As she regained her balance, she was caught under her right arm by the accused. The accused spoke to her in English. Although she had learned some English in school, she was "so scared and * * * surprised" that she did not know what was said, except that there was mention of yen. She was then pulled to the front of the latrine and pushed in. The accused entered and closed the door.

Tomobe tried to get away from the accused, but he was "very big." She was "scared" and "had no strength to go out." While the accused did not punch, kick, or otherwise inflict bodily harm upon her, he fondled her person against her protests. She kept saying "No" in Japanese as loudly as she could. She pushed the accused away, but he was "so strong that [she] was unable to hold him away."

In the meantime, Okano, having seen Tomobe pulled into the latrine, reported to the manager of the shop. He immediately went to the latrine and opened the door. He heard Tomobe saying "No," and he saw the accused holding her. However, just then O'Rourke tapped him on the shoulder and he made no further effort to interfere. Instead, he went to a police box, located approximately forty feet from the latrine, and reported the matter to the Japanese policemen. They hastened to the latrine. One of the policemen opened the door, and in Japanese called out to the accused to stop. In the same language, the accused replied that it was all right. Then he was forcibly removed from the latrine, and taken to the police box.

At the trial, the accused admitted fondling Tomobe, as set out in the specification. However, he denied that he acted unlawfully. He testified that when he saw Tomobe, he thought she was a prostitute since the area was known to be frequented by them. He "propositioned" her, and after some negotiation they agreed on a price of 500 yen. Tomobe showed him the latrine; he previously did not know of its existence. Inside Tomobe helped him in his efforts to "make love to her." Although he was "under the influence," he was generally aware of what he was doing. When the police entered the latrine, he thought that they wanted to arrest the girl as a prostitute. He told them that it was all right because he was anxious to protect her.

*   *   *

Before giving his instructions, the law officer discussed them with both counsel in a recorded out-of-court hearing. Each counsel submitted requests for specific instructions. With some modification, one of the three offered by the prosecution was accepted; the two submitted by the defense were rejected. The defense requests are as follows:

* * *

> "In order to constitute an offense, the accused must think victim is not consenting because he must intend not only to have carnal knowledge of the woman but to do so by force.
>
> "The guilt or innocence of the accused depends on the circumstances as they appear to him."

* * *

Turning to the second request, the accused argues that this instruction sought, in essence, to present a defense of mistake of fact. It is axiomatic that, before a failure to instruct on a defense may be alleged as ground for error, the evidence must show that the defense was reasonably raised. United States v. Sandoval, 4 USCMA 61, 15 CMR 61. We assume for the purposes of this case that sufficient evidence appears in the record from which it may reasonably be inferred the accused believed that Tomobe consented to his "proposition." However, the question still to be answered is whether the instruction requested is legally correct. The accused stresses the similarity of the requested instruction to that in McQuirk v. State, 84 Ala. 435, 4 So. 775. In that case the accused was charged with rape. The evidence showed that the prosecutrix was weakminded. The defendant maintained that he believed she had consented to the act. He requested the following instruction which was denied by the trial judge:

> "If the jury believe, from the evidence, that the conduct of the prosecutrix was such towards the defendant, at the time of the alleged rape, as to create in the mind of the defendant the honest and reasonable belief that she had consented, or was willing for defendant to have connection with her, they must acquit the defendant."

On appeal the conviction was reversed because of the failure of the trial judge to give the requested instruction.

It is immediately apparent that the requested instruction in this case is markedly different from that in McQuirk. It fails to qualify the accused's belief by requiring that it be reasonable and honest. * * * This omission is substantial. The requested instruction also assumes too much. When consent is in issue, whether or not it was given is a question of fact for the court. It, not the accused, must determine whether the woman's conduct was such as to lead the accused to believe she had consented to his acts. The accused's personal evaluation of the circumstances is but one factor to be considered by the court; it is not conclusive. There are other objectionable elements in the request * * * but we need not further elaborate upon them. There may be occasions when a request to instruct is technically defective but still sufficiently challenging in content to require the law officer to instruct on the subject matter in spite of the defect. * * * However, nothing in the instant request suggested a material issue that was not adequately covered in the general instructions.

The decision of the board of review is affirmed.

BROSMAN, Judge (concurring in part and dissenting in part):

* * * Here the evidence seems to me to have raised reasonably the possibility that the accused believed the prosecutrix was acceding to his overtures. The principal opinion suggests that such a belief, to be effective, must be both reasonable and honest. For this its author cites United States v. Perruccio, 4 USCMA 28, 15 CMR 28, where an unreasonable—and thus negligent—mistake of fact was deemed no defense to a prosecution for negligent homicide. On the other hand, a mistake of fact may be negligent and yet negate the intent or knowledge required for conviction of certain offenses. United States v. Lampkins, 4 USCMA 31, 15 CMR 31. Within which category do rape and assault with intent to commit rape fall?

Rape—like unpremeditated murder—has ordinarily been treated as requiring only a general criminal intent. Thus, drunkenness, even in excessive degree, would probably not constitute a defense to this crime—that is, as serving to belie the accused's necessary intent. However, assault with intent to commit rape would seem to occupy a quite different position—since the very designation of the offense indicates the requirement of a specific intent. Clearly, then, drunkenness could operate to negate the intent required for conviction of such an assault. An *unreasonable* mistake of fact could perhaps not serve to deny criminal liability for a consummated rape. But could it negative the prerequisites for a finding of guilt of assault with intent to commit rape just as an unreasonable mistake of fact is said to destroy liability for larceny by false pretenses?
* * *

Assault with intent to commit rape demands proof of an assault on the prosecutrix accompanied by an intent to have unlawful sexual intercourse by force and without her consent—a purpose to overcome any resistance by force. Manual for Courts-Martial United States, 1951, paragraph 213d(1) (c). If the woman consents to the application of force to her body, there would presumably be no assault in the first instance. Of course, if she had consented to sexual intercourse—that is, if her "will" favored such a result—she would also ordinarily have consented to that fondling which frequently precedes the act of coition. Thus, acts like those before us here would not partake of their usual character of a battery. See Manual, supra, paragraph 207a, page 371.

Ignorance or mistake of fact—if reasonable—normally provides a defense to an accused. Manual, paragraph 154a(3). Ignorance of law usually constitutes no excuse—although it may negate the existence of the specific intent required in certain offenses. Idem, paragraph 154a(4). While consent in some areas may be a matter of law * * * I would suppose that the type of consent with which we are now dealing is "factual" in nature, and that a mistake as to the woman's attitude would constitute one of fact. Thus, if the accused believed reasonably that the Japanese girl here was consenting to his proposals, he would be exonerated, I should think, even from the crime of assault. On the other hand, an unreasonable mistake on his part would not affect his liability for assault, in violation of the Uniform Code, Article 128, 50 U.S.C.A. § 722.

But if an assault is to be found here—on the theory there was neither consent nor a reasonable mistake with regard thereto—does not the accused's mistake reenter the picture? One possibility is that the trier of fact may conclude that the girl did not consent, and that no reasonable man would have thought she did, but that the accused—because of drunkenness or some variety of mild sexual complex which destroyed his realism—genuinely believed that she was acquiescent. His purpose simply was to enjoy sexual relations with her under the circumstances presented to him. Those circumstances he unreasonably construed to amount to an invitation on her part. However, he did not intend coitus under any other circumstances. This might be because (a) he did not desire intercourse without full consent; or (b) because he was just not the sort of person who worries about hypothetical problems. When an accused fondles a woman against a background of the frame of mind just mentioned, I would suppose him to be wanting in that variety of criminal purpose required for assault with intent to rape. One may well lack an intention to overcome resistance when nothing is present which seems to suggest the possibility of its presence.

It may be regarded as anomalous to conclude that an accused may be exonerated from guilt of assault with intent to commit rape because of an unreasonable mistake, whereas he could have been convicted lawfully of rape had penetration been effected under the same misapprehension. It is to be observed, however, that the anomaly is no greater than that involved in holding that an assault with intent to murder requires a specific intent to kill, whereas the crime of murder may be made out with a lesser intent. See United States v. Woodson, 3 USCMA 372, 12 CMR 128. The fact of the matter is that a specific intent is, by definition, required for the present finding. The evidence, in my view, raised the possibility that a mistake of fact on the accused's part precluded that intent.

*   *   *

Regardless of whether the offered—and denied—instruction was entirely accurate in phrasing, it is manifest that the law officer was put on notice to see to it that the court-martial was instructed correctly on mistake of fact.

* * *

It follows from what has been said that, as to mere assault, the accused is not entitled to an instruction on mistake of fact, unless the possibility of a *reasonable* mistake was raised by the evidence. On the other hand, as to assault with intent to rape, he is so entitled *regardless* of reasonableness. * * *

I would reverse the decision of the board of review and order a rehearing.

NOTE

The position taken by Judge Brosman in the instant case is generally regarded as the traditional rule. See generally, Howard, The Reasonableness of Mistake in the Criminal Law, 4 U.Queens L.J. 45 (1961). This is, in part, inconsistant with the rule that generally a defendant must be at least reckless with regard to all of those things which are necessary to guilt, isn't it?

PROPOSED FEDERAL CRIMINAL CODE (1971)

§ 304. Ignorance or Mistake Negating Culpability

A person does not commit an offense if when he engages in conduct he is ignorant or mistaken about a matter of fact or law and the ignorance or mistake negates the kind of culpability required for commission of the offense.

---

b. IGNORANCE OR MISTAKE OF LAW

PROPOSED FEDERAL CRIMINAL CODE (1971)

§ 304. Ignorance or Mistake Negating Culpability

[For text of this section, see above.]

§ 609. Mistake of Law

Except as otherwise expressly provided, a person's good faith belief that conduct does not constitute a crime is an affirmative defense if he acted in reasonable reliance upon a statement of the law contained in:

    (a) a statute or other enactment;

    (b) a judicial decision, opinion, order or judgment;

    (c) an administrative order or grant of permission; or

(d) an official interpretation of the public servant or body charged by law with responsibility for the interpretation, administration or enforcement of the law defining the crime.

Comment

This section sets forth those circumstances under which a person is excused from criminal liability for his conduct because he mistakenly believed his conduct did not constitute a crime. The defense is not available for infractions where proof of culpability is generally not required. Mistake of law is an affirmative defense; it must be established by a preponderance of the evidence. See § 103(3). Note that the reliance must be "reasonable," and that good faith is explicitly required. In most instances, it would be unreasonable for a layman to fail to consult a lawyer, and would not be in good faith if he failed to make full disclosure to him of all relevant facts. * * *

An alternative preferred by a substantial body of opinion in the Commission would limit the defense to situations where knowledge of the law might be regarded as especially relevant to culpability, e. g., tax and draft evasion, conflict of interest. This approach is premised on the view that " * * * to admit the excuse at all would be to encourage ignorance * * *." Holmes, The Common Law 41 (Howe ed. 1963). Consequently, it is argued, mistake of law ought only be a defense where knowledge of the law is an element of the offense. It is argued for the view embodied in the text, however, that it does not "encourage ignorance" since it explicitly requires a good faith effort by the accused to inform himself from usually reliable sources, and puts the burden of proof on the defendant.

NOTES

1. The study draft of the proposed federal code did not contain the words "good faith" that now appear before "belief." What, if anything, did the insertion of these words add to the section?

2. For general discussions, see Hall, Ignorance and Mistake in Criminal Law, 33 Ind.L.J. 1, 14–44 (1957); Hall and Seligman, Mistake of Law and Mens Rea, 8 U.Chi.L.Rev. 641 (1941); Keedy, Ignorance and Mistake in the Criminal Law, 22 Harv.L.Rev. 81, 88–96 (1908); Mueller-Rappard, The Mistake of Law as a Defense, 36 Temple L.Q. 261 (1963); Perkins, Ignorance and Mistake in Criminal Law, 88 U.Pa.L.Rev. 35, 36–53 (1939); Ryu and Silving, Error Juris: A Comparative Study, 24 U.Chi.L.Rev. 421 (1957).

LAMBERT v. CALIFORNIA

Supreme Court of the United States, 1957.
355 U.S. 225, 78 S.Ct. 240, 2 L.Ed.2d 228.

[The opinion in this case is reprinted at page 442.]

HUNTER v. STATE

Supreme Court of Tennessee, 1928.
158 Tenn. 63, 12 S.W.2d 361.

CHAMBLISS, J. This appeal is from a conviction of embezzlement by a public officer, under section 6574, Shan. Code. Hunter was trustee of Hamilton county, and he failed to account for $31,-239.48 of public funds. His defense is and was that he acted, in appropriating to his own use these funds, under the belief, supported by the advice of counsel, that chapter 101 of the Acts of 1921, passed prior to his election, and in effect during his term, known as the Salary Law, was unconstitutional, leaving in force the former law which vested all fees of the office in the trustee. * * *

In effect, the sole question for consideration is whether or not belief in the unconstitutionality of an act of the Legislature, supported by the advice of counsel, is competent to rebut such proof of criminal intent, if any, as is essential under the embezzlement statute to a conviction of a public officer who has converted and appropriated public funds to his personal use.

* * *

The authorities uniformly recognize and give effect to this distinction between mistakes of fact and ignorance of the law, sometimes excusing the accused in the first case, but refusing always to do so in the latter. The claim of belief in the unconstitutionality of a law comes, of course, within the latter class. It is a plea of ignorance of the law which is never admissible to excuse crime.

* * *

In the noted case of U. S. v. Anthony, 24 Fed.Cas. p. 829, No. 14459, in which Susan B. Anthony was convicted of voting illegally, the United States Circuit Court for the Northern District of New York, affirming the judgment, rejected the insistence of the defendant that the state Constitution, which denied to her the right to vote, contravened the Federal Constitution and was therefore void, and held that she could not, when prosecuted, defend on the ground of her belief in the unconstitutionality of the state law. Said the court, "Miss Anthony knew that she was a woman, and that the Constitution of this State prohibits her from voting. She intended to violate that provision—intended to test it, perhaps, but certainly, intended to violate it. * * * There was no ignorance of any fact. * * *

She takes the risk, and she cannot escape the consequences. It is said, and authorities are cited to sustain the position, that there can be no crime unless there is a culpable intent, and that, to render one criminally responsible a vicious will must be present. * * * To constitute a crime, it is true that there must be a criminal intent, but it is equally true that knowledge of the facts of the case is always held to supply this intent. * * * No system of criminal jurisprudence can be sustained upon any other principle." This language might readily be paraphrased and made to fit the case before us. It enunciates the rule and draws the distinction here applicable. Moreover, we have here a case not so much of ignorance of the law, either as to existence or interpretation, as of conscious and purposeful repudiation of its authority. The plaintiff in error, committed by his obligation of office to its observance, has challenged the power of the General Assembly to enact it, and has usurped the exclusive prerogative of the courts to adjudge its invalidity. This no man may do with impunity.

It results that we find no error, and the judgment is affirmed.

NOTE

In recent years efforts have been made to defend on the grounds that the defendants did not have the required mens rea because they acted out of a belief that another and higher law so required. Thus, in United States v. Berrigan, 283 F.Supp. 336 (D.Md.1968), aff'd 417 F.2d 1002 (4th Cir. 1969), cert. denied 397 U.S. 909, 90 S.Ct. 907, 25 L.Ed.2d 90, where the defendants were charged, inter alia, with destruction of the property or the United States in the course of a "raid" on a local draft board, the argument was offered that the defendants sincerely believed the American war effort in Viet Nam was illegal under international law and that their actions were intended to prevent further criminal acts in support of that war. In accord with the principle that motive is neither an element of, nor a defense to, criminal conduct, such defenses have been rejected by the courts. Equally unsuccessful have been attempts to offer what is commonly known as the "Nurnberg Defense"—based on the trial of Nazi war criminals in 1946—which essentially posits that it cannot be a crime to refuse to participate in what were termed at Nurnberg crimes against peace and humanity. See 9 Harv.Inter.L.J. 169 (1968).

MODEL PENAL CODE (TENT. DRAFT NO. 4, 1955)

Comment to § 2.02, p. 131.

[T]he general principle that ignorance or mistake of law is no excuse is usually greatly overstated; it has no application when the circumstances made material by the definition of the offense include a legal element. * * * The law involved is not the law defining the offense; it is some other legal rule that characterizes the attendant circumstances that are material to the offense.

RICHARDSON v. UNITED STATES

United States Court of Appeals for the District of Columbia, 1968.
131 U.S.App.D.C. 168, 403 F.2d 574.

EDGERTON, Senior Circuit Judge. Appellant was charged with robbery (count one), assault with a dangerous weapon (count two), and carrying a dangerous weapon (count three). A jury found him guilty as charged on count one, guilty of simple assault on count two and not guilty on count three.

The complaining witness Snowden testified that appellant and another held him up at gunpoint and took $98 from his wallet. Appellant testified that Snowden, who had recently been convicted of a gambling offense, owed him a $270 gambling debt which he had several times unsuccessfully tried to collect. He admitted reaching into Snowden's wallet and removing $138 without his consent, but denied having a gun. His mother corroborated his story of the gambling debt and testified that Snowden was a known gambler.

The chief ground of this appeal is the trial court's denial of appellant's request for the following standard instruction:

Evidence has been introduced that the defendant believed that he had a right to take the property he is alleged to have stolen.

If a person takes the property of another, but does so in the good faith belief that he has a right to take the property, the specific intent essential to the crime of robbery is lacking.

The Government must prove beyond a reasonable doubt that the defendant acted with the specific intent to steal. If you have a reasonable doubt whether or not the defendant acted with a specific intent to steal, you must find him not guilty.

I.

A defendant is not guilty of robbery unless he has a specific intent to take the property of another. Jackson v. United States, 121 U.S. App.D.C. 160, 348 F.2d 772 (1965). Viewing the evidence most favorably to the defendant, as we must where he appeals from the denial of a favorable instruction, he believed in good faith that he was entitled to the money. If so, he did not have that specific intent. We therefore find that the requested instruction should have been given.[2]

The government's position seems to be that no instruction on a claim of right is necessary unless the defendant had a legally enforceable right to the property he took. But specific intent depends upon

2. Accord: State v. Steele, 150 Wash. 466, 273 P. 742 (1929). The majority rule in cases involving a forceful taking of money under color of a liquidated debt is that the requisite specific intent for robbery is lacking.

a state of mind, not upon a legal fact. If the jury finds that the defendant believed himself entitled to the money, it cannot properly find that he had the requisite specific intent for robbery. * * *

The government urges affirmance for policy reasons, claiming that a reversal of this robbery conviction would encourage violent takings and would frustrate the policy of the law that a successful gambler may not recover his winnings from the loser. But "The taking and carrying away of the property of another in the District of Columbia without right to do so" is a misdemeanor. D.C.Code (1967 ed.) § 22–1211. Since this section can be violated without specific intent, it provides a deterrent to self-help by a winning gambler without rejecting the principle that specific intent turns on the actor's state of mind and not upon an objective fact.

*   *   *

Reversed.

NOTE

The court in the instant case rejected the following argument made by the appellee:

*   *   *

Cases on claim of right as a defense to robbery involve three general types of situations: (1) where a defendant has a liquidated, legally enforceable claim against a complainant; (2) where he has a legal claim but for an unliquidated amount; and (3) where as a loser at gambling he retakes his losses from a winner or as a winner he takes his winnings from a loser. In the first type, where the forceful taking is under color of a liquidated, legally enforceable claim, most courts hold that there is no robbery on the theory that the requisite intent to steal is lacking. * * *

In contrast to the majority rule for liquidated claims, the cases do not allow a claim of right defense for an unliquidated claim. The rationale in these cases is that it violates public policy to allow a defendant to bypass the courts and determine for himself the value of a claim which may not even be valid.

Our research has located only one case corresponding to the fact situation at bar, that is, where the winner at gambling forcefully extracts his winnings from the loser. State v. Steele, 150 Wash. 466, 273 Pac. 742 (1929). The lower court had denied a defense request for an instruction that if the property involved was taken under an honest belief of entitlement, however ill-founded that belief was, the requisite intent for robbery was absent. The Supreme Court ruled the instruction should have been given. That the wager may have been won by dishonest means did not matter, the court said, because if the defendants nonetheless entertained a good faith belief of entitlement, there was no intent to steal.

Where the loser retakes his losses, the cases are divided. In Texas if losses incurred in a fair gambling transaction are voluntarily surrendered, the loser retaking by force is guilty of robbery even though he believes he is entitled to retake. Murphy v. State, 133 Tex.Cr. 504, 109 S.W.2d 488 (1937). Blair v. State, 34 Tex. Cr. 488, 31 S.W. 368 (1895). This criminal doctrine is in the context of a civil rule which leaves the parties in *status quo*—the winner cannot recover his winnings nor can the loser recover his losses voluntarily surrendered. * * *

In our view, a rule that the forceful taking of what is clearly another person's property because the assailant had a belief mistaken as a matter of law that he had a right to it not only would serve to offer encouragement to violence and thus endanger life but would also frustrate the clear policy of the civil law of this jurisdiction that a gambler cannot recover his winnings from the loser. Where the claim is barred by law, more is involved than the policy also applicable here that disputes should be settled in court, not by force.[9] A good faith, although mistaken, belief of a right to property as a defense to robbery could not easily be limited to a case with some sympathetic defense appeal where a gambler has "welched" on a bet. Suppose A agreed to pay B $10,000 if B turned over to A evidence of a sordid incident in A's past life. After B did so A refused to pay. Believing he is entitled to the $10,000, B extracts it from A at gunpoint. In our view, it is absurd to say that because of this belief in the validity of an illegal contract (as is the gambling contract at bar), B is not guilty of robbery. Or suppose A, a poor man, really believes he is entitled to take money by force from B, a rich man, because of his need and the disparity in their economic positions. As a practical matter, we submit, the law cannot tolerate such a defense, and neither should it permit the same defense in the case at bar.

Brief for Appellee at 7–10, Richardson v. United States, 131 U.S.App.D.C. 168, 403 F.2d 574 (1968).

LONG v. STATE

Supreme Court of Delaware, 1949.
65 A.2d 489.

PEARSON, Judge, delivering the opinion of the court:

The defendant Long was married to his first wife in Wilmington, and resided there with her for thirty years prior to their separation in

9. In a discussion rejecting claim of right to collect on a debt as a defense to robbery, the following appears in 135 Am.St.Reps. at 487:
"But assuming * * * [the creditor took only the amount to which he was entitled], an accord with the principle that such was his right would land us just a couple of thousand years back. There would be no longer need for courts of justice. Every creditor would carry his court of appeal in his hip pocket! And if the demand of one's debt is not robbery, what is it? * * * A man has a sum of money on his person, and is stopped by two or more of his creditors, each of whom levels a revolver at him and demands payment of his claim. If he hasn't enough for all, it would be as perfectly consistent to charge him with giving a fraudulent preference to the one who first took his money vi et armis as to say that such taking is not robbery."

October 1945. On September 21, 1946, he went to Arkansas. He had been pensioned from the police force, and had been in bad health for a number of years. He testified that he went to Arkansas on account of his health because he "thought it would be a better climate"; also that he went there to obtain a divorce; and that he intended "to leave Delaware permanently and take up a permanent domicile in Arkansas". His health improved there. He returned to Wilmington for a few days in November "for business reasons" and spent the Christmas holidays in Wilmington. On December 3, he renewed his Delaware automobile registration for six months ending June 30, 1947. He remained in Arkansas for the statutory period of residence required for divorce in that state, and instituted divorce proceedings against his wife in the Chancery Court of Garland County. On January 7, 1947, that court entered a decree of absolute divorce. The decree recites publication of a notice and the mailing of a registered letter with a copy of the complaint to defendant's wife, a nonresident of Arkansas. She did not appear in the proceeding. She testified before the lower court here that she was not "served with any divorce papers" and did not receive any mail or a registered letter from Arkansas. On the same day the divorce decree was granted, defendant left Arkansas and returned to Wilmington where he has since resided. While in Wilmington during the Christmas holidays of 1946, he had been offered a job in a hospital there. He accepted this job after the divorce decree was granted and began work on January 13, 1947. On January 25, he was married to a second wife in Wilmington. This marriage was the subject of the bigamy prosecution under Rev.Code of Del. Sec. 5254.

*   *   *

* * * [E]rror is assigned for the refusal of the lower court to receive evidence relating to adultery of defendant's first wife, and relating to defendant's mistake in applying law to the facts with respect to the validity of the Arkansas divorce. In his brief, defendant makes the following statement of facts in this connection:

"Prior to the defendant's decision to go to Arkansas he discussed the question of securing a divorce with a Delaware attorney (not his present attorney). Shortly prior to that time he had been advised by certain men, * * * that they had lived in adultery with defendant's wife. The evidence would have borne out these facts and shown with specificity by the men themselves that they had registered at certain Wilmington hotels and the names under which they had registered and that sexual relations were had. These facts were known to the Delaware attorney. In his discussion with the Delaware attorney he stated he was 'fed up with Wilmington' and that his health had been bad and that he wanted to get away. He also stated, upon being advised that he could get a divorce in Delaware, that he did not want to further embarrass his children by getting a divorce on the ground of adultery, especially since a number of them had just come out of the service and were attempting to make their way in Wilmington.

"He was advised by the Delaware attorney to go to Arkansas for the divorce and that it would be 'just as good as if obtained in Delaware.' He was advised and knew that he could secure a divorce in Delaware for approximately one-tenth of the total cost in Arkansas. * * *

"* * * After he had returned from Arkansas he decided to remarry, which marriage is the basis for the present prosecution. Before deciding on marriage, he went to the same Delaware attorney and inquired whether he was free to remarry and whether the divorce was good in view of the fact that he had returned to Delaware and changed his intention of living in Arkansas for an indefinite period of time. He was advised that the divorce was good and that he was free to remarry. He then made arrangements with the Reverend Harris for the marriage. Reverend Harris, due to hearsay statements he had read in the newspapers, was suspicious of the validity of the divorce in Arkansas. The Reverend Harris decided, after conferring with the defendant, to visit the Delaware attorney himself and, upon doing so, was advised that the divorce was good and the defendant was free to remarry.

"The defendant conferred a final time with his attorney before applying for a marriage application and defendant's Delaware counsel appeared with him and signed his second marriage application as guarantor in the Office of the Clerk of the Peace for New Castle County. He also offered evidence to the Clerk of the Peace that he was legally divorced and free to remarry."

The evidence of defendant's consulting an attorney and following his advice was refused on * * * [the ground] that defendant's mistake was one of law, and is a case "to which the maxim 'ignorantia juris non excusat' applies." * * *

We turn now to the ground that this is a case to which the ignorance of law maxim applies. In many crimes involving a *specific* criminal intent, an honest mistake of law constitutes a defense if it negatives the specific intent. State v. Pullen, 3 Pennewill, 184, 50 A. 538 (larceny); State v. Collins, 1 Marv. 536, 41 A. 144 (embezzlement); see also Perkins: Ignorance and Mistake in Criminal Law, 88 Univ. of Pa.Law Rev. 35, 45, 46. As to crimes not involving a specific intent, an honest mistake of law is usually, though not invariably, held not to excuse conduct otherwise criminal. (Perkins article, pp. 41–45 and cases cited.) A mistake of law, where not a defense, may nevertheless negative a general criminal intent as effectively as would an exculpatory mistake of fact. Thus, mistake of law is disallowed as a defense in spite of the fact that it may show an absence of the criminal mind. The reasons for disallowing it are practical considerations dictated by deterrent effects upon the administration and enforcement of the criminal law, which are deemed likely to result if it were allowed as a general defense. As stated in the Perkins article, supra, p. 41: " * * *

But if such ignorance were available as a defense in every criminal case, this would be a constant source of confusion to juries, and it would tend to encourage ignorance at a point where it is peculiarly important to the state that knowledge should be as widespread as is reasonably possible. In the language of one of the giants of the profession, this is a point at which 'justice to the individual is rightly outweighed by the larger interests on the other side of the scales.' " Quoting from Holmes: The Common Law, p. 48.

Similar considerations are involved when we disallow ignorance or mistake of law as a defense to a defendant who engages in criminal conduct (even though not obviously immoral or anti-social) where his ignorance or mistake consists merely in (1) unawareness that such conduct is or might be within the ambit of any crime; or (2) although aware of the existence of criminal law relating to the subject of such conduct, or to some of its aspects, the defendant erroneously concludes (in good faith) that his particular conduct is for some reason not subject to the operation of any criminal law. But it seems to us significantly different to disallow mistake of law where (3) together with the circumstances of the second classification, it appears that before engaging in the conduct, the defendant made a bona fide, diligent effort, adopting a course and resorting to sources and means at least as appropriate as any afforded under our legal system, to ascertain and abide by the law, and where he acted in good faith reliance upon the results of such effort. It is inherent in the way our legal system functions that the criminal law consequences of any particular contemplated conduct cannot be determined in advance with certainty. Not until after the event, by final court decision, may the consequences be definitely ascertained. Prior to the event, the ultimate that can be ascertained about the legal consequences consists of predictions of varying degrees of probability of eventuation. Hence, in the sense in which we are concerned with the expression, a "mistake of law" of the second or third classification refers to the failure of predictions of legal consequences to come to pass. No matter how logical, plausible and persuasive may be the bases for a prediction (assumptions, abstract legal rules, reasoning, etc.,) a mistake of law arises if the prediction does not eventuate; and there is no mistake of law if the prediction eventuates.

With these thoughts in mind, let us examine how the considerations which justify the rejection of a mistake of the first and second classifications operate with respect to a mistake of the third classification. The objection of tending to "encourage ignorance" of the law would hardly seem applicable. The very conditions of the third classification include a diligent effort, in good faith, by means as appropriate as any available under our legal system, to acquire knowledge of the relevant law. The objection of difficulties of proof, including facilitation of subterfuge, is applicable, if at all, in a far less degree than in the case of mistakes of the first and second classifications. For them, the facts are essentially confined to the defendant's subjective state of mind. The conditions of the third classification are not so limited. They include an affirmative showing of effort to abide by the law, tested by objective standards rather than the defendant's subjective state of mind.

Any deterrent effects upon the administration of the criminal law which might result from allowing a mistake of the third classification as a defense seem greatly outweighed by considerations which favor allowing it. To hold a person punishable as a criminal transgressor where the conditions of the third classification are present would be palpably unjust and arbitrary. Most of the important reasons which support the prohibition of ex post facto legislation are opposed to such a holding. It is difficult to conceive what more could be reasonably expected of a "model citizen" than that he guide his conduct by "the law" ascertained in good faith, not merely by efforts which might seem adequate to a person in his situation, but by efforts as well designed to accomplish ascertainment as any available under our system. We are not impressed with the suggestion that a mistake under such circumstances should aid the defendant only in inducing more lenient punishment by a court, or executive clemency after conviction. The circumstances seem so directly related to the defendant's behavior upon which the criminal charge is based as to constitute an integral part of that behavior, for purposes of evaluating it. No excuse appears for dealing with it piecemeal. We think such circumstances should entitle a defendant to full exoneration as a matter of right, rather than to something less, as a matter of grace. Unless there be aspects of the particular crime involved which give rise to considerations impelling a contrary holding,—some special, cogent reasons why "justice to the individual is rightly outweighed by the larger interests on the other side of the scales"—a mistake of the third classification should be recognized as a defense.

We find nothing about the crime of bigamy under our statute which calls for a contrary holding. As previously decided, an absence of general criminal intent is a defense to this crime. As to the acts involved in the crime, remarriage is obviously neither immoral nor anti-social in our culture. These aspects lie in the circumstance that the defendant has a spouse living from whom a divorce has not been obtained which our courts will recognize as valid. The matters to which a mistake of law might relate are legal questions concerning marriage and divorce. It is a gross understatement to say that such questions are more frequently perplexing than obvious to a layman. For these reasons, the defense seems appropriate and we hold it available in prosecutions for bigamy.   *   *   *

Here, from the evidence rejected by the lower court, the jury might have found substantially as follows: (1) that prior to his second marriage, defendant consulted a reputable Delaware attorney for the purpose of ascertaining whether such marriage would be lawful or unlawful in Delaware, and so that he might abide by the law; (2) that the attorney advised him that the proposed remarriage would not be unlawful; (3) that he relied on this advice, honestly believing his remarriage lawful; (4) that his efforts to ascertain the law were at all times diligent and in good faith, not by way of subterfuge, and such that there was no better course for ascertaining the law than that which he followed; and hence, that he made a full disclosure to the attorney of the relevant circumstances as well as of what he proposed to do, and that he had no substantial reason to believe that the advice received was ill-founded, such as circumstances reasonably indicating that the attorney was incompetent to give advice about this matter, or had not given the question sufficient consideration, or that the advice was lacking in candor.   Assuming that the Arkansas decree be held invalid here, such findings would constitute a defense to the present charge as a mistake of law of the third classification.   They would meet the test of bona fide, diligent efforts, as well designed to accomplish ascertainment of the law as any available under our system.   The conditions indicated furnish safeguards against pretext and fraud.   The defendant would have the burden of demonstrating that his efforts were well nigh exemplary.   It would not be enough merely for him to say that he had relied on advice of an attorney, unless the circumstances indicated that his conduct throughout in seeking to ascertain the law and in relying on advice received manifested good faith and diligence beyond reproach.   We see no occasion to assume that recognizing such a defense would foster dishonest practices among attorneys.   These might well be expected to be deterred by the availability of disciplinary measures for non-professional conduct.   Moreover, although erroneous advice might save a defendant from criminal responsibility for acts in reliance on it, the same acts would in many instances incur substantial civil responsibility and financial loss.   The risk of possible disingenuous resort to the defense does not seem to us sufficient to warrant withholding it from those acting in good faith.   Accordingly, the evidence should have been submitted to the jury under proper instructions.

A new trial should be awarded for the reasons set forth in this opinion.

An order accordingly will be entered.

---

c.   INTOXICATION

UNITED STATES v. WILLIAMS

United States District Court for the District of Maryland, 1971.
332 F.Supp. 1.

HERBERT F. MURRAY, District Judge.   In this case the defendant was charged in a two-count indictment under Title 18, U.S.C.A.

Sections 2113(a) and (b) with robbery of a branch of the Maryland National Bank in Cambridge, Maryland on December 4, 1970. [The relevant portions of the statute were as follows:

§ 2113.   Bank robbery and incidental crimes

(a) Whoever, by force and violence, or by intimidation, takes, or attempts to take, from the person or presence of another any property or money or any other thing of value belonging to, or in the care, custody, control, management, or possession of, any bank, credit union, or any savings and loan association   *   *   *

Shall be fined not more than $5,000 or imprisoned not more than twenty years, or both.

(b) Whoever takes and carries away, with intent to steal or purloin, any property or money or any other thing of value exceeding $100 belonging to, or in the care, custody, control, management, or possession of any bank, credit union, or any savings and loan association, shall be fined not more than $5,000 or imprisoned not more than ten years, or both   *   *   *]

The case was tried non-jury on September 13 and 14, 1971.

The basic facts are not in dispute. In a stipulation signed by government counsel, the defendant and his counsel, it was agreed that on the date set out in the indictment, the defendant went into the bank in Cambridge, Maryland and requested a loan from a branch officer of the bank. The officer declined to grant the defendant a loan. Thereafter the defendant walked up to Mrs. Martina Bennett, a teller, and handed to her a note stating "This is a stickup". Mrs. Bennett gave him all her cash, and defendant then left the bank with the money. It was also stipulated that Mrs. Bennett was intimidated by defendant giving her the note and for that reason turned over to defendant the funds in her drawer. An audit made immediately after the robbery showed the defendant had taken $4,727 of the bank's money.

While defendant thus does not contest the fact that a robbery occurred and he committed it, his counsel urges upon the Court that an essential element of the crime is lacking. It is contended that the two sections of the bank robbery statute on which the counts in the indictment are based both require a specific intent to steal, and that at the time of the robbery defendant was so intoxicated from alcohol and drugs that he was incapable of forming such specific intent.

The threshold legal questions thus are whether voluntary intoxication can negative specific intent as an element of crime and, if so, whether the offenses charged in either or both counts of the indictment require proof of specific intent. If specific intent is an element of the offense in either count of the indictment, the factual question then arises as to whether on all the evidence the degree of defendant's intoxication was such as to create a reasonable doubt that defendant had a specific intent to steal when the robbery took place.

It is clear from the cases that while voluntary intoxication is ordinarily no defense to crime, it may have that effect if specific intent is an element of the crime. * * *

The rule has also been adopted by the American Law Institute. Model Penal Code, Tentative Draft No. 9, Section 2–08.

Thus in the area of criminal responsibility as affected by voluntary intoxication, a distinction must be drawn between so-called "general intent" to commit a crime and a "specific intent" to do a particular criminal act.

These terms are often used in the cases but seldom defined. * *

Did Congress in the several subsections of the bank robbery statute create "general intent" crimes or "specific intent" crimes? Some cases uncritically lump all subsections of the statute under the "specific intent" label. Other cases ascribe more careful draftsmanship to the Congress, and find a specific intent an element of the crime only in those subsections of the statute where the language "with intent" is used.

Thus, in United States v. DeLeo, 422 F.2d 487 (1st Cir. 1970), cert. den. 397 U.S. 1037, 90 S.Ct. 1355, 25 L.Ed.2d 648 (1970), the indictment was under 18 U.S.C.A. Sections 2113(a) and (d). On appeal the defendant contended that the crime was of the common law larceny genus requiring allegation and proof of specific intent. The Court rejected this argument, stating at pages 490–491:

> "Six specific crimes are set out in Section 2113. Felonious intent is specifically incorporated in the definition of two of them: entering a federally insured institution with intent to commit a felony (a—second paragraph), and taking property with intent to steal or purloin (b). However, it is not made part of the crimes of taking by force and violence or by intimidation (a—first paragraph); knowingly receiving stolen property (c); assaulting or putting in jeopardy the life of a person by a dangerous weapon (d); or killing a person, or forcing a person to accompany him, while in the course of committing one of the other offenses or avoiding apprehension or confinement for any of them (e).
>
> "This differentiation shows careful draftsmanship. Entering and taking can be innocent acts, and therefore require felonious intent to constitute crime; receiving stolen property can be innocent, unless done knowingly. However, the other offenses described acts which, when performed, are so unambiguously dangerous to others that the

requisite mental element is necessarily implicit in the description. * * *

The Court in the present case concludes as a matter of law * * that the act of the defendant, which he admits of taking by intimidation from the presence of another money belonging to the bank, constitutes a violation of subsection (a) of the statute as charged in Count I of the indictment. The Court rejects as a defense to the crime charged in Count I of the indictment any voluntary intoxication of the defendant.

As to Count II of the indictment, the Court feels that historically and legally the contention of the defendant is correct, and that a specific intent to steal is an element of the crime. The Court on a review of all the evidence in the case is satisfied beyond a reasonable doubt that defendant when he took and carried away money belonging to the bank exceeding $100 in value did so with the intent to steal or purloin.

The Court in finding as a fact that defendant had the intent to steal is not unmindful of the fact that there was substantial evidence to show that defendant had imbibed significant quantities of alcohol and drugs, but the Court from all the evidence finds beyond a reasonable doubt that he both had the capacity to and did intend to steal when he took the bank's money. The basis for the Court's finding in this regard requires some reference to the evidence of defendant's taking of alcohol and drugs and his condition at the time of the robbery.

In testifying on his own behalf, defendant claimed that as a result of an argument with his wife he started drinking with a companion around 9:00 A.M. on December 3, 1970, the day before the robbery and over the next fourteen hours the two consumed three fifths of whiskey, of which defendant had about half. During this period defendant also took 6 or 7 "yellow jackets" or barbiturate pills. Between midnight on December 3 and the occurrence of the robbery around 1:00 P.M. on December 4, defendant claims that he and a companion drank an additional one or one and a half fifths of whiskey, of which defendant had all but half a pint. In addition, sometime in this latter period defendant took some LSD pills, with the result that he had only "spotty" recollection of events the morning of the robbery. Defendant does recall going into the bank and talking with the branch officer, and leaving the bank stuffing money under his jacket, but disclaims any recollection of confronting the teller, presenting her with a "stickup" note and actually receiving from her over $4,000 in cash.

The witnesses who actually observed the defendant on the day of the robbery indicate he had been drinking but not that he was drunk. A cab driver named Hopkins who drove the defendant at 6:00 A.M. to redeem his watch and then to a drive-in said his eyes were red and he had been drinking. His speech was "heavy" and he did not seem to walk normally.

Mrs. Florence Brannock, a teller in the bank, spoke briefly with defendant when he asked for the loan department and directed him to the branch officer. She felt he smelled strongly of cheap wine or alcohol and that his speech while understandable was not normal— it was a little "slurred" or "thick".

Branch Officer John Bramble testified that * * * he could smell a strong odor of alcohol on the defendant's breath and felt he was under the influence of liquor and that he also appeared somewhat nervous. After declining to grant the defendant a loan, the witness watched the defendant walk towards the lobby of the bank and could not remember anything unusual about the defendant's walk.

Mrs. Martina Bennett * * * noticed nothing unusual about the defendant's appearance and did not smell any alcohol. When he was standing before her he did not appear to waver, but his eyes did appear sleepy. She watched him walk away from her counter and down a flight of four steps leading to the lobby entrance.

*   *   *

The testimony as to acts of the defendant closest in time to the robbery was given by the owner of a small store in Cambridge, George Heist. His store is located about two blocks from the bank. He recalled that the defendant came into his store about noon and asked for a piece of paper to figure a bill. The defendant reached for a sales pad but the witness did not want the defendant to use the pad and gave him a piece of paper instead. The defendant turned around with his back to the witness and put the piece of paper on top of some stocking boxes and started to write. Apparently dissatisfied, he balled up the piece of paper and threw it on the floor. Defendant reached again for the witness' sales pad, which the witness again refused to give him, tearing off a piece of old calendar paper instead. Defendant again turned around and wrote some more, and then left the store.

The witness said that the defendant while in his store seemed coherent, didn't stagger, and acted normally except for trying to take his sales pad twice. However, because the defendant "seemed a little high on something" he decided, after the defendant left the store, to read what was on the balled up piece of paper. It read "This is a stick". Although defendant on leaving the store walked away from and not towards the bank, the witness appropriately concluded a robbery might be in prospect and got a policeman to whom he gave a description of the defendant. Later he heard the fire whistle blow about 1:00 P.M., which was a signal that the bank had been robbed.

Dr. Leonard Rothstein, a private psychiatrist called by defendant, had an interview examination with defendant on May 24, 1971 and also talked to defendant's wife. The defendant gave the doctor a history of abusing alcohol since age 19, and told the doctor he was drinking beer all day before the robbery and took some "yellow jackets" in the evening, and some LSD in the morning before the robbery. Dr. Rothstein found no significant evasiveness in the defendant and no discrepancies between defendant's account and his wife's.

On the basis of defendant's account to him and his examination the doctor expressed the opinion that at the time of the offense the defendant had no psychosis or structural alteration in the brain. However, the doctor concluded from what the defendant told him of his ingestion of alcohol and drugs that the higher centers governing the making of judgments, control of behavior and retention of experience in memory had been affected. While the defendant knew what he was doing, his judgment about the appropriateness of his actions and his ability to control them were severely impaired. From the history the doctor concluded the defendant had taken the alcohol and drugs voluntarily and with knowledge from previous experience of their probable effect. In response to a hypothetical question asked on cross examination by counsel for the government, the doctor admitted that if the defendant had not taken alcohol and drugs before the offense, he would at the time have had no psychiatric illness and would have had the capacity to conform his conduct to the requirements of the law.

Dr. William Fitzpatrick, who had examined the defendant on July 15, 1971 at the request of the government, was called as an expert psychiatric witness by the defense. He related a personal history and account of the offense given him by the defendant very similar to that related by defendant's own expert, Dr. Rothstein. He found the defendant of normal intelligence with no evidence of psychosis or structural brain disorder. From the history he judged defendant to be a passive dependent personality of the type more likely to abuse alcohol than the average person. Although from defendant's own account he was an episodic heavy user of alcohol and drugs, he did not find evidence that he was an alcoholic or a drug addict. He felt that because defendant was a passive dependent type he had a condition something short of total mental health. However, had the defendant not taken alcohol and drugs at time of the offense, he would not consider that defendant lacked criminal responsibility or capacity to conform his conduct to the requirements of the law. Although the doctor did not know the quantity of alcohol or drugs defendant consumed before the offense, he assumed the defendant was intoxicated at the time and that his intoxication was self-induced with knowledge on the part of the defendant that he would get drunk if he drank. He admitted that if he assumed a lesser degree of intoxication he would have to alter his opinion, but his opinion that defendant at the time of the offense could not conform his conduct to the requirements of the law was based on assumed intake of large quantities of alcohol. However, the doctor honestly disclaimed any opinion on whether defendant could specifically intend to rob a bank.

In expressing their conclusions, both psychiatrists obviously had in mind the ALI formulation [of the insanity defense] contained in Model Penal Code, Section 4.01, approved in this circuit in United States v. Chandler, 393 F.2d 920 (1968). [Under this formulation, "a person is not responsible for criminal conduct if at the time of such conduct as a result of mental disease or defect he lacks substantial capacity either to appreciate the criminality of his conduct or to conform his conduct to the requirements of law."]   However, defense counsel disclaimed any contention that this standard was applicable in determining the issue of the criminal responsibility of this defendant. In this connection it is noted that Section 2.08(3) of the Model Penal Code provides "Intoxication does not, in itself, constitute mental disease within the meaning of Section 4.01."

As then Circuit Judge Burger stated in Heideman v. United States, 104 U.S.App.D.C. 128, 259 F.2d 943, at p. 946 (1958): "Drunkenness, while efficient to reduce or remove *inhibitions*,* does not readily negate *intent*.* "   (* Footnotes omitted)

The Court believes that the defendant had taken alcohol and drugs to the point of being "under the influence" but that he was not so intoxicated as not to understand what he was doing or to not have the intention to steal from the bank. There is a marked difference between the accounts of the persons who observed defendant and defendant's own account as to his condition. It appears from a witness called by the defense that he was able to write a "stickup" note shortly before the robbery, to go into the bank, hold a coherent conversation about a loan, present the note, obtain over $4,000 in cash, none of which has been returned, and make good his escape. The Court concludes beyond a reasonable doubt that defendant had the intent to steal from the bank as required for conviction under Count II, and that he is in any event guilty under Count I of the indictment. If an intent to steal is an element of the offense charged in Count I, the Court finds that intent proved as to Count I also. The Court therefore finds the defendant guilty as charged in both counts of the indictment.

NOTES

1. Hutchison, Tuchie, Gray and Steinberg, A Study of the Effects of Alcohol on Mental Functions, 7 Crim.L.Q. 343 (1965) describe the ability to identify oneself, relate certain items of personal history, and to orient oneself as to time and place as "the usual basis of the average person's appraisal of whether a person is mentally impaired." Id. at 348. In the authors' experiment, these abilities remained unimpaired by intoxication although other mental processes were impaired.

Most of the experimental work, the authors observe, deals with the impairment of physical actions by intoxication. Given this deficiency, the authors describe an experiment "undertaken to provide data relevant to the task of the expert witness" called to testify as to the state of mind of an accused who was intoxicated at the time of the offense. Eight individuals drank whiskey until their blood alcohol was approximately 1.0 parts per 1,000 (ascertained by a Breathalyzer). The subjects were then given a battery of tests, and their performance while intoxicated was compared with their performance while sober. The results, concluded the authors, showed that the effects of drinking upon mental functions are not uniform. No effect was noted upon the subjects' ability to relate their personal histories or to orient themselves as to time and place. Nor was their ability to repeat a sequence of digits spoken by the examiner impaired. But other functions were adversely affected, including attention (as measured by the subjects' ability to repeat in reverse order a sequence of digits spoken by the examiner) and learning efficiency (as measured by the subjects' ability, after the examiner has read off a short list of word pairs, to accurately give the second word of each pair as the examiner gives the first). Also affected was the subjects' abstract thinking capacity, as measured by their ability to abstract essential likenesses or common properties from apparently dissimilar objects or events, i. e., "In what way are good and evil alike?" This ability, the authors note, "is not only a reliable measure of general intelligence but is recognized as 'a measure of the logical character of the subject's thinking processes.'" Id. at 349. The subjects' ability to recognize certain pictures that had been shown to them during the period of intoxication was not significantly impaired, but they did demonstrate a significantly reduced ability to recall the title they had given the picture (in response to the examiner's request) earlier.

To what extent does this information assist in evaluating the criminal liability of someone like Williams? If it can be assumed that Williams' intoxication was at least no less than that of the subjects of the Hutchison, et al. study, does the study suggest that Williams did not have the specific intent required by the robbery statute? Hutchison, et al. describe their findings as supporting the clinical observation that impairment of mental functioning can occur at relatively low concentrations of blood alcohol. But is this impairment of the kind or degree that might reasonably be expected to affect criminal liability by showing the nonexistence of a specific intent?

2. It is generally held that intoxication from substances other than alcohol have the same effect upon criminal liability as alcohol intoxication. Is this appropriate? Consider the following from Commonwealth v. Campbell, 445 Pa. 388, 284 A.2d 798, 801 (1971):

> Defendant contends that the law with respect to voluntary intoxication is [as it is] because human experience has shown the effects of taking alcohol are predictable, but not predictable with LSD [and therefore LSD intoxication should be permitted to result in complete acquittal]. The expert testimony in this case (if believed * * *) showed * * * that LSD produces widely varying results among different persons and even different results with the same person on different occasions. This distinction of nonpredictability of effect on the human body is devoid of any adequate legal justification based upon legal precedent, or reason, or policy

considerations for a radical change and departure from our law of criminal responsibility. The very fact that the effects of a voluntary, nonmedical use of a hallucinogenic drug are predictably unforeseeable should require Courts to decide in the public interest that this is not legally sufficient to completely exculpate a person from murder or any criminal act.

3. What arguments could be made for or against the enactment of the following statute:

Effect of Intoxication Upon Criminal Liability.

(a) Except under the circumstances described in subsection (b), no person shall be convicted of an offense committed while intoxicated if it is found that [Alternative A: except for such intoxication he would not have committed the offense.] [Alternative B: his intoxication so reduces his culpability that given general community standards of accountability and blameworthiness he should not be held liable.]

(b) If a person, contemplating the commission of an offense, becomes intoxicated as a means of causing or enabling himself to commit the offense, he shall be liable for that offense without regard to subsection (a).

PROPOSED FEDERAL CRIMINAL CODE (1971)

§ 502. Intoxication

(1) Defense Precluded. Except as provided in subsection (3), intoxication is not a defense to a criminal charge. Intoxication does not, in itself, constitute mental disease within the meaning of section 503. Evidence of intoxication is admissible whenever it is relevant to negate or to establish an element of the offense charged.

(2) Recklessness. A person is reckless with respect to an element of an offense even though his disregard thereof is not conscious, if his not being conscious thereof is due to self-induced intoxication.

(3) When a Defense. Intoxication which (a) is not self-induced, or (b) if self-induced, is grossly excessive in degree, given the amount of the intoxicant, to which the actor does not know he is susceptible, is an affirmative defense if by reason of such intoxication the actor at the time of his conduct lacked substantial capacity either to appreciate its criminality or to conform his conduct to the requirements of law.

(4) Definitions. In this section:

(a) "intoxication" means a disturbance of mental or physical capacities resulting from the introduction of alcohol, drugs or other substances into the body;

(b) "self-induced intoxication" means intoxication caused by substances which the actor knowingly introduces into his body, the tendency of which to cause intoxication he knows or ought to know, unless he introduces them pursuant to medical advice or under such circumstances as would otherwise afford a defense to a charge of crime.

Comment

This section largely codifies existing law as to when or whether intoxication is a defense to a criminal charge. * * *

The Congress and the Advisory Committee on the Federal Rules of Criminal Procedure should give consideration to requiring pretrial notice of these defenses.

NOTE

Probably the most difficult issue posed by the Proposed Federal Code as well as by other model statutory formulations relates to the question of whether intoxication should be permitted to "disprove" recklessness when that is sufficient for guilt. Present law is generally stated as in accord with the position of the Proposed Federal Code. See W. LaFave and A. Scott, Criminal Law 346–47 (1972). The commentary to the Model Penal Code defends this position as follows:

> Those who oppose a special rule [making intoxication unavailable to "disprove" recklessness] draw strength initially from the presumptive disfavor of any special rules of liability. * * * [They] draw further strength from the proposition that it is precisely the awareness of the risk in recklessness that is the essence of its moral culpability—a culpability dependent on the magnitude of the specific risk advertently created. When that risk is greater in degree than that which the actor perceives at the time of getting drunk, as is frequently the case, the result of a special rule is bound to be a liability disproportionate to culpability. * * *
>
> The case thus made is worthy of respect, but there are strong considerations on the other side. We mention first the weight of the prevailing law * * *. Beyond this, there is the fundamental point that awareness of the potential consequences of excessive drinking on the capacity of human beings to gauge the risks incident to their conduct is by now so dispersed in our culture that we believe it fair to postulate a general equivalence between the risks created by the conduct of the drunken actor and the risks created by his conduct in becoming drunk. Becoming so drunk as to destroy temporarily the actor's power of perception and of judgment is conduct which plainly has no affirmative social value to counterbalance the potential danger. The actor's moral culpability lies in engaging in such conduct. Added to this are the impressive difficulties posed in litigating the foresight of any particular actor at the time when he imbibes and the relative rarity of cases where intoxication really does engender unawareness as distinguished from imprudence. These considerations lead us to propose, on balance, that the Code declare that unawareness of a risk of which the actor would have been aware had he been sober be declared immaterial.

Model Penal Code § 2.08, comment (Tent.Draft No. 9, 1959).

C. RESULTS AND THE REQUIREMENT OF CAUSATION

A number of crimes, including but by no means restricted to the homicide offenses, require proof of the occurrence of a result and of a causal relationship between the defendant's acts and that result. Problems of causation—especially of so-called "proximate" causation—present some of the most perplexing matters with which the substantive criminal law must deal.

WEINREB, COMMENT ON BASIS OF CRIMINAL LIABILITY; CULPABILITY; CAUSATION, IN 1 WORKING PAPERS OF THE NATIONAL COMMISSION ON REFORM OF FEDERAL CRIMINAL LAWS

142–43 (1970).

The principles governing attribution of consequences to a person's conduct for purposes of criminal liability are not ordinarily stated collectively as a coherent body of doctrine. Still less often have such principles been codified. * * *

If anything but for which an event would not have occurred is a cause of the event, there are any number of "causes" of every event. The presence of oxygen in the air and the physical properties of paper are as much causes, in that sense, of the burning of a piece of paper as is touching a lit match to the paper. When we select a cause as *the cause,* the selection is based on some principle that reflects our interests. By making the selection, we focus our attention on some aspect of the situation, usually one which we think is under our control, so that we can assure or prevent a repetition of the occurrence. If someone drops a cup and it breaks, we are more likely to say "You should be more careful," than to say "I wish the floor were not so hard"; but if an infant drops the cup, we are likely to say "We'll have to get him a plastic cup," instead of "He really must not drop things." As a crude and preliminary approximation of ordinary speech and understanding it is fair to say that we distinguish the cause of an event from the (necessary) conditions of an event according to our interests, which usually but not always means that we single out as the "cause" some element of the situation which we can control and describe as "conditions" other necessary elements. Some necessary conditions are taken so much for granted—for example, the presence of oxygen in the air, the physical properties of paper—that unless some curious feature of the situation focuses our attention on them, we do not mention them even as conditions. Without some frame of reference, the question, "What is (are) the cause(s) of X?" is as meaningless as the question, "What are all the conditions but for which X would not have occurred?" Ordinarily the frame of reference is clear and is supplied by commonsense out of common experience.

The inadequacy of principles of causation in the criminal law reflects uncertainty about the basis of criminal liability in situations where results are important to liability. We are not certain whether the assailant who gives the hemophiliac a light blow that causes a bruise from which the hemophiliac dies should be punished for assault or homicide; or whether all the senators should be punished as Caesar's murderers even though any dozen could have stayed away from the Forum on the fateful day without changing the result.

PEOPLE v. HEBERT

California District Court of Appeal, 1964.
228 Cal.App.2d 514, 39 Cal.Rptr. 539.

SHINN, Presiding Justice. Henry Hebert was charged with the murder of Charles Swallow, pleaded not guilty, and after a trial by jury was convicted of involuntary manslaughter, a lesser included offense. Probation was denied and he was sentenced to the state prison. Defendant was represented by the Public Defender. Appeal is brought from the judgment in propria persona.

Defendant was a patron in a Venice bar, drinking beer but not intoxicated, when the victim entered at about 11 p. m. According to all the witnesses who testified on the subject, Swallow appeared to be either drunk or ill; the barmaid refused him service. He sat on a stool near defendant and an argument arose between them. It was established that defendant, while standing, hit Swallow in the face with his fist while Swallow was sitting on a bar stool, and that the assault was without sufficient provocation. When hit, the victim was knocked to the floor. Defendant testified that Swallow asked him for a quarter, which was refused, and Swallow said "All I done for you niggers, I can't get anything out of you" and defendant said "That is where you are wrong, man." Swallow shoved him, put his hand into his coat pocket and said "I ought to cut your throat"; Swallow did not fall off the bar stool but that after he was hit another patron said "watch that knife," grabbed Swallow around the waist and pulled him off the stool. This other patron did not testify, nor was any knife found. No one actually saw Swallow fall, but several witnesses heard him fall. There was sufficient evidence to prove that the victim was knocked off the bar stool by the force of defendant's blows and that his head hit the wooden barroom floor with what one witness described as a loud "thud."

Officers arrived about ten minutes later. Swallow was lying on the floor on his back, but apparently conscious. Officers assisted him to a sitting position and thought he was not seriously injured, but was intoxicated. They partly carried, partly dragged him to a patrol car and took him to the police station for booking for being intoxicated in a public place. Thelma McCord, the barmaid, testified that the two officers dragged Swallow from the place where he lay on the floor to the sidewalk; one officer lifted Swallow by holding onto his belt in the rear; the other lifted at his head; Swallow's feet were dragging; at the sidewalk the officers dropped him on his face; the drop was 12 to 14 inches; he was perfectly limp. The two officers testified that they partly carried, partly dragged Swallow to the sidewalk, sat him down in a sitting position and then laid him gently on his back; they did not drop him.

The officers arrived at the station with the victim about 35 minutes after the altercation. According to the officers, during the booking procedure and just after Swallow was searched and he was standing with his hands high against a wall, he was observed to fall over backwards with his arms at his sides and "completely rigid as though a plank were falling"; his buttocks hit the floor first and then the back of his head; his head bounced about six inches off the floor and fell back, striking the floor a second time. The floor was concrete with an asphalt tile covering. Immediately after hitting the floor he started bleeding from one ear and within a few seconds from both ears. He was removed to a hospital where he died that morning.

The determinative question on the trial was whether defendant's act of striking decedent and knocking him to the floor was a proximate cause of death.

Dr. Kade, autopsy surgeon for the Los Angeles County Coroner's office, testified that there were three areas of injury to the head, each caused by a separate impact; one to the nasal area, causing a fracture of the nasal bones; one to the left rear of the skull, causing severe hemorrhaging; and a third to the right rear portion of the skull, causing additional fracturing and hemorrhaging. The nasal fracture was apparently due to the direct blows of defendant; the injury to the left rear of the skull was the most serious and the injury was more consistent with the decedent's having struck his head on the wooden barroom floor than with his falling and striking his head on the concrete floor at the police station. In the opinion of the witness, the injury to the left rear of the skull was received as the result of decedent's being knocked off the bar stool. Both these injuries to the brain caused hemorrhaging, and either one, in Dr. Kade's opinion, would have resulted in a loss of consciousness. It was the opinion of Dr. Kade that the injury to the right side of decedent's head was caused at the police station when decedent suddenly lost consciousness and fell backward. The opinion of Dr. Kade was stated on cross-examination as follows: "In my opinion, death was caused by the two blows to the rear of the head. Whether the injury causing the fracture of the nasal bone would have been enough to cause death in and of itself, is difficult for me to establish, since there were these two additional injuries to the back of the head."

The witness was questioned further on cross-examination: "Q You feel at this time, Doctor, that it is difficult for you to say that the damage to the nasal area and the front of the skull there, that that would have been sufficient in and of itself to have brought about death; is that right? A Well, it is difficult to say because it is a conjectural question. It is like saying, if a boat is on fire and there is an explosion on board and the boat sinks would the fire have been enough to destroy the boat by itself had there not been an explosion. It is trying to infer what would have happened or could have happened if something else didn't happen. But the something else did happen and so I would be hesitant to conjecture about what could or might have happened under other circumstances." And when questioned further on cross-examination, he answered as follows: "Q Well, when you stated earlier, Doctor, that you felt it would be speculative or conjectural for you to say that the damage to the front part of the skull was sufficient in itself to be fatal, did you mean that you felt it was conjectural, too conjectural or speculative for you to testify under oath that such damage could cause death in and of itself? A No, I did not. It is my opinion that it easily could have, but I did not wish to state it as an absolute certainty that it would have definitely and unequivocally have caused death as an inevitable result in and of itself. It is my opinion that the greatest likelihood, the greatest medical probability is that it would have been sufficient to cause death. But I hesitate to state it as an absolute certainty."

The statement of the doctor that death resulted from the blows on the rear portions of the skull is clear enough. His opinion with respect to the probable consequences of the blow which fractured the nasal bones was an expression of his belief that the blow "easily could have" and that according "to the greatest medical probability" would have been sufficient to cause death. The force of this opinion was not destroyed by the stated qualification that he was not saying that death would have been the inevitable result of the blow or would have followed as an absolute certainty. The opinions expressed with respect to the probable consequences of the blow to the face, considered with the opinion that the major brain hemorrhage resulted from the fall on the barroom floor left no doubt that the opinion of the doctor was that the injuries in the barroom were probably fatal.

The evidence of the several injuries, the blow to the face, the fall in the barroom, the incident on the sidewalk and the fall in the police station presented the critical question as to the proximate cause of the death.

Upon this issue the primary factual question was whether the injuries received in the barroom would have resulted in death. Defendant was responsible for all the injuries inflicted in the barroom and if the jury had found those injuries to have been so severe as to have resulted in death the fact that other injuries were suffered later would have been immaterial. The only support for a finding of the jury that the injuries in the barroom were fatal would have been the opinion expressed by Dr. Kade. The jury was not required to give full effect to his opinion, and could have doubted that the fatal injuries were suffered in the barroom incident. It is of common knowledge that a blow which causes a broken nose does not ordinarily cause death. The picture of deceased taken at the police station merely showed him lying on his back with his head on the floor. There was evidence that his head bounced after hitting the floor. It was a matter of pure speculation which side of the skull hit the floor first. Moreover, the opinion of the doctor that the most serious fall was the one in the barroom was inconsistent with the fact that it was the fall in the police station that caused immediate bleeding from both ears. If it was doubted that the first injuries would have produced a fatal result and that death would have resulted despite the injuries received in the police station, the question necessarily arose whether defendant was responsible for the consequences of the later fall. It was, therefore, vitally important that the jury be adequately and correctly instructed on the doctrine of proximate cause.

The court instructed that in order to find the defendant guilty of either murder or involuntary manslaughter the jury must find that the injury inflicted by defendant was a proximate cause of the death and that "The proximate cause of an injury is that cause which, in natural and continuous sequence, unbroken by any efficient intervening cause, produces the injury, and without which the result would not have occurred. It is the efficient cause—the one that necessarily sets in operation the factors that accomplish the injury."

The court also instructed as follows: "You are instructed that to be a legal cause of death, a defendant's act must be its proximate cause, not merely its possible cause. A defendant's act may be considered the proximate cause of the death of another though it is not the immediate cause, if it is the ultimate cause. But where there is a supervening cause the defendant's act cannot be considered a proximate cause. The fact, if it be a fact, that the deceased or some other person or persons were guilty of negligence, which was a contributory cause of the death involved in the case, is not deemed to be a supervening cause and is no defense to a criminal charge if the defendant's own conduct was a proximate cause of the death." We are of the opinion that these instructions were wholly inadequate.

It has been the practice for many years to instruct in the language of the first quoted instruction, but we do not believe it was a satisfactory or sufficient instruction to give in the present case where the question of proximate cause was an intricate and difficult one to be resolved by the jury. We do not say the instruction misstates the law, but only that in the present case it was unclear and confusing as a statement of the doctrine of proximate cause.   *   *   *

There have been many attempts to phrase an all-purpose definition of proximate cause, but we think that in ordinary circumstances all the definitions have had their roots in the doctrine of foreseeability. We think the jury should have been instructed in clear and simple language as to the measure of the responsibility of defendant for the acts which caused Swallow's death.   He was responsible not only for the injuries inflicted in the barroom, but for any later injuries to Swallow that were reasonably foreseeable, and which he would not have sustained if in a normal condition.   The issue here was clearcut and vital and should have been submitted to the jury upon the test of foreseeability.   Instead of being submitted in this simple form, the issue was confused by the use in the first instruction of the terms "natural and continuous sequence," "efficient intervening cause" and "necessarily sets in operation the factors that accomplish the result."   And in the second quoted instruction, we find "superseding cause" added. The jury was given no definition of "efficient intervening cause" or "supervening cause."   These are vague and confusing terms, at best, and the jury should not have been left to guess at their meaning and their application to the facts.   What test was the jury to apply in determining their meaning?   Do the terms "intervening" and "supervening" mean the same thing, or have they different meanings?   What would be an "efficient intervening cause" or "supervening cause" that would break the chain of causation?   Would the chain remain unbroken even though the later event was one that was extraordinary and unpredictable?   The instructions did not answer these questions.

We cannot doubt that in an effort to understand the full purport of the instructions the minds of the jurors would have been distracted from the question of foreseeability of future injury.   They were told to look for an "efficient intervening cause" or a "supervening cause" as if it made no difference whether after-occurring causes were reasonably foreseeable.   The fall in the police station, judged from appearances, was extremely serious, as evidenced by the bleeding from both ears.   The jury could well have believed that except for that fall death would not have occurred.   Of course, the question was not whether that particular event might occur, but whether any serious injury was likely to occur because of Swallow's condition.   Defendant had a duty to anticipate the common and ordinary consequences of his act, and these he was responsible for.   They could be said to be the direct consequences.   But the fall in the police station could have been found to be an extraordinary and abnormal occurrence, not reasonably foreseeable as a result of the first injuries.   The failure of the court to instruct that defendant would have been responsible for the consequences of the injuries received after Swallow was taken from the barroom only if further injury was reasonably to be anticipated, and the giving of instructions that enabled the jury to hold him responsible for later injuries even if the same were not reasonably foreseeable was prejudicial and reversible error.

The judgment is reveresd.

NOTE

The court suggests that "supervening" and "intervening" were not adequately defined. But R. Perkins, Criminal Law 698 (2nd ed. 1969) has suggested that "superceding cause" be defined as a factor that intervenes between the defendant's act and the result in question in such a way that legally speaking it is "the cause." Thus a superceding cause is simply one that has the legal effect of breaking the chain of proximate causation between the defendant's act and the result of death. Supervening cause, as used by the trial court in this case, could be given the same definition.

McLaughlin, Proximate Cause, 39 Harv.L.Rev. 149, 159–60 (1925) defines "intervening" force as follows:

> An intervening force is a force which is neither operating in the defendant's presence, nor at the place where the defendant's act takes effect at the time of the defendant's act, but comes into effective operation at or before the time of the damage. Thus where a fire is started in a then existing wind, the wind is not an intervening force, but a condition existing at the time of the defendant's act.

An "intervening cause" could be similarly defined. If a "supervening cause" must be an "intervening cause," this only means that it must be something that comes into operation at or before the time of the damage. For example, in the instant case if Swallow was intoxicated at the time he was struck by the defendant, his intoxication was a "condition existing at the time of the defendant's act," not an intervening factor, and therefore it could not break the chain of proximate causation between the defendant's blow and Swallow's death.

MODEL PENAL CODE

(Tent. Draft No. 4, 1955).

Section 2.03. Causal Relationship Between Conduct and Result; Divergence Between Result Designed or Contemplated and Actual Result or Between Probable and Actual Result

(1) Conduct is the cause of a result when:

(a) it is an antecedent but for which the result in question would not have occurred; and

(b) the relationship between the conduct and result satisfies any additional causal requirements plainly imposed by law.

(2) When purposely or knowingly causing a particular result is a material element of an offense, the element is not established if the actual result is not within the purpose or the contemplation of the actor unless:

(a) the actual result differs from that designed or contemplated, as the case may be, only in the respect that a different person or different property is injured or affected or that the injury or harm designed or contemplated would have been more serious or more extensive than that caused; or

(b) the actual result involves the same kind of injury or harm as that designed or contemplated and is not too accidental in its occurrence to have a just bearing on the actor's liability or on the gravity of his offense. [Alternative: and it occurs in a manner which the actor knows or should know is rendered substantially more probable by his conduct.]

(3) When recklessly or negligently causing a particular result is a material element of an offense, the element is not established if the actual result is not within the risk of which the actor is aware, or in the case of negligence, of which he should be aware unless:

(a) the actual result differs from the probable result only in the respect that a different person or different property is injured or affected or that the probable injury or harm would have been more serious or more extensive than that caused; or

(b) the actual result involves the same kind of injury or harm as the probable result and is not too accidental in in its occurrence to have a just bearing on the actor's liability or on the gravity of his offense. [Alternative: and it occurs in a manner which the actor knows or should know is rendered substantially more probable by his conduct.]

Commentary

Section 2.03. Causal relationship between conduct and result; Divergence between result designed or contemplated and actual result or between probable and actual result

1. This section is concerned with offenses that are so defined that causing a particular result is a material element of the offense, as in the case of homicide, theft, etc. It undertakes to define the causality relationship that should generally be required to establish liability for such offenses and to deal with inevitable problems incident to variations between the actual result of conduct and the result sought or contemplated by the actor or probable under the circumstances of the action. These problems are now faced as issues of "proximate causation" and they present enormous difficulty, especially in homicide, because of the vague meaning of that term. Rather than seek to systematize variant and sometimes inconsistent rules in different areas in which the problem has arisen, the section undertakes a fresh approach to what appear to be the central issues.

2. Paragraph 1(a) treats but-for cause as the causality relationship that normally should be regarded as sufficient, in the view

that this is the simple, pervasive meaning of causation that is relevant for purposes of penal law. When concepts of "proximate causation" disassociate the actor's conduct and a result of which it was a but-for cause, the reason always inheres in the judgment that the actor's culpability with reference to the result, i. e., his purpose, knowledge, recklessness or negligence, was such that it would be unjust to permit the result to influence his liability or the gravity of the offense of which he is convicted. Since this is so, the draft proceeds upon the view that problems of this kind ought to be faced as problems of the culpability required for conviction and not as problems of "causation."

Paragraph 1(b) contemplates, however, that this general position may prove unacceptable in dealing with particular offenses. In that event, additional causal requirements may be imposed explicitly, such, for example, as a temporal limitation with respect to causing death.

3.   Paragraphs (2) and (3) are drafted on the theory stated. They assume that liability requires purpose, knowledge, recklessness or negligence with respect to the result which is an element of the offense and deal explicitly with variations between the actual result and that designed, contemplated or threatened, as the case may be, stating when the variation is considered immaterial.

4.   Paragraph (2) is addressed to the case where the culpability requirement with respect to the result is purpose or knowledge, i. e. where purposely or knowingly causing a specified result is a material element of the offense. Here if the actual result is not within the purpose or the contemplation of the actor, the culpability requirement is not established, except in the circumstances set forth in sub-paragraphs (a) and (b).

Sub-paragraph (a) deals with the situation where the actual result differed from the result designed or contemplated only in the respect that a different person or different property was injured or affected or that the injury or harm designed or contemplated was more serious or more extensive than that caused. Such variations between purpose or contemplation and result are made immaterial, as almost certainly would be the view under existing law.

Sub-paragraph (b) deals with the situation where the actual result involved the same kind of injury or harm as that designed or contemplated but the precise injury inflicted was different or occurred in a different way. Here the draft makes no attempt to catalogue the possibilities, e. g., to deal with the intervening or concurrent causes, natural or human; unexpected physical conditions; distinctions between the infliction of mortal or non-mortal wounds. It deals only with the ultimate criterion by which the significance of such possibilities ought to be judged, presenting two alternative formulations. The first proposes that the question to be faced is whether the actual result is "too accidental in its occurrence to have a just bearing on the actor's liability or on the gravity of his offense." The alternative proposes that the issue turn on whether the actual result "occurs in a manner which the actor knows or ought to know is rendered substantially more probable by his conduct."

It may be useful in appraising either treatment of the problem to note that what will usually turn on the determination will not be the criminality of a defendant's conduct but rather the gravity of his offense. Since the actor, by hypothesis, has sought to cause a criminal result or has been reckless or negligent with respect to such a result, he will be guilty of some crime under a well-considered penal code even if he is not held for the actual result, i. e. he will be guilty of attempt, assault or some offense involving risk creation, such as reckless driving. Thus the issue in penal law is very different than in torts. Only in form is it, in penal law, a question of the actor's liability. In substance, it is a question of the severity of sentence which the Court is authorized or obliged to impose. Its practical importance thus depends on the disparity in sentence for the various offenses that may be involved, e. g. the sentences for an attempted and completed crime.

How far a Model Code ought to attribute importance in the grading of offenses to the actual result of conduct, as distinguished from results attempted or threatened, presents an issue of some difficulty which is of general importance in the Code. It may be said, however, that distinctions of this order are to some extent essential, at least when the severest sanctions are involved. For juries will not lightly find convictions that will lead to the severest types of sentences unless the resentments caused by the infliction of important injuries have been aroused. Whatever abstract logic may suggest, a prudent legislator cannot disregard these facts of life in the enactment of a penal code.

It may be added that attributing importance to the actual result does not substantially detract from the deterrent efficacy of the law, at least in dealing with cases of purposeful misconduct. One who attempts to kill and thus expects to bring about the result punishable by the gravest penalty, is unlikely to be influenced in his behavior by the treatment that the law provides for those who fail in such attempts; his expectation is that he is going to succeed. See Michael and Wechsler, A Rationale of the Law of Homicide, 37 Columbia L. Rev. 1261, 1294–1298.

Viewed in these terms, it may be said that either the proposed or the alternative formulation should suffice for the exclusion of those situations where the actual result is so remote from the actor's purpose or contemplation that juries can be expected to believe that it should have no bearing on the actor's liability for the graver offense or, stated differently, on the gravity of the offense of which he is convicted. If, for example, the defendant attempted to shoot his wife and missed, with the result that she retired to her parents' country home and then was killed in falling off a horse, no one would think that the defendant should be held guilty of murder, though he did intend her death and his attempt to kill her was a but-for cause of her encounter with the horse. Both court and jury would regard the actual result as "too accidental in its occurrence to have a just bearing on the actor's liability or on the gravity of his offense." Alternatively, they would regard the actual result as one which did not occur in a manner that the actor knew or should have known was rendered substantially more probable by his conduct when he attempted to shoot his wife to death.

It is in closer cases that a difference in result might be expected. Thus, if the defendant in the case supposed had shot his wife and in the hospital she had contracted a disease which was medically unrelated to the wound (though related to her presence in the hospital), her death from the disease may well be thought to have been rendered substantially more probable by the defendant's conduct, as presumably he should have known. Yet juries might regard it as a too unusual result to justify convicting him of murder. The advantage of putting the issue squarely to the jury's sense of justice is that it does not attempt to force a result which the jury may resist. It also leaves the principle flexible for application to the infinite variety of cases likely to arise. The argument for the alternative is, on the other hand, that flexibility will involve inequality of application; that if the actual result was foreseen or foreseeable as a substantial probability, there can be no injustice in holding the actor responsible for its occurrence, nor is there any reason to expect that jury action will nullify such a rule.

In the Reporter's view, either formulation is acceptable. What is important is to free the law from the encrusted precedents on "proximate causation", offering a principle that will permit both courts and juries to begin afresh in facing problems of this kind.

5. Paragraph (3) deals with the case where recklessness or negligence is the required kind of culpability and where the actual result is not within the risk of which the actor was aware, or, in the case of negligence, of which he should have been aware. The principles proposed to govern are the same as in the case where purposely or knowingly causing the specified result is the material element of the crime. If the actual result differed from the probable result only in the respect that a different person or different property was injured or affected, the variation is declared to be inconsequential. In other situations, if the actual result involved the same kind of injury or harm as the probable result, the question asked is whether it was too accidental in its occurrence to have just bearing on the actor's liability or on the gravity of his offense or, if the alternative is preferred, whether the result occurred in a manner which the actor knew

or should have known was rendered substantially more probable by his conduct. The governing considerations are the same as in the situation dealt with by paragraph (2).

WEINREB, COMMENT ON BASIS OF CRIMINAL LIABILITY; CULPABILITY; CAUSATION, IN 1 WORKING PAPERS OF THE NATIONAL COMMISSION ON REFORM OF FEDERAL CRIMINAL LAWS

144-46 (1970).

The basic provision of the Model Penal Code adopts "but for" causation as the general test; it is both necessary and, unless "additional causal requirements" are specifically imposed, sufficient. This provision does not clearly state the accepted rule or easily lead to the correct result in cases of "concurrent causation."

Even though all of the senators may have intended to kill Caesar and all of them stabbed him, under the Model Penal Code's formulation none would be criminally liable for his death since (so I shall assume) he would have died even though any one of them had held back his knife. Even a senator who stabbed Caesar through the heart would not be liable, since, so Anthony tells us (act 3, scene 2) "sweet Caesar's blood" was streaming from all the wounds.

The Model Penal Code's reliance on "but for" causation as ordinarily enough for liability ignores the cases in which it is not essential to liability. There are situations in which, for purposes of the criminal law, we are properly "interested" in more than one cause of an occurrence, even though none of them alone is necessary or more than one of them are alone sufficient. The paradigm is a situation in which each of two or more persons engages in conduct that fully satisfies the definition of a crime but in which there is only "one" harmful consequence.

A and B simultaneously shoot at X, both intending to kill him. The bullets enter X's body at the same time. Each wound is sufficient to cause death and would alone cause death in the same amount of time. X dies from the joint effect of both wounds.

* * *

Additional sections of the Model Penal Code's formulation deal with cases in which the actual result is not intended or is not within the risk created by the actor's conduct, by providing that there is no causal relation in such cases unless either the actual and the intended or probable results differ only in respects generally irrelevant to the criminal law (the specific person or property injured; the greater seriousness of the intended or probable harm) or the actual result is similar to ("involves the same kind of injury or harm as") the intended or probable result, and "is not too remote or accidental in its occurrence to have a [just] bearing on the actor's liability or on the gravity of his offense." This formulation breaks down in precisely those cases in which difficulties arise, those covered by the last clause. Of the alternative formulations, that which omits the word "just" states the problem without resolving it (by use of the question-begging word "too"); that which includes the word "just" (in addition to using the word "too") refers to an inapt standard for resolving it— that the connection between a result and conduct but for which the result would not have occurred is remote or accidental does not, unless the words "remote" and "accidental" are given special (question-begging) meaning, affect the justice of holding the actor liable for his conduct.

Illustrative of an alternative to the Model Penal Code's reliance on "but for" causation as the basic test, is the following, drafted for consideration in the Federal Code:

> A causal connection between a person's conduct and an occurrence does not exist if:
>
> (a) the person's conduct was not sufficient to cause the occurrence without the cooperation of one or more events or the conduct of one or more persons; and
>
> (b) without the cooperation of the person's conduct, another event or the conduct of another person was sufficient to cause the occurrence.

Such a provision, which does not attempt to state what causation is but only what, in some circumstances, it is not, leads to the correct result in many cases of concurrent causation by providing that a person's conduct is not the cause of a result if someone else's conduct or some other event is both necessary and sufficient to produce the result. Where conduct is not sufficient to cause an occurrence and there is present and identifiable other conduct or some event which is sufficient to cause the occurrence, common understanding would probably regard the latter as the cause. However, the provision, at best, offers no guidance in the case of sequential, as opposed to concurrent causes. (If A shoots X, as a result of which X goes to the hospital, and while he is there (i) the hospital burns down, or (ii) the wound becomes infected, or (iii) a doctor stabs X inadvertently, or (iv) a doctor stabs X deliberately, and X dies, in which of the four cases should A be liable for X's death?) Even though the provision attempts to say only when causation is not present, it is readily perceived as indicating when causation is present. If we understand the provision to refer only to concurrent and not sequential causes, it is only because, without relying on the provision, we have a sense of when an act or event causes an occurrence. (If the provision is not so understood, A would, or at least might, be liable for X's death in all of the cases described, which would surely be the wrong result at least in case (iv) and possibly in others as well.)

The provision gives limited guidance, and even that only because of our independent understanding of the very concept of causation which the provision attempts partially to illuminate.

PROPOSED FEDERAL CRIMINAL CODE

(1971).

§ 305.   Causal Relationship Between Conduct and Result

Causation may be found where the result would not have occurred but for the conduct of the accused operating either alone or concurrently with another cause, unless the concurrent cause was clearly sufficient to produce the result and the conduct of the accused clearly insufficient.

Comment

Rules governing causation have never been specified in federal criminal statutes.   The major problem in enunciating such rules is presented by situations in which two or more factors "cause" the result.   This section is a modified "but for" test with a proviso that excludes those situations in which the concurrent cause was clearly sufficient to produce the result and the accused's conduct clearly insufficient.   An alternative approach would be to have no specific provision on causation, leaving the matter to judge-made law.   While the proposed section may not be useful in all cases where causation must be explained, it is intended to be an aid to uniformity and clarification whenever it does apply.

NOTES

1.   Weinreb, Comment on Basis of Criminal Liability; Culpability; Causation, in 1 Working Papers of the National Commission on Reform of Federal Criminal Laws 147 (1970) explained the Proposed Federal Code's position as follows:

> The drafters of the basic provisions on liability have been unable to develop an explanatory formula of causation which is both accurate and meaningful.   All such formulae, whether cast in terms of what is necessary or sufficient to establish a causal relationship or, more tentatively, in terms of what is relevant to the existence of a causal relationship, flounder in precisely those cases where the existence of the relationship is in doubt.   To omit a section defining causation generally will simply acknowledge the absence of any such general provision in Federal criminal law.

2.   In R. v. Jordan, 40 Crim.App. 158 (Eng.1956), the defendant's conviction of murder (sentence, death) was quashed on the basis of new evidence indicating that the victim died not from the defendant's perforation of his intestine but from pneumonia which resulted from medical treatment which was "palpably wrong" and "not normal." Id. at 157, 158.   The court's judgment was based upon the testimony of two medical witnesses who apparently had not been involved in the treatment of the deceased.   Fol-

lowing the court's action a medical board of inquiry found that the treatment had been "devoted and exemplary". Williams, Causation in Homicide, [1957] Crim.L.Rev. (Eng.) 429, 430, 510. An interesting critical piece on *Jordan* is Camps & Havard, Causation in Homicide—A Medical View, [1957] Crim.L.Rev. (Eng.) 576 which concludes:

> In future when victims of homicidal assaults survive long enough to receive hospital treatment it may well become a routine of the defence to impeach the medical treatment in order to show that the treatment was 'not normal.' There must be a strong body of opinion to agree with the old authorities that the point is legally irrelevant providing a wound has been given which is dangerous to life and the treatment has been adopted bona fide by competent medical attendants. The consequence of this change in the substantive law of homicide may be greater than has been appreciated. In particular, the courts may find themselves involved in protracted, undesirable, and, it is respectfully submitted, unnecessary investigations into the medical treatment of victims of homicidal assaults. Id. at 585.

If Jordan is absolved of murder as a result of the acts of the medical personnel should they be charged with some form of negligent homicide? If not, why?

3. In many American jurisdictions, the common law rule that one may not be convicted of murder unless the victim died within a year and one day from the time the fatal blow was given or the cause of death administered is applied. See, e. g., Louisville, E. & St. L. R. Co. v. Clarke, 152 U.S. 230, 239 (1894). In Commonwealth v. Ladd, 402 Pa. 164, 166 A.2d 501 (1966) the Pennsylvania Supreme Court interpreted the requirement as only a common law rule of evidence which the court was empowered to change, and abandoned it. Seeing the purpose of the requirement as preventing prosecutions in which the passage of time would make it too difficult to accurately ascertain the cause of death, the court concluded that advances in crime detection and medicine were such that the interest in accuracy would be served by putting no restriction upon the time within which prosecutions might be brought and requiring "proof of causation of conventional quality" at the trial. Musmanno, J. dissented, arguing that despite advances in crime detection and medicine there remains a real danger of unjustified prosecutions if the year and a day requirement was removed. He pointed to specifically the facts of the case—the victim had died of pneumonia thirteen months after being assaulted by the defendant—as demonstrating the difficult issues the rule was designed to withdraw from courts' consideration.

Should other courts and legislatures follow this lead?

COMMONWEALTH v. FEINBERG

Supreme Court of Pennsylvania, 1969.
433 Pa. 558, 253 A.2d 636.

JONES, Justice. Appellant Max Feinberg owned and operated a cigar store in the skid-row section of Philadelphia. One of the products he sold was Sterno, a jelly-like substance composed primarily of methanol and ethanol and designed for cooking and heating purposes. Sterno was manufactured and sold in two types of containers, one for home use and one for industrial use. Before September, 1963, both types of Sterno contained approximately 3.75% methanol, or wood alcohol, and 71% ethanol, or grain alcohol; of the two types of alcohols, methanol is far more toxic if consumed internally. Beginning in September of 1963, the Sterno company began manufacturing a new type of industrial Sterno which was 54% methanol. The cans containing the new industrial Sterno were identical to the cans containing the old industrial Sterno except in one crucial aspect: on the lids of the new 54% methanol Sterno were imprinted the words "Institutional Sterno. Danger. Poison. For use only as a Fuel. Not for consumer use. For industrial and commercial use. Not for home use." A skull and crossbones were also lithographed on the lid. The carton in which the new Sterno cans were packaged and shipped did not indicate that the contents differed in any respect from the old industrial Sterno.

According to its records, Sterno Corporation sent only one shipment of the new Sterno to the Philadelphia area; that shipment went to the Richter Paper Company and was received on December 17, 1963. Charles Richter, president of the firm, testified that his company in turn, made only one sale of the new industrial Sterno, and that was to appellant. Richter testified that his records indicated that appellant received the Sterno on December 21 and, since Richter had not opened any of the cartons, he was unaware that he was selling appellant a new type of industrial Sterno. On December 27, Richter received a call from appellant informing him that the cartons contained a new type of Sterno and that appellant wished to return the portion of his order that he had not sold. The unused cartons were picked up by Richter's deliveryman the next day.

Meanwhile, between December 21 and December 28, appellant had sold approximately 400 cans of the new industrial Sterno. Between December 23 and December 30, thirty-one persons died in the skid-row area as a result of methanol poisoning. In many of the cases the source of the methanol was traced to the new industrial Sterno. Since appellant was the only retail outlet of this type of Sterno in Philadelphia, he was arrested and indicted on thirty-one counts charging involuntary manslaughter and on companion bills charging violations of the Pharmacy Act (Act of September 27, 1961, P.L. 1700, § 1 et seq., 63 P.S. § 390–1 et seq.)

Appellant was convicted on seventeen counts of involuntary manslaughter and on twenty-five counts of violating the Pharmacy Act by Judge Charles L. Guerin, sitting without a jury. Judge Guerin held that appellant had violated the Pharmacy Act and that, therefore, he was guilty of a misdemeanor-manslaughter in each of the seventeen cases. Five of the manslaughter convictions were appealed to the Superior Court which affirmed four of them, although on a different theory. Commonwealth v. Feinberg, 211 Pa.Super. 100, 234 A.2d 913 (1967). In writing for a six-judge majority, Judge Montgomery held that appellant had not violated the Pharmacy Act and, therefore, was not guilty of a misdemeanor-manslaughter, but that the evidence justified the conclusion that appellant was guilty of involuntary manslaughter. * * *

The second issue in this case is whether appellant is guilty of involuntary manslaughter in each or any of the four appeals presently before us. The Penal Code defines involuntary manslaughter as a death "happening in consequence of an unlawful act, or the doing of a lawful act in an unlawful way * * *." (Act of June 24, 1939, P.L. 872, § 703, 18 P.S. § 4703) Since we have determined that appellant did not violate the Pharmacy Act in selling the new industrial Sterno, the second portion of this statutory definition must be controlling. When a death results from the doing of an act lawful in itself but done in an unlawful manner, in order to sustain a conviction for manslaughter the Commonwealth must present evidence to prove that the defendant acted in a rash or reckless manner. The conduct of the defendant resulting in the death must be such a departure from the behavior of an ordinary and prudent man as to evidence a disregard of human life or an indifference to the consequences. Furthermore, there must be a direct causal relationship between the defendant's act and the deceased's death. Commonwealth v. Root, 403 Pa. 571, 170 A.2d 310, 82 A.L.R.2d 452 (1961).

We have searched in vain for cases from this Commonwealth involving factual situations similar to the one now before us. We have, however, found four cases from other jurisdictions which are on point. In the leading case, Thiede v. State, 106 Neb. 48, 182 N. W. 570 (1921), the defendant gave the deceased moonshine containing methanol, the drinking of which resulted in his death. While noting that the defendant had violated the state prohibition laws, the court refused to rest the manslaughter conviction on this statutory violation, holding that the manufacturing and distribution of moonshine was merely malum prohibitum and not malum per se. The court continued, "We cannot go so far as to say that [dispensing moonshine], prompted perhaps by the spirit of good-fellowship, though prohibited by law, could ever, by any resulting consequence, be converted into the crime of manslaughter; *but, where the liquor by reason of its extreme potency or poisonous ingredients,* is dangerous to use as an intoxicating beverage, where the drinking of it is capable of producing direct physical injury, other than as an ordinary intoxicant, and of perhaps endangering life itself, *the case is different, and the question of negligence enters; for, if the party furnishing the liquor knows, or was apprised of such facts that he should have known, of the danger, there then appears from his act a recklessness which is indifferent to results.* Such recklessness in the furnishing of intoxicating liquors, in violation of law, may constitute such an unlawful act as, if it results in causing death, will constitute manslaughter." (106 Neb. at 57, 58, 182 N.W. at 573.) (Emphasis added.)

We conclude, after studying the record, that appellant fits within the black-letter rule laid down in *Thiede* and that the Commonwealth has made out all the elements necessary to warrant a conviction for involuntary manslaughter. First, the record establishes that appellant sold the Sterno with the knowledge that at least some of his customers would extract the alcohol for drinking purposes. * * * Second, appellant was aware, or should have been aware, that the Sterno he was selling was toxic if consumed. The new industrial Sterno was clearly marked as being poisonous. Even the regular Sterno is marked "Caution. Flammable. For Use only as a Fuel" and if consumed internally may have serious consequences. * * *

Appellant presses several contentions for our consideration. First, he claims that the Commonwealth has not established the necessary causal link between the sale of the Sterno and the deaths, citing Commonwealth v. Root, supra. We cannot agree. First, appellant sold the Sterno knowing, or having reason to know, that some of his customers would consume it. Second, some of his customers did consume the new industrial Sterno and died as a result. The Commonwealth's expert toxicologist testified that in several of the cases death could only have resulted from consumption of the new as opposed to the regular Sterno. Since appellant was the only retail outlet for the new Sterno in Philadelphia, these persons must have died from drinking Sterno purchased in appellant's store. Third, *Root* does not help the appellant. *Root* involved a drag racing situation. The decedent died when he negligently passed the defendant on a two-lane road and collided with a truck. This Court held that the defendant could not be held criminally responsible for the deceased's death because there was no direct causal connection between the defendant's act in engaging in a drag race and the deceased's death. The court in *Thiede,* in answering an argument similar to the one now made by appellant, stated: "Defendant contends that the drinking of liquor, by deceased was his voluntary act and served as an intervening cause, breaking the causal connection between the giving of the liquor by defendant and the resulting death. The drinking of the liquor, in consequence of defendant's act, was, however, what the defendant contemplated. Deceased, it is true, may have been negligent in drinking, but, where the defendant was negligent, then the contributory negligence of the deceased will be no defense in a criminal action." (106 Neb. at 58, 59, 182 N.W. at 574)

* * *

NOTES

1.   Defendant attempted to force a police car off the road. A chase ensued and another police car, requested by radio to aid, collided with a bus
causing the death of an officer.   Defendant was convicted of involuntary
manslaughter and appealed on the grounds that, although he was driving
with wilful and wanton disregard of the safety of others, this was not the
proximate cause of the officer's death.   The trial judge had instructed the
jury that defendant's conduct need not have been "the" direct cause but
that it was sufficient for conviction if it were found to be "a" cause.   The
appellate court reversed on the grounds that, although such a definition of
causation might be satisfactory for purposes of civil liability, a more direct relationship was required to sustain a conviction.   People v. Scott, 29
Mich.App. 549, 185 N.W.2d 576 (1971).

2.   In Commonwealth v. Atencio, 345 Mass. 627, 189 N.E.2d 223 (1963),
the defendants were convicted of manslaughter due to the death of a friend
killed in the course of a game of "Russian roulette".   Defendants had
each spun the revolver, which contained one bullet, pointed it at his own head,
and pulled the trigger before the deceased did the same with fatal results.
In affirming the conviction, the court rejected the contention that the deceased's voluntary act should constitute a bar to conviction as it might to
a civil suit for damages.   Their participation in the "game" helped bring
about the death.   The court considered distinguishable cases involving
drag racing in which the driver of the noncolliding car had been held not
responsible for the death of his competitor.   Without approving those decisions the court noted that in drag racing, unlike Russian roulette, some
skill was involved.

3.   It should be noted with respect to drag racing deaths that convictions, even of the noncolliding competitor, have been upheld when the victim was a third person uninvolved in the race.

4.   If, in the *Scott* case, note 1 supra, it had been the defendant's car
rather than that of the pursuing officer, which had crashed and caused a
death would there be any doubt as to his culpability?   See Tegethoff v.
State, 220 So.2d 399 (Fla.Dist.Ct.App.1969).   Is this because no other actor
intervened or because the crash may be viewed as a natural result of such
conduct?   Wasn't police pursuit, with its attendant dangers, a natural result of Scott's conduct?   Would holding Scott responsible for the results of
the officer's mishap serve to deter such flight?   Would it violate our sense
of fairness?   Would holding the officer liable for the results of his apparently reckless pursuit deter such pursuit?   Would it violate our sense of fairness?

5.   Is *Atencio*, note 2, supra, to be distinguished from *Scott* because the
chances of a fatal result in Russian roulette are greater than in high speed
auto chases?   Because of the comparative lack of social utility of the two activities?   Because the driving skills of the pursuing officer in *Scott,* or the
lack thereof, are a variable for which the defendant should not be held responsible?   Is the *Scott* court's reliance on *Root* (described in *Feinberg*)
well-placed given the voluntary participation of the decedent there?

D. COMPLICITY

The law of "parties" is the doctrinal device by which the criminal law defines the outer limits of liability for activity indirectly related to a crime. At common law, participants in—or "parties to—felonies [d] were categorized as follows:

Principal in the First Degree	One who, with the requisite state of mind, performed the criminal act or directly caused the criminal result, either with his own hand, with an instrument or a non-human agent, or by means of an innocent human agent.
Principal in the Second Degree	One who was actually or constructively present at the scene of the crime and who, with the required state of mind, aided, counseled, commanded, or encouraged the principal in the first degree.
Accessory Before the Fact	One neither actually nor constructively present at the scene of the crime who, with the requisite state of mind, ordered, counseled, encouraged or otherwise aided and abetted the principal in the first degree.
Accessory After the Fact	One who, with knowledge of the commission of an offense by an offender, concealed the offender or gave him some other assistance to prevent his detection, arrest, trial, or punishment.

All participants in misdemeanors were simply principals. Concealment or assistance of a misdemeanant did not give rise to criminal liability at all.

Initially, all participants in a felony were subject to the same penalty without regard to which category they fell into. But it was soon recognized that the involvement of an accessory after the fact rendered him significantly less culpable than other participants. This category was set aside as a separate offense, independent of the felony of the individual aided or concealed, and penalty was assigned to it that was less severe than that assigned to the offense committed by the assisted felon. Although no jurisdiction still retains unmodified the common law of parties, statutory changes have been widely varied.

---

d. Treason was the sole exception. All participants in treason were regarded as principals.

Most, however, retain the basic notion of the common law of parties, that all who aid or abet the commission of a serious offense are subject to the same punishment as the person who actually commits it.

Clearly the law of parties (or its modern statutory progeny) is significant insofar as it defines the liability of those whose activity is only indirectly related to the offense. At common law, however, the law of parties had other implications. Jurisdictional complexities arose because of the common law rule that an accessory was punishable only where his act of accessoryship was committed, not where the final offense was committed. Strict attitudes towards pleading resulting in holdings that a defendant must be charged with the specific form of liability that the proof showed at trial; one charged as a principal in the first degree could not be convicted if the proof at trial showed that he was an accessory before the fact. (This was not expanded, however, to distinguish between the two degrees of principals.) Finally, the liability of an accessory was tied to that of the principal. Thus an accessory could not be tried before the principal and anything which prevented the conviction of the principal also prevented conviction of the accessory. This was even expanded to the point of holding that reversal of the principal's conviction required reversal of the conviction of the accessory.

Many of the procedural implications of the law of parties have been modified by statutes, and other offenses have been created in many jurisdictions to supplement that defining the accessory after the fact as guilty of an offense as a means of dealing with those whose actions impede official investigation of crime. The emphasis on the following material, then, is upon the law of parties as it defines the outer limits of liability for conduct other than that consisting of the criminal act itself or conduct directly causing the criminal result.

---

1. LIABILITY AS AN AIDER AND ABETTOR OR INCITOR

---

18 UNITED STATES CODE

§ 2. Principals

(a) Whoever commits an offense against the United States or aids, abets, counsels, commands, induces or procures its commission, is punishable as a principal.

(b) Whoever willfully causes an act to be done which if directly performed by him or another would be an offense against the United States, is punishable as a principal.

CALIFORNIA PENAL CODE

§ 30. Classification

CLASSIFICATION OF PARTIES TO CRIME. The parties to crimes are classified as:

1. Principals; and,

2. Accessories.

§ 31. Principals defined

WHO ARE PRINCIPALS. All persons concerned in the commission of a crime, whether it be felony or misdemeanor, and whether they directly commit the act constituting the offense, or aid and abet in its commission, or, not being present, have advised and encouraged its commission, and all persons counseling, advising, or encouraging children under the age of fourteen years, lunatics or idiots, to commit any crime, or who, by fraud, contrivance, or force, occasion the drunkenness of another for the purpose of causing him to commit any crime, or who, by threats, menaces, command, or coercion, compel another to commit any crime, are principals in any crime so committed.

PROPOSED FEDERAL CRIMINAL CODE

(1971).

§ 401. Accomplices

(1) Liability Defined. A person may be convicted of an offense based upon the conduct of another person when:

(a) acting with the kind of culpability required for the offense, he causes the other to engage in such conduct; or

(b) with intent that an offense be committed, he commands, induces, procures, or aids the other to commit it or, having a legal duty to prevent its commission, he fails to make proper effort to do so; or

(c) he is a co-conspirator and his association with the offense meets the requirements of either of the other paragraphs of this subsection.

A person is not liable under this subsection for the conduct of another person when he is either expressly or by implication made not accountable for such conduct by the statute defining the offense or related provisions, because he is a victim of the offense or otherwise.

(2) Defenses Precluded. Except as otherwise provided, in any prosecution in which the liability of the defendant is based upon the conduct of another person, it is no defense that:

(a) the defendant does not belong to the class of persons who, because of their official status or other capacity or characteristic, are by definition of the offense the only persons capable of directly committing it; or

(b) the person for whose conduct the defendant is being held liable has been acquitted, has not been prosecuted or convicted or has been convicted of a different offense, or is immune from prosecution, or is otherwise not subject to justice.

§ 1002. Criminal Facilitation

(1) Offense. A person is guilty of criminal facilitation if he knowingly provides substantial assistance to a person intending to commit a crime which is, in fact, a felony, and that person, in fact, commits the crime contemplated, or a like or related felony, employing the assistance so provided. The ready lawful availability from others of the goods or services provided by a defendant is a factor to be considered in determining whether or not his assistance was substantial. This section does not apply to a person who is either expressly or by implication made not accountable by the statute defining the felony facilitated or related statutes.

(2) Defense Precluded. Except as otherwise provided, it is no defense to a prosecution under this section that the person whose conduct the defendant facilitated has been acquitted, has not been prosecuted or convicted, has been convicted of a different offense, is immune from prosecution, or is otherwise not subject to justice.

(3) Grading. Facilitation of a Class A felony is a Class C felony. Facilitation of a Class B or Class C felony is a Class A misdemeanor.

NOTE

The Study Draft's section dealing with criminal facilitation is discussed in Comment, A New Crime: Criminal Facilitation, 18 Loyola L.Rev. 103 (1972).

----

a. THE EXTENT OF PARTICIPATION NECESSARY

STATE v. COBB

Supreme Court of Missouri, 1969.
444 S.W.2d 408.

STORCKMAN, Judge. A jury convicted the defendant Harold Cobb of burglary in the second degree and stealing in connection therewith * * *. He attacks the sufficiency of the evidence to support the verdict * * *.

On February 27, 1967, at approximately 4:25 a. m., in response to a burglar alarm, a police patrol car was dispatched to a drug store owned and operated by Bingaman's No. 1 United Super Market, Inc., which was located at the State Fair Shopping Center in Sedalia. It had been raining and the pavement was wet. The evidence most favorable to the verdict shows that when the patrol car arrived at the parking lot the police officers, James Tuttle and Charles Shepherd, saw a GTO Pontiac automobile occupied by the defendant and three other persons about 20 feet from the north door of the drug store, sometimes referred to as Bing's or Bing's No. 1. The lights on the Pontiac were completely off and it was moving slowly. As the patrol car entered the parking lot, the Pontiac accelerated and was driven rapidly from the parking lot. As it turned left on Limit Avenue, the rear end "fishtailed" and the car skidded into a ditch; it then came back across the highway and stalled in the middle of the road and crossways of it.

The police officers stopped their patrol car near the stalled Pontiac and ordered the occupants to get out on the driver's side. Ernest Greer was driving and left the car first. The defendant Cobb was riding on the right side of the front seat and got out next. A boy by the name of Herbert Horton and a girl whose name was once given as Courtney Bell were in the back seat and got out last. As the occupants of the Pontiac were getting out, a second patrol car occupied by officers Robert Lewis and James Curry arrived and assisted in searching the occupants, handcuffing them, and taking them to the police station.

An investigation at the drug store disclosed that a window beside the front door had been broken. The dimensions of the window were estimated by some witnesses as 6 feet by 4 feet and by others as 3 feet wide by 8 or 10 feet high. Approximately half or ¾ths of the glass had been broken out of the window. The opening was large enough to admit a man's body. There were fragments of glass both inside and outside the building. A heavy metal container or basket for carrying four gallons of milk was found on the walk immediately in front of the broken window. There were fragments of glass in the container.

A number of bottles containing prescription drugs which were on a shelf when the store was closed the night before were missing. The missing articles were found in a carton on the floor of the Pontiac automobile behind the right front seat occupied by the defendant Cobb. The drug items were identified at the trial as being the property of the owner of the store and as having been stolen from the store.

The GTO Pontiac was a two-door sports model with bucket seats in front. To permit a person to leave or enter the back seat, one of the side doors had to be opened and then the back of the front seat pushed forward. If the door was not opened first, the back of the front seat when pushed forward would strike and get caught on the door handle.

The defendants Cobb and Greer were the only witnesses for the defense. Their testimony tended to show that they and two other men left Kansas City for Jefferson City in two automobiles at about

8:30 p. m. on the day before the burglary was committed. The men were accompanied by four girls, two of whom were students at Lincoln University. After they arrived in Jefferson City, they spent some time at a cafe drinking 3.2 beer since the students were not required to check into the University until midnight. On the return trip to Kansas City, the occupants of the GTO Pontiac were the defendants Greer and Cobb, Herbert Horton, and Courtney Bell who was referred to as a sixteen-year old girl.

According to the testimony of Cobb and Greer, Horton was driving the GTO, Greer was on the right side of the front seat, and Cobb and the girl were in the rear seat. Cobb testified that he did not know what time they left Jefferson City, that he went to sleep shortly thereafter and was aware of nothing that happened until he was awakened by lights of the patrol car flashing on the stalled GTO in Sedalia and Horton saying that everybody must get out.

Greer testified that he, too fell asleep on the return trip but that Horton awakened him in Sedalia and told him he was going to look for a girl he knew there. Greer went back to sleep and after an hour or two Horton again awakened him and asked for money to get sandwiches and coffee. They were at a filling station and Greer went in and relieved himself, returned to the car, again fell asleep, and the next time he woke up was when the officers told him to get out of the car. Greer denied that he was the driver of the Pontiac and testified that the car belonged to a friend of Horton's but the testimony as to ownership was quite vague and uncertain.

The defendant Cobb testified that he was twenty-seven years old at the time of the trial. It is not a vital factor in the case, but there is some indication in the record that Horton and the girl as well as Greer, were under seventeen when the crime was committed.

The appellant contends that the state failed to prove that he burglarized the store or that he aided or abetted or associated himself with the venture in any way and, therefore, the verdict and judgment are contrary to the evidence and against the greater weight of the credible evidence. He relies mainly on State v. Irby, Mo., 423 S.W.2d 800, for the proposition that something more than mere presence at the scene of the crime must be shown in order to convict; on State v. Castaldi, Mo., 386 S.W.2d 392, for the proposition that evidence that the accused had an opportunity to commit a crime or which merely raises a suspicion or gives rise to conjecture is insufficient to support a judgment of conviction; and on State v. Butler, Mo., 310 S.W.2d 952, for the proposition that some form of affirmative participation must be shown. These rules are well recognized but more than mere presence and an opportunity to commit the crime are involved in this case.

The presence of the accused at the place of the commission of a criminal offense may be considered along with other incriminating evidence to determine if the total circumstances raise a reasonable inference that the accused was a participant or an aider or abettor in the crime. * * * Evidence fairly showing any form of affirmative participation in a crime is sufficient to support a conviction. * * * Even in cases where the evidence is wholly circumstantial, the evidence tending to support the verdict must be considered as true, contrary evidence must be disregarded, and every reasonable inference in support of the verdict must be indulged. * * * For present purposes we must disregard entirely the testimony of Cobb and Greer that Cobb was asleep at the time the burglary and stealing occurred.

* * *

An inference of guilt is permissible from the unexplained possession of property recently stolen in a burglary and the inference exists both as to the offense of burglary and of stealing. * * * However, the jury determines the credibility of the defendant's explanation of his possession of the stolen property, and even though such explanation was not impeached, the jury was entitled to disbelieve it and draw an inference unfavorable to him based on his possession. * * * Quite understandably, the jury did not believe the defendant's story that he slept through the din that must have attended the breaking of the large window of the drug store with a 10-pound metal milk carrier approximately 20 feet from the automobile, the disturbance of depositing the stolen drugs in the rear portion of the two-door GTO Pontiac, and the unusual movements of rapid acceleration, fishtailing and skidding of the car. We hold that the evidence was sufficient to make a case for the jury and it supports the verdict returned.

* * *

DONNELLY, Judge (dissenting).

I would apply the following rules to the facts in this case:

(1) A recent, unexplained, and exclusive possession of stolen property will support an inference of the guilt of the possessor.

(2) To "create an inference of guilt, the term 'exclusive' does not mean that the possession must be separate from all others * * *." State v. Oliver, 355 Mo. 173, 176, 195 S.W.2d 484, 486.

(3) However, in situations where joint possession is claimed, there must be *other* evidence to connect defendant with the offense. State v. Oliver, supra; State v. Crawford, 59 Utah 39, 201 P. 1030.

In my opinion, the "other evidence" adduced in this case is not sufficient to show defendant *participated in the burglary.*

I respectfully dissent.

SEILER, J., concurs.

NOTES

1. Was it ever made clear to the jury what extent of participation they must infer from the unexplained possession of the stolen goods in order to

find the defendant guilty? Suppose Cobb had not been asleep; would he be liable for the crimes? If neither the appellate court nor the trial court ever address themselves to the extent of participation necessary for a finding of guilt, can this failure be justified by the existence of the permissible inference of guilt from possession of the stolen items?

2. To what extent—or under what circumstances—may a passenger in an automobile involved in a fatal accident be liable for the death of the victim on the theory that he aided and abetted the driver? See, e. g., Flippen v. State, 211 Tenn. 507, 365 S.W.2d 895 (1963).

3. Is there any helpful way to describe in general terms what nature of activity related to an offense committed by another will give rise to liability for aiding and abetting? Is the matter one of describing the acts of the potential aider and abettor, or is it one of describing the requisite impact (or likely impact) upon the principal? Consider Perkins, Parties to Crime, 89 U.Pa.L.Rev. 581, 598 (1941), who makes the following comment concerning the encouragement necessary for liability as a principal in the second degree: "Guilt or innocence of the abettor * * * is not determined by the quantum of his advice or encouragement. If it is rendered to induce another to commit the crime and actually has this effect, no more is required." Cf. Commonwealth v. Pierce, 437 Pa. 266, 263 A.2d 350 (1970). Is it accurate to say that there is guilt as an aider and abettor if one, with the requisite state of mind, does any act within the meaning of the general principle that an act is required for criminal liability, or fails to act under circumstances making that failure sufficient for liability under general principles, and there is a resulting significant impact upon the principal in the commission of the crime? Must some impact, (i. e., a "result" factually and proximately caused by the alleged aider and abettor) be proved, or is it sufficient that the accused's act would generally tend to cause such an impact?

STATE v. SPILLMAN

Supreme Court of Arizona, 1970.
105 Ariz. 523, 468 P.2d 376.

HAYS, Justice. Defendant Erich Spillman was charged by information with two counts of forcible rape of Marguerite Basko. Count II of the complaint alleged that defendant raped Margie Basko * * * and Count I charged that defendant aided and abetted another rape of Miss Basko by one Gilbert Felix * * *. Trial on both charges was held in the Maricopa County Superior Court, at which the jury returned a verdict of guilty to Count I. The jury was unable to reach a verdict on Count II. The trial court sentenced defendant to a term of not less than five nor more than seven years at the Arizona State Prison. Defendant appeals from this conviction and sentence.

* * *

The information filed against Gilbert Felix was identical to that filed against defendant, that is, Count II of rape and Count I of aiding and abetting a rape. Felix was tried separately from and subsequent to defendant. At the time of Felix' trial, Count I, the aiding and abetting charge was dropped, and the jury subsequently found Felix not guilty of rape. In this appeal, defendant Spillman contends that his conviction of aiding and abetting Felix' rape cannot stand for the reason that Felix, the actual perpetrator of the alleged rape, was acquitted. The argument is made that where, as here, there is no question as to the identity of the party allegedly committing the forcible rape, the acquittal of the principal establishes that no forcible rape took place at all, thus invalidating the conviction for aiding and abetting. We do not agree.

* * *

Aiding and abetting is an independent and distinct substantive offense, and it is not necessary to try and convict the perpetrator of a criminal act before an aider and abettor can be tried. * * * But where a principal has been acquitted of a criminal act, can his accomplice, in a separate trial, be convicted of aiding and abetting that criminal act? We hold that he can.

The State is never required to prove more than the allegations contained in an information in order to sustain the conviction of an aider and abettor. Where, as here, a principal and an aider and abettor are jointly charged in the same information, and the aider and abettor is tried first, there can be no truthful allegation that the principal has been convicted of the crime. What is required at the trial of the aider and abettor is proof, complete and convincing, of the guilt of the principal. Justice demands that the principal crime be fully proved, since the guilt of the aider and abettor depends upon the commission of the principal crime. Thus, whether or not the principal is convicted or acquitted in a separate trial can have no bearing on the trial of the aider and abettor, if the evidence shows the latter guilty. Society is no less injured by the illegal acts of the aider and abettor even though the principal himself escapes conviction. In order to convict an aider and abettor, justice demands no more than the information properly charge and the evidence convincingly show that a crime was committed by the principal. * * * We hold that defendant's conviction * * * was not made invalid by the fact that Gilbert Felix was later acquitted of rape.

* * *

[The conviction was reversed on the grounds that the evidence as to defendant's complicity was insufficient.]

NOTE

Compare United States v. Prince, 430 F.2d 1324 (4th Cir. 1970), reversing a conviction for aiding and abetting a hunting companion in taking a rail bird from a boat powered by a motor in violation of federal law on the ground that while the appeal was pending the companion was tried as a principal and acquitted. What arguments can be made for the result in *Prince*? Is the acquittal of the principal logically inconsistent with the guilt of the aider and abettor? Does not the verdict in the principal's trial simply establish that on this occasion the prosecution failed to meet its especially high burden of proof of the principal's guilt, a determination in no way conclusive as to the actual guilt of the principal? What policy would be served by granting an alleged aider and abettor the "windfall" of acquittal?

---

b. THE STATE OF MIND NECESSARY

WYATT v. UNITED STATES

United States Court of Appeals, Tenth Circuit, 1968.
388 F.2d 395.

HILL, Circuit Judge. * * * [A]ppellant Chandler attacks the sufficiency of the evidence to sustain his conviction * * * [of] aiding and abetting in the sale of non-tax-paid liquor to Agent Carpenter * * *.

Carpenter, an undercover agent and the Government's witness, testified that on August 14 he went to "Sonny Boy's" place in Guthrie, Oklahoma, and there he contacted Sonny Boy and asked him if he could buy some whiskey. Sonny Boy, not having any whiskey, directed him to go see Quinnon Chandler. Carpenter testified that he did go to the residence of Quinnon Chandler. Further: "When I arrived, I walked up to the front door and knocked and was invited into the house. Inside the house I observed Chester Chandler and Quinnon Chandler, they said they were glad to see me and told me to come out in the garage and see what they had. I walked out into the garage with Quinnon Chandler and Chester Chandler and observed seventeen and one-half gallons of moonshine whiskey inside the garage. After a brief conversation, I agreed to purchase six gallons of whiskey that night. After the agreement was made, Quinnon Chandler took two gallons, Chester Chandler took the four gallons in the case and placed them in the front of my vehicle, which was a Corvair with a trunk in the front. After the six gallons of whiskey was placed in the, in my vehicle, I asked Quinnon Chandler how much I owed him for the six gallons of whiskey, and he replied $36.00. I then paid Quinnon Chandler $36.00 for the six gallons of non-tax-paid whiskey, non-tax paid spirits." To be guilty of the crime of "aiding and abetting" one does not have to have an active stake in the outcome of the crime but merely participate therein. * * * Clearly and without any doubt, appellant Chandler participated here to the extent of helping his brother carry the illegally sold alcohol to the purchaser's car.

* * *

Affirmed.

STATE v. GLADSTONE

Supreme Court of Washington, 1970.
78 Wash.2d 306, 474 P.2d 274.

HALE, Justice. A jury found defendant Bruce Gladstone guilty of aiding and abetting one Robert Kent in the unlawful sale of marijuana. Deferring imposition of sentence, the court placed defendant on probation. He appeals * * * contending that the evidence as a matter of law was insufficient to sustain a verdict of guilty. His point, we think, is well taken.

* * *

Gladstone's guilt as an aider and abettor in this case rests solely on evidence of a conversation between him and one Douglas MacArthur Thompson concerning the possible purchase of marijuana from one Robert Kent. There is no other evidence to connect the accused with Kent who ultimately sold some marijuana to Thompson.

* * *

The conversation between defendant and Thompson occurred at defendant's residence. Douglas MacArthur Thompson, a 25-year-old student at the University of Puget Sound in Tacoma and an employee of the Internal Revenue Service of the United States, had done some investigative work for the government. From time to time, the Tacoma Police Department engaged him to investigate the use, possession and sale of narcotics, principally marijuana, among college students. When working for the Tacoma Police Department, he operated under the control and direction of the department's narcotics detail.

Thompson testified that Lieutenant Seymour and Detective Gallwas of the narcotics detail asked him to attempt a purchase of marijuana from Gladstone. During the evening of April 10, 1967—between 10 and 11 o'clock—the two officers and Thompson drove in a police car to the vicinity of defendant's apartment. Thompson went to Gladstone's door alone, beyond the hearing and out of the sight of the two officers. He knocked at the door and Gladstone responded. Thompson asked Gladstone if he would sell him some marijuana. Describing this incident, Thompson testified as follows:

Well, I asked—at the time Gladstone told me that he was—he did not have enough marijuana on hand to sell me any, but he did know an individual who had quite a sufficient quantity and that was very willing to sell and he named the individual as Robert Kent, or Bob Kent as he put it, and he gave me directions to the residence and he—due to the directions I asked him if, you know, if he could draw me a map and he did.

When Thompson said he asked Gladstone to draw the map for him, he added, "I'm not sure whether he did give me the exact address or not, he told me where the residence was." He said that Gladstone then with pencil and paper sketched the location of Kent's place of residence. Thompson had no prior knowledge of where Kent lived, and did not know if he might have marijuana or that he had ever possessed it.

The two officers then took Thompson to Kent's residence where marijuana was purchased. The actual purchase was made by Thompson directly from Kent while Officer Gallwas and Lieutenant Seymour stayed in the police car. Kent was subsequently arrested and convicted of selling Thompson approximately 8 ounces of marijuana—the very sale which defendant here was convicted of aiding and abetting.

That ended the prosecution's case. Even if it were accorded all favorable inferences, there appears at this point a gap in the evidence which we feel as a matter of law is fatal to the prosecution's cause. Neither on direct examination nor under cross-examination did Thompson testify that he knew of any prior conduct, arrangements or communications between Gladstone and Kent from which it could be even remotely inferred that the defendant had any understanding, agreement, purpose, intention or design to participate or engage in or aid or abet any sale of marijuana by Kent. Other than to obtain a simple map from Gladstone and to say that Gladstone told him Kent might have some marijuana available, Thompson did not even establish that Kent and the defendant were acquainted with each other. Testimony of the brief conversation and Gladstone's very crude drawing consisting of 8 penciled lines indicating where Kent lived constitute the whole proof of the aiding and abetting presented.

* * *

If all reasonable inferences favorable to the state are accorded the evidence, it does not, in our opinion, establish the commission of the crime charged. That vital element—a nexus between the accused and the party whom he is charged with aiding and abetting in the commission of a crime—is missing. The record contains no evidence whatever that Gladstone had any communication by word, gesture or sign, before or after he drew the map, from which it could be inferred that he counseled, encouraged, hired, commanded, induced or procured Kent to sell marijuana to Douglas Thompson as charged, or took any steps to further the commission of the crime charged. He was not charged with aiding and abetting Thompson in the purchase of marijuana, but with Kent's sale of it.

* * *

[E]ven without prior agreement, arrangement or understanding, a bystander to a robbery could be guilty of aiding and abetting its commission if he came to the aid of a robber and knowingly assisted him in perpetrating the crime. But regardless of the modus operandi and with or without a conspiracy or agreement to commit the crime and whether present or away from the scene of it, there is no aiding and abetting unless one " 'in some sort associate himself with the venture, that he participate in it as in something that he wishes to bring about, that he seek by his action to make it succeed.' " Nye & Nissen v. United States, 336 U.S. 613, 619, 69 S.Ct. 766, 769, 93 L.Ed. 919 (1949).

Although an aider and abettor need not be physically present at the commission of the crime to be held guilty as a principal, his conviction depends on proof that he did something in association or connection with the principal to accomplish the crime. Learned Hand, J., we think, hit the nail squarely when, in United States v. Peoni, 100 F.2d 401, 402 (2d Cir. 1938), he wrote that, in order to aid and abet another to commit a crime, it is necessary that a defendant

> in some sort associate himself with the venture, that he participate in it as in something that he wishes to bring about, that he seek by his action to make it succeed. All the words used—even the most colorless, "abet"—carry an implication of purposive attitude towards it.

*   *   *

Another case—and one nearly identical with the instant case—affirms the foregoing principles. In Morei v. United States, 127 F.2d 827 (6th Cir. 1942), undercover narcotic agents approached the defendant, a physician, and asked him to sell them narcotics. The doctor told the agents he had none, but gave the agents the name of another party and advised the agent to tell the latter that the doctor had sent him. The doctor added that "he will take care of you." The agents did arrange a purchase of illegal narcotics from the person to whom the doctor had referred them, and the doctor was thereupon charged with aiding and abetting in the sale.

After tracing the common-law distinction between a principal in the second degree and an accessory before the fact and pointing out that an aider and abettor must at least procure, counsel or command another to commit the felony actually committed, the court said, at 830:

> It is not necessary that there should be any direct communication between an accessory before the fact and the principal felon; it is enough if the accessory direct an intermediate agent to procure another to commit the felony, without naming or knowing of the person to be procured. *A person is not an accessory before the fact, unless there is some sort of active proceeding on his part; he must incite, or procure, or encourage the criminal act, or assist or enable it to be done, or engage or counsel, or command the principal to do it.* Halsbury, supra, § 531. [9 Halsbury, Laws of England § 531 (1909)]. *   *   *
>
> *   *   * It is not to be assumed that Congress, in defining as a principal, one who "procures the commission of

an offense," and using almost the identical language by which the common law defined aiders, abettors, and accessories, was providing for a new crime theretofore unknown. If the criterion for holding that one is guilty of procuring the commission of an offense, is that the offense would not have been committed except for such a person's conduct or revelation of information, it would open a vast field of offenses that have never been comprehended within the common law by aiding, abetting, inducing or procuring. * * *

* * * [T]he only thing Dr. Platt did was to give Beach the name of Morei as a man from whom he might secure heroin to dose horses in order to stimulate them in racing. This is not the purposive association with the venture that, under the evidence in this case, brings Dr. Platt within the compass of the crime of selling or purchasing narcotics, either as principal, aider and abettor, or accessory before the fact. (Italics ours.)

* * *

It would be a dangerous precedent indeed to hold that mere communications to the effect that another might or probably would commit a criminal offense amount to an aiding and abetting of the offense should it ultimately be committed.

There being no evidence whatever that the defendant ever communicated to Kent the idea that he would in any way aid him in the sale of any marijuana, or said anything to Kent to encourage or induce him or direct him to do so, or counseled Kent in the sale of marijuana, or did anything more than describe Kent to another person as an individual who might sell some marijuana, or would derive any benefit, consideration or reward from such a sale, there was no proof of an aiding and abetting, and the conviction should, therefore, be reversed as a matter of law. Remanded with directions to dismiss.

HAMILTON, Justice (dissenting).

* * *

The statutory language and the overt action it contemplates does * * * give rise to the requirement that the aider or abettor entertain a conscious intent, i. e., knowledge and intent that his action will instigate, induce, procure or encourage perpetration of the primary crime. * * *

The question to be resolved, then, in the instant case is whether the evidence sustains the jury's conclusion that the appellant entertained the requisite intent to render him culpable as an aider or abettor.

* * *

Although the evidence in the case is conflicting, the jury was entitled to believe * * * that prior to the evening of April 10, 1967, when Thompson talked to appellant, *Thompson and the Tacoma Police Department were unaware of Kent or his association with marijuana;* * * * *that Thompson approached Kent and told him "Gladstone had sent me" whereupon Kent invited him to a room and sold him some marijuana for $30 * * *.*

Based upon the * * * inferences reasonably derivable therefrom, I am satisfied that the jury was fully warranted in concluding that appellant, when he affirmatively recommended Kent as a source and purveyor of marijuana, entertained the requisite conscious design and intent that his action would instigate, induce, procure or encourage perpetration of Kent's subsequent crime of selling marijuana to Thompson. Furthermore, insofar as an element of preconcert be concerned, certainly the readiness with which the passwords, "Gladstone had sent me," gained a stranger's late evening entree to Kent's domain and produced two illegal sales strongly suggests, if not conclusively establishes, the missing communal nexus which the majority belabors.

NOTE

Perkins, Parties to Crime, 89 U.Pa.L.Rev. 581, 603–04 (1941), in discussing the liability as an accessory before the fact of one conducting a lawful business who becomes aware that one purchasing his wares or services intends to use them in the commission of a crime, concludes as follows: "[T]he gravity of the social harm resulting from the unlawful conduct is used to determine whether mere knowledge of the intended use will be sufficient * * *. A seller who completes the sale of goods after correctly divining that the purchaser is buying them as an agent of an armed combination attempting to overthrow the government, thereby 'voluntarily aids the treason'. * * * But the mere knowledge of one party to transaction that the other intends later to make an unlawful use of the property will not of itself be sufficient * * * if [the offense] is of a relatively minor nature. * * * It is otherwise, even as to such an offense, if the one charged as an inciter has not only had knowledge of the intended offense but has gone out of his way to promote it, as by packing the goods sold in an unusual manner to conceal their identity." How can such a position be defended on policy grounds?

---

c. RENUNCIATION OR WITHDRAWAL

COMMONWEALTH v. HUBER

Court of Quarter Sessions, Montgomery County, Pennsylvania, 1958.
15 D. & C.2d 726.

GROSHENS, J. Defendant was indicted * * * on the charge of accessory before the fact to robbery, and on * * * the charge of accessory after the fact to robbery.

At the trial before the Hon. Harold G. Knight, sitting without a jury, defendant was found guilty of accessory before the fact.

Defendant's motions for a new trial and in arrest of judgment are now before the court for disposition. In support of his motions, defendant contends in his brief: (a) That the Commonwealth failed to prove his guilt beyond a reasonable doubt, and (b) that defendant withdrew from any plan or scheme of robbery so as to make him not guilty as an accessory before the fact.

* * *

The happening of the robbery was not in dispute at the trial, as counsel for defendant admitted in open court that a robbery had taken place. The issue was narrowed down to defendant's connection with the robbery.

To prove defendant's implications the Commonwealth called the two police officers who investigated the case and one of the principals to the robbery. Both police officers testified defendant freely admitted to them three days after the robbery that he had furnished the rifle used in the robbery and the naptha type fluid used on the victim, that he knew a "hold-up" was planned, that he had been asked to accompany the principals which he refused to do, that defendant had gone to the police station on the night of the robbery where he learned that the robbery had taken place and that he went forthwith to the home of one of the principals to get his rifle back.

One of the three principals, Ernest Farr, testified that defendant knew of the plan and that defendant furnished the rifle and naptha (ether).

Defendant took the stand in his own defense and corroborated much of the Commonwealth's evidence. For example defendant testified concerning his rifle and his knowledge of its proposed use in a conversation with John Goodwin, one of the principals:

" 'Sure, you can borrow it,', and I asked him what he was going to do with it, and he said:

" 'I am going to rob somebody.' "

By the Court:

"Q. Going to what?

"A. He said he was going to rob somebody.

"Q. Rob somebody?

"A. That's it."

By Mr. Pearlstine:

"Q. And then what did you say to him about that?

"A. I just laughed right then, and then Landis, Dave Landis came in and I hadn't had a chance to talk to him again till we got down to my place.

"Q. Did Goodwin at that time say anything about you going with him or where they were going or anything like that or what they planned to?

"A. Yes, at that time he asked me to go along.

"Q. What did you say?

"A. I said no I had a date at first; and then he was persistent and it seemed like he wanted me to go and I says: *'No I ain't going to get involved in anything like that'* (Italics supplied)

"Q. Did you or not think he was serious at the time?

"A. No, I did not."

* * *

Certainly, the Commonwealth's evidence of aid given by this defendant, supported as it is by defendant's own testimony, amply supports the finding of guilt. The defense of withdrawal remains but to be considered.

The aid given by defendant to the principals in the perpetration of the robbery was supplying the rifle and the naptha type fluid which were indubitably used by the principals. To "aid" literally means to "help". A rifle, for instance, may be of great help to a robber. A pointed rifle is one of the oldest and most effective methods to cow a person into the quick and docile relinquishment of his wallet. Hence, a person who supplies an avowed robber with a rifle which is shortly thereafter used by the robber in a robbery may be said to have aided the robber.

The fact that this defendant was asked to participate in the robbery as a principal, and that he refused, does not constitute such a withdrawal as would relieve him of criminal liability as an accessory before the fact. Had this defendant demanded and received back his rifle, or had he reported the principals to the police in time to thwart the robbery, then he could be said to have withdrawn successfully. Having placed the rifle in the hands of John Goodwin who, according to defendant's own testimony, told defendant "he was going to rob somebody", defendant committed himself to a sequence of events from which he could only extricate himself by getting his rifle out of the hands of John Goodwin before the robbery, or by thwarting the robbery in some other way. The "aid" in this case was the rifle. Therefore, to effectively withdraw made it incumbent upon defendant to get the rifle out of the hands of John Goodwin, or the equivalent thereof. He did neither of these things. He did, however, go to the police station where he learned of the perpetration of the robbery. He then rushed posthaste to get his rifle, not to withdraw from the crime, but to get incriminating evidence out of the possession of a principal who was then the object of a police investigation.

* * *

[D]efendant's motions for a new trial and in arrest of judgment are dismissed, and defendant is ordered to appear for sentence at miscellaneous court on Friday, March 28, 1958.

NOTES

1.   Suppose Huber had sought Goodwin to get the rifle back, but was unable to find him despite thorough search?   Suppose he had retrieved the rifle because he learned of increased police surveillance of prime robbery targets, but the others nevertheless committed the robbery using a knife one of them already had?

2.   The Study Draft of the Proposed Federal Criminal Code (1970) contained this portion of § 401 which was left out of the final version

> (3) Affirmative Defense of Renunciation and Withdrawal.   It is an affirmative defense in a prosecution under subsection (1) that, under circumstances manifesting a voluntary and complete renunciation of his culpable intent, the defendant attempted to prevent the commission of the offense by taking affirmative steps which substantially reduced the likelihood of the commission thereof.   A renunciation is not "voluntary and complete" if it is motivated in whole or in part by (a) a belief that circumstances exist which increase the probability of detection or apprehension of the defendant or an accomplice or which make more difficult the consummation of the offense, or (b) a decision to postpone the offense until another time or to substitute another victim or another but similar objective.

Was this desirable?   How might it be justified?

There was no equivalent provision in § 1002, Criminal Facilitation. How could this be justified, if the above provision in § 401 was appropriate?

---

2.   LIABILITY FOR CONDUCT AFTER THE COMMISSION OF AN OFFENSE

---

18 UNITED STATES CODE

§ 3.   Accessory after the fact

Whoever, knowing that an offense against the United States has been committed, receives, relieves, comforts or assists the offender in order to hinder or prevent his apprehension, trial or punishment, is an accessory after the fact.

Except as otherwise expressly provided by any Act of Congress, an accessory after the fact shall be imprisoned not more than one-half the maximum term of imprisonment or fined not more than one-half the maximum fine prescribed for the punishment of the principal, or both; or if the principal is punishable by death, the accessory shall be imprisoned not more than ten years.

§ 4. Misprision of felony

Whoever, having knowledge of the actual commission of a felony cognizable by a court of the United States, conceals and does not as soon as possible make known the same to some judge or other person in civil or military authority under the United States, shall be fined not more than $500 or imprisoned not more than three years, or both.

UNITED STATES v. FOY

United States Court of Appeals for the Seventh Circuit, 1969.
416 F.2d 940.

KERNER, Circuit Judge.   Defendant was indicted for violation of 18 U.S.C.A. § 1071, harboring and concealing a person from arrest.   A jury found defendant guilty and from this conviction he appeals.

On October 19, 1967 an appeal bond of Bernard Francis Ryan was revoked and a bench warrant was issued for his arrest.   The next morning, F.B.I. agents drove to an apartment building in Chicago, Illinois in which a friend of Ryan's, Leona Phebus, lived.   Ryan was known to frequent her residence.   When the agents arrived, they saw Ryan's car outside.   Two agents entered the front of the building while two other agents entered through the rear.   Four minutes elapsed from the time the agents knocked on the door until Leona Phebus let them in.   In the apartment the agents met the defendant Foy.   Phebus and Foy were told that the agents had an arrest warrant for Ryan based on the revocation of his bond.   The agents also told them that if they failed to tell the whereabouts of Ryan they would be guilty of harboring and concealing a fugitive.   Both Foy and Phebus told the agents that they had not seen Ryan since the previous afternoon.   The agents were allowed to search the entire apartment but they could not find Ryan.   Two agents left to try another place but later called back to say that Ryan was not at the other place.   Then, one of the agents at the Phebus apartment found Ryan on a ledge outside the bedroom window.   He was ordered to come in and was arrested.   Phebus and Foy were both indicted for harboring and concealing Ryan.   Phebus pled guilty but refused to testify at the trial of Foy.   The court was asked to issue a writ of habeas corpus ad testificandum for production of Ryan but the court refused.

Since there was no evidence that Foy told Ryan to hide on the ledge, the essential question before the court is whether Foy's statement that he had not seen Ryan since the previous afternoon and did not know where he was, violated 18 U.S.C.A. § 1071.

18 U.S.C.A. § 1071 provides:

> Whoever harbors or conceals any person for whose arrest a warrant * * * has been issued under the provisions

of any law of the United States, so as to prevent his discovery and arrest, after notice or knowledge of the fact that a warrant * * * has been issued * * * shall be fined.
* * *

In United States v. Shapiro, 113 F.2d 891, 130 A.L.R. 147 (2nd Cir. 1940), the court having before it 18 U.S.C.A. § 246, the predecessor of § 1071, held that the words "harbor" and "conceal" must be construed narrowly, not to include all forms of assistance. "These are active verbs, which have the fugitive as their object." 113 F.2d at 892. The court concluded that weekly payments of $250 to the fugitive, the purpose of the payments being to allow him to evade arrest, did not come within the proscribed behavior. The court in United States v. Biami, 243 F.Supp. 917 (E.D.Wis.1965), held that the refusal to admit the police officers into the apartment where the fugitive was, constituted harboring and concealing under § 1071. Here, the agents were admitted into the apartment and were allowed to completely search it. There was no evidence that defendant took any action "to hide, secrete or keep out of sight" or "to lodge, to care for after secreting the offender" as the terms conceal and harbor are defined in United States v. Thornton, 178 F.Supp. 42, 43 (E.D.N.Y.1959). In *Thornton* the defendant left Denver, Colorado with the fugitive because FBI notices that the fugitive was wanted were posted in a Denver hotel, traveled with the fugitive to Brooklyn, New York and rented a room in his name for himself and the fugitive in Brooklyn. The court in United States v. Giampa, 290 F.2d 83 (2nd Cir. 1961), held that defendant's conduct in leasing an apartment in his name for the fugitive, shopping for food for the fugitive and refusing to let Federal narcotics agents into the apartment constituted a violation of § 1071. Here, the false statement of defendant that he did not know where Ryan was, without any further acts of concealment, did not impose a real barrier to the discovery of Ryan. While there are many negative or passive acts which would fall within the statutory prohibition, we do not think that a failure to disclose the location of a fugitive is the type of assistance contemplated by "harbor and conceal" as used in § 1071. The statute proscribes acts calculated to obstruct the efforts of the authorities to effect arrest of the fugitive, but it does not impose a duty on one who may be aware of the whereabouts of the fugitive, although having played no part in his flight, to reveal this information on pain of criminal prosecution.

The government relies heavily on Stamps v. United States, 387 F. 2d 993 (8th Cir. 1967), claiming that the facts are identical with those in the case before us. While in *Stamps* the court was not confronted with the issue of sufficiency of the evidence, the defendant, there, committed various acts calculated and determined to prevent the arrest of the fugitive: one, defendant refused to let officers in the apartment; two, after police had left, defendant removed the fugitive from the apartment and placed him in the apartment of a neighbor; and three, after the fugitive had left the building, defendant picked him up in a car and tried to drive away. We do not think the facts in *Stamps* lend any support to the government's argument in the case before us.

For the foregoing reasons we reverse.

Reversed.

KNOCH, Senior Circuit Judge (dissenting).

I am very reluctant to disagree with my colleagues; yet I believe that we should draw some distinction between mere mute refusal to assist the officers and deliberate misstatements of fact designed to mislead the police so as to prevent the fugitive's discovery and arrest. On the specific circumstances of this case, I would affirm.

NOTES

1. How, on policy grounds, might the interpretation of the words "harbor" and "conceal" used by the court in the instant case be defended? Would the result have been the same if there had been proof that Foy was aware of Ryan's guilt and Foy was charged as an accessory after the fact under 18 U.S.C.A. § 3? Cf. State v. Young, 7 Ohio App.2d 194, 220 N.E.2d 146 (1966). But contrast People v. Duty, 269 Cal.App.2d 97, 74 Cal.Rptr. 606 (1969); McClain v. State, 10 Md.App. 106, 268 A.2d 572 (1970). If he was charged with misprision of felony under 18 U.S.C.A. § 4? Should the words "receives" and assists" (in 18 U.S.C.A. § 3) and "conceals" (in 18 U.S.C.A. § 4) be interpreted in the same manner as "harbours" and "conceals" in 18 U.S.C.A. § 1071?

2. Goldberg, Misprision of Felony: An Old Concept in a New Context, 52 A.B.A.J. 148, 149–50 (1966):

> Unfortunately, the courts have interpreted "conceals" [in statutes making misprision of felony an offense, such as 18 U.S.C.A. § 4] as requiring a positive act, thus effectively emasculating the statute by merging it into the general accessory provisions of the law. The history of misprision of felony strongly suggests that this interpretation is erroneous. The Supreme Court of Vermont in 1907 defined the offense in its traditional sense:
>
>> Misprision of felony is * * * a criminal neglect either to prevent a felony from being committed or to bring the offender to justice after its commission, but without such previous concert with or subsequent assistance of him as will make the concealer an accessory before or after the fact.[17]
>
> Thus defined, misprision of felony would be a very salutary influence in our distressed society. If limited by its terms to serious crimes, perhaps only serious crimes against the person, few injustices are likely to result. Then Chief Justice Marshall's concern that "It may be the duty of a citizen to accuse every offender, and

17. Vermont v. Wilson [67 Atl. 553,] 533 [(1907)].

to proclaim every offence which comes to his knowledge; but the law which would punish him in every case for not performing this duty is too harsh for man" [19] need not deter legislators from passing a much-needed law. In the case which elicited Marshall's compassion, the defendant had advanced money to his son-in-law in an attempt to save him from the consequences of forgery. The law which would punish such behavior and even require a man to report his family's peculations to the police *is* too harsh. Restricting the operation of the law to serious crimes (and perhaps exempting certain degrees of consanguinity) ought to remove this objection.

Exceptions must also be made for conflicting legal duties. A lawyer is legally obliged not to divulge information confidentially revealed to him by his client regarding a committed felony. Nor may a doctor broadcast his patient's confidential communications, nor a clergyman his parishioner's. Misprision of felony statutes must allow for these obligations to be respected without fear of lawbreaking.

It may finally be objected that a legal duty to report criminal acts to the authorities would be so novel in most American jurisdictions that even responsible citizens would unavoidably break the law. But all Americans are familiar with their legal duty to report serious traffic accidents to the police. It is about time we consider violent assault on persons as important as automobile crashes.

3. The tendency in recent legislative revision has been to replace accessory-after-the-fact statutes and misprision crimes with offenses defined in terms of interfering with law enforcement activity. Consider the extent to which the following sections of the Proposed Federal Criminal Code adequately serve the purposes which ought to be served:

§ 1303. Hindering Law Enforcement

(1) Offense. A person is guilty of hindering law enforcement if he intentionally interferes with, hinders, delays or prevents the discovery, apprehension, prosecution, conviction or punishment of another for an offense by:

(a) harboring or concealing the other;

(b) providing the other with a weapon, money, transportation, disguise or other means of avoiding discovery or apprehension;

(c) concealing, altering, mutilating or destroying a document or thing, regardless of its admissibility in evidence; or

(d) warning the other of impending discovery or apprehension other than in connection with an effort to bring another into compliance with the law.

(2) Grading. Hindering law enforcement is a Class C felony if the actor:

(a) knows of the conduct of the other and such conduct constitutes a Class A or Class B felony; or

19. Marbury v. Brooks, 7 Wheat. 556, 575–76 (1822).

(b) knows that the other has been charged with or convicted of a crime and such crime is a Class A or Class B felony.

Otherwise hindering law enforcement is a Class A misdemeanor.

§ 1304. Aiding Consummation of Crime

(1) Offense. A person is guilty of aiding consummation of crime if he intentionally aids another to secrete, disguise, or convert the proceeds of a crime or otherwise profit from a crime.

(2) Grading. Aiding consummation of a crime:

(a) is a Class C felony if the actor knows of the conduct of the other and such conduct constitutes a Class A or Class B felony; and

(b) is a Class A misdemeanor if the actor knows of the conduct of the other and such conduct constitutes a Class C felony or a Class A misdemeanor.

Otherwise aiding consummation of a crime is a Class B misdemeanor.

§ 1353. False Reports to Security Officials

(1) Offense. A person is guilty of a Class B misdemeanor if he:

(a) gives false information to a law enforcement officer with intent to falsely implicate another; or

(b) falsely reports to a law enforcement officer or other security official the occurrence of a crime of violence or other incident calling for an emergency response when he knows that the incident did not occur. "Security official" means fireman or other public servant responsible for averting or dealing with emergencies involving public safety.

The comment to the Proposed Draft of Section 1353 contained the following:

A significant issue * * * is whether there should be criminal sanctions at all for false reports to officials other than the type dealt with in subsection (1)(b), in view of the dangers presented in making criminal the conduct of persons who thoughtlessly make reports and in view of the potential of official abuse. These dangers might be lessened if the prohibition were limited to written (or even signed) statements, if it is required that notice of the statute be given to a reporting individual, and if distinctions were made among kinds of investigators in order to avoid application of the section to a casual street encounter. The potential for official abuse could also be lessened by requiring corroboration of the falsity of the statement and of the fact the statement was made.

E.   OTHER ASPECTS OF LIABILITY FOR THE ACTS OF ANOTHER

1.   VICARIOUS LIABILITY

COMMONWEALTH v. KOCZWARA

Supreme Court of Pennsylvania, 1959.
397 Pa. 575, 155 A.2d 825, certiorari denied 363 U.S. 848,
80 S.Ct. 1624, 4 L.Ed.2d 1731.

COHEN, Justice.   This is an appeal from the judgment of the Court of Quarter Sessions of Lackawanna County sentencing the defendant to three months in the Lackawanna County Jail, a fine of five hundred dollars and the costs of prosecution, in a case involving violations of the Pennsylvania Liquor Code.

John Koczwara, the defendant, is the licensee and operator of an establishment on Jackson Street in the City of Scranton known as J. K.'s Tavern.   At that place he had a restaurant liquor license issued by the Pennsylvania Liquor Control Board.   The Lackawanna County Grand Jury indicted the defendant on five counts for violations of the Liquor Code.   The first and second counts averred that the defendant permitted minors, unaccompanied by parents, guardians or other supervisors, to frequent the tavern on February 1st and 8th, 1958; the third count charged the defendant with selling beer to minors on February 8th, 1958; the fourth charged the defendant with permitting beer to be sold to minors on February 8th, 1958,   *   *   *.

At the conclusion of the Commonwealth's evidence, count three of the indictment, charging the sale by the defendant personally to the minors, was removed from the jury's consideration by the trial judge on the ground that there was no evidence that the defendant had personally participated in the sale or was present in the tavern when sales to the minors took place.   Defense counsel then demurred to the evidence as to the other three counts.   The demurrer was overruled.   Defendant thereupon rested without introducing any evidence and moved for a directed verdict of acquittal.   The motion was denied, the case went to the jury and the jury returned a verdict of guilty as to each of the remaining three counts: two counts of permitting minors to frequent the licensed premises without parental or other supervision, and the count of permitting sales to minors.

Upon the conclusion of the trial, defendant filed a motion in arrest of judgment.   After argument before the court *en banc*, the motion was overruled by Judge Hoban, who sentenced the defendant to pay the costs of prosecution, a fine of five hundred dollars and to undergo imprisonment in the Lackawanna County Jail for three months.

* * *

Defendant raises two contentions, both of which, in effect, question whether the undisputed facts of this case support the judgment and sentence imposed by the Quarter Sessions Court. Judge Hoban found as fact that "in every instance the purchase [by minors] was made from a bartender, not identified by name, and service to the boys was made by the bartender. There was *no* evidence that the defendant was present on any one of the occasions testified to by these witnesses, nor that he had any personal knowledge of the sales to them or to other persons on the premises." We, therefore, must determine the criminal responsibility of a licensee of the Liquor Control Board for acts committed by his employees upon his premises, without his personal knowledge, participation, or presence, which acts violate a valid regulatory statute passed under the Commonwealth's police power.

While an employer in almost all cases is not criminally responsible for the unlawful acts of his employees, unless he consents to, approves, or participates in such acts, courts all over the nation have struggled for years in applying this rule within the framework of "controlling the sale of intoxicating liquor." See Annotation, 139 A.L.R. 306 (1942). At common law, any attempt to invoke the doctrine of *respondeat superior* in a criminal case would have run afoul of our deeply ingrained notions of criminal jurisprudence that guilt must be personal and individual.[1] In recent decades, however, many states have enacted detailed regulatory provisions in fields which are essentially noncriminal, e. g., pure food and drug acts, speeding ordinances, building regulations, and child labor, minimum wage and maximum hour legislation. Such statutes are generally enforceable by light penalties, and although violations are labelled crimes, the considerations applicable to them are totally different from those applicable to true crimes, which involve moral delinquency and which are punishable by imprisonment or another serious penalty. Such so-called statutory crimes are in reality an attempt to utilize the machinery of criminal administration as an enforcing arm for social regulations of a purely civil nature, with the punishment totally unrelated to questions of moral wrongdoing or guilt. It is here that the social interest in the

---

1. The distinction between *respondeat superior* in tort law and its application to the criminal law is obvious. In tort law, the doctrine is employed for the purpose of settling the incidence of loss upon the party who can best bear such loss. But the criminal law is supported by totally different concepts. We impose penal treatment upon those who injure or menace social interests, partly in order to reform, partly to prevent the continuation of the anti-social activity and partly to deter others. If a defendant has personally lived up to the social standards of the criminal law and has not menaced or injured anyone, why impose penal treatment?

general well-being and security of the populace has been held to outweigh the individual interest of the particular defendant. The penalty is imposed despite the defendant's lack of a criminal intent or mens rea.

Not the least of the legitimate police power areas of the legislature is the control of intoxicating liquor. As Mr. Justice B. R. Jones recently stated in In re Tahiti Bar, Inc., 1959, 395 Pa. 355, 360, 150 A.2d 112, 115, "There is perhaps no other area of permissible state action within which the exercise of the police power of a state is more plenary than in the regulation and control of the use and sale of alcoholic beverages." It is abundantly clear that the conduct of the liquor business is lawful only to the extent and manner permitted by statute. Individuals who embark on such an enterprise do so with knowledge of considerable peril, since their actions are rigidly circumscribed by the Liquor Code.

Because of the peculiar nature of this business, one who applies for and receives permission from the Commonwealth to carry on the liquor trade assumes the highest degree of responsibility to his fellow citizens. As the licensee of the Board, he is under a duty not only to regulate his own personal conduct in a manner consistent with the permit he has received, but also to control the acts and conduct of any employee to whom he entrusts the sale of liquor. Such fealty is the *quid pro quo* which the Commonwealth demands in return for the privilege of entering the highly restricted and, what is more important, the highly *dangerous* business of selling intoxicating liquor.

In the instant case, the defendant has sought to surround himself with all the safeguards provided to those within the pale of criminal sanctions. He has argued that a statute imposing criminal responsibility should be construed strictly, with all doubts resolved in his favor. While the defendant's position is entirely correct, we must remember that we are dealing with a statutory crime within the state's plenary police power. In the field of liquor regulation, the legislature has enacted a comprehensive Code aimed at regulating and controlling the use and sale of alcoholic beverages. The question here raised is whether the legislature *intended* to impose vicarious criminal liability on the licensee-principal for acts committed on his premises without his presence, participation or knowledge.

This Court has stated, as long ago as Commonwealth v. Weiss, 1891, 139 Pa. 247, 251, 21 A. 10, 11 L.R.A. 530, that "whether a criminal intent, or a guilty knowledge, is a necessary ingredient of a statutory offense * * * is a matter of construction. It is for the legislature to determine whether the public injury, threatened in any particular matter, is such, and so great as to justify an absolute and indiscriminate prohibition." * * *

In the Liquor Code, Section 493, the legislature has set forth twenty-five specific acts which are condemned as unlawful, and for which penalties are provided in Section 494. Subsections (1) and (14) of Section 493 contain the two offenses charged here. In neither of these subsections is there any language which would require the prohibited acts to have been done either knowingly, wilfully or intentionally, there being a significant absence of such words as "knowingly, wilfully, etc." That the legislature intended such a requirement in other related sections of the same Code is shown by examining Section 492(15), wherein it is made unlawful to *knowingly* sell any malt beverages to a person engaged in the business of illegally selling such beverages. The omission of any such word in the subsections of Section 494 is highly significant. It indicates a legislative intent to eliminate both knowledge and criminal intent as necessary ingredients of such offenses. To bolster this conclusion, we refer back to Section 491 wherein the Code states, "It shall be unlawful (1) For any person, by himself *or by an employe or agent*, to expose or keep for sale, or directly or *indirectly* * * * to sell or offer to sell any liquor within this Commonwealth, except in accordance with the provisions of this act and the regulations of the board." The Superior Court has long placed such an interpretation on the statute. Commonwealth v. Speer, 1945, 157 Pa.Super. 197, 42 A.2d 94.[4]

As the defendant has pointed out, there is a distinction between the requirement of a mens rea and the imposition of vicarious absolute liability for the acts of another. It may be that the courts below, in relying on prior authority, have failed to make such a distinction.[5] In any case, we fully recognize it.[6] Moreover, we find that the intent of the legislature in enacting this Code was not only to eliminate the common law requirement of a mens rea, but also to place a very high degree of responsibility upon the holder of a liquor license to make certain that neither he nor anyone in his employ commit any of the prohibited acts upon the licensed premises. Such a burden of care is imposed upon the licensee in order to protect the public from the

4. It is established that a liquor license may be legally suspended or revoked for violations of the Code committed by employees of the licensee even though there is no evidence that the licensee knew of such violations. McGrath v. Pennsylvania Liquor Control Board, 1958, 185 Pa.Super. 187, 137 A.2d 812; Southern Outing Club of Pittsburgh Liquor License Case, 1950, 166 Pa.Super. 555, 72 A.2d 600.

5. We must also be extremely careful to distinguish the present situation from the question of *corporate* criminal liability, such as was involved in Commonwealth v. Liberty Products Company, 1925, 84 Pa.Super. 473. For a penetrating inquiry into this latter subject, see Mens Rea And The Corporation, 19 U.Pitt.L.Rev. 21 (1957).

6. For an extremely interesting and incisive analysis of the mens rea requirement in criminal offenses, see Mueller, On Common Law Mens Rea, 42 Minn.L.Rev. 1043 (1958). While we sympathize fully with the author's eloquent plea for a return to the moral implications of criminal guilt, we await further determinations by the Supreme Court of the United States as to whether the rationale of Lambert v. People of State of California, 1957, 355 U.S. 225, 78 S.Ct. 240, 2 L.Ed.2d 228, will be extended to all statutory offenses which have been interpreted as not requiring a criminal mens rea. See also Allen, Book Review, 66 Yale L.J. 1120 (1957); Mueller, Mens Rea And The Law Without It, 58 W.Va. L.Rev. 34 (1955).

potentially noxious effects of an inherently dangerous business. We, of course, express no opinion as to the *wisdom* of the legislature's imposing vicarious responsibility under certain sections of the Liquor Code. There may or may not be an economic-sociological justification for such liability on a theory of deterrence. Such determination is for the legislature to make, so long as the constitutional requirements are met.

Can the legislature, consistent with the requirements of due process, thus establish absolute criminal liability? Were this the defendant's first violation of the Code, and the penalty solely a minor fine of from $100–$300, we would have no hesitation in upholding such a judgment. Defendant, by accepting a liquor license, must bear this financial risk. Because of a prior conviction for violations of the Code, however, the trial judge felt compelled under the mandatory language of the statute, Section 494(a), to impose not only an increased fine of five hundred dollars, but also a three month sentence of imprisonment. Such sentence of imprisonment in a case where liability is imposed vicariously cannot be sanctioned by this Court consistently with the law of the land clause of Section 9, Article I of the Constitution of the Commonwealth of Pennsylvania., P.S.[7]

The Courts of the Commonwealth have already strained to permit the legislature to carry over the civil doctrine of *respondeat superior* and to apply it as a means of enforcing the regulatory scheme that covers the liquor trade. We have done so on the theory that the Code established petty misdemeanors involving only light monetary fines. It would be unthinkable to impose vicarious criminal responsibility in cases involving true crimes. Although to hold a principal criminally liable might possibly be an effective means of enforcing law and order, it would do violence to our more sophisticated modern-day concepts of justice. Liability for all true crimes, wherein an offense carries with it a jail sentence, must be based exclusively upon personal causation. It can be readily imagined that even a licensee who is meticulously careful in the choice of his employees cannot supervise every single act of the subordinates. A man's liberty cannot rest on so frail a reed as whether his employee will commit a mistake in judgment. See Sayre, Criminal Responsibility For Acts of Another, 43 Harv.L.Rev. 689 (1930).

This Court is ever mindful of its duty to maintain and establish the proper safeguards in a criminal trial. To sanction the imposition of imprisonment here would make a serious change in the substantive criminal law of the Commonwealth, one for which we find no justification. We have found *no* case in any jurisdiction which has permitted a *prison term* for a vicarious offense. The Supreme Court of the United States has had occasion only recently to impose due process

7. Sec. 9. " * * * nor can he be deprived of his life, liberty or prop- erty, unless by the judgment of his peers or the law of the land."

limitations upon the actions of a state legislature in making unknowing conduct criminal. Lambert v. People of State of California, 1957, 355 U.S. 225, 78 S.Ct. 240, 2 L.Ed.2d 228. Our own courts have stepped in time and again to protect a defendant from being held criminally responsible for acts about which he had no knowledge and over which he had little control. We would be utterly remiss were we not to so act under these facts.

In holding that the punishment of imprisonment deprives the defendant of due process of law under these facts, we are not declaring that Koczwara must be treated as a first offender under the Code. He has clearly violated the law for a second time and must be punished accordingly. Therefore, we are only holding that so much of the judgment as calls for imprisonment is invalid, and we are leaving intact the five hundred dollar fine imposed by Judge Hoban under the subsequent offense section.

* * *

Judgment, as modified, is affirmed.

BELL, MUSMANNO and McBRIDE, JJ., file separate dissenting opinions.

* * *

MUSMANNO, Justice (dissenting).

The Court in this case is doing what it has absolutely no right to do. It is laying aside its judicial robes and officiating as members of the General Assembly. It is declaring a crime which has no existence in the statute books, it is imposing a penalty which is not authorized by the criminal code.

* * *.

If it is wrong to send a person to jail for acts committed by another, is it not wrong to convict him at all? There are those who value their good names to the extent that they see as much harm in a degrading criminal conviction as in a jail sentence. The laceration of a man's reputation, the blemishing of his good name, the wrecking of his prestige by a criminal court conviction may blast a person's chances for honorable success in life to such an extent that a jail sentence can hardly add much to the ruin already wrought to him by the conviction alone.

* * *

COMMONWEALTH v. ALI

Supreme Court of Pennsylvania, 1970.
438 Pa. 463, 265 A.2d 796.

POMEROY, Justice. At a non-jury trial, appellant was convicted of having issued a worthless check in violation of § 854 of the Penal Code of June 24, 1939, P.L. 872, 18 P.S. § 4854. His motions in arrest of judgment and for a new trial were denied and he was sentenced to imprisonment for a term of 60 days to 23 months. On appeal to the Superior Court, his judgment of sentence was affirmed in a per curiam decision to which Judge Spaulding filed a dissenting opinion which Judge Hoffman joined. 214 Pa.Super. 512, 257 A.2d 370 (1969). We granted allocatur.

The worthless check upon which the prosecution was based was issued to the Totem Lumber Company in the amount of $349.95. The basic facts surrounding presentation of the check were not disputed. They are that on September 9, 1966, appellant signed a blank check and gave it to his employee, one Garmusa; that Mr. Garmusa took the check to the Totem Lumber Company for the purpose of purchasing supplies for appellant; that at the Lumber Company, the amount of the check was filled in by or at the direction of Garmusa, and accepted by the Lumber Company for materials delivered to Garmusa; and that the materials delivered to Garmusa were itemized on a sales slip, which showed a total cost of $349.95. The check was twice returned by the drawee bank for insufficient funds and was never paid.

Appellant testified that on the preceding day, September 8, he had ordered paint, lumber and nails by telephone from one Nick Grande, an employee of Totem Lumber Co.; that Grande told him that the total cost of the materials would be about $80 but that as Grande could not determine the exact amount, appellant could send a signed, blank check with the man who would pick up the materials, and the check could be completed at the time the materials were called for; and that he had signed a blank check and given it to Garmusa for this purpose. Appellant denied ordering or receiving any materials other than paint, lumber and nails costing about $80. Called by the Commonwealth in rebuttal, Grande denied requesting appellant to send a blank check, and stated that he could not recall whether appellant had personally placed an order over the telephone. Garmusa did not testify.

Upon this evidence, the trial court found that all elements of the crime had been established by the Commonwealth and found appellant guilty. We do not agree.

Under § 854 of the Penal Code the three essential elements of the crime of issuing a worthless check are: (1) making, drawing, uttering or delivering a check; (2) intent to defraud; and (3) knowledge at the time of making the check that the maker or drawer has insufficient funds for the payment thereof in, or credit with, the bank or other entity upon which the check is drawn. Under the second paragraph of § 854, the making, drawing, uttering or delivering of a check, payment of which is refused by the drawee,[1] "shall be prima facie

___

1. Although "drawee" is used in § 854 to refer both to the entity or person upon whom the check is drawn and the person to whom it is payable, the term "drawee" technically refers only to the former while the latter is properly the "payee". Drawee is used in this opinion only in its technical sense.

evidence of intent to defraud and of knowledge of insufficient funds in, or credit with" the drawee, unless the check (together with any interest or protest fees) is made good within ten days after the maker receives notice that the check has not been paid. Thus the Commonwealth may establish a prima facie case of guilt of this crime by introducing evidence that (1) the defendant was the maker of a worthless check, and (2) that he did not make it good within ten days of receipt of notice that it had not been paid. It seems likely that the trial court relied upon this statutory scheme of proof in finding appellant guilty, since there was no direct evidence either of his intent to defraud or of his knowledge of insufficient funds.[2]

In our opinion, however, the Commonwealth did not sustain its burden of proving that appellant made or drew a worthless check. While appellant signed the instrument, he did not himself complete it by filling in the amount of $349.95. Making a check or other negotiable instrument is more than merely signing it; it is issuing a completed instrument, or an incomplete instrument with authority in another to complete it. In order for the finder of fact to determine that appellant made the check in the amount of $349.95, evidence was required that he authorized the check to be so completed. No such evidence was introduced; the only testimony on the subject was that of appellant himself that he intended and expected the check to be made out for approximately $80. It may be folly and negligent to sign a blank check or other negotiable instrument and entrust it to another for completion, and doing so may very well entail liability to a holder in due course,[3] but it does not per se render the maker guilty of a crime. The prima facie evidence provision of the second paragraph of § 854 does not help the Commonwealth here, and direct evidence of authority was therefore necessary. Since it was not adduced, and the only evidence was that there was no authority, the elements of the crime were not made out.

The order of the Superior Court is reversed, the judgment of sentence is vacated, and the motion in arrest of judgment is granted and the defendant is discharged.

BELL, C. J., did not participate in the decision of this case.

2. Under our view of this case we need not determine whether the effect of the second paragraph of § 854 is merely to enable the Commonwealth to withstand a demurrer to the evidence where it produces no direct evidence of intent or knowledge, or whether it is to create an issue for the finder of fact on these two elements even in the face of contrary evidence, and we express no opinion on this question.

3. See, e. g., §§ 3–115, 3–406 and 3–407 of the Uniform Commercial Code, 12A P.S. §§ 3–115, 3–406 and 3–407. Section 3–115 places the burden on the maker to prove that the terms of the instrument as completed by another were unauthorized, but this civil standard of proof is not governing in a criminal prosecution.

NOTES

1. If Koczwara himself had made the sale would the court have had difficulty in affirming the conviction and sentence? Even if the minors appeared to be of age and presented apparently valid evidence in proof thereof?

2. Is there any question as to Koczwara's liability if he had known of his agent's practice of selling to minors? Cf. Commonwealth v. Feinberg, 433 Pa. 558, 253 A.2d 636 (1969) (convictions for involuntary manslaughter arising from death of thirty-one skid-row denizens due to drinking industrial Sterno sold, in some cases, by appellant's agent in his absence, upheld given finding that appellant stocked the same for sale knowing that purchasers would ingest it).

3. Does the statute in *Koczwara,* like that in *Ali,* require for conviction a finding that the defendant acted with knowledge of wrong-doing? If not, and if Koczwara would have been held responsible if he had made the sale, albeit in good faith reliance on the appearance, assertions and identification of the minor customers, what values are served by limiting his liability where he acts through an agent? To what extent, if any, are legitimate objectives of the criminal law sacrificed by such a limitation? Is the problem here that the liability is vicarious or that it is strict?

4. A Pennsylvania statute requires, in absolute terms, that every judicial officer who collects fines for violations of the motor vehicle code make a sworn report of these to the state Department of Revenue. Failure to do so may be punished by a fine of $500 plus costs, imprisonment for up to 60 days, or both. Is the prosecution required to prove a mens rea despite the absence of any reference to such in the statute? Does the fact that this is a crime of omission affect your analysis? Does the *Koczwara* discussion of "police regulations" aid the resolution of the question? See Commonwealth v. Bready, 220 Pa.Super. 157, 286 A.2d 654 (1971).

---

2. CRIMINAL LIABILITY OF ORGANIZATIONS AND THEIR AGENTS

Among the problems presented by use of traditional concepts of criminal liability in an increasingly organized society are those concerning the criminal liability of a corporation or other organization and the criminal liability of members of such organizations for crimes involving the organization. These materials raise questions regarding the extent to which criminal liability in this context serves traditional (or other) functions of imposing such liability, and the extent to which imposing it may run counter to traditional limitations upon the imposition of criminal liability.

McCOLLUM v. STATE

Court of Criminal Appeals of Texas, 1957.
165 Tex.Cr.R. 241, 305 S.W.2d 612.

DAVIDSON, Judge. In view of appellant's argument and citation of additional authorities in his motion for rehearing, we now withdraw our original opinion and substitute therefor the following:

This is a conviction for the pollution of public waters, which is prohibited by Art. 698b, Vernon's P.C., with punishment assessed at a fine of $110.

The Hess Terminal was a tank storage depot for the loading of ships, barges, and tank cars adjacent to and along the Houston Ship Channel. Appellant was the vice-president of the company and in complete charge of its operation.

According to the testimony of the state's witness who reported the fact to appellant, oil was found escaping from Hess Terminal into the Ship Channel, thereby polluting those public waters. Appellant promised, then, to take all necessary steps to prevent further pollution. Shortly thereafter, oil was again found in the channel of such nature and in such amount as to constitute pollution of public waters, under the statute, and to warrant the conclusion that the operation of boats thereon was endangered.

While there was some dispute in the evidence, the conclusion is reached that the evidence is sufficient to warrant the trial court's ruling that the oil actually escaped into the channel from Hess Terminal because of defective or improper operation of a separator designed to prevent such escape.

Appellant did not testify as a witness in his own behalf.

James, who was the superintendent of the Hess Terminal and appellant's subordinate, testified as to the prior efforts of the company not only to salvage escaping oil but to prevent pollution of the channel waters by the installation and operation of the separator. He denied any knowledge of the escaped oil, involved in this prosecution, from the separator or premises of Hess Terminal.

It will be noted that there is an absence of any testimony showing that appellant was actually in charge of the operation or maintenance of the separator or that he was in any manner personally connected with the oil escaping from the premises of the company and the resultant pollution of the channel or that he knowingly permitted such pollution.

On the other hand, it is established that appellant was the head of the company and, as such, was responsible for its operation and maintenance by and through delegated subordinates or employees.

This conviction is against appellant, personally. It is not a proceeding against Hess Terminal.

The question for determination, then, turns upon whether—under the facts stated—appellant may be adjudged guilty of the pollution of the channel waters.

In support of his contention that the facts do not warrant the conclusion of guilt, he poses this question:

Suppose the pollution here shown had caused damage to the person or property of another, who, as a result thereof, sues both Hess Terminal and him to recover the damage, would the instant facts authorize a judgment against him, personally, for the damage sustained?

The position taken is that the question should be answered in the negative because the undisputed facts show that appellant was the general manager in charge of the Hess Terminal plant and had delegated the operations of the plant to subordinates who, in turn, delegated their functions to other employees.

Appellant insists that he could not be personally liable for the defective operation of the sump or separator causing the pollution and, since he had delegated the operation of the separator to subordinates, he could not be held criminally responsible for his subordinates' failure to act.

In support of the position taken, appellant cites the case of S. H. Kress & Co. v. Selph, Tex.Civ.App., 250 S.W.2d 883, writ refused, n. r. e. That case appears to be directly in point and covers a very similar state of facts. It sustains this appellant's contention that a civil suit for damages could not be successfully maintained against him for damages that might have been sustained by another because of the pollution here shown.

We have reached the conclusion, here, that inasmuch as the facts fail to show any personal connection on the part of the appellant with the pollution or the maintenance or operation of the separator, he cannot be held liable, criminally, for the acts of his subordinates or employees in the absence of a showing that he was connected therewith in some manner recognized by law, whereby one may be criminally liable for the acts of another or others. Myers v. State, 148 Tex.Cr.R. 77, 184 S.W.2d 924, is deemed also in point, and supports our holding here.

The statute under which this prosecution was conducted prohibits pollution of public waters by corporations and companies. The conclusion here reached does not foreclose the right of the state to proceed against the Hess Terminal.

It is now determined that the facts do not warrant the conviction in the instant case.

Accordingly, appellant's motion for rehearing is granted, the judgment of affirmance is set aside, and the judgment of the trial court is now reversed and the cause remanded.

NOTES

1. The president of defendant corporation gave $4,500 of corporate funds to the president of the local union representing some of defendant's employees. The Government charged this transaction violated the Taft-Hartley Act, 29 U.S.C.A. § 186(a) & (b), which makes it a crime for an employer to pay any money to an official of a union representing its employees. The two individuals claimed that they were social friends, that the money was a loan for the purchase of a new home and that the corporation received a note in exchange for the loan. No effort was made to collect the note. May the corporation be convicted of "wilfully" violating the law? Was the president acting within the scope of his employment. How should that phrase be defined for this purpose? United States v. Carter, 311 F.2d 934 (6th Cir. 1963).

2. What goals of the criminal law are furthered by the imposition of criminal liability on a corporation given the fact that the only possible punishment is a fine which may be passed on to either the stockholders or customers, both of which groups are likely to be innocent of any wrongdoing?

3. If financial penalties are seen as efficacious, why wouldn't civil suits for damages resulting from the "criminal" conduct of the corporation serve the same purpose as well or better than the generally small—relative to the assets of many corporations—fines, which can be imposed?

4. Would not punishment of the responsible individual more effectively achieve legitimate goals of the criminal law without raising the problems incident to vicarious liability? Who would be the appropriate individual in a situation such as that presented in *McCollum*?

5. The Proposed Federal Criminal Code (1971) contains the following resolution of the major issues illustrated by the preceding cases.

§ 402. Corporate Criminal Liability

(1) Liability Defined. A corporation may be convicted of:

(a) any offense committed by an agent of the corporation within the scope of his employment on the basis of conduct authorized, requested or commanded, by any of the following or a combination of them:

[(a) any offense committed in furtherance of its affairs on the basis of conduct done, authorized, requested, commanded, ratified or recklessly tolerated in violation of a duty to maintain effective supervision of corporate affairs, by any of the following or a combination of them:]

(i) the board of directors;

(ii) an executive officer or any other agent in a position of comparable authority with respect to the formulation of corporate policy or the supervision in a managerial capacity of subordinate employees;

(iii) any person, whether or not an officer of the corporation, who controls the corporation or is responsibly involved in forming its policy;

(iv) any other person for whose act or omission the statute defining the offense provides corporate responsibility for offenses;

(b) any offense consisting of an omission to discharge a specific duty of affirmative conduct imposed on corporations by law;

(c) any misdemeanor committed by an agent of the corporation within the scope of his employment; or

(d) any offense for which an individual may be convicted without proof of culpability, committed by an agent of the corporation within the scope of his employment.

(2) Defense Precluded. It is no defense that an individual upon whose conduct liability of the corporation for an offense is based has been acquitted, has not been prosecuted or convicted or has been convicted of a different offense, or is immune from prosecution, or is otherwise not subject to justice.

§ 403. Individual Accountability for Conduct on Behalf of Organizations

(1) Conduct on Behalf of Organization. A person is legally accountable for any conduct he performs or causes to be performed in the name of an organization or in its behalf to the same extent as if the conduct were performed in his own name or behalf.

(2) Omission. Except as otherwise expressly provided, whenever a duty to act is imposed upon an organization by a statute or regulation thereunder, any agent of the organization having primary responsibility for the subject matter of the duty is legally accountable for an omission to perform the required act to the same extent as if the duty were imposed directly upon himself.

(3) Accomplice of Organization. When an individual is convicted of an offense as an accomplice of an organization, he is subject to the sentence authorized when a natural person is convicted of that offense.

(4) Default in Supervision. A person responsible for supervising relevant activities of an organization is guilty of an offense if he manifests his assent to the commission of an offense for which the organization may be convicted by his willful default in supervision within the range of that responsibility which contributes to the occurrence of that offense. Conviction under this subsection shall be of an offense of the same class as the offense for which the organization may be convicted, except that if the latter offense is a felony, conviction under this subsection shall be for a Class A misdemeanor.

§ 409. General Provisions for Chapter 4

(1) Definitions. In this Chapter:

(a) "organization" means any legal entity, whether or not organized as a corporation or unincorporated association, but does not include an entity organized as or by a governmental agency for the execution of a governmental program;

(b) "agent" means any partner, director, officer, servant, employee, or other person authorized to act in behalf of an organization.

(2) Unincorporated Associations. Nothing in this Chapter shall limit or extend the criminal liability of an unincorporated association.

It is interesting to note that the bracketed provision in § 402(1)(a) was the one recommended in the 1970 Study Draft. What do you see as the merits of the alternative formulations? Recognition of the unusual problems involved in devising effective sanctions for organizations was reflected in the Study Draft's section 405 which provided, in part:

(1) Organization. When an organization is convicted of an offense, the court may, in addition to or in lieu of imposing other authorized sanctions, do either or both of the following:

(a) require the organization to give appropriate publicity to the conviction by notice to the class or classes of persons or sector of the public interested in or affected by the conviction, by advertising in designated areas or by designated media, or otherwise;

(b) direct the Attorney General, United States Attorney, or other attorney designated by the court to institute supplementary proceedings in the case in which the organization was convicted of the offense to determine, collect and distribute damages to persons in the class which the statute was designed to protect who suffered injuries by reason of the offense, if the court finds that the multiplicity of small claims or other circumstances make restitution by individual suit impractical.

The Final Report retreats somewhat from this position. It omits (1)(b) because of separate congressional consideration of class actions by consumers, and offers (1)(a) only as a bracketed alternative to the following provision:

§ 3007. Special Sanction for Organizations

When an organization is convicted of an offense, the court may require the organization to give notice of its conviction to the persons or class of persons ostensibly harmed by the offense, by mail or by advertising in designated areas or by designated media or otherwise.

The Report comment explains that a "broader sanction envisioning 'publicity,' rather than 'notice,' was rejected as inappropriate with respect either to organizations or to individuals, despite its possible deterrent effect, since it came too close to the adoption of a policy approving social ridicule as a sanction."

IV. THE INCHOATE CRIMES

The offenses of attempt, solicitation, and conspiracy are all "inchoate" in that they consist of incompleted activity related to other acts, usually criminal acts. Part IV deals with these three offenses and defenses to them. Conspiracy raises a number of special problems, largely because in addition to serving as an inchoate offense conspiracy may (when conviction is sought for conspiracy as well as completed offenses) serve as a means of aggravating the actual or potential punishment for other crimes or may be used to attach liability to one individual for crimes committed by others.

MODEL PENAL CODE COMMENT TO ARTICLE 5, 24–26

(Tent. Draft No. 10, 1960).

Introduction

This Article undertakes to deal systematically with attempt, solicitation and conspiracy to commit crimes, conduct which has in common that it is designed to culminate in the commission of a substantive offense but either has failed to do so in the discrete case or has not yet achieved its culmination because there is something that the actor or another still must do. The offenses are inchoate in this sense.

These, to be sure, are not the only crimes which are so defined that their commission does not rest on proof of the occurrence of the evil that it is the object of the law to prevent; many specific, substantive offenses also have a large inchoate aspect. This is true not only with respect to crimes of risk-creation, such as reckless driving, or specific crimes of preparation, like those of possession with unlawful purpose. It is also true, at least in part, of crimes like larceny, forgery, kidnaping and even arson, not to speak of burglary, where a purpose to cause greater harm than that which is implicit in the actor's conduct is an element of the offense. It may be thought, indeed, that murder is the only crime which by its definition calls for proof that the full evil that the law endeavors to prevent has come to pass. This reservation notwithstanding, attempt, solicitation and conspiracy have such generality of definition and of application as inchoate crimes that it is useful to bring them together in the Code and to confront the common problems they present.

Since these offenses always presuppose a purpose to commit another crime, it is doubtful that the threat of punishment for their commission can significantly add to the deterrent efficacy of the sanction—which the actor by hypothesis ignores—that is threatened

244

for the crime that is his object. There may be cases where this does occur, as when the actor thinks the chance of apprehension low if he succeeds but high if he should fail in his attempt, or when reflection is promoted at an early stage that otherwise would be postponed until too late, which may be true in some conspiracies. These are, however, special situations. Viewed generally, it seems clear that general deterrence is at most a minor function to be served in fashioning provisions of the penal law addressed to these inchoate crimes; that burden is discharged upon the whole by the law dealing with the substantive offenses.

Other and major functions of the penal law remain, however, to be served. They may be summarized as follows:

First: When a person is seriously dedicated to commission of a crime, there is obviously need for a firm legal basis for the intervention of the agencies of law enforcement to prevent its consummation. In determining that basis, there must be attention to the danger of abuse; equivocal behavior may be misconstrued by an unfriendly eye as preparation to commit a crime. It is no less important, on the other side, that lines should not be drawn so rigidly that the police confront insoluble dilemmas in deciding when to intervene, facing the risk that if they wait the crime may be committed while if they act they may not yet have any valid charge.

Second: Conduct designed to cause or culminate in the commission of a crime obviously yields an indication that the actor is disposed towards such activity, not alone on this occasion but on others. There is a need, therefore, subject again to proper safeguards, for a legal basis upon which the special danger that such individuals present may be assessed and dealt with. They must be made amenable to the corrective process that the law provides.

Third: Finally, and quite apart from these considerations of prevention, when the actor's failure to commit the substantive offense is due to a fortuity, as when the bullet misses in attempted murder or when the expected response to solicitation is withheld, his exculpation on that ground would involve inequality of treatment that would shock the common sense of justice. Such a situation is unthinkable in any mature system, designed to serve the proper goals of penal law. See Section 1.02, Tentative Draft No. 4 (1955).

A. ATTEMPTS

According to Sayre, Criminal Attempts, 41 Harv.L.Rev. 821 (1928), until quite recently there was no generalized doctrine that attempts to commit crime were, in themselves, criminal. Although

some few early convictions for unsuccessful efforts to commit especially heinous crimes are reported, these, according to Professor Sayre,
were based on an earlier doctrine that the intention is to be taken for
the deed (*voluntas reputabitur pro facto*). The danger of imposing
liability upon mere intent was too great to permit resort to this maxim
often. Professor Sayre dates the modern doctrine of attempts from
Rex v. Scofield, Cald. 397 (1784) where it was declared that "[t]he
intent may make an act, innocent in itself, criminal; nor is the *completion* of an act, criminal in itself, necessary to constitute criminality." Id. at 400. Many issues vital to the law of attempts seem unsettled and resistant to ready resolution. Perhaps the relative youth
of the doctrine explains this; perhaps the difficulties are inherent
in efforts to criminalize in the absence of a prohibited result.

Model Penal Code, Comment to § 5.01, 26 (Tent. Draft No. 10, 1960):

> 1. *The Definition of Attempt.* The literature and de-
> cisions dealing with the definition of a criminal attempt re-
> flect ambivalence as to how far the governing criterion should
> be found in the dangerousness of the actor's conduct, mea-
> sured by objective standards, and how far in the dangerous-
> ness of the actor, as a person manifesting a firm disposition
> to commit a crime. Both criteria may lead, of course, to the
> same disposition of a concrete case. When they do not, we
> think, for reasons stated in the *Introduction,* that the proper
> focus of attention is the actor's disposition, and the draft is
> framed with this in mind. Needless to say, we are in full
> agreement that the law must be concerned with conduct, not
> with evil thoughts alone. The question is what conduct,
> when engaged in with a purpose to commit a crime or to ad-
> vance towards the attainment of a criminal objective, should
> suffice to constitute a criminal attempt?
>
> In fashioning an answer we must keep in mind that in at-
> tempt, as distinct from solicitation and conspiracy, it is not
> intrinsic to the actor's conduct that he has disclosed his crim-
> inal design to someone else; nor is there any natural line that
> is suggested by the situation—like utterance or agreement.
> The law must deal with the problem presented by a single in-
> dividual and must address itself to conduct that may fall
> anywhere upon a graded scale from early preparation to the
> final effort to commit the crime.
>
> We think, therefore, that it is useful to begin with any
> conduct designed to effect or to advance towards the attain-
> ment of the criminal objective and to ask when it ought *not*
> to be regarded as a crime, either because it does not ade-
> quately manifest the dangerousness of the actor or on other
> overriding grounds of social policy. The formulations in this
> section are intended as responses to this question.

1. THE ACT: BEYOND MERE PREPARATION

MODEL PENAL CODE

(Proposed Official Draft, 1962).

Section 5.01. Criminal Attempt

(1) *Definition of Attempt.* A person is guilty of an attempt to commit a crime if, acting with the kind of culpability otherwise required for commission of the crime, he:

> (a) purposely engages in conduct which would constitute the crime if the attendant circumstances were as he believes them to be; or

> (b) when causing a particular result is an element of the crime, does or omits to do anything with the purpose of causing or with the belief that it will cause such result without further conduct on his part; or

> (c) purposely does or omits to do anything which, under the circumstances as he believes them to be, is an act or omission constituting a substantial step in a course of conduct planned to culminate in his commission of the crime.

(2) *Conduct Which May Be Held Substantial Step Under Subsection (1) (c).* Conduct shall not be held to constitute a substantial step under Subsection (1) (c) of this Section unless it is strongly corroborative of the actor's criminal purpose. Without negativing the sufficiency of other conduct, the following, if strongly corroborative of the actor's criminal purpose, shall not be held insufficient as a matter of law:

> (a) lying in wait, searching for or following the contemplated victim of the crime;

> (b) enticing or seeking to entice the contemplated victim of the crime to go to the place contemplated for its commission;

> (c) reconnoitering the place contemplated for the commission of the crime;

> (d) unlawful entry of a structure, vehicle or enclosure in which it is contemplated that the crime will be committed;

> (e) possession of materials to be employed in the commission of the crime, which are specially designed for such unlawful use or which can serve no lawful purpose of the actor under the circumstances;

> (f) possession, collection or fabrication of materials to be employed in the commission of the crime, at or near

the place contemplated for its commission, where such possession, collection or fabrication serves no lawful purpose of the actor under the circumstances;

(g) soliciting an innocent agent to engage in conduct constituting an element of the crime.

(3) *Conduct Designed to Aid Another in Commission of a Crime.* A person who engages in conduct designed to aid another to commit a crime which would establish his complicity under Section 2.06 if the crime were committed by such other person, is guilty of an attempt to commit the crime, although the crime is not committed or attempted by such other person.

(4) *Renunciation of Criminal Purpose.* When the actor's conduct would otherwise constitute an attempt under Subsection (1) (b) or (1) (c) of this Section, it is an affirmative defense that he abandoned his effort to commit the crime or otherwise prevented its commission, under circumstances manifesting a complete and voluntary renunciation of his criminal purpose. The establishment of such defense does not, however, affect the liability of an accomplice who did not join in such abandonment or prevention.

Within the meaning of this Article, renunciation of criminal purpose is not voluntary if it is motivated, in whole or in part, by circumstances, not present or apparent at the inception of the actor's course of conduct, which increase the probability of detection or apprehension or which make more difficult the accomplishment of the criminal purpose. Renunciation is not complete if it is motivated by a decision to postpone the criminal conduct until a more advantageous time or to transfer the criminal effort to another but similar objective or victim.

Section 5.05. Grading of Criminal Attempt, Solicitation and Conspiracy; Mitigation in Cases of Lesser Danger; Multiple Convictions Barred

(1) *Grading.* Except as otherwise provided in this Section, attempt, solicitation and conspiracy are crimes of the same grade and degree as the most serious offense which is attempted or solicited or is an object of the conspiracy. An attempt, solicitation or conspiracy to commit a [capital crime or a] felony of the first degree is a felony of the second degree.

(2) *Mitigation.* If the particular conduct charged to constitute a criminal attempt, solicitation or conspiracy is so inherently unlikely to result or culminate in the commission of a crime that neither such conduct nor the actor presents a public danger warranting the grading of such offense under this Section, the Court shall exercise its power under Section 6.12 to enter judgment and impose sentence for a crime of lower grade or degree or, in extreme cases, may dismiss the prosecution.

(3) *Multiple Convictions.* A person may not be convicted of more than one offense defined by this Article for conduct designed to commit or to culminate in the commission of the same crime.

———

MODEL PENAL CODE, COMMENT TO § 5.01(1), 39–48

(Tent. Draft No. 10, 1960).

The General Distinction between Preparation and Attempt. Paragraph (c) deals with the most difficult problem in defining attempt liability: the formulation of a general standard for distinguishing acts of preparation from acts constituting the attempt. If the "last proximate act" is not required in order for there to be an attempt, and if— as is generally assumed—every act done with intent to commit a crime is not to be made criminal, it becomes necessary to establish a means of inclusion and exclusion. Some of the approaches which have been tried or suggested are as follows:

(a) *The physical proximity doctrine.* Some courts purport to be guided by principles which state in general terms that the overt act required for an attempt must be proximate to the completed crime, or that the act must be one directly tending toward the completion of the crime, or that the act must amount to the commencement of the consummation. Such opinions often admit that each case must be decided on its own facts and examine in detail the act's remoteness from the completed crime, emphasizing time, distance and the number of necessary acts as yet undone. A stringent view of the physical proximity test holds that the actor's conduct does not proceed beyond preparation until the actor has the power—or at least the apparent power —to complete the crime forthwith. The physical proximity test is not in itself inconsistent with principles of attempt liability: other things being equal, the further the actor progresses toward completion of the offense, the greater is the dangerousness of character manifested and the need for preventative arrest. But the standard is a vague one and emphasizes only one aspect of the actor's behavior. The physical proximity test does not provide much guidance in answering the crucial problem of how close is close enough for attempt liability.

(b) *The dangerous proximity doctrine.* A test which incorporates the physical proximity approach within it, but which proceeds beyond it, is the doctrine given impetus by the writings and opinions of Mr. Justice Holmes. In order to determine whether a given act constitutes an attempt the following factors are considered: the gravity of the offense intended, the nearness of the act to completion of the crime, and the probability that the conduct will result in the offense intended. The greater the gravity and probability, and the nearer the act to the crime, the stronger is the case for calling the act an attempt. The test is based on the assumption that the purpose of punishing attempts is to deter undesirable behavior and that until the actor's conduct becomes sufficiently dangerous there is not adequate reason for deterring it. The assumption, as it relates to the law of attempts, is not, in our view, the right foundation for the liability. The primary purpose of punishing attempts is to neutralize dangerous individuals and not to deter dangerous acts. Since the dangerousness of the actor's conduct has some relation to the dangerousness of the actor's personality, and to the need for preventative arrest, the test is not entirely irrelevant. But the basic orientation of the dangerous proximity doctrine is so at odds with the principles of attempt liability on which the draft is based that we cannot embrace it as a working *rationale*. The shortcomings of the physical proximity test are also applicable.

(c) *The indispensable element approach.* One variation of the several proximity tests emphasizes any indispensable aspect of the criminal endeavor over which the actor has not yet acquired control. Some decisions seem to stand for the proposition that, if the successful completion of a crime requires the assent or action of some third person, that assent or action must be forthcoming before the actor can be guilty of an attempt. Thus if *A* and *B* plan to defraud a life insurance company by pretending that *A*, the insured, is dead, and if *C*, the beneficiary, must file a formal claim before any proceeds can be paid, it has been held that the acts of *A* and *B* cannot amount to an attempt to defraud the insurance company until *C* files a claim or agrees to file a claim. And one court has held that giving counterfeit matter to another, in order that he may "pass" it, does not constitute an attempt to "pass" on the giver's part until the other makes an effort to pass the counterfeit matter to an innocent third party. If the actor seeks to influence a juror by asking a third party to approach the juror, the cases split on whether the actor has attempted to corrupt a juror. The reasoning of the courts which refuse to find an attempt here because of the need for the third party's cooperation is similar to that applied in cases which hold that solicitation does not constitute an attempt because completion of the crime requires action by the party solicited.

An analogous group of cases supports the view that a person cannot be guilty of an attempt if he lacks a means essential to completion of the offense. Thus it has been held that one cannot be guilty of an attempt to introduce whiskey into a forbidden territory until he acquires the whiskey; that a person cannot attempt an assault with a dangerous weapon until he acquires the weapon; that one cannot attempt to illegally manufacture whiskey until he acquires the necessary apparatus; and that one cannot attempt to vote illegally until he obtains a ballot.

This approach is subject to the same general objections as the proximity tests of which it is a variation.

(d) *The probable desistance test.* Oriented largely toward the dangerousness of the actor's conduct but giving slightly more emphasis to the actor's personality is the rule which provides that the actor's conduct constitutes an attempt if, in the ordinary and natural course of events, without interruption from an outside source, it will result in the crime intended. Apart from any question as to the suitability of the means employed for achieving the criminal end contemplated (considered in connection with "impossibility"), this test seems to require, in order for there to be an attempt, a judgment in each case that the actor had reached a point where it was unlikely that he would have voluntarily desisted from his efforts to commit the crime. But in cases applying this test no inquiry is made into the personality of the particular offender before the court. The question is whether *anyone* who went so far would stop short of the final step.

The recently enacted Wisconsin Criminal Code adopts a variation of the probable desistance test in classifying as an attempt "acts toward the commission of the crime which demonstrate unequivocally, under all the circumstances, that [the actor formed an intent to commit the crime] and would commit the crime except for the intervention of another person or some other extraneous factor."

Accepting for the time being the underlying assumption that probability of desistance (or actual abandonment of the criminal endeavor) sufficiently negatives dangerousness as to warrant immunity from attempt liability, still this test does not appear to provide a workable standard. Is there a sufficient empirical basis for making predictions in various types of cases as to whether desistance is probable at various points along the way? The opinion has been voiced that one who undertakes a criminal endeavor and performs an act pursuant to that purpose is not likely to stop short of the final step. And in actual operation the probable desistance test is linked entirely to the nearness of the actor's conduct to completion, this being the sole basis of unsubstantiated judicial appraisals of the probabilities of desistance. The test as applied appears to be little more than the physical proximity approach.

(e) *The abnormal step approach.* One commentator, recognizing the role of attempts in revealing dangerous personalities, defines an attempt as a step toward crime which goes beyond the point where the normal citizen would think better of his conduct and desist. Despite its proper orientation, this approach has several serious deficiencies. First, with respect to some crimes—and probably with respect to most crimes—any step toward the crime is a departure from the conduct of the normal citizen. Thus as to these crimes the approach would effect a major revolution in attempt liability—making it an attempt to do any act for the purpose of committing such crimes. Second, there may be some offenses where the normal citizen does not stop at all. To tie attempt liability to the normal citizen in this

case is to raise the whole problem of unpopular laws and their enforcement. It seems untenable that normalcy in violation or near-
violation should constitute a defense to an attempt charge. Finally,
who is to judge where the normal citizen will stop and what kind of
proof will be appropriate for such a determination? The test is
oriented toward singling out dangerous personalities but it is virtually
impossible of application.

(f) *The res ipsa loquitur test*. Taking an entirely different approach to the preparation-attempt problem is the view which holds
that an attempt is committed when the actor's conduct manifests an
intent to commit a crime. The conduct would be considered in relation to all the surrounding circumstances exclusive of representations made by the actor about his intentions; but presumably representations of the actor which negative a criminal intent would be
admissible to disprove the intention imputed. The object of this
approach is to subject to attempt liability conduct which unequivocally
demonstrates that the actor is being guided by a criminal purpose.
There are two lines of thought upon which this view can be sustained.

The first goes to the problem of proof. Assuming that any act
done for the purpose of committing a crime is an act which demonstrates dangerousness, why not make all such acts attempts? One
answer is that such a law would allow prosecutions for acts which are
externally equivocal and would create a risk that innocent persons
would be convicted. It is assumed that the conduct involved is non-
causal, so at the outset there is the opportunity to charge a crime
where nothing is amiss. There is no corpus delicti to verify the fact
that somebody has caused some sort of trouble. Moreover, there is
a further difference between the conduct involved in an attempt case
and the conduct questioned in a case involving the completed crime.
In the latter the last proximate act must be proved. For an attempt
conviction this is not necessary; if immunity for preparation is eliminated almost any act would do. Thus, with respect to any substantive
crime, the chances are that more steps will have to be proved if the
completed crime is involved than if it is the attempt which is charged.
Finally, there is the problem, if preliminary acts toward the crime are
externally equivocal, of establishing the necessary purpose. Recourse
must be had to statements made by the actor before, during, and after
the acts in question. The first two kinds of statements are not reliable
because the actor may have been bluffing or he may have entertained
an idea or inclination without really acting upon it, the act in question
being motivated by a noncriminal purpose. Statements made after the
act, usually in the form of a confession, are not always considered
reliable.

The *res ipsa* rule on preparation-attempt may be viewed entirely
as a matter of procedure, as a device to prevent liability based solely
on confessions and other representations of purpose because of the

risks they raise when considered with the other probative weaknesses incident to attempt liability.   And whether the requirement of unequivocality is considered part of the substantive definition of attempt or as a separate rule of evidence, it can be realistically administered only by means of a procedural mechanism—*i.e.*, by excluding from the jury, in whole or in part, the actor's incriminating representations of purpose.   If it is problems of proof which are the basis of the preparation-attempt distinction, then the *res ipsa* approach has considerable merit.

There is considerable support in the cases for the proposition that the preparation-attempt distinction is the result of difficulty in proving purpose.   There are cases which make explicit reference to the necessity for unequivocal behavior.   And it has been said, with some frequency, that the overt act must manifest the intent to commit the crime.   Moreover, many courts which adopt a stringent view as to what constitutes an attempt reveal their actual motivation by openly expressing concern over the inadequate proof of criminal intent.

A second point of departure in considering the *res ipsa* test is its relation to the manifested dangerousness of the actor.   If an act unequivocally demonstrates a criminal purpose, does this show something more about the dangerousness of the actor's personality than an act done with a criminal purpose which must be established "independently"?   The assumption underlying an affirmative answer is that there is some relationship between the actor's state of mind and the external appearance of his acts.   While the actor's behavior is externally equivocal the criminal purpose in his mind is likely to be unfixed—a subjective equivocality.   But once the actor must desist or perform acts which he realizes would incriminate him if all external facts were known, then in all probability a firmer state of mind exists. Subjective equivocality seems inconsistent with an act which unequivocally demonstrates a criminal purpose.   A hunter might buy extra supplies to facilitate an escape in the event he resolves to kill his companion, a question as yet unsettled in his mind.   But when he buys poison which has no reasonable use under the circumstances other than the murder of his companion, the chances are that the debate has been resolved and the actor's purpose is fixed on murder.

The basis for our rejection of the *res ipsa* or unequivocality test can best be explained in connection with a consideration of the test proposed in the instant paragraph.

(g) *Substantiality and corroboration.*   In addition to criminal purpose, the proposed paragraph, together with Subsection 5.01(2), sets forth two requirements which distinguish attempt from preparation: (1) the act must be "a *substantial* step in a course of conduct" planned to accomplish the criminal result, and (2) the act must be "strongly corroborative" of criminal purpose in order for it to constitute such a "substantial step."

Whether a particular act is a substantial step is obviously a matter of degree. To this extent the present paragraph retains the element of imprecision found in most of the other approaches to the preparation-attempt problem. There are, however, several differences to be noted:

First, this formulation shifts the emphasis from what remains to be done—the chief concern of the proximity tests—to what the actor *has already done*. The fact that further major steps must be taken before the crime can be completed does not preclude a finding that the steps already undertaken are substantial. It is expected, in the normal case, that this approach will broaden the scope of attempt liability.

Second, although it is intended that the requirement of a substantial step will result in the imposition of attempt liability only in those instances in which some firmness of criminal purpose is shown, no finding is required as to whether the actor would probably have desisted prior to completing the crime. Potentially the probable desistance test could reach very early steps toward crime—depending upon how one assesses the probabilities of desistance—but since in practice this test follows closely the proximity approaches, rejection of probable desistance will not narrow the scope of attempt liability.

Finally, the requirement of proving a substantial step generally will prove less of a hurdle for the prosecution than the *res ipsa loquitur* approach, which requires that the actor's conduct must itself manifest the criminal purpose. The difference will be illustrated in connection with the present section's requirement of corroboration. Here it should be noted that, in the present formulation, the two purposes to be served by the *res ipsa loquitur* test are, to a large extent, treated separately. Firmness of criminal purpose is intended to be shown by requiring a substantial step, while problems of proof are dealt with by the requirement of corroboration (although, under the reasoning previously expressed, the latter will also tend to establish firmness of purpose).

In addition to assuring firmness of purpose, the requirement of a substantial step will remove very remote preparatory acts from the ambit of attempt liability and the relatively stringent sanctions imposed for attempts. On the other hand, by broadening liability to the extent suggested, apprehension of dangerous persons will be facilitated and law enforcement officials and others will be able to stop the criminal effort at an earlier stage—thereby minimizing the risk of substantive harm—without providing immunity for the offender.

DUPUY v. STATE

Supreme Court of Tennessee, 1959.
204 Tenn. 624, 325 S.W.2d 238.

PREWITT, Justice.   The defendant below, James Russell Dupuy, was convicted under an indictment charging him with attempt to procure a miscarriage on a young woman named June Harris.   This appeal in error resulted.

* * *

The facts appearing in the record are that the defendant, Dupuy, was a druggist and pharmacist in the City of Memphis, and his business establishment was located on Linden Circle.

It seems that Dupuy had a good reputation as an individual and as a pharmacist.

The police of Memphis suspected him of violating the law as to abortion and that they anonymously heard that he was producing miscarriages.

In furtherance of the plan of the police to apprehend the defendant they selected a young woman to get in the confidence of the defendant and set up a situation to find him guilty of violating the law.

This young woman, June Harris, was selected by the officers but she was not pregnant at the time.   It seems that this young woman went into the place of business of the defendant two or three times, and finally solicited his help; that the defendant finally agreed to come to her assistance and that they went to a room taking along various instruments owned by the defendant.   When they got into the room the officers, who were waiting close by, came upon the defendant and arrested him.

It appears that the defendant had all of his instruments ready on the table and that the woman left the room before any attempt was made to touch her body, or it seems that the defendant never got within five feet of her.   About this time the officers came upon the scene and arrested the defendant.

* * *

It appears that in this case this young woman never allowed the man to touch her either with his hands or his instruments.   While his conduct is very reprehensible and he would no doubt have carried out this attempt had he not been thwarted in his efforts by the arrival of the police.

It has been suggested that since the female here was not in fact pregnant that the commission of the attempt was impossible.

The State relies upon the case of Rafferty v. State, 91 Tenn. 655, 659, 16 S.W. 728, 729, in which the Court said:

> "Hayes v. State [15 Lea 64] was approved and followed in the late case of Clark v. State, 86 Tenn. 511, 8 S.W. 145, wherein it was decided that one who feloniously opened the cash-drawer of another, believing it to contain money or other valuables, and intending to steal the same, was guilty of an attempt to commit larceny, and punishable as for a felony, though the drawer proved to be entirely empty."

The holding in the above case is a complete answer to this proposition. The intent was there and the overt act was there.

We have no such case here. While the defendant had completed his plan to do this crime the element of attempt does not appear in this record. The proof shows that he did not use any of the instruments and did not touch the body of the girl in question. Under such facts we do not think that the defendant is guilty under the statute.

We seem to have no Tennessee case directly in point. We quote the following from 14 Am.Jur. Sec. 68, page 816:

> "In a general way, however, it may be said that preparation consists in devising or arranging the means or measures necessary for the commission of the offense and that the attempt is the direct movement toward the commission after the preparations are made. Even though a person actually intends to commit a crime, his procurement of the instrumentalities adapted to that end will not constitute an attempt to commit the crime in the absence of some overt act."

For example the procurement by a prisoner of tools adapted to breaking jail does not render him guilty of an attempt to break jail.

* * *

It follows that we find a full preparation to do the act with the criminal intent but the overt act is wholly lacking.

It results that the judgment of the conviction must be reversed and remanded.[a]

NOTE

In the recent past vagrancy statutes would commonly be employed to justify the arrest and punishment of persons apprehended in circumstances

a. Compare People v. Berger, 131 Cal. App.2d 127, 280 P.2d 136 (Dist.Ct.App. 1955) where the facts appear to be identical to those in *Dupuy* except that the accused's accomplice who was to perform the abortion admitted that this was her intention upon her arrest. The court held that while the sterilization of instruments might be too equivocal an act to constitute an attempt, when the intent with which the act was performed was established it became sufficient to support a conviction for an attempt to commit an abortion.

in which a conviction for "attempt" would be difficult to obtain. In Papachristou v. Jacksonville, reprinted at page 99, Mr. Justice Douglas acknowledged the usefulness of such statutes to the police and, in footnote 15, offered
the following table as evidence of the frequency with which they were invoked.

The table below contains nationwide data on arrests for "vagrancy" and
for "suspicion" in the three-year period 1968–1970.

Year*	Vagrancy		Suspicion		Combined Offenses	
	Total rptd. arrests	Rate per 100,000	Total rptd. arrests	Rate per 100,000	Total rptd. arrests	Rate per 100,000
1968	99,147	68.2	89,986	61.9	189,133	130.1
1969	106,269	73.9	88,265	61.4	194,534	135.3
1970	101,093	66.1	70,173	46.3	171.266	113.0
3 year averages	102,170	69.6	82,808	56.5	184,978	126.1

*Reporting agencies represent population of: 1968—145,306,000; 1969—
143,815,000; 1970—151,604,000.

Source: FBI Annual Crime Reports, 1968–1970.

Despite, or perhaps because of, heavy police reliance on such statutes, the
city ordinance challenged in *Papachristou* was unanimously held void for
vagueness in language which sounds a death knell for all similar statutory
provisions.

If traditional vagrancy statutes are not to be available to police efforts
to "nip crime in the bud," should laws making it criminal to possess tools
commonly employed in, or capable of being used for, burglary be enacted?
Given the commonplace nature of many instruments which can be and are
employed in burglaries such a statute would, to withstand challenge, have to
contain some further element of criminality. One that is commonly employed
is that they be possessed with intent to commit burglary but that possession
is to be deemed presumptive evidence of such intent. E. g., Iowa Code Ann.
§ 708.7 (1950), which was upheld in State v. Von Voltenburg, 260 Iowa 200,
147 N.W.2d 869 (1967). There the defendant, upon being interrogated by
a watchman who stopped him in an alley at 2:15 A.M., dropped a paper bag
containing a pry bar and a screwdriver. When arrested he was found to
have a butter knife on his person. His conviction under the statute was affirmed, the court holding that since the presumption was not conclusive no unconstitutional burden was placed on the accused. Another technique is to
make possession a crime if it is without lawful excuse and to require the defendant to carry the burden of proving lawful excuse. E. g., Conn.Gen.Stat.
Ann. § 53–71 (1968), which was held unconstitutional in State v. Nales, 28
Conn.Supp. 28, 248 A.2d 242 (1968). The court held that placing the burden on the accused violated his Fifth Amendment privilege against self-incrimination, and that the presumption from mere possession in the night was
irrational. In 1969 Connecticut adopted a new penal code and provided that
possession would be a misdemeanor if "under circumstances manifesting an

intent to use   *   *   *   in the commission of an offense of such character".
Conn.Gen.Stat.Ann. § 53a–106.   Still another technique is that selected by
Texas which makes possession of such instruments "under circumstances
evincing an intent to use   *   *   *   in the commission of burglary" a felony
if the possessor has been convicted of a felony—a one bite at the apple notion.   Vernon's Ann.Tex.P.C. art. 1402(b) (Penal Code) (1953).   This was
upheld against a vagueness challenge in Logan v. State, 448 S.W.2d 462
(Tex.Crim.App.1970).

Without some such statute are not the police and prosecutors at a serious disadvantage in their efforts to prevent the commission of crimes? Even
if the authority to "stop and frisk", Terry v. Ohio, 392 U.S. 1, 88 S.Ct. 1868,
20 L.Ed.2d 889 (1968), permits early intervention in such situations and
thereby the probable prevention of the specific burglary, what of the accused's future activities?   Is not a major objective of the criminal law the
identification of persons who are appropriate subjects for correction and/or
restraint?

----

2. THE STATE OF MIND REQUIRED

MODEL PENAL CODE, COMMENT TO § 5.01, 27–30

(Tent. Draft No. 10, 1960).

3.   *5.01(1).   The Requirement of Purpose.*   As previously stated, the proposed definition of attempt follows the conventional pattern of limiting this inchoate crime to purposive conduct.   In the
language of the courts, there must be "intent in fact" or "specific intent" to commit the crime allegedly attempted.   Nonetheless a problem of drafting is presented in endeavoring to explain the nature of
the requisite purpose.

This section adopts the view that the actor must have for his
purpose to engage in the criminal conduct or accomplish the criminal
result which is an element of the substantive crime but that his purpose need not encompass all the surrounding circumstances included
in the formal definition of the substantive offense.   As to them, it is
sufficient that he acts with the culpability that is required for commission of the crime.   Suppose, for example, that it is a federal offense to kill or injure an FBI agent and that recklessness or even negligence with respect to the identity of the victim as an agent suffices
for commission of the crime.   There would be an attempt to kill or injure such an agent under the present formulation if the actor with
recklessness or negligence as to the official position of the victim
attempts to kill or injure him.   Under paragraph (b) the killing or
injuring would be the required purpose; the fact that the victim is
an agent would be only a circumstance as to which the actor had
"the kind of culpability otherwise required for commission of the
crime."

It is difficult to say what the result would be in this kind of case under prevailing principles of attempt liability. However, the proposed formulation imposes attempt liability in a group of cases where the normal basis of such liability is present—purposive conduct manifesting dangerousness—and allows the policy of the substantive crime, respecting recklessness or negligence as to surrounding circumstances, to be applied to the attempt to commit that crime.

With rare exceptions, the necessity for showing intent has not given rise to many difficulties in applying prevailing attempt principles. * * *

Under paragraph (b), liability for an attempt may be founded upon the actor's belief that his conduct will cause a particular result which is an element of the crime. If, for example, the actor's purpose were to demolish a building and, knowing and believing that persons in the building would be killed by the explosion, the actor nonetheless detonated a bomb, there would be an attempt to kill even though it was no part of the actor's purpose—i. e., he did not consciously desire—that the building's inhabitants should be killed. Again, it is difficult to say what the decision would be under prevailing attempt principles in a case of this kind. It might be held that the actor did not specifically intend to kill the inhabitants of the building; on the other hand, the concept of "intent" has always been an ambiguous one and might be thought to include results which are believed by the actor to be the inevitable consequences of his conduct.

The inclusion of such conduct as a basis for liability under paragraph (b) is based on the conclusion that the manifestation of dangerousness is as great—or very nearly as great—as in the case of purposive conduct. In both instances a deliberate choice is made to bring about the consequence forbidden by the criminal laws, and the actor has done all within his power to cause this result to occur. The absence in one instance of any desire for the forbidden result is not, under these circumstances, a sufficient basis for differentiating between the two types of conduct involved.

It should be emphasized that this extension of paragraph (b) beyond the area of purposive behavior does *not* result in the inclusion of reckless conduct. Indeed, as previously noted, the additional ground of liability may well be within the common law concept of intentional behavior. Certain types of non-causal reckless conduct are encompassed by § 201.11 of the Code, Tentative Draft No. 9 (1959).

THACKER v. COMMONWEALTH

Supreme Court of Appeals of Virginia, 1922.
134 Va. 767, 114 S.E. 504.

WEST, J. This writ of error is to a judgment upon the verdict of a jury finding John Thacker, the accused, guilty of attempting to murder Mrs. J. A. Ratrie, and fixing his punishment at two years in the penitentiary.

The only assignment of error is the refusal of the trial court to set aside the verdict as contrary to the law and the evidence.

The accused, in company with two other young men, Doc Campbell and Paul Kelly, was attending a church festival in Alleghany county, at which all three became intoxicated. They left the church between 10 and 11 o'clock at night, and walked down the county road about 1½ miles, when they came to a sharp curve. Located in this curve was a tent in which the said Mrs. J. A. Ratrie, her husband, four children, and a servant were camping for the summer. The husband, though absent, was expected home that night, and Mrs. Ratrie, upon retiring, had placed a lighted lamp on a trunk by the head of her bed. After 11 o'clock she was awakened by the shots of a pistol and loud talking in the road near by, and heard a man say, "I am going to shoot that God-damned light out;" and another voice said, "Don't shoot the light out." The accused and his friends then appeared at the back of the tent, where the flaps of the tent were open, and said they were from Bath county and had lost their way, and asked Mrs. Ratrie if she could take care of them all night. She informed them she was camping for the summer, and had no room for them. One of the three thanked her, and they turned away, but after passing around the tent the accused used some vulgar language and did some cursing and singing. When they got back in the road, the accused said again he was going to shoot the light out, and fired three shots, two of which went through the tent, one passing through the head of the bed in which Mrs. Ratrie was lying, just missing her head and the head of her baby, who was sleeping with her. The accused did not know Mrs. Ratrie, and had never seen her before. He testified he did not know any of the parties in the tent, and had no ill will against either of them; that he simply shot at the light, without any intent to harm Mrs. Ratrie or any one else; that he would not have shot had he been sober, and regretted his action.

The foregoing are the admitted facts in the case.

An attempt to commit a crime is composed of two elements: (1) The intent to commit it; and (2) a direct, ineffectual act done towards its commission. The act must reach far enough towards the accomplishment of the desired result to amount to the commencement of the consummation.

The law can presume the intention so far as realized in the act, but not an intention beyond what was so realized. The law does not presume, because an assault was made with a weapon likely to produce death, that it was an assault with the intent to murder. And where it takes a particular intent to constitute a crime, that particular intent must be proved either by direct or circumstantial evidence, which would warrant the inference of the intent with which the act was done.

When a statute makes an offense to consist of an act combined with a particular intent, that intent is just as necessary to be proved as the act itself, and must be found as a matter of fact before a conviction can be had; and no intent in law or mere legal presumption, differing from the intent in fact, can be allowed to supply the place of the latter.

In discussing the law of attempts, Mr. Clark in his work on Criminal Law says, at page 111:

"The act must be done with the specific intent to commit a particular crime. This specific intent at the time the act is done is essential. To do an act from general malevolence is not an attempt to commit a crime, because there is no specific intent, though the act according to its consequences may amount to a substantive crime. To do an act with intent to commit one crime cannot be an attempt to commit another crime, though it might result in such other crime. To set fire to a house and burn a human being who is in it, but not to the offender's knowledge, would be murder, though the intent was to burn the house only; but to attempt to set fire to the house under such circumstances would be an attempt to commit arson only and not an attempt to murder. A man actuated by general malevolence may commit murder, though there is no actual intention to kill; to be guilty of an attempt to murder there must be a specific intent to kill."

Mr. Bishop, in his Criminal Law, vol. 1 (8th Ed.), at section 729, says:

"When the law makes an act, whether more or less evil in itself, punishable, though done simply from general malevolence, if one takes what, were all accomplished, would be a step towards it, yet if he does not mean to do the whole, no court can justly hold him answerable for more than he does. And when the thing done does not constitute a substantive crime, there is no ground for treating it as an attempt. So that necessarily an act prompted by general malevolence, or by a specific design to do something else, is not an attempt to commit a crime not intended. * * * When we say that a man attempted to do a given wrong, we mean that he intended to do specifically it, and proceeded a certain way in the doing. The intent in the mind covers the thing in full; the act covers it only in part. Thus (section 730) to commit murder, one need not intend to take life, but to be guilty of an attempt to murder, he must so intend. It is not sufficient that his act, had it proved fatal, would have been murder. Section 736. We have seen that the unintended taking of life may be murder, yet there can be no attempt to murder without the specific intent to commit it—a rule the latter branch whereof appears probably in a few of the states to have been interfered with by statutes (citing Texas cases). For example, if one from a housetop recklessly throws down a billet of wood upon the sidewalk where persons are constantly passing, and it falls upon a person passing by and kills him, this would be the common-law murder, but if, instead of killing, it inflicts only a slight injury, the party could not be convicted of an assault with attempt to commit murder, since, in fact, the murder was not intended."

The application of the foregoing principles to the facts of the instant case shows clearly, as we think, that the judgment complained of is erroneous. While it might possibly be said that the firing of the shot into the head of Mrs. Ratrie's bed was an act done towards the commission of the offense charged, the evidence falls far short of proving that it was fired with the intent to murder her.

However averse we may be to disturb the verict of the jury, our obligation to the law compels us to do so.

The judgment complained of will be reversed, the verdict of the jury set aside, and the case remanded for a new trial therein, if the commonwealth shall be so advised.

Reversed.

---

3. THE "DEFENSE" OF IMPOSSIBILITY

BOOTH v. STATE

Court of Criminal Appeals of Oklahoma, 1964.
398 P.2d 863.

NIX, Judge. John Fletcher Booth, Jr., was charged by information in the District Court of Oklahoma County with the crime of Receiving Stolen Property, and was found guilty of the lesser crime of Attempt to Receive Stolen Property. The jury assessed his penalty at

Two Years in the Oklahoma State Penitentiary, and to pay a fine in the amount of $150.00. From said judgment and sentence the defendant appeals.

The record before this Court reveals that this case arose out of a circumstance as testified to by a self-admitted, well-known thief bearing the name of Charley Stanford, whose FBI "rap sheet" covers 8 pages of arrests extending over a period of 15 years. He was obviously braggadocio about his convictions and related from the witness stand that he had been arrested approximately 300 times on everything in the book, short of murder and rape. He admitted serving 4 terms in the penitentiary, and having been committed to a mental institution twice. He testified, in substance, that in the early morning hours he was walking in the parking lot at the YMCA in Oklahoma City and sighted a topcoat in a parked automobile. That he jimmied the window and removed the coat, took it to his home at 308 N.E. 8th Street, where he retired until about 7:00 at which time he proceeded down to a pay telephone where he called his attorney (the defendant herein). He testified that he advised him he had the coat he had ordered, and agreed to let him have the coat for $20.00. Arrangements were made for the defendant to meet him at the thief's home at approximately 11:00 A.M. where the transfer was to be made. He returned home, and a friend came by and invited him to go get a drink. He started from his house to his friend's car and was arrested by Lt. Anthony of the Oklahoma City Police Department. He was wearing the stolen coat at the time of his arrest. Lt. Anthony took Stanford to the police station, and asked him where he had gotten the coat and he confessed getting it from the car in the YMCA parking lot.

Lt. Anthony testified, in substance, that he received an anonymous telephone call at approximately 7:00 A.M. on the morning of the day in question, and proceeded to the YMCA and located the owner of the vehicle that had been burglarized. They went then to the vehicle and observed the wing glass had been broken, pried open, and a gray cashmere coat and some shirts were missing. Officer Anthony proceeded to the 300 block on N.E. 8th and saw an ex-convict by the name Charley Stanford leaving his house wearing a gray cashmere coat. Anthony then and there arrested Stanford for Burglary and took him to the police station. He then called Mr. Gothard to the police station, where he identified the coat as his and asked Lt. Anthony for the coat, but was advised that they needed it as evidence. Officer Anthony, Officer Reading and Stanford proceeded to 308 N.E. 8th taking the recovered coat with them. After arriving, they took their position behind a closet door containing "peep-holes" and waited for the arrival of defendant Booth. According to the testimony of Anthony, the following transpired:

* * *

"A.   Booth entered the house, and   *   *   *   I heard Charlie Stanford say, 'John, I got the coat which you wanted.' 'I need the twenty dollars right away.' And Mr. Booth said, 'This is child support month, Charlie, come to my office later and I will give you a check.'

*   *   *

well, Booth picked up the coat in his arms and there was conversation of and he warned him that the thing was 'hot'.

"Q.   Who warned who?

"A.   Charlie Stanford warned John Booth that the thing was 'hot'.

"Q.   That the coat was 'hot'?

"A.   Yes, that's the way he termed it.

"Q.   What did Mr. Booth say?

"A.   He said, 'well, I know how to handle things like this, don't worry about it, Charlie.'

*   *   *

"Q.   Then what happened?

"A.   At this point they went into a rest-room and what went on in there, I didn't hear. Then they came back out, and Booth went to his car and put the coat in the turtle-back of his car and then returned to the house and that is about all that occurred.

After taking Stanford to the police station, Anthony obtained a search warrant and then maintained a surveillance of Booth's house until he arrived. He then entered the premises, arrested Booth, and again recovered the coat.

Though defendant Booth was charged with Receiving Stolen Property, at the conclusion of the evidence and after the state and defendant had rested their case, the trial judge gave the following instruction:

"You are instructed that under the law of this case you are at liberty to consider only the included offense of whether the defendant John Fletcher Booth may be guilty of the crime of Attempt to Receive Stolen Property. In this regard you are instructed, an attempt to commit a crime is defined as being the compound of two elements.

"(1) The intent to commit a crime. (2) A direct ineffectual act done towards its commission.

"Preparation alone to an attempt to commit a crime is not sufficient. * * *"

No doubt this instruction was given based upon the theory that once stolen property has been recovered by the police it loses its character as stolen property.

*   *   *

The general rule evidently adopted by the trial court is stated in 76 C.J.S. Receiving Stolen Goods § 5, pg. 7, as follows:

"In order to convict of receiving stolen goods, the goods in question must have retained their stolen character at the time they were received by accused; if they were stolen, they continue to be stolen goods until they are recovered by their owner or some one for him. Hence, where the actual physical possession of stolen goods has been recovered by the owner or his agent and afterwards carried to the receiver either by the original thief or the instrumentality through which the thief originally intended to convey it, at the express direction of the owner or his agent, for the purpose of entrapping the receiver, his receiving of the goods is not a receiving of stolen goods."

* * *

The law seems to be clear on this point, leaving the only question to be decided as whether or not the defendant could be convicted of an attempt to receive stolen property in such cases. It is the defendant's contention that if he could not be convicted of the substantive charge, because the coat had lost its character as stolen property; neither could he be convicted of an attempt because the coat was not in the category of stolen property at the time he received it.

The briefs filed in the case, and extensive research has revealed that two states have passed squarely on the question—New York and California. It is definitely one of first impression in Oklahoma.

The New York Court, in passing upon the question, laid down the following rule in the case of People v. Jaffe, 185 N.Y. 497, 78 N.E. 169, 6 L.R.A.,N.S., 263, on the following facts:

"A clerk stole goods from his employer under an agreement to sell them to accused, but before delivery of the goods the theft was discovered and the goods were recovered. Later the employer redelivered the goods to the clerk to sell to accused, who purchased them for about one-half of their value, believing them to have been stolen.

"Held that the goods had lost their character as stolen goods at the time defendant purchased them, and that his criminal intent was insufficient to sustain a conviction for an attempt to receive stolen property, knowing it to have been stolen."

The Jaffe case, supra, was handed down in 1906, and has prevailed as the law in New York state 58 years without modification * * *

The State of California has passed upon the question several times and up until 1959, they followed the rule laid down in the Jaffe case, supra.

In 1959, in the case of People v. Camodeca, 52 Cal.2d 142, 338 P.2d 903, the California Court abandoned the Jaffe rationale that a person accepting goods which he believes to have been stolen, but which was not in fact stolen goods, is not guilty of an attempt to receive stolen goods, and imposed a liability for the attempt, overruling its previous holding to the contrary in the above cited cases. The Camodeca case, supra, was affirmed in People v. Rojas, 55 Cal.2d 252, 10 Cal.Rptr. 465, 358 P.2d 921, 85 A.L.R.2d 252, 1961.

Though the instant case, insofar as it pertains to the specific crime of attempting to receive stolen property is one of first impression in Oklahoma. This Court held in the Nemecek v. State, 72 Okl.Cr. 195, 114 P.2d 492, 135 A.L.R. 1149, involving attempting to receive money by false pretenses:

> "An accused cannot be convicted of an attempt to commit
> a crime unless he could have been convicted of the crime it-
> self if his attempt had been successful. Where the act, if
> accomplished, would not constitute the crime intended, there
> is no indictable attempt."

In the Nemecek case, supra, the Court quotes with approval, In re Schurman, 40 Kan. 533, 20 P. 277; wherein the Kansas Court said:

> "With reference to attempt, it has also been said that 'if all
> which the accused person intended would, had it been done,
> constitute no substantive crime, it cannot be a crime, under
> the name "attempt," to do, with the same purpose, a part of
> this thing.' "

The two paramount cases of latest date; Rojas of Calif.1961, supra, and [People v.] Rollino, [37 Misc.2d 14, 233 N.Y.S.2d 580 (1962)]; present two rationales directly contrary to each other relative to an attempt to receive stolen property after it had been recovered by the police.

Before adhering too closely to either rationale, it is deemed ad-visable to briefly discuss the development of the "attempt to commit crimes" and the complexity pertaining thereto.

*   *   *

That attempts were indictable as such was restated and definitively determined in Rex. v. Higgins, 2 East 5 (1801). Fifty-six years later, the question of "impossibility" was raised for the first time in Regina v. McPherson, Dears. & B. 197, 201, (1857), when Baron Bramwell said:

> " *   *   * The argument that a man putting his hand into
> an empty pocket might be convicted of an attempt to steal
> appeared to me at first plausible; but suppose a man, believ-
> ing a block of wood to be a man who was his deadly enemy,

struck it a blow intending to murder, could he be convicted of attempting to murder the man he took it to be?"

Subsequently, in Regina v. Collins, 9 Cox C.C. 497, 169 Eng.Rep. 1477 (1864), the Court expressly held that attempted larceny was not made out by proof that the defendant pickpocket actually inserted his hand into the victim's pocket with intent to steal. Chief Justice Cockburn, declaring, at page 499:

> "We think that an attempt to commit a felony can only be made out when, if no interruption had taken place, the attempt could have been carried out successfully, and the felony completed of the attempt to commit which the party is charged."

This very broad language, encompassing as it did all forms of "impossibility", was subsequently rejected by the English courts and it was held that the inability of the pickpocket to steal from an empty pocket did not preclude his conviction of an attempted larceny. Regina v. Ring, 17 Cox C.C. 491, 66 L.T.(N.S.) 306 (1892).

In this country it is generally held that a defendant may be charged with an attempt where the crime was not completed because of "physical or factual impossibility", whereas a "legal impossibility" in the completion of the crime precludes prosecution for an attempt. (Smith, "Two Problems in Criminal Attempts", 70 Harvard Law Review, 422.)

What is a "legal impossibility" as distinguished from a "physical or factual impossibility" has over a long period of time perplexed our courts and has resulted in many irreconcilable decisions and much philosophical discussion by legal scholars in numerous articles and papers in law school publications and by text-writers. See, for example: * * * [Arnold, Criminal Attempts—the Rise and Fall of an Abstraction, 40 Yale L.J. 53 (1930); Curren, Criminal and Non-Criminal Attempts, 19 Geo.L.J. 185, 316 (1931); Keedy, Criminal Attempts at Common Law, 102 U.Pa.L.Rev. 464 (1954); Ryu, Contemporary Problems of Criminal Attempts, 32 N.Y.U.L.Rev. 1170 (1957); Sayre, Criminal Attempts, 41 Harv.L.Rev. 821 (1928); Strahorn, The Effect of Impossibility on Criminal Attempts, 78 U.Pa.L.Rev. 962 (1930).]

The reason for the "impossibility" of completing the substantive crime ordinarily falls into one of two categories: (1) Where the act if completed would not be criminal, a situation which is usually described as a "legal impossibility", and (2) where the basic or substantive crime is impossible of completion, simply because of some physical or factual condition unknown to the defendant, a situation which is usually described as a "factual impossibility".

The authorities in the various states and the text-writers are in general agreement that where there is a "legal impossibility" of completing the substantive crime, the accused cannot be successfully charged with an attempt, whereas in those cases in which the "factual impossibility" situation is involved, the accused may be convicted of an attempt. Detailed discussion of the subject is unnecessary to make it clear that it is frequently most difficult to compartmentalize a particular set of facts as coming within one of the categories rather than the other. Examples of the so-called "legal impossibility" situations are:

(a) A person accepting goods which he believes to have been stolen, but which were not in fact stolen goods, is not guilty of an attempt to receive stolen goods. (People v. Jaffe, 185 N.Y. 497, 78 N.E. 169, 9 L.R.A.,N.S., 263).

(b) It is not an attempt to commit subornation of perjury where the false testimony solicited, if given, would have been immaterial to the case at hand and hence not perjurious. (People v. Teal, 196 N.Y. 372, 89 N.E. 1086, 25 L.R.A.,N.S., 120).

(c) An accused who offers a bribe to a person believed to be a juror, but who is not a juror, is not guilty of an attempt to bribe a juror. (State v. Taylor, 345 Mo. 325, 133 S.W.2d 336).

(d) An official who contracts a debt which is unauthorized and a nullity, but which he believes to be valid, is not guilty of an attempt to illegally contract a valid debt. (Marley v. State, 58 N.J.L. 207, 33 A. 208).

(e) A hunter who shoots a stuffed deer believing it to be alive is not guilty of an attempt to shoot a deer out of season. (State v. Guffey, 262 S.W.2d 152 (Mo.App.)).

Examples of cases in which attempt convictions have been sustained on the theory that all that prevented the consummation of the completed crime was a "factual impossibility" are:

(a) The picking of an empty pocket. (People v. Moran, 123 N.Y. 254, 25 N.E. 412, 10 L.R.A. 109; Commonwealth v. McDonald, 5 Cush. 365 (Mass.); People v. Jones, 46 Mich. 441, 9 N.W. 486).

(b) An attempt to steal from an empty receptacle. (Clark v. State, 86 Tenn. 511, 8 S.W. 145) or an empty house (State v. Utley, 82 N.C. 556).

(c) Where defendant shoots into the intended victim's bed, believing he is there, when in fact he is elsewhere. (State v. Mitchell, 170 Mo. 633, 71 S.W. 175).

(d) Where the defendant erroneously believing that the gun is loaded points it at his wife's head and pulls the trigger. (State v. Damms, 9 Wis.2d 183, 100 N.W.2d 592, 79 A.L.R.2d 1402).

(e) Where the woman upon whom the abortion operation is performed is not in fact pregnant. (Commonwealth v. Tibbetts, 157 Mass. 519, 32 N.E. 910; People v. Huff, 339 Ill. 328, 171 N.E. 261; and Peckham v. United States, 96 U.S. App.D.C. 312, 266 F.2d 34).

Your writer is of the opinion that the confusion that exists as a result of the two diverse rationales laid down in the Rollino case (NY) supra, and the Rojas case (Calif) supra, was brought about by the failure to recognize the distinction between a factual and a legal impossibility to accomplish the crime. In the Camodeca case (Calif) supra, the facts revealed a prevention of the crime because of a factual situation as stated on page 906, 338 P.2d:

"In the present case there was not a legal but only a factual impossibility of consummating the intended offense * * *."

In the Rojas case, supra, wherein was adopted the departure from the Jaffe case, by saying:

"The situation here is materially like those considered in People v. Camodeca."

The Rojas case was definitely not materially the same. In the Rojas case the facts reveal a legal and not factual impossibility.

In the case at bar the stolen coat had been recovered by the police for the owner and consequently had, according to the well-established law in this country, lost its character as stolen property. Therefore, a legal impossibility precluded defendant from being prosecuted for the crime of Knowingly Receiving Stolen Property.

It would strain reasoning beyond a logical conclusion to hold contrary to the rule previously stated herein, that,

"If all which the accused person intended would, had it been done, constituted no substantive crime, it cannot be a crime under the name 'attempt' to do, with the same purpose, a part of this thing."

If a series of acts together will not constitute an offense, how can it be said that one of the acts alone will constitute an indictable offense? Bishop Crim.Law § 747.

The rule is well stated by the English Court in the case of R. v. Percy, Ltd., 33 Crim.App.R. 102 (1949):

"Steps on the way to the commission of what would be a crime, if the acts were completed, may amount to attempts to commit that crime, to which, unless interrupted, they would have led; but steps on the way to the doing of something, which is thereafter done, and which is no crime, cannot be regarded as attempts to commit a crime."

The defendant in the instant case leaves little doubt as to his moral guilt. The evidence, as related by the self-admitted and perpetual law violator indicates defendant fully intended to do the act with which he was charged. However, it is fundamental to our law that a man is not punished merely because he has a criminal mind. It must be shown that he has, with that criminal mind, done an act which is forbidden by the criminal law.

Adhering to this principle, the following example would further illustrate the point.

A fine horse is offered to A at a ridiculously low price by B, who is a known horse thief. A, believing the horse to be stolen, buys the same without inquiry. In fact, the horse had been raised from a colt by B and was not stolen. It would be bordering on absurdity to suggest that A's frame of mind, if proven, would support a conviction of an attempt. It would be a "legal impossibility".

Our statute provides that defendant must attempt to *Knowingly* Receive Stolen Property before a conviction will stand. How could one know property to be stolen when it was not? The statute needs to be changed so it would be less favorable to the criminal.

J. C. Smith, a Reader in Law, University of Nottingham, B.A., Cambridge, 1949, LL. Bl, 1950, M. A., 1954, said in an article (70 Harvard Law Review 422) supporting the Jaffe case, supra, and the above reasoning:

> "If it appears wrong that the accused should escape unpunished in the particular circumstances, then it may be that there is something wrong with the substantive law and his act ought to be criminal. But the remedy then is to alter the substantive crime. Otherwise "there is no ACTUS REUS because 'the accident has turned up in his favour' " and the accused ought to be acquitted. When a man has achieved all the consequences which he set out to achieve and those consequences do not, in the existing circumstances, amount to an ACTUS REUS it is in accordance both with principle and authority that that man should be held not guilty of any crime."

We earnestly suggest that the Legislature revise the law on Attempts in accordance with The * * * "Model Penal Code", * * * Article 5.01 * * *.

In view of our statutory law, and the decisions herein related, it is our duty to Reverse this case, with orders to Dismiss, and it is so ordered. However, there are other avenues open to the County Attorney which should be explored.

JOHNSON, P. J., and BUSSEY, J., concur.

MODEL PENAL CODE, COMMENT TO § 5.01, 30–32

(Tent. Draft No. 10, 1960).

Rejection of the "Impossibility" Defense. The purpose of this paragraph is to reverse the results in cases where attempt convictions have been set aside on the ground that it was legally impossible for the actor to have committed the crime contemplated. * * *

The basic rationale of these decisions is that, judging the actor's conduct in the light of the actual facts, what he intended to do did not amount to a crime. This approach, however, is unsound in that it seeks to evaluate a mental attitude—"intent" or "purpose"—not by looking to the actor's mental frame of reference, but to a situation wholly at variance with the actor's beliefs. In so doing, the courts exonerate defendants in situations where attempt liability most certainly should be imposed. In all of these cases (1) criminal purpose has been clearly demonstrated, (2) the actor has gone as far as he could in implementing that purpose, and (3) as a result, the actor's "dangerousness" is plainly manifested.

* * *

Of course, it is still necessary that the result desired or intended by the actor constitute a crime. If, according to his beliefs as to facts and legal relationships, the result desired or intended is not a crime, the actor will not be guilty of an attempt even though he firmly belives that his goal is criminal.[22]

The basic premise here is that the actor's mind is the best proving ground of his dangerousness. In connection with the discussion which follows of the general application of the impossibility doctrine in the law of criminal attempts, consideration will be given to the proposition that the nature of the actor's mistaken beliefs may negative dangerousness. This factor has not played any role in the impossibility cases discussed above.

---

4. THE "DEFENSE" OF ABANDONMENT

PEOPLE v. STAPLES

California Court of Appeal, 1970.
6 Cal.App.3d 61, 85 Cal.Rptr. 589.

REPPY, Associate Justice. Defendant was charged in an information with attempted burglary (Pen.Code, §§ 664, 459). Trial by

---

22. Thus it has been held that there is no attempt to suborn a witness if the testimony sought is immaterial and would not, if given, constitute perjury. People v. Teal, 196 N.Y. 372, 89 N.E. 1086 (1909) * * *.

jury was waived, and the matter submitted on the testimony contained in the transcript of the preliminary hearing together with exhibits. Defendant was found guilty. Proceedings were suspended before pronouncement of sentence, and an order was made granting defendant probation. The appeal is from the order which is deemed a final judgment. (Pen.Code, § 1237.)

In October 1967, while his wife was away on a trip, defendant, a mathematician, under an assumed name, rented an office on the second floor of a building in Hollywood which was over the mezzanine of a bank. Directly below the mezzanine was the vault of the bank. Defendant was aware of the layout of the building, specifically of the relation of the office he rented to the bank vault. Defendant paid rent for the period from October 23 to November 23. The landlord had 10 days before commencement of the rental period within which to finish some interior repairs and painting. During this prerental period defendant brought into the office certain equipment. This included drilling tools, two acetylene gas tanks, a blow torch, a blanket, and a linoleum rug. The landlord observed these items when he came in from time to time to see how the repair work was progressing. Defendant learned from a custodian that no one was in the building on Saturdays. On Saturday, October 14, defendant drilled two groups of holes into the floor of the office above the mezzanine room. He stopped drilling before the holes went through the floor. He came back to the office several times thinking he might slowly drill down, covering the holes with the linoleum rug. At some point in time he installed a hasp lock on a closet, and planned to, or did, place his tools in it. However, he left the closet keys on the premises. Around the end of November, apparently after November 23, the landlord notified the police and turned the tools and equipment over to them. Defendant did not pay any more rent. It is not clear when he last entered the office, but it could have been after November 23, and even after the landlord had removed the equipment. On February 22, 1968, the police arrested defendant. After receiving advice as to his constitutional rights, defendant voluntarily made an oral statement which he reduced to writing.

Among other things which defendant wrote down were these:

"Saturday, the 14th * * * I drilled some small holes in the floor of the room. Because of tiredness, fear, and the implications of what I was doing, I stopped and went to sleep.

"At this point I think my motives began to change. The actual [sic] commencement of my plan made me begin to realize that even if I were to succeed a fugitive life of living off of stolen money would not give the enjoyment of the life of a mathematician however humble a job I might have.

"I still had not given up my plan however. I felt I had made a certain investment of time, money, effort and a certain pschological [sic] commitment to the concept.

"I came back several times thinking I might store the tools in the closet and slowly drill down (covering the hole with a rug of linoleum square). As time went on (after two weeks or so). My wife came back and my life as bank robber seemed more and more absurd."

* * *

There was definitely substantial evidence entitling the trial judge to find that defendant's acts had gone beyond the preparation stage.

The instant case provides an out-of-the-ordinary factual situation * * * Usually the actors in cases falling within that category of attempts are intercepted or caught in the act. Here, there was no direct proof of any actual interception. But it was clearly inferable by the trial judge that defendant became aware that the landlord had resumed control over the office and had turned defendant's equipment and tools over to the police. This was the equivalent of interception.

The inference of this nonvoluntary character of defendant's abandonment was a proper one for the trial judge to draw. However, it would seem that the character of the abandonment in situations of this type, whether it be voluntary (prompted by pangs of conscience or a change of heart) or nonvoluntary (established by inference in the instant case), is not controlling. The relevant factor is the determination of whether the acts of the perpetrator have reached such a stage of advancement that they can be classified as an attempt. Once that attempt is found there can be no exculpatory abandonment. "One of the purposes of the criminal law is to protect society from those who intend to injure it. When it is established that the defendant intended to commit a specific crime and that in carrying out his intention he committed an act that caused harm or sufficient danger of harm, it is immaterial that for some collateral reason he could not complete the intended crime." (People v. Camodeca, 52 Cal.2d 142, 147, 338 P.2d 903, 906.)

The order is affirmed.

NOTE

Consider the following discussion in Model Penal Code, Comments to § 5.01(4) 69–70 (Tent.Draft No. 10, 1960):

Renunciation of Criminal Purpose. There is uncertainty under the present law whether abandonment of a criminal effort, after the bounds of preparation have been surpassed, will constitute a defense to a charge of attempt. In passing on this issue it is customary to distinguish between "voluntary" and "involuntary" abandonments.

An "involuntary" abandonment occurs where the actor ceases his criminal endeavor because he fears detection or apprehension, or because he decides he will wait for a better opportunity, or because his powers or instruments are inadequate for completing the crime. There is no doubt that such an abandonment does not exculpate the actor from attempt liability otherwise incurred.

By a "voluntary" abandonment is meant a change in the actor's purpose not influenced by outside circumstances, what may be termed repentance or change of heart. Lack of resolution or timidity may suffice. A reappraisal by the actor of the criminal sanctions hanging over his conduct would presumably be a motivation of the voluntary type as long as the actor's fear of the law is not related to a particular threat of apprehension or detection. Whether voluntary abandonments constitute a defense to an attempt charge is far from clear, there being few decisions squarely facing the issue.

If assault cases are not considered, the prevailing view—contrary to the general conceptions of the commentators—is in favor of allowing voluntary desistance as a defense. Supplementing these "express" statements are opinions which impliedly accept this view by emphasizing the fact that desistance in the particular case was involuntary or by giving effect to voluntary desistance in classifying the actor's discontinued conduct as "preparation". Also supporting this position is the widespread statutory definition of attempt—one who "does any act toward the commission of such crime, but fails or is prevented or intercepted in the perpetration thereof"—which, by enumerating involuntary causes of failure, may be taken to exclude voluntary desistance. A similar implication is present in the oft-quoted judicial doctrine that an attempt requires an act which would, in the natural course of things, if not interrupted by an intervening cause independent of the will of the actor, consummate the offense. The bulk of the decisions squarely denying the defense are cases involving assaults, and these are distinguishable. Whether they are correct need not be decided here; it is enough to note that something in the way of a substantive offense had been committed and immunity was accordingly withheld.

It must be noted that even where voluntary desistance is not itself a defense, an abandonment by the actor may result in exoneration if the abandonment negatives a criminal intent. Where the charge is assault with intent to rape and the evidence shows that the accused apparently had it within his power to complete the offense, proof of a voluntary abandonment will weigh heavily in favor of the accused. One state makes it conclusive evidence that defendant did not intend to rape.

The present subsection does not utilize the "voluntary-involuntary" terminology of the prior cases but reaches much the same result by allowing abandonment as a defense only where the circumstances manifest "renunciation of [the actor's] criminal purpose." The requirement of "renunciation" of purpose involves two elements: (1) that the abandonment of the criminal effort originate with the actor and not be forced upon him by some external circumstance such as police intervention; and (2) that the abandonment be permanent and complete rather than temporary or contingent—*e. g.*, a decision by the actor to wait for a better opportunity to commit the crime would not manifest renunciation of criminal purpose.

The basis for allowing the defense involves two related considerations.

First, renunciation of criminal purpose tends to negative dangerousness. As previously indicated, much of the effort devoted to excluding early "preparatory" conduct from criminal attempt liability is based on the desire not to punish where there is an insufficient showing that the actor has a firm purpose to commit the crime contemplated. In cases where the actor has gone beyond the line drawn for preparation, indicating *prima facie* sufficient firmness of purpose, he should be allowed to rebut such a conclusion by showing that he has plainly demonstrated his lack of firm purpose by completely renouncing his purpose to commit the crime.

This line of reasoning, however, may prove unsatisfactory where the actor has proceeded far toward the commission of the contemplated crime, or has perhaps committed the "last proximate act." It may be argued that, whatever the inference to be drawn where the actor's conduct was in the area near the preparation-attempt line, in cases of further progress the inference of dangerousness from such an advanced criminal effort outweighs the countervailing inference arising from abandonment of the effort. However, it is in this latter class of cases that the second of the two policy considerations comes most strongly into play.

A second reason for allowing renunciation of criminal purpose as a defense to an attempt charge is to encourage actors to desist from pressing forward with their criminal designs, thereby diminishing the risk that the substantive crime will be committed. While, under the proposed subsection, such encouragement is held out at all stages of the criminal effort, its significance becomes greatest as the actor nears his criminal objective and the risk that the crime will be completed is correspondingly high. At the very point where abandonment least influences a judgment as to the dangerousness of the actor—where the last proximate act has been committed but the resulting crime can still be avoided—the inducement to desist stemming from the abandonment defense achieves its greatest value.

It is possible, of course, that the defense of renunciation of criminal purpose may add to the incentives to take the *first* steps toward crime. Knowledge that criminal endeavors can be undone with impunity may encourage preliminary steps that would not be undertaken if liability inevitably attached to every abortive criminal undertaking that proceeded beyond preparation. But this is not a serious problem. First, any consolation the actor might draw from the abandonment defense would have to be tempered with the knowledge that the defense would be unavailable if the actor's purposes were frustrated by external forces before he had an opportunity to abandon his effort. Second, the encouragement this defense might lend to the actor taking preliminary steps would be a factor only where the actor was dubious of his plans and where, consequently, the probability of continuance was not great.

On balance, it is concluded that renunciation of criminal purpose should be a defense to a criminal attempt charge because, as to the early stages of an attempt, it significantly negatives dangerousness of character, and, as to later stages, the value of encouraging desistance outweighs the net dangerousness shown by the abandoned criminal effort. And, because of the importance of encouraging desistance in the final stages of the attempt, the defense is allowed even where the last proximate act has occurred but the criminal result can be avoided—*e. g.*, where the fuse has been lit but can still be stamped out. If, however, the actor has gone so far that he has put in motion forces which he is powerless to stop, then the attempt has been completed and cannot be abandoned. In accord with existing law, the actor can gain no immunity for this completed effort (*e. g.*, firing at the intended victim and missing); all he can do is desist from making a second attempt.

*　　*　　*

In considering the significance to be attached to abandonment of a criminal attempt, one solution which was rejected was provision for reduction of penalty in the event of such abandonment. Insofar as encouragement of desistance is concerned, reductions in sanction would have to be very great in order to have a substantial impact on those already engrossed in a criminal attempt; indeed it is unlikely that anything short of complete immunity would suffice. And in dealing with the question of dangerousness, it seems that, once liability is established, sanctions should be linked to neutralizing the actor's dangerousness and determined on a broad basis with reference to the requirements of the particular offender. An automatic reduction in the case of abandonment would be inconsistent with this approach.

––––––––

PROPOSED FEDERAL CRIMINAL CODE (1971)

§ 1005.　General Provisions Regarding Sections 1001 to 1004

*　　*　　*

(3) Renunciation Defense.

(a) Attempt. In a prosecution under section 1001 it is an affirmative defense that, under circumstances manifesting a voluntary and complete renunciation of his criminal intent, the defendant avoided the commission of the crime attempted by abandoning his criminal effort and, if mere abandonment was insufficient to accomplish such avoidance, by taking further and affirmative steps which prevented the commission thereof.

B. SOLICITATION

GERVIN v. STATE

Supreme Court of Tennessee, 1963.
212 Tenn. 653, 371 S.W.2d 449.

DYER, Judge. This appeal in error is from a verdict and judgment convicting Gervin, the appellant here and defendant below, of an attempt to commit murder * * *.

The question to be decided is whether or not an indictment which alleges criminal solicitation is sufficient in law to aver an attempt to commit a felony * * *. This question necessarily involves the primary consideration of common law, criminal solicitation as an attempt.

We hold that such an indictment is not legally sufficient, and that mere criminal solicitation does not constitute an attempt to commit murder * * *.

Robert George Gervin was arraigned and convicted under an indictment, the pertinent parts of which read:

"The Grand Jurors * * * present that Robert George Gervin * * * unlawfully and feloniously did commit and otherwise attempt to commit a felony * * * that is to say, the defendant with intent to feloniously and with malice aforethought commit murder in the first degree, did hire, persuade, try to persuade, and otherwise procure another to attempt to kill and murder another * * * contrary to the statute and against the peace and dignity of the State."

The defendant moved to quash the indictment, challenging the sufficiency of the averments. The motion to quash was overruled by the trial court, and this is assigned as error on appeal. Numerous other assignments of error are made which we do not reach as the one question is determinative.

The terms "attempt" and "solicitation" as used in criminal law are often confused and frequently these terms are merged. Nevertheless attempts and solicitation are distinct by definition. 25 L.R.A. 434 (1894).

"An attempt is an act done with the intent of committing a crime, but which fails of completion. To constitute an attempt, the defendant must, (1) with the intent to commit a specific crime, (2) do an overt act directed to its commission, which goes beyond mere preparation, and is apparently suitable for that purpose, but (3) which fails to result in the commission of the intended crime. 1 Wharton, Criminal Law and Procedure, Sec. 71 at 151-2 (1957)."

Common law, criminal solicitation is defined to include any words or devices by which a person is "requested, urged, advised, counseled, tempted, commanded or otherwise enticed to commit a crime." Perkins, Criminal Law 505 (1957).

It is evident from the above definitions that the indictment in question is couched in terms of criminal solicitation while averring an attempt to commit a felony. This, we hold, is not permissable in Tennessee.

The weight of American authority holds, as a general proposition, that mere criminal solicitation of another to commit a crime does not constitute an attempt.

The weight of authority is, of course, not determinative, but the reasons for that position are compelling.

The definitions of attempts and solicitation are not only different, but these offenses are analytically distinct. The gist of criminal solicitation is incitement. The body of the crime is the act of solicitation, and any additional conduct is incidental and collateral. Curran, Solicitations: A Substantive Crime, 17 Minn.L.Rev. 499, 503 (1932–33).

An attempt, on the other hand, requires three elements; (1) an intent to commit a specific crime; (2) an overt act; and (3) failure to consummate the crime. 1 Wharton, op. cit. supra Sec. 71 at 151–152. In attempts, the intent must be to commit the contemplated crime. The intent required in solicitation is the intent to have the crime committed with the purpose of communicating that intent to another. Blackburn, Solicitation to Crimes, 40 W.Va.L.Q. 135 (1933–34). But in relation to attempts, solicitation only supplies a wrongful intent. Solicitation to Commit Murder as an Attempt to Commit, 40 U.Mo.Bull.L.Ser. 45 (1928). Consequently, if the solicitor does not plan to take an active part in effecting the crime, and the solicitation is held an attempt, the requirement of a specific intent may be violated. See Perkins, op. cit. supra at 509.

To constitute an attempt there must also be an act of perpetration, that is, an overt act. However solicitation is preparation rather than perpetration. This being true, to call solicitation an attempt is to delete the element of an overt act. The element of an overt act is, however, necessary and serves a useful purpose as pointed out in State v. Mandel, 78 Ariz. 226, 278 P.2d 413 (1954).

> The fundamental reason for an overt act is that until such act occurs, there is too much uncertainty that a design is to be apparently carried out. Until that time the situation is equivocal. 278 P.2d at 415–416.

We are reluctant to hold, and indeed our cases indicate we cannot, that at the stage of preparation the attempt will be carried out and that the situation is unequivocal. At this point there are too many contingencies, such as the willingness of the solicitant to carry out the design, to say the dye [sic] is cast. But to hold solicitation an attempt this would be necessary.

Not only would the merging of attempts and solicitations do violence to the respective concepts, but there are other reasons which are grounded in policy. There is not the same degree of heinousness in solicitation as in attempts, nor is solicitation as likely to result in a completed crime, there not being the same dangerous proximity to success as found in attempts.

In most areas of the law degrees of culpability and fault are recognized and different penalties are prescribed. We can see no good reason why there should be an exception made here. * * *

The latest decision in point is Valley v. State, 203 Tenn. 80, 309 S.W.2d 374 (1958). The defendant was indicted under T.C.A. § 39-603 for an assault with the intent to commit a felony, that is, have unnatural relations with a 14 year old boy. The testimony of the victim tended to prove that the defendant actually had made propositions to the boy and on one occasion had tried unsuccessfully to touch the boy.

This court said that although a technical assault was not made out the defendant was still guilty as the statute under which he was prosecuted also covered attempts. The court held this was at least an attempt.

Chief Justice Neil dissented upon the basis that since no overt act was shown the evidence was insufficient to sustain a conviction for an attempt.

We do not think this case stands for the proposition that solicitation is an attempt. At most the case indicates that solicitation in addition to some other conduct which transcends preparation may constitute an attempt. Interpreting this case as we do, we are cognizant of the contrary interpretation in Miller, Criminal Law and Procedure—1958 Tennessee Survey, 11 Vand.L.Rev. 1226, 1228–1229 (1958).

A reading of the decision in the Valley case indicates that the court was impressed that the defendant had tried to touch the victim. This is strengthened by the fact that the court quoted only that part of the testimony which dealt with the attempted touching. Further, we think it significant that the dissent was based on no overt act being shown. Therefore any difference of opinion within the court appears to have been grounded on whether there was or was not an overt act, and not over the question of whether or not solicitation is an attempt.

* * *

In reaching our conclusion in this case, we are mindful of the formidable opposition to making any distinction between attempts and criminal solicitation. One authority takes the position that the policy of attempt statutes should be expanded to cover solicitation, because solicitation involves the same consideration attempts do, and any distinction is artificial. Arnold, Criminal Attempts—The Rise and Fall of an Abstraction, 40 Yale L.J. 53, 76–77 (1931–32).

* * *

The appellee's contention implies that if solicitation cannot be punished as an attempt the solicitor may go free though guilty of reprehensible conduct. If this was the case we would be inclined to agree with the appellee. However, we think the crime of solicitation may be punished as an independent crime although we find no evidence of it ever having been done in this state. We therefore must turn to our statutes or to the common law.

* * *

At common law, solicitation to commit a crime, which by statute or common law is a felony, is a substantive crime. Furthermore so much of the common law as has not been abrogated or repealed by statute is in full force and effect in Tennessee. Finding no local statute which abrogates the offense of common law solicitation, we must conclude it is an indictable offense in Tennessee. And being an indictable offense, solicitation to commit a felony is treated as a misdemeanor. * * *

The trial court, therefore, erred in failing to sustain the defendant's motion to quash the indictment.

The cause is reversed and remanded.

MODEL PENAL CODE (PROPOSED OFFICIAL DRAFT, 1962)

Section 5.02. Criminal Solicitation

(1) *Definition of Solicitation.* A person is guilty of solicitation to commit a crime if with the purpose of promoting or facilitating its commission he commands, encourages or requests another person to engage in specific conduct which would constitute such crime or an attempt to commit such crime or which would establish his complicity in its commission or attempted commission.

(2) *Uncommunicated Solicitation.* It is immaterial under Subsection (1) of this Section that the actor fails to communicate with the person he solicits to commit a crime if his conduct was designed to effect such communication.

(3) *Renunciation of Criminal Purpose.* It is an affirmative defense that the actor, after soliciting another person to commit a crime persuaded him not to do so or otherwise prevented the commission of the crime, under circumstances manifesting a complete and voluntary renunciation of his criminal purpose.

PROPOSED FEDERAL CRIMINAL CODE
(STUDY DRAFT 1970)

§ 1003. Criminal Solicitation

(1) Offense. A person is guilty of criminal solicitation if he commands, induces, entreats, or otherwise attempts to persuade another person to commit a particular crime which is, in fact, a felony, whether as principal or accomplice, with intent to promote or facilitate the commission of that crime, and under circumstances strongly corroborative of that intent.

(2) Defense. It is a defense to a prosecution under this section that, if the criminal object were achieved, the defendant would be a victim of the offense or the offense is so defined that his conduct would be inevitably incident to its commission or he otherwise would not be guilty under the statute defining the offense or as an accomplice * * *.

(3) Defense Precluded. It is no defense to a prosecution under this section that the person solicited could not be guilty of the offense because of lack of responsibility or culpability, or other incapacity or defense.

(4) Renunciation and Withdrawal. It is an affirmative defense to a prosecution under this section that the defendant, after soliciting another person to commit a felony, persuaded him not to do so or otherwise prevented the commission of the felony, under circumstances manifesting a complete and voluntary renunciation of the defendant's criminal intent. A renunciation is not "voluntary and complete" if it is motivated in whole or in part by (a) a belief that a circumstance exists which increases the probability of detection or apprehension of the defendant or another or which makes more difficult the consummation of the crime or (b) a decision to postpone the crime until another time or to substitute another victim or another but similar objective.

(5) Grading. Criminal solicitation shall be subject to the penalties provided for attempt in section 1001(4).

* * *

NOTES

1. The drafters of the Model Penal Code and the Draft of the New Federal Criminal Code take a rather more serious view of those who solicit crime than does the Tennessee Supreme Court in *Gervin*. The Comments to § 5.02, Model Penal Code, Tent.Draft No. 10 at 82 (1960), acknowledge the existence of views such as those expressed in *Gervin* but continue: "Against this is the view that a solicitation is, if anything, more dangerous than a direct attempt, since it may give rise to that cooperation among criminals that is a special hazard. Solicitation may, indeed, be thought of as an attempt to conspire. Moreover, the solicitor, working his will through one or

more agents, manifests an approach to crime more intelligent and masterful than the efforts of his hireling." It goes on to note that " * * * the imposition of liability for criminal solicitation may be an important means by which the leadership of a movement deemed criminal may be suppressed." [4] The citations offered in support of this statement illustrate the major concern that civil libertarians have with the criminalization of solicitation.

How great is the danger that such statutes will be employed to stifle First Amendment rights either directly or by its "chilling effect"? Cf. Speiser v. Randall, 357 U.S. 513, 78 S.Ct. 1332, 2 L.Ed.2d 1460 (1958). Is either MPC § 5.02 or Proposed Federal Criminal Code § 1003 consistent with the "clear and present danger" doctrine? Need they be?

2. If a general solicitation statute poses serious dangers to First Amendment rights, would it be preferable to have statutes aimed at more specific evils. An example of such is N.J.Stat.Ann. 2A:148–10 which reads as follows:

> Any person who, in public or private, by speech, writing, printing or otherwise, advocates, encourages, justifies, praises or incites:
>
> a. The unlawful burning or destruction of public or private property; or
>
> b. Assaults upon any of the armed forces of the United States, the national guard, or the police force of this or any other state or of any municipality; or
>
> c. The killing or injuring of any class or body of persons or of any individual—
>
> Is guilty of a high misdemeanor.

See State v. Cappon, 118 N.J.Super. 9, 285 A.2d 287 (1971) (at the end of a Puerto Rican Day parade in Newark defendant cried "get those motherfuckers" and bottles began to be hurled at nearby police officers) and State v. Hopson, 109 N.J.Super. 382, 263 A.2d 205 (1970) (in the course of a demonstration concerning grievances at a local high school defendant's son was arrested, whereupon she uttered words "of the general purport of, 'get the cops,' and 'Free the black boy.' "). Turner v. La Belle, 251 F.Supp. 443 (D.C.Conn.1966) involved a prosecution under a virtually identical Connecticut statute. There, four leaders of civil rights groups in Hartford sought to restrain enforcement of the statute against them. They had led a demonstration of support in the Hartford Ghetto shortly after the Watts riots. One defendant allegedly said " * * * treat every cop as your enemy

---

4. Political agitation. Masses Pub. Co. v. Patten, 246 Fed. 24 (2d Cir. 1917); United States v. Nearing, 252 Fed. 223 (S.D.N.Y.1918); United States v. Galleanni, 245 Fed. 977 (D.Mass.1917); People v. Most, 171 N.Y. 423, 64 N.E. 175 (1902) (based on breach of peace statute); Rex v. Bowman, 76 J.P. 271 (Central Crim.Ct.1912); Rex v. Antonelli & Barberi, 70 J.P. 4 (Central Crim.Ct.1905); The Queen v. Most, 7 Q.B.D. 244 (C.C.R.1881); R. v. M'Carthy, Holland, and O'Dwyer, [1903] 2 Irish Rep. 146 (1902).

Labor agitation. State v. Schleifer, 99 Conn. 432, 121 Atl. 805 (1923); State v. Quinlan, 86 N.J.L. 120, 91 Atl. 111 (Sup.Ct.1914), aff'd per curiam, 87 N.J.L. 333, 93 Atl. 1086 (Ct.Err. & App. 1915); State v. Boyd, 86 N.J.L. 75, 91 Atl. 586 (1914), rev'd on other grounds, 87 N.J.L. 560, 94 Atl. 807 (Ct.Err. & App.1915); Rex v. O'Brien, [1914] So. Afr.L.R. (Trans.Prov.Div.) 287.

* * * until America wakes up." Another was alleged to have told the small crowd: "If I can't be imported back, then kill me, kill me, or I'll kill you" and "anyone that's black is so very angry that he wants to fight, that he wants to shoot, well then, only look to the left, to the blue shirts."

3. Another way of limiting the reach of solicitation statutes is that adopted by the Proposed Federal Criminal Code which, in its Final Draft, adds the following clause at the end of § 1003(1)

"and the person solicited commits an overt act in response to the solicitation."

The Comment explains:

"the solicitee either has not yet agreed (although he has committed an overt act, such as coming back for further discussions) or he has agreed but no overt act has been committed sufficient to make the crime a conspiracy. * * * An overt act is required so that criminality depends on something besides speech."

C. CONSPIRACY

1. MODEL STATUTORY FORMULATIONS

MODEL PENAL CODE (PROPOSED OFFICIAL DRAFT, 1962)

Section 5.03. Criminal Conspiracy

(1) *Definition of Conspiracy.* A person is guilty of conspiracy with another person or persons to commit a crime if with the purpose of promoting or facilitating its commission he:

(a) agrees with such other person or persons that they or one or more of them will engage in conduct which constitutes such crime or an attempt or solicitation to commit such crime; or

(b) agrees to aid such other person or persons in the planning or commission of such crime or of an attempt or solicitation to commit such crime.

(2) *Scope of Conspiratorial Relationship.* If a person guilty of conspiracy, as defined by Subsection (1) of this Section, knows that a person with whom he conspires to commit a crime has conspired with another person or persons to commit the same crime, he is guilty of conspiring with such other person or persons, whether or not he knows their identity, to commit such crime.

(3) *Conspiracy With Multiple Criminal Objectives.* If a person conspires to commit a number of crimes, he is guilty of only one conspiracy so long as such multiple crimes are the object of the same agreement or continuous conspiratorial relationship.

* * *

(5) *Overt Act.* No person may be convicted of conspiracy to commit a crime, other than a felony of the first or second degree, unless an overt act in pursuance of such conspiracy is alleged and proved to have been done by him or by a person with whom he conspired.

(6) *Renunciation of Criminal Purpose.* It is an affirmative defense that the actor, after conspiring to commit a crime, thwarted the success of the conspiracy, under circumstances manifesting a complete and voluntary renunciation of his criminal purpose.

(7) *Duration of Conspiracy.* For purposes of Section 1.06 (4):

> (a) conspiracy is a continuing course of conduct which terminates when the crime or crimes which are its object are committed or the agreement that they be committed is abandoned by the defendant and by those with whom he conspired; and

> (b) such abandonment is presumed if neither the defendant nor anyone with whom he conspired does any overt act in pursuance of the conspiracy during the applicable period of limitation; and

> (c) if an individual abandons the agreement, the conspiracy is terminated as to him only if and when he advises those with whom he conspired of his abandonment or he informs the law enforcement authorities of the existence of the conspiracy and of his participation therein.

Section 5.04. Incapacity, Irresponsibility or Immunity of Party to Solicitation or Conspiracy

(1) Except as provided in Subsection (2) of this Section, it is immaterial to the liability of a person who solicits or conspires with another to commit a crime that:

> (a) he or the person whom he solicits or with whom he conspires does not occupy a particular position or have a particular characteristic which is an element of such crime, if he believes that one of them does; or

> (b) the person whom he solicits or with whom he conspires is irresponsible or has an immunity to prosecution or conviction for the commission of the crime.

(2) It is a defense to a charge of solicitation or conspiracy to commit a crime that if the criminal object were achieved, the actor would not be guilty of a crime under the law defining the offense or as an accomplice under Section 2.06(5) or 2.06(6)(a) or (b).

PROPOSED FEDERAL CRIMINAL CODE (1971)

§ 1004. Criminal Conspiracy

(1) Offense. A person is guilty of conspiracy if he agrees with one or more persons to engage in or cause the performance of conduct which, in fact, constitutes a crime or crimes, and any one or more of such persons does an act to effect the objective of the conspiracy. The agreement need not be explicit but may be implicit in the fact of collaboration or existence of other circumstances.

(2) Parties to Conspiracy. If a person knows that one with whom he agrees has agreed or will agree with another to effect the same objective, he shall be deemed to have agreed with the other, whether or not he knows the other's identity.

(3) Duration of Conspiracy. A conspiracy shall be deemed to continue until its objectives are accomplished, frustrated or abandoned. "Objectives" includes escape from the scene of the crime, distribution of booty, and measures, other than silence, for concealing the crime or obstructing justice in relation to it. A conspiracy shall be deemed to have been abandoned if no overt act to effect its objectives has been committed by any conspirator during the applicable period of limitations.

(4) Defense Precluded. It is no defense to a prosecution under this section that the person with whom such person is alleged to have conspired has been acquitted, has not been prosecuted or convicted, has been convicted of a different offense, is immune from prosecution, or is otherwise not subject to justice.

(5) Liability as Accomplice. Accomplice liability for offenses committed in furtherance of the conspiracy is to be determined as provided in section 401.

(6) Grading. Conspiracy shall be subject to the penalties provided for attempt in section 1001(3).

(7) Jurisdiction. There is federal jurisdiction over an offense defined in this section as prescribed in section 203.

2. ELEMENTS OF THE OFFENSE

a. AGREEMENT

(1) GENERAL REQUIREMENT OF AGREEMENT

BENDER v. STATE

Supreme Court of Delaware, 1969.
253 A.2d 686.

WOLCOTT, Chief Justice. This is an appeal from a conviction of robbery and conspiracy to commit robbery. William L. Bender, Frank Lightcap and Kenneth Lloyd were jointly indicted, tried and convicted on the two charges. All three appeal. Basically, the question raised is the sufficiency of the State's evidence to support the convictions.

The State's case was as follows:

On June 28, 1967, at about 6:30 p. m., Eli Byler was walking with David Detweiler at Ninth and Shipley Streets in Wilmington. Byler was approached by Lloyd who asked for a cigarette and for money. Byler refused and started to walk away. At this point, Bender and Lightcap came up. Lloyd then threatened Byler with a glass bottle he had in his hand.

Byler began to run and was chased by the three defendants. He was caught from behind by Lightcap and was held from behind by more than one person. His wallet was taken from his pocket and money removed from it by Lloyd. Thereupon, all three defendants, Lightcap, Lloyd and Bender, fled the scene.

Appellants argue that there was insufficient evidence of robbery as to Bender to submit to the jury, and that there was no evidence as to conspiracy to commit robbery as to any of the appellants. Accordingly, they seek a reversal and a remand for new trial as to Lloyd and Lightcap on the robbery charge, and a judgment of acquittal as to Bender on the robbery charge, and as to all three on the conspiracy charge.

We think, however, that under the evidence, the State proved without question that Byler was the victim of a robbery and that all three of the defendants participated in it. No other conclusion seems credible when it is considered that all were present when Byler was threatened by Lloyd. When Byler sought to flee, all three defendants pursued him. At least two of them held him from behind while, presumably, Lloyd removed his wallet. All three defendants then ran off together.

* * *

With respect to the conspiracy charge, the State, of course, produced no evidence of a prior agreement among the defendants to commit this robbery. The State contends that the presence of the three defendants on the scene and their concerted action in committing the crime justify the conclusion that they had agreed among themselves.

A conspiracy is the combination of two or more persons to commit a crime. It is not necessary that there be a formal agreement in advance of the crime. The basic requirement is that there be an unlawful combination, and that the parties have a common design or purpose. If a person understands the unlawful nature of the acts taking place, and nevertheless assists in any manner in the carrying out of the common scheme, he thereupon becomes a conspirator to commit the offense.

We think there is sufficient evidence of the joint participation in this crime of these defendants to warrant the inference that they had the common design or purpose of robbing Byler. The matter was therefore properly submitted to the jury which found them guilty.

The judgments below are affirmed.

NOTE

Conspiracy doctrine permits the state to intervene long before the defendants have taken any action which brings them close to the achievement of their criminal purpose. It permits this intervention on the basis of conduct, other than the agreement, which may be extremely equivocal as an expression of criminal purpose. Therefore, it is clear that the establishment of an agreement is essential to the rationale for conspiracy prosecutions. The existence of the agreement presumably allays any concerns we might have about possible misidentification of the accused. It has been asserted that:

> " * * * The act of agreeing with another to commit a crime * * * is concrete and unambiguous; it does not present the infinite degrees and variations possible in the general category of attempts. The danger that truly equivocal behavior may be misinterpreted as preparation to commit a crime is minimized; purpose must be relatively firm before the commitment involved in agreement is assumed."

Wechsler, Jones, & Korn, The Treatment of Inchoate Crimes in the Model Penal Code of The American Law Institute: Attempt, Solicitation, and Conspiracy, 61 Colum.L.Rev. 957, 958 (1961). How consistent is this position with that of the Arkansas Supreme Court:

> "Appellant seems to take the position that there must be direct evidence of a conspiracy, common design or purpose, and of the intent of the conspirators or joint actors to engage therein. In this he is mistaken. We have long recognized * * * that it is not necessary that an unlawful combination, conspiracy or concert of action to commit an unlawful act be shown by direct evidence, and that it may be proved by circumstances. * * * It may be in-

ferred, even though no actual meeting among the parties is proved, if it be shown that two or more persons pursued by their acts the same unlawful object, each doing a part, so that their acts, though apparently independent, were in fact connected."

Griffin v. State, 248 Ark. 1223, 1225, 455 S.W.2d 882, 884 (1970).

Probably in large part because of the difficulty of establishing the fact of an agreement, the prosecution has traditionally been permitted considerable leeway in proving this element of the offense.

----

(2) OBJECTIVE OF THE AGREEMENT

STATE v. BOWLING

Court of Appeals of Arizona, 1967.
5 Ariz.App. 436, 427 P.2d 928.

MOLLOY, Judge. The defendants in this action appeal from convictions upon two counts of an indictment rendered against them by a grand jury. Both were charged in count one of this indictment with conspiracy to commit an act " * * * injurious to the public morals or unlawfully perverting or obstructing justice or due administration of the laws * * * " and in count two of receiving a bribe, while a member of the Arizona State Legislature, " * * * upon an understanding that their official opinions, judgments and actions should be influenced thereby * * * ".

The facts giving rise to these charges are substantially without dispute. A resident of Pima county by the name of Jerry Hanson, the co-proprietor of a tavern, was desirous of obtaining a new liquor license for his business, which would permit the sale of additional types of liquor. He had a conversation with Bowling, one of the defendants, who was at the time a member of the House of Representatives of the Arizona State Legislature, about assistance in obtaining such license. Bowling informed Hanson that he might be able to assist him, and arranged a meeting between Hanson, himself, and the other defendant, Cook, who was also a member of the Arizona House of Representatives. Hanson testified that Cook was introduced to him only as a legislator, while Bowling testified that Cook was introduced as a real estate broker. At this meeting, Hanson was informed that it would cost approximately $5,000 for the license over and above regular license fees and at a subsequent meeting, it was agreed that Hanson would pay $4,200, over and above the normal license fees, if the liquor license was obtained for him.

An application for such a license was duly submitted and a personal conference with Mr. John Duncan, Superintendent of Liquor Licenses and Control for the State of Arizona, followed, with Hanson, Bowling and Cook all speaking in behalf of the issuance of the license. The statements made in support of issuing the license were in the nature of character references for Hanson and his father, who was a partner in the tavern, and included the argument that such a license was needed because two families were to be supported from this one business. There was no showing in the evidence of any inducements being offered to Mr. Duncan to issue the license nor of any improper persuasions advanced. The testimony is undisputed that Hanson was fully qualified under applicable law for the issuance of the license and that the location as to which the license application pertained fulfilled all of the legal requirements for such a license.

About a month after the conversation with Duncan, Cook contacted Hanson to inform him that the license had been issued, and Cook together with Bowling, brought the license to Hanson's home, where Hanson gave them $4,200 in cash. Bowling testified that all of this money was received and retained by Cook; Cook did not take the stand during the trial.

Numerous questions are raised on appeal, but it is our judgment that this proceeding must be disposed of on the basis of the contention that the trial court erred in refusing to direct a verdict of acquittal at the close of the State's case as to both counts of the indictment.

Count one of the indictment charges a crime under A.R.S. § 13–331. This statute, insofar as pertinent here, reads as follows:

"A.   It is unlawful for two or more persons to conspire to:

*   *   *   *   *   *   *   *   *   *

"5.   Commit any act injurious to the public health or public morals.

"6.   Pervert or obstruct justice or due administration of laws.

"B.   A person who violates any provision of this section shall be punished by imprisonment in the state prison for not to exceed one year, or by a fine not exceeding one thousand dollars.

"C.   No conspiracies other than those enumerated in this section are punishable criminally."

From this statute, the following language was selected to charge that the defendants: " *   *   *   did unlawfully conspire with each other to obtain a Series No. 6 Arizona State Liquor License for one JERRY HANSON from JOHN A. DUNCAN, the Superintendent of the Arizona State Department of Liquor Licenses and Control, *   *   * such act being injurious to the public morals or unlawfully perverting or obstructing justice or due administration of the laws *   *   *."

Initially, the appellants challenge the language charged in the indictment—that they conspired to commit an act "injurious to public morals"—on the grounds that it is unconstitutionally indefinite. * *

In considering a Utah statute with similar wording, the Supreme Court of the United States said:

> "Standing by itself, it would seem to be warrant for conviction for agreement to do almost any act which a judge and jury might find at the moment contrary to his or its notions of what was good for health, morals, trade, commerce, justice or order."

Musser v. State of Utah, 333 U.S. 95, 68 S.Ct. 397, 398, 92 L.Ed. 562 (1948).

The Supreme Court of the United States remanded the *Musser* case to the Utah Supreme Court to consider whether the language of this statute was unconstitutionally vague. The United States Supreme Court suggested that there was a possibility that under Utah statutory or case law the broad language of the statute might have been limited so as to give the required degree of specificity thereto.

The Supreme Court of Utah, however, was unable to point to any limitations upon the subject language and came to the conclusion that this statute, making it a crime to conspire to commit an act " * * * injurious * * * to public morals * * *" was unconstitutional:

> "No language in this or any other statute of this state or other law thereof or any historical fact or surrounding circumstance connected with the enactment of this statute has been pointed to as indicating that the legislature intended any limitation thereon other than that expressed on the face of the words used. We are therefore unable to place a construction on these words which limits their meaning beyond their general meaning. The conviction of the defendants thereunder cannot be upheld. This part of the statute is therefore void for vagueness and uncertainty under the Fourteenth Amendment to the Federal Constitution."

State v. Musser, 118 Utah 537, 223 P.2d 193, 194 (1950).

Likewise, we know of no statutory or case law in this state which limits the broad sweep of that which is encompassed within the words " * * * injurious to * * * public morals * * *". Common-law crimes have not survived in this state, and unless certain conduct is singled out by criminal statute, conduct is not a crime no matter how reprehensible.

We are aware that if a criminal statute refers by name to a common-law crime, the elements of that common-law crime may give sufficient definiteness to statutory language. However, we know of no common-law crime which bears analogy to the committing of an act "injurious to public morals."

In our view, these key words are even more vague and indefinite than the language "obscene or indecent," which was struck down by our Supreme Court in State v. Locks [97 Ariz. 148, 397 P.2d 949 (1964)]. We follow the specific holding of State v. Musser, supra, in declaring that this language is not sufficiently definite to satisfy due process requirements.

The State has contended that California, from whence our state adopted the statutory language under which these defendants were charged, has upheld the statute as to constitutionality. The cases cited are: Lorenson v. Superior Court, 35 Cal.2d 49, 216 P.2d 859 (1950); People v. Sullivan, 113 Cal.App.2d 510, 248 P.2d 520 (1952); Calhoun v. Superior Court, 46 Cal.2d 18, 291 P.2d 474 (1955); and Davis v. Superior Court, 175 Cal.App.2d 8, 345 P.2d 513 (1959). An examination of these decisions, however, will disclose no reliance upon that portion of the statute pertaining to acts injurious to the "public morals." These decisions all lean upon the words "to pervert or to obstruct justice or the due administration of the laws", as illustrated in the following language in *Lorenson:*

> "Considering the well-settled meaning at common law of the words 'to pervert or obstruct justice, or the due administration of the laws', the other and more specific provisions in the Penal Code concerning 'Crimes Against Public Justice', and the relative certainty of words employed in statutes which have been held valid, it cannot be said that subsection 5 of section 182 of the Penal Code is unconstitutional."

216 P.2d at 866.

In each of the four California cases, there was at least one specific criminal statute as to which the charges of conspiracy related. Here the State points to no criminal statute which the defendants are charged to have conspired to violate. Hence, under these California decisions, this charge can be sufficiently specific only if it charges a conspiracy to commit an act which would constitute the common-law crime "to pervert or obstruct justice, or the due administration of laws." *Lorenson* undertakes to define this common-law misdemeanor in this language:

> "Section 182 defines as criminal conspiracy acts committed with the purpose ' * * * to pervert or obstruct justice, or the due administration of the laws.' [G]enerally speaking, conduct which constitutes an offense against public justice, or the administration of law includes *both malfeasance and nonfeasance by an officer in connection*

with the administration of his public duties, and also *anything done by a person in hindering or obstructing an officer in the performance of his official obligations.* Such an offense was recognized at common law and generally punishable as a misdemeanor. Now, quite generally, it has been made a statutory crime, and, under some circumstances, a felony. Burdick, Law of Crimes [1946], vol. 1, p. 382, et seq.; 20 Cal.Jur. 347–354." (Emphasis added) 216 P.2d at 865.

In *Davis*, in rejecting the contention that the "obstruction of justice" statute was unconstitutional on its face, the court said:

"The constitutionality of the California statute, however, rests upon the fact that three cases have charted boundaries to its otherwise limitless sea of criminality." 345 P.2d at 517.

These California decisions leave open the possibility that the remaining language in count one of the subject indictment—"unlawfully perverting or obstructing justice or due administration of the laws"—properly charges a criminal offense. In this regard, the appellants do not directly attack this charging language upon constitutional grounds, but rather on the basis of lack of proof. In considering this argument, we have concluded that unless the acceptance of $4,200 by the defendants constituted a violation of this law, there was no proof submitted to the jury meriting a conviction on the conspiracy charge.

* * *

It seems clear that these defendants, Bowling and Cook, or any other person, could have recommended to Mr. Duncan the issuance of a license to any particular applicant, for any legitimate reason, without violating criminal law, and, in fact, this is not disputed by the State in this action. But the State contends that the acceptance of the $4,200 renders that which would otherwise be legal conduct into a perversion or obstruction of justice and/or due administration of laws. No pertinent authority is cited.

We see no justification for characterizing the defendants' conduct as a perversion or obstruction of "justice or due administration of laws," assuming that these concepts are made sufficiently definite by reference to the common law. The act charged as to which there was alleged to have been a conspiracy was the obtaining of the license for Hanson. The selection of Hanson by Duncan for the receipt of one of the quota licenses was not, in and of itself, a "malfeasance" or a "nonfeasance" nor a failure to perform "official obligations." (In the language of *Lorenson.*) The conduct of the defendants simply does not fit the charging language in count one of the indictment. Any conspiratorial conduct of the defendants, if criminal at all under the then existing law, most closely approached being a conspiracy to violate a bribery statute, a charge not made, nor, as we shall see, supportable in the evidence. The fact that conduct may be highly reprehensible in the eyes of the courts does not justify the court in distorting language of a criminal statute to fit the conduct. A verdict should have been directed for the defendants on count one.

NOTE

Modern criminal codes, proposed and adopted, require that the objective of a conspiracy be a crime specifically defined in the code. See, e. g., Smith-Hurd Ill.Ann.Stat. ch. 38, § 8–2(a); McKinney Consol.Laws of N.Y. (Penal Law) §§ 105.00, 105.05, 105.10 & 105.15; Proposed New Federal Criminal Code § 1004(1); and MPC § 5.03 (1).

---

(3) DEFENSES BASED ON THE REQUIREMENT OF AN AGREEMENT

It is generally held that a criminal conspiracy must involve an actual agreement between at least two "guilty" persons. Thus if it appears that for some reason, all but one of the alleged conspirators are innocent or for some other reason could not be convicted of the criminal conspiracy, the remaining person may not be convicted. It is a "defense," in other words, to show that there is no one else who could be convicted of the conspiracy. This section deals with situations controlled by this rule.

REGLE v. STATE

Court of Special Appeals of Maryland, 1970.
9 Md.App. 346, 264 A.2d 119.

MURPHY, Chief Judge. On September 28, 1968, Sergeant Frank Mazzone, a Maryland State Police officer working under cover, was advised by other police officers that Michael Isele, a police informer, had informed them that he had been invited by the appellant Regle to participate in a robbery. Mazzone immediately contacted Isele, whom he previously knew, and together they went to see the appellant. Isele introduced Mazzone to the appellant as a prospective participant in the planned robbery. After some discussion, the appellant invited Mazzone to participate in the robbery. While appellant did not then specify the place to be robbed, he indicated to Mazzone that Richard Fields had been involved with him in planning the robbery, and that he would also participate in the crime. Appellant, Mazzone, and Isele then met with Fields and the robbery plan was outlined by appellant and Fields. The need for guns was discussed and appellant and Fields spoke of the necessity of killing two employees at O'Donnell's restaurant, the situs of the proposed robbery. The four men then drove in Isele's car to appellant's home where appellant phoned Kent Chamblee for the purpose of purchasing a shotgun. Thereafter, the men drove to Chamblee's home, purchased the gun from him, and tested it in his presence. While Chamblee knew that the shotgun was to be used "for a job," he did not accompany the others when they then drove to the restaurant to perpetrate the robbery. Upon arriving there, Mazzone told appellant that he first wanted to "case" the restaurant. This being agreed, Mazzone and Isele went into the restaurant while appellant and Fields went to a nearby bar to await their return. Once inside the restaurant, Mazzone contacted police headquarters and requested assistance. Thereafter, he and Isele left the restaurant and rejoined appellant and Fields. While several police cars promptly responded to the scene, Mazzone found it necessary, in the interim, to reveal his identity as a police officer and to arrest appellant and Fields at gunpoint. At the same time he also arrested Isele in order "to cover him." After the arrest, appellant made an incriminating statement to the effect that he and Fields had planned the robbery and that he had invited Isele to participate in the crime.

Appellant, Fields, and Chamblee were thereafter jointly indicted for conspiracy to rob with a dangerous and deadly weapon and for carrying a deadly weapon openly with intent to injure. Appellant was separately tried by a jury, found guilty on both counts, and sentenced to twenty years on the conspiracy charge, and two years, concurrent, on the weapons offense.

The docket entries indicate that the conspiracy indictment against Chamblee was *nol prossed* prior to appellant's trial. It also appears that at his trial appellant established through the testimony of a police officer that Fields had been examined by State psychiatrists at the Clifton Perkins State Hospital and found "not guilty by reason of being insane at the time of the alleged crime." The State did not rebut the officer's testimony, although the record indicates that two of the State psychiatrists who had examined Fields were then present in court.

Against this background, appellant contends that since the indictment against Chamblee was *nol prossed,* only he and Fields were charged as conspirators; and that because Fields was found insane at the time of the commission of the crime and thus was not a person legally capable of engaging in a criminal conspiracy, his own conviction cannot stand since one person alone cannot be guilty of the crime of conspiracy.

Conspiracy—a common law misdemeanor in Maryland—is defined as a combination by two or more persons to accomplish a criminal or unlawful act, or to do a lawful act by criminal or unlawful means. Jones v. State, 8 Md.App. 370, 259 A.2d 807. The gist of the offense is the unlawful combination resulting from the agreement, rather than the mere agreement itself, and no overt act is required to constitute the crime. Wilson v. State, 8 Md.App. 653, 262 A.2d 91. In other words, as succinctly stated by the Supreme Court of New Jersey in State v. Carbone, 10 N.J. 329, 91 A.2d 571, 574, the "gist of the offense of conspiracy lies, not in doing the act, nor effecting the purpose for which the conspiracy is formed, nor in attempting to do them, nor in inciting others to do them, but in the forming of the scheme or agreement between the parties." Concert in criminal purpose, it is said, is the salient factor in criminal conspiracy. Criminal conspiracy is a partnership in crime—"It is the coalition of manpower and human minds enhancing possibilities of achievement aimed at the objective that present a greater threat to society than does a lone offender." Clark and Marshall Crimes (6th Edition) Section 9.00. In short, it is *the existence* of the conspiracy which creates the danger. Dennis v. United States, 341 U.S. 494, 511, 71 S.Ct. 857, 95 L.Ed. 1137.

As one person cannot conspire or form a combination with himself, it is essential in proving the existence of a criminal conspiracy to show "the consent of two or more minds," Bloomer v. State, 48 Md. 521, 536, viz., it must be shown that at least two persons had a meeting of the minds—a unity of design and purpose—to have an agreement. Wilson v. State, supra; Jones v. State, supra. A formal agreement need not, however, be established; it is sufficient if the minds of the parties meet understandingly, so as to bring about an intelligent and deliberate agreement to do the acts contemplated. As the crime of conspiracy is one requiring a specific intent, and necessarily involves at the least two guilty parties, the required criminal intent must exist in the minds of two or more parties to the conspiracy.

In view of these principles, it is the well settled general rule that one defendant in a prosecution for conspiracy cannot be convicted where all of his alleged coconspirators, be they one or more, have been acquitted or discharged under circumstances that amount to an acquittal. The validity of the general rule has been consistently recognized by the Court of Appeals. See State v. Buchanan, 5 H & J 317; Bloomer v. State, supra; Hurwitz v. State, 200 Md. 578, 92 A.2d 575. We recognized the rule in Wilson v. State, supra (footnote 9). The rationale underlying the rule appears clear: that it is illogical to acquit all but one of a purported partnership in crime; that acquittal of all persons with whom a defendant is alleged to have conspired is repugnant to the existence of the requisite corrupt agreement; and that regardless of the criminal animus of the one defendant, there must be someone with whom he confected his corrupt agreement, and where all his alleged coconspirators are not guilty, a like finding as to him must be made. See 91 A.L.R.2d, at p. 703. But "It is only where one is convicted and another or others are acquitted, resulting in a repugnancy upon the record, that the convicted conspirator may be discharged." Berry v. State, 202 Ind. 294, 173 N.E. 705 cited with approval in Hurwitz v. State, supra.

Generally speaking, it would appear that so long as the disposition of the case against a coconspirator does not remove the basis for the charge of conspiracy, a single defendant may be prosecuted and convicted of the offense, even though for one reason or another his coconspirator is either not tried or not convicted. See the exhaustive collection of cases at 72 A.L.R. 1180–1192 and 91 A.L.R.2d 700–733. Consistent with this rule, the authorities all agree that the death of one conspirator does not of itself prevent the conviction of the other, where the conspiracy between them is shown by the evidence. In Hurwitz v. State, supra, a case in which all but one of the conspirators were granted immunity from prosecution on a ground not inconsistent with their participation in the conspiracy, the court held that such grant of immunity was not equivalent to acquittal and would not require reversal of the conviction of the one remaining conspirator. The same rule has been applied where one of two conspirators enjoyed diplomatic immunity and therefore could not be prosecuted for the conspiracy. Farnsworth v. Zerbst, 98 F.2d 541 (5th Cir.). In Adams v. State, 202 Md. 455, 97 A.2d 281, it was held that conviction of one defendant in a conspiracy case was proper despite failure to convict any of the other conspirators where it was alleged and shown that there were persons unknown to the prosecution with whom the convicted defendant had conspired. And while the cases are generally divided on the question whether the entry of a *nolle prosequi* as to one of two alleged conspirators compels an acquittal of the remaining conspirator, the better reasoned view would appear to support the proposition that it does not, at least where the *nolle prosequi* was not entered without the coconspirator's consent after the trial had begun (which then would have amounted to an acquittal and precluded reindictment). See Greathouse v. State, 5 Md.App. 675, 249 A.2d 207. In *Hurwitz*, it was held that the entry of a "stet" to a coconspirator's indictment was not tantamount to an acquittal and did not compel the discharge of the only remaining conspirator.[1]

Some cases suggest that the rule that acquittal of all save one of the alleged conspirators results in the acquittal of all applies only to acquittals on the merits. See Farnsworth v. Zerbst, supra. Other cases—while recognizing that acquittals are not always tantamount to a declaration of innocence—nevertheless conclude that an acquittal is in effect a judicial determination, binding on the State, that the acquitted defendant was not a participant in a criminal conspiracy. See United States v. Fox, 130 F.2d 56 (3rd Cir.); State v. Smith, 117 Ark. 384, 175 S.W. 392. The State urges that where the acquittal

---

1. By the Maryland stet procedure, the prosecutor indicates that he does not choose *at that time* to further prosecute the indictment.

of one of the alleged conspirators is based solely on the fact that he was insane at the time of the crime, the remaining conspirator should nonetheless be held responsible for the offense. The State relies on Jones v. State, 31 Ala.App. 504, 19 So.2d 81, a case in which the defendant, convicted of murder, maintained that the actual killing was done by his brother and that because his brother was insane at the time of the crime, and hence innocent of the offense, he (the defendant) must likewise be exonerated. The court, after characterizing the defendant as "a co-conspirator and an aider and abettor in the homicide," said (p. 83):

> " * * * the insanity [of appellant's brother] would not exculpate the appellant if he conspired with the principal or aided or abetted him in the killing of deceased * * *. If appellant so conspired or aided or abetted in the homicide, the mental irresponsibility of [his brother] could not be invoked to exonerate said appellant. One may or could use an insane person as the agent of destruction—or conspire with such person to accomplish the homicide—just as guilty as with a person of sound mind. The fact, if true, that the coconspirator or principal in the crime is not amenable to justice because of mental irresponsibility does not exempt the other from prosecution. Pruitt v. State, 91 Tex.Cr.R. 189, 237 S.W. 572; People v. Armstrong, 299 Ill. 349, 132 N.E. 547; Conley v. People, 170 Ill. 587, 48 N.E. 911; 22 C.J.S. Criminal Law §§ 85, 101."

We think the cases relied upon by the *Jones* court to support its conclusion stand for the proposition that it is no defense to one who participates either as a principal or aider or abettor in the actual commission of the substantive criminal offense that the principal offender was insane at the time of the crime. The principle would appear similar to the rule that a coconspirator may be convicted of any crime committed by any member of a conspiracy to do an illegal act if the act is done in furtherance of the purpose of the conspiracy. The conspiracy being established, the fact that the member who committed the crime was insane at the time would thus not exonerate the others from complicity in the commission of the substantive offense. See State v. Alton, 139 Mont. 479, 365 P.2d 527.

We do not find these cases controlling of the primary question before us, namely, whether *under an indictment for conspiracy*, one conspirator may be convicted of the offense where the only other conspirator was shown to be insane at the time the agreement between them was concluded. Conspiracy to commit a crime is a different offense from the crime that is the object of the conspiracy. One necessarily involves joint action; the other does not. By its nature, conspiracy is a joint or group offense requiring a concert of free wills, and the union of the minds of at least two persons is a prerequisite to the commission of the offense. The essence of conspiracy is, therefore, a mental confederation involving at least two persons; the crime is indivisible in the sense that it requires more than one guilty person; and where the joint intent does not exist, the basis of the charge of conspiracy is necessarily swept away. See Feder v. United States, 257 F. 694 (2nd Cir.). In short, the guilt of both persons must concur to constitute that of either. It is upon this premise that the authorities all agree that if two persons are charged as conspirators and one is an entrapper, or merely feigns acquiescence in the criminal intent, there is no punishable conspiracy because there was no agreement on the part of the one to engage in a criminal conspiracy.[2] Delaney v. State, 164 Tenn. 432, 51 S.W.2d 485; Woo Wai v. United States, 223 F. 412 (9th Cir.); State v. Dougherty, 88 N.J.L. 209, 96 A. 56; Solomon v. State, 168 Tenn. 180, 76 S.W.2d 331; Odneal v. State, 117 Tex.Cr.R. 97, 34 S.W.2d 595. For like reasons, we hold that where only two persons are implicated in a conspiracy, and one is shown to have been insane at the time the agreement was concluded, and hence totally incapable of committing any crime, there is no punishable criminal conspiracy, the requisite joint criminal intent being absent.

The evidence in the record before us plainly shows that appellant and Fields planned to commit a robbery at O'Donnell's restaurant. There is some evidence in the record to suggest that Chamblee may also have been a conspirator, although the State made little effort at the trial to establish his involvement in the conspiracy. Since an insane person is mentally incapable of forming a criminal intent, Bradford v. State, 234 Md. 505, 514, 200 A.2d 150, it is clear that if Fields was actually insane at the time of the offense, he could not be found guilty of engaging in a criminal conspiracy. It does not appear however, that Fields was ever tried and acquitted of the conspiracy charge. But the only evidence in the record—the testimony of the police officer—is that Fields was found by State psychiatrists upon examination to have been insane at the time of the commission of the offense. While such testimony is hardly the equivalent of the expert medical evidence required to prove insanity, see Millard v. State, 8 Md.App. 119, 261 A.2d 227, the trial judge, in his charge to the jury, stated as a fact that Fields "was found to be insane." Assuming this to be the true situation, it is unlikely that Fields will ever be brought to trial on the conspiracy charge.

As to Chamblee, the docket entries indicate the entry of a *nolle prosequi* to his conspiracy indictment. We cannot ascertain, therefore, whether, in the circumstances in which it was entered, the *nolle prosequi* operated as an acquittal or not. See Greathouse v. State, supra. It appears, however, from colloquy between counsel and with

---

2. This would not be true, however, if after elimination of the alleged entrapper, there are at least two other parties to the conspiracy.

the court that Chamblee was permitted to plead to a lesser offense than conspiracy, possibly with the understanding that he would not thereafter be charged with that offense.

In his advisory instructions to the jury, the trial judge, after fully defining the crime of conspiracy, stated that under Maryland law where only two parties are involved in the alleged conspiracy, and one is found not guilty, "the other could not be tried because one person cannot conspire except with another to commit a crime." He further advised the jury that there has to be "an outright finding of not guilty" but such was not the case with Fields who was merely found to be insane and for that reason not brought to trial. With reference to Chamblee, the trial judge instructed that he had not been found not guilty of conspiracy; that he did not believe that Chamblee had been prosecuted for that offense.

While appellant made no objection to the court's instructions, on the state of the record before us we think they constituted "plain error * * * material to the rights of the accused" under Maryland Rule 756 g. See Parker v. State, 4 Md.App. 62, 241 A.2d 185. We thus deem it essential in the interest of justice that appellant's conspiracy conviction be reversed and that the State be afforded the opportunity to retry the case in light of the principles of law which we consider relevant and controlling. If, upon retrial, the State intends to charge only Fields and appellant as conspirators, and the evidence properly shows that Fields was legally insane at the time the agreement to perpetrate the robbery was concluded, then even though Fields has not been acquitted of the offense of conspiracy by a judicial determination that he was insane, nevertheless the requisite *joint* criminal intent being absent, appellant cannot properly be convicted of engaging with Fields in a criminal conspiracy. If Fields is shown so to be insane, but the facts show that the conspiracy indictment against Chamblee was not *nol prossed* under circumstances amounting to an acquittal (see Greathouse v. State, supra), then the State may undertake to adduce evidence showing that Chamblee was a conspirator, with appellant, in the plan to commit the robbery.

MODEL PENAL CODE, COMMENT TO § 5.03(1), 102

(Tent. Draft No. 10, 1960).

2. *The Conspiratorial Relationship.*

Unilateral Approach of the Draft. The definition of the Draft departs from the traditional view of conspiracy as an entirely bilateral or multilateral relationship, the view inherent in the standard formulation cast in terms of "two or more persons" agreeing or combining to commit a crime. Attention is directed instead to each individual's culpability by framing the definition in terms of the conduct which suffices to establish the liability of any given actor, rather than the conduct of a group of which he is charged to be a part—an approach which in this comment we have designated "unilateral."

One consequence of this approach is to make it immaterial to the guilt of a conspirator whose culpability has been established that the person or all of the persons with whom he conspired have not been or cannot be convicted. Present law frequently holds otherwise, reasoning from the definition of conspiracy as an agreement between two or more persons that there must be at least two guilty conspirators or none.

----

b. OVERT ACT REQUIREMENT

At common law, no overt act was required for a criminal conspiracy. All of the conspirators were criminally liable at the moment the agreement was completed. In a number of jurisdictions, however, statutes have added the requirement of an overt act. Sometimes an overt act is required for some but not all criminal conspiracies, i. e., for conspiracies to commit less serious crimes. In those situations in which an overt act is required, only one such act need be committed, and only one of the conspirators need commit it in order to render all of the conspirators guilty. But the difficult question is determining whether a specific act committed by one of the parties to the agreement is a sufficient act to complete the conspiracy.

PEOPLE EX REL. CONTE v. FLOOD

Supreme Court of New York, 1966.
53 Misc.2d 109, 277 N.Y.S.2d 697.

MEMORANDUM

MARIO PITTONI, Justice. Relator, Dino Conte, has petitioned to be released pursuant to a Writ of Habeas Corpus on the ground that he has been illegally incarcerated since September 4, 1966. The reason given for such release is that pursuant to Section 250 of the Correction Law, as amended, he was entitled to 10 days per month for "good time". Relator Conte says that the pertinent part of Section 250 of the Correction Law became effective as to crimes committed after June 1, 1964 and his crime of conspiracy was consummated after June 1, 1964.

Count One of the indictment, to which Relator Conte pleaded guilty, charges him with violating Section 580–a of the Penal Law which reads as follows:

"If two or more persons conspire to commit the crime of
* * * extortion, and if some act besides the agreement to

commit such crime be done to effect the object of the agreement by one or more of such persons, each of them is guilty of a felony."

Count One of the indictment, to which he pleaded guilty, alleges that Relator Conte and others "between the 1st day of May, 1964 to the 15th day of July, 1964 did * * * combine * * * conspire and agree together to extort money * * * from Irving Holzman", and that they committed certain overt acts in pursuance and furtherance of the conspiracy.

The first alleged overt act is no overt act at all. It merely states that during the 2½ month period involved the conspirators threatened Irving Holzman and members of his family with physical harm. This is not an overt act required under Sections 580–a and 583 of the Penal Law. It must be a specific, affirmative, independent, identified overt act done to further the object of the conspiracy.

The second overt act is that the conspirators "did on or about the 8th day of June, 1964 assault one Ruth Holzman * * * by * * * striking her with a * * * pistol * * *".

The third overt act is that the conspirators "did on or about the 2nd day of July, 1964 have a telephone conversation with Irving Holzman * * *".

The fourth overt act is that the conspirators "on or about the 30th day of June, 1964 * * * did make a telephone call to Dolores Billing * * *".

The fifth alleged overt act is a general statement of conversations among the conspirators within the 2½ month period of the conspiracy. But it is "hornbook" law that conversations among co-conspirators in forming and planning the conspiracy are not overt acts in furtherance of the conspiracy, as meant by "overt acts" in Sections 580–a and 583 of the Penal Law.

As one can see, the only valid overt acts alleged in the indictment took place on three dates: June 8, 1964, June 30, 1964 and July 2, 1964, all after the important or key date involved in this proceeding, June 1, 1964. It is well established that the crime of conspiracy is not complete until the commission of an overt act. Clearly, therefore, the conspiracy in our case was not completed or consummated till after June 1, 1964.

Assuming, arguendo, that an overt act were not necessary to complete or consummate the crime of conspiracy, we would be bound to interpret or construe the statutes involved herein "according to the fair import of their terms, to promote justice and effect the objects of the law" (Section 21 of Penal Law). A crime which starts before June 1, 1964 and ends after June 1, 1964 is committed after June 1, 1964.

Be that as it may, as previously pointed out, a conspiracy under Sections 580-a and 583 of the Penal Law is not completed and is no crime until an overt act in furtherance of that conspiracy has been committed.

It follows that the benefit of Section 250 of the Correction Law effective June 1, 1964 applies to Relator Conte, who was sentenced on December 10, 1965, and his legal period of incarceration has already run its course.

The writ is *sustained*.

---

c. THE STATE OF MIND REQUIRED

Obviously, all of the parties to a conspiracy must know that they are entering into an agreement, i. e., they must intend to agree. But a more difficult problem is raised by the question of what state of mind each member must have towards the criminal objective. As in the *Lauria* case in this section, a person may enter into an agreement knowing that he is agreeing to do something that will assist in the commission of a crime. But that may not be enough. It may be necessary to prove that he actually desired that the crime be successfully committed. As the two cases in this section make clear, courts are not agreed on when, if ever, it is necessary to prove that a particular alleged conspirator desired the commission of the crime.

CLEAVER v. UNITED STATES

United States Court of Appeals for the Tenth Circuit, 1956.
238 F.2d 766.

LEWIS, Circuit Judge. * * *

Defendants next challenge the conviction upon the ground that the trial court did not adequately charge the jury relative to the law pertaining to the testimony of accomplices; specific complaint is made that the court did not inform the jury that two of the government's witnesses, Thomas Sullivan and James Webster, were accomplices. Sullivan admitted and testified to his participation in the crime from its inception to his arrest in Tulsa, Oklahoma, where he passed some of the stolen money orders. He, of course, was an accomplice. Webster, however, did not participate in the planning or the commission of the burglary, although he was present during a number of the conversations among the various conspirators. Mere knowledge, approval of or acquiescence in the object or the purpose of the conspiracy, without an intention and agreement to cooperate in the crime is insufficient to constitute one a conspirator.

PEOPLE v. LAURIA

California Court of Appeal, 1967.
251 Cal.App.2d 471, 59 Cal.Rptr. 628.

FLEMING, Associate Justice. In an investigation of call-girl activity the police focused their attention on three prostitutes actively plying their trade on call, each of whom was using Lauria's telephone answering service, presumably for business purposes.

On January 8, 1965, Stella Weeks, a policewoman, signed up for telephone service with Lauria's answering service. Mrs. Weeks, in the course of her conversation with Lauria's office manager, hinted broadly that she was a prostitute concerned with the secrecy of her activities and their concealment from the police. She was assured that the operation of the service was discreet and "about as safe as you can get." It was arranged that Mrs. Weeks need not leave her address with the answering service, but could pick up her calls and pay her bills in person.

On February 11, Mrs. Weeks talked to Lauria on the telephone and told him her business was modelling and she had been referred to the answering service by Terry, one of the three prostitutes under investigation. She complained that because of the operation of the service she had lost two valuable customers, referred to as tricks. Lauria defended his service and said that her friends had probably lied to her about having left calls for her. But he did not respond to Mrs. Weeks' hints that she needed customers in order to make money, other than to invite her to his house for a personal visit in order to get better acquainted. In the course of his talk he said "his business was taking messages."

On February 15, Mrs. Weeks talked on the telephone to Lauria's office manager and again complained of two lost calls, which she described as a $50 and a $100 trick. On investigation the office manager could find nothing wrong, but she said she would alert the switchboard operators about slip-ups on calls.

On April 1 Lauria and the three prostitutes were arrested. Lauria complained to the police that this attention was undeserved, stating that Hollywood Call Board had 60 to 70 prostitutes on its board while his own service had only 9 or 10, that he kept separate records for known or suspected prostitutes for the convenience of himself and the police. When asked if his records were available to police who might come to the office to investigate call girls, Lauria replied that they were whenever the police had a specific name. However, his service didn't "arbitrarily tell the police about prostitutes on our board. As long as they pay their bills we tolerate them." In a subsequent voluntary appearance before the Grand Jury Lauria testified he had always cooperated with the police. But he admitted he knew some of his customers were prostitutes, and he knew Terry was a prostitute because he had personally used her services, and he knew she was paying for 500 calls a month.

Lauria and the three prostitutes were indicted for conspiracy to commit prostitution, and nine overt acts were specified. Subsequently the trial court set aside the indictment as having been brought without reasonable or probable cause. (Pen.Code, § 995.) The People have appealed, claiming that a sufficient showing of an unlawful agreement to further prostitution was made.

To establish agreement, the People need show no more than a tacit, mutual understanding between coconspirators to accomplish an unlawful act. Here the People attempted to establish a conspiracy by showing that Lauria, well aware that his codefendants were prostitutes who received business calls from customers through his telephone answering service, continued to furnish them with such service. This approach attempts to equate knowledge of another's criminal activity with conspiracy to further such criminal activity, and poses the question of the criminal responsibility of a furnisher of goods or services who knows his product is being used to assist the operation of an illegal business. Under what circumstances does a supplier become a part of a conspiracy to further an illegal enterprise by furnishing goods or services which he knows are to be used by the buyer for criminal purposes?

The two leading cases on this point face in opposite directions. In United States v. Falcone, 311 U.S. 205, 61 S.Ct. 204, 85 L.Ed. 128, the sellers of large quantities of sugar, yeast, and cans were absolved from participation in a moonshining conspiracy among distillers who bought from them, while in Direct Sales Co. v. United States, 319 U.S. 703, 63 S.Ct. 1265, 87 L.Ed. 1674, a wholesaler of drugs was convicted of conspiracy to violate the federal narcotic laws by selling drugs in quantity to a codefendant physician who was supplying them to addicts. The distinction between these two cases appears primarily based on the proposition that distributors of such dangerous products as drugs are required to exercise greater discrimination in the conduct of their business than are distributors of innocuous substances like sugar and yeast.

In the earlier case, *Falcone,* the sellers' knowledge of the illegal use of the goods was insufficient by itself to make the sellers participants in a conspiracy with the distillers who bought from them. Such knowledge fell short of proof of a conspiracy, and evidence on the volume of sales was too vague to support a jury finding that respondents knew of the conspiracy from the size of the sales alone.

In the later case of *Direct Sales,* the conviction of a drug wholesaler for conspiracy to violate federal narcotic laws was affirmed on a showing that it had actively promoted the sale of morphine sulphate in quantity and had sold codefendant physician, who practiced in a small town in South Carolina, more than 300 times his normal requirements of the drug, even though it had been repeatedly warned of the dangers of unrestricted sales of the drug. The court contrasted the restricted goods involved in *Direct Sales* with the articles of free commerce involved in *Falcone:* "All articles of commerce may be put to illegal ends," said the court. "But all do not have inherently the same susceptibility to harmful and illegal use. * * * This difference is important for two purposes. One is for making certain that the seller knows the buyer's intended illegal use. The other is to show that by the sale he intends to further, promote and cooperate in it. This intent, when given effect by overt act, is the gist of conspiracy. While it is not identical with mere knowledge that another purposes unlawful action, it is not unrelated to such knowledge. * * * The step from knowledge to intent and agreement may be taken. There is more than suspicion, more than knowledge, acquiescence, carelessness, indifference, lack of concern. There is informed and interested cooperation, stimulation, instigation. And there is also a 'stake in the venture' which, even if it may not be essential, is not irrelevant to the question of conspiracy." (319 U.S. at 710–713, 63 S.Ct. at 1269–1270.)

While *Falcone* and *Direct Sales* may not be entirely consistent with each other in their full implications, they do provide us with a framework for the criminal liability of a supplier of lawful goods or services put to unlawful use. Both the element of *knowledge* of the illegal use of the goods or services and the element of *intent* to further that use must be present in order to make the supplier a participant in a criminal conspiracy.

Proof of *knowledge* is ordinarily a question of fact and requires no extended discussion in the present case. The knowledge of the supplier was sufficiently established when Lauria admitted he knew some of his customers were prostitutes and admitted he knew that Terry, an active subscriber to his service, was a prostitute. In the face of these admissions he could scarcely claim to have relied on the normal assumption an operator of a business or service is entitled to make, that his customers are behaving themselves in the eyes of the law. Because Lauria knew in fact that some of his customers were prostitutes, it is a legitimate inference he knew they were subscribing to his answering service for illegal business purposes and were using his service to make assignations for prostitution. On this record we think the prosecution is entitled to claim positive knowledge by Lauria of the use of his service to facilitate the business of prostitution.

The more perplexing issue in the case is the sufficiency of proof of *intent* to further the criminal enterprise. The element of intent may be proved either by direct evidence, or by evidence of circumstances from which an intent to further a criminal enterprise by supplying lawful goods or services may be inferred. Direct evidence of participation, such as advice from the supplier of legal goods or services to the user of those goods or services on their use for illegal purposes, such evidence as appeared in a companion case we decide today, People v. Roy, 59 Cal.Rptr. 636, provides the simplest case. When the intent to further and promote the criminal enterprise comes from the lips of the supplier himself, ambiguities of inference from circumstance need not trouble us. But in cases where direct proof of complicity is lacking, intent to further the conspiracy must be derived from the sale itself and its surrounding circumstances in order to establish the supplier's express or tacit agreement to join the conspiracy.

In the case at bench the prosecution argues that since Lauria knew his customers were using his service for illegal purposes but nevertheless continued to furnish it to them, he must have intended to assist them in carrying out their illegal activities. Thus through a union of knowledge and intent he became a participant in a criminal conspiracy. Essentially, the People argue that knowledge alone of the continuing use of his telephone facilities for criminal purposes provided a sufficient basis from which his intent to participate in those criminal activities could be inferred.

In examining precedents in this field we find that sometimes, but not always, the criminal intent of the supplier may be inferred from his knowledge of the unlawful use made of the product he supplies. Some consideration of characteristic patterns may be helpful.

1.   Intent may be inferred from knowledge, when the purveyor of legal goods for illegal use has acquired a stake in the venture. (United States v. Falcone, 2 Cir., 109 F.2d 579, 581.)   For example, in Regina v. Thomas, (1957), 2 All.E.R. 181, 342, a prosecution for living off the earnings of prostitution, the evidence showed that the accused, knowing the woman to be a convicted prostitute, agreed to let her have the use of his room between the hours of 9 p. m. and 2 a. m. for a charge of £3 a night. The Court of Criminal Appeal refused an appeal from the conviction, holding that when the accused rented a room at a grossly inflated rent to a prostitute for the purpose of carrying on her trade, a jury could find he was living on the earnings of prostitution.

In the present case, no proof was offered of inflated charges for the telephone answering services furnished the codefendants.

2.   Intent may be inferred from knowledge, when no legitimate use for the goods or services exists. The leading California case is People v. McLaughlin, 111 Cal.App.2d 781, 245 P.2d 1076, in which the court upheld a conviction of the suppliers of horse-racing information by wire for conspiracy to promote bookmaking, when it had been established that wire-service information had no other use than to supply information needed by bookmakers to conduct illegal gambling operations.

In Rex v. Delaval (1763) 3 Burr. 1434, 97 E.R. 913, the charge was unlawful conspiracy to remove a girl from the control of Bates, a musician to whom she was bound as an apprentice, and place her in the hands of Sir Francis Delaval for the purpose of prostitution. Lord Mansfield not only upheld the charges against Bates and Sir Francis, but also against Fraine, the attorney who drew up the indentures of apprenticeship transferring custody of the girl from Bates to Sir Francis. Fraine, said Lord Mansfield, must have known that Sir Francis had no facilities for teaching music to apprentices so that it was impossible for him to have been ignorant of the real intent of the transaction.

In Shaw v. Director of Public Prosecutions, [1962] A.C. 220, the defendant was convicted of conspiracy to corrupt public morals and of living on the earnings of prostitution, when he published a directory consisting almost entirely of advertisements of the names, addresses, and specialized talents of prostitutes. Publication of such a directory, said the court, could have no legitimate use and serve no other purpose than to advertise the professional services of the prostitutes whose advertisements appeared in the directory. The publisher could be deemed a participant in the profits from the business activities of his principal advertisers.

Other services of a comparable nature come to mind: the manufacturer of crooked dice and marked cards who sells his product to gambling casinos; the tipster who furnishes information on the movement of law enforcement officers to known lawbreakers. (Cf. Jackson v. State of Texas, 164 Tex.Cr.R. 276, 298 S.W.2d 837 (1957), where the furnisher of signaling equipment used to warn gamblers of the police was convicted of aiding the equipping of a gambling place.) In such cases the supplier must necessarily have an intent to further the illegal enterprise since there is no known honest use for his goods.

However, there is nothing in the furnishing of telephone answering service which would necessarily imply assistance in the performance of illegal activities. Nor is any inference to be derived from the use of an answering service by women, either in any particular volume of calls, or outside normal working hours. Night-club entertainers, registered nurses, faith healers, public stenographers, photographic models, and free lance substitute employees, provide examples of women in legitimate occupations whose employment might cause them to receive a volume of telephone calls at irregular hours.

3. Intent may be inferred from knowledge, when the volume of business with the buyer is grossly disproportionate to any legitimate demand, or when sales for illegal use amount to a high proportion of the seller's total business. In such cases an intent to participate in the illegal enterprise may be inferred from the quantity of the business done. For example, in *Direct Sales,* supra, the sale of narcotics to a rural physician in quantities 300 times greater than he would have normal use for provided potent evidence of an intent to further the illegal activity. In the same case the court also found significant the fact that the wholesaler had attracted as customers a disproportion-

ately large group of physicians who had been convicted of violating the Harrison Act. In Shaw v. Director of Public Prosecutions, [1962] A.C. 220, almost the entire business of the directory came from prostitutes.

No evidence of any unusual volume of business with prostitutes was presented by the prosecution against Lauria.

Inflated charges, the sale of goods with no legitimate use, sales in inflated amounts, each may provide a fact of sufficient moment from which the intent of the seller to participate in the criminal enterprise may be inferred. In such instances participation by the supplier of legal goods to the illegal enterprise may be inferred because in one way or another the supplier has acquired a special interest in the operation of the illegal enterprise. His intent to participate in the crime of which he has knowledge may be inferred from the existence of his special interest.

Yet there are cases in which it cannot reasonably be said that the supplier has a stake in the venture or has acquired a special interest in the enterprise, but in which he has been held liable as a participant on the basis of knowledge alone. Some suggestion of this appears in *Direct Sales,* supra, where both the knowledge of the illegal use of the drugs and the intent of the supplier to aid that use were inferred. In Regina v. Bainbridge (1959), 3 W.L.R. 656 (CCA 6), a supplier of oxygen-cutting equipment to one known to intend to use it to break into a bank was convicted as an accessory to the crime. In Sykes v. Director of Public Prosecutions [1962] A.C. 528, one having knowledge of the theft of 100 pistols, 4 submachine guns, and 1960 rounds of ammunition was convicted of misprision of felony for failure to disclose the theft to the public authorities. It seems apparent from these cases that a supplier who furnishes equipment which he *knows* will be used to commit a serious crime may be deemed from that knowledge alone to have intended to produce the result. Such proof may justify an inference that the furnisher intended to aid the execution of the crime and that he thereby became a participant. For instance, we think the operator of a telephone answering service with positive knowledge that his service was being used to facilitate the extortion of ransom, the distribution of heroin, or the passing of counterfeit money who continued to furnish the service with knowledge of its use, might be chargeable on knowledge alone with participation in a scheme to extort money, to distribute narcotics, or to pass counterfeit money. The same result would follow the seller of gasoline who knew the buyer was using his product to make Molotov cocktails for terroristic use.

Logically, the same reasoning could be extended to crimes of every description. Yet we do not believe an inference of intent drawn from knowledge of criminal use properly applies to the less serious crimes classified as misdemeanors. The duty to take positive action to dissociate oneself from activities helpful to violations of the criminal law is far stronger and more compelling for felonies than it is for misdemeanors or petty offenses. In this respect, as in others, the distinction between felonies and misdemeanors, between more serious and less serious crime, retains continuing vitality. In historically the most serious felony, treason, an individual with knowledge of the treason can be prosecuted for concealing and failing to disclose it. (Pen.Code, § 38; 18 U.S.Code, § 2382.) In other felonies, both at common law and under the criminal laws of the United States, an individual knowing of the commission of a felony is criminally liable for concealing it and failing to make it known to proper authority. (4 Blackstone 121; Sykes v. Director of Public Prosecutions [1962] A.C. 528; 18 U.S.Code, § 4.) But this crime, known as misprision of felony, has always been limited to knowledge and concealment of felony and has never extended to misdemeanor. A similar limitation is found in the criminal liability of an accessory, which is restricted to aid in the escape of a principal who has committed or been charged with a *felony*. (Pen.Code, § 32.) We believe the distinction between the obligations arising from knowledge of a felony and those arising from knowledge of a misdemeanor continues to reflect basic human feelings about the duties owed by individuals to society. Heinous crime must be stamped out, and its suppression is the responsibility of all. Backun v. United States, 4 Cir., 112 F.2d 635, 636, 637. Venial crime and crime not evil in itself present less of a danger to society, and perhaps the benefits of their suppression through the modern equivalent of the posse, the hue and cry, the informant, and the citizen's arrest, are outweighed by the disruption to everyday life brought about by amateur law enforcement and private officiousness in relatively inconsequential delicts which do not threaten our basic security. The subject has been summarized in an English text on the criminal law: "Failure to reveal a felony to the authorities is now authoritatively determined to be misprision of felony, which is a common-law misdemeanor; misprision of treason is punishable with imprisonment for life. * * * No offence is committed in failing to disclose a misdemeanour. * * *

" 'To require everyone, without distinction, as to the nature and degree of the offence, to become an accuser, would be productive of inconvenience in exposing numbers to penal prosecutions, multiplying criminal charges, and engendering private dissension. It may sometimes be more convenient that offences should be passed over, than that all should indiscriminately be made the subject of prosecution; and a law would be considered to be harsh and impolitic, if not unjust, which compelled every party injured by a criminal act, and, still more so, to compel everyone who happened to know that another had been so injured, to make a public disclosure of the circumstances. Here, therefore, there is reason for limiting the law against mere misprisions to the concealment of such crimes as are of an aggravated complexion.' " (Criminal Law, Glanville Williams (2d ed.) p. 423.)

With respect to misdemeanors, we conclude that positive knowledge of the supplier that his products or services are being used for criminal purposes does not, without more, establish an intent of the supplier to participate in the misdemeanors. With respect to felonies, we do not decide the converse, viz. that in all cases of felony knowledge of criminal use alone may justify an inference of the supplier's intent to participate in the crime. The implications of *Falcone* make the matter uncertain with respect to those felonies which are merely prohibited wrongs. See also Holman v. Johnson, 98 E.R. 1120, (1775) (sale and delivery of tea at Dunkirk known to be destined for smuggling into England not an illegal contract). But decision on this point is not compelled, and we leave the matter open.

From this analysis of precedent we deduce the following rule: the intent of a supplier who knows of the criminal use to which his supplies are put to participate in the criminal activity connected with the use of his supplies may be established by (1) direct evidence that he intends to participate, or (2) through an inference that he intends to participate based on, (a) his special interest in the activity, or (b) the aggravated nature of the crime itself.

When we review Lauria's activities in the light of this analysis, we find no proof that Lauria took any direct action to further, encourage, or direct the call-girl activities of his codefendants and we find an absence of circumstances from which his special interest in their activities could be inferred. Neither excessive charges for standardized services, or the furnishing of services without a legitimate use, nor an unusual quantity of business with call girls, are present. The offense which he is charged with furthering is a misdemeanor, a category of crime which has never been made a required subject of positive disclosure to public authority. Under these circumstances, although proof of Lauria's knowledge of the criminal activities of his patrons was sufficient to charge him with that fact, there was insufficient evidence that he intended to further their criminal activities, and hence insufficient proof of his participation in a criminal conspiracy with his codefendants to further prostitution. Since the conspiracy centered around the activities of Lauria's telephone answering service, the charges against his codefendants likewise fail for want of proof.

In absolving Lauria of complicity in a criminal conspiracy we do not wish to imply that the public authorities are without remedies to combat modern manifestations of the world's oldest profession. Licensing of telephone answering services under the police power, together with the revocation of licenses for the toleration of prostitution, is a possible civil remedy. The furnishing of telephone answering service in aid of prostitution could be made a crime. (Cf. Pen.Code, § 316, which makes it a misdemeanor to let an apartment with knowledge of its use for prostitution.) Other solutions will doubtless occur to vigilant public authorities if the problem of call-girl activity needs further suppression.

The order is affirmed.

MODEL PENAL CODE, COMMENT TO 5.03, 107–10

(Tent. Draft No. 10, 1960).

The Requirement of Purpose. The purpose requirement is crucial to the resolution of the difficult problems presented when a charge of conspiracy is leveled against a person whose relationship to a criminal plan is essentially peripheral. Typical is the case of the person who sells sugar to the producers of illicit whiskey. He may have little interest in the success of the distilling operation and be motivated mainly by the desire to make the normal profit of an otherwise lawful sale. To be criminally liable, of course, he must at least have knowledge of the use to which the materials are being put, but the difficult issue presented is whether knowingly facilitating the commission of a crime ought to be sufficient, absent a true purpose to advance the criminal end. In the case of vendors conflicting interests are also involved: that of the vendors in freedom to engage in gainful and otherwise lawful activities without policing their vendees, and that of the community in preventing behavior that facilitates the commission of crimes. The decisions are in conflict, although many of those requiring purpose properly emphasize that it can be inferred from such circumstances as, for example, quantity sales, the seller's initiative or encouragement, continuity of the relationship, and the contraband nature of the materials sold. The considerations are the same whether the charge be conspiracy or complicity in the substantive crime, and the Institute has resolved them, in the complicity provisions of the Code, in favor of requiring a purpose to advance the criminal end. Under the proposed Draft, the same purpose requirement that governs complicity is essential for conspiracy: the actor must have "the purpose of promoting or facilitating" the commission of the crime.

The requirement of purpose would also play a crucial role in the case where a charge of conspiracy is based on membership in an organization having both lawful and criminal objectives, as in the Communist cases. The defendant's membership and dues may encourage and assist the organization in pursuing all its objects, legal and illegal. He would not be guilty of conspiracy, however, unless he had the purpose of promoting or facilitating the attainment of a criminal objective. Of course, knowledge of that objective and conscious assistance may justify an inference of such purpose, but they would not be independently sufficient to establish liability.

*   *   *

It is worth noting, futher, that as related to those elements of substantive crimes that consist of proscribed conduct or undesirable results of conduct, the Draft requires purposeful behavior for guilt of conspiracy, regardless of the state of mind required by the definition of the substantive crime. If the crime is defined in terms of prohibited conduct, such as the sale of narcotics, the actor's purpose must be to promote or facilitate the engaging in such conduct by himself or another. If it is defined in terms of a result of conduct, such as homicide, his purpose must be to promote or facilitate the production of that result.

Thus, it would not be sufficient, as it is under the attempt draft, if the actor only believed that the result would be produced but did not consciously plan or desire to produce it. For example—to use the same illustration as the comments on attempt—if two persons plan to destroy a building by detonating a bomb, though they know and believe that there are inhabitants in the building who will be killed by the explosion, they are nevertheless guilty only of a conspiracy to destroy the building and not of a conspiracy to kill the inhabitants. While this result may seem unduly restrictive from the viewpoint of the completed crime, it is necessitated by the extremely preparatory behavior that may be involved in conspiracy. Had the crime been completed or had the preparation progressed even to the stage of an attempt, the result would be otherwise. As to the attempt, knowledge or belief that the inhabitants would be killed would suffice. As to the completed crime, the complicity draft covers the matter, despite its general requirement of a purpose to promote or facilitate the commission of the crime, by the special provision of Section 2.06(4). This provides that where causing a particular result is an element of a crime, a person is an accomplice in the crime if he was an accomplice in the behavior that caused the result and shared the same purpose or knowledge with respect to the result that is required by the definition of the crime.

A fortiori, where recklessness or negligence suffices for the actor's culpability with respect to a result element of a substantive crime —where, for example, homicide through negligence is made criminal —there could not be a conspiracy to commit that crime. This should be distinguished, however, from a crime defined in terms of conduct that creates a risk of harm, such as reckless driving or driving above a certain speed limit. In this situation the conduct rather than any result it may produce is the element of the crime, and it would suffice for guilt of conspiracy that the actor's purpose is to promote or facilitate such conduct—for example, if he urged the driver of the car to go faster and faster.

3. LIABILITY OF ONE COCONSPIRATOR FOR CRIMES OF OTHER CONSPIRATORS

PINKERTON v. UNITED STATES

Supreme Court of the United States, 1946.
328 U.S. 640, 66 S.Ct. 1180, 90 L.Ed. 1489, rehearing denied
329 U.S. 818, 67 S.Ct. 26, 91 L.Ed. 697.

Mr. Justice DOUGLAS delivered the opinion of the Court.

Walter and Daniel Pinkerton are brothers who live a short distance from each other on Daniel's farm. They were indicted for violations of the Internal Revenue Code. The indictment contained ten substantive counts and one conspiracy count. The jury found Walter guilty on nine of the substantive counts and on the conspiracy count. It found Daniel guilty on six of the substantive counts and on the conspiracy count. Walter was fined $500 and sentenced generally on the substantive counts to imprisonment for thirty months. On the conspiracy count he was given a two year sentence to run concurrently with the other sentence. Daniel was fined $1,000 and sentenced generally on the substantive counts to imprisonment for thirty months. On the conspiracy count he was fined $500 and given a two year sentence to run concurrently with the other sentence. The judgments of conviction were affirmed by the Circuit Court of Appeals. 151 F.2d 499.

* * *

A single conspiracy was charged and proved. Some of the overt acts charged in the conspiracy count were the same acts charged in the substantive counts. Each of the substantive offenses found was committed pursuant to the conspiracy. Petitioners therefore contend that the substantive counts became merged in the conspiracy count, and that only a single sentence not exceeding the maximum two-year penalty provided by the conspiracy statute (Criminal Code § 37, 18 U.S.C. § 88, 18 U.S.C.A. § 88) could be imposed. Or to state the matter differently, they contend that each of the substantive counts became a separate conspiracy count but since only a single conspiracy was charged and proved, only a single sentence for conspiracy could be imposed. They rely on Braverman v. United States, 317 U.S. 49, 63 S.Ct. 99, 87 L.Ed. 23.

In the Braverman case the indictment charged no substantive offense. Each of the several counts charged a conspiracy to violate a different statute. But only one conspiracy was proved. We held that a single conspiracy, charged under the general conspiracy statute, however diverse its objects may be, violates but a single statute and no penalty greater than the maximum provided for one conspiracy may be imposed. That case is not apposite here. For the offenses charged and proved were not only a conspiracy but substantive offenses as well.

Nor can we accept the proposition that the substantive offenses were merged in the conspiracy. There are, of course, instances where a conspiracy charge may not be added to the substantive charge. One is where the agreement of two persons is necessary for the completion of the substantive crime and there is no ingredient in the conspiracy which is not present in the completed crime. See United States v. Katz, 271 U.S. 354, 355, 356, 46 S.Ct. 513, 514, 70 L.Ed. 986; Gebardi v. United States, 287 U.S. 112, 121, 122, 53 S.Ct. 35, 37, 77 L.Ed. 206, 84 A.L.R. 370. Another is where the definition of the substantive offense excludes from punishment for conspiracy one who voluntarily participates in another's crime. Gebardi v. United States, supra. But those exceptions are of a limited character. The common law rule that the substantive offense, if a felony, was merged in the conspiracy, has little vitality in this country. It has been long and consistently recognized by the Court that the commission of the substantive offense and a conspiracy to commit it are separate and distinct offenses. The power of Congress to separate the two and to affix to each a different penalty is well established. Clune v. United States, 159 U.S. 590, 594, 595, 16 S.Ct. 125, 126, 40 L.Ed. 269. A conviction for the conspiracy may be had though the substantive offense was completed. See Heike v. United States, 227 U.S. 131, 144, 33 S.Ct. 226, 228, 57 L.Ed. 450, Ann.Cas.1914C, 128. And the plea of double jeopardy is no defense to a conviction for both offenses. Carter v. McClaughry, 183 U.S. 365, 395, 22 S.Ct. 181, 193, 46 L.Ed. 236. It is only an identity of offenses which is fatal. See Gavieres v. United States, 220 U.S. 338, 342, 31 S.Ct. 421, 422, 55 L.Ed. 489. Cf. Freeman v. United States, 6 Cir., 146 F.2d 978. A conspiracy is a partnership in crime. United States v. Socony-Vacuum Oil Co., 310 U.S. 150, 253, 60 S.Ct. 811, 858, 84 L.Ed. 1129. It has ingredients, as well as implications, distinct from the completion of the unlawful project. As stated in United States v. Rabinowich, 238 U.S. 78, 88, 35 S.Ct. 682, 684, 685, 59 L.Ed. 1211:

"For two or more to confederate and combine together to commit or cause to be committed a breach of the criminal laws is an offense of the gravest character, sometimes quite outweighing, in injury to the public, the mere commission of the contemplated crime. It involves deliberate plotting to subvert the laws, educating and preparing the conspirators for further and habitual criminal practices. And it is characterized by secrecy, rendering it difficult of detection, requiring more time for its discovery, and adding to the importance of punishing it when discovered."

And see Sneed v. United States, 5 Cir., 298 F. 911, 912, 913; Banghart v. United States, 4 Cir., 148 F.2d 521.

Moreover, it is not material that overt acts charged in the conspiracy counts were also charged and proved as substantive offenses. As stated in Sneed v. United States, supra, 298 F. at page 913, "If the overt act be the offense which was the object of the conspiracy, and is also punished, there is not a double punishment of it." The agreement to do an unlawful act is even then distinct from the doing of the act.

It is contended that there was insufficient evidence to implicate Daniel in the conspiracy. But we think there was enough evidence for submission of the issue to the jury.

There is, however, no evidence to show that Daniel participated directly in the commission of the substantive offenses on which his conviction has been sustained, although there was evidence to show that these substantive offenses were in fact committed by Walter in furtherance of the unlawful agreement or conspiracy existing between the brothers. The question was submitted to the jury on the theory that each petitioner could be found guilty of the substantive offenses, if it was found at the time those offenses were committed petitioners were parties to an unlawful conspiracy and the substantive offenses charged were in fact committed in furtherance of it.

Daniel relies on United States v. Sall [116 F.2d 745 (3rd Cir. 1940)]. That case held that participation in the conspiracy was not itself enough to sustain a conviction for the substantive offense even though it was committed in furtherance of the conspiracy. The court held that, in addition to evidence that the offense was in fact committed in furtherance of the conspiracy, evidence of direct participation in the commission of the substantive offense or other evidence from which participation might fairly be inferred was necessary.

We take a different view. We have here a continuous conspiracy. There is here no evidence of the affirmative action on the part of Daniel which is necessary to establish his withdrawal from it. Hyde v. United States, 225 U.S. 347, 369, 32 S.Ct. 793, 803, 56 L.Ed. 1114, Ann.Cas.1914A, 614. As stated in that case, "Having joined in an unlawful scheme, having constituted agents for its performance, scheme and agency to be continuous until full fruition be secured, until he does some act to disavow or defeat the purpose he is in no situation to claim the delay of the law. As the offense has not been terminated or accomplished, he is still offending. And we think consciously offending,—offending as certainly, as we have said, as at the first moment of his confederation, and consciously, through every moment of its existence." Id., 225 U.S. at page 369, 32 S.Ct. at page 803. And so long as the partnership in crime continues, the partners act for each other in carrying it forward. It is settled that "an overt act of one partner may be the act of all without any new agreement specifically directed to that act." United States v. Kissel, 218 U.S. 601, 608, 31 S.Ct. 124, 126, 54 L.Ed. 1168. Motive or intent may be proved by the acts or declarations of some of the conspirators in furtherance of the common objective. Wiborg v. United States, 163 U.S. 632, 657, 658, 16 S.Ct. 1127, 1137, 1197, 46 L.Ed. 289. A scheme to use the mails to defraud, which is joined in by more than one person, is a conspiracy. Yet all members are responsible, though only one did the mailing. The governing principle is the same when the substantive offense is committed by one of the conspirators in furtherance of the unlawful project. The criminal intent to do the act is established by the formation of the conspiracy. Each conspirator instigated the commission of the crime. The unlawful agreement contemplated precisely what was done. It was formed for the purpose. The act done was in execution of the enterprise. The rule which holds responsible one who counsels, procures, or commands another to commit a crime is founded on the same principle. That principle is recognized in the law of conspiracy when the overt act of one partner in crime is attributable to all. An overt act is an essential ingredient of the crime of conspiracy under § 37 of the Criminal Code, 18 U.S.C. § 88, 18 U.S.C.A. § 88. If that can be supplied by the act of one conspirator, we fail to see why the same or other acts in furtherance of the conspiracy are likewise not attributable to the others for the purpose of holding them responsible for the substantive offense.

A different case would arise if the substantive offense committed by one of the conspirators was not in fact done in furtherance of the conspiracy, did not fall within the scope of the unlawful project, or was merely a part of the ramifications of the plan which could not be reasonably foreseen as a necessary or natural consequence of the unlawful agreement. But as we read this record, that is not this case.

Affirmed.

Mr. Justice JACKSON took no part in the consideration or decision of this case.

Mr. Justice RUTLEDGE, dissenting in part.

The judgment concerning Daniel Pinkerton should be reversed. In my opinion it is without precedent here and is a dangerous precedent to establish.

Daniel and Walter, who were brothers living near each other, were charged in several counts with substantive offenses, and then a conspiracy count was added naming those offenses as overt acts. The proof showed that Walter alone committed the substantive crimes. There was none to establish that Daniel participated in them, aided and abetted Walter in committing them, or knew that he had done so. Daniel in fact was in the penitentiary, under sentence for other crimes, when some of Walter's crimes were done.

There was evidence, however, to show that over several years Daniel and Walter had confederated to commit similar crimes concerned with unlawful possession, transportation, and dealing in whiskey, in fraud of the federal revenues. On this evidence both were convicted of conspiracy. Walter also was convicted on the substantive counts on the proof of his committing the crimes charged. Then, on that evidence without more than the proof of Daniel's criminal agreement with Walter and the latter's overt acts, which were also the substantive offenses charged, the court told the jury they could find Daniel guilty of those substantive offenses. They did so.

I think this ruling violates both the letter and the spirit of what Congress did when it separately defined the three classes of crime, namely, (1) completed substantive offenses; (2) aiding, abetting or counseling another to commit them; and (3) conspiracy to commit them. Not only does this ignore the distinctions Congress has prescribed shall be observed. It either convicts one man for another's crime or punishes the man convicted twice for the same offense.

* * *

The court's theory seems to be that Daniel and Walter became general partners in crime by virtue of their agreement and because of that agreement without more on his part Daniel became criminally responsible as a principal for everything Walter did thereafter in the nature of a criminal offense of the general sort the agreement contemplated, so long as there was not clear evidence that Daniel had withdrawn from or revoked the agreement. Whether or not his commitment to the penitentiary had that effect, the result is a vicarious criminal responsibility as broad as, or broader than, the vicarious civil liability of a partner for acts done by a co-partner in the course of the firm's business.

Such analogies from private commercial law and the law of torts are dangerous, in my judgment, for transfer to the criminal field. Guilt there with us remains personal, not vicarious, for the more serious offenses. It should be kept so. The effect of Daniel's conviction in this case, to repeat, is either to attribute to him Walter's guilt or to punish him twice for the same offense, namely, agreeing with Walter to engage in crime. Without the agreement Daniel was guilty of no crime on this record. With it and no more, so far as his own conduct is concerned, he was guilty of two.

4. IMPOSSIBILITY

STATE v. MORETTI

Supreme Court of New Jersey, 1968.
52 N.J. 182, 244 A.2d 499, certiorari denied 393 U.S. 952,
89 S.Ct. 376, 21 L.Ed.2d 363.

PROCTOR, J. Defendants John J. Moretti, Marietta Schmidt, and Lawrence Gianettino were convicted in the Essex County Court of conspiracy to commit an unlawful abortion on Sylvia Swidler. N.J.S. 2A:98–1, 2, N.J.S.A.; N.J.S. 2A:87–1, N.J.S.A.[1] Gianettino died short-

---

1. The pertinent provisions of these statutes are:

        * * *

N.J.S. 2A:87–1, N.J.S.A.:

"Any person who, maliciously or without lawful justification, with intent

ly after the trial. On the appeal of Moretti and Schmidt, the Appellate Division affirmed the conviction with one judge dissenting. 97 N.J.Super. 418, 235 A.2d 226 (App.Div.1967). Moretti and Schmidt appealed to this Court   *   *   *.

On the evidence the jury could find that Mrs. Schmidt arranged with Moretti, a physician, to have an abortion performed on Mrs. Swidler. The abortion was to be performed by Gianettino, an inspector for the New Jersey State Board of Barber Examiners. Unknown to the defendants, Mrs. Swidler was a special investigator for the Essex County Prosecutor's Office. Gianettino appeared at about eleven o'clock one evening at the Swidler home pursuant to an appointment with Mrs. Swidler. She paid him $600 in marked money and they went upstairs to her bedroom where the abortion was to be performed. As Gianettino removed instruments to perform the abortion from a bag he had brought with him, the police who had been secreted in the house arrested him. The State concedes that Mrs. Swidler was not pregnant.

It has been held that under our statute an essential element of the crime of abortion is that the woman be pregnant. The defendants contend that since it was impossible to commit an abortion upon Mrs. Swidler because she was not pregnant, they cannot be convicted of a criminal conspiracy to commit an abortion. The argument runs that if no violation of the law was to be accomplished by the act of the defendants, they cannot be held for conspiracy to do that act. The majority of the Appellate Division rejected this argument, while the dissenting judge found it to be ground for reversing the convictions.

The crime of conspiracy is distinct from the substantive offense which the conspirators plotted to commit. The essence of the statutory crime of conspiracy is the joining together of the conspirators with an unlawful intent. It is this unlawful purpose upon which they agreed which makes a conspiracy punishable once any overt act is committed in furtherance of it. As Justice Heher said for this Court in State v. Carbone, 10 N.J. 329, 338, 91 A.2d 571, 575 (1952): "The union is invested with a potentiality for evil that renders the plan criminal in itself, and punishable as such if an act be done to effect its object." Here, there can be no doubt that if, as the jury found, there was an agreement among the defendants, its purpose was to commit an unlawful abortion and the conspirators took substantial steps in an endeavor to accomplish this end. That, unknown to them, Mrs. Swidler was not in a condition to be aborted in no way negates their clearly manifested intent to commit a criminal act. Such concerted intent, coupled with an overt act, is punishable whether or not the contemplated crime is consummated. That a factor unknown to the conspirators makes it impossible for them to complete their intended

to cause or procure the miscarriage of a pregnant woman, administers or prescribes or advises or directs her to take or swallow any poison, drug, medicine or noxious thing, or uses any instrument or means whatever, is guilty of a high misdemeanor.
*   *   *."

crime in no way lessens the degree of culpability involved in the criminal combination. People v. Nathanson, 389 Ill. 311, 318, 59 N.E.2d 677, 680, certiorari denied, 325 U.S. 872, 65 S.Ct. 1412, 89 L.Ed. 1990 (1945) (holding that in a prosecution for conspiracy to commit an abortion it was not necessary to prove the woman's pregnancy); Craven v. United States, 22 F.2d 605 (1st Cir. 1927), certiorari denied 276 U.S. 627, 48 S.Ct. 321, 72 L.Ed. 729 (1928) (holding that the defendant could be convicted of conspiring with others to smuggle imported liquor even though he had been deceived by the substitution of liquor of domestic origin).

The case has been argued as though, for purposes of the defense of impossibility, a conspiracy charge is the same as a charge of attempting to commit a crime. It seems that such an equation could not be sustained, however, because, as discussed above, a conspiracy charge focuses primarily on the *intent* of the defendants, while in an attempt case the primary inquiry centers on the defendants' *conduct* tending toward the commission of the substantive crime. The crime of conspiracy is complete once the conspirators, having formed the intent to commit a crime, take any step in preparation; mere preparation, however, is an inadequate basis for an attempt conviction regardless of the intent. Thus, the impossibility that the defendants' conduct will result in the consummation of the contemplated crime is not as pertinent in a conspiracy case as it might be in an attempt prosecution. However, we need not pursue this point since we are satisfied that even if we treat the present appeal as an attempt case the defense of impossibility does not shield the defendants.

*   *   *

[The court's review of impossibility in the law of attempt is omitted.]

In the present case, the defendants' intent to commit an abortion on Mrs. Swidler is clear; believing her to be pregnant, they did all that was in their power to bring about the criminal result they desired. That, had the police not intervened, they would have been thwarted in attaining this end by the unknown fact that Mrs. Swidler was not pregnant does not in one whit diminish the criminal quality of their agreement. The consequence the defendants intended was a result which, if successful, would have been a crime. We hold that when the consequences sought by a defendant are forbidden by the law as criminal, it is no defense that the defendant could not succeed in reaching his goal because of circumstances unknown to him. See Marley v. State, 58 N.J.L. 207, 212, 33 A. 208 (1895) where our former Supreme Court recognized that criminal liability would attach to a person "designing to perpetrate a crime, when he cannot effect it by reason of the existence of some fact unknown to him at the time." Accordingly, we conclude that the defendants could be convicted of conspiracy to perform an abortion on Mrs. Swidler notwithstanding the absence of pregnancy.

NOTE

Many courts would distinguish between "factual" impossibility—involved in *Moretti*—and "legal" impossibility. Review the material in the section on attempt distinguishing between the two types of impossibility. If A and B agreed to buy certain goods from C, believing them to be stolen goods, but in fact the goods that C had shown A and B were goods that were being used by C with the permission of the owner, are A and B liable for conspiracy to receive stolen goods? A court that distinguishes between factual and legal impossibility would say "no," because even if the agreement was fully carried out, i. e., A and B received the goods involved, no crime would have been committed.

---

5. THE DEFENSE OF ABANDONMENT

As the case in this section suggests, abandonment may have some impact upon a defendant's liability in the conspiracy situation. But this impact may be limited. Once the agreement has become complete (and an overt act, if required, has been committed), abandonment of the agreement will not have any effect upon the defendant's guilt for the crime of conspiracy. But if it is legally effective, such an abandonment will prevent the defendant from being liable for offenses committed by other members of the conspiracy.

PEOPLE v. BROWN

Supreme Court of Illinois, 1962.
26 Ill.2d 308, 186 N.E.2d 321.

DAILY, Justice. An indictment returned to the criminal court of Cook County jointly charged Fred Brown, Leonard McGarry, James Washington and Charles Gunn with the murder of Richard Hunter, who was shot to death in the course of an attempted robbery. Washington and McGarry pleaded guilty to the crime, whereas Brown and Gunn, who waived a jury, were found guilty after a bench trial and each was sentenced to the penitentiary for a term of 14 years. This writ of error is prosecuted by Brown, to whom we shall refer as defendant, and as grounds for reversal he contends that he was not proved guilty beyond a reasonable doubt, that he had withdrawn from the robbery plan in such a manner as to avoid liability for its consequences, and that he was denied a fair and impartial trial due to the incompetency of his appointed counsel and to the admission of evidence relating to another crime.

The victim of the homicide was among those present on July 12, 1959, at a party being held in a basement apartment of a building located at 4601 S. Michigan Avenue in Chicago. Gambling seems to have been the principal activity at the "party," while the "apartment" appears to have been in the nature of an unlicensed tavern. Around

3:30 A.M. four men, later identified as defendant and those indicted with him, entered the premises. Washington and McGarry produced guns, under circumstances later to be detailed, announced that it was a stickup and ordered those present to lie on the floor. Decedent, however, jumped on McGarry's back and was shot by Washington, the fatal bullet first passing through McGarry's body. In the confusion the robbers were able to flee from the premises.

Defendant and Washington were apprehended in Nashville, Tennessee, and were delivered into the custody of Chicago police on August 17, 1959. At this time defendant made several oral statements and signed a written statement wherein he consistently acknowledged that he and his codefendants had first met in a tavern in South Chicago on the night in question and that they had driven to the Michigan Avenue address in furtherance of an express plan to rob those at the party. In addition, he consistently stated at all times prior to trial that he had looked through a window when they arrived at the apartment, that he then advised his companions he was not going in because there were too many people, and that he then took a taxi back to South Chicago. In his written statement he said he next saw his co-defendants an hour later in South Chicago, that McGarry was then suffering from a gunshot wound in the back, and that McGarry had been taken to defendant's room and ministered to.

At the trial, however, defendant deviated materially from his prior statements and testified there had been no plan or conversation relating to a robbery and that he had gotten into the car with the others merely for the purpose of going to the party. He stated that just as they reached the entrance of the building McGarry announced he was "going to make him some money," whereupon defendant said he didn't want any part of it and took a taxi back to South Chicago.

The chief witness for the prosecution was defendant's co-conspirator, Leonard McGarry. Although completely irreconcilable with his subsequent testimony, McGarry also testified there had been no preconceived plan or intention of committing a robbery and stated he and his companions had set out for the apartment solely for the purpose of gambling. Gunn, it was stated, had lost money at the party earlier and wanted to win it back. According to McGarry, he and his three companions went into the apartment and found about 25 persons present. He said that Gunn walked in first and went to the bar, that Washington remained behind at the door, and that he and the defendant walked to the middle of the room at a point four to five feet equidistant from Gunn and Washington. One Jimmy Jones, who had driven the men to the apartment, remained outside in the car.

McGarry said that after looking around for a moment he remarked there were "too many people," and that defendant thereupon replied: "Yes, forget it, let's go." At this, to use McGarry's words "most of us turned to go," but defendant asked him to wait and walked across the floor to a washroom. Immediately after defendant went into the other room, still according to McGarry, Washington pulled his gun, shouting as he did so, and when people started running about McGarry drew his pistol, fired a shot into the ceiling and announced that it was a "stickup." The witness said he then vaulted over the bar and demanded the money there and that defendant, "looking surprised," came out of the rest room at this time. Several patrons attempted to seize defendant but, McGarry testified, defendant fought them off and ran out the front door shouting that "one had got away." It was following this that Hunter was fatally shot as he grappled with McGarry. Concluding his testimony, McGarry stated that he staggered to the car, that he lost consciousness, and that his next recollection was being taken to defendant's house.

Fletcher Henderson, who was present at the party, appeared as a witness for the prosecution and pointed out defendant as one of the robbers. However, it appears he had been unable to identify defendant when called upon to do so on two occasions before the trial. Another prosecution witness, Helen Wilson, who was tending bar in the apartment, testified that defendant had had a drink at the bar, prior to the shooting, and that she had not seen him after the melee occurred. Gunn, who was jointly tried with defendant, testified on cross-examination that he was the last to arrive at the apartment where the murder took place, that defendant, Washington and McGarry were already present in the front room, and that he, the witness, had protested when Washington pulled a gun.

Defendant's initial contention that he is not guilty of murder because he had abandoned and withdrawn from the criminal enterprise of his companions must fail in two respects. We held in People v. Rybka, 16 Ill.2d 394, 406, 158 N.E.2d 17, 23, that it is "the communication of intent to withdraw and not the naked fact of withdrawal that determines whether one who advised, encouraged or incited another to commit a crime is to be released from liability as an accessory before the fact." To this need may be added the further requirement that the withdrawal must be timely, that is to say it must be "such as to give his coconspirators a reasonable opportunity, if they desire, to follow his example and refrain from further action before the act is committed," and it must be possible for the trier of fact "to say that the accused had wholly and effectively detached himself from the criminal enterprise before the act with which he is charged is in the process of consummation or has become so inevitable that it cannot reasonably be stayed." * * *

Stated otherwise, withdrawal may not be effectively made from a felony murder when the "transaction which immediately begets it has actually been commenced." People v. Nichols, 230 N.Y. 221, 129 N.E. 883, 886.

In the instant case, while there may have been "communication" by defendant to McGarry, the evidence in the record does not satisfactorily show communication to Washington and Gunn who were admittedly four to five feet away in a noisy crowded room. Indeed,

Washington was standing behind defendant and McGarry and his conduct in drawing a gun when he did strongly militates against the argument that he had been apprised of the alleged abandonment by defendant.   However, even if it could be said that communication to Washington and Gunn is a matter in which reasonable doubt should be resolved for defendant, we are of the opinion the attempt at withdrawal came too late.   Not only was there insufficient time given to provide the co-conspirators a reasonable opportunity to withdraw, but the criminal enterprise which begot the murder had already commenced.   When defendant and his companions, at least two of whom were armed, entered the apartment they passed beyond mere preparation in their common plan to rob those present, and defendant, by his presence, was efficiently encouraging and aiding the others.   Cf. People v. Chapman, 224 N.Y. 463, 121 N.E. 381.

Nor is it of any consequence that defendant had fled the premises before the murder of Hunter took place.   Defendant knew his companions were armed and is deemed to have known they would use their weapons if resistance was met.   Where conspirators contemplate that violence may be necessary to enable them to carry out their conspiracy or common purpose, all are liable for the acts done in furtherance of the common object, and where death results from the prosecution of the common object, all are equally guilty of murder, whether or not each is actually present.   People v. Rybka, 16 Ill.2d 394, 158 N. E.2d 17;   People v. Suddeth, 374 Ill. 132, 28 N.E.2d 268.

NOTE

The Final Draft of the Proposed New Federal Criminal Code would provide in section 1005(3)(b) for an affirmative defense of renunciation to a conspiracy charge "that, under circumstances manifesting a voluntary and complete renunciation of his criminal intent, the defendant prevented the commission of * * * the crime or crimes contemplated by the conspiracy."

6.   PROSECUTORIAL ADVANTAGES IN THE USE OF CONSPIRACY

KRULEWITCH v. UNITED STATES

Supreme Court of the United States, 1949.
336 U.S. 440, 69 S.Ct. 716, 93 L.Ed. 790.

[Petitioner's conviction for violation of the Mann Act was reversed because the trial court's admission of a co-conspirator's hearsay declaration made more than six weeks after the alleged conspiracy's termination was held to be error on the grounds that a statement made at that time could not properly be viewed as made in furtherance of the conspiracy or in furtherance of an implied subsidiary conspiracy to avoid detection and punishment.]

Mr. Justice JACKSON, concurring in the judgment and opinion of the Court.

This case illustrates a present drift in the federal law of conspiracy which warrants some further comment because it is characteristic of the long evolution of that elastic, sprawling and pervasive offense. Its history exemplifies the "tendency of a principle to expand itself to the limit of its logic." [1] The unavailing protest of courts against the growing habit to indict for conspiracy in lieu of prosecuting for the substantive offense itself, or in addition thereto,[2] suggests that loose practice as to this offense constitutes a serious threat to fairness in our administration of justice.

The crime comes down to us wrapped in vague but unpleasant connotations. It sounds historical undertones of treachery, secret plotting and violence on a scale that menaces social stability and the security of the state itself. "Privy conspiracy" ranks with sedition and rebellion in the Litany's prayer for deliverance. Conspiratorial movements do indeed lie back of the political assassination, the *coup d'état*, the *putsch*, the revolution, and seizures of power in modern times, as they have in all history.[7]

But the conspiracy concept also is superimposed upon many concerted crimes having no political motivation. It is not intended to question that the basic conspiracy principle has some place in modern criminal law, because to unite, back of a criminal purpose, the strength, opportunities and resources of many is obviously more dangerous and more difficult to police than the efforts of a lone wrongdoer. It also may be trivialized, as here, where the conspiracy consists of the concert of a loathsome panderer and a prostitute to go from New York to Florida to ply their trade (see 145 F.2d 76 for details) and it would appear that a simple Mann Act prosecution would vindicate the majesty of federal law. However, even when

1. The phrase is Judge Cardozo's—The Nature of the Judicial Process, p. 51.

2. The Conference of Senior Circuit Judges, presided over by Chief Justice Taft, in 1925 reported:
"We note the prevalent use of conspiracy indictments for converting a joint misdemeanor into a felony; and we express our conviction that both for this purpose and for the purpose—or at least with the effect—of bringing in much improper evidence, the conspiracy statute is being much abused.
"Although in a particular case there may be no preconcert of plan, excepting that necessarily inherent in mere joint action, it is difficult to exclude that situation from the established definitions of conspiracy; yet the theory which permits us to call the aborted plan a greater offense than the completed crime supposes a serious and substantially continued group scheme for cooperative law breaking.

We observe so many conspiracy prosecutions which do not have this substantial base that we fear the creation of a general impression, very harmful to law enforcement, that this method of prosecution is used arbitrarily and harshly. Further the rules of evidence in conspiracy cases make them most difficult to try without prejudice to an innocent defendant." Annual Report of the Attorney General for 1925, pp. 5–6.

7. See Senturia, Conspiracy, Political, IV Encyc.Soc.Sci. 238 (1931).

On conspiracy principles German courts, on May 30, 1924, adjudged the Nazi Party to be a criminal organization. It also held in 1928 that the Leadership Corps of the Communist Party was a criminal organization and in 1930 entered judgment of criminality against the Union of Red Front Fighters of the Communist Party. See note 15.

appropriately invoked, the looseness and pliability of the doctrine present inherent dangers which should be in the background of judicial thought wherever it is sought to extend the doctrine to meet the exigencies of a particular case.

Conspiracy in federal law aggravates the degree of crime over that of unconcerted offending. The act of confederating to commit a misdemeanor, followed by even an innocent overt act in its execution, is a felony and is such even if the misdemeanor is never consummated.[9] The more radical proposition also is well-established that at common law and under some statutes a combination may be a criminal conspiracy even if it contemplates only acts which are not crimes at all when perpetrated by an individual or by many acting severally.[10]

Thus the conspiracy doctrine will incriminate persons on the fringe of offending who would not be guilty of aiding and abetting or of becoming an accessory, for those charges only lie when an act which is a crime has actually been committed.

The interchangeable use of conspiracy doctrine in civil as well as penal proceedings opens it to the danger, absent in the case of many crimes, that a court having in mind only the civil sanctions will approve lax practices which later are imported into criminal proceedings. In civil proceedings this Court frankly has made the end a test of the means, saying, "To require a greater showing would cripple the Act," United States v. Griffith, 334 U.S. 100, in dispensing with the necessity for specific intent to produce a result violative of the statute. Further, the Court has dispensed with even the necessity to infer any definite agreement, although that is the gist of the offense. "It is elementary that an unlawful conspiracy may be and often is formed without simultaneous action or agreement on the part of the conspirators. * * *" United States v. Masonite Corp., 316 U.S. 265, 275. One might go on from the reports of this and lower courts and put together their decisions condoning absence of proof to demonstrate that the minimum of proof required to establish conspiracy is extremely low, and we may expect our pronouncements in civil cases to be followed in criminal ones also.

Of course, it is for prosecutors rather than courts to determine when to use a scatter-gun to bring down the defendant, but there are

---

9. 18 U.S.C.A. § 371. Until recently, the punishment for such a felony could have been far in excess of that provided for the substantive offense. However, the Act of June 25, 1948, c. 645, 62 Stat. 683, 701, provides that in such a case the punishment for the conspiracy shall not exceed the maximum provided for such misdemeanor.

10. This is the federal law applicable to antitrust prosecutions. For the history of this conception and its perversion, particularly in labor cases, see Sayre, Criminal Conspiracy, 35 Harv. L.Rev. 393. On the abuse of conspiracy see O'Brian, Loyalty Tests and Guilt by Association, 61 Harv.L.Rev. 592, and Note, The Conspiracy Dilemma: Prosecution of Group Crime or Protection of Individual Defendants, 62 Harv.L.Rev. 276.

procedural advantages from using it which add to the danger of unguarded extension of the concept.

An accused, under the Sixth Amendment, has the right to trial "by an impartial jury of the State and district wherein the crime shall have been committed." The leverage of a conspiracy charge lifts this limitation from the prosecution and reduces its protection to a phantom, for the crime is considered so vagrant as to have been committed in any district where any one of the conspirators did any one of the acts, however, innocent, intended to accomplish its object.[19] The Government may, and often does, compel one to defend at a great distance from any place he ever did any act because some accused confederate did some trivial and by itself innocent act in the chosen district. Circumstances may even enable the prosecution to fix the place of trial in Washington, D. C., where a defendant may lawfully be put to trial before a jury partly or even wholly made up of employees of the Government that accuses him. Cf. Frazier v. United States, 335 U.S. 497.

When the trial starts, the accused feels the full impact of the conspiracy strategy. Strictly, the prosecution should first establish *prima facie* the conspiracy and identify the conspirators, after which evidence of acts and declarations of each in the course of its execution are admissible against all. But the order of proof of so sprawling a charge is difficult for a judge to control. As a practical matter, the accused often is confronted with a hodgepodge of acts and statements by others which he may never have authorized or intended or even known about, but which help to persuade the jury of existence of the conspiracy itself. In other words, a conspiracy often is proved by evidence that is admissible only upon assumption that conspiracy existed. The naive assumption that prejudicial effects can be overcome by instructions to the jury, cf. Blumenthal v. United States, 332 U.S. 539, 559, all practicing lawyers know to be unmitigated fiction. See Skidmore v. Baltimore & Ohio R. Co., 167 F.2d 54.

The trial of a conspiracy charge doubtless imposes a heavy burden on the prosecution, but it is an especially difficult situation for the defendant. The hazard from loose application of rules of evidence is aggravated where the Government institutes mass trials.[20] Moreover, in federal practice there is no rule preventing conviction on un-

19. Hyde v. United States, 225 U.S. 347. Mr. Justice Holmes, on behalf of himself and Justice Hughes, Lurton and Lamar, wrote a vigorous protest which did not hesitate to brand the doctrine as oppressive and as "one of the wrongs that our forefathers meant to prevent." 225 U.S. 347, 387.

20. An example is afforded by Allen v. United States, 4 F.2d 688. At the height of the prohibition frenzy, seventy-five defendants were tried on charges of conspiracy. A newspaper reporter testified to going to a drinking place where he talked with a woman, behind the bar, whose name he could not give. There was not the slightest identification of her nor showing that she knew or was known by any defendant. But it was held that being back of the bar showed her to be a co-conspirator and, hence, her statements were admissible against all. He was allowed to relate incriminating statements made by her.

corroborated testimony of accomplices, as there are in many jurisdictions, and the most comfort a defendant can expect is that the court can be induced to follow the "better practice" and caution the jury against "too much reliance upon the testimony of accomplices." Caminetti v. United States, 242 U.S. 470, 495.

A co-defendant in a conspiracy trial occupies an uneasy seat. There generally will be evidence of wrongdoing by somebody. It is difficult for the individual to make his own case stand on its own merits in the minds of jurors who are ready to believe that birds of a feather are flocked together. If he is silent, he is taken to admit it and if, as often happens, co-defendants can be prodded into accusing or contradicting each other, they convict each other. There are many practical difficulties in defending against a charge of conspiracy which I will not enumerate.[b]

BLAKEY, ASPECTS OF THE EVIDENCE GATHERING PROCESS IN ORGANIZED CRIME CASES: A PRELIMINARY ANALYSIS, IN TASK FORCE REPORT: ORGANIZED CRIME

80, 81–83 (1967).

The utility of conspiracy theory in the prosecution of organized crime is manifest. No other single substantive legal tool has been as effective in bringing organized crime to book. Nevertheless, a dispassionate examination and analysis of its origin, development and use today leaves a feeling of uneasiness. An almost direct relation seems to exist between its present efficiency and its potential threat to individual liberty.

The exact origin of conspiracy theory in the common law apparently is not known. While it first received legislative recognition as early as 1305,[4] it did not reach full maturity until the 17th century when the criminal law experienced perhaps its greatest growth largely at the hands of the infamous Star Chamber. In 1611, the Star Chamber in the *Poulterers Case* [5] held for the first time that an unexecuted agreement was itself punishable. Emphasis was thus shifted from the substantive crime to the agreement which preceded it. There-

---

b. Despite Justice Jackson's expressions of concern and because of the advantages he recites, conspiracy doctrine has proven an especially favored weapon in the arsenal of federal prosecutors. In recent years it has been extensively employed in efforts to stem the flow of illicit drugs and, with greater notoriety, in the prosecution of various groups of political dissidents. With respect to the latter significant First Amendment issues have been presented since the discussions which will often evidence the illegal agreement may also be viewed as exercises of the right of free speech. Neither juries nor judges have proven very sympathetic to such prosecutorial efforts. For a particularly careful and detailed examination of the difficulties involved in such prosecutions see United States v. Spock, 416 F.2d 165 (1st Cir. 1969).

4. Ordinance of Conspirators, 1305, 33 Edw. 1.

5. 9 Co.Rep. 55b, 77 Eng.Rep. 813 (Star Chamber 1611).

after, the history of conspiracy theory aptly illustrated, as Mr. Justice Jackson has pointed out, "the tendency of a principle to expand itself to the limit of its logic."

Writing in 1842, Chief Justice Shaw in the leading case of Commonwealth v. Hunt [7] summed up the historical development of conspiracy law and gave to the concept its classic definition: "a combination of two or more persons, by some concerted action, to accomplish some criminal or unlawful purpose, or to accomplish some purpose, not in itself criminal or unlawful, by criminal or unlawful means."

The development of conspiracy theory in the law constituted an acute recognition by society of the special danger presented by group crime. Division of labor, specialization, anonymity, complexity of organization, continuity of operation, insulation from the normal investigative techniques of law enforcement, enhanced ability to corrupt the processes of law enforcement, and the accumulation of capital and skills are all made possible. There is no question that multiple-party, conspiratorial organized crime presents to society a challenge materially different from incident crime. Conspiracy theory is the attempt of the law to take the measure of that difference.

* * *

Conspiracy theory itself differs little from jurisdiction to jurisdiction. A conspiracy is thought to constitute a continuing crime. Criminal liability thus remains viable during the entire life of any organized criminal activity. While each co-conspirator must be aware of the existence of con-conspirators, he need not know their identity or the exact outlines of the criminal organization. Indeed, it is not necessary that any expressed communication take place between the conspirators. Criminal liability attaches to those on the periphery and reaches into the center of the conspiracy touching the chief figures no matter how hard they might seek to insulate thmselves from overt criminal activity. All members of a criminal organization are thus equally liable for the crime of conspiracy. In addition, concerted criminal activity carries with it vicarious substantive criminal liability. Every party to a conspiracy is liable for any offense committed by a co-conspirator reasonably contemplated by the conspiracy and committed in furtherance of it. Management-level members of a criminal combine may thus be held responsible not only for the crime of conspiracy but also for substantive offenses committed by others in furtherance of it.

All of this may be concretely illustrated by the investigation, prosecution and conviction for compulsory prostitution of Charles "Lucky" Luciano, the head of a criminal syndicate in New York City in the late 1930's. Over a period of years, Luciano gained monopoly control over prostitution in New York. Luciano himself did not

7. 45 Mass. (4 Met.) 111, 123 (1842).

take an active part in the daily operation of the business. His organization included such diverse functionaries as "strong arm enforcers," "protection collectors," "booking agents," "keepers of the houses" and the prostitutes themselves. Indeed, Luciano's combine was so large and well set up that it is clear that he did not know all of the people in his organization. In addition, the organization's activities were not limited solely to vice aspects of the business. If arrested, the girls were supplied bail, counsel, and other help in escaping punishment. Ultimately, Luciano's substantive conviction for compulsory prostitution rested on evidence which established his role in the overall conspiracy.

The list of major and minor organized crime figures convicted by utilizing conspiracy theory is long. Indeed, there is no question that existing conspiracy theory is equal to the challenge of organized crime. The failure of the criminal law to meet the challenge of organized crime must be sought elsewhere.

STUDY DRAFT OF A PROPOSED FEDERAL CRIMINAL CODE (1970)

§ 1005. Organized Crime Leadership. (Alternative I)

(1) Offense. A person is guilty of leading organized crime if he knowingly organizes, manages, directs, supervises, or finances a criminal syndicate, or knowingly employs violence or intimidation to promote or facilitate its criminal objectives, or with intent to promote or facilitate its criminal objectives furnishes legal, accounting, or other managerial assistance, or intentionally promotes or facilitates its criminal objectives by any act or omission of a public servant in violation of his official duty. No person shall be convicted under this section on the basis of accomplice liability unless he aids or participates in one of the ways herein specified.

(2) Definitions. A criminal syndicate is an association of ten or more persons for engaging on a continuing basis in crimes of the following character: illicit trafficking in narcotics or other dangerous substances, liquor, weapon, or stolen goods; gambling; prostitution; extortion; engaging in a criminal usury business; counterfeiting; bankruptcy or insurance frauds by arson or otherwise; and smuggling. If more than ten persons are so associated, any group of ten or more associates is a "criminal syndicate" although it is or was only a part of a larger association. Association, within the meaning of this section, exists among persons who collaborate in carrying on the criminal operation although:

(a) associates may not know each other's identity;

(b) membership in the association may change from time to time; and

(c) associates may stand in a wholesaler-retailer or other arm's length relationship in an illicit distribution operation.

(3) Grading.   The offense is a Class A felony if the number of associates exceeds twenty-five or if the activity of the association embraces Class A or B felonies.   Otherwise the offense is a Class B felony.

(4) Attorney General's Certification.   No prosecution shall be instituted under this section unless the Attorney General certifies that the nature and scope of the criminal association is of national concern and warrants invocation of the extraordinary sanctions herein provided.

(5) Jurisdiction.   There is federal jurisdiction over an offense defined in this section when any crime engaged in by the association is a federal crime.[c]

Comment

Traditional conspiracy notions of an agreement of two or more to commit a crime seem outdated when applied to an organized criminal business characterized by specialization of function, continuity of operation with changing personnel and a system of internal laws. Obviously, provisions such as this section which make for severe penalties against leaders of criminal syndicates will not alone solve the problem of organized crime; but it may be a significant step forward. An alternative approach is to provide extended sentences for ordinary crimes committed through large criminal syndicates, as in proposed § 3203.   A current Senate bill, The Organized Crime Control Act of 1969 (S. 30), adopts the sentencing procedure.   Arguments favoring that alternative include: the factors which warrant imposition of more severe penalties than in the case of an ordinary offender relate more to issues involved in treatment than issues involved in the determination of criminal liability; the sentencing process permits greater flexibility with respect to proof and to changing circumstances, i. e., organized crime moves, from time-to-time, into new fields of operation; consideration of some of these factors at the trial may unduly prejudice determination of guilt as to the underlying crime.
*   *   *

Arguments favoring this section include: circumstances which warrant imposition of the severe penalties prescribed should be specifically defined by the Congress, and their availability should result from jury findings made in the usual manner and under traditional standards; definition as a specific crime may raise the level of deterrence.

c. This section was deleted from the final draft.

V. SPECIFIC OFFENSES: CRIMES AGAINST PROPERTY

A. LARCENY

Larceny involves the misappropriation or attempted misappropriation of property without any threat of harm to the person of another. At common law it consisted of the taking and asportation (carrying away) of personal property in the possession of another against the will of the other and by means of a trespass with the intent to permanently deprive the other of his interests in the property. Modern codes generally retain the offense as defined at common law, either as the separate offense of larceny or as one form of theft. The following materials illustrate the meaning commonly given the various elements in the definition of larceny.

ROGERS v. STATE

Supreme Court of Arkansas, 1970.
458 S.W.2d 369.

FOGLEMAN, Justice. Appellant was convicted of the larceny of a boat and trailer belonging to Maxwell's Esso Station. His appeal questions the sufficiency of the evidence to support the jury verdict. Viewing it in the light most favorable to the state, we find it sufficient.

Morris Maxwell, proprietor of the station, kept boats and motors as stock-in-trade. On the night preceding February 5, 1970, he left one boat resting on a trailer chained to a light pole on the north side of the station. About 2:30 a. m. on February 5, Officers Paul Wood and Harold Flowers were patrolling the street in front of the station and saw a Thunderbird automobile backed up to the boat and a man standing behind the auto. They drove their patrol car to the next driveway on the street and watched the car at the station. When they saw this car pull out from the station, they pursued it to a driveway of a fire station on another street and blocked the Thunderbird there as the driver attempted to turn it around. The driver was identified by Paul Wood as the defendant and the person seen behind the vehicle at Maxwell's station. The officers looked into this automobile and saw a pair of bolt cutters lying on the right front floorboard. There was a trailer hitch on the rear of this vehicle. The defendant was arrested and searched. He had a small, cheap .22 caliber gun in a coat pocket. The officers then returned to the Maxwell station with the defendant in custody. There they found that the boat had been moved from its previous position and the chain by which it was secured to the lamp post cut.

331

The bolt cutters and chain were taken to the police station and on February 6 delivered by the Chief of Police to Paul McDonald, who was in charge of the State Police Firearms Identification Laboratory. McDonald testified that when a tool is manufactured, machine marks are left which are identifiable in the marks made by that tool. It was his opinion that the severed link of the chain had been cut by that particular set of cutters. It was stipulated that the boat and trailer were never removed from Maxwell's premises.

The principal argument advanced by appellant is that the evidence fails to show that the defendant ever had such possession and control of the boat and trailer adverse to the owner to constitute the crime of larceny. This argument is based upon the fact that the tongue of the trailer supporting the boat was only lifted off a block upon which it rested, and that no evidence showed that the trailer was ever hitched to defendant's automobile. We find this argument invalid.

We have said that the requisite element of asportation in larceny cases may be found from the slightest removal of goods from the place where they were left by the owner. The fact that the property was not actually removed from the owner's premises does not make the thief's dominion over it incomplete nor preclude a finding that there was an asportation. Banks v. State, 133 Ark. 169, 202 S.W. 43. In cases from other jurisdictions, it has been held that: moving a safe in a building five feet before the owner arrived is an asportation, Caruso v. State, 205 Tenn. 211, 326 S.W.2d 434 (1958); removal only a hair's breadth is sufficient, Gettinger v. State, 13 Neb. 308, 14 N.W. 403 (1882); the slightest change of location is sufficient, Lundy v. State, 60 Ga. 143 (1878); the least removal of a thing from the place it was located is sufficient, Wombles v. Commonwealth, 317 S.W.2d 169 (Ky.Ct.App.1958); the act of asportation is complete when the property taken is moved from its original position regardless of however slight may be the change of position, Blakeney v. State, 31 Ala. App. 154, 13 So.2d 424 (1942), reversed for error in instructions, Blakeney v. State, 244 Ala. 262, 13 So.2d 430 (1943).

It was reasonable for the jury to infer that appellant, with larcenous intent, cut the chain by which the boat and trailer had been fastened to the light pole, and removed them from their original position where they were supported by a concrete block in order to fasten the tongue of the trailer to the hitch on his vehicle. The evidence was sufficient to show asportation and felonious intent.

The judgment is affirmed.

RAY v. UNITED STATES

Court of Appeals of the District of Columbia, 1967.
229 A.2d 161.

MYERS, Associate Judge. After trial by the court, appellant was found guilty of petit larceny of United States property in violation of 18 U.S.C.A. § 641.[1]

Appellant was employed by a professional mover who was an independent contractor of the United States government. On the day of the alleged larceny, appellant's duties were to transport and deliver several chairs and a typewriter from a storage area in the city to the warehouse area of the Department of Commerce. After part of his load had been transferred from the truck to the warehouse, appellant was seen carrying an adding machine covered with wrapping paper out of the storage room of the warehouse. His explanation was that he was temporarily moving the adding machine to free space on a skid, thus permitting him to keep his entire load together. Although testimony differed as to how far he carried the machine, it is clear he never went beyond the warehouse area or carried the machine outside the building. On these facts, we feel the trial judge erred as a matter of law in his finding of guilt beyond a reasonable doubt.

Larceny from the United States is merely a codification of common law larceny, with the owner specified in the statute. As such it retains the common law elements of asportation and intent. While we are mindful that the slightest moving or taking may constitute an asportation when viewed with other circumstances, appellant had the government's permission, as a normal incident of his employment duties, to move and carry certain articles in and around the warehouse area. This he had done on previous occasions. Under principles of agency, he had the implied permission to touch, move and carry other articles in the same area to facilitate the proper performance of his duties. He would be guilty of larceny only if his possession of the adding machine was clearly adverse and contrary to the interest of its rightful owner, the United States. Since it was without doubt within appellant's scope of employment to pick up and carry articles for the purpose of rearranging items stored, some other act on the part of appellant would be necessary to allow a reasonable inference of criminal intent. Although intent is generally a question for the trier of fact, we find no substantial evidence from which criminal intent could be inferred here, and, without intent, the element of asportation in this case fails for want of adequate showing.

Reversed with directions to enter a judgment of acquittal.

1. The information charged that he did "unlawfully embezzle, steal, purloin and knowingly convert to his own use and use of another, and without authority sell, convey and dispose of an adding machine, a thing of value of the United States and of a department or agency thereof."

NOTES

1. The essential elements of larceny, the oldest and most important of the acquisitive offenses, are that the offender, by trespass, takes and carries away another's personal property with intent to steal it.

In *Rogers* the only dispute was whether the defendant had taken and carried away the property—that is, whether the asportation requirement had been satisfied. The element of trespass was present not because the station was not open for business at 2:30 a. m. but because all that is needed is a taking from the possession of the owner without his consent. The result would have been the same if these actions had been performed during business hours. One of the more difficult theoretical problems with respect to the trespass requirement is where the owner has voluntarily surrendered actual possession as where an employer has given some property to an employee for his use in the employer's business. In such situations the courts have solved the problem by creating the fiction of constructive possession so that the employee is said to have mere custody and his taking is deemed to be trespassory, i. e., from the employer's possession.

Taking (caption) and carrying away (asportation) have traditionally been viewed as separate elements. The former refers to the thief's exercise of control over the property, either directly or through an innocent third party, the latter to some movement, however slight, of the property. In practice the distinction is unimportant and in some states it has been abandoned. Thus, Vernon's Tex.Code Ann. Art. 1412 (Penal) provides:

> To constitute 'taking' it is not necessary that the property be moved any distance from the place of taking; it is sufficient that it has been in the possession of the thief, though it may not be moved out of the presence of the person deprived of it * * *.

It should be noted that the requisite larcenous intent, which was inferred in *Rogers*, is an intent to steal which has been defined in the Model Penal Code Section 223(1) as:

> (a) to withhold property of another permanently or for so extended a period as to appropriate a major portion of its economic value, or with intent to restore only upon payment of reward or other compensation; or (b) to dispose of the property so as to make it unlikely that the owner will recover it.

The intent and the larcenous conduct must coincide. Normally, there will be little difficulty with this requirement since intent may be readily inferred from conduct. However, where, as in *Ray*, the conduct is consistent with the continued possession by the owner such an inference would not be reasonable. As may be seen from the MPC definition, if the taker is unaware that the property is that of another or believes that he has a claim of right to it the intent requirement is not satisfied. The existence of such states of mind is made an affirmative defense by MPC section 223.1(3). Thus, the unexplained possession of recently stolen property is commonly said to permit the inference that the possessor committed the crime by which the property was taken from its owner. A rather special problem is where the property is taken with intent merely to use it temporarily, as in joyriding. This has frequently been treated as a separate and less serious offense.

2. The taking of the property must be "trespassory." If it is without the consent of the person from whom the property is taken, it is of course trespassory. But even a taking with permission is trespassory if the permission was obtained by means of misrepresentation. In such cases, there may be a problem as to whether the offense is larceny or false pretenses; see the discussion following Pollard, infra.

3. Larceny is a crime against possession. All that is necessary, therefore, is that the offender take the property from one who has a possessory interest superior to that of the offender. Thus it is larceny even to take property from one who has himself obtained the property by larceny. Moreover, one can commit larceny by taking his own property, as if one takes his automobile from the possession of a mechanic who has repaired it and as a result under local law has a lien on it which gives him the right to retain it until he is paid for the repairs.

4. Only personal property with some value and capable of being possessed can be the subject of larceny at common law. Thus land and things attached to it, or services cannot be the subject of larceny. The same is true of intangibles (such as access to the performance of a play) and documents and instruments, which are regarded as "merged" with the land or intangible rights they represented.

VIRGIN ISLANDS v. WILLIAMS

United States Court of Appeals for the Third Circuit, 1970.
424 F.2d 526.

HASTIE, Chief Judge. This case presents the question whether larceny as defined by the Virgin Islands Code can be committed without an intent to deprive the owner permanently of his property.

The five juvenile appellants have been convicted of petit larceny under 14 V.I.C. §§ 1081, 1084. It was stipulated at the beginning of the hearing that the defendants had taken five horses from a pasture in St. Croix, ridden them to another part of the island several miles away, returned them to the general area from which they had been taken and released them. One horse subsequently died of injuries sustained during this unauthorized excursion.

At the close of the prosecution's case and again after all the evidence had been presented, the defendants moved to dismiss the complaint on the basis that there was no proof of an intent to deprive the owners of the horses permanently. The court denied the motion ruling that the Virgin Islands Code does not require proof of such an intent to establish larceny.

Section 1081 of title 14, Virgin Islands Code, defines larceny as " * * * the unlawful taking, stealing, carrying, leading, or driving away the personal property of another." This definition contains no mention of any requisite intent. In these circumstances, the process of interpretation begins with the consideration that the specific intent to deprive the owner permanently of his property is an essential ele- ment of the crime of larceny at common law. Absent a clear indica- tion of legislative purpose, we are reluctant to assume that the omis- sion of any mention of intent in the statute which makes "larceny" a crime was intended to eliminate that important and long-accepted element from the crime. * * *

In the tradition of Anglo-American law the crime of larceny is a major felony and as such is not intended to cover the less serious wrong of temporary appropriation of another's property. In the Virgin Islands larceny is deemed such a serious crime that, if the value of the stolen property exceeds $100, the wrongdoer is subject to imprisonment for up to ten years. 14 V.I.C. § 1083. In these circum- stances, as had been said at common law, a "momentary loss of pos- session is not what has been guarded against with such severe penal- ties. What the law means to prevent is the loss of it wholly and for- ever * * * ." Holmes, The Common Law 71 (1881).

At least one situation of temporary appropriation of property is treated separately by the Virgin Islands Code, and less severe penal- ties are provided. The unauthorized use of a motor vehicle, however valuable, or bicycle with no intent permanently to deprive the owner of possession is a lesser crime, distinct from larceny. 14 V.I.C. § 1381. One convicted under that section " * * * shall be fined not more than $500 or imprisoned not more than 1 year, or both." We are un- able to believe that the Territorial Legislature intended that the "joy- rider" who wrongfully takes even a valuable horse from its pasture for an unauthorized ride should be punishable ten times more severely than one who similarly appropriates an automobile.

If the legislature of the Virgin Islands determines, as it has for motor vehicles and bicycles, that the unauthorized temporary taking of horses is a sufficiently serious wrong, it may properly make such misappropriation criminal. But it has not yet done so.

The judgment will be reversed.

NOTES

1. Does the state of mind required for larceny require that the defendant affirmatively desire the permanent deprivation of the owner's interest? That he know or have a firm belief unaccompanied by a substantial doubt that such deprivation will occur? Or is it sufficient that he was aware of a certain risk that the deprivation would occur? In Commonwealth v. Salerno, 356 Mass. 642, 255 N.E.2d 318 (1970) the defendant had apparently taken a parked car from Worcester, Massachusetts. He drove it to Leominster, Massachusetts where it was used the next morning as the "get-away" car in an armed robbery. That afternoon the car was found, apparently abandoned, in a parking lot behind a Leominster theater. In affirming the defendant's conviction for theft of the car, the court commented, "One who takes property without the authority of the owner and so uses or disposes of it as to show indifference whether the owner recovers possession may be found to intend to deprive the owner of it permanently." Compare W. LaFave and A. Scott, Handbook on Criminal Law 637 (1972), who suggest that the state of mind required is the "intent to deprive the owner of his possession of the property either permanently or for an unreasonable length of time, or [the intent] to use it in such a way that the owner will probably be thus deprived of his property." Would the court in Salerno have come out as it did if it had applied this requirement? Which is preferable?

Generally, of course, if the person taking property intended at the time of the taking to restore the property to the other, the taking was not larceny. But if he merely intended to pay the owner the value of the property, the taking was larceny unless the other person had placed the property for sale. One who takes property from another openly in the belief that he is entitled to it because of a debt owned by the person from whom the property is taken does not commit larceny; he believes that the other person has no rights in the property and therefore he cannot intend to deprive the "victim" of any such rights.

One who takes property with the intent to return it does not commit larceny simply because he hopes for or expects a reward for the return. But if he intends to return it only upon receipt of a reward, there is sufficient risk that the property will be lost to make the action larceny. Similarly, one who takes property intending to sell it back to the owner or to pledge it commits larceny, because this also involves a high risk of permanent loss of the property.

2. Samuels, Permanently to Deprive, New Law Journal, March 21, 1968, at 281:

> Why should not dishonest borrowing amount to stealing? The reasons given by the Criminal Law Revision Committee are in para. 56 of their report. Borrowing is essentially different from stealing. It would constitute a considerable extension of the criminal law, when there is no existing serious evil. It might have undesirable social consequences. Quarrelling neighbours and families would be able to threaten one another with prosecution. Students and young people sharing accommodation who might be tempted to borrow one another's property in disregard of a prohibition by

the owner would be in danger of acquiring a criminal record. It would be difficult for the police to avoid being involved in wasteful and undesirable investigations into alleged offences which had no social importance. It is difficult to see how the provision could be framed in a way which would satisfactorily exclude trivial cases and meet these objections. * * *

The counter-arguments in favour of making dishonest borrowing a criminal offence are, it is submitted, overwhelming. The reform of the law of theft should be moving towards the concept of dishonest economic deprivation and away from the traditional concept of a physical taking with intent permanently to deprive. The new code should be expressed in terms of simple and comprehensive general principle, and it should not be necessary to have to make special provision for taking and driving away aeroplanes and for removing Goyas, a provision anyway rightly recognising that dishonest borrowing should be criminal. The complete usurpation clause is difficult to construe, complicated, and anyway an admission that the permanently to deprive concept is by itself inadequate. The jury are unlikely to be enlightened by such a clause being put to them in the summing up in every theft case, as presumably it would have to be. My lecture notes in my car are "taken" when my car is criminally taken and driven away. The car and the notes are recovered, after the lecture. Is this complete usurpation? Naturally in order to be criminal the borrowing would have to be dishonest, and the defence of claim of right or subjectively reasonable belief that the owner would have consented if he has been asked would apply. The man in the street readily recognises "pinching" when he sees it, he does not require or accept the permanently to deprive concept. At the time of taking the thief is not always too sure whether he is going to retain or return the stuff. As for the dishonest student borrowing without authority to the grave inconvenience of a colleague, why should he be protected and privileged? Perhaps an exception should be made for "borrowing" the mascot of a rival college in a student rag, though the student rag is not dishonest. The suggestion that neighbours and families would threaten one another with prosecution is naive. Is knowledge of the subtleties of the criminal law so widespread? And are the police no longer to be trusted to be capable of exercising their discretion not to prosecute in their traditionally responsible manner? It is a crime for a boy of 11 to take an apple from an orchard, but there are few prosecutions. The existence of a civil remedy for the owner against the unauthorised borrower is more of a theoretical than a practical argument. The concept of permanently to deprive is not found in Canada and many other common law jurisdictions.

R. v. COCKBURN

Court of Appeal, Criminal Division, 1967.
[1968] 1 All E.R. 466.

WINN, L.J., delivered the following judgment of the court: The appellant was employed as manager of a shop of Peter Dominic, Ltd., wine merchants in Halifax. He was dismissed on Apr. 17, not for any matter connected with this charge. The next day the area manager carried out a check of the cash at the shop, and found that about £107 was missing. The appellant then and subsequently maintained that he certainly knew nothing about any shortage to the extent of £107; he had not taken any such amount at all, but he somewhat belatedly admitted that he did take £50 from the till on the previous Saturday. He said that he had intended to cover that £50 withdrawal by a cheque, but it was discovered on the Monday before he had time to put the cheque in. It appears that the appellant was helped by his own daughter in a most remarkably loose and rash fashion in as much as she gave him from time to time bunches of blank cheques which she had signed on her own bank account with authority from her to fill them in with any amount that he might require, and to put those cheques into his employers' till against money that he took from the till. He said that his practice was to put a note into the till when he did not immediately put a cheque, but as and when he found himself with a cheque and at the till he would put one of his daughter's cheques in the till. It is right to say that all his daughter's cheques had been met up to the relevant date, a total of nine of them, some given in payment of her account and some with the daughter's authority in the manner that I have indicated. He apparently was receiving an allowance of about £10 a week from a trust fund left by his late wife, but he was not operating any bank account of his own at the material time.

The point raised by counsel for the appellant is that it is a good defence in law to a charge of larceny of a sum of money if the defendant is able to satisfy the jury, or if it remains open in the minds of the jury as a reasonable possibility, that he intended to replace the money taken with its currency equivalent and had resources available to him which would enable him to make that replacement. The court is quite satisfied that that submission of counsel is founded on, and very ill-founded on, a passage in a report of R. v. Williams [1] which was before the Court of Criminal Appeal in 1953, when the court was presided over by LORD GODDARD, C. J., and PARKER and BYRNE, JJ., were the other two members of the court. There is in the Weekly Law Reports a passage [2] which this court sincerely hopes will for the future be disregarded entirely by the Bar and all others who have occasion from time to time to refer to R. v. Williams [1]. There is no correspond-

1. [1953] 1 All E.R. 1068; [1953] 1 Q.B. 660.

ing passage in the Law Reports [3], or in the Criminal Appeal Reports [4], and I venture to think that beyond peradventure LORD GODDARD himself must have checked those reports, the Law Reports and the Criminal Appeal Reports, and taken good care to see that the passage which I am about to read did not appear in those official reports. The passage reads as follows [2]:

> "It is one thing if a person with good credit and plenty of money uses somebody else's money which may be in his possession and which may have been entrusted to him or which he may have had the opportunity of taking, merely intending to use those coins instead of some of his own which he has only to go to his room or to his bank to obtain. No jury would then say that there was any intent to defraud or any fraudulent taking, it is quite another matter if the person who takes the money is not in a position to replace it at the time but only has a hope or expectation that he will be able to do so in the future   *   *   * "

I venture to think that quite probably, LORD GODDARD, C. J., felt about that passage what I myself not only feel but now say: that it is an extremely dangerous and misleading statement. It does not appear in the other reports that I have mentioned.

The fact of the matter, however, is this: that whereas larceny may vary very greatly indeed to the extent, one might say, of the whole heavens between grave theft and a taking which, whilst technically larcenous, reveals no moral obloquy and does no harm at all, it is nevertheless quite essential always to remember what are the elements of larceny and what are the complete and total elements of larceny, that is to say, taking the property of another person against the will of that other person without any claim of right so to do, and with the intent at the time of taking it permanently to deprive the owner of it. If coins, half a crown, a 10s. note, a £5 note, whatever it may be, are taken in all the circumstances which I have already indicated with the intention of spending or putting away somewhere those particular coins or notes, albeit not only hoping but intending and expecting reasonably to be able to replace them with their equivalent, nevertheless larceny has been committed because with full appreciation of what is being done, the larcenous person, the person who commits the offence, has taken something which he was not entitled to take, had no claim of right to take, without the consent of the owner, and is in effect trying to force on the owner a substitution to which the owner has not consented.

*   *   *

Appeal against conviction dismissed. Sentence varied.

2. [1953] 2 W.L.R. 937 at p. 942.   4. (1953), 37 Cr.App.Rep. 71.

3. [1953] 1 Q.B. 660.

B. EMBEZZLEMENT

Embezzlement, unlike larceny, was not a crime at common law but was created by an early English statute. It is committed when one who has possession of another's property by virtue of a relationship of trust fraudulently appropriates that property to a use inconsistent with the trust.

STATE v. WILLIAMS

Supreme Court of Iowa, 1970.
179 N.W.2d 756.

BECKER, Justice. Defendant was indicted and tried for the crime of embezzlement by bailee, section 710.4, Code of Iowa, 1966.[1] Jury verdict of guilty was returned, defendant's post trial motions were overruled and he was sentenced to the State Penitentiary for a term not exceeding five years. He appeals. We reverse.

The embezzlement charge is an outgrowth of a business arrangement between defendant, his father and Liberty Livestock Farms, a partnership owned by Dwaine Clark and Dr. Joe Graham. Both Earl Williams, defendant's father and Dwaine Clark, one of the partners, were deceased at time of trial.

The parties mentioned entered into an agreement under which the partnership was to deliver 35 head of Hampshire open gilt hogs and 2 boars to defendant and his father for breeding purposes. Defendant and his father were to keep the hogs long enough to farrow and raise two litters of pigs. Thereafter the partnership was to receive one hog from each litter plus the return of the hogs originally delivered.

The 35 gilts and two boars were delivered as agreed to the farm owned by defendant's father and operated by defendant. Defendant took delivery of the animals.

The contract provided the gilts were to be large enough to breed and the boars large enough for service. One of the State's witnesses notes that he talked to defendant after the hogs were delivered and received complaints that the hogs were too small. Defendant claims the hogs were too small and were returned.

The contract contemplated defendant and his father would have the hogs on their farm for over a year. Delivery was made February

---

1. "Embezzlement by bailee. Whoever embezzles or fraudulently converts to his own use, or secretes with intent to embezzle or fraudulently convert to his own use, money, goods, or property delivered to him, or any part thereof, which may be the subject of larceny, shall be guilty of larceny and punished accordingly."

24, 1967. Frank Madera told of visiting defendant's farm and seeing the hogs in early April 1967. Dwaine Clark died May 27, 1967. His son-in-law, Leo Seuferer, took over the management of the partnership, discovered the contract for 35 gilts and two boars in the active file but took no further action until February 3, 1968, when he went to defendant's farm to check on the animals. Neither defendant nor his father was at home. Seuferer looked around the premises but saw no hogs. Two days later he reached defendant on the telephone and asked how the hogs were getting along. Defendant said they were doing fine. Seuferer then said he had been at the farm the previous Saturday and did not see any hogs on the farm. The telephone then went dead and Seuferer could not immediately reestablish connections.

Later the same evening Seuferer again called defendant and said he wanted to pick up the animals belonging to Liberty Livestock Farms. Defendant said he and his father did not have the animals, they had only been on the farm about a week when they were picked up. Defendant said he had been thinking about another deal when Seuferer had called earlier in the evening.

Defendant acknowledges the above telephone calls but denies the substance of the conversation. He denied he hung up on the first conversation and said that during the second conversation he told Seuferer Dwaine Clark had picked up the hogs.

Defendant did not produce the hogs and Seuferer then took the matter to the county attorney. The result was the instant indictment.

The first line of defense was that the State did not generate a jury question on all essential elements of the crime charged. The affirmative portion of the defense was that the hogs were returned to their rightful owners. Defendant contends the hogs were too small for proper breeding when delivered. His father was dissatisfied and called Dwaine Clark. Defendant's wife testified Dwaine Clark and a trucker came and took the hogs away while defendant was working in the fields. She was in the house. Earl Williams, defendant's father, went out and helped load the animals.

Since Dwaine Clark, the manager of the partnership that owned the hogs, died May 1967, shortly after the hogs were delivered and Earl Williams, defendant's father, died July 20, 1968, three weeks before defendant was indicted, the only person active in the contract, and still alive, was defendant. No evidence was produced as to how the partnership kept track of its hogs, what books were kept on financial transactions or what, if any, evidence the partnership papers contained as to whether the hogs in question had or had not been returned. In this regard the sole evidence was by James Clark and Leo Seuferer. Both said to the best of their knowledge no hogs had been returned but they did not know what, if anything, Dwaine Clark might have done about the hogs in April 1967. Seuferer said he found the contract under which the hogs were delivered in the active files maintained by Dwaine Clark at the time of his death in May 1967. Dr. Graham was an inactive partner and knew nothing about the matter.

*   *   *

Embezzlement was not a crime at common law, 2 Burdick, Law of Crime, § 574, p. 351; 29A C.J.S. Embezzlement § 2, p. 4. In Iowa embezzlement and all other crimes are wholly statutory. State v. Wallace, 259 Iowa 765, 772, 145 N.W.2d 615.

Chapter 710, Code, 1966, deals with embezzlement in several sections which define distinct and separate crimes; i. e., embezzlement by public officers, § 710.1; by bailee, § 710.4; by agents, § 710.9; et cetera. These crimes are similar but not subject to identical rules, State v. Cavanaugh, 214 Iowa 457, 460, 236 N.W. 96.

The different crimes of embezzlement covering different situations are noted here because of a rule laid down in State v. Bryan, 40 Iowa 379, 381, 382:

"The crime with which the defendant is charged, is that of converting the money which came into his hands as treasurer to his own use. The rule is too well established to require citation of authorities to verify it, that conversion may be shown either by direct proof of the fact of conversion, or by proof of a demand and refusal. Where the fact of conversion is sought to be proved by evidence of a demand and refusal, it may always be met and neutralized by evidence showing an excuse for this refusal; and when the excuse shown is sufficient, then the evidence of a demand and refusal does not establish the fact of conversion. *   *   *

"But this doctrine does not apply to the crime of embezzlement as defined by the next section of our statute, (Code, 3909). (Now § 710.5, at that time § 710.3, embezzlement by bailee had not been enacted.) There the doctrine relied upon by appellant's counsel and vindicated by the authorities they cite applies."

The State's brief relies on the above rule: " *   *   * The State showed that appellant signed an agreement to lease certain hogs, the hogs were delivered to appellant and when the lease expired a demand was made on appellant to return the hogs and the hogs were never returned. Obviously the State sustained its burden in proving the elements of the crime in question and the case was properly submitted to the jury." If the rule applies to embezzlement by bailee there is sufficient evidence for a jury case. This rule, under which the State need only show receipt of the property, demand and refusal to redeliver, is peculiar to embezzlement by public officials. State v. Bryan, supra, so states. Reference to section 710.1 relating to public officials will show the wealth of prohibited acts provided in the section and a rational basis for the rule.

In cases charging embezzlement by persons other than public officials a different rule applies. Ordinarily, fraudulent conversion to defendant's use must be shown. Cf. Footnote 1. See also, 2 Burdick, Law of Crime, § 575, p. 353: " * * * the accused must have fraudulently converted the property; and under most statutes, there must be an intent to defraud."

We have had little occasion in the past to consider the quantum of proof of conversion required necessary in cases of this kind. In similar cases there has always been proof of some overt act of defendant which is inconsistent with the rights of the true owner of the property; State v. Dykes (Iowa, 1968), 158 N.W.2d 154 (sale of corn at other than designated elevator); State v. Christiansen, 231 Iowa 525, 1 N.W.2d 623 (admitted collection of monies retained by agent and kept by him); State v. Schumacher, 162 Iowa 231, 143 N. W. 1110 (use of company funds to purchase grain options); State v. Boggs, 166 Iowa 452, 147 N.W. 934 (pledge of nonowned contract as security for personal loan); State v. Rowell, 172 Iowa 208, 154 N.W. 488 (commingling and use of funds by agent. The funds belonged to the principal). Other cases to the same effect could be cited. In each case, where conviction has been sustained there has been some evidence, direct or circumstantial, of wrongful conversion. We can find no such evidence here.

The subject, as it relates to demand and refusal, is best covered by Perkins on Criminal Law, Second Ed., chapter 4 (D), p. 293, where he quotes People v. Ward (1901), 134 Cal. 301, 304, 66 P. 372, 373:

" 'A demand, followed by a refusal *if the other essential facts exist,* is evidence of embezzlement, and sometimes indispensable evidence of it; *but it is the fraudulent and felonious conversion of the money or other property that constitutes the offense,* and that may often be proved without a demand' " (Emphasis supplied.)

Except in the case of public officials our statutes ordinarily require a showing of conversion of the property to the use of the embezzler. This may be done by circumstantial evidence and the State is entitled to all reasonable inferences to be taken from the factual circumstances shown. Here the State relied entirely on circumstantial evidence to prove defendant converted the property to his own use.

*   *   *

We know of no other case with a similar factual situation; i. e., where the accused defendant was one of two joint bailees either of whom could have disposed of the bailed property. There is no direct evidence that either bailee actually did so act. The possible activity of the deceased father is simply not met as an issue in the State's case. This alone is a fatal weakness under the foregoing rule long recognized in this court.

Nor is there any substantial evidence to eliminate the very real possibility that the bailor Dwaine Clark did not come and take the hogs away. The jury's obvious rejection of defendant's contention in this regard is not enough "to exclude a reasonable doubt that defendant was innocent of the charge". The negative factor of rejection of defendant's story does not relieve the State of its affirmative burden to prove its case. Defendant's evidence is to be considered but here it did not add to the weight of the State's case. There was no effort, beyond the finding of the papers with the "active files", to show the partnership still charged defendant and his father with possession of the hogs at the time of Clark's death.

The books of the partnership may or may not have been sufficiently detailed to show the location and number of hogs to which the partnership claimed ownership. If such evidence was available it was not produced. In the absence of such evidence and because of the death of Mr. Clark, the jury was left to speculate as to what the active partner did or did not do between the date of delivery of the hogs and the date of his death. As in the case of the possible activity of defendant's father, this dearth of evidence constitutes a fatal weakness in the State's case.

The rule applicable to public officials as to demand and nondelivery is inapplicable here. The record is completely silent as to what happened to the hogs. The evidence permits rational hypothesis inconsistent with defendant's guilt. As was asked in State v. Daves, 259 Iowa 584, 591, 144 N.W.2d 879, 884:

"The evidence is circumstantial. Can we say it is sufficient to allow the jury to find every rational hypothesis of innocence has been negatived as required by the cases? State v. Whisler, 231 Iowa 1216, 3 N.W.2d 525, 527; State v. Sigman, 220 Iowa 146, 149, 261 N.W. 538; State v. Bricker, 178 Iowa 297, 306–307, 159 N.W. 873; State v. Vandewater, not reported in Iowa, 176 N.W. 883, 884." As in State v. Daves, supra, the answer must be negative under the record made.

What has been said here makes moot the other points relied upon by defendant. The motion for directed verdict made at the close of all the evidence should have been sustained.

Reversed.

MOORE, C. J., and MASON, RAWLINGS, LeGRAND and UHLENHOPP, JJ., concur.

LARSON, STUART and REES, JJ., dissent.

NOTES

1. As the instant case makes clear, embezzlement requires conversion of the property. Unlike the caption and asportation necessary for larceny,

conversion requires no movement of the property. On the other hand, a mere movement that would suffice for asportation may not, depending on the circumstances, amount to conversion.

2. Embezzlement requires that at the time of conversion, the property be in the rightful possession of the defendant. But a person with some right of access to and control over property may have only "custody" rather than "possession". If he misappropriates the property, the offense is larceny rather than embezzlement. Whether a person has custody or possession of property depends upon how extensive is the authority given him to deal with it. Employees who use their employer's property during the performance of their jobs generally have only custody, unless especially broad power is given to them. A bank teller, for example, has sufficient authority to deal with his employer's money to justify classifying his power over it as possession. Lost property is regarded as "constructively" in the possession of the owner, so one who finds it and misappropriates it is guilty of larceny. Abandoned property, however, is regarded as having no owner.

UNITED STATES v. POWELL

United States District Court for the Eastern District of Virginia, 1968.
294 F.Supp. 1353, affirmed 413 F.2d 1037 (4th Cir. 1969).

KELLAM, District Judge. Charged under Title 18 § 641 of U.S.C.A. with embezzlement of funds of the United States Post Office Department aggregating $1,393.56, entrusted to his care as a postal clerk, Langston B. Powell entered a plea of not guilty, waived jury trial and was found guilty by the Court. * * *

Defendant contends the evidence fails to show (a) a criminal intent, and (b) a fraudulent appropriation of the money by him. In substance, defendant admits the funds in question came into his hands in his capacity as a postal employee, and that when an audit of the funds was made the funds were missing. But, he says he thereafter made good on the shortage, and there has been no showing "there was a fraudulent appropriation of the money by the defendant." That is, the government has not shown what he did with the funds. Defendant says the prosecution must establish how he spent the money, whether in high living, gambling, etc.

The offense charged in the indictment is that defendant did "embezzle certain funds of the United States Post Office Department * * * in the care and custody" of defendant. Embezzlement is the fraudulent or felonious conversion or appropriation of property which has rightfully or lawfully come into the hands of the converter. It is defined in Moore v. United States, 160 U.S. 268, 269, 16 S.Ct. 294, 295, 40 L.Ed. 422, in these words:

Embezzlement is the fraudulent appropriation of property by a person to whom such property has been entrusted, or into whose hands it has lawfully come. It differs from larceny in the fact that the original taking of the property was lawful, or with the consent of the owner, while in larceny the felonious intent must have existed at the time of the taking.

* * * Embezzlement presupposes that the money or property came to the possession of the accused lawfully and/or with the consent of the owner, and that a fiduciary relationship exists between the owner and accused. The elements are (1) a trust or fiduciary relationship, (2) that the property claimed embezzled is embraced within the meaning of the statute, (3) that it came into the possession or care of accused by virtue of his employment, (4) it is property of another, (5) that his dealing therewith constituted a fraudulent conversion or appropriation of same to his own use, and (6) such was with the intent to deprive the owner thereof.

When one wrongfully and intentionally embezzles or misappropriates the property of another which is lawfully in his possession to his own use, the offense is complete. The mere fact he intends subsequently to return the property or to make restitution to the rightful owner does not relieve his wrongful act; nor does it destroy the criminal nature of the act or excuse him. Hence, the mere fact that defendant at a subsequent date made restitution of the amount of the shortage does not wipe out the offense.

Accused offered no explanation of the shortage except to say he did not use the funds for his personal use. * * *

The motion for judgment of acquittal is denied. Upon the evidence heard by the court, the defendant is adjudged guilty as charged.

NOTE

As the instant case states, it is generally regarded as the law that the defendant must, at the time of the conversion, have had an "intent to defraud". The instant case to the contrary, it has been stated that converting property with the intent to return it is not embezzlement, at least if the person had a substantial ability to return it. See W. LaFave and A. Scott, Criminal Law § 89 (1972). But intending to restore equivalent property does not prevent a conversion from being embezzlement, even if the property taken is money and the defendant intended to return other, equally good, money. This, of course, explains the result in the instant case. But does it make sense?

C. FALSE PRETENSES

As you have seen larceny involves a misappropriation of another's property against his will and embezzlement the misappropriation of another's property rightfully in the possession of the offender. But what was to be done where the owner gave ownership (title) and not just possession of the property to the offender due to misplaced reliance on some deed or word of the latter? An easy example would be where the owner sells the property in exchange for counterfeit money. At common law there was an offense of cheating by false tokens which covered such conduct. It did not, however cover the situation where the property is given because of promises by the offender. This gap was largely closed by the statutory development of the crime of false pretenses which involved the fraudulent causing of another to part with ownership of property by means of false representations of fact known to the offender to be false.

POLLARD v. STATE

Supreme Court of Mississippi, 1971.
244 So.2d 729.

ROBERTSON, Justice. The appellant, Norman Pollard, was indicted, tried and convicted in the Circuit Court of Lee County, of the crime of false pretense (giving a bad check), and was sentenced to serve a term of three years in the State Penitentiary and to pay a fine of $250.00.

The appellant assigned as error: the granting of State's Instruction No. 1; the refusal to direct a verdict for the defendant * * *

Appellant had a sideline of buying used cars, repairing and improving them, and then selling them at a profit. He was a young married man with no capital and operated on a shoestring. He had been doing business for some months with Ronald Michael and Charles Baxter, of B & M Motors, Inc., Baldwyn, Mississippi.

On September 5, 1968, Pollard gave B & M Motors a $2,550.00 check for three used cars. September 5th was on Thursday, and Pollard testified that he asked Ronald Michael to hold the check until the following week. The proof showed that the check was held until the following Tuesday, September 10th, when it was deposited to the account of B & M Motors. Michael explained that B & M Motors was charged a flat exchange fee of $5.00 whether he deposited $1,000.00 or $50,000.00, so he usually waited until after the auction sale on Monday to make his deposit. The $2,550.00 check of Pollard was returned because of insufficient funds.

At the November, 1968, term of Circuit Court, Pollard was indicted for the crime of false pretense, (the giving of a bad check for $2,550.00 and receiving value for the check in the form of three used cars). The one indispensable element of this offense is the receiving of value for the check at the very time it is delivered. In other words, the seller parts with something of value on the belief that the check is good at that particular time. * * *

The gravamen of the offense was succinctly stated in Jackson v. State, 251 Miss. 529, 170 So.2d 438 (1965):

> "So an essential element of the offense under section 2153 is the making and delivering of the check to another person for value, *and thereby obtaining from such other person money, goods, or other property of value.*" (Emphasis added). 251 Miss. at 531, 170 So.2d at 439.

It would appear that the transaction between Pollard and B & M Motors was a credit sale, and not an exchange for value based on the belief that Pollard's check was good at that particular moment.

If Pollard is to be believed, he was doing business on a hold-check basis, received the cars on Thursday and his check was deposited the following Tuesday. This would indicate a credit sale.

If Michael is to be believed, he frequently allowed dealers to take cars one day and mail in a check several days later. He testified that he had followed this practice with Pollard on two or three occasions. This also would indicate a credit sale based on Michael's confidence in the purchaser generally. Michael had followed this procedure with Pollard just a week before. Pollard had taken delivery of two used cars on August 24, 1968, and his check to B & M Motors was dated August 27, 1968. Michael's uncertain testimony about this transaction was:

> "A   I'm saying it is a possibility that—it's been a long time, Mr. Parker, that he could have bought the cars, come by my place and bought the cars, verbally bought them, and said that when I send after the cars or when somebody brings them to me I'll send the check back or I'll put the check in the mail. There is that possibility, which I do that on numerous occasions.
>
> "Q   You have done that for him on numerous occasions, is that right?
>
> "A   No, probably a couple of times, but I do that with all of my dealers. *I had no reason to doubt the man wouldn't send me the check.*
>
> "Q   In fact you had no reason to doubt that he wouldn't send you the $2550 check?
>
> "A   I didn't—
>
> "Q   Isn't that a fact?
>
> "A   I thought the check was good when he gave it to me, I'll tell that.
>
> "Q   You had delivered his cars before that hadn't you?
>
> "A   I'm not sure when they delivered the cars on the $2550 check.

"Q   That's all my questions.

*   *   *   *   *   *   *   *   *   *

"A   I believe he took those cars that day, Mr. McCreary
I believe took those cars down there, I'm not sure."
(Emphasis added).

This Court said in Grenada Coca Cola Co. et al. v. Davis, 168
Miss. 826, 151 So. 743 (1934):

"The so-called bad check law does not cover the obtaining
of goods where the goods had already been delivered, had
passed completely out of the possession of the seller and
away from his hands and premises in a previously completed
transaction or transactions, *although those transactions
may have been at previous hours on the same day. There
must be an exchange for the check at the time of delivery.*
The bad check law is severe enough without extending it by
construction so as to include past deliveries, to say nothing
of the question of the constitutional validity of such a statute
if it were so construed." (Emphasis added.)   168 Miss. at
832, 151 So. at 744.

In the later case of Broadus v. State, 205 Miss. 147, 38 So.2d
692 (1949), this Court again interpreted the bad check law:

"In the case at bar, the pressing machinery had been delivered to the agent of Broadus and the agent had completely
removed them from the possession and premises of Fowler
and had departed from Roses Hill for Escatawpa, and had
been gone for some thirty minutes before Broadus came
up and delivered the check to Fowler in payment for same.
When Fowler let the machinery leave his possession and
control without demanding and receiving the purchase price,
he extended credit for same, Broadus did not obtain the
machinery with the check, for he had already, before that
time, obtained the machinery. He obtained nothing with the
check. The check was given in discharge of a pre-existing
debt. The bad check law has no application here." 205
Miss. at 150–151, 38 So.2d at 693.

The court should have directed a verdict for the Defendant Pollard.

*   *   *

Judgment reversed and defendant discharged.

GILLESPIE, P. J., and RODGERS, JONES and INZER, JJ.,
concur.

NOTES

1.   Although the English statute creating the crime of false pretenses was limited to obtaining "money, goods, wares, or merchandises," modern statutes are often broader and cover things which are not the subject of larceny.   Thus it may be false pretenses to acquire written instruments and documents relating to land or legal rights, title to real property, board and lodging, labor, or services.

2.   A major problem, created by the haphazard historical development of the property acquisition offenses, is distinguishing "larceny by trick" from false pretenses.   The traditional distinction turns upon what the victim passes to the offender.   If the victim transfers mere possession to the offender in response to the misrepresentation, the offense is larceny by trick.   If, on the other hand, title as well as possession is passed, the offense is false pretenses.   Whether title or mere possession is passed depends upon the intent of the victim.

3.   The misrepresentation must be of "present or past fact."   Thus it is not false pretenses to obtain money by a promise to do something in the future, even if that promise is not kept.   It is not even the offense of false pretenses if, at the time the promise is made, the promisor does not intend to keep it, although arguably he is misrepresenting his state of mind, a "present fact."

4.   The misrepresentation must be the cause of the victim's transferring title to the offender.   Thus the offense is not committed if the victim is not in fact deceived but rather transfers the property for some other reason.   Nor is it committed if the victim is deceived but this false impression does not play a significant role in his decision to give the property to the other.

5.   It should be noted in connection with *Pollard* that "bad check" laws were enacted because of difficulties encountered in fitting this activity within the traditional requirement that in obtaining property by false pretenses there must be reliance by the victim on a false representation with respect to a past or present fact.   Cf. Chaplin v. United States, 157 F.2d 697 (D.C.Cir. 1946).   Unlike the statute in *Pollard* most such laws do not require that property be obtained as a result of the check.   It is sufficient that the check be given with the requisite state of mind; usually knowledge of insufficient funds and an intent to defraud.

STATE v. MILLS

Supreme Court of Arizona, 1964.
96 Ariz. 377, 396 P.2d 5.

LOCKWOOD, Vice Chief Justice.   Defendants appeal from a conviction on two counts of obtaining money by false pretenses in violation of A.R.S. §§ 13–661.A.3. and 13–663.A.1.[1]

---

1.   A.R.S. § 13–661.A.   (1956) defines "theft" to include:
"3.   Knowingly and designingly, by any false or fraudulent representa-
tion or pretense, defrauding any other person of money, labor or property, whether real or personal."

The material facts, viewed " *   *   * in the light most favorable to sustaining the conviction," *   *   * are as follows: Defendant William Mills was a builder and owned approximately 150 homes in Tucson in December, 1960. Mills conducted his business in his home. In 1960 defendant Winifred Mills, his wife, participated in the business generally by answering the telephone, typing, and receiving clients who came to the office.

In December 1960, Mills showed the complainant, Nathan Pivowar, a house at 1155 Knox Drive and another at 1210 Easy Street, and asked Pivowar if he would loan money on the Knox Drive house. Pivowar did not indicate at that time whether he would agree to such a transaction. Later in the same month Nathan Pivowar told the defendants that he and his brother, Joe Pivowar, would loan $5,000 and $4,000 on the two houses. Three or four days later Mrs. Mills, at Pivowar's request, showed him these homes again.

Mills had prepared two typed mortgages for Pivowar. Pivowar objected to the wording, so in Mills' office Mrs. Mills, retyped the mortgages under Pivowar's dictation. After the mortgages had been recorded on December 31, 1960, Pivowar gave Mills a bank check for $5,791.87, some cash, and a second mortgage formerly obtained from Mills in the approximate sum of $3,000. In exchange Mills gave Pivowar two personal notes in the sums of $5,250.00 and $4,200.00 and the two mortgages as security for the loan.

Although the due date for Mills' personal notes passed without payment being made, the complainant did not present the notes for payment, did not demand that they be paid, and did not sue upon them. In 1962 the complainant learned that the mortgages which he had taken as security in the transaction were not first mortgages on the Knox Drive and Easy Street properties. These mortgages actually covered two vacant lots on which there were outstanding senior mortgages. On learning this, Pivowar signed a complaint charging the defendants with the crime of theft by false pretenses.

On appeal defendants contend that the trial court erred in denying their motion to dismiss the information. They urge that a permanent taking of property must be proved in order to establish the crime of theft by false pretenses. Since the complainant had the right to sue on the defendants' notes, the defendants assert that complainant cannot be said to have been deprived of his property permanently.

Defendants misconceive the elements of the crime of theft by false pretenses. Stated in a different form, their argument is that although the complainant has parted with his cash, a bank check, and a second mortgage, the defendants intend to repay the loan.

Defendants admit that the proposition of law which they assert is a novel one in this jurisdiction. Respectable authority in other states persuades us that their contention is without merit. A creditor has a right to determine for himself whether he wishes to be a secured or an unsecured creditor. In the former case, he has a right to know about the security. If he extends credit in reliance upon security which is falsely represented to be adequate, he has been defrauded even if the debtor intends to repay the debt. His position is now that of an unsecured creditor; at the very least, an unreasonable risk of loss has been forced upon him by reason of the deceit. This risk which he did not intend to assume has been imposed upon him by the intentional act of the debtor, and such action constitutes an intent to defraud.

*   *   *

The cases cited by defendants in support of their contention are distinguishable from the instant case in that they involved theft by larceny. Since the crime of larceny is designed to protect a person's possessory interest in property whereas the crime of false pretenses protects one's title interest, the requirement of a permanent deprivation is appropriate to the former. Accordingly, we hold that an intent to repay a loan obtained on the basis of a false representation of the security for the loan is no defense.

NOTES

1. The court in the instant case suggests that the state of mind required for false pretenses is not the same as that required for larceny. But this is doubtful. Most commentators regard the "intent to defraud" required for false pretenses as identical to the intent to permanently deprive needed for larceny. Is it arguable that the defendant in *Mills* intentionally subjected the victim to such an unreasonable risk of loss that he intended to permanently deprive as well as to defraud? Consider also the discussion in R. v. Cockburn, supra.

2. The defendant must also know of the falsity of his representation. If he believes it is accurate, he is not guilty no matter how unreasonable his belief may be. But the more unreasonable the purported belief is, the less likely it is that the defendant honestly entertained it. It is probably not necessary that the defendant consciously believe the misrepresentation to be false; it is sufficient if he does not know whether it is true or false but asserts it as true.

D.   THEFT

Dissatisfaction with the complexities inherent in the various traditional property acquisition offenses has lead many legislatures to modify common law offenses. The prevailing pattern has been to consolidate some or all of the common law property acquisition offenses into a single offense, titled Theft. (Theft itself has no significance in the traditional language of the criminal law.) The following is the proposed theft section of the Proposed Federal Criminal Code (1971):

§ 1731. Consolidation of Theft Offenses

(1) Construction. Conduct denominated theft in sections 1732 to 1734 constitutes a single offense designed to include the separate offenses heretofore known as larceny, stealing, purloining, embezzlement, obtaining money or property by false pretenses, extortion, blackmail, fraudulent conversion, receiving stolen property, and the like.

(2) Charging Theft. An indictment or information charging theft under sections 1732 to 1734 which fairly apprises the defendant of the nature of the charges against him shall not be deemed insufficient because it fails to specify a particular category of theft. The defendant may be found guilty of theft under such an indictment or information if his conduct falls under any of sections 1732 to 1734, so long as the conduct proved is sufficiently related to the conduct charged that the accused is not unfairly surprised by the case he must meet.

§ 1732. Theft of Property

A person is guilty of theft if he:

(a) knowingly takes or exercises unauthorized control over, or makes an unauthorized transfer of an interest in, the property of another with intent to deprive the owner thereof;

(b) knowingly obtains the property of another by deception or by threat with intent to deprive the owner thereof, or intentionally deprives another of his property by deception or by threat; or

(c) knowingly receives, retains or disposes of property of another which has been stolen, with intent to deprive the owner thereof.

§ 1733. Theft of Services

A person is guilty of theft if:

(a) he intentionally obtains services known by him to be available only for compensation, by deception, threat, false token or other means to avoid payment for the services; or

(b) having control over the disposition of services of another to which he is not entitled, he knowingly diverts those services to his own benefit or to the benefit of another not entitled thereto.

Where compensation for services is ordinarily paid immediately upon their rendition, as in the case of hotels, restaurants, and comparable establishments, absconding without payment or making provision to pay is prima facie evidence that the services were obtained by deception.

§ 1735. Grading of Theft Offenses Under Sections 1732 to 1734

(1) Class B Felony. Theft under sections 1732 to 1734 is a Class B felony if the property or services stolen exceed $100,000

in value or are acquired or retained by a threat to commit a Class A or Class B felony or to inflict serious bodily injury on the person threatened or on any other person.

(2) Class C Felony. Theft under sections 1732 to 1734 is a Class C felony if:

(a) the property or services stolen exceed $500 in value;

(b) the property or services stolen are acquired or retained by threat and (i) are acquired or retained by a public servant by a threat to take or withhold official action, or (ii) exceed $50 in value;

(c) the property or services stolen exceed $50 in value and are acquired or retained by a public servant in the course of his official duties;

(d) the property stolen is a firearm, ammunition, explosive or destructive device or an automobile, aircraft or other motor-propelled vehicle;

(e) the property consists of any government file, record, document or other government paper stolen from any government office or from any public servant;

(f) the defendant is in the business of buying or selling stolen property and he receives, retains or disposes of the property in the course of that business;

(g) the property stolen consists of any implement, paper, or other thing uniquely associated with the preparation of any money, stamp, bond, or other document, instrument or obligation of the United States;

(h) the property stolen consists of a key or other implement uniquely suited to provide access to property the theft of which would be a felony and it was stolen to gain such access; or

(i) the property is stolen from the United States mail and is first class mail or air mail.

(3) Class A Misdemeanor. All other theft under sections 1732 to 1734 is a Class A misdemeanor, unless the requirements of subsection (4) or (5) are met.

(4) Class B Misdemeanor. Theft under sections 1732 to 1734 of property or services of a value not exceeding $50 shall be a Class B misdemeanor if:

(a) the theft was not committed by threat;

(b) the theft was not committed by deception by one who stood in a confidential or fiduciary relationship to the victim of the theft; and

(c) the defendant was not a public servant or an officer or employee of a financial institution who committed the theft in the course of his official duties.

The special classification provided in this subsection shall apply if the offense is classified under this subsection in the charge or if at sentencing, the required factors are established by a preponderance of the evidence.

(5) Infraction. Theft under section 1733 of services of a value not exceeding $10 shall be an infraction if the defendant was not a public servant who committed the theft in the course of his official duties. The special classification provided in this subsection shall apply if the offense is classified under this subsection in the charge or if, at sentencing, the required factors are established by a preponderance of the evidence.

§ 1741. Definitions for Theft and Related Offenses

In sections 1731 to 1741:

(a) "deception" means: (i) creating or reinforcing a false impression, including false impressions as to fact, law, status, value, intention or other state of mind; but deception as to a person's intention to perform a promise shall not be inferred from the fact alone that he did not substantially perform the promise unless it is part of a continuing scheme to defraud; or (ii) preventing another from acquiring information which would affect his judgment of a transaction; or (iii) failing to correct a false impression which the actor previously created or reinforced, or which he knows to be influencing another to whom he stands in a fiduciary or confidential relationship; or (iv) failing to correct an impression which the actor previously created or reinforced and which the actor knows to have become false due to subsequent events; or (v) failing to disclose a lien, adverse claim or other impediment to the enjoyment of property which he transfers or encumbers in consideration for the property obtained or in order to continue to deprive another of his property, whether such impediment is or is not valid, or is or is not a matter of official record; or (vi) using a credit card, charge plate, or any other instrument which purports to evidence an undertaking to pay for property or services delivered or rendered to or upon the order of a designated person or bearer (A) where such instrument has been stolen, forged, revoked or cancelled, or where for any other reason its use by the actor is unauthorized, and (B) where the actor does not have the intention and ability to meet all obligations to the issuer arising out of his use of the instrument; or (vii) any other scheme to defraud. The term "deception" does not, however, include falsifications as to matters having no pecuniary significance, or puffing by statements unlikely to deceive ordinary persons in the group addressed. "Puffing" means an exaggerated commendation of wares in communications addressed to the public or to a class or group;

(b) "deprive" means: (i) to withhold property or to cause it to be withheld either permanently or under such circumstances that a major portion of its economic value, or its use and benefit, has, in fact, been appropriated; or (ii) to withhold property or to cause it to be withheld with the intent to restore it only upon the payment of a reward or other compensation; or (iii) to dispose of property or use it or transfer any interest in it under circumstances that make its restoration, in fact, unlikely.

* * *

(e) "obtain" means: (i) in relation to property, to bring about a transfer or purported transfer of an interest in the property, whether to the actor or another; or (ii) in relation to services, to secure performance thereof;

(f) "property" means any money, tangible or intangible personal property, property (whether real or personal) the location of which can be changed (including things growing on, affixed to, or found in land and documents although the rights represented thereby have no physical location), contract right, chose-in-action, interest in or claim to wealth, credit, or any other article or thing of value of any kind. "Property" also means real property the location of which cannot be moved if the offense involves transfer or attempted transfer of an interest in the property;

(g) "property of another" means property in which a person other than the actor or in which a government has an interest which the actor is not privileged to infringe without consent, regardless of the fact that the actor also has an interest in the property and regardless of the fact that the other person or government might be precluded from civil recovery because the property was used in an unlawful transaction or was subject to forfeiture as contraband. Property in possession of the actor shall not be deemed property of another who has a security interest therein, even if legal title is in the creditor pursuant to a conditional sales contract or other security agreement. "Owner" means any person or a government with an interest in property such that it is "property of another" as far as the actor is concerned;

(k) "threat" means an expressed purpose, however communicated, to (1) cause bodily injury in the future to the person threatened or to any other person; or (ii) cause damage to property; or (iii) subject the person threatened or any other person to physical confinement or restraint; or (iv) engage in other conduct constituting a crime; or (v) accuse anyone of a crime; or (vi) expose a secret or publicize an asserted fact, whether true or false, tending to subject a person living or deceased, to hatred, contempt, or ridicule or to impair another's credit or business repute; or (vii) reveal any information sought to be concealed by the person threatened; or (viii) testify or provide information or withhold testimony or information with respect to another's legal claim or defense; or (ix) take or withhold official action as a public servant, or cause a public servant to take or withhold official action; or (x) bring about or continue a strike, boycott, or other similar collective action to obtain property or deprive another of his property which is not demanded or received for the benefit of the group which the actor purports to represent; or (xi) cause anyone to be dismissed from his employment, unless the property is demanded or obtained for lawful union purposes; or (xii) do any other act which would not in itself substantially benefit the actor or a group he represents but which is calculated to harm another person in a substantial manner with respect to his health, safety, business, employment, calling, career, financial condition, reputation, or personal relationship. Upon a charge of theft, the receipt of property in consideration for taking or withholding official action shall be deemed to be theft by threat regardless of whether the owner voluntarily parted with his property or himself initiated the scheme.

Note that section 1732 supra provides that theft shall include the knowing receipt of stolen property with the intent to deprive the owner thereof. The crime of receiving stolen property traditionally requires proof that the property was stolen by another; actual receipt by the defendant; that the defendant knew at the time of receipt that it was stolen; and that his intent was to deprive the owner of it. It should be obvious that proof of the recipient's knowledge as to the stolen nature of the property can be an extremely difficult task. As a result, the law has evolved so that proof of possession of recently stolen property permits, in the absence of a satisfactory explanation, the inference that the person in possession knew the property had been stolen. This extremely important rule was challenged and upheld in Barnes v. United States, 412 U.S. 837, 93 S.Ct. 2357, 37 L.Ed.2d 380 (1973).

E. ROBBERY

Robbery is an offense against both the security of the person and of interests in property. It consists of the taking and asportation of personal property from the person or the presence of another against his will by means of violence or placing the other in fear of personal safety with the intent to permanently deprive him of his interest in the property. It was apparently the initial common law property offense, although it was defined somewhat more narrowly.

PEOPLE v. HELLER

Appellate Court of Illinois, 1971.
131 Ill.App.2d 799, 267 N.E.2d 685.

SCOTT, Justice. Defendant was indicted and tried by a jury in Tazewell County for armed robbery and robbery. He was found guilty of robbery and sentenced to the penitentiary for a term of four to twelve years. The charge arises out of an incident that occurred on October 21, 1969, in a tavern in Creve Coeur, Illinois, known as the Harbor Lights. The complaining witness, Peter Horvath, was tending bar on the night in question in the Harbor Lights, the same being a tavern, pool hall and restaurant establishment owned by Horvath's mother. He testified that early in the morning at approximately 2:30 or 3:00 A.M., two men came into the establishment, played three games of pool, ordered and ate "three chili dogs" taking them approximately twenty to twenty-five minutes. No one else was in the establishment. He identified defendant as one of the two men. He stated that defendant's accomplice gave him a $10.00 bill to change and while he was looking for change the accomplice struck him on the right temple knocking him down. He testified that defendant and his accomplice then took money from the cash register in the amount of approximately $100.00 and the defendant removed a gun from a small drawer near the register, the gun apparently being the property of Horvath or his mother. The defendant then pointed the gun at him and said twice that he would kill him. The two men then left the store.

* * *

Defendant next contends the court erred in failing to direct a verdict to the charge of armed robbery. The contention here is that the failure to so direct a verdict, acting together with an erroneous instruction given by the court and inflammatory remarks made by the State's Attorney, prejudiced the defendant and caused the jury to reach a compromise verdict. The instructions given by the court will be commented on later in this opinion.

The testimony establishes that the gun did not come into play until and at the same time the money was taken from the cash register. Defendant contends the gun was no more than a part of the property taken. This is not accurate for the testimony shows the gun was pointed at Horvath and that the defendant threatened to kill him. Defendant nonetheless claims, not without merit, that the weapon was not used in the commission of the crime nor in perfecting an escape. The substance of the argument is that despite the obvious intimidation of Horvath with the gun and despite the use of the gun while the robbery was in effect, this should not change the crime from robbery to armed robbery.

The question immediately arises as to whether the act of using the gun cannot be considered along with the robbery as a continuous series of events constituting a single occurrence. People v. Watson, 110 Ill.App.2d 343, 249 N.E.2d 293.

To sustain a conviction for robbery the force or threat of force must proceed or be contemporaneous with the taking of the property, People v. Jones, 290 Ill. 603, 125 N.E. 256, yet it is acknowledged by the authorities that the taking of property may be peaceful but the departure with the same may be forceful. In People v. Jones, supra, defendant apparently lifted the wallet of the complaining witness, who was intoxicated. The latter then accused the defendant of taking his wallet and defendant responded by striking him and knocking him out. The court there said:

"There was no evidence of a struggle to retain possession of the pocketbook, but only an accusation of the theft after it occurred, which the plaintiff in error resented by assaulting the accuser."

In 58 A.L.R. 656, that authority says:

"Though the decisions are not without conflict, the general rule requires that, in the offense of robbery, force or putting in fear be employed before, or at the time of, the taking of property, and does not permit a charge of robbery to be sustained by showing a retention of property, or an attempt to escape, by force or putting in fear." Citing People v. Jones, supra.

No case directly in point has been suggested by either party and People v. Jones cannot, we believe, be quoted as placing Illinois within that general rule.

In People v. Brown, 76 Ill.App.2d 362, 222 N.E.2d 227, a case involving a simple robbery, the court held that force exerted after the taking was sufficient to sustain the robbery charge. The complaining witness was asleep in an elevated train in the city of Chicago. He awoke and saw a man with his wallet taking money from it. He reached for his wallet and was struck by a second man and knocked back into his seat. The three men, all accomplices, left the train with his money. The court in denying defendant's contention that robbery had not been proven stated:

"The series of events—the taking of the wallet, the attempt to recover it by Dickerson, and the striking of Dickerson * * *—constituted a single incident or occurrence or the 'res gestae' of the crime."

In People v. Chambliss, 69 Ill.App.2d 459, 217 N.E.2d 422, the force took place after the taking of a wallet and after the complaining witness chased the thief after he had felt someone take his wallet from his pocket. The court quotes with approval from 46 Am.Jur., Robbery, Sec. 21, where it is stated:

"Thus, if a struggle *immediately ensues* to keep possession of the property and the thief overcomes the resistance * * * the violence is sufficient to constitute the act a robbery."

The court there referred to the force applied after the taking as the "res gestae of the crime."

We feel that the use of a dangerous weapon at any point of a robbery, so long as it can reasonably be said to be a part of a single occurrence or incident—or put another way, a part of the "res gestae of the crime", will constitute armed robbery.

In the case at bar we believe there was sufficient evidence to go to the jury on the question of armed robbery. So long as the assailant wielded a gun it is impossible to say what further resistance the victim may have put forth. No error was committed by the lower court in permitting the jury to consider the armed robbery count and certainly under these circumstances the defendant was not prejudiced.

NOTE

Robbery is not consolidated into theft in the Proposed Federal Criminal Code but rather is retained as a separate offense in the following provision:

§ 1721. Robbery

(1) Offense. A person is guilty of robbery if, in the course of committing a theft, he inflicts or attempts to inflict bodily injury upon another, or threatens or menaces another with imminent bodily injury.

(2) Grading. Robbery is a Class A felony if the actor fires a firearm or explodes or hurls a destructive device or directs the force of any other dangerous weapon against another. Robbery is a Class B felony if the robber possesses or pretends to possess a firearm, destructive device or other dangerous weapon, or menaces another with serious bodily injury, or inflicts bodily injury upon another, or is aided by an accomplice actually present. Otherwise robbery is a Class C felony.

(3) Definitions. In this section:

(a) an act shall be deemed "in the course of committing a theft" if it occurs in an attempt to commit theft, whether or not the theft is successfully completed, or in immediate flight from the commission of, or an unsuccessful effort to commit, the theft;

(b) "dangerous weapon" means a weapon the possession of which under the circumstances indicates an intent or readiness to inflict serious bodily injury.

PARNELL v. STATE

Court of Criminal Appeals of Oklahoma, 1964, 389 P.2d 370

BUSSEY, Judge: Plaintiff in Error, Rex Parnell, was charged by information in District Court Case #19773, with Robbery By Fear, as defined by Title 21 § 791, O.S.A.

To this information the defendant entered a plea of not guilty and was tried by a jury on the 3rd day of December, 1962, who found him guilty and fixed his punishment at Five (5) Years in the State Penitentiary at McAlester, Oklahoma.

A timely appeal was perfected in this Court; in substance, the record discloses the following material facts:

On the 28th day of April, 1962, Rex Parnell, accompanied by Floyd Kritser and and Bill Kritser, went to the home of the prosecuting witness, Mrs. Cora McDonald, an 84 year old woman, living at 609 South Atlanta, Tulsa, Oklahoma. After conversation with Mrs. McDonald, and her brother, Mr. Wimberly, a retired banker, residing in Independence, Missouri, Parnell and his companions agreed to do certain repair work in the attic of the home, for the sum of $25.00, but being unable to secure the necessary materials to make said repairs, they returned the following Monday, the 30th day of April, 1962. At this time Mrs. McDonald was alone; two of them worked in the attic and the third man remained in the dining room during the approximate two hour period of time which it took to complete the repair work in the attic; and using in said repair work, lumber and material of the reasonable value of $12.00. After having completed the work in the attic, Parnell presented a bill in the sum of $600.00. What occurred at this point may best be summarized in the language of the prosecuting witness:

DIRECT EXAMINATION: CORA McDONALD by MR. JACK-MAN.

"* * *

"A. Mr. Parnell came in and sat down and told me what my bill was.

"Q. Okay. Now, who else was there?

"A. Kritser was still sitting there.

"Q. Still sitting in the rocking chair?

"A. In the rocking chair.

"Q. What did Mr. Parnell say to you, Mrs. McDonald?

"A. He said 'Your bill is $600.00.' I said, 'Oh no. It couldn't be $600.00.' I don't—now, I'm not sure that I said, 'You said it would be $25.00'. I don't know that I said that. I said, 'It couldn't be.' 'Yes, it's $600.00.' I said, 'I don't have that much.' 'Well, what do you have?'

"Q. What did he say?

"A. 'What do you have? What can you pay?'

"Q. So what did you do then?

"A. I went and got the $300.00 and handed it to him and he counted it.

"* * *

"Q. Okay, why did you pay them the $300.00, Mrs. McDonald?

"A. Why did I?

"Q. Yes, Ma'am.

"A. I wish you'd tell me that. I was just so frightened that I didn't know what to do. One of them was on one side of me and one on the other and between me and the door. I've read of cases like that and—

"THE COURT: Wait, Wait, don't tell that—

* * *

CROSS EXAMINATION: BY MR. ARDIS:
"* * *

"Q. Okay. Did Mr. Parnell ever say anything to you that was impolite?

"A. No.

"Q. Was he polite to you?

"A. Yes he was.

"Q. Did even the boy that sat in the rocking chair, one of the brothers that sat in the rocking chair, was he polite to you?

"A. Yes.

"Q. And did he make conversation about various things, about things that you had done, etc.

"A. Yes.

"Q. And were they in any way impolite to you at all?

"A. No. The only time there was a rough note sounded at all was Mr. Parnell, when I gave him the $300.00, said 'I'm still stuck for $63.00 for material.' I don't know why he said $63.00, but that's what he said, and a little—just like that. 'I'm still stuck.'

"Q. Well, did he in any way lay a hand on you at that time?

"A. No he didn't.

"Q. Did he in any way say, 'You pay me this money or else'?

"A. No.

"Q. Well what were you afraid of?

"A. He said, 'When—when can you pay the rest of this?' He did say that. 'When can you pay the rest of this?'

"Q. All right. Now, what did you tell him?

"A. I said, 'I don't have any money.' Then I said— * * * 'Well, maybe I can go to this little store over here and cash a check.' Knowing that when he got away I'd call the police, and I did. I called the police.

"Q. But you first paid him some money?

"A. Yes. I paid him $300.00.

"Q. And let me ask you this, why didn't you call the police before you paid him the $300.00?

"A. You tell me. I was frightened.

"Q. From what, Mrs. McDonald?

"A. *Well, I was shocked at such a—at such a thing, asking $600.00 for a job that they had promised to do for $25.00.*

"Q. Okay, now you were shocked?

"A. Yes, and frightened.

"Q. But you were not afraid; is that right?

"A. *Yes, I was afraid. I was afraid of those two men.*

"Q. Now, in what way had they hindered you or bothered you?

"A. *They asked $600.00 for a job that they promised to do for $25.00 and I knew that meant something bad, they were planning something bad, or they wouldn't have done such a thing as that.* (Emphasis ours)

" * * *

"Q. But these two boys that were in the room and this defendant did not in any way lay a hand on you?

"A. No.

"Q. Is that right?

"A. Yes.

"Q. Did they in any way yell at you or threaten you?

"A. No.

"Q. Did they in any way prevent you from going to the outside?

"A. Only by fear. I was afraid.

"Q. Answer the question please, did they prevent you from
going to the outside?

"A. No.

" *　*　*

Title 21 § 791, O.S.A., provided:

"Robbery is a wrongful taking of personal property in the possession of another, from his person or immediate presence, and
against his will, accomplished by means of force or fear."

Title 21 § 792, O.S.A., provides:

"To constitute robbery, the force or fear must be employed either
to obtain or retain possession of the property, or to prevent or
overcome resistance to the taking. If employed merely as a
means of escape, it does not constitute robbery."

Title 21 § 794, O.S.A., provides:

"The fear which constitutes robbery may be either:

"1. The fear of an unlawful injury, immediate or future, to the
person or property of the person robbed or of any relative of
his, or member of his family; or,

"2. The fear of an immediate and unlawful injury to the person
or property of anyone in the company of the person robbed, at
the time of the robbery."

While we believe that Mrs. Cora McDonald was in a state of
shock and fear after the accused, Rex Parnell, made demand upon her
for the sum of $600.00 (a sum grossly in excess of the sum agreed
upon), we do not believe that the mere request of a larger amount
than was actually due defendant, unaccompanied by some act, gesture
deed or word, threatening unlawful injury, either to the person of
Mrs. Cora McDonald or her property, is sufficient to constitute that
degree of coercion or intimidation required under our statutes. For
as was stated in Davis v. Commonwealth, Ky., 54 S.W. 959; Syllabus
#1:

"Where a person parts with money upon a mere demand made
in a rough, positive voice, with an oath, the taking is not robbery; the menace not being such as to excite reasonable apprehension of danger."

In construing statutes similar to our own, the Supreme Court of
Illinois, in Syllabus #2, Steward v. People, 224 Ill. 434, 79 N.E. 636,
stated the rule which we will follow here:

"To constitute the crime of robbery there must be violence or
intimidation of such a character as that the injured party is put

in fear of such a nature as in reason and common experience is likely to induce a person to part with his property against his will, and temporarily suspend the power of exercising his will."

It can thus be seen that some act, word, gesture or deed calculated to produce fear or injury to property or person must be established by competent evidence. And it must further appear that as a result of said act, word, gesture or deed the victim was in such a state of fear that he parted with his property.

For as was stated in United States v. Baker, D.C., 129 F.Supp. 684:

"Intimidation in the law of robbery means putting in fear, and the fear must arise from the conduct of the accused rather than the mere temperamental timidity of the victim. The fear need not be so great as to result in great terror, panic, or hysteria."

Under the facts here presented, in view of the authorities above cited we are of the opinion that the evidence was wholly insufficient to support the verdict of the Jury and accordingly reverse and remand this cause, with instructions to dismiss.

Reversed and remanded.

NOTE

Common law robbery requires a threat of immediate death or great bodily injury to the victim, a member of family or a relative, or someone in the victim's company at the time. Threats to do damage to property will not suffice, with the exception of a threat to destroy the victim's dwelling house.

W. LaFave and A. Scott, Criminal Law 94, p. 700 (1972) state that the "correct" rule is that robbery is committed if the victim is actually frightened by the defendant into parting with his property, even if an ordinary person would not have been so frightened. The fact that another person would not have been frightened is, of course, evidence from which it can be inferred that the victim was not in fact frightened. If this approach had been taken in the instant case, what would have been the outcome of the appeal? If Mrs. McDonald was not frightened, why would she have given up the $300? Is it possible that she believed she was legally obligated to pay $600, and her fear was over her financial situation rather than of harm from the defendant? Is it likely?

F. EXTORTION

Extortion was a misdemeanor at common law consisting of the unlawful collection by an official of an unlawful fee under color of his office. Thus it was an offense against the administration of justice. But in modern codes extortion has often been expanded (sometimes under the label of blackmail) to include obtaining property by means of a threat not sufficient to constitute robbery, including threats to do future (i. e., not immediate) bodily injury, to injure property, to accuse the victim of a crime, or to reveal certain types of information concerning the victim.

STATE v. HARRINGTON

Supreme Court of Vermont, 1969.
260 A.2d 692.

HOLDEN, Chief Justice. The respondent John B. Harrington has been tried and found guilty of the offense of threatening to accuse Armand Morin of Littleton, New Hampshire, of the crime of adultery. The indictment charges that the threat was maliciously made with the intent to extort $175,000 and to compel Morin to do an act against his will in violation of 13 V.S.A. § 1701.[a]

At the outset the respondent acknowledges that there is no serious conflict in the material evidence presented to the jury. The main effort of his appeal challenges the jurisdiction and the sufficiency of the evidence to sustain the conviction.

At the time of the alleged offense the respondent was engaged in the general practice of law in a firm with offices in Burlington, Vermont. Early in March, 1968, he was consulted by Mrs. Norma Morin, the wife of the alleged victim, Armand E. Morin. Mrs. Morin had separated from her husband because of his recent and severe physical abuse. Prior to their separation they owned and operated the Continental 93 Motel in Littleton, New Hampshire, where the Morins maintained a residential apartment. The respondent learned the marital estate of the parties had a net value of approximately $500,000. Mrs. Morin reported to the respondent that her husband had also been guilty of numerous marital infidelities with different women at the motel. Mrs. Morin also disclosed that she had been guilty of marital misconduct which apparently had been condoned.

During the first conference the respondent advised Mrs. Morin that, because of her residence in New Hampshire, she could not undertake divorce proceedings in Vermont for at least six months and for her to obtain a divorce in New Hampshire it would be necessary that she obtain counsel from that state. Mrs. Morin indicated she wished to retain Mr. Harrington to represent her.

On one of the subsequent conferences a friend of Mrs. Morin's, who accompanied her to the respondent's office, suggested that an effort should be made to procure corroborative evidence of Mr. Morin's marital misconduct. To this end, the floor plan of the motel was discussed and a diagram prepared. At this time a scheme was designed to procure the services of a girl who would visit the motel in an effort to obtain corroborative evidence of Morin's infidelity.

a. A person who maliciously threatens to accuse another of a crime or offense, or with an injury to his person or property, with intent to extort money or other pecuniary advantage, or with intent to compel the person so threatened to do an act against his will, shall be imprisoned in the state prison not more than two years or fined not more than $500.00.

After some screening, a Mrs. Mazza, who had been suggested by the respondent, was selected to carry out the assignment. The respondent explained to Mrs. Mazza the purpose of her employment and the results she was expected to accomplish and provided her with a "cover story" to explain her registration and presence as a guest at the Continental 93 Motel. Warning Mrs. Mazza against enticement and entrapment, the respondent instructed the employee to be "receptive and available," but not aggressive. The agreement with Mrs. Mazza was that she would be paid one hundred dollars at the time she undertook the assignment and one hundred dollars when her mission was completed.

Mrs. Morin was without funds at the time. A contingent fee agreement was signed by Mrs. Morin and the firm of Harrington and Jackson, by the respondent. The agreement was dated March 5, 1968 and provided that in the event a satisfactory property settlement was obtained, the respondent's firm was to receive twelve and a half percent of the settlement, in addition to reimbursement for expenses advanced by counsel. Electronic listening and recording equipment was ordered and delivered by air.

On the afternoon of March 6 the respondent and two office associates traveled to St. Johnsbury in two vehicles. Mrs. Mazza continued on to Littleton unaccompanied. She registered on arrival at the Continental 93 Motel under the name of Jeanne Raeder. She called the respondent at St. Johnsbury from a public telephone and informed him of her room number and location. Mrs. Mazza later delivered the key to her room to the respondent to enable him to procure a duplicate. The respondent, representing that he was a book salesman, registered at the motel and procured a room directly above that occupied by Mrs. Mazza. He was accompanied by a junior associate and an investigator,—both employed by the respondent's law firm.

During the next day Mrs. Mazza attracted Mr. Morin's attention. The sequence of events which followed led to an invitation by Morin for her to join him at his apartment for a cocktail. Mrs. Mazza accepted. Later she suggested that they go to her room because Mr. Morin's young son was asleep in his quarters. Morin went to Mrs. Mazza's room about midnight. Soon after the appointed hour the respondent and his associates entered the room. With one or more cameras, several photographs were taken of Morin and Mrs. Mazza in bed and unclothed. Morin grabbed for one camera and broke it.

During the time of her stay at the motel Mrs. Mazza carried an electronic transmitter in her handbag. By means of this device, her conversations with Morin were monitored by the respondent and his associates.

The respondent and his companions checked out of the motel at about one in the morning. Before doing so, there was a brief confrontation with Morin. According to Morin's testimony, the respondent demanded $125,000. Morin testified—"at that time I made him an offer of $25,000 to return everything he had, and in a second breath I retracted the offer."

The following day the respondent conferred with Mrs. Morin and reported the events of the trip to New Hampshire. He asked Mrs. Morin to consider reconciliation over the weekend. On March 11, 1968, Mrs. Morin informed the respondent she decided it was too late for reconciliation. With this decision, the respondent dictated, in the presence of Mrs. Morin, a letter which was received in evidence as State's Exhibit 1. The letter was addressed to Armand Morin at Littleton, New Hampshire, and was placed in the United States mail at Burlington the same day.

The communication is designated personal and confidential. The following excerpts are taken from the full text:

"—Basically, your wife desires a divorce, and if it can be equitably arranged, she would prefer that the divorce be as quiet and as undamaging as possible.

This letter is being written in your wife's presence and has been completely authorized by your wife. The offer of settlement contained herein is made in the process of negotiation and is, of course, made without prejudice to your wife's rights.

It is the writer's thinking that for the children's sake, for your sake, and for Mrs. Morin's sake, that neither the courts in New Hampshire nor in Vermont should become involved in this potentially explosive divorce. If a suitable 'stipulation or separation agreement' can be worked out, the writer would recommend a Mexican, Stipulation-Divorce.   *   *   *

Mrs. Morin is willing to give up the following:

1. All of her marital rights, including her rights to share in your estate.

2. All of her right, title, and interest, jointly or by reason of marital status, that she has in and to, any or all property of the marriage   *   *   *. Furthermore, any such settlement would include the return to you of all tape recordings, all negatives, all photographs and copies of photographs that might in any way, bring discredit upon yourself. Finally, there would be an absolute undertaking on the part of your wife not to divulge any information of any kind or nature which might be embarrassing to you in your business life, your personal life, your financial life, of your life as it might be affected by the Internal Revenue Service, the United States Customs Service, or any other governmental agency.—"

The letter goes on to specify the terms of settlement required by Mrs. Morin, concerning custody of the minor child, her retention of an automobile and the disposition of certain designated personal effects. It further provides:

"5.   Mrs. Morin would waive all alimony upon receipt of One Hundred Seventy Five Thousand Dollars ($175,000)—."

The sum of $25,000 is specified to be paid at the signing of the separation agreement, with the balance due according to a schedule of payments over the period of eighteen months.

The letter continues:

"* * * Unless the writer has heard from you on or before March 22, we will have no alternative but to withdraw the offer and bring immediate divorce proceedings in Grafton County. This will, of course, require the participation by the writer's correspondent attorneys in New Hampshire. If we were to proceed under New Hampshire laws, without any stipulation, it would be necessary to allege, in detail, all of the grounds that Mrs. Morin has in seeking the divorce. The writer is, at present, undecided as to advising Mrs. Morin whether or not to file for 'informer fees' with respect to the Internal Revenue Service and the United States Customs Service. In any event, we would file, alleging adultery, including affidavits, alleging extreme cruelty and beatings, and asking for a court order enjoining you from disposing of any property, including your stock interests, during the pendency of the proceeding.

* * *

With absolutely no other purpose than to prove to you that we have all of the proof necessary to prove adultery beyond a reasonable doubt, we are enclosing a photograph taken by one of my investigators on the early morning of March 8. The purpose of enclosing the photograph as previously stated, is simply to show you that cameras and equipment were in full operating order.—"

It was stipulated that the letter was received by Morin in Littleton, New Hampshire "in the due course of the mail."

Such is the evidence upon which the respondent was found guilty. * * *

Turning to the other grounds advanced in the motion for acquittal, the respondent maintains his letter (State's Exhibit 1) does not constitute a threat to accuse Morin of the crime of adultery. He argues the implicit threats contained in the communication were "not to accuse of the CRIME of adultery but to bring an embarrassing, reputation-ruining divorce proceeding, in Mr. Morin's county of residence unless a stipulation could be negotiated." (Brief of Respondent-Appellant, p. 13.)

In dealing with a parallel contention in State v. Louanis, 79 Vt. 463, 467, 65 A. 532, 533, the Court answered the argument in an opinion by Chief Judge Rowell. "The statute is aimed at blackmailing, and a threat of any public accusation is as much within the reason of the statute as a threat of a formal complaint, and is much easier made, and may be quite as likely to accomplish its purpose. There is nothing in the statute that requires such a restricted meaning of the word 'accuse'; and to restrict it thus, would well nigh destroy the efficacy of the act."

The letter, marked "personal and confidential," makes a private accusation of adultery in support of a demand for a cash settlement. An incriminating photograph was enclosed for the avowed purpose of demonstrating "we have all of the proof necessary to prove adultery beyond a reasonable doubt." According to the writing itself, cost of refusal will be public exposure of incriminating conduct in the courts of New Hampshire where the event took place.

In further support of motion for acquittal, the respondent urges that the totality of the evidence does not exclude the inference that he acted merely as an attorney, attempting to secure a divorce for his client on the most favorable terms possible. This, of course, was the theory of the defense.

*   *   *

At the time of the writing, the respondent was undecided whether to advise his client to seek "informer fees." One of the advantages tendered to Morin for a "quiet" and "undamaging" divorce is an "absolute undertaking" on the part of the respondent's client not to inform against him in any way. The Internal Revenue Service, the United States Customs Service and other governmental agencies are suggested as being interested in such information. Quite clearly, these veiled threats exceeded the limits of the respondent's representation of his client in the divorce action. Although these matters were not specified in the indictment, they have a competent bearing on the question of intent. State v. Louanis, supra, 79 Vt. at 467, 65 A. 532.

Apart from this, the advancement of his client's claim to the marital property, however well founded, does not afford legal cause for the trial court to direct a verdict of acquittal in the background and context of his letter to Morin. A demand for settlement of a civil action, accompanied by a malicious threat to expose the wrongdoer's criminal conduct, if made with intent to extort payment, against his will, constitutes the crime alleged in the indictment.

The evidence at hand establishes beyond dispute the respondent's participation was done with preconceived design. The incriminating evidence which his letter threatens to expose was wilfully contrived and procured by a temptress hired for that purpose. These factors in the proof are sufficient to sustain a finding that the respondent acted maliciously and without just cause, within the meaning of our criminal statutes. State v. Muzzy, 87 Vt. 267, 269, 88 A. 895; Compare, State v. Sylvester, 112 Vt. 202, 206, 22 A.2d 505. The sum of the evidence supports the further inference that the act was done with intent to extort a substantial contingent fee to the respondent's personal advantage.

* * * The evidence of guilt is ample to support the verdict and the trial was free from errors in law.

Judgment affirmed.

NOTES

1. As the instant case demonstrates, modern extortion statutes are generally far broader in their coverage than the common law offense. Many statutes are broader than the Vermont statute applied in the instant case. Thus some cover threats to injure the victim's family or relatives and even threats to disclose disgraceful secrets or defects of the victim or his family or relatives. Others prohibit any threats to publish defamatory materials or to injure the personal character or business reputation of the victim or others.

Most statutes—like the statute in the instant case—require only that a threat of a given nature be made with the specific intent indicated. Others, however, require that the property actually be obtained by means of these threats. The crime defined by these statutes is significantly broader than robbery for several reasons. First, the threat need not be of immediate harm to suffice for extortion, although it must for robbery. Second, the threatened harm that is sufficient for extortion is generally much broader than is necessary for robbery; see above. Third, robbery requires that the property be obtained from the person or presence of the victim; extortion has no such requirement.

A very similar statutory offense is that of blackmail. Under some statutory schemes a distinction between the two offenses is made on the basis that for extortion the accused must be a public official whereas blackmail involves private citizens.

Although extortion and blackmail are distinguishable from the crime of false pretenses inasmuch as there may be neither misrepresentations nor an intent to defraud involved, it has been suggested, see, e. g., Proposed Federal Criminal Code § 1731(1) (1971) (reprinted at page —— supra), that they be included in the consolidated theft offense. Does the employment of threats, particularly those of future violence, invade a distinct social interest to the extent that it is more appropriate to treat this crime as equivalent to robbery?

2. What interest deserving protection is threatened by attempts to obtain money in exchange for a promise not to reveal the truth? Should the result be the same if the accused had not participated in the creation of the compromising situation? Is it extortion if law enforcement officials require a drug offender to "make" a certain number of cases for them in order to avoid prosecution?

VI. SPECIFIC OFFENSES: CRIMES AGAINST THE HABITATION

A. BURGLARY

Burglary was one of two common law felonies designed to protect the interest of the security of the habitation. Arson was the other. Burglary consisted of a breaking and entry of the dwelling of another in the nighttime with the intent to commit a felony in the dwelling. Modern statutes often modify the crime of burglary by removing the requirement of a breaking, expanding the type of buildings protected, and eliminating the requirement that the offense be committed in the nighttime. The intent to commit even misdemeanor theft is often made a sufficient intent for the offense.

HOUCHIN v. STATE

Court of Criminal Appeals of Oklahoma, 1970.
473 P.2d 925.

BUSSEY, Judge. Clifford Rhea Houchin was charged, tried and convicted in the District Court of Oklahoma County with the crime of Burglary in the Second Degree After Former Convictions of Felonies, and from the judgment and sentence fixing his punishment at ten years imprisonment in the state penitentiary, he appeals.

Briefly stated, the evidence discloses that Houchin, hereinafter referred to as defendant, removed a box containing a television set from the trunk of a car belonging to Dorothy Davis. He was observed placing this television set in the trunk of his car and arrested by Officer Kerlick. The evidence further discloses that the trunk of the Davis' car was not closed because of the height of the box containing the television set, and that it had been secured by a nylon cord which was broken when the defendant opened the trunk.

It is first contended by the defendant that the evidence was not sufficient to support the verdict of the jury for the reason that there was no "breaking and entering" as contemplated by the provisions of 21 O.S. § 1435, the same providing:

> "Every person who breaks and enters any building or any part of any building, room, booth, tent, railroad car, automobile, truck, trailer, vessel or other structure or erection in which any property is kept, with intent to steal therein or to commit any felony, is guilty of burglary in the second degree."

372

We are of the opinion that this assignment of error is without merit. In Lumpkin v. State, 25 Okl.Cr. 108, 219 P. 157 (1923), this Court stated, and has continued to follow, the following rule:

> "It is a familiar principle that a breaking, necessary to constitute the crime of burglary, may be by any act of physical force, however slight, by which obstruction to entering is forcibly removed and the opening and closing of a door to enter a building may constitute a breaking　*　*　*"

In the instant case it is apparent that the nylon cord which was broken when the defendant opened the trunk, served the purpose of a lock or latch, the breaking of which to gain entry falls squarely within the purview of 21 O.S. § 1435, supra.[1]

It is next contended that there was no evidence of entry as required by 21 O.S. § 1435 and for that reason his Demurrers and Motions to Dismiss were improperly overruled. We are of the opinion that this assignment of error is also without merit, for it is readily apparent that the box containing the television set was in the trunk of Mrs. Davis' automobile and that in order to remove the box from said trunk and place it in his own vehicle, the defendant, of necessity, had to place his hands inside the trunk.

*　　*　　*

The judgment and sentence appealed from is accordingly affirmed.

NOTES

1. At common law, burglary requires that the thing entered be a "dwelling", i. e., a structure used by someone as a residence. It is not necessary that the resident be present at the time, and his temporary absence does not cause the structure to lose its character as a dwelling. But if no one has yet lived in the structure, it is not a dwelling, even if it was constructed for purposes of residence. And if the resident left with no intent to return, the structure is no longer a dwelling. As the instant case demonstrates, however, modern statutes have often expanded the crime of burglary to include entry into structures other than dwellings and even things other than structures.

The common law required the dwelling to be "of another". Since burglary was an offense against the dwelling, however, this does not require that ownership be in someone other than the defendant. All that is necessary is that the structure be used as a dwelling by another.

Entry constitutes burglary at common law only if it is by means of an opening created by a breaking. Breaking is actual or constructive. Actual breaking requires only some use of force; pushing open a door held shut by

---

I. In Landry v. State, 96 Tex.Cr.R. 417, 258 S.W. 172, which involved a prosecution for burglary, the court found that the requisite "breaking" was present where the defendant, in order to obtain entrance to a garage, unfastened a wire in order that the door might be opened.

friction is sufficient. Constructive breaking occurs if entry is through the chimney or is accomplished by use of fraud, threats, or intimidation.

As the instant case again demonstrates, modern statutes sometimes modify or dispense with this requirement. The entry is required to be "of the house". But it is sufficient if it is of any portion of the house. Thus breaking to gain entry of a locked closet is burglary. But simply breaking into a locked suitcase found in the house is not the offense.

There must be entry for the burglary to be complete, but it is sufficient if any portion of the offender's body is inside the structure, even momentarily. It is also sufficient if a tool or inanimate object is inserted or otherwise placed in the structure, *if* it is placed in it for the purpose of accomplishing the crime that the offender intends. It is not sufficient if the instrument is inserted for purposes of gaining entry.

At common law, the entry is required to be at nighttime, defined as that period during which the countenance of a person cannot be discerned by natural light. Again, this is often modified by statute. Daytime burglary is often covered by modern statutes, although it may be a less serious offense than nighttime burglary. Nighttime is often defined by statute in terms of sunset to sunrise.

For an entry to be burglary at common law, it is necessary that at the time of the entry the defendant intended to commit a felony in the dwelling. It was not sufficient that, after he entered, he decides to commit the felony. The Oklahoma statute applied in the instant case, which provides that entry with the intent to commit a felony or misdemeanor theft is burglary, is typical of a large number of modern burglary statutes.

2. The Proposed Federal Criminal Code (1971) would provide:

§ 1711. Burglary

(1) Offense. A person is guilty of burglary if he willfully enters or surreptitiously remains in a building or occupied structure, or a separately secured or occupied portion thereof, when at the time the premises are not open to the public and the actor is not licensed, invited or otherwise privileged to enter or remain, as the case may be, with intent to commit a crime therein.

(2) Grading. Burglary is a Class B felony if:

(a) the offense is committed at night and is knowingly perpetrated in the dwelling of another; or

(b) in effecting entry or while in the premises or in immediate flight therefrom, the actor inflicts or attempts to inflict bodily injury or physical restraint on another, or menaces another with imminent serious bodily injury, or is armed with a firearm, destructive device or other weapon the possession of which under the circumstances indicates an intent or readiness to inflict serious bodily injury.

Otherwise burglary is a Class C felony.

§ 1719. **Definitions for Sections 1711 to 1719**

In sections 1711 to 1719:

(a) "occupied structure" means a structure or vehicle:

(i) where any person lives or carries on business or other calling; or

(ii) which is used for overnight accommodation of persons.

Any such structure or vehicle is deemed to be "occupied" regardless of whether a person is actually present;

* * *

(e) "night" means the period between 30 minutes past sunset and 30 minutes before sunrise.

Notice that the above proposal abandons common law requirements that there be a "breaking", that it be at night and that it be into a dwelling. How would you explain these changes in the definition of the prohibited conduct? Is the resulting expansion of criminalization desirable? Can there be any justification for retaining burglary as a separate offense? Is there any conduct which we wish to deter which could not be punished in the absence of a burglary provision?

B.   ARSON

Arson was committed at common law by the malicious burning of a dwelling (or some building used in connection with it) belonging to or occupied by another. Modern criminal codes generally retain the offense in this form, although many have expanded it to cover the burning of structures other than residential dwellings.

STATE v. NIELSON

Supreme Court of Utah, 1970, 25 Utah 2d 11, 474 P.2d 725

ELLETT, Justice. The defendant was convicted by a jury of the crime of second-degree arson and of being an habitual criminal. Thereafter he was sentenced to serve concurrent terms in the Utah State Prison of "not less than one year and not more than ten years" for second-degree arson and "not less than fifteen years" for being an habitual criminal. He appeals and assigns various errors which he claims were made at the trial.

* * *

1.   The crime of arson was not made out because no part of the building was burned.

* * *

As to the contention that no part of the building was burned, the proof was ample to support a finding that the defendant set a fire in the Logan jail and that drapes, furniture, and so forth were consumed and that some acoustical ceiling tile was glowing red with heat, although no flames developed.

The law is well established that a charring of fibers of a part of a building is all that is required to constitute a burning sufficient to make the crime of arson. See cases collected in the annotation in 1 A.L.R. at page 1163. It is not necessary that the building be destroyed. Any charring is sufficient.

The legal question is presented as to whether acoustical tile is a part of the building. We cannot see any reason to make a distinction between a wood panel ceiling and an acoustical tile ceiling. Each is an integral part of the building. The assignments relating to the burning of the building are not well taken.

*   *   *

The judgment is   *   *   *   affirmed.

NOTE

Common law arson required that the structure burned be the dwelling af another. This was defined as the same phrase in the law of burglary.

As the instant case indicates, arson does not require the destruction of the structure or even that extensive damage be done to it. Mere "charring"—some damage to the fiber of the material of the structure—is sufficient. But discoloration from heat or smoke—"scorching"—is not enough. Moreover, the damage must have been caused by fire. If a structure is destroyed by an explosion, this is not arson unless the explosion caused a fire which, in turn, burned the structure.

The common law offense requires that the burning be "malicious", but this means only that it must be intentional or not accidental or merely caused by negligence. No ill will or hatred towards the structure or the resident is necessary.

VII. SPECIFIC OFFENSES: CRIMES AGAINST THE PERSON

A. ASSAULT AND BATTERY

The crime of assault, a misdemeanor at common law, has been defined in a wide variety of ways. Some jurisdictions define the offense as an attempt to commit a battery. Under such a definition, the defendant must intend to commit a battery and engage in some activity designed to effectuate that intent. If, as is sometimes the case, the definition also requires the present ability to commit a battery, it is also necessary that there have been no inherent impediment to success. But under this definition, the reaction of the victim is of no legal significance. Probably a majority of jurisdictions include in the definition of assault threatening conduct engaged in with intent to injure or frighten the victim which does create in the victim a reasonable apprehension of immediate physical harm.

A battery is a successful assault, consisting of any application of force to the person of another. Modern American jurisdictions often distinguish between "simple" assaults and batteries and "aggravated" crimes of that nature. The latter consist of assaults and batteries performed under specified circumstances and carry a higher penalty.

PEOPLE v. ABRAMS

Supreme Court of Illinois, 1971.
48 Ill.2d 446, 271 N.E.2d 37.

PER CURIAM. A jury in the circuit court of Cook County found each of the 11 defendants guilty of violating one or more of the statutes or ordinances under which complaints had been filed. The defendant Arnold Abrams was convicted of selling liquor without a license in violation of the Municipal Code of the City of Chicago and was fined $200. The defendant Florence Levinsohn, convicted on two complaints of aggravated assault and on two complaints of battery, received a sentence of two months on each charge. The sentences were ordered to run concurrently. She was also convicted of disorderly conduct and of interfering with a police officer in the performance of his duties, both violations of the Municipal Code, and fined $200 and $100 respectively on these charges. Convictions of disorderly conduct were entered against the other defendants * * *.

On the evening of April 8, 1967, the Chicago Peace Council and the Student Mobilization Committee to End the War in Vietnam sponsored a "send-off" party which was held at the home of Mr.

and Mrs. Arnold Abrams in Chicago. The party's object was to raise funds for the transportation of the groups' representatives to New York City, where a march protesting the war in Vietnam was to be held on April 15. Leaflets announcing the date, place, time, charge for admission, and purpose of the proposed party had been placed at several public locations in the neighborhood. The leaflets bore the request "R.S.V.P." and two telephone numbers were given.

Sergeant Lewis Smith of the Chicago Police Department obtained one of the announcements on April 8 and brought it to the attention of Lieutenant Cassidy at the 21st District Police Station. Early that evening the lieutenant informed Officers Andrew Alinovich and Donald Duffy of the party, gave them the announcement and instructions to go to the Abramses' house in order, according to testimony given by the police at trial, to make an "investigation and surveillance" and to "discover what was going on there." The two officers, who were not in uniform, arrived at the Abramses' house at about 9:15 P.M. They entered the house and purchased two tickets of admission at a table set up just inside the entranceway to the house. The officers did not identify themselves at this time nor were they asked to do so. Upon entering the officers observed two signs taped to a door in the entry hall which read: "Ice 75¢—drinks free," "Cups 30¢—beer free," and "No drinks served to minors under 21 years of age." They remained in the house for about 10 minutes. They said they observed odors of alcohol on the breaths and from drinking cups of a number of young persons who appeared to be underage.

Upon returning to their car Officers Alinovich and Duffy resumed normal patrol activity for about an hour and then returned to the district station at 10:30 P.M. There they met with Lieutenant Cassidy and Sergeant Smith. After a discussion of "probable violations" of law, the lieutenant instructed Alinovich and Duffy to return to the house. The record is not clear concerning the purpose of this second visit to the Abramses' house. It cannot be determined whether the officers were instructed to make arrests or whether they were only to continue their investigation. The two officers left the station, and about one-half hour later by pre-arrangement met three other officers near the Abramses' house. After a brief discussion, the five officers proceeded directly to the house, arriving at approximately 11:50 P.M. No attempt was made at any time to procure a search or an arrest warrant.

As the officers reached the admission table inside the door, they were stopped by either the defendant Florence Levinsohn or by Mrs. Alice Peurala, and were asked if they were police officers. They identified themselves as officers and were then informed that their presence was not desired. Several persons were congregated at the table, including the defendants Mrs. Abrams and Mrs. Levinsohn. The officers were asked if they had a search warrant and were told they could not enter without a warrant. Officer Alinovich testified that he informed Mrs. Levinsohn that a crime had been committed in his presence and that, therefore, no warrant was necessary. According to Alinovich's testimony, the offense he referred to involved a youth seated at the admission table. At his request the youth handed Alinovich a styrofoam cup, which the officer said contained an alcoholic beverage. The evidence is conflicting as to whether the cup was on the table or in the boy's hand when first noticed by Alinovich: When the cup was handed to the officer a minor scuffle developed. Alinovich testified that Mrs. Levinsohn, claiming the cup belonged to her, reached for the cup and in her efforts to take it struck him several times. According to the testimony of the officers, Alinovich handed the cup to officer Hines and then Mrs. Levinsohn struck Hines. Mrs. Abrams and Mrs. Levinsohn testified, however, that when Mrs. Levinsohn reached for the cup, Officer Hines took hold of her. Mrs. Abrams then, they said, pulled Mrs. Levinsohn behind her. Throughout this incident, Mrs. Abrams and others standing near the door were insisting that the officers leave the house until they had obtained a search warrant.

* * *

[The court's very extensive discussion of the fourth amendment issue and of the constitutionality of the ordinances relating to disorderly conduct and interfering with a police officer in the performance of his duties, is omitted.]

A contention of the defendant Florence Levinsohn is that the complaints which charged her with aggravated assault and with battery were fatally defective in that they failed to charge the respective offenses. Section 111-3 of the Code of Criminal Procedure, consistently with the requirement of our constitution that an accused be apprised of the nature and cause of the accusation (Ill.Const. art. II, sec. 9, S.H.A.; see also People v. Heard, Ill., 266 N.E.2d 340), provides in part: "(a) A charge shall be in writing and allege the commission of an offense by: * * * (3) Setting forth the nature and elements of the offense charged." (Ill.Rev.Stat.1969, ch. 38, par. 111-3(a) (3).) Where the nature and elements of the offense with which the accused is intended to be charged are not set forth in the complaint, it fails to state an offense and is subject to dismissal under section 114-1(a) (8) of the Code of Criminal Procedure. (Ill. Rev.Stat.1969, ch. 38, par. 114-1(a) (8).) It is sufficient to allege an offense in the language of a statute if the words so far particularize the offense that by their use alone an accused is informed with reasonable certainty of the precise offense with which he is charged (People v. Mills, 40 Ill.2d 4, 237 N.E.2d 697), or by specifically alleging all the facts which constitute the crime. See People v. Vraniak, 5 Ill.2d 384, 389, 125 N.E.2d 513; People v. Barnes, 314 Ill. 140, 145, 145 N.E. 391.

Two of the complaints charged that Mrs. Levinsohn committed the offense of "aggravated assault" against Officers Andrew Alinovich and Kenneth Hines. They alleged that she, knowing Alinovich and Hines to be police officers engaged in official duties, "did without lawful authority strike the officer(s) about the arms and body," thereby placing them in reasonable apprehension of receiving a battery. The statute defining this offense provides in part: "(a) A person commits an aggravated assault, when, in committing an assault, he: * * * (6) Knows the individual assaulted to be a peace officer * * * while such officer is engaged in the execution of any of his official duties." (Ill.Rev.Stat.1969, ch. 38, par. 12–2(a)(6).) To commit an assault, including an aggravated assault, one without lawful authority must engage "in conduct which places another in reasonable apprehension of receiving a battery." (Ill.Rev.Stat.1969, ch. 38, par. 12–1.) Assault is an offense distinct from battery. If there has been any touching or other form of physical contact with the victim, a battery has been committed and not an assault, assuming the presence of the other requirements for a battery. The Comments to section 12–1 of the Criminal Code (assault) observe: "It should be emphasized that an assault does not involve a touching. If a touching occurs, by any means, it is a battery." (See Committee Comments, S. H.A. ch. 38, § 12–1.) Too, the Comments to the section which defines aggravated assault note: "If there is a touching the offense would not come within this section but should be prosecuted under the attempt, battery, or aggravated battery section." (Committee Comments, S.H.A. ch. 38, § 12–2.) Considering this, it must be concluded that the assault complaints failed to charge the offense of aggravated assault. The conduct alleged that the officers had been struck and therefore assault was not charged. The complaints were fatally defective and the judgments of conviction thereunder must be reversed. See People v. Heard, Ill., 266 N.E.2d 340; People v. Billingsley, 67 Ill.App.2d 292, 297–301, 213 N.E.2d 765.

Considering the complaints which assertedly charge the defendant Levinsohn with battery we note that the statute defining the offense states: "(a) A person commits battery if he intentionally or knowingly without legal justification and by any means, (1) causes bodily harm to an individual or (2) makes physical contact of an insulting or provoking nature with an individual." (Ill.Rev.Stat. 1969, ch. 38, par. 12–3.) The complaints here alleged that the defendant Levinsohn committed the offense of battery against Officers Alinovich and Hines in that she "knowingly and intentionally and without legal justification made physical contact with complainant herein without the consent of said complainant." It is, of course, essential that a complaint allege all the material facts constituting the offense charged. (See People v. Vraniak, 5 Ill.2d 384, 389, 125 N.E.2d 513; People v. Strong, 363 Ill. 602, 605, 2 N.E.2d 942.) The complaints here did not charge either that the physical contact was of an insulting or provoking nature or caused bodily harm, the alternative elements of the offense. Thus, the complaints for battery were also fatally defective and the judgments of conviction thereunder must be reversed.

* * *

For the reasons given, the judgments of conviction against the defendant Florence Levinsohn for aggravated assault and for battery are reversed. The remaining judgments of the circuit court of Cook County are reversed and the causes remanded for a new trial.

Reversed in part, and reversed and remanded in part.

UNDERWOOD, Chief Justice (dissenting in part):

I disagree with the majority's finding that the complaints charging defendant Levinsohn with aggravated assault are fatally defective and do not charge an offense. These complaints alleged that, knowing Alinovich and Hines to be police officers engaged in official duties, defendant "did without lawful authority strike the officer(s) about the arms and body" thereby placing them in reasonable apprehension of receiving a battery. Examination of the relevant statutes as stated in the majority opinion reveals that the statutory language varies from that used in the complaint only in that defendant's conduct, which created the reasonable apprehension, is described. Since this conduct involved touching, however, the majority finds that it no longer constituted assault. Sole reliance for this curious result is placed on the Committee Comments to § 12—1 and § 12—2 of the Criminal Code. (S.H.A., ch. 38, §§ 12—1, 12—2, pp. 697 and 700.) These comments are clearly intended only to emphasize the fact that no touching is required for assault or aggravated assault, while physical contact is required for battery. They cannot reasonably be read, in my opinion, to preclude prosecution for assault where touching is involved. This point becomes even more apparent when one considers the majority's treatment of the complaint charging Levinsohn with battery against the same two police officers. The rejection of this complaint because it did not allege that the physical contact complained of was of an insulting or provoking nature, or that it caused bodily harm, clearly indicates that all intentional physical contact without legal justification does not constitute a battery. No element of the offense of aggravated assault is absent from the complaint in question. The additional allegation of physical contact is, at most, unnecessary surplusage which does not constitute a fatal defect, and ought to be so treated. People v. Adams, 46 Ill.2d 200, 204, 263 N.E.2d 490; People v. Figgers, 23 Ill.2d 516, 179 N.E.2d 626; People v. Crawford, 23 Ill.2d 605, 179 N.E.2d 667.

DAVIS and RYAN, JJ., join in this dissent.

OTT v. STATE

Court of Special Appeals of Maryland, 1971.
11 Md.App. 259, 273 A.2d 630.

ANDERSON, Judge. Appellant, Harry Clifford Ott, was convicted in the Criminal Court of Baltimore by a jury of the crime of common law assault, and was sentenced to a term of one year under the jurisdiction of the Department of Correctional Services.

It is contended in this appeal that:

* * *

2) that the evidence was insufficient to sustain the conviction, and that the State failed to prove the necessary *mens rea* to establish the guilt of the appellant.

From the evidence adduced by the State, on February 18, 1969, Leo Zimmerman, a constable with the Peoples' Court of Baltimore City, accompanied by Edward Connor, a collection agent, went to the home of Harry C. Ott and Maxine Ott, his wife, located at 2057 Druid Park Drive. He had in his possession a writ of *fieri facias* (commonly called a fi-fa) issued by Chief Judge Tippett of the Peoples' Court of Baltimore City for the purpose of collecting a judgment. Zimmerman and Connor arrived at the Ott home at approximately 2:20 p. m. and were admitted by Mrs. Ott. Zimmerman showed her his badge and explained to her that he was there to execute a writ, or it could be settled by payment of the debt to Mr. Connor. Present in the home at the time was David Perry, a son of Mrs. Ott by a former marriage. About ten minutes after their arrival, Mr. Ott arrived on the premises. He became loud and disorderly and, although Zimmerman showed him his badge and the writ, he refused to listen and informed them that no matter who they were they had better get out or he was going to kill them. Zimmerman told Connor to call the police and after Connor left he tried to calm Ott down, but Ott refused to listen and said he would throw them out. Connor returned and told Zimmerman that he had called the police. When Ott heard the police had been summoned, he said: "You better all get out of here or I'm going to make you get out. I'm going to kill you all." He then ran upstairs and returned with a gun in his pocket with the butt protruding out and his hand on the butt. At that time, he said: "I'm going to kill all of you if you don't get out of here." As he said this, his stepson grabbed his hand and after a struggle disarmed him. Zimmerman testified he was frightened as was everyone else in the room. At this time the police arrived and upon being informed what had happened, the officer asked the stepson where the gun was, and Perry gave it to the police officer and appellant was placed under arrest.

The witness, Edward Connor, supported in detail the testimony of the witness Zimmerman. He testified that appellant refused to listen to any explanation about the writ but became very loud and abusive and threatened to kill them. He observed appellant with the gun in his pocket and his hand on the pistol grip and at that time appellant's stepson grabbed his hand and wrestled the gun away from him. When the police wagon arrived, he ran out and called them in real quick.

Baltimore City Police Officer Richard Bernhartz testified that when he arrived appellant was very emotional, nervous and excited and was hollering. After receiving certain information, he requested the gun and Perry, Ott's stepson, got the gun and turned it over to him. When the chamber was opened, the gun contained one bullet.

This concluded the State's case. At this time the State confessed a plea of not guilty to the first count of the indictment (assault with intent to murder) and the court denied the defendant's motion for judgment of acquittal to the second count (common law assault).

Appellant's first witness was his wife, Maxine Ott. She testified that at the time of the alleged assault she was under the care of her doctor for a heart condition. She denied that she was the one who admitted Zimmerman and Connor and was under the impression that they had pushed their way in after her son had opened the door. She stated that Connor had threatened to take all her possessions and had yelled at her causing her to feel faint. She further stated that her husband arrived home at this time and ordered the two men out of the house. She said at this time it looked like Constable Zimmerman was reaching for his gun and at this point her husband ran upstairs and got a gun. She denied hearing her husband make any threats.

Appellant, testifying in his own behalf, stated that when he returned home he found Zimmerman and Connor inside the house and that Connor was standing over his wife yelling at her. He told both men to get out, and when he thought Zimmerman was reaching for his gun he ran upstairs to get his gun, claiming he thought the two men might be hold-up men. On cross-examination he admitted to numerous other convictions of assault and disorderly conduct.

Appellant's final witness was his stepson, David Perry. He testified it was he who admitted Zimmerman and Connor to the house; that Zimmerman said something about being a constable and having a writ in his hand and asked if Mr. Ott was home. When told he was not, he said he had a matter of importance to discuss with him about furniture, and as the door was partly opened, Zimmerman completed opening the door and, together with Connor, walked in. As they entered the house, his mother, Mrs. Ott, came though the doorway from the dining room and the two men began talking with her. During the discussion the talking was louder than usual but he did not understand much about it as they were all talking at once. However, his mother did say that she was sick and had a heart condition.

About 5 or 10 minutes after they arrived, his stepfather, Mr. Ott, arrived. Upon his arrival, the first thing he did was to rush up to where the discussion was taking place and tell them "to get the hell out of the house." He saw the smaller man reach inside his jacket and at that time Mr. Ott turned and ran up the steps. He ran up after him but Ott got back first. He had a gun in his hand when he got to the bottom of the steps and stuck it in his pocket. He managed to take the gun away from him. It had one bullet in it.

On cross-examination he admitted that he knew Zimmerman was a constable and that the conversation between Zimmerman, Connor and his mother was normal conversation up to the time of appellant's arrival, and while it was a little louder than usual, it was not sufficient to upset anyone. He stated that it was only after Mr. Ott arrived that the discussion became very loud. He admitted that Zimmerman and Connor tried to explain to appellant why they were there but Ott refused to listen.

On redirect examination he stated that "the loud talk and all" was Harry Ott's fault.

Appellant then renewed his motion for judgment of acquittal, which was denied.

I

* * *

Assault has been defined as any attempt to apply the least force to the person of another. The attempt is made when there is any action or conduct reasonably tending to create apprehension in another and that the person engaged therein is about to apply such force to him. An apparent intention to inflict a battery and an apparent ability to carry out such intention is sufficient. A specific purpose to inflict a particular injury is not necessary. General malevolence or recklessness is sufficient; but mere negligence does not suffice. Williams v. State, 4 Md.App. 643, 244 A.2d 619; Hochheimer, Crimes and Criminal Procedure, Sec.Ed. §§ 253, 254, 256.

The exhibition of a gun to a victim in such a manner as to cause apprehension that it would be used to inflict harm upon him is an assault. Tender v. State, 2 Md.App. 692, 237 A.2d 65.

From the evidence in this case the jury could find appellant guilty of assault. After threatening to kill Connor and Zimmerman appellant ran upstairs and returned with a revolver which was clearly visible and renewed his threat. His actions and conduct tended to create apprehension in Zimmerman and with a weapon in his possession appellant had an apparent ability to carry out his threats. Zimmerman testified he was frightened and the jury could well so find.

We further point out that it is not necessary that there be a specific purpose to do a particular injury in order to prove the necessary *mens rea*. General malevolence or recklessness is sufficient. Williams v. State, supra. The jury could infer general malevolence from appellant's threats to kill coupled with his obtaining the gun.

We find the evidence sufficient to sustain the conviction.

NOTE

As is indicated by the *Abrams* opinion, assault and battery are separate and distinct offenses. It is generally agreed that the unlawful application of force to the person of another is a battery but assault is more difficult to define. An attempted battery which fails will, in most jurisdictions, be deemed an assault. But what if the accused has pointed the gun at his victim and pulled the trigger but unknown to either the gun is unloaded? In a minority of jurisdictions this is not an assault because the accused did not have "present ability" to commit a battery. Yet it would seem that the accused is a proper subject for the criminal sanction. Is he distinguishable from the accused who has pointed the gun and pulled the trigger knowing it to be unloaded but intending to frighten his victim? Under statutes such as that involved in *Abrams,* and in a majority of American jurisdictions, such conduct is an assault since it "places another in reasonable apprehension of receiving a battery". What should be the result if the victim was not conscious of the accused's attempt to frighten him?

B.   KIDNAPPING AND FALSE IMPRISONMENT

The common law misdemeanor of kidnapping consisted of the forcible abduction of another and the transportation of the victim to another country. Current statutes have greatly modified this offense in several ways. First, the seriousness of the crime has been increased. In many jurisdictions, at least some forms of kidnapping are categorized with the most serious felonies. Second, the extent to which the victim must be affected has been modified. Transportation to another country is not required; movement of any sort is often sufficient. In some jurisdictions, mere detention (if done with the requisite intent) is sufficient. Finally, some forms of kidnapping have been formulated so as to require detention or movement of the victim for certain specific purposes, such as the infliction of bodily harm, the obtaining of money or property, or the commission of some sexual offense.

PEOPLE v. ADAMS

Court of Appeals of Michigan, 1971.
34 Mich.App. 546, 192 N.W.2d 19.

LEVIN, Judge. The defendant, Otis L. Adams, appeals his conviction of kidnapping.

Kidnapping is now a statutory, not a common-law crime. The relevant portion of our statute makes it unlawful to "wilfully, maliciously and without lawful authority * * * forcibly or secretly confine or imprison any other person within this state against his will." But every forcible confinement is not the capital offense of kidnapping.

Our kidnapping statute, like most, is so all-encompassing in its literal breadth that unless its operative effect is confined by objective standards it would be void for overbreadth.

Where a kidnapping statute does not in terms require a "carrying away" of the victim, an asportation requirement or, as a substitute, the element of secrecy, has been judicially read into and made a part of the definition of the crime.

There are two basic kidnapping patterns. In one, the victim is seized and removed to another place; in the other, the victim is confined in the place where he is found. In the first, an asportation or movement of the victim is an essential element; in the second, movement is not an element, but secrecy of the confinement is required.

In this case the people do not charge that the victim was secretly confined. The information charged the defendant Otis Adams with "forcibly confining and imprisoning" his victim—the word "secretly" in the statutory phrase "forcibly or secretly confine" was omitted when the charge was drawn.

To save the Michigan kidnapping statute, insofar as it applies to nonsecret confinements, from a declaration of unconstitutionality because of overbreadth we read it as requiring an asportation. A confinement (other than a secret confinement) without a movement of the victim is not kidnapping. And, for reasons which we will spell out, every movement of the victim of an assaultive crime incidental to the commission of that crime is not kidnapping; the asportation must have a significance independent of the assault in order to manifest the capital and separate offense of kidnapping.

In this case the victim, a prison official, was seized in Jackson State Prison by Adams and other inmates and moved from one part of the prison to another. The seizure and movement occurred in the presence of prison guards; the exact location of both the victim and of the defendant Adams was at all times known to prison guards who had the place cordoned off and surrounded by overwhelming armed force. It is not claimed that Adams ever intended to remove his victim from the prison or that he intended to attempt to effect an escape. This is not the usual hostage pattern, nor is it the usual kidnapping pattern.

I.

Facts

On the morning of October 18, 1965, Adams consumed substantial quantities of alcohol and barbiturates in the company of several other inmates of Jackson Prison. Their conversation turned to the grievances—real or imagined—which they felt against the prison administration.

Shortly after 11:00 a. m., Adams and inmate Edward Whitehead went to the main dining hall of the prison where lunch was being served. Adams cut into the serving line ahead of other inmates and was told by a guard to go to the end of the line. Adams directed some verbal abuse at the guard, then proceeded with Whitehead to the prison's 4-block, a cell block in the northwest portion of the prison. Adams' conduct aroused the attention of two unarmed prison guards who followed him to 4-block.

Because this was the lunch hour, several hundred prisoners were milling about 4-block. The presence of Adams and Whitehead, plus a third inmate, Alvin Shaw, all of whom were highly agitated, as well as the two guards and the hundreds of milling prisoners, led to a disturbance of uncertain proportions.

At this time Inspector Joseph Dembosky, the highest ranking uniformed prison officer, was notified of the disturbance in 4-block. He immediately proceeded to the area and thrust himself into the center of the milling crowd.

Before Inspector Dembosky could take any action, he was seized from behind by inmate Whitehead, who held a knife to his throat. Adams also produced a knife which he used to wave back the prisoners pressing in on Inspector Dembosky and Whitehead. At the trial Inspector Dembosky testified that at this point he said, "Can't we talk about this?" Another witness testified that Dembosky said, "Can't we go somewhere and talk about this?" Adams, Whitehead and Shaw, all of whom had knives, then accompanied Dembosky at knifepoint out of 4-block into the prison yard.

There were approximately one thousand inmates in the yard as Dembosky, Whitehead, Shaw and Adams left 4-block. Inspector Dembosky testified that he felt that there was danger of a riot if the party remained in the yard. He suggested that they go to the prison gymnasium to talk things over. Instead, he was forced to accompany Whitehead, Shaw, and Adams to the prison hospital, which was roughly 1500 feet from the entrance to 4-block. During their journey to the hospital, the armed inmates repeatedly shouted warnings to the heavily-armed tower guards that Inspector Dembosky would be killed if they were fired upon.

Shortly before reaching the hospital building, the group was joined by another inmate, Milton Thomas, who was also armed. Together, immediately after entering the hospital, they seized two guards, a prison doctor, and an inmate elevator operator named Hubbard. Shaw, Whitehead, Thomas, and Adams, together with Inspector Dembosky and the other victims, then proceeded to the doctor's lounge on the fifth floor of the hospital.

Adams and his cohorts erected barricades around the lounge. Over an intercom, they repeatedly demanded to see various prison officials, as well as the warden, to air their grievances. They also demanded to see a newspaper reporter. There were repeated warnings that Inspector Dembosky would be killed if they were fired upon.

During the hours that followed, the armed inmates displayed contradictory behavior toward their captives. The physician was released when Adams ascertained that he had a heart condition. Thomas told the warden to notify the pregnant wife of one of the captive guards that he would not be harmed. Contrastingly, inmate Hubbard was severely beaten by Adams, then released as an example of Adams' serious intentions.

A number of prison officials visited the fifth floor landing to discuss grievances. A newspaper reporter summoned to the scene was occupied for almost three hours in recording these grievances. Adams repeatedly expressed his fear of being shot by guards when he left the fifth floor.

After about 5½ hours, Shaw, Whitehead, Thomas, and Adams were persuaded to abandon their barricaded position. Upon being given assurances that they would not be shot, they released their captives unharmed. They then proceeded to the deputy warden's office, where they surrendered their weapons.

The reprehensible nature of Adams' action does not alter our duty to determine whether the evidence against him is sufficient to support his conviction for kidnapping Inspector Dembosky.

II.

The statute and its overbreadth

* * *

What is immediately obvious about the language of our kidnapping statute is the extraordinary range of conduct it might proscribe.

In the phrase "forcible confinement or imprisonment," the word "imprisonment" is clearly a narrower term than "confinement"; every "imprisonment" would be a "confinement." The word "forcible" adds little, if anything, to the word "confine." "Confine," in the sense in which it is used in this statute, clearly speaks of an involuntary restraint of the liberty of the individual, which, of necessity, is brought about by the use of some force. Similarly, as to the words "against his will." If the confinement was voluntary, it would mean that the victim was confined although he was free to leave—an obvious contradiction of terms.

Since "confine" in this context strongly implies force of some kind, the offense is complete when the actor "wilfully, maliciously and without lawful authority" confines the victim. And, since in the ordinary case there is likely to be no question of lawful authority (and besides, lawful authority negatives "malice"), and since the wilfulness required by law does not enlarge the requirement of malice, *violation of the terms of the statute occurs whenever the actor "maliciously confines" any other person.*

"Malice, in its common acceptation, means ill will toward some person. In its legal sense, it applies to a wrongful act committed intentionally against that person, without legal justification or excuse." Bonkowski v. Arlan's Department Store (1970), 383 Mich. 90, 99, 174 N.W.2d 765, 768.

*   *   *

Accordingly, freed of its tautology, the kidnapping statute, simply put, makes it kidnapping to *intentionally confine another person without legal justification or excuse.*

It will be observed that the statute makes no reference to the duration or circumstances of the confinement. Literally construed, the statute leads to absurd results. The trespasser who momentarily locks a caretaker in his cottage is placed on the same footing as the professional criminal who invades a home, seizes the occupants at gunpoint, transports them to a secret hideout, and holds them for ransom. The robber who orders his victim to stand motionless while his wallet is removed is guilty of the same crime as the robber who forces his victim to drive for miles to a deserted location, where he is terrorized and abandoned. A group of college students who invade a dean's office, wrongfully confining its occupants, commit the same offense as a gang of rapists who seize a woman and remove her from her family to a place of isolation.

Shopkeepers who wrongfully detain suspected shoplifters, cabdrivers who purposely deliver passengers to the wrong destinations, tavernkeepers who bar exits until bar bills have been paid, all may be subject to civil damage actions, but a sensible penology rebels at the classification of such acts as capital offenses.

*   *   *

[The Court's discussion of the problems posed by statute under the void-for-vagueness doctrine (see section II.D.2. supra) is omitted. The Court concluded that a literal reading of the statute would expose perpetrators of virtually every crime against the person to capital sanctions in the discretion of prosecutors, judges and juries. To avoid such results and thereby preserve the statute the court turned to an analysis of its substance.]

III.

Substantive law of kidnapping

At common law, kidnapping required an asportation of the victim out of the country. Kidnapping was a misdemeanor, and was viewed merely as an aggravated form of false imprisonment; the aggravating factor was the removal of the victim from the sovereign's protection.[20]

Kidnapping statutes in the United States have abolished the requirement that a national or a regional boundary be breached.

Modification of the asportation element of the common-law crime was not the only American statutory departure from the common law. Public revulsion against the wave of carefully-planned and often brutal kidnappings for ransom of the 1920's and 1930's resulted in the imposition of heavy penalties,[23] including the death penalty, for kidnappers, and passage of the Federal Kidnapping Act, the so-called Lindbergh Law. It was in 1931 that Michigan imposed a maximum sentence of life imprisonment for kidnapping.

Another characteristic of kidnapping legislation has been its failure to distinguish between the crimes of kidnapping and false imprisonment. Michigan, along with most States, does not have a separate false imprisonment statute.

These matters aside, the principal question that has perplexed American courts in construing kidnapping legislation has been the degree of asportation required to transform an assault, robbery, or other crime into kidnapping. Torn between the common-law rule that a most significant asportation was required, and the obvious legislative intention to broaden the scope of the offense, the courts, virtually without exception, endorsed the idea that any asportation, however slight, was sufficient to constitute kidnapping.

Representative of this formulation were the opinions of the California Supreme Court in People v. Chessman (1951), 38 Cal.2d 166, 192, 238 P.2d 1001, 1017, and People v. Wein (1958), 50 Cal.2d 383, 399, 400, 326 P.2d 457, 466. In *Chessman,* the defendant forced his victim to move 22 feet to his automobile, where he sexually assaulted her. The Court held that, "It is the fact, not the distance, of forcible removal which constitutes kidnapping in this state." In *Wein,* the Court applied the *Chessman* standard to uphold the kidnapping conviction of a defendant who forced his victims to move from room in their

20. For discussions of the common law crime of kidnapping, see Perkins on Criminal Law (2d ed.), p. 176; Note, A Rationale of the Law of Kidnapping, 53 Colum.L.Rev. 540 (1953).

23. See Model Penal Code, Tentative Draft No. 11, comment p. 11, fn. 1: "Kidnapping (or some category of it) is punishable by life imprisonment or death in all States except Alaska (10 years), Connecticut (50 years), Minnesota (40 years), New Hampshire (25 years), and North Dakota (20 years). Where kidnapping is divided into de-

grees, even simple kidnapping is punishable by life imprisonment, in some States, and the maximum in other States is commonly 10–25 years."

* * *

Modern legislation, as an inducement to the felon to release his victim unharmed, reserves the capital offense of kidnapping for cases where the victim is not voluntarily released free of serious physical injury. See, e. g., New York Penal Law, McKinney's Consol.Laws, c. 40, § 135.00 et seq.; Model Penal Code, § 212, et seq.; Study Draft of a New Federal Criminal Code, § 1631.

own homes during a series of robberies and rapes. These holdings came under sharp criticism,[27] but were accurate reflections of the state of the law until quite recently.

The first significant departure from the "any asportation" requirement came in another California case, Cotton v. Superior Court (1961), 56 Cal.2d 459, 464, 15 Cal.Rptr. 65, 68, 364 P.2d 241, 244. A labor dispute led to the invasion of a farm worker's camp by union members. Several braceros were assaulted and dragged about the camp during the ensuing riot. The California Supreme Court ruled that the assailants could not be convicted of kidnapping, saying that "all 'asportation' in the instant case would appear to be only incidental to the assault and rioting." The Court declared that it should avoid "absurd consequences" in application of the kidnapping laws; it warned that a literal reading of the California statute "could result in a rule that every assault could also be prosecuted for kidnapping." The Court ignored, it did not overrule, *Chessman* and *Wein,* but the significance of *Cotton* was not lost on the commentators.

A few years after *Cotton* was decided, the New York Court of Appeals articulated a new approach to the asportation requirement. In People v. Levy (1965), 15 N.Y.2d 159, 164, 256 N.Y.S.2d 793, 796, 204 N.E.2d 842, 844, the defendants accosted the victims, who had just arrived at their home in an automobile. One of the defendants took the wheel, and the victims, husband and wife, were driven about city streets for twenty minutes, covering twenty-seven blocks. During this journey the victims were robbed of money and jewelry.

The defendants were convicted by a jury of kidnapping under the New York statute, which provided that a person who "confines" another with intent to "cause him   *   *   *   to be confined" against his will is guilty of kidnapping. The Court of Appeals reversed. Central to the Court's holding was its concern that the broad statutory definition, "could literally overrun several other crimes, notably robbery and rape, and in some circumstances assault, since detention and sometimes confinement, against the will of the victim, frequently accompany these crimes   *   *   *   It is a common occurrence in robbery, for example, that the victim be confined briefly at gunpoint or bound and detained, or moved into and left in another room or place.

"It is unlikely that these restraints, sometimes accompanied by asportation, which are incidents to other crimes and have long been treated as integral parts of other crimes, were intended by the Legislature in framing its broad definition of kidnapping to constitute a separate crime of kidnapping, even though kidnapping might sometimes be spelled out literally from the statutory words." The Court

27. See Model Penal Code, Tentative Draft No. 11, p. 14, fn. 9 as to *Chessman*. *Wein* was termed the *reductio ad absurdum* case in Packer, The Case for Revision of the Penal Code, 13 Stan.L.Rev. 252, 259, fn. 41 (1961).

overruled a contrary prior decision [31] and held that the kidnapping statute was to be limited in its application "to 'kidnapping' in the conventional sense in which that term has now come to have acquired meaning."

Left unresolved in *Levy* was the precise degree of asportation necessary to constitute "kidnapping in the conventional sense." The opinion did, however, revive the requirement that some meaningful asportation must accompany the crime. In a subsequent case the Court of Appeals declared that "the direction of the criminal law has been to limit the scope of the kidnapping statute, with its very substantially more severe penal consequences, to true kidnapping situations and not to apply it to crimes which are essentially robbery, rape or assault and in which some confinement or asportation occurs as a subsidiary incident." People v. Lombardi (1967), 20 N.Y.2d 266, 270, 282 N.Y.S. 2d 519, 521, 229 N.E.2d 206, 208. But, in a still more recent case, the Court held that "the more complicated nature of the asportation" pursued in the defendant's efforts to kill the victim, removed the case from the *Levy-Lombardi* rule.

The reasoning of the New York Court of Appeals was not accepted by other courts. Several jurisdictions expressly rejected the idea that a substantial asportation was necessary under broadly-worded kidnapping statutes.

In 1969, by a 6-to-1 decision the California Supreme Court overruled its prior constructions in the *Chessman-Wein* line of cases. People v. Daniels (1969), 71 Cal.2d 1119, 1139, 80 Cal.Rptr. 897, 910, 459 P.2d 225, 238, clearly repudiates the doctrine that any asportation of the victim is sufficient to constitute kidnapping. There the victims had been forced to move about in their apartments during the commission of crimes of robbery and rape. The Court declared:

> "We hold that the intent of the Legislature   *   *   *   was to exclude from [the statute's] reach not only 'standstill' robberies   *   *   *   but also those in which the movements of the victim are merely incidental to the commission of the robbery and do not substantially increase the risk of harm over and above that necessarily present in the crime of robbery itself."

A few months ago the California Supreme Court elaborated on its decision in *Daniels*. See People v. Timmons (1971), 4 Cal.3d 411, 93 Cal.Rptr. 736, 482 P.2d 648, where the Court held that the defendant's acts in entering the robbery victims' automobile and directing them to drive it some five city blocks, in order to facilitate the robbery, did not constitute kidnapping since the acts did not "substan-

---

31. People v. Florio, * * * In *Florio* a girl was enticed into an automobile and driven from Manhattan to an iso-   lated spot in Queens where she was raped.

tially" increase "the risk that the victim may suffer significant physical injuries over and above those to which a victim of the underlying
crime [robbery] is normally exposed." Similarly, see People v. Smith
(1971), 4 Cal.3d 426, 93 Cal.Rptr. 743, 482 P.2d 655, where the Court
held that the crime of kidnapping had not been committed where, in
the course of robbing a hotel, the defendant caused the night clerk to
move about the office and up to a second floor room.

Having reviewed the authorities in some detail, we approach decision.

IV.

The asportation requirement and the standard by which it is applied

We hold that, except in those relatively rare cases where the victim is intentionally locked in the place where he is found and
there secretly isolated and confined, a reasonable construction of our
kidnapping statute requires an asportation of the victim before the
crime of kidnapping is complete. Still to be answered is the extent of
the asportation required.

We believe that the history of kidnapping jurisprudence in this
country demonstrates the futility of attempting to calculate the requisite asportation in terms of linear measurement. The harm sought to
be prevented is not movement of the victim, but his removal from one
place to another and attendant increased risks to the victim. The actual distance the victim is transported does not necessarily correspond
with the invasion of his physical interest. An asportation of 50 feet
may in some cases expose the victim to precisely those abuses which
kidnapping statutes are designed to prevent; in other cases, an asportation of 500 feet may alter the victim's situation not at all.

We have concluded that under the kidnapping statute a movement
of the victim does not constitute an asportation unless it has significance independent of the assault. And, unless the victim is removed from the environment where he is found, the consequences of
the movement itself to the victim are not independently significant
from the assault—the movement does not manifest the commission
of a separate crime—and punishment for injury to the victim must be
founded upon crimes other than kidnapping.

A comprehensive scheme for dealing with this offense rests within the province of the legislature, not the courts. The standard we apply today does, however, discriminate with some certainty between conduct which ought clearly to be punished under the kidnapping statute and conduct which falls within the scope of other crimes.[36]

36. While, as Judge Gillis points out, this case does not involve movement of a victim incident to a robbery or rape, it does involve movement inci-dent to a felonious assault which, too, is a separate crime. Indeed, under Michigan law there is little reason to charge kidnapping where the movement is incidental to an armed robbery or a rape because both of those offenses are punishable by life sentences and in Michigan all

V.

The standard applied to the facts of this case

To define "environment" restrictively, *e. g.,* the mere geographic location of the victim, would be to return to the "any movement" concept. The relevant environment is the totality of the surroundings, animate and inanimate.

Applying these criteria to the assault on Inspector Dembosky, we conclude that Adams did not commit the crime of kidnapping. The movement of Inspector Dembosky did not remove him from the prison environment. As his duties customarily took him throughout the entire prison, it cannot be said that moving him from the confused, threatening situation in 4-block to the fifth floor hospital was independently significant from the assault.

The purpose of the movement was neither to avoid detection nor to expose Inspector Dembosky to an increased risk of harm. He was moved to reduce the risk of escalation by providing a cooling-off period. When he was first assaulted the inspector asked, "Can't we talk about this?" And, when the group moved off, he suggested that they go to the prison gymnasium. Instead he was required to accompany the assailants to the fifth floor of the prison hospital. This case is not like a case of street assault where the victim is seized on a thoroughfare and pulled into a dark alley or into an automobile to prevent detection so that the assault can be completed in greater privacy; such a movement might have significance independent of the assault.

The evidence does not support a contention that the movement to the fifth floor of the hospital exposed the inspector to an increased risk of harm because it made his rescue more difficult. Adams and the other men were armed with knives. There is no evidence, no reason to suppose or infer that they were less likely to use their knives if a confrontation with rescuers had occurred at 4-block than at the fifth floor landing of the hospital. Might not the presence at 4-block of hundreds of milling men have made rescue there more difficult? Might not one of the three agitated, perhaps still intoxicated and narcotized, assailants reacted mortally on the spur of the moment to a taunting challenge from an unseen voice in the milling throng? Un-

---

sentences, with few exceptions, run concurrently. It is only where the other offense is punishable by a sentence less than life that there is likely to be an issue whether movement incidental to the commission of that offense constituted the separate crime of kidnapping.

Accordingly, the likelihood is that in Michigan kidnapping will be charged for a street assault most frequently where the assailant failed to consummate his objective, the prosecutorial purpose in charging kidnapping being to aggravate the penalty for the unsuccessful attempt. The degree of asportation that should be required to justify a kidnapping prosecution in such a case is beyond the scope of this opinion.

der the circumstances we are satisfied that the evidence does not support a finding that the movement had significance adverse to Inspector Dembosky independent of the continuing assault.[39]

The inspector was seized in Jackson Prison. It is an atypical place, an armed enclosure that no one can enter or leave without passing through guarded entranceways. Movement from one building to another in Jackson Prison, for purposes of the kidnapping statute, is not significantly different than movement from one room to another in a building, especially where, as here, the movement was under surveillance of armed guards who had the enclosure protected and there was no intention on the part of Adams or the other felons themselves to leave or to remove Inspector Dembosky from the prison.

The movement of Inspector Dembosky did not make the apprehension of the felons less likely, nor did the movement make it less likely that the inspector would be released unharmed. It provided a cooling-off period—which Inspector Dembosky himself wisely sought. It provided time for these impetuous, desperate men to reflect and to draw back from worse folly.

Adams' conduct was highly dangerous and indefensible. The prison and prosecutorial authorities are understandably anxious to see that he is severely punished. Prison guards and officials like Inspector Dembosky mingle with frustrated, assaultive desperate men. An assault upon any of them is a serious breach of discipline; punishment should be clear, certain and severe.

Michigan, unlike other jurisdictions, does not have a specific statute making assault by a prisoner on a prison guard or official a crime carrying special penalties. In Michigan, assault upon a prison guard is treated no differently than assault outside of prison walls. The maximum penalties are relatively mild for the kind of aggravated conduct indulged in by Adams and his confederates. That is a good reason for the legislature to amend the penal code to provide adequate sanctions for an assault by a prisoner. It is not a reason for transforming, without legislative authorization, what under present law may

---

39. It is important in this case to make clear what we do not decide as well as what we hold so that our opinion is not misread.

The taking of a hostage may be the offense of kidnapping. In the hostage situation, if the victim is removed from the environment where he is found, the removal will generally have significance adverse to the victim independent of the assault and the offense of kidnapping will be completed upon his removal from the environment. Even if the victim is not so removed, if the actor intends to remove him from the environment where he is found and commits an overt act going beyond mere preparation, that would be attempted kidnapping. If the victim is seized with intent "to extort money or other valuable thing" or to hold the victim "to service against his will" that too may be kidnapping even though there has been no asportation * * *

Nor do we express any opinion as to when a seizure of a person on the street incidental to the commission or attempted commission of another offense (e. g., rape, robbery) becomes the separate offense of kidnapping. * * *

be nothing more than a felonious assault, into an offense which carries with it a possible life sentence.

Criminal statutes, in contrast with the common law, may not be expanded to meet new problems beyond the contemplation of the legislature when the statute was enacted.[42]

Reversed.

J. H. GILLIS, Presiding Judge (dissenting).

Unlike my Colleagues, I am satisfied that there was sufficient evidence from which the jury could lawfully find defendant Adams guilty of kidnaping. Accordingly, I would affirm defendant's conviction.

In my view, the majority misapply the teachings of such cases as People v. Levy, People v. Lombardi and People v. Daniels. And, as a result, the majority reach what I consider to be an absurd result. This case is not one in which the restraint and forcible movement of Inspector Dembosky can be characterized solely as "incident[s] to other crimes and * * * integral parts of other crimes." People v. Levy, 15 N.Y.2d at 164–165, 256 N.Y.S.2d at 796, 204 N.E.2d at 844. This case does not involve movement of the victim incident to robbery (People v. Levy, *supra*; People v. Daniels, *supra*); nor does it involve asportation incident to rape (People v. Lombardi, *supra*; People v. Daniels, *supra*).

42. In the construction of criminal statutes a court is not at liberty to evolve the law much the same as if the court were developing the common law. It is the prerogative of the legislature, not the courts, to define a new crime. "There is no crime whatever punishable by our laws except by virtue of a statutory provision." In the Matter of Lamphere (1886), 61 Mich. 105, 108, 27 N.W. 882, 883.

"The spirit of the doctrine which denies to the federal judiciary power to create crimes forthrightly admonishes that we should not enlarge the reach of enacted crimes by constituting them from anything less than the incriminating components contemplated by the words used in the statute. And where Congress borrows terms of art in which are accumulated the legal tradition and meaning of centuries of practice, it presumably knows and adopts the cluster of ideas that were attached to each borrowed word in the body of learning from which it was taken and the meaning its use will convey to the judicial mind unless otherwise instructed. In such case, absence of contrary direction may be taken as satisfaction with widely accepted definitions, not as a departure from them." Morissette v. United States (1951), 342 U.S. 246, 263, 72 S.Ct. 240, 249, 96 L.Ed. 288, 300.

* * *

An asportation is the gist of the offense of kidnapping. If we sustain a conviction for kidnapping on evidence that the victim of the confinement has been held a "substantial" period of time and exposed to "serious" risk of harm even though there was not an asportation having significance independent of the assault, then most every assaultive crime can be the capital offense of kidnapping if the prosecutor so charges and a jury so finds.

We acknowledge that we have, indeed, by our construction of Michigan's kidnapping statute defined the crime. But we have done so in the context that the Michigan Supreme Court has not defined the crime and, unless defined, the statute would be void for overbreadth. It is the traditional role of the judiciary to pass on the constitutionality of a statute and to construe it, if possible, to preserve its constitutionality.

In People v. Miles (1969), 23 N.Y.2d 527, 539, 540, 297 N.Y.S.2d 913, 922, 245 N.E.2d 688, 694, 695, the New York Court of Appeals explained the *Levy-Lombardi* rationale as follows:

> "In the *Levy* and *Lombardi* cases, and especially in the *Levy* case, the restraint and asportation were parts of the crimes ultimately committed. The robbery and the rapes could not be committed in the forms planned without the limited asportations there involved. Indeed, in any robbery, there is a restraint of 'false imprisonment' and in every rape there is a similar restraint and often removal in some limited sense. It is this kind of factual merger with the ultimate crime of the preliminary, preparatory, or concurrent action that the rule is designed to recognize, and thus prevent unnatural elevation of the 'true' crime to be charged.

*   *   *   *   *   *   *   *   *   *

> "Moreover, *the rule has no purpose of ignoring as independent crimes alternative or optional means used in committing another crime which, by the gravity and even horrendousness of the means used, constitute and should constitute a separately cognizable offense.*

*   *   *   *   *   *   *   *   *   *

> "In short, the *Levy-Lombardi* rule was designed to prevent gross distortion of lesser crimes into a much more serious crime by excess of prosecutorial zeal. *It was not designed to merge 'true' kidnappings into other crimes merely because the kidnappings were used to accomplish ultimate crimes of lesser or equal or greater gravity.*" (Emphasis supplied.)

Nothing in this record suggests to me an excess of prosecutorial zeal. Accordingly, the *Levy-Lombardi* rule is inapposite. In my view, Adams' conduct could lawfully be considered "true" kidnaping.

In People v. Congdon (1889), 77 Mich. 351, 354, 43 N.W. 986, the Michigan Supreme Court noted that the gist of the offense under the kidnaping statute is the involuntariness of the seizure. Similarly, the United States Supreme Court has stated that "the involuntariness of seizure and detention   *   *   *   is the very essence of the crime of kidnaping." Chatwin v. United States (1946), 326 U.S. 455, 464, 66 S.Ct. 233, 237, 90 L.Ed. 198, 203. On the facts as recited in the majority opinion, it clearly appears that the jury could find that Inspector Dembosky had been involuntarily seized.

Moreover, "the gravity and even horrendousness", People v. Miles, 23 N.Y.2d at 539, 297 N.Y.S.2d at 922, 245 N.E.2d at 694, of Adams' conduct serves to distinguish this case from mere false imprisonment. Inspector Dembosky was confined against his will for a substantial period of time. He was exposed to serious risk of harm. Thus, Inspector Dembosky was subjected to the very abuses the kidnaping statute is intended to prevent. It follows that we should not, as a matter of law, refuse to characterize defendant Adams' conduct as kidnaping. At least, on this record, the jury should be permitted to so find.

I have discovered but two cases which factually resemble this case of *Adams*. In each, a prison guard was forcibly seized and held against his will within the prison by inmates. Jury convictions of kidnaping were affirmed in both cases on the law and the facts. The evidence was held sufficient to justify the verdicts. See State v. Randall (1960), 137 Mont. 534, 353 P.2d 1054, and State v. Frodsham (1961), 139 Mont. 222, 362 P.2d 413. See, also, People v. Shaw (1968), 11 Mich.App. 255, 160 N.W.2d 761. Such should be the result in this case.

Defendant's other contentions are without merit. His conviction should be affirmed.

C. RAPE

Rape consists, as it did at common law, of an act of intercourse with a woman not the wife of the perpetrator against her will and accomplished by actual or constructive force. At common law, a girl under the age of ten was legally incapable of consenting to intercourse, so any such act with her constituted rape. Modern statutes defining the crime of "statutory" rape generally set a significantly higher age at which a girl may give legally effective consent to intercourse. At common law rape was a felony, and it is also under contemporary statutes.

STATE v. HORNE

Supreme Court of Utah, 1961, 12 Utah 2d 162, 364 P.2d 109

CALLISTER, Justice. Defendant was convicted of the forcible rape of a female over the age of 18 years, sentenced to prison for 10 years to life, and he appeals.

The rape was alleged to have occurred sometime during the early morning hours of June 15, 1960. The prosecutrix was a married woman, 21 years of age, and was living, at the time, with her two young children in a trailer house located in a trailer court in Clearfield, Utah. Her husband was in the armed services and stationed overseas.

The defendant, an unmarried man of 23, lived in the home of his parents which was located about 100 yards from the trailer court. He and the prosecutrix were acquainted, and he had been a visitor to her trailer house on previous occasions. He admits having had intercourse with the prosecutrix, but denies the act was accomplished by force or violence, but on the contrary was with her consent.

In State v. Mills,[2] this court stated:

" * * * If the State's evidence is so 'inherently improbable,' as to be unworthy of belief, so that upon objective analysis it appears that reasonable minds could not believe beyond a reasonable doubt that the defendant was guilty, the jury's verdict cannot stand. Conversely, if the State's evidence is such that reasonable minds could believe beyond a reasonable doubt that the defendant was guilty, the verdict must be sustained."

With the foregoing principle in mind, we examine the State's evidence in the instant case, which is substantially as follows:

The prosecutrix testified that on the night of June 14, 1960, she retired to her bed in the trailer at about 10:30 p. m., leaving both doors and all of the windows open and unlocked. She had placed her two-year-old daughter in bed with her and her three-year-old son in an adjacent bedroom. Some time after midnight she was awakened when the defendant rang her doorbell. He identified himself and, without invitation, entered the trailer. As to what then transpired, the prosecutrix testified:

"A. He opened the refrigerator and looked in the refrigerator and asked me if I had any coke in the house, and I said no, I didn't have any. He asked me why, and I said I didn't keep any in the house. And he was still in the kitchen at this time.

"Q. And where were you? A. I was still in the bedroom.

"Q. Then what happened after he went to the refrigerator? A. He closed the refrigerator, and then he turned on the light in the kitchen.

"Q. Did you have any further conversation with him? A. Yes, I thought he was looking for Bonnie, because he had come to my house the night before looking for her.

"Q. Did you make any statement to him with regard to Bonnie? A. I told him Bonnie wasn't there. That she was at home.

"Q. Did he say anything in response to that? A. He said he wasn't looking for Bonnie. That he was looking for me.

"Q. All right. What happened then, Mrs. ———? A. Then he walked back into the bedroom.

"Q. Did he make a statement at that time? A. Well, I told him to go away. To go home. That I didn't want anything to do with him. And he said that he wasn't going to go away, and go home.

2.   122 Utah 306, 249 P.2d 211, 212.

"Q. After he had stated that he wasn't going to go home, what happened, if anything, after that? A. He took off his pants.

"Q. Did he make any statement at that time? A. I asked him what he was doing, and he said he was going to make love to me.

"Q. Then what did he do? A. Then he climbed on the bed.

"Q. Where were your children at this time? A. My little girl was at the head of the bed, on the right of me. My little boy was asleep in the other bedroom.

"Q. Will you relate the events then, after he came to the bed, Mrs. ———? As you best remember them? A. He kept trying to put his hands on me, and kept trying to put his mouth on me. And I kept pushing him away, and struggling with him. My little girl woke up and she started to cry, and she kept saying she wanted a drink of water, and finally I told Larry: 'Please, I have to go to the bathroom.' I thought if I got to the bathroom that he'd think I had locked the door and he'd leave, but there wasn't a lock on the bathroom door.

"I was in the bathroom about 10 or 15 minutes, and he kept telling me to come out, and I told him I wasn't going to, and then he opened the bathroom door. He found out it wasn't locked, and he came to the bathroom door and opened it, and he pulled me out of the bathroom and back into the bedroom.

"Q. What happened after you were taken back to the bedroom? A. Well, we struggled for quite awhile more, and Larry kept throwing me on the bed, and I would manage to get away from him, and then he would pull me back, and I couldn't get away from him.

"Q. Was anything happening to your clothing during this time, Mrs. ———? A. Oh, he pulled my slip down, down to my waist, and he tried to take my pants off, and I had ahold of my pants with my one hand, and he pulled them off of me. I couldn't hold them up.

"Q. And after he had your pants off, what happened then? A. Then he threw me back on the bed. And I was so tired and my little girl kept crying for a drink of water, and at one time my head hit her in the stomach, and I said. 'Stop it. You're hurting my little girl,' and he said: 'I'm not hurting you. If you'd quit fighting me,' he said: 'then none of this would happen.'

"Q. Did you continue to struggle? A. Yes, I did. I begged him to let me go, and he wouldn't. He wouldn't leave me alone.

"Q. What happened after that, Mrs. _____? A. Well, after this he got me on the bed, and I don't know exactly how he got me pinned down. I couldn't move, but anyway I kept trying to push him off, and I pulled his hair and I hit him, and it didn't do any good. He acted like he didn't feel anything. And then he had intercourse with me.

"Q. Will you tell us how that was done? A. What do you mean by that?

"Q. Tell us how he accomplished the act of intercourse with you. A. Well, he had my legs pinned down some way. I can't remember just how. It's pretty much of a blur, the memory of it, but I couldn't move. And finally he let me go, and I went into the living room."

Prosecutrix, on direct examination, further testified that after defendant left she went back to bed, but did not sleep. She arose about 6 a. m., and at approximately 6:30 a. m., visited a friend, Thelma, who occupied a nearby trailer. She told Thelma that the defendant had raped her. Later, about 3:00 p. m., she visited a doctor and advised him of the alleged rape. Still later at 7 p. m., she informed the police.

Thelma was called as a witness and corroborated the early morning conversation related by the prosecutrix. The doctor whom she visited in the afternoon did not testify. The officer who answered the summons of the prosecutrix was called as a witness and, after verifying the receipt of the complaint, identified a bed sheet, pair of green panties, and a folder of matches which had been given to him by the prosecutrix.

Upon cross-examination, the prosecutrix testified that the defendant arrived at her trailer around 1 a. m. and did not leave until about 4 a. m. That at no time did she turn on a light, although light switches were easily within her reach. She stated that approximately one-half an hour elapsed, during which period the defendant made advances minus his pants, between the time the defendant arrived and the time she went to the bathroom. In order to get from the bed to the bathroom she had to pass the open rear door. She did not attempt to leave by this door because, "I wasn't going to leave my two children in the house with him there." However, she stated that the defendant had not in any way molested the children.

Further, on cross-examination, the prosecutrix admitted going out with other men and having entertained one man in her trailer for several hours. Other than the alleged rape by the defendant, she denied having had intercourse with anyone other than her husband.

Defendant, on the witness stand, admitted that at the outset the prosecutrix resisted his advances and asked him not to commit the act. She told him she was afraid of becoming pregnant. However, he testified that the prosecutrix, after returning from the bathroom, voluntarily engaged in the act of intercourse.

The old rule of "resistance to the utmost" is obsolete. The law does not require that the woman shall do more than her age, strength, the surrounding facts, and all attending circumstances make it reasonable for her to do in order to manifest her opposition. However, in determining the sufficiency of the evidence, there must be considered the ease of assertion of the forcible accomplishment of the sexual act, with impossibility of defense except by direct denial, or of the proneness of the woman, when she finds the fact of her disgrace discovered or likely of discovery to minimize her fault by asserting force or violence, which had led courts to hold to a very strict rule of proof in such cases.

Did the prosecutrix in this case do what was reasonable in light of her age and strength, the facts and attending circumstances to manifest her oppositon? We think not.

It is of highest significance that the prosecutrix, during the three-hour period defendant was in her bedroom, made no outcry. This despite the fact that all doors and windows were open and there were occupied trailers within 20 to 30 feet from hers. Her three-year-old son, sleeping in the adjacent bedroom was not disturbed.

The prosecutrix did not attempt to leave the trailer to seek help, although she had ample opportunity. When she went to the bathroom the defendant, according to her testimony, had already removed his pants and had made indecent proposals and advances. Yet, she did not avail herself of the opportunity to seek help. It is the natural impulse of every honest and virtuous female to flee from threatened outrage. Her explanation that she did not want to leave the children alone with the defendant is a rather weak one, to say the least. It would have taken less than a minute to rouse her neighbors. Furthermore, she left the defendant with the children for 10 to 15 minutes while she was in the bathroom.

There was no evidence of marks or bruises upon either party. This, after an alleged struggle which lasted three hours! There was no evidence of any threats made to either the prosecutrix or her children.

The green panties introduced into evidence had a torn elastic band, but otherwise were intact. The materiality of the bed sheet introduced into evidence is not shown in the record. The defendant admitted the act of intercourse.

True, in corroboration of her story, the prosecutrix made complaint to her friend, Thelma, at 6:30 a. m., more than two and one-half hours after alleged rape. However, had she truly been outraged, it would seem more likely that complaint would have been made immediately after the defendant left.   It was not until 7 o'clock in the evening that she notified the police.

* * *

We have carefully evaluated the testimony of the prosecutrix and conclude that it is so inherently improbable as to be unworthy of belief and that, upon objective analysis, it appears that reasonable minds could not believe beyond a reasonable doubt that the defendant was guilty.   The jury's verdict cannot stand.

Reversed.

NOTE

Rape consists of unlawful sexual intercourse with a female person without her consent.   Traditionally, intercourse between a husband and wife has been regarded as "lawful", and it has been held that a husband cannot commit rape by having forced intercourse with his wife.   Of course, under the law of parties a husband may be guilty of the rape of his wife by virtue of having aided and abetted someone else in having forcible intercourse with her.

Intercourse requires only the penetration of the vagina by the penis. Emission is not necessary.

It is commonly held that the victim of a sexual attack need not resist at all if such resistance is prevented by the attacker's threats of death or serious bodily injury.   Would this rule have any application to the instant case?   Is there any basis in the evidence for concluding that the prosecutrix did not flee or resist more vigorously because she feared that the defendant would retaliate with force likely to cause her serious bodily injury?

If the woman is unconscious, as from fainting or intoxication, intercourse with her constitutes rape.   Submission induced by fraud, however, will cause intercourse to be rape only if the fraud is such as to cause the woman to believe that the act is other than sexual intercourse or that the male with whom she has intercourse is her husband.   Thus it is rape for a male to have intercourse with a woman after representing to her that she will be penetrated only by an inanimate instrument as part of a medical treatment.   But representing that intercourse is psychologically therapeutic and thereby gaining the woman's consent does not amount to rape because the woman is not deceived as to the nature of the activity.

A woman's consent is not legally valid—and intercourse pursuant to it constitutes rape if she has been incapacitated by mental illness, mental deficiency, or age from giving consent.

The ease of false accusations of rape and the difficulty of defending against such accusations has led to the development in a minority of jurisdictions of a requirement that the prosecutrix's testimony be corroborated by other evidence.   The result has been to reduce dramatically the number of convictions.   This is because rape is commonly committed out of view of other persons, often in surroundings, such as an alley, which will not show signs of a struggle, and accompanied by threats which lead the woman not to resist for reasonable fear of her physical safety thus precluding such corroboration as bruises and torn clothing.   In response there is growing pressure to eliminate or minimize such requirements.   See, e. g., Note, "The Rape Corroboration Requirement: Repeal Not Reform", 81 Yale L.J. 1365 (1972).

PEOPLE v. HERNANDEZ

Supreme Court of California, 1964.
61 Cal.2d 529, 39 Cal.Rptr. 361, 393 P.2d 673.

PEEK, Justice. By information defendant was charged with statutory rape. (Pen.Code, § 261, subd. 1.) Following his plea of not guilty he was convicted as charged by the court sitting without a jury and the offense determined to be a misdemeanor.

Section 261 of the Penal Code provides in part as follows: "Rape is an act of sexual intercourse, accomplished with a female not the wife of the perpetrator, under either of the following circumstances: 1. Where the female is under the age of 18 years; * * *."

The sole contention raised on appeal is that the trial court erred in refusing to permit defendant to present evidence going to his guilt for the purpose of showing that he had in good faith a reasonable belief that the prosecutrix was 18 years or more of age.

The undisputed facts show that the defendant and the prosecuting witness were not married and had been companions for several months prior to January 3, 1961—the date of the commission of the alleged offense. Upon that date the prosecutrix was 17 years and 9 months of age and voluntarily engaged in an act of sexual intercourse with defendant.

In support of his contention defendant relies upon Penal Code, § 20, which provides that "there must exist a union, or joint operation of act and intent, or criminal negligence" to constitute the commission of a crime. He further relies upon section 26 of that code which provides that one is not capable of committing a crime who commits an act under an ignorance or mistake of fact which disapproves any criminal intent.

Thus the sole issue relates to the question of intent and knowledge entertained by the defendant at the time of the commission of the crime charged.

Consent of the female is often an unrealistic and unfortunate standard for branding sexual intercourse a crime as serious as forcible rape. Yet the consent standard has been deemed to be required by important policy goals. We are dealing here, of course, with statutory rape where, in one sense, the lack of consent of the female is not an element of the offense. In a broader sense, however, the lack of consent is deemed to remain an element but the law makes a conclusive presumption of the lack thereof because she is presumed too innocent and naive to understand the implications and nature of her act. The law's concern with her capacity or lack thereof to so understand is explained in part by a popular conception of the social, moral and personal values which are preserved by the abstinence from sexual indulgence on the part of a young woman. An unwise disposition of her sexual favor is deemed to do harm both to herself and the social mores by which the community's conduct patterns are established. Hence the law of statutory rape intervenes in an effort to avoid such a disposition. This goal, moreover, is not accomplished by penalizing the naive female but by imposing criminal sanctions against the male, who is conclusively presumed to be responsible for the occurrence.

The assumption that age alone will bring an understanding of the sexual act to a young woman is of doubtful validity. Both learning from the cultural group to which she is a member and her actual sexual experiences will determine her level of comprehension. The sexually experienced 15-year old may be far more acutely aware of the implications of sexual intercourse than her sheltered cousin who is beyond the age of consent. A girl who belongs to a group whose members indulge in sexual intercourse at an early age is likely to rapidly acquire an insight into the rewards and penalties of sexual indulgence. Nevertheless, even in circumstances where a girl's actual comprehension contradicts the law's presumption, the male is deemed criminally responsible for the act, although himself young and naive and responding to advances which may have been made to him.[1]

The law as presently constituted does not concern itself with the relative culpability of the male and female participants in the prohibited sexual act. Even where the young woman is knowledgeable it does not impose sanctions upon her. The knowledgeable young man, on the other hand, is penalized and there are none who would claim that under any construction of the law this should be otherwise. However, the issue raised by the rejected offer of proof in the instant case goes to the culpability of the young man who acts *without* knowledge that an essential factual element exists and has, on the other hand, a positive, reasonable belief that it does not exist.

The primordial concept of *mens rea*, the guilty mind, expresses the principle that it is not conduct alone but conduct accompanied by certain specific mental states which concerns, or should concern the law. In a broad sense the concept may be said to relate to such im-

---

1. The inequitable consequences to which we may be led are graphically illustrated by the following excerpt from State v. Snow (Mo.1923) 252 S.W. 629 at page 632:

"We have in this case a condition and not a theory. This wretched girl was young in years but old in sin and shame. A number of callow youths, of otherwise blameless lives * * * fell under her seductive influence. They flocked about her, * * * like moths about the flame of a lighted candle and probably with the same result. The girl was a common prostitute * * *. The boys were immature and doubtless more sinned against than sinning. They did not defile the girl. She was a mere 'cistern for foul toads to knot and gender in.' Why should the boys, misled by her, be sacrificed? What sound public policy can be subserved by branding them as felons? Might it not be wise to ingraft an exception in the statute?"

portant doctrines as justification, excuse, mistake, necessity and mental capacity, but in the final analysis it means simply that there must be a "joint operation of act and intent," as expressed in section 20 of the Penal Code, to constitute the commission of a criminal offense. The statutory law, however, furnishes no assistance to the courts beyond that, and the casebooks are filled to overflowing with the courts' struggles to determine just what state of mind should be considered relevant in particular contexts. In numerous instances culpability has been completely eliminated as a necessary element of criminal conduct in spite of the admonition of section 20 to the contrary. * * * More recently, however, this court has moved away from the imposition of criminal sanctions in the absence of culpability where the governing statute, by implication or otherwise, expresses no legislative intent or policy to be served by imposing strict liability. * * *

Statutory rape has long furnished a fertile battleground upon which to argue that the lack of knowledgeable conduct is a proper defense. The law in this state now rests, as it did in 1896, with this court's decision in People v. Ratz, 115 Cal. 132, at pages 134 and 135, 46 P. 915, at page 916, where it is stated: "The claim here made is not a new one. It has frequently been pressed upon the attention of courts, but in no case, so far as our examination goes, has it met with favor. The object and purpose of the law are too plain to need comment, the crime too infamous to bear discussion. The protection of society, of the family, and of the infant, demand that one who has carnal intercourse under such circumstances shall do so in peril of the fact, and he will not be heard against the evidence to urge his belief that the victim of his outrage had passed the period which would make his act a crime." The age of consent at the time of the Ratz decision was 14 years, and it is noteworthy that the purpose of the rule, as there announced, was to afford protection to young females therein described as "infants." * * *

The rationale of the Ratz decision, rather than purporting to eliminate intent as an element of the crime, holds that the wrongdoer must assume the risk; that, subjectively, when the act is committed, he consciously intends to proceed regardless of the age of the female and the consequences of his act, and that the circumstances involving the female, whether she be a day or a decade less than the statutory age, are irrelevant. There can be no dispute that a criminal intent exists when the perpetrator proceeds with utter disregard of, or in the lack of grounds for, a belief that the female has reached the age of consent. But if he participates in a mutual act of sexual intercourse, believing his partner to be beyond the age of consent, with reasonable grounds for such belief, where is his criminal intent? In such circumstances he has not consciously taken any risk. Instead he has subjectively eliminated the risk by satisfying himself on reasonable evidence that the crime cannot be committed. If it occurs that he has been misled, we cannot realistically conclude that for such reason alone the intent with which he undertook the act suddenly becomes more heinous.

While the specific contentions herein made have been dealt with and rejected both within and without this state, the courts have uniformly failed to satisfactorily explain the nature of the criminal intent present in the mind of one who in good faith believes he has obtained a lawful consent before engaging in the prohibited act. As in the Ratz case the courts often justify convictions on policy reasons which, in effect, eliminate the element of intent. The Legislature, of course, by making intent an element of the crime, has established the prevailing policy from which it alone can properly advise us to depart.

We have recently given recognition to the legislative declarations in sections 20 and 26 of the Penal Code, and departed from prior decisional law which had failed to accord full effect to those sections as applied to charges of bigamy. (People v. Vogel, supra, 46 Cal.2d 798, 299 P.2d 850.) We held there that a good faith belief that a former wife had obtained a divorce was a valid defense to a charge of bigamy arising out of a second marriage when the first marriage had not in fact been terminated. Pertinent to the instant contention that defendant's intent did not suddenly become more criminal because it later developed that he had been misled by the prosecutrix, are the following comments appearing in Vogel at page 804 of 46 Cal.2d, at page 854 of 299 P.2d: "Nor would it be reasonable to hold that a person is guilty of bigamy who remarries in good faith in reliance on a judgment of divorce or annulment that is subsequently found not to be the 'judgment of a competent Court' * * *. Since it is often difficult for laymen to know when a judgment is not that of a competent court, we cannot reasonably expect them always to have such knowledge and make them criminals if their bona fide belief proves to be erroneous." Certainly it cannot be a greater wrong to entertain a bona fide but erroneous belief that a valid consent to an act of sexual intercourse has been obtained.

Equally applicable to the instant case are the following remarks, also appearing at page 804 of 46 Cal.2d, at page 855 of 299 P.2d of the Vogel decision: "The severe penalty imposed for bigamy, the serious loss of reputation conviction entails, * * * and the fact that it has been regarded for centuries as a crime involving moral turpitude, make it extremely unlikely that the Legislature meant to include the morally innocent to make sure the guilty did not escape."

We are persuaded that the reluctance to accord to a charge of statutory rape the defense of a lack of criminal intent has no greater justification than in the case of other statutory crimes, where the

Legislature has made identical provision with respect to intent. " 'At common law an honest and reasonable belief in the existence of circumstances, which, if true, would make the act for which the person is indicted an innocent act, has always been held to be a good defense. * * * So far as I am aware it has never been suggested that these exceptions do not equally apply to the case of statutory offenses unless they are excluded expressly or by necessary implication.' " (Matter of Application of Ahart, 172 Cal. 762, 764–765, 159 P. 160, 161–162, quoting from Regina v. Tolson, [1889] 23 Q.B.D. 168, s. c., 40 Alb.L.J. 250.) Our departure from the views expressed in Ratz is in no manner indicative of a withdrawal from the sound policy that it is in the public interest to protect the sexually naive female from exploitation. No responsible person would hesitate to condemn as untenable a claimed good faith belief in the age of consent of an "infant" female whose obviously tender years preclude the existence of reasonable grounds for that belief. However, the prosecutrix in the instant case was but three months short of 18 years of age and there is nothing in the record to indicate that the purposes of the law as stated in Ratz can be better served by foreclosing the defense of a lack of intent. This is not to say that the granting of consent by even a sexually sophisticated girl known to be less than the statutory age is a defense. We hold only that in the absence of a legislative direction otherwise, a charge of statutory rape is defensible wherein a criminal intent is lacking.

For the foregoing reasons People v. Ratz, supra, 115 Cal. 132, 46 P. 915, and People v. Griffin, supra, 117 Cal. 583, 49 P. 711 are overruled, and People v. Sheffield, 9 Cal.App. 130, 98 P. 67 is disapproved to the extent that such decisions are inconsistent with the views expressed herein.

Some question has been raised that the offer of proof of defendant's reasonable belief in the age of the prosecutrix was insufficient to justify the pleading of such belief as a defense to the act. It is not our purpose here to make a determination that the defendant entertained a reasonable belief. Suffice to state that the offer demonstrated a sufficient basis upon which, when fully developed, the trier of fact might have found in defendant's favor. We conclude that it was reversible error to reject the offer.

The judgment is reversed.

NOTES

1. Other courts considering the same issue as is raised in the instant case have rejected the California Supreme Court's conclusion. E. g., State v. Superior Court, 104 Ariz. 440, 454 P.2d 982 (1969); Eggleston v. State, 4 Md.App. 124, 241 A.2d 433 (1968); People v. Doyle, 16 Mich. App. 242, 167 N.W.2d 907 (1969) ("Current social and moral values make more realistic the California view that a reasonable and honest mistake of

age is a valid defense to a charge of statutory rape * * * but this court is bound to follow the law presently in effect.") ; State v. Moore, 105 N.J. Super. 567, 253 A.2d 579 (1969) ; State v. Fulks, 83 S.D. 433, 160 N.W. 2d 418 (1968). See generally, Annot., 8 A.L.R.3rd 1100 (1966). The cases seldom discuss any constitutional issues which might be raised by interpreting statutory rape statutes as to provide for no defense based upon mistake of age. Why might this be? But see Commonwealth v. Moore, 269 N.E.2d 636 (Mass.1971), in which the defendant was charged with "carnally knowing and abusing" a minor. The victim testified she had an identification card showing her age as eighteen and that she told the defendant she was that age. In addition, the victim had been convicted of prostitution and placed on probation; apparently the police officers, the lawyer representing her, the trial court judge, and the probation officer assumed she was eighteen. Nevertheless, the court held that no affirmative defense of mistake of age was available and that this "strict" liability did not deny the defendant due process of law.

2. Despite the California Supreme Court's decision in People v. Vogel, 46 Cal.2d 798, 299 P.2d 850 (1956) bigamy has often been regarded as imposing strict liability in regard to that element requiring proof of the existence of a prior spouse. See Moore, Bigamy, A Crime Though Unwittingly Committed, 30 U.Cin.L.Rev. 35 (1961) ; Annot., 56 A.L.R.2d 905 (1957). The Supreme Court seems to have approved, or at least not disapproved. See Williams v. North Carolina, 325 U.S. 226, 238, 65 S.Ct. 1092, 1099, 89 L.Ed. 1577 (1945). Is this appropriate? Explain. Would it be significant if the statute specifically provided, as many do, for a defense consisting of proof that the prior spouse had been absent for a specified number of years during which time the defendant had no knowledge that the spouse was alive?

3. Consider the treatment of the issues raised in the instant case by the following sections of the Proposed Federal Criminal Code (1970):

§ 1641. Rape

(1) Offense. A male who has sexual intercourse with a female not his wife is guilty of rape if:

(a) he compels her to submit by force, or by threat of imminent death, serious bodily injury, or kidnapping, to be inflicted on any human being;

(b) he has substantially impaired her power to appraise or control her conduct by administering or employing without her knowledge intoxicants or other means with intent to prevent resistance; or

(c) the victim is less than ten years old.

(2) Grading. Rape is a Class A felony if in the course of the offense the actor inflicts serious bodily injury upon the victim, or if his conduct violates subsection (1) (c), or if the victim is not a voluntary companion of the actor and has not previously permitted him sexual liberties. Otherwise rape is a Class B felony.

§ 1645.   Corruption of Minors

(1) Offense.   A male who has sexual intercourse with a female not his wife or any person who engages in deviate sexual intercourse with another or causes another to engage in deviate sexual intercourse is guilty of an offense if the other person is less than sixteen years old and the actor is at least five years older than the other person.

(2) Grading.   The offense is a Class C felony, except when the actor is less than twenty-one years old, in which case it is a Class A misdemeanor.

§ 1648.   General Provisions for Sections 1641 to 1647

(1) Mistake as to Age.   In sections 1641 to 1647: (a) when the criminality of conduct depends on a child's being below the age of ten, it is no defense that the actor did not know the child's age, or reasonably believed the child to be older than ten; (b) when criminality depends on the child's being below a critical age older than ten, it is an affirmative defense that the actor reasonably believed the child to be of the critical age or above.

*   *   *

(3) Prompt Complaint.   No prosecution may be instituted or maintained under sections 1641 to 1647 unless the alleged offense was brought to the notice of public authority within three months of its occurrence or, where the alleged victim was less than sixteen years old or otherwise incompetent to make complaint, within three months after a parent, guardian or other competent person specifically interested in the victim, other than the alleged offender, learned of the offense.

*   *   *

[(5) Testimony of Complainants.   No person shall be convicted of any felony under sections 1641 to 1645 upon the uncorroborated testimony of the alleged victim.   Corroboration may be circumstantial.   In a prosecution before a jury for an offense under sections 1641 to 1647, the jury shall be instructed to evaluate the testimony of a victim or complaining witness with special care in view of the emotional involvement of the witness and the difficulty of determining the truth with respect to alleged sexual activities carried out in private.]

The earlier Study Draft had contained the following additional provision:

(3) Sexually Promiscuous Complainants.   It is an affirmative defense to prosecution under sections 1645 * * * that the alleged victim had, prior to the time of the offense charged, engaged promiscuously in sexual relations with others.

This was deleted from the final draft, according to the comment, because it attempted "to reduce an issue of credibility to a fixed rule."

NOTE ON MORALS OFFENSES

There is a wide variety of offenses with roots in early English law that have in common only the fact that all are defined as crimes because the conduct prohibited has been viewed as infringing the broad interest of the state in maintaining the general public health, safety, and morality.

Prominent among these are prohibitions of certain consensual sexual conduct. Fornication—usually defined as intercourse between a man and woman not lawfully married—was not a common law offense, although the common law did prohibit any open and notorious lewdness and indecency, including open and notorious cohabitation. Most American jurisdictions criminalize fornication and even more have prohibitions on adultery which is usually defined as illicit sexual relations in which at least one of the persons is married to someone other than the sexual partner. However, such laws are rarely enforced and modern codes tend to omit such provisions. In contrast, laws against incest—sexual relations between individuals related within the degrees of consanguinity or affinity within which marriage is prohibited—are enforced but almost exclusively in cases in which the "victim" is a minor daughter. In such situations, of course, the laws against statutory rape would normally also be available as a basis for prosecution.

Two other sex related offenses should be mentioned: prostitution and sodomy. Prostitution which is prohibited in all American jurisdictions, usually is defined as engaging in, or offering to engage in, sexual conduct for hire. In United States v. Moses, 12 Crim.L.Rptr. 2198 (D.C.Super.Ct. 1972), the court struck down a statute prohibiting solicitation for purposes of prostitution because it found that the state had an insufficient interest to support a blanket prohibition against prostitution and solicitation for prostitution. Central to the Court's concern was the developing right of the individual to control the use and function of his or her own body which as the "right of privacy" led to the virtual elimination of all state prohibitions on abortion in Roe v. Wade, U.S., 93 S.Ct. 705, 35 L.Ed.2d 147 (1973).

Roe v. Wade may prove to be of great importance with respect to state laws against sodomy which commonly prohibit some or all of the following forms of sexual conduct: oral-genital relations; anal intercourse; and bestiality. Commonly such laws do not exempt such sexual contact between husband and wife although prosecutions in such circumstances are very rare. For a critique of such laws and an explication of their vulnerability to constitutional challenge see Barnett, *Sexual Freedom and the Constitution* (N.M. Press 1973).

D. HOMICIDE

WOLFGANG, A SOCIOLOGICAL ANALYSIS OF CRIMINAL HOMICIDE

Federal Probation, Vol. 25, No. 4 (March, 1961) pages 48, 49, 53.

[R]esearch was conducted in Philadelphia, using all criminal homicides recorded by the Philadelphia Homicide Squad from January 1, 1948 through December 31, 1952. Excusable and justifiable homicides were excluded from the study and concentration was only on criminal cases listed by the police.   *   *   *

During the period from 1948 through 1952 there were 588 cases of criminal homicide in Philadelphia; i.e., there were 588 victims. Because several people were sometimes involved in killing one person, there were 621 offenders arrested by the police and taken into custody. In terms of a mean annual rate per 100,000 population in the city, the victim rate was 5.7 and the offender rate 6.0. This is neither high nor low. Compared with 18 other cities across the country, each of which had a population of a quarter of a million or more in 1950, Philadelphia ranks ninth, with the range between Miami having a victim rate of 15.1 and Milwaukee having a low of 2.3.   *   *   *

Some Basic Findings: Race, Sex, and Age

Research has shown that although criminal homicide is largely an unplanned act, there are nonetheless in the act regular uniformities and patterns. We have found, as previous research has noted, that there is a statistically significant association between criminal homicide and the race and sex of both victim and offender. Negroes and males involved in homicide far exceed their proportions in the general population and rates for these two groups are many times greater than for whites and females. The rate per 100,000 by race and sex of offenders reveals the following rank order of magnitude: Negro males (41.7), Negro females (9.3), white males (3.4), and white females (.4). Although Negroes of either sex, and males of either race, are positively related to criminal slayings, the association between race and homicide is statistically more significant than that between sex and homicide.   *   *   *

Among offenders, the age group 20–24 predominates with a rate of 12.6 per 100,000, while the highest rate for victims is in the age group 25–34. In short, victims are generally older than their offenders; the median age of the former being 35.1 years and of the latter 31.9 years. The importance of the race factor here is striking in view of the fact that the *lowest* 5-year age-specific rates for Negro males and females are similar to, or higher than the *highest* of such rates for white males and females, respectively. Although males of both races more frequently commit criminal homicide during their twenties than during any other period of life, Negro males in their early sixties kill as frequently as do white males in their early twenties.

*   *   *

Place Where Crimes Occur

The place where the crime occurred is also important. The most dangerous single place is the highway (public street, alley, or field), although more slayings occur in the home than outside the home. Men kill and are killed most frequently in the street, while women kill most often in the kitchen but are killed in the bedroom. For victims and offenders of each race and sex group significant differences have been noted. Most cases of Negro males who kill Negro males involve a stabbing in a public street; most cases of white males who kill white males involve a beating in a public street. * * *

Presence of Alcohol

Either or both the victim and offender had been drinking immediately prior to the slaying in nearly two-thirds of the cases. The presence of alcohol in the homicide situation appears to be significantly associated with Negroes—either as victims or as offenders—and, separately, with Negro male and female victims. Particular caution must be exercised in evaluating the presence of alcohol in these homicides, since drinking—particularly on Saturday night, the time of highest incidence of homicide—is an integral part of the mores of most groups involved in this crime. A significantly higher proportion of weekend homicides than of homicides occurring during the remainder of the week had alcohol present (in either the victim, the offender, or both). An association between alcohol, weekend slayings, and the payment of wages on Friday was indicated and crudely confirmed by the available data. We have, therefore, suggested that when the socioeconomic group most likely to commit homicide almost simultaneously receives its weekly wages, purchases alcohol, and meets together socially, it is not unlikely that the incidence of homicide should also rise.

Previous Police Record and Victim-Offender Relationships

Contrary to many past impressions, an analysis of offenders in criminal homicide reveals a relatively high proportion who have a previous police or arrest record. Of total offenders, nearly two-thirds have a previous arrest record, and of total victims, almost half have such a record. Having a previous record is also associated with males both among victims and offenders, and is obvious from the fact that more *male victims* have such a record than do *female offenders*. Moreover, when an offender has a previous record, he is more likely to have a record of offenses against the person than against property; and when he has a record of offenses against the person, he is more likely than not to have a record of having committed a serious assault offense, such as aggravated assault or assault with intent to kill. A greater proportion of Negro male and female victims have a previous arrest record than do white male and female offenders, respectively.
* * *

Criminal homicide usually results from a vaguely defined altercation, domestic quarrel, jealousy, argument over money, and robbery. These five police-recorded "motives" are involved in 8 out of 10 cases. Most of the identified victim-offender relationships may be classified as "primary group" relations, or those that include in-

timate, close, frequent contacts.   Close friends and relatives accounted for over half of the contacts, and the combined categories which involve primary group contacts constitute 59 percent of all victim-
offender relationships among males, but significantly as much as 84
percent among females.   Because white males were killed more frequently than Negro males during the commission of a robbery, the
former were also more frequently strangers to their slayers than the
latter.

Mate slayings have been given special attention.   Of the 100
husband-wife homicides, 53 victims were wives and 47 were husbands.
The number of wives killed by their husbands constitutes 41 percent
of all women killed, whereas husbands slain by their wives make up
only 11 percent of all men killed.   Thus, when a woman commits
homicide, she is more likely than a man to kill her mate; and when
a man is killed by a woman, he is most likely to be killed by his wife.
Husbands are often killed by their wives in the kitchen with a butcher
knife, but nearly half of the wives are slain in the bedroom.   More
male than female offenders in these spouse slayings were found guilty,
were convicted of more serious degrees of homicide, and committed
suicide.

In 94 percent of the cases, the victim and offender were members of the same race, but in only 64 percent they were of the same
sex.   Thus, the ratio of intra- to interracial homicide is 15.2 to 1;
but the ratio of intra- to intersex homicide is only 1.8 to 1.   In general, it may be said that victims were homicidally assaulted most
frequently by males of their own race, and least frequently by females
of another race.

In 32 cases involving 57 offenders and 6 victims, a felony, in
addition to the killing, was perpetrated at the time of the slaying.
In most cases the other felony was robbery, and white males accounted for a larger proportion of these felony-murders than they did
among all homicides in general.

Victim-Precipitated Homicide

The term *victim-precipitated* homicide has been introduced to
refer to those cases in which the victim is a direct, positive precipitator
in the crime—the first to use physical force in the homicide drama.
After establishing a theoretical and legal basis for analysis, the Philadelphia data reveal several factors significantly associated with the
150 victim-precipitated homicides, which is 26 percent of all homicides.   These factors are: Negro victims and offenders, male victims,
female offenders, stabbings, victim-offender relationships involving
male victims and female offenders, mate slayings, husbands who were
victims in mate slayings, alcohol, victims with a previous arrest record,
particularly an arrest record of assault.   Thus, in most of these cases,
the role and characteristics of the victim and offender are reversed,

the victim assumes the role of determinant, and the victim makes a definite contribution to the genesis of his own victimization.

Recently, I have extended the meaning of victim precipitated homicide to include a sociological and psychoanalytic discussion of these 150 victims as being bent on suicide. Although it is impossible to verify an assumption of subconscious suicide wishes among these victims, empirical data from broad social factors combine with psychological and sociological data suggesting that victims in many cases present themselves as willing targets for violent aggression leading to homicide.

*   *   *

Court Dispositions

Finally, analysis has been made of the tempo of legal procedures, of court disposition, designation of the degree of homicide, insanity, and sentences imposed by the court. Two-thirds of the offenders were arrested on the same day that the crime was committed, and over half appeared in court for trial within 6 months after the crime. Two-thirds of those taken into police custody, and over three-quarters of those who experienced a court trial were declared guilty. Proportionately, Negroes and males were convicted more frequently than whites and females; but previous analysis of the nature of these cases reveals that Negroes and males had in fact committed more serious offenses   *   *   *[.]

Of the 387 offenders convicted and sentenced, 30 percent were guilty of murder in the first degree, 29 percent of murder in the second degree, 36 percent of voluntary manslaughter, and 15 percent of involuntary manslaughter. Less than 3 percent of the offenders were declared insane by the courts   *   *   *[.]

NOTE

Of what, if any, value is this type of information in formulating or working with the substantive law of homicide? Should an effort be made to differentiate for legal purposes any of the categories of offenders described by Wolfgang? To what extent do the categories created by the statutes in the next section do this? Is the Wolfgang material helpful in determining the extent to which reliance should be placed upon severity of penalty—or upon criminal penalties at all—in preventing killings?

---

1. STATUTORY FORMULATIONS

PENN. STAT. ANN. TITLE 18 (1963)

§ 4701. Murder of the first and second degree

All murder which shall be perpetrated by means of poison, or by lying in wait, or by any other kind of willful, deliberate and premeditated killing, or which shall be committed in the perpetration of, or attempting to perpetrate any arson, rape, robbery, burglary, or kidnapping, shall be murder in the first degree. All other kinds of murder shall be murder in the second degree.   *   *   *

Whoever is convicted of the crime of murder of the first degree is guilty of a felony and shall be sentenced to suffer death in the manner provided by law, or to undergo imprisonment for life, at the discretion of the jury trying the case, which shall, in the manner hereinafter provided, fix the penalty.   *   *   *

Whoever is convicted of the crime of murder of the second degree is guilty of a felony, and shall, for the first offense, be sentenced to undergo imprisonment by separate or solitary confinement not exceeding twenty (20) years, or fined not exceeding ten thousand dollars, or both, and for the second offense, shall undergo imprisonment for the period of his natural life.

§ 4703. Voluntary and involuntary manslaughter

Whoever is convicted of voluntary manslaughter is guilty of a felony, and shall be sentenced to pay a fine not exceeding six thousand dollars ($6,000), and to undergo imprisonment, by separate or solitary confinement at labor or simple imprisonment, not exceeding twelve (12) years, and in the discretion of the court, to give security for good behavior during life, or for any less time, according to the nature and enormity of the offense.

Whoever is convicted of involuntary manslaughter, happening in consequence of an unlawful act, or the doing of a lawful act in an unlawful way, is guilty of a misdemeanor, and shall be sentenced to pay a fine not exceeding two thousand dollars ($2,000), or to undergo imprisonment not exceeding three (3) years, or both.

CALIFORNIA PENAL CODE (1970)

§ 187. Murder defined

MURDER DEFINED. Murder is the unlawful killing of a human being, with malice aforethought.

§ 188. Malice, express malice, and implied malice defined

MALICE DEFINED. Such malice may be express or implied. It is express when there is manifested a deliberate intention unlawfully to take away the life of a fellow creature. It is implied, when no considerable provocation appears, or when the circumstances attending the killing show an abandoned and malignant heart.

§ 189. Murder; degrees

All murder which is perpetrated by means of a bomb, poison, lying in wait, torture, or by any other kind of willful, deliberate, and premeditated killing, or which is committed in the perpetration of, or attempt to perpetrate, arson, rape, robbery, burglary, mayhem, or any act punishable under Section 288 [prohibiting "any lewd or lascivious act * * * upon or with the body, or any part or member thereof, of a child under the age of fourteen years, with the intent of arousing, appealing to, or gratifying the lust or passions or sexual desires of such person or of such child * * *"], is murder of the first degree; and all other kinds of murders are of the second degree.

As used in this section, "bomb" includes any device, substance, or preparation, other than fixed ammunition or fireworks regulated under * * * the Health and Safety Code, which is designed to cause an explosion and is capable of causing death or serious bodily injury.

§ 190.   Murder; punishment; discretion of jury

Every person guilty of murder in the first degree shall suffer death, or confinement in the state prison for life, at the discretion of the court or jury trying the same, and the matter of punishment shall be determined [in a separate proceeding before the court or a jury], and every person guilty of murder in the second degree is punishable by imprisonment in the state prison from five years to life.

§ 192.   Manslaughter; voluntary, involuntary, and in driving a vehicle defined; construction of section

Manslaughter is the unlawful killing of a human being, without malice. It is of three kinds:

1.   Voluntary—upon a sudden quarrel or heat of passion.

2.   Involuntary—in the commission of an unlawful act, not amounting to felony; or in the commission of a lawful act which might produce death, in an unlawful manner, or without due caution and circumspection; provided that this subdivision shall not apply to acts committed in the driving of a vehicle.

3.   In the driving of a vehicle—

(a) In the commission of an unlawful act, not amounting to felony, with gross negligence; or in the commission of a lawful act which might produce death, in an unlawful manner, and with gross negligence.

(b) In the commission of an unlawful act, not amounting to felony, without gross negligence; or in the commission of a lawful act which might produce death, in an unlawful manner, but without gross negligence.

This section shall not be construed as making any homicide in the driving of a vehicle punishable which is not a proximate result of the commission of an unlawful act, not amounting to felony, or of the commission of a lawful act which might produce death, in an unlawful manner.

§ 193. Manslaughter; punishment

Manslaughter is punishable by imprisonment in the state prison for not exceeding 15 years, except that a violation of subsection 3 of Section 192 of this code is punishable as follows: In the case of a violation of subdivision (a) of said subsection 3 the punishment shall be either by imprisonment in the county jail for not more than one year or in the state prison for not more than five years, and in such case the jury may recommend by their verdict that the punishment shall be by imprisonment in the county jail; in the case of a violation of subdivision (b) of said subsection 3, the punishment shall be by imprisonment in the county jail for not more than one year. In cases where, as authorized in this section, the jury recommends by their verdict that the punishment shall be by imprisonment in the county jail, the court shall not have authority to sentence the defendant to imprisonment in the state prison, but may nevertheless place the defendant on probation as provided in this code.

PROPOSED FEDERAL CRIMINAL CODE (1971)

Homicide

§ 1601. Murder

A person is guilty of murder, a Class A felony, if he:

(a) intentionally or knowingly causes the death of another human being;

(b) causes the death of another human being under circumstances manifesting extreme indifference to the value of human life; or

(c) acting either alone or with one or more other persons, commits or attempts to commit treason, offenses defined in sections 1102 [Participating in or Facilitating War Against the United States Within Its Territory] or 1103 [Armed Insurrection] espionage, sabotage, robbery, burglary, kidnapping, felonious restraint, arson, rape, aggravated involuntary sodomy, or escape and, in the course of and in furtherance of such crime or of immediate flight therefrom, he, or another participant, if there be any, causes the death of a person other than one of the participants; except that in any prosecution under this paragraph in which the defendant was not the only participant in the underlying crime, it is an affirmative defense that the defendant:

(i) did not commit the homicidal act or in any way solicit, command, induce, procure, counsel or aid the commission thereof; and

(ii) was not armed with a firearm, destructive device,
dangerous weapon or other weapon which under the circumstances indicated a readiness to inflict serious bodily injury; and

(iii) reasonably believed that no other participant was
armed with such a weapon; and

(iv) reasonably believed that no other participant intended to engage in conduct likely to result in death or serious bodily injury.

Paragraphs (a) and (b) shall be inapplicable in the circumstances
covered by paragraph (b) of section 1602.

§ 1602.   Manslaughter

A person is guilty of a Class B felony if he:

(a) recklessly causes the death of another human being; or

(b) causes the death of another human being under circumstances which would be murder, except that he causes the death under the influence of extreme emotional disturbance for which there
is reasonable excuse.   The reasonableness of the excuse shall be determined from the viewpoint of a person in his situation under the
circumstances as he believes them to be.   An emotional disturbance is
excusable, within the meaning of this paragraph, if it is occasioned
by any provocation, event or situation for which the offender was not
culpably responsible.

§ 1603.   Negligent Homicide

A person is guilty of a Class C felony if with criminal negligence
he causes the death of another human being.

NOTES

1.   As an alternative to what became § 1601(c) in the Proposed Federal Criminal Code, the Study Draft proposed the following expansion of what
became § 1601(b) :

(b) causes the death of another human being under circumstances manifesting extreme indifference to the value of human
life.   Such indifference is presumed if the actor is engaged in the
commission of, or an attempt to commit, or flight after committing
or attempting to commit, a Class A or B felony or a felony involving force or danger to human life.   An accomplice of such actor in
the commission of or attempt to commit such felony is deemed an
accomplice in the conduct causing the death.   A participant in such
felony is deemed to have caused a death resulting from resistance

to the commission of the felony or from prevention or an attempt to prevent flight of a participant, whether or not the killing is committed by a participant.

2. The California statute and the Proposed Federal Criminal Code define murder as the killing of a "human being." In Keeler v. Superior Court, 2 Cal.3d 619, 87 Cal.Rptr. 481, 470 P.2d 617 (1970), the California Supreme Court held, over dissent, that "human being" did not include an unborn but viable fetus. In the case before it, there was little doubt that the defendant had assaulted a woman with the intention of aborting the fetus. Is this appropriate? Why, or why not?

The California statute was subsequently amended to cover the killing of a fetus, unless this was done by an abortion performed pursuant to the state's abortion act.

3. For general treatments of the law of homicide, see R. Moreland, Law of Homicide (1952); Danforth, The Model Penal Code and Degrees of Homicide, 11 Am.U.L.Rev. 147 (1962); Parker, The Evolution of Criminal Responsibility, 9 Alberta L.Rev. 47 (1970); Perkins, The Law of Homicide, 36 J.Crim.L. & C. 391 (1946); Wechsler and Michael, A Rationale of the Law of Homicide, 37 Colum.L.Rev. 701, 1261 (1937). For a discussion emphasizing Canadian law, see Hooper, Some Anomalies and Developments in the Law of Homicide, 3 U.B.C.L.Rev. 55 (1967). English law is covered in Royal Commission on Capital Punishment 1949–1953, Report 25–72 (1953).

---

2. THE STATE OF MIND REQUIRED FOR MURDER: MALICE AFORETHOUGHT

PEOPLE v. MORRIN

Michigan Court of Appeals, 1971.
31 Mich.App. 301, 187 N.W.2d 434.

LEVIN, Judge. Leslie Taylor Morrin was convicted of first-degree murder by a jury in Monroe County Circuit Court. At the trial he testified that he killed the victim in self-defense. His evidence, coupled with the jury's unquestioned right to reject the claim of self-defense, provided sufficient evidence to sustain a verdict finding that he committed the crime of second-degree murder by killing another human being with malice aforethought.

*   *   *

I.

Morrin killed William Abell, a 53-year-old unmarried male. Abell died from some combination of eight blows to the head inflicted by Morrin with a large pair of tongs.

There were no witnesses to the killing or the events that preceded it. Morrin's testimony is the only affirmative evidence concerning the circumstances of the killing.

Morrin was 37 years old at the time of the killing. He was a mill-wright by trade. On March 27, 1967, at approximately 8:30 A.M., he completed seventeen hours of work in Oregon, Ohio. He testified that after eating breakfast he went to a union hall in nearby Toledo, Ohio, to talk to the union's business agent. Finding that the agent was not there, he stopped at a nearby bar, where he periodically phoned the union hall to see if the business agent had returned. Morrin drank seven or eight glasses of beer before 1:00 P.M., when he learned the agent was gone for the day.

While sitting in the bar, Morrin was approached by Abell, a com-plete stranger. Abell asked for a ride to Erie, Michigan, which was near Morrin's home in Monroe, Michigan. After Morrin learned that the business agent was unavailable, he and Abell left together.

When they reached Erie, Abell asked to be taken to a specific lo-cation. Morrin agreed, and proceeded at Abell's direction to traverse a number of quite remote, unpaved roads. Ultimately the car became mired in a mudhole. Abell alighted to push while Morrin attempted to extricate the vehicle by rocking the wheels. Their joint efforts succeeded, and the car was freed, whereupon Abell reentered the car.

At this point, Morrin testified, Abell pulled out a knife. Grab-bing Morrin by the hair, he held the knife to his throat. Morrin of-fered to let Abell have all the money in his possession. Abell said that Morrin would first have to commit an oral sexual act upon him.

With Abell still holding the knife at Morrin's throat, they slid out of the car, whereupon Morrin was forced to assume a kneeling position, facing Abell. Abell directed Morrin to remove his (Abell's) trousers, but when Morrin did not move Abell partially removed them himself. Abell then commanded Morrin to commit the sexual act. When Morrin still did not move, Abell grasped him by the back of the head to pull him forward.

Morrin testified that he then struck Abell in the testicles. Rising to his feet, Morrin started to flee before he saw Abell advancing on him with the knife. Morrin then grabbed a large pair of tongs from the back seat of the car. (The tongs apparently were one of the tools of his trade and he customarily took them on trips to and from work.) A struggle then ensued and the two men exchanged blows. Finally, as Morrin swung the tongs, they entered Abell's rectum. Abell fell forward slightly and Morrin struck him several more times with the tongs. When Abell fell to the ground, Morrin seized Abell's knife and threw it away. (The knife was not found.) Morrin then ran to his car and drove away. He drove straight home, stopping once at a gasoline station. He told the attendant that he had been in a scuf-fle.

Upon reaching home, he was in a distraught and hysterical state. His wife called his sister who immediately came over. Morrin said that he had hurt someone, perhaps killed him. He was crying and somewhat incoherent. He kept repeating the words, "if he hadn't disgusted me so." He took his sister out to the car to convince her he was telling the truth. His sister washed the blood off the car and also washed the tongs which were in the back seat.

Morrin and his sister drove back to the place of the fight to see whether Abell was alive. The sister drove. It took them some time to find the exact place. Morrin alone got out of the car and found that Abell was, indeed, dead. They then returned home. It was agreed that they would do nothing immediately but would take some action the next morning.

The sister then returned to her home and phoned an attorney who then phoned the police. The police picked up the sister who took them to Abell's body. Morrin said that the next morning, without having heard from his sister, he decided to turn himself in. He met the police on the way to his sister's home.

This was substantially the evidence upon which the case went to the jury. The prosecution introduced numerous photographs of the deceased taken at the scene. Morrin produced two character witnesses. Throughout the trial, the prosecutor repeatedly emphasized the bizarre rectal wound suffered by Abell; he claimed that the wound was inflicted after Abell was already dead.

The jury was instructed on the elements of first-degree murder, second-degree murder, and manslaughter, as well as self-defense.

II.

Homicide, the killing of one human being by another, may be innocent or criminal. There are two categories of innocent homicide; they are called justifiable homicide and excusable homicide. Homicide is "justifiable" if it is authorized (*e.g.*, self-defense) or commanded (*e.g.*, execution of a death sentence) by law. Homicide is "excusable" if the death is the result of an accident and the actor was not criminally negligent.

A person who kills another is guilty of the crime of murder if the homicide is committed with malice aforethought. Malice aforethought is the intention to kill, actual or implied, under circumstances which do not constitute excuse or justification or mitigate the degree of the offense to manslaughter. The intent to kill may be implied where the actor actually intends to inflict great bodily harm or the natural tendency of his behavior is to cause death or great bodily harm. (The common-law felony-murder rule is an example of implied intent or implied malice aforethought.)

Thus, as "malice aforethought" is now defined, a killing may be murder even though the actor harbored no hatred or ill will against the victim and even though he "acted on the spur of the moment." Whatever may be the philological origin of the words "malice aforethought," today "each word has a different significance in legal usage than in ordinary conversation."

The nature of malice aforethought is the source of much of the confusion that attends the law of homicide. The cause of this confusion has been the evolution of malice aforethought from an independently significant element of murder to a "term of art" whose significance is largely historical and procedural.

The precise roots of malice aforethought are uncertain. Common-law courts spoke of "malice prepense" as early as the 13th century. The requirement that malice aforethought be established in all murder prosecutions represented the common law's recognition that a rational legal system will punish certain homicides (for example, those that are intentional) while excusing others (accidental homicides, for example).

From the beginning malice aforethought was defined principally in functional terms. We know what it did; it both distinguished criminal from innocent homicide and murder from manslaughter. Yet what it was, the precise state of mind which it described, eluded symmetrical definition.

The common-law courts were faced with a difficult problem: malice aforethought was a requisite element of murder, but one so elusive that in many cases it resisted direct proof. Their solution was to create a presumption of malice. As early as the 16th century proof that the accused person killed the victim gave rise to a "presumption" that the act was done with malice aforethought. Once it was established that the accused killed the victim, the burden was upon the accused to prove circumstances of justification, excuse, or mitigation.

This rule, firmly rooted in English law, has taken hold in a great many American jurisdictions, including Michigan * * *.

The merits of the rule are that it relieves the prosecution from the necessity of proving the nonexistence of circumstances of excuse, justification, and mitigation—frequently an impossible burden—and instead allocates the burden of proving such circumstances to the defendant, who, arguably, has greater ability to do so than the prosecution.

* * *

There is also, however, a grave drawback to this presumptive device. This defect arises in connection with jury instructions, to instruct a jury that malice is presumed from the fact of killing is to invite confusion concerning the ultimate burden of proof in the trial. The prosecution must always prove the defendant guilty beyond a reasonable doubt; a rule of law that shifts the burden of proof with respect to "malice" tends to cloud the dimensions of the prosecution's ultimate burden.

It was this danger which led the House of Lords in 1935 to repudiate instructions that charged jurors that they are to presume malice from the mere fact of killing.[21] Speaking of the presumption of innocence as a "golden thread" running through the common law, the Court rejected a formulation that required the jurors to find a defendant guilty unless he discharged his burden of rebutting the presumption of malice.

The Court did not rule that malice must be proved by evidence independent of the killing itself. The fact of homicide still *permits* the jury to find malice aforethought. But it in no sense *compels* such a finding, even absent any evidence of excuse, justification or mitigation on the part of the defendant.

> "All that is meant is that if it is proved that the conscious act of the prisoner killed a man and nothing else appears in the case, there is evidence upon which the jury may, not must, find him guilty of murder." Woolmington v. The Director of Public Prosecutions, [1935] AC 462, 480.

The Michigan Supreme Court recognized at an early date the importance of categorizing malice aforethought as a permissible inference rather than a presumption.

* * *

Consider that the term "malice aforethought" is supposed to signify both what murder is: the presence of an essential element of the offense (intent to kill, actual or implied), and what it isn't: the absence of certain defenses (excuse and justification)—but not other defenses [24]—and, as well, the absence of circumstances which would mitigate the seriousness of the offense reducing it to manslaughter. Add that the term "malice aforethought" does not mean malice as used in ordinary speech,[25] and forethought is not required, and it becomes clear that it is well-nigh impossible to communicate to jurors

---

21. Woolmington v. The Director of Public Prosecutions, [1935] A.C. 462, 472. * * *

24. Coercion, mistake, insanity, among others are possible defenses, but they would not necessarily negative malice aforethought taken to mean intent to kill, actual or implied, neither excused nor justified.

25. Since "malice," as that word is used in ordinary speech, is not an issue, it is misleading to continue to speak to juries of ill will, corruption or malignancy of heart and depravity of the soul. It is, of course, arguable that where the issue is first-degree or second-degree murder, a court might describe one who premeditates and deliberates and decides to kill as being corrupt, malignant or depraved. But the issue is whether the actor deliberated or premeditated, not whether he was corrupt, malignant or depraved. Similarly, those words can be used to distinguish the "non-malignant" conduct of a person who accidentally kills his victim or who acted in self-defense or under circumstances of mitigation; however, again, the true issue would not be whether the actor was corrupt, malignant or depraved but whether he was justified in acting as he did in self-defense or whether it was an accident or there were circumstances of mitigation.

in the arcane jargon of malice aforethought the mental state required. No doubt many jurors are confused, and many, in error but understandably, make up their own working definition out of their own appreciation of what malice aforethought "must" mean.

* * *

The new penal codes, in defining the crime of murder, eliminate the word "malice." Although Michigan has not remolded its penal code along these lines, a restatement of the common law need not wait upon legislative action. Murder is a common-law crime: "Neither murder nor manslaughter is defined by our statutes, and the definition of murder remains the same as at common law." 3 Gillespie, Michigan Criminal Law and Practice, § 1637, p. 1969. If the language of the common law is misleading it should be clarified. It is the duty of the common-law courts to speak clearly in language that jurors can understand, not to persist in the lazy repetition of words which have lost all capacity to convey relevant thoughts and which are frequently misleading.

The problem of formulating suitable instructions on malice aforethought does not lend itself to ready solution. Although the formulation of jury instructions is outside the scope of this opinion, defendants charged with murder will either deny that they killed the victim or direct their defense toward the proof of facts inconsistent with malice aforethought, claiming either that they did not intend to kill or, even if it is found that they did, that the homicide was justified, excusable, or committed under circumstances of mitigation.

In People v. Dunn (1925), 233 Mich. 185, 197, 206 N.W. 568, 572, the Supreme Court of Michigan observed:

"In practical application legal refinements of definition over which those learned in the law often differ are of scant aid to a jury.

" 'If the jurors are told what constitutes legal justification or excuse, and what circumstances will reduce the killing to manslaughter, they have all the law they need to determine whether the particular homicide is murder or not, without the mention of the word malice.' 13 R.C.L. 773."

Courts might well emphasize that juries can convict of murder only when they are convinced beyond a reasonable doubt that (1) the defendant intended (actually or impliedly) to kill and (2) circumstances of justification, excuse or mitigation do *not* exist. A judge could, for example, charge that the defendant is guilty of the crime of murder if the jurors find, beyond a reasonable doubt, that he killed the victim and that he actually intended to kill the victim or (where relevant), although he did not actually intend to kill, he actually intended to inflict great bodily harm or engaged in behavior the natural tendency of which is to cause death or great bodily harm, unless (where relevant) the jurors have a reasonable doubt whether (i) circumstances of mitigation are present, in which event the offense is reduced from murder to manslaughter, or (ii) the killing was accidental, or (iii) the defendant justifiably acted in self-defense.

We have addressed ourselves to this perplexing question in order to make clear the nature of the presumption of malice aforethought, to caution against misdirection of jurors regarding the "presumption", and to show why in the instant case there was adequate evidence to sustain a conviction for common-law, *i. e.,* second-degree, murder. The fact that Morrin killed his victim was not in dispute. From this fact, the jury was permitted to infer that the killing was committed with malice aforethought. Morrin's testimony concerning self-defense sought to nourish a reasonable doubt in the minds of the jurors as to the existence of this inferential fact. The jury, nevertheless, chose to draw the requisite inference and exercised its prerogative to disbelieve Morrin's exculpatory testimony.

NOTE

The United States Supreme Court has held that a conviction under a statute authorizing the inference of one fact from another must be scrutinized to prevent conviction upon insufficient proof. Reliance upon such an inference violates the due process clause of the Fifth and Fourteenth Amendments "unless it can be said with substantial assurance that the presumed fact is more likely than not to flow from the proved fact on which it is made to depend." Leary v. United States, 395 U.S. 6, 37, 89 S.Ct. 1532, 23 L.Ed.2d 57 (1969). See also, e. g., Turner v. United States, 396 U.S. 398, 90 S.Ct. 642, 24 L.Ed.2d 610 (1970). Does this cast any doubt upon the appropriateness of the approach of the court in the instant case? Is the approach consistent with the presumption of innocence? See State v. Cuevas, 53 Hawaii 110, 488 P.2d 322 (1971) striking down an instruction placing upon the defendant the burden of proving the absence of "malice aforethought" once the act of killing has been proved.

----

a.   GROSS RECKLESSNESS

COMMONWEALTH v. MALONE

Supreme Court of Pennsylvania, 1948.
354 Pa. 180, 47 A.2d 445.

MAXEY, Chief Justice. This is an appeal from the judgment and sentence under a conviction of murder in the second degree. William H. Long, age 13 years, was killed by a shot from a 32-caliber revolver held against his right side by the defendant, then aged 17 years. These youths were on friendly terms at the time of the homicide. The defendant and his mother while his father and brother were in the U. S. Armed Forces, were residing in Lancaster, Pa., with the family of William H. Long, whose son was the victim of the shooting.

On the evening of February 26th, 1945, when the defendant went to a moving picture theater, he carried in the pocket of his raincoat a revolver which he had obtained at the home of his uncle on the preceding day. In the afternoon preceding the shooting, the decedent procured a cartridge from his father's room and he and the defendant placed it in the revolver.

After leaving the theater, the defendant went to a dairy store and there met the decedent. Both youths sat in the rear of the store ten minutes, during which period the defendant took the gun out of his pocket and loaded the chamber to the right of the firing pin and then closed the gun. A few minutes later, both youths sat on stools in front of the lunch counter and ate some food. The defendant suggested to the decedent that they play "Russian Poker." Long replied: "I don't care; go ahead." The defendant then placed the revolver against the right side of Long and pulled the trigger three times. The third pull resulted in a fatal wound to Long. The latter jumped off the stool and cried: "Oh! Oh! Oh!" and Malone said: "Did I hit you, Billy? Gee, Kid, I'm sorry." Long died from the wounds two days later.

The defendant testified that the gun chamber he loaded was the first one to the right of the firing chamber and that when he pulled the trigger he did not "expect to have the gun go off." He declared he had no intention of harming Long, who was his friend and companion. The defendant was indicted for murder, tried and found guilty of murder in the second degree and sentenced to a term in the penitentiary for a period not less than five years and not exceeding ten years. A new trial was refused and after sentence was imposed, an appeal was taken.

* * *

The killing of William H. Long by this defendant resulted from an act intentionally done by the latter, in reckless and wanton disregard of the consequences which were at least sixty per cent certain from his thrice attempted discharge of a gun known to contain one bullet and aimed at a vital part of Long's body. This killing was, therefore, murder, for malice in the sense of a wicked disposition is evidenced by the intentional doing of an uncalled-for act in callous disregard of its likely harmful effects on others. The fact that there was no motive for this homicide does not exculpate the accused. In a trial for murder proof of motive is always relevant but never necessary.

STATE v. CHALMERS

Supreme Court of Arizona, 1966.
100 Ariz. 70, 411 P.2d 448.

LOCKWOOD, Justice. * * * The facts of the case are as follows: The defendant was driving his Chevrolet automobile at approximately 12:30 a. m. on April 24, 1963 in a northerly direction on Oracle Road near the intersection of Wetmore Road which is located in Pima County, Arizona. Oracle Road is a two lane highway at and near the location where the collision shortly thereafter occurred.

The Chevrolet car was traveling at a speed estimated between eighty and one hundred miles per hour. It passed several other cars moving in the same direction, and in order to do so crossed into the left or southbound lane. Two vehicles which were moving in a southerly direction were forced to leave the roadway because the Chevrolet car was in the southbound lane. The first southbound vehicle was a pickup truck with a camper body, and the second was a Pima County Sheriff's patrol car. The Chevrolet car swerved back into the right lane after forcing the patrol car off the road, and again into the left lane where it shortly thereafter collided with two vehicles moving in a southerly direction in the southbound or left lane.

As a result of the collision two passengers in one of the cars involved in the collision were killed, the driver and one other passenger were injured. The driver of the second car involved was also injured. [Defendant was convicted on two counts charging second degree murder based upon the deaths of the two passengers. He appealed from these convictions.] * * * At the time the appeal was taken, this Court was committed to the proposition that wanton and reckless conduct, in utter disregard of the safety of others and of himself, on the part of a person driving a motor vehicle, was sufficient to supply the willful and unlawful intention to inflict bodily injury upon another if such occurred. Brimhall v. State, 31 Ariz. 522, 255 P. 165, 53 A.L.R. 231 (1927). However, in State v. Balderrama, 97 Ariz. 134, 397 P.2d 632 (1964) we expressly overruled Brimhall so far as it held that evidence of negligent conduct may be sufficient to prove the criminal intent with which an act is done. This being so, in a prosecution for murder, the element of malicious intent may not be shown by a proof of gross negligence in the operation of a motor vehicle which produces the death of another person.

In view of the fact that the crime of manslaughter in the driving of a vehicle may occur by the commission of an unlawful act not amounting to a felony and *without gross negligence,* it is obvious that a mere showing that there was no considerable provocation for the killing of a human being under such circumstances cannot supply the implied malicious intent to constitute murder.

There remains the Legislative provision that in the crime of murder malice may be implied "when the circumstances attending the killing show an abandoned and malignant heart." This term also occurs in many other jurisdictions in defining the offense of murder. However, we have found no case which would indicate that gross negligence alone would constitute such conduct as appears to be contemplated when referring to *"an abandoned and malignant heart."* The latter phrase seems to mean conduct by the use of a weapon or other appliance likely to produce death, and by the brutal and blood-thirsty use of such instrumentality. Daniels v. State, 197 Ga. 754, 30 S.E.2d 625 (1944); People v. Endner, 73 Cal.App.2d 20, 165 P.2d 712 (1946), (evidence of a long course of physical abuse of the victim, defendant's mother, and evidence of a severe beating which caused her death); People v. Lamothe, 222 Cal.App.2d 314, 35 Cal.Rptr. 122 (1963), (evidence that defendant had slapped and beat his stepdaughter, a sixteen-month old baby, to such an extent that she died from a brain injury, and that defendant had frequently struck and thrown the child on the floor, rendering her unconscious.)

* * *

In the instant case, there is sufficient evidence for the jury to find gross negligence and utter disregard of the safety or welfare of any persons who might have been in the vicinity of defendant's car at the time of the collision. There was no evidence in the record tending to show that defendant had by the use of any weapon indulged in vicious or brutal conduct which might support a finding of "an abandoned and malignant heart." There was no evidence that defendant deliberately used his Chevrolet car for the purpose of a weapon to inflict injury upon another. Nor is there evidence tending to show that defendant had used any other instrumentality as a weapon for indulging in vicious or brutal conduct, which could support a finding of "an abandoned and malignant heart." As stated in Balderrama, supra, criminal neglect can supply the place of intent only where the legislative power has expressly so provided. It therefore follows that under all the facts the defendant was not guilty of murder. Nor, under the holding in Balderrama, supra, could he be guilty of an assault with a deadly weapon. Even though defendant failed to raise this issue on appeal, it is such fundamental error as to require a reversal in any event. It may be that because of the utter disregard of the defendant for the consequences of his operation of an automobile which could and did cause a senseless tragedy in loss of life and in personal injuries, he should be subject to severe criminal responsibilities. However, as stated in Balderrama, supra, if there is an inadequacy of the present laws dealing with criminal responsibility in cases of this kind the remedy lies with the Legislature.

Judgment of the lower court is reversed and the case remanded for further proceedings in accordance with this opinion.

UDALL, Justice (specially concurring).

I concur in the majority opinion as to the law set forth but disagree with the application of the facts of this matter to that law. Because of the complete agreement by other members of this Court, I do not desire to file a dissent in this matter but would like to express my views as to why the jury verdict should be upheld.

* * *

The majority opinion concludes that "[t]here was no evidence in the record tending to show that defendant had by the use of any weapon indulged in vicious or brutal conduct which might support a finding of 'an abandoned and malignant heart.'" This conclusion supplants the determination of the jury which, after hearing the evidence, rendered a verdict convicting defendant of second degree murder. The jury was instructed and found that defendant's conduct distinctly manifested "an abandoned and malignant heart" necessary to convict him of murder.

* * *

The facts would indicate the accident was not the typical automobile accident where a driver makes a gross error of judgment and is thus tried for manslaughter. Rather, the conduct surpasses the usual vehicle manslaughter case and demonstrates characteristics of wanton conduct and an abandoned and malignant heart. The jury found that the accused should have known of the plain and obvious likelihood that death or great bodily injury could have resulted from driving his automobile in such a manner.

NOTES

1. Compare Gibson v. State, 476 P.2d 362 (Okl.Cr.App.1970) in which the defendant, while being transported to jail in a car driven by a police officer, lunged across the front seat of the car and grabbed the steering wheel. This caused the vehicle to veer across the center line of the highway, where it struck another vehicle killing the driver of the police car. Defendant's conviction for murder was upheld on the ground that his actions could have been found to come within the statutory definition of murder which included "an act imminently dangerous to others and evincing a depraved mind, regardless of human life."

2. In attempting to reconcile Malone and Chalmers, is it relevant that the instrument used in Chalmers was a motor vehicle? In evaluating whether the statistical risk of death created by the defendant (and of which he was aware) was sufficient to give rise to liability for murder, is it proper to consider the general social utility of the instrument? Thus, in order to commit murder by use of a motor vehicle might one have to create a greater risk of death by one's use of the car than would be necessary if the instrument used was a firearm, because of the general greater social utility assigned to motor vehicles?

b. INTENT TO DO PHYSICAL HARM

PEOPLE v. GEIGER

Court of Appeals of Michigan, 1968.
10 Mich.App. 339, 159 N.W.2d 383.

BURNS, Judge.   Defendant appeals from a circuit court jury conviction of manslaughter.

Sometime after 11 p. m., May 6, 1965, defendant confronted his estranged wife, Sharon Geiger, in the parking lot of a bar in Prudenville, Michigan, as she was about to enter the bar with Joan Greening.   Joan Greening testified that she and Mrs. Geiger had had only one drink at another bar prior to meeting the defendant, that Mrs. Geiger's health appeared normal and that she observed no black and blue marks or abrasions upon Mrs. Geiger that evening.   Joan Greening further testified that she was told by the defendant to wait for Mrs. Geiger in the bar, but that she waited in the parking lot and observed the defendant talking to his wife and trying to force her into the car; he then "threw" her into the car and drove away.

State police officers who had interrogated the defendant after the alleged offense testified that defendant told them the couple drove to the Prudenville elementary school playing field.   They argued and got out of the car.   Defendant struck his wife "two or three times" with his open hand and pushed her to the ground in such a manner that she bumped her head against the car.   When Mrs. Geiger failed to get up and appeared unconscious, defendant picked her up and placed her in his car.   He then allegedly attempted to clean her after driving a short distance to a house trailer which the Geigers had rented until May 1, 1965.

Early in the morning on May 7, defendant left his wife in the trailer and drove to James Meigs' house where defendant had been residing while he and his wife were separated.   Meigs was awakened around 3:15 a. m., at which time defendant persuaded Meigs to help move the automobile which Mrs. Geiger had driven to the bar.   After taking the vehicle to Mrs. Geiger's parents' home, defendant finally replied to Meigs' inquiries as to what was going on; defendant stated that he might be "facing a murder rap."

Between 3:30 a. m. and 4:30 a. m., May 7, defendant aroused his employer, asked for $100 and was given $50 in order to get away for a few days.

Defendant apparently returned to the house trailer, placed his wife in the front seat of his car and put a blanket over her.   He drove south for approximately 186 miles and at 7:30 a. m. or 8 a. m., stopped at the Addison Community Hospital, Addison, Michigan, where his wife was pronounced dead.

* * *

Defendant was charged with first-degree murder, but the jury was instructed only as to second-degree murder and manslaughter. Defendant contends that the instructions regarding second-degree murder should not have been submitted to the jury because there were no proofs showing malice.

Malice has been defined as "an intent to cause the very harm that results *or some harm of the same general nature, or an act done in wanton or wilful disregard of the plain and strong likelihood that some such harm will result*." (Emphasis supplied.) People v. Hansen (1962), 368 Mich. 344, 350, 118 N.W.2d 422, 425. Consistent with this definition, it follows that an assault by blows without a weapon may, under certain circumstances, permit a jury to infer an intent to kill. Wellar v. People (1874), 30 Mich. 16; People v. Collins (1942), 303 Mich. 34, 5 N.W.2d 556; also, see 22 A.L.R.2d 854.

On pages 19 and 20 of 30 Mich. of the *Wellar* Case, supra, Justice Campbell said:

"In determining whether a person who has killed another without meaning to kill him is guilty of murder or manslaughter, the nature and extent of the injury or wrong which was actually intended, must usually be of controlling importance.

"It is not necessary in all cases that one held for murder must have intended to take the life of the person he slays by his wrongful act. It is not always necessary that he must have intended a personal injury to such person. But it is necessary that *the intent with which he acted shall be equivalent in legal character to a criminal purpose aimed against life.* Generally the intent must have been to commit either a specific felony, or at least an act involving all the wickedness of a felony. And if the intent be directly to produce a bodily injury, it must be such an injury as may be expected to involve serious consequences, either periling life or leading to great bodily harm. There is no rule recognized as authority which will allow a conviction of murder where a fatal result was not intended, *unless the injury intended was one of a very serious character which might naturally and commonly involve loss of life, or grievous mischief.*" (Emphasis supplied.)

"The intent to kill must undoubtedly be established, as an inference of fact, to the satisfaction of the jury; but they may draw that inference, as they draw all other inferences, from any fact in evidence which, to their minds, fairly proves its existence. Intentions can only be proved by acts, as juries cannot look into the breast of the criminal. And where any act is knowingly committed which naturally and usually leads to certain consequences, a jury certainly has the right, in the exercise of ordinary sagacity, to draw the inference that such results are intended." People v. Scott (1859), 6 Mich. 287, 296.

The question before this Court is: was there evidence from which a jury could infer defendant's alleged intent to produce great bodily injury with the attendant likelihood that death would result therefrom?

It was legally possible for the jury in this case to find that the nature and extent of Sharon Geiger's injuries were reflective of an intent equivalent to a criminal purpose aimed against life. This consideration standing alone would be insufficient to establish malice, but the extent and nature of the injuries is not set against a solitary backdrop. Defendant "forced" or "pushed" the deceased into his car shortly before he severely beat her. After the beating decedent's unconsciousness and general physical appearance, as revealed to the jury from photographs and the autopsy report, showed a need for medical attention. Notwithstanding this need, defendant failed to immediately take his wife to a local hospital; instead he waited approximately 6 to 8 hours, during which time he travelled over 180 miles. Although by no means conclusive, defendant's statement to James Meigs that he "might be facing a murder rap" would give a jury additional insight into defendant's intent. An inference of intent to kill could be drawn from these and other facts presented in this case.

---

3. FIRST DEGREE MURDER: THE PREMEDITATED KILLING

STATE v. SNOWDEN

Supreme Court of Idaho, 1957.
79 Idaho 266, 313 P.2d 706.

McQUADE, Justice. This is an appeal by the defendant, who had entered a plea of guilty to an information charging him with the crime of murder in the first degree. At all times during the proceedings the defendant was represented by counsel. The district court, after hearing evidence to determine the degree of the crime and mitigating circumstances, if any, held the offense was murder in the first degree, and entered judgment sentencing the defendant to death.

The victim, Cora Lucyle Dean, was stabbed to death September 22, 1956, in Garden City, Idaho. The evidence showed the following sequence of events:

Defendant Snowden had been playing pool and drinking in a Boise pool room early in the evening. With a companion, one Carrier, he visited a club near Boise, then went to nearby Garden City. There the two men visited a number of bars, and defendant had several drinks. Their last stop was the HiHo Club.

Witnesses related that while defendant was in the HiHo Club he met and talked to Cora Lucyle Dean. The defendant himself said he hadn't been acquainted with Mrs. Dean prior to that time, but he had "seen her in a couple of the joints up town." He danced with Mrs. Dean while at the HiHo Club. Upon departing from the tavern, the two left together.

In statements to police officers, that were admitted in evidence, defendant Snowden said after they left the club Mrs. Dean wanted him to find a cab and take her back to Boise, and he refused because he didn't feel he should pay her fare. After some words, he related:

"* * * she got mad at me so I got pretty hot and I don't know whether I back handed her there or not. And, we got calmed down and decided to walk across to the gas station and call a cab. * * *"

They crossed the street, and began arguing again. Defendant said:

"* * * She swung and at the same time she kneed me again. I blew my top."

Defendant said he pushed the woman over beside a pickup truck which was standing near a business building. There he pulled his knife—a pocket knife with a two-inch blade—and cut her throat.

The body, which was found the next morning, was viciously and sadistically cut and mutilated. An autopsy surgeon testified the voice box had been cut, and that this would have prevented the victim from making any intelligible outcry. There were other wounds inflicted while she was still alive—one in her neck, one in her abdomen, two in the face, and two on the back of the neck. The second neck wound severed the spinal cord and caused death. There were other wounds all over her body, and her clothing had been cut away. The nipple of the right breast was missing. There was no evidence of a sexual attack on the victim; however, some of the lacerations were around the breasts and vagina of the deceased. A blood test showed Mrs. Dean was intoxicated at the time of her death.

Defendant took the dead woman's wallet. He hailed a passing motorist and rode back to Boise with him. There he went to a bowling alley and changed clothes. He dropped his knife into a sewer, and threw the wallet away. Then he went to his hotel and cleaned up again. He put the clothes he had worn that evening into a trash barrel.

After hearing the testimony of police officers and other witnesses, the trial court determined the killing was murder in the first degree and there were no circumstances in mitigation of the offense or of the punishment to be inflicted. The defendant was sentenced to death. This appeal is from that judgment.

*   *   *

The second assignment of error of the defendant is based upon the finding of the court that the defendant's acts in taking the life of Cora Lucyle Dean were willful, deliberate, and premeditated. I. C. § 18–4003 requires first degree homicide to be perpetrated by any kind of willful, deliberate, and premeditated killing * * *[.] The test to determine if the killing was willful, deliberate, and premeditated has been set out in State v. Shuff, 9 Idaho 115, 72 P. 664, 668, wherein the court stated:

> "* * * The unlawful killing must be accompanied with a deliberate and clear intent to take life, in order to constitute murder of the first degree. The intent to kill must be the result of deliberate premeditation. It must be formed upon the pre-existing reflection, and not upon a sudden heat of passion sufficient to preclude the idea of deliberation. * * *"

The court further stated in this case while approving an instruction:

> "* * * That instruction reads as follows, to wit: 'From these definitions the jury will see that any unlawful killing of a human being, with malice aforethought, is murder; but if nothing further characterizes the offense it is murder of the second degree. To constitute the higher offense there must be superadded, to the general definition above given, willfulness, deliberation, and premeditation. By willfulness is meant that it was of purpose, with the intent that, by the given act, the life of the party should be taken. It must be deliberate and premeditated. By this it is not meant that the killing must have been conceived or intended for any particular length of time. It is sufficient if it was done with reflection and conceived beforehand. And in this view, as I have said before, the deliberate purpose to kill and the killing may follow each other as rapidly as successive impulses or thoughts of the mind. It is enough that the party deliberate before the act—premeditate—the purpose to slay before he gave the fatal blow. But while the purpose, the intent, and its execution may follow thus rapidly upon each other, it is proper for the jury to take into consideration the shortness of such interval in considering whether such sudden and speedy execution may not be attributed to sudden passion and anger, rather than to deliberation and premeditation, which must characterize the higher offense. * * *."

The Supreme Court of Arizona held in the case of Macias v. State, 283 P. 711, 715:

"* * * There need be no appreciable space of time between the intention to kill and the act of killing. They may be as instantaneous as successive thoughts of the mind. It is only necessary that the act of killing be preceded by a concurrence of will, deliberation, and premeditation on the part of the slayer, and, if such is the case, the killing is murder in the first degree * * *."

In the present case, the trial court had no other alternative than to find the defendant guilty of willful, deliberate, and premeditated killing with malice aforethought in view of the defendant's acts in deliberately opening up a pocket knife, next cutting the victim's throat, and then hacking and cutting until he had killed Cora Lucyle Dean and expended himself. The full purpose and design of defendant's conduct was to take the life of the deceased.

The fourth assignment of error is directed at the imposition of the penalty of death upon the defendant. * * * It is abuse of discretion we are dealing with, and in particular the alleged abuse of discretion in prescribing the punishment for murder in the first degree as committed by the defendant. To choose between the punishments of life imprisonment and death there must be some distinction between one homicide and another. This case exemplifies an abandoned and malignant heart and sadistic mind, bent upon taking human life. It is our considered conclusion, from all the facts and circumstances, the imposition of the death sentence was not an abuse of discretion by the trial court.

The judgment is affirmed.

NOTE

1. What is the relationship, if any, between the premeditation formula and the death penalty? In McGautha v. California, 402 U.S. 183, 91 S.Ct. 1454, 28 L.Ed.2d 711 (1971) the petitioners had been convicted of first degree murder in California and Ohio and sentenced to death. Petitioner McGautha was convicted under the California statute, reprinted at page 416, supra, of a death caused by a shooting during the commission of a robbery by McGautha; McGautha apparently fired the fatal shot. Petitioner Crampton was convicted under Ohio law of killing his wife "purposely, and * * * of deliberate and premeditated malice." Ohio Rev. Code § 2901.01 (1954). Both statutes permitted, but did not require, the trial jury to impose a death sentence upon a defendant convicted of first degree murder. Neither statute authorized the death penalty upon the conviction of any other homicide crime. Both petitioners argued that by granting the jury this broad discretion without providing guidelines or limitations upon the ability of the jury to impose the death penalty, the

statutes deprived them of life without due process of law. Rejecting this argument, the Court reasoned as follows:

In order to see petitioners' claim in perspective, it is useful to call to mind the salient features of the history of capital punishment for homicides under the common law in England, and subsequent statutory developments in this country. This history reveals continual efforts, uniformly unsuccessful, to identify before the fact those homicides for which the slayer should die. Thus, the laws of Alfred, echoing Exodus 21:12–13, provided: "Let the man who slayeth another wilfully perish by death. Let him who slayeth another of necessity or unwillingly, or unwilfully, as God may have sent him into his hands, and for whom he has not lain in wait be worthy of his life and of lawful bot if he seek an asylum." Quoted in 3 J. Stephen, Histroy of the Criminal Law of England 24 (1883).

*   *   *

During all this time there was no clear distinction in terminology or consequences among the various kinds of criminal homicide. All were *prima facie* capital, but all were subject to the benefit of clergy, which after 1350 came to be available to almost any man who could read. Although originally those entitled to benefit of clergy were simply delivered to the bishop for ecclesiastical proceedings, with the possibility of degradation from orders, incarceration, and corporal punishment for those found guilty, during the 15th and 16th centuries the maximum penalty for clergyable offenses became branding on the thumb, imprisonment for not more than one year, and forfeiture of goods. 1 Stephen, supra, at 459–464. By the statutes of 23 Hen. 8, c. 1, §§ 3, 4 (1531), and 1 Edw. 6, c. 12, § 10 (1547), benefit of clergy was taken away in all cases of "murder of malice prepensed." 1 Stephen, supra, at 464–465; 3 id., at 44. During the next century and a half, however, "malice prepense" or "malice aforethought" came to be divorced from actual ill will and inferred without more from the act of killing. Correspondingly, manslaughter, which was initially restricted to cases of "chance medley," came to include homicides where the existence of adequate provocation rebutted the inference of malice. 3 id., at 46–73.

The growth of the law continued in this country, where there was rebellion against the common-law rule imposing a mandatory death sentence on all convicted murderers. Thus, in 1794, Pennsylvania attempted to reduce the rigors of the law by abolishing capital punishment except for "murder of the first degree," defined to include all "willful, deliberate and premeditated" killings, for which the death penalty remained mandatory. Pa.Laws 1794, c. 1777. This reform was soon copied by Virginia and thereafter by many other States.

This new legislative criterion for isolating crimes appropriately punishable by death soon proved as unsuccessful as the concept of "malice aforethought." Within a year the distinction between the degrees of murder was practically obliterated in Pennsylvania. Other States had similar experiences. The result was characterized in this way by Chief Judge Cardozo, as he then was:

"What we have is merely a privilege offered to the jury to find the lesser degree when the suddenness of the intent, the vehemence of the passion, seems to call irresistibly for the exercise of mercy. I have no objection to giving them this dispensing power, but it should be given to them directly and not in a mystifying cloud of words." What Medicine Can Do For Law, in Law and Literature 70, 100 (1931).

At the same time, jurors on occasion took the law into their own hands in cases which were "willful, deliberate, and premeditated" in any view of that phrase, but which nevertheless were clearly inappropriate for the death penalty. In such cases they simply refused to convict of the capital offense. * * *

In order to meet the problem of jury nullification, legislatures did not try, as before, to refine further the definition of capital homicides. Instead they adopted the method of forthrightly granting juries the discretion which they had been exercising in fact. * * * Tennessee was the first State to give juries sentencing discretion in capital cases, but other States followed suit, as did the Federal Government in 1897. * * *

In light of history, experience, and the present limitations of human knowledge, we find it quite impossible to say that committing to the untrammeled discretion of the jury the power to pronounce life or death in capital cases is offensive to anything in the Constitution. The States are entitled to assume that jurors confronted with the truly awesome responsibility of decreeing death for a fellow human will act with due regard for the consequences of their decision and will consider a variety of factors, many of which will have been suggested by the evidence or by the arguments of defense counsel. For a court to attempt to catalog the appropriate factors in this elusive area could inhibit rather than expand the scope of consideration, for no list of circumstances would ever be really complete. The infinite variety of cases and facets to each case would make general standards either meaningless "boiler-plate" or a statement of the obvious that no jury would need.

If Furman v. Georgia, 408 U.S. 238, 92 S.Ct. 2726, 33 L.Ed.2d 346 (1972) means that as a practical matter the death penalty may no longer be imposed for any homicide offenses, is there any longer a need to differentiate between "first" and "second degree" murders?

2. Is premediation, under any definition, an appropriate criterion with which to select those cases in which the maximum penalty—whatever it is—may be imposed? Consider the following:

The Significance of Deliberation and Impulse

Whether and to what extent homicidal behavior was preceded by deliberation is plainly of evidential value in determining what the actor knew and intended when he acted. The more extensive the deliberation, the more probable it is that at least the more palpable risks created by the homicidal act were clearly perceived, and at least its more immediate consequences intended. From this point of view, however, gradations in homicidal behavior from the purely impulsive to the completely deliberate bear directly upon the question whether the actor created the homicidal risk inadvertently or advertently and, if advertently, whether or not he intended to kill, and only indirectly upon his character. The difficult question is whether the impulsiveness or deliberateness of his behavior has direct and independent significance in relation to his character. Assuming that other factors indicative of his character, such as knowledge, intent and motive are the same, of what additional importance is it that his act was the product of or was preceded by more or less deliberation? It may be argued that the more carefully considered and the less impulsive the act is, the more it indicates basic perversion of the actor's conceptions of good and evil. But it is surely not self-evident that the man who acts on wrong principles is a more dangerous man than one who acts without considering what is good. There are, moreover other objections to this view of the significance of deliberation. In the first place, it ignores that passion may influence deliberation as well as lead to action without deliberation, so that deliberate as well as impulsive action may be contrary to the actor's real notions of good and evil. In the second place, it does not embrace either deliberation about means rather than ends or acts which are preceded by but are not in accord with the results of deliberation. And yet it is extremely difficult in most cases to discover in what terms the actor deliberated or what was the relationship between deliberation and act. These objections are not avoided by stating the significance of deliberation in another way. Thus it may be said that reflection prior to action indicates that the actor lacks the sort of desires that will prevent such an act, since reflection is the opportunity to bring such desires into play, an opportunity which, by hypothesis, is not afforded by impulsive action; whereas action without reflection does not permit of that inference because if the actor had deliberated he might not have acted as he did. But in order to draw from these premises the conclusion that the man who acts deliberately is more dangerous than the man who acts impulsively, it must be asserted that the probability that the former's deliberations will result in wrong judgments is greater than the probability that the latter will not reflect before acting. This proposition also requires proof. The truth is, we think, that deliberation has no independent significance in relation to character and that the importance usually accorded it properly belongs to other factors which are its concomitants such, for example, as lapse of time, or to still other factors which it evidences, such as knowledge and intent. When the matter is viewed in that way, no difficulty is experienced in dealing with cases in which deliberation itself results in the intensification of passion, as it may when the enormity of an injury done the actor or the value of an end to be served by a homicidal act becomes apparent only after thought.

Wechsler and Michael, A Rationale of the Law of Homicide, 37 Colum.L. Rev. 701, 1261, 1282–84 (1937).

PEOPLE v. ANDERSON

Supreme Court of California, 1968.
70 Cal.2d 15, 73 Cal.Rptr. 550, 447 P.2d 942.

TOBRINER, Justice.   Defendant was indicted for the murder
of Victoria Hammond, a 10-year-old girl, in 1962.   The jury found
defendant guilty of first degree murder, found that he was sane, and
fixed the penalty at death.

The Facts.

Defendant, a San Jose cab driver, had been living for about eight
months with a Mrs. Hammond and her three children, Cynthia, aged
17, Kenneth, aged 13, and the victim, Victoria, aged 10.   On the morning of the day of the murder, December 7, 1962, Mrs. Hammond left
for work at 7:30 a. m., leaving only Victoria at home with the defendant.   Defendant was still in bed.   He had been home from work
for the previous two days, during which time he had been drinking
heavily, and apparently he did not go to work on the day of the murder.

The owner of a nearby liquor store testified that defendant purchased a quart of whisky from him sometime between 1 and 2 p. m.
on December 7, 1962.   The only other witness who testified as to
defendant's whereabouts that day prior to the discovery of the murder was the victim's 13-year-old brother Kenneth.

Kenneth testified that he arrived home from school at 3:30 p. m.
on December 7.   He found the front door locked, which was not unusual, so he went around to the back of the house and down to the
basement.   Kenneth stayed there awhile working with his micro-
scope.   In a short time he heard noise coming from upstairs in the
house which sounded like boxes and other things being moved around,
like someone was cleaning up.   He then heard the shower water running.   A police officer later verified that a person in the basement
could hear water running in the shower and movement in Victoria's
bedroom.

Kenneth testified further that he then came up from the basement and went to the back porch screen door.   The screen door was
locked, which also was not unusual, so Kenneth jerked on it so the
hook would pop out.   Kenneth then went from the back porch directly into his bedroom to change his clothes.   He then returned
through the back porch to the kitchen door which was also locked.
Kenneth knocked on the door and the defendant opened it.   Kenneth
testified that the defendant was wearing slacks only.   Kenneth went
into the kitchen and asked defendant for $1.00 for a teen club dance
he intended to attend that evening.   Defendant obtained a dollar for
him out of the pocket of another pair of slacks hanging on the knob
of a bedroom door.   When Kenneth noticed the blood on the kitchen
floor and asked defendant about it, the defendant told Kenneth that

he had cut himself. This explanation apparently satisfied Kenneth, as he finished dressing and left the house sometime before 4 p. m.

Kenneth testified that no one else was at his house when he was there between 3:30 and 4 p. m. He further testified that about 6:30 he realized that he had forgotten his wallet and returned home. As he approached the front door, his mother came out and asked to see the cut on his arm, and Kenneth explained that he had no cut. His mother then asked defendant about the blood she had noticed and defendant told her that Victoria had cut herself, but that the mother should not worry, as the cut was not serious. After defendant told her that Victoria was at a friend's for dinner, the mother wanted to take Kenneth with her to get Victoria. Kenneth went back to his room to get a jacket. Because he had a "weird" feeling, he looked into Victoria's room. He found her nude, bloody body under some boxes and blankets on the floor near her bed. Kenneth ran out of the room screaming that defendant had killed her. Mrs. Hammond, after seeing Victoria's body, went next door to phone the police.

Mrs. Hammond testified that she returned home from work at 4:45 p. m. The front door was locked, she rang the doorbell, and defendant answered. Mrs. Hammond noticed blood on the couch in the living room, and when she asked defendant about it, he told her that Kenneth had cut himself playing with a knife and that he was at a teenage dance. Mrs. Hammond then went to the grocery store and returned about 5:30 p. m. She testified that at both times she arrived home defendant was drinking a highball. She also testified as to examining Kenneth's arm for a cut when he returned home for his wallet and as to defendant's subsequent explanation that Victoria had been cut, but not seriously. Mrs. Hammond discovered Victoria's body after Kenneth came out of Victoria's room.

A classmate of Victoria, who was the last person to see Victoria alive, testified that she left Victoria in front of the Hammond house about 3:45 p. m. after the two of them had walked home from school.

When the police arrived at 7 p. m. the shades were down on all the windows and the doors were locked. Defendant finally opened the front door for one of the officers who arrested and handcuffed defendant. The arresting officer testified that defendant was wearing slacks, no shirt or shoes, and that there was no blood on him.

The arresting officer found Victoria's body on the floor near her bed. He found defendant's blood-spotted shorts on a chair in the living room, and a knife and defendant's socks, with blood encrusted on the soles, in the master bedroom. The evidence established that the victim's torn and bloodstained dress had been ripped from her, that her clothes, including her panties out of which the crotch had been ripped, were found in various rooms of the house, that there were bloody footprints matching the size of the victim's leading from the master bedroom to Victoria's room, and that there was blood in almost every room including the kitchen, the floor of which appeared to have been mopped.

The TV cameraman who covered the murder story for channel 11, the officer who drove defendant to the police station, and the officer who "observed" defendant for four hours at the station the night of December 7, 1962, all testified that defendant did not appear intoxicated. The officers who talked to defendant testified, however, that they smelled alcohol on his breath; a blood test taken at 7:45 p. m. indicated that the alcohol content in defendant's blood was .34 percent, which was more than necessary for an automobile driver to be classified as "under the influence."

Over 60 wounds, both severe and superficial, were found on Victoria's body. The cuts extended over her entire body, including one extending from the rectum through the vagina, and the partial cutting off of her tongue. Several of the wounds, including the vaginal lacerations, were post mortem. No evidence of spermatozoa was found in the victim, on her panties, or on the bed next to which she was found.

The prosecution contended that the murder was sexually motivated. The defendant, who pleaded not guilty and not guilty by reason of insanity, presented no defense whatsoever.

(a) *The evidence is insufficient to support a finding of premeditation and deliberation.*

It is well established that the brutality of a killing cannot in itself support a finding that the killer acted with premeditation and deliberation. "If the evidence showed no more than the infliction of multiple acts of violence on the victim, it would not be sufficient to show that the killing was the result of careful thought and weighing of considerations."

Given the presumption that an unjustified killing of a human being constitutes murder of the second, rather than of the first, degree, and the clear legislative intention to differentiate between first and second degree murder, we must determine in any case of circumstantial evidence whether the proof is such as will furnish a *reasonable foundation* for an inference of premeditation and deliberation * * * or whether it "leaves only to *conjecture and surmise* the conclusion that defendant either arrived at or carried out the intention to kill as the result of a concurrence of deliberation and premeditation." (Italics added.) * * *

As we noted in People v. Bender, supra, 27 Cal.2d 164, 183, 163 P.2d 8, we find no indication that the Legislature intended to give the words "deliberate" and "premeditated" other than their ordinary dictionary meanings. Moreover, we have repeatedly pointed out that the legislative classification of murder into two degrees would be meaningless if "deliberation" and "premeditation" were construed as requiring no more reflection than may be involved in the mere formation of a specific intent to kill. * * *

Thus we have held that in order for a killing with malice aforethought to be first rather than second degree murder, " '[t]he intent to kill must be * * * formed upon a *pre-existing* reflection' * * [and have] been the subject of actual deliberation or *forethought*. * * *'" (People v. Thomas, supra, 25 Cal.2d at pp. 900–901, 156 P. 2d 7, at p. 18.)   (Italics added.)   We have therefore held that "a verdict of murder in the first degree * * * [on a theory of a wilful, deliberate, and premeditated killing] is proper only if the slayer killed 'as a result of careful thought and weighing of considerations; as a *deliberate* judgment or plan; carried on coolly and steadily, [especially] according to a *preconceived design*.' * * *'"

The type of evidence which this court has found sufficient to sustain a finding of premeditation and deliberation falls into three basic categories: (1) facts about how and what defendant did *prior* to the actual killing which show that the defendant was engaged in activity directed toward, and explicable as intended to result in, the killing—what may be characterized as "planning" activity; (2) facts about the defendant's *prior* relationship and/or conduct with the victim from which the jury could reasonably infer a "motive" to kill the victim, which inference of motive, together with facts of type (1) or (3), would in turn support an inference that the killing was the result of "a pre-existing reflection" and "careful thought and weighing of considerations" rather than "mere unconsidered or rash impulse hastily executed" (People v. Thomas, supra, 25 Cal.2d 880, at pp. 898, 900, 901, 156 P.2d 7, at p. 14); (3) facts about the nature of the killing from which the jury could infer that the *manner* of killing was so particular and exacting that the defendant must have intentionally killed according to a "preconceived design" to take his victim's life in a particular way for a "reason" which the jury can reasonably infer from facts of type (1) or (2).

Analysis of the cases will show that this court sustains verdicts of first degree murder typically when there is evidence of all three types and otherwise requires at least extremely strong evidence of (1) or evidence of (2) in conjunction with either (1) or (3). As will become clear from the following analysis of representative cases, the present case lacks evidence of any of the three types.

In People v. Hillery, supra, 62 Cal.2d 692, 44 Cal.Rptr. 30, 401 P.2d 382, the jury could reasonably infer that the defendant engaged in the following "extended course of conduct": defendant parked his car near the victim's (a 15-year-old girl's) house, entered the house surreptitiously, seized the victim while she was sewing and covered her head with a towel and slip to prevent outcry or identification, cut a length of cord in another room to secure her hands behind her, took the victim's scissors, dragged her to a nearby irrigation ditch where her body was subsequently found, engaged in a struggle with the victim, and then plunged the scissors directly into her chest. (Id. at p. 704, 44 Cal.Rptr. 30, 401 P.2d 382.)

Hillery represents a case of very strong type (1) evidence: the defendant's surreptitious conduct, subjection of his victim to his complete control, and carrying off of his victim to a place where others were unlikely to intrude, can be described as "planning" activity directly related to the killing. Moreover, there is also strong evidence of type (3): directly plunging a lethal weapon into the chest evidences a deliberate intention to kill as opposed to the type of "indiscriminate" multiple attack of both severe and superficial wounds which defend- ant engaged in in the instant case.

In People v. Kemp (1961) 55 Cal.2d 458, 11 Cal.Rptr. 361, 359 P. 2d 913, the defendant entered his victim's apartment through a win- dow after removing the screen, found the victim alone in bed, tied stockings around her neck and hands, gagged her with a washcloth, and then raped and strangled her. In *Kemp,* as in *Hillery,* defendant's surreptitious coming upon the victim and calculated efforts to prevent her from identifying her assailant or crying out for help, together with the deliberate manner of killing—evidence of types (1) and (3) —point to a killing which is the result of "preconceived design" as op- posed to "an explosion of violence." People v. Anderson, supra, 63 Cal.2d at p. 360, 46 Cal.Rptr. 763, at p. 768, 406 P.2d 43, at p. 48.)

The present case is strikingly similar to People v. Granados, su- pra, 49 Cal.2d 490, 319 P.2d 346, in which this court reduced a ver- dict of first degree murder to second degree murder on the ground that the evidence was insufficient to show either premeditation and deliberation or that the killing occurred in the course of an attempted violation of section 288 of the Penal Code. The evidence of premed- itation and deliberation in *Granados,* while clearly insufficient to sus- tain the verdict of first degree murder on that theory, was stronger than in the present case in which we find no evidence from which the jury could *reasonably* infer that defendant acted " '*with a deliberate and clear intent to take life.*' " * * *

In *Granados,* defendant lived in a common law relationship with the mother of his victim, a 13-year-old girl. After taking the de- ceased and her brother to a real estate office, defendant gave the brother a note requesting money to take to his mother who worked nearby. When the brother returned home with the requested money he saw defendant at the rear of the house. As he started to enter the house, defendant came running to him and asked him to get some alcohol for his sister (decedent) who had fainted. The brother no- ticed blood on one of defendant's hands and that defendant had the other hand behind his back.

The brother unsuccessfully looked for some alcohol. Defendant then suggested they get a doctor and an ambulance. The brother then noticed that defendant's hand had been washed. Defendant then drove the brother to a drugstore, gave him 50 cents for some alcohol, and told him he would wait for him. The defendant drove away and did not return for the brother.

Defendant then called the mother and told her the victim had poisoned herself. The mother returned to the house with a friend who found the victim's body in the bedroom lying on the floor. Her skirt was pulled up exposing her private parts, there were bloodstains on the wall, floor, and decedent's head, and a machete covered with blood was lying in a corner of the living room behind a small heater.

Defendant testified that on the day of the killing the girl was helping him clean the house and that he asked her if she was a virgin, to which she replied that it was none of his business. Defendant said that she had never answered him in that way and that he therefore struck her with his hand, but did not remember striking her with the machete.

Decedent's mother testified that she had warned defendant that the next time he bothered her daughter, she would tell the police, and that defendant in reply threatened to kill her and both her children if she did.

The prosecution argued that the murder was sexually motivated. This court, per Justice McComb, held that the evidence was insufficient as a matter of law to support a verdict of first degree murder. (49 Cal.2d at p. 497, 319 P.2d 346.)

Applying the standards developed above to *Granados,* we find that the only evidence of (1) defendant's behavior prior to the killing which could be described as "planning" activity related to a killing purpose was defendant's sending the victim's brother on an errand and apparently returning home alone with the decedent. Such evidence is highly ambiguous in terms of the various inferences it could support as to defendant's purpose in so behaving. The evidence of (2) defendant's prior behavior with the victim (alleged sexual molestation and his question as to her virginity) is insufficient to support a reasonable inference that defendant had a "motive" to kill the girl, which could in turn support an inference that the striking with the machete was the result of a "preconceived design" and "forethought." Finally, the evidence of (3) the manner of killing (brutal hacking) does not support a reasonable inference of deliberately placed blows, which could in turn support an inference that the act of killing was premeditated rather than "hasty and impetuous."

Justice Carter dissented in *Granados* on the ground that the following evidence was sufficient to sustain a finding of premeditation and deliberation: the nature of the instrument, the condition of the body, defendant's sending the brother on an errand immediately prior to the time of the killing, and defendant's prior threats against the

girl and her family.   (49 Cal.2d at pp. 498–499, 319 P.2d 346.)   Justice Carter's dissent demonstrates that there was some evidence of
premeditation and deliberation in *Granados,* albeit insufficient.   Here,
on the other hand, we do not have any evidence of either (1) any
conduct by defendant prior to the killing which would indicate that
he was planning anything, felonious or otherwise, or (2) any behavior towards Victoria from which the jury could reasonably infer
that defendant had a "motive" or desire to sexually attack and/or
kill her.   The evidence of (3), the manner of killing and the condition of the body, is the same in both cases: the only inference which
the evidence reasonably supports in either case is that the killing resulted from a "random," violent, indiscriminate attack rather than
from deliberately placed wounds inflicted according to a preconceived
design.   * * *

Finally, the defendant in *Granados,* as here, attempted to "cover
up" the crime by lying to the brother and the mother of the victim.
Although this type of evidence may possibly bear on defendant's state
of mind *after* the killing, it is irrelevant to ascertaining defendant's
state of mind immediately prior to, or during, the killing.   Evasive
conduct shows fear: it cannot support the double inference that defendant planned to hide his crime at the time he committed it and
that therefore defendant committed the crime with premeditation
and deliberation.

The judgment is modified by reducing the degree of the crime
to murder of the second degree and, as so modified, is affirmed.   The
cause is remanded to the trial court with directions to arraign and
pronounce judgment on defendant in accordance with the foregoing
ruling.

TRAYNOR, C. J., and PETERS and PEEK, JJ., concur.

BURKE, Justice (dissenting).   * * *   I believe there is credible evidence from which the jury could find a premeditated homicide,
e. g. the locking of the doors (whether before or after the actual killing is a matter of conjecture), the duration of the assault, the pursuit
through many rooms with a quantity of blood being left in each room,
the extensive stabbings many of which would have sufficed as fatal,
the removal of the murder weapon from one room and the apparent
repeated use of it in other rooms.

NOTES

1.   Does the approach of the California Supreme Court in the instant
case create a satisfactory criterion for distinguishing those killers that
should be dealt with most severely?   For example, the court cites People v.
Hillery and People v. Kemp as examples of adequate proof of premeditation.   Were the defendants in those cases sufficiently different from the
defendants in the instant case and People v. Granados (also discussed in
the instant case) to justify treating them more severely?   Does it matter
that the most important aspect of this increased severity might be the pos-

sibility of the death penalty? How might the answers to these questions differ if the death penalty were abolished in the jurisdiction?

2. To what extent might dissatisfaction with the premeditation criterion be based upon its perceived unsatisfactoriness when applied to "psychologically abnormal" offenders? If this is important, should the distinction between the degrees of homicide be tailored to distinguish among psychologically abnormal offenders, or should they be premised upon "normal" offenders and some other doctrine (see section VIII.F of this text) be developed to permit consideration of psychological abnormality? Does the answer depend upon how many "psychologically normal" people commit killings that the law might want to classify as the most serious offense? If so, how many are there? See generally, Brenner, The Impulsive Murder and the Degree Device, 22 Fordham L.Rev. 274 (1953); 21 Md.L.Rev. 349 (1961).

3. Does premeditation require an intent to kill? If one carefully considers the legal and moral implications of engaging in an act creating an extremely high risk of death of others, could he be guilty of first degree murder under a scheme defining first degree murder as a "deliberate and premeditated killing"?

-----

4. FELONY MURDER

-----

a. THE BASIC DOCTRINE

PEOPLE v. PHILLIPS

Supreme Court of California, 1966.
64 Cal.2d 574, 51 Cal.Rptr. 225, 414 P.2d 353.

TOBRINER, Justice. [Defendant, a doctor of chiropractic, had been convicted of second degree murder. The prosecution relied in part upon the theory that the death of the victim, one of defendant's patients, had been caused by defendant's commission of the felony of grand theft by obtaining money falsely representing his ability to cure cancer. The California statutes defining the homicide offenses appear at page 416, supra.]

Defendant challenges the propriety of the trial court's instructions to the jury. The court gave the following   *   *   *   instruction on murder in the second degree:

[T]he unlawful killing of a human being with malice aforethought, but without a deliberately formed and premeditated intent to kill is murder of the second degree:

*   *   *

(3) If the killing is done in the perpetration of or attempt to perpetrate a felony such as Grand Theft. If death occurs in the perpetration in a course of conduct amounting to Grand Theft, which course of conduct is a proximate cause of the unlawful killing of a human being, such course of conduct constitutes murder in the second degree, even though the death was not intended.

Despite defendant's contention that the Penal Code does not expressly set forth any provision for second degree felony murder and that, therefore, we should not follow any such doctrine here, the concept lies embodied in our law. * * * [T]he cases hold that the perpetration of some felonies, exclusive of those enumerated in [the Penal Code section defining first degree murder] may provide the basis for a murder conviction under the felony murder rule.

NOTES

1. The traditional semantic framework for felony murder has been that the intent necessary for the underlying felony supplies the malice aforethought necessary for murder. Of course, where a statute makes a felony murder first degree murder, the underlying felony must be regarded as not only supplying malice aforethought but also as an adequate alternative to whatever other factors might raise a killing from second to first degree murder.

2. Throughout the materials dealing with felony murder (and its manslaughter equivalent), keep in mind the following queries: To what extent does the felony murder doctrine make a real difference, i. e., to what extent could the results achieved by use of the felony murder doctrine also be achieved by other methods? What, if any, constitutional attacks might be made upon the felony murder doctrine or its application to a specific set of facts? What should be the appropriate attitude of a court in interpreting statutes dealing with felony murder? For example, could the court in Phillips have read the statute as not applying the felony murder doctrine? If so, should it have done so? Why, or why not?

PEOPLE v. STAMP

California Court of Appeals, 1969.
2 Cal.App.3d 203, 82 Cal.Rptr. 598, certiorari denied
400 U.S. 819, 91 S.Ct. 36, 27 L.Ed.2d 46.

COBEY, Associate Justice. These are appeals by Jonathan Earl Stamp, Michael John Koory and Billy Dean Lehman, following jury verdicts of guilty of robbery and murder, both in the first degree. Each man was given a life sentence on the murder charge together with the time prescribed by law on the robbery count.

Defendants appeal their conviction of the murder of Carl Honeyman who, suffering from a heart disease, died between 15 and 20

minutes after Koory and Stamp held up his business, the General
Amusement Company, on October 26, 1965, at 10:45 a. m. Lehman,
the driver of the getaway car, was apprehended a few minutes after
the robbery; several weeks later Stamp was arrested in Ohio and
Koory in Nebraska.

* * *

On this appeal appellants primarily rely upon their position that
the felony-murder doctrine should not have been applied in this case
due to the unforeseeability of Honeyman's death.

THE FACTS

Defendants Koory and Stamp, armed with a gun and a black-
jack, entered the rear of the building housing the offices of General
Amusement Company, ordered the employees they found there to go
to the front of the premises, where the two secretaries were working.
Stamp, the one with the gun, then went into the office of Carl Honeyman, the owner and manager. Thereupon Honeyman, looking very
frightened and pale, emerged from the office in a "kind of hurry."
He was apparently propelled by Stamp who had hold of him by an
elbow.

The robbery victims were required to lie down on the floor while
the robbers took the money and fled out the back door. As the robbers, who had been on the premises 10 to 15 minutes, were leaving,
they told the victims to remain on the floor for five minutes so that
no one would "get hurt."

Honeyman, who had been lying next to the counter, had to use it
to steady himself in getting up off the floor. Still pale, he was short
of breath, sucking air, and pounding and rubbing his chest. As he
walked down the hall, in an unsteady manner, still breathing hard
and rubbing his chest, he said he was having trouble "keeping the
pounding down inside" and that his heart was "pumping too fast for
him." A few minutes later, although still looking very upset, shaking,
wiping his forehead and rubbing his chest, he was able to walk in a
steady manner into an employee's office. When the police arrived,
almost immediately thereafter, he told them he was not feeling very
well and that he had a pain in his chest. About two minutes later,
which was 15 to 20 minutes after the robbery had occurred, he collapsed on the floor. At 11:25 he was pronounced dead on arrival at
the hospital. The coroner's report listed the immediate cause of
death as heart attack.

The employees noted that during the hours before the robbery
Honeyman had appeared to be in normal health and good spirits. The
victim was an obese, sixty-year-old man, with a history of heart
disease, who was under a great deal of pressure due to the intensely
competitive nature of his business. Additionally, he did not take good
care of his heart.

Three doctors, including the autopsy surgeon, Honeyman's physician, and a professor of cardiology from U.C.L.A., testified that although Honeyman had an advanced case of atherosclerosis, a progressive and ultimately fatal disease, there must have been some immediate upset to his system which precipitated the attack. It was their conclusion in response to a hypothetical question that but for the robbery there would have been no fatal seizure at that time. The fright induced by the robbery was too much of a shock to Honeyman's system. There was opposing expert testimony to the effect that it could not be said with reasonable medical certainty that fright could ever be fatal.

SUFFICIENCY OF THE EVIDENCE RE CAUSATION

* * *

A review of the facts as outlined above shows that there was substantial evidence of the robbery itself, that appellants were the robbers, and that but for the robbery the victim would not have experienced the fright which brought on the fatal heart attack.

APPLICATION OF THE FELONY-MURDER RULE

* * *

There is no requirement that the killing occur, "while committing" or "while engaged in" the felony, or that the killing be "a part of" the felony, other than that the few acts be a part of one continuous transaction. Thus the homicide need not have been committed "to perpetrate" the felony. There need be no technical inquiry as to whether there has been a completion or abandonment of or desistence from the robbery before the homicide itself was completed.

The doctrine is not limited to those deaths which are foreseeable. Rather a felon is held strictly liable for *all* killings committed by him or his accomplices in the course of the felony. As long as the homicide is the direct causal result of the robbery the felony-murder rule applies whether or not the death was a natural or probable consequence of the robbery. So long as a victim's predisposing physical condition, regardless of its cause, is not the *only* substantial factor bringing about his death, that condition, and the robber's ignorance of it, in no way destroys the robber's criminal responsibility for the death. So long as life is shortened as a result of the felonious act, it does not matter that the victim might have died soon anyway. In this respect, the robber takes his victim as he finds him.

REX v. LUMLEY

Central Criminal Court, 1911.
22 Cox Crim.C. 635.

[Charles Lumley, a physician, was charged with the murder of Mabel Gorringe. The evidence tended to show that the defendant had performed an illegal abortion upon the victim, and that she had died as a result of this operation. The following is a portion of the trial court's instruction on the felony murder doctrine.]

AVORY, J. (in the course of his summing up) directed the jury as follows: If the evidence satisfies you beyond reasonable doubt that the prisoner did, in fact, either use an instrument or other means, for the purpose and with the intention of procuring abortion, and that death resulted from that act, then you must ask yourselves the further question: When he did the act, did he contemplate, or must he as a reasonable man have contemplated, that death was likely to result, or must he as a reasonable man have contemplated that grievous bodily harm was likely to result? If, in your opinion, he must as a reasonable man have contemplated either of those consequences, then your duty is to find him guilty of murder. If you are of the opinion, and are driven to the conclusion by the evidence, that he did the act which is charged against him, but that he had not at the time in contemplation, and would not as a reasonable man have contemplated, that either death or grievous bodily harm would result, but thought that by his own skill as a medical man he could perform this operation without any risk of either death or grievous bodily harm, then you would be justified in convicting him of manslaughter.

NOTES

1. Although it is frequently said that a felon is not liable for murder if during the felony he causes a death in an unforeseeable manner because the felonious activity is not the "proximate cause" of the death, e. g., W. LaFave and A. Scott, Criminal Law 264 (1972), American case law support for this proposition is sparse. Most of the support is dicta[a] in cases holding defendants liable for what is determined to have been a foreseeable death. E. g., State v. Glover, 330 Mo. 709, 50 S.W.2d 1049 (1932) (defendant who set fire to drug store to collect insurance liable for felony-murder of fireman killed fighting the blaze on the ground that he had reason to anticipate that members of the fire department would endanger themselves fighting the fire). See Ward v. State, 109 S.W.2d 207 (Tex.Crim.App.1937) in which the defendant caused fire to be set to a building; a person in an upper room was killed in the fire. "The testimony," concluded the court, "excludes the idea that the principals knew, or should have known, that any person was in the building at the time the arson was consummated." Defendant also denied any knowledge of this fact. He was charged with murder under a

---

a. "Dicta" is that part of a court's opinion that is not necessary to its decision in the case before it. Thus it is not part of the decision and law announced by the court.

statute in the arson section of the penal code providing that "Where death is occasioned by any offense described in this * * * chapter the offender is guilty of murder." The conviction was upheld, although the court commented that in the absence of the statute it would have grave doubt that the defendant would be liable for murder "unless the death in question was the natural and reasonable consequence of [the] arson * * *." Should the existence of such a statute preclude application of a "proximate cause" requirement of foreseeability?

2. What is the purpose of the felony-murder rule? Consider the following statement by Chief Justice Traynor of the California Supreme Court:

> The purpose of the felony-murder rule is to deter felons from killing negligently or accidentally by holding them strictly liable for killings they commit. * * *

> It is contended * * * that another purpose of the felony-murder rule is to prevent the commission of robberies [and other felonies]. Neither the common-law rationale of the rule nor the Penal Code supports this contention. In every robbery there is a possibility that the victim will resist and kill. The robber has little control over such a killing once the robbery is undertaken * * *. To impose an additional penalty for the killing would discriminate between robbers, not on the basis of any difference in their own conduct, but solely on the basis of the response by others that the robber's conduct happened to induce. An additional penalty for a homicide * * * [caused in this manner] would deter robbery haphazardly at best. To "prevent stealing, the law would do better to hang one thief in every thousand by lot." (Holmes, The Common Law, p. 58.)

People v. Washington, 62 Cal.2d 777, 44 Cal.Rptr. 442, 402 P.2d 130, 133 (1965).

3. The President's Commission on Crime in the District of Columbia examined the circumstances of selected samples of serious crimes committed in the District of Columbia. Consider the following conclusions as they may relate to the appropriateness of a felony-murder rule, or as to the selection of offenses as to which any such rule should apply:

> Of the 172 murders committed between 1963 and 1964, twenty-four (or 14 percent) were felony murders. Seventeen (10 percent) were incidental to robberies, and seven (4 percent) were incidental to rapes.

President's Commission on Crime in the District of Columbia, Report 45 (1966)

> Of 151 rapes committed during 1964, thirty-eight (25 percent) involved assailants armed with dangerous weapons. Twenty-seven of these were armed with knives.

Id. at 54.

> Of 297 robberies committed in December, 1965, 120 (40 percent) involved armed perpetrators. 86 were armed with guns and 16 with knives. Seventy-five (25 percent) of the victims were injured; no figure as to the number killed was given. Injuries occurred in

ten (11 percent) of 91 holdups or armed robberies; injuries occurred in thirty (45 percent) of the "yokings" (strong-arm robbery, usually involving assault from the back).

Id. at 64.

4. Must the death be caused by the felonious aspect of the defendant's conduct for the felony-murder doctrine to take effect? See Moynahan v. State, 140 Tex.Crim. 540, 146 S.W.2d 376 (1941) in which the defendant was charged with felony-murder for a death arising out of an automobile accident which occurred while the defendant allegedly was intoxicated. Driving while intoxicated was a felony under state law. The conviction was reversed on the basis of the prosecutor's following argument to the jury: "It makes no difference how carefully the defendant was driving his car; he could have been driving it five miles an hour, and if he was drunk at the time of the collision he is guilty of murder." The "correct statement of the settled law of the state," the court held, was embodied in the trial court's instruction that the defendant "would not be guilty of murder if he was operating the same in the manner that it would be operated by one not under the influence of intoxicating liquor." Suppose at the time the accident occurred the defendant was driving at five miles an hour because he realized he was intoxicated and wanted to be especially careful. Would he be liable for murder on the theory that if he had not been intoxicated he would have driven faster and not been at the intersection at the same time as the deceased? Compare Ross v. State, 314 S.W.2d 592 (Tex.Crim.App.1958) affirming a conviction for felony-murder arising out of a motor vehicle accident occurring when the defendant was allegedly intoxicated despite what a dissenting judge described as "not the least suggestion in [the] record that the intoxication of the appellant caused him to run into the motorcycle [upon which the deceased was riding]."

5. The felony-murder rule has been specifically abolished in England by statute. See Homicide Act, 1957, 5 & 6 Eliz. II, c. 11, § 1. The Supreme Court of Iowa has interpreted its statute to require "a purpose or intent to kill," even where the killing is caused in the perpetration of felonies enumerated in the statute. Robbins v. State, 8 Ohio St. 131 (1857); State v. Farmer, 156 Ohio St. 214, 102 N.E.2d 11 (1951). But cf. State v. Salter, 149 Ohio St. 264, 78 N.E.2d 575 (1948).

IN RE ALLEN

Court of Appeals of New York, 1912.
205 N.Y. 158, 98 N.E. 470.

WILLARD BARTLETT, J. Some time in November, 1910, one Jacob Kuhn and the appellant, Ralph Friedman, entered into a conspiracy to obtain money feloniously and by force, in the nighttime, from the person or custody of George A. Schuchart, a grocer in the city of Rochester. The conspiracy was carried into effect between half past 9 and half past 10 o'clock in the evening of November 15, 1910. One of the conspirators waited in the street outside the store;

the other entered the store to perform the more active part of the contemplated robbery or larceny. A struggle ensued within between the grocer and his assailant during which three revolver shots were fired, one of which inflicted a mortal wound upon Mr. Schuchart. The appellant, Friedman, who claims to have been the one who waited outside, testified that he entered the door upon hearing the three shots and found Kuhn and Mr. Schuchart there engaged in a personal encounter. He states that he reached his arm over to knock the revolver up, when a fourth shot was fired which penetrated his left wrist. The conspirators then fled, leaving Mr. Schuchart dying upon the floor of his grocery. * * * The proof * * * suffices to uphold the conviction even if the killing was unintentional, on the ground that the homicide was committed by persons engaged in a common attempt to commit a felony.

At the close of the charge, counsel for the defendant asked the court to instruct the jury as follows: "If the jury believe that the defendant, Friedman, and Kuhn did confederate and agree together to enter the store of Schuchart and take money from it by stealth, and that the scope and plan of execution of their unlawful enterprise did not involve the use of force or violence which might result in the taking of human life, then the defendant is not responsible for the act of Kuhn in taking human life if they find that the defendant did not shoot and kill Schuchart."

It is contended that the refusal to charge this request was error. I think not. The learned trial judge had previously charged the jury correctly on this subject, as follows: "If they [Friedman and Kuhn] went to the store of Schuchart merely to steal his money, that would not necessarily mean that their errand was of a dangerous, homicidal character, or that it necessarily involved the use of violence which might result in the taking of human life unlawfully. But if they confederated together to commit a felony at Schuchart's store, then it is left to you to say whether or not they intended the natural and probable consequence of their act, and each one would be responsible for the acts of the other in carrying out their joint enterprise."

If the natural and probable consequence of the common enterprise was the killing of Mr. Schuchart in case of resistance on his part, the defendant was liable for murder in the first degree, although he did not do the actual killing. The request assumes that, if the appellant did not fire the fatal shot, he could escape liability unless the conspiracy expressly contemplated the use of such force or violence as might cause death. This is an erroneous view of the law. An express agreement by intending robbers not to kill in carrying out a plan of robbery would not save any of the conspirators from responsibility for a homicide by one of them in committing or attempting to

commit the robbery, if such killing was the natural and probable result of the robbery or attempt to rob in such a contingency as actually
occurred in this case.

* * *

Judgment of conviction affirmed.

NOTES

1. Is the result in the instant case consistent with general principles
of complicity? If not, how can the difference be justified? Is the felony
murder rule an exception to the "act" requirement as well as to the "state
of mind" requirement of murder?

2. Suppose that A and B agree to assault C with their fists. During
the affray, B, upon an "impulse," pulls a gun and shoots C. C dies. Is this
sufficient to convict A of the death of C on a felony-murder theory? Cf.
People v. Raybourn, 72 Ill.App.2d 379, 219 N.E.2d 711 (1966). Would it be
relevant that A did or did not know that B had a gun? Would the result
differ if B had planned all along to shoot C during the fight, but did not
reveal this to A? Would it differ if B had not intended to kill C when the
fight began and had assured A of this, but formed the intent to kill when,
during the fight, C revealed to B that he was the person who had earlier
stolen certain property belonging to B?

----

b. LIMITATION OF THE DOCTRINE TO "DANGEROUS" FELONIES

PEOPLE v. SATCHELL

Supreme Court of California, 1971.
6 Cal.3d 28, 98 Cal.Rptr. 33, 489 P.2d 1361.

SULLIVAN, Justice. * * * [D]efendant John M. Satchell
was charged * * * with murder * * *. The jury * * *
found him guilty of murder of the second degree. Defendant appeals
from the judgment of conviction.

* * *

The facts relevant to our determination can be briefly stated.
On July 2, 1969, defendant and the victim Jordan became engaged
in a heated argument on a public street in San Francisco. The argument progressed beyond mere harsh language when defendant shoved
Jordan. The latter then withdrew some distance down the street;
defendant went to his automobile, which was parked nearby and got
in. A few minutes later Jordan returned and walked over to defendant's car. The argument then resumed, but it was abruptly terminated when defendant emerged from the car holding a sawed-off
shotgun, shot Jordan once in the chest, and then drove off. Jordan
died of the shotgun wound.

At trial defendant took the stand and testified that he had shot Jordan, with whom he had had no prior acquaintance, in self-defense when the latter threatened him and made movements which defendant interpreted as efforts to draw a weapon.   A defense witness testified that Jordan had a gun in his hand at the time of the shooting, which gun was taken from the victim after defendant had departed.

The trial court instructed the jury on the definition of murder and malice and the degrees of murder, but it eliminated first degree murder from the consideration of the jury by indicating that none of the felonies enumerated in section 189 of the Penal Code was here involved and by not instructing on premeditation. The jury was fully instructed on second degree murder, however, and the following instruction on second degree felony murder was given: "The unlawful killing of a human being, whether intentional, unintentional or accidental, which occurs as a direct causal result of the commission of or attempt to commit a felony inherently dangerous to human life, namely, the crime of *possession of a concealable firearm by a felon,* and where there was in the mind of the perpetrator the specific intent to commit such crime, is murder of the second degree. The specific intent to commit *the crime of possession of a concealable firearm by a felon* and the commission of or attempt to commit such crime must be proved beyond a reasonable doubt."

The trial court went on to give a series of instructions defining and explaining the crime of possession of a concealable firearm by a felon.   (Pen.Code, § 12021; see Pen.Code, § 12001.)[5]

Defendant moved for a new trial on the ground that the second degree felony-murder instruction should not have been given, but the motion was denied. He appeals from the judgment of conviction on the same ground among others. We have concluded that his contention must be sustained.

In the case of People v. Washington (1965) 62 Cal.2d 777, at page 783, 44 Cal.Rptr. 442, 446, 402 P.2d 130, 134, this court struck

---

5. Section 12021 of the Penal Code at the time here pertinent provided: "Any person who is not a citizen of the United States and any person who has been convicted of a felony under the laws of the United States, of the State of California, or any other state, government, or country, or who is addicted to the use of any narcotic drug, who owns or has in his possession or under his custody or control any pistol, revolver, or other firearm capable of being concealed upon the person is guilty of a public offense, and shall be punishable by imprisonment in the state prison not exceeding 15 years, or in a county jail not exceeding one year or by a fine not exceeding five hundred dollars ($500), or by both."

Section 12001 of the Penal Code at the time here pertinent provided in relevant part: " 'Pistol,' 'revolver,' and 'firearm capable of being concealed upon the person' as used in this chapter shall apply to and include any device, designed to be used as a weapon, from which is expelled a projectile by the force of any explosion, or any other form of combustion, and which has a barrel less than 12 inches in length. * * *" The sawed-off shotgun involved in this case had a barrel 11¾ inches in length.

the keynote which has guided all our subsequent consideration of cases involving the felony-murder doctrine. Acknowledging the substantial body of legal scholarship which has concluded that the doctrine not only "erodes the relation between criminal liability and moral culpability" but also is usually unnecessary for conviction, we went on to say of it: "Although it is the law in this state (Pen.Code, § 189), *it should not be extended beyond any rational function that it is designed to serve.*" (Italics added.)

Applying this principle to various concrete factual circumstances, we have sought to insure that the "highly artificial concept" (People v. Phillips (1966) 64 Cal.2d 574, 582, 51 Cal.Rptr. 225, 414 P.2d 353) of strict criminal liability incorporate in the felony-murder doctrine be given the narrowest possible application consistent with its ostensible purpose—which is to deter those engaged in felonies from killing negligently or accidentally * * *.[12]

In the instant case it is clear that the victim was killed by defendant while he was engaged in the commission of a felony other than the six enumerated in section 189 of the Penal Code. Thus, in determining whether the felony-murder doctrine is properly applicable the threshold inquiry is whether the felony in which defendant was engaged was a "felony inherently dangerous to human life" within the meaning of People v. Phillips, *supra*, 64 Cal.2d 574, 51 Cal.Rptr. 225, 414 P.2d 353, and People v. Williams [(1965), 63 Cal.2d 452, 47 Cal.Rptr. 7, 406 P.2d 647]. If the felony in question was not such an inherently dangerous felony, the felony-murder instruction given was without legal foundation and the judgment must be reversed if the giving of that instruction was prejudicial.

At the outset it is clear that this court has unequivocally held on more than one occasion that the offense set forth in section 12021 is a felony capable of supporting a second degree felony-murder instruction. * * * It is equally clear, however—in light of our continuing concern that the felony-murder doctrine not be extended beyond its rational function—that those decisions cannot be invested with a vitality independent from the developing concept of inherent danger * * *. Rather, our task today is to assess the cited decisions as they relate to that concept and determine whether or not the conclusion announced by them is consistent therewith and should endure. "[T]he branch cannot bear fruit by itself, except it abides in the vine." (John XV, 4.)

12. In *Williams* we stated that the ostensible purpose of the felony-murder rule "may be well served with respect to felonies such as robbery or burglary, but it has little relevance to a felony which is not inherently dangerous. If the felony is not inherently dangerous it is highly improbable that the potential felon will be deterred; he will not anticipate that any injury or death might arise solely from the fact that he will commit the felony." (63 Cal.2d at pp. 457–458, fn. 4, 47 Cal.Rptr. at p. 10, 406 P.2d at p. 650.)

It is useful to consider the subject decisions within the chronological development of the principle of inherent danger. That principle * * * was first stated as positive law in People v. Ford, *supra* (1964), 60 Cal.2d 772, at page 795, 36 Cal.Rptr. 620 at page 635, 388 P.2d 892 at page 907: "A homicide that is a direct causal result of the commission of *a felony inherently dangerous to human life* (other than the six felonies enumerated in Pen.Code, § 189) constitutes at least second degree murder." (Italics added.) That case itself involved a violation of section 12021, and this court, looking to the facts of the particular case and relying on the prior (i. e., pre-*Ford*) decision in People v. Robillard (1960), 55 Cal.2d 88, 98, 10 Cal.Rptr. 167, 358 P.2d 295, concluded that that offense was inherently dangerous to human life and could properly support a second degree felony-murder instruction. This conclusion was followed in People v. Schader (1965), 62 Cal.2d 716, 732, 44 Cal.Rptr. 193, 401 P.2d 665, * * * again looking to the facts of the particular case which involved the armed holdup of a store by a previously convicted felon.

However, in 1965 we held that, in assessing whether a felony was inherently dangerous within the meaning of *Ford*, "we look to the elements of the felony in the abstract, not the particular 'facts' of the case." (People v. Williams, supra (1965), 63 Cal.2d 452, 458, fn. 5, 47 Cal.Rptr. 7, 10, 406 P.2d 647, 650.) There the victim, an illegal supplier of methedrine, was killed with a knife during an affray which resulted after defendants demanded that he pay a debt either in methedrine or in money. The jury was given a second degree felony-murder instruction based upon the crime of conspiracy to possess methedrine without a prescription. We held that the instruction was erroneous because the subject felony, viewed in the abstract "is surely not, as such, inherently dangerous." (63 Cal.2d at p. 458, 47 Cal.Rptr. at p. 10, 406 P.2d at p. 650.)[16]

The teaching of *Williams* was applied and explained in People v. Phillips, supra (1966) 64 Cal.2d 574, 51 Cal.Rptr. 225, 414 P.2d 353. There the defendant, a chiropractor, was tried for murder following the death from cancer of a patient whom he dissuaded from surgery and purported to treat through chiropractic methods. The jury was given a second degree felony-murder instruction based upon the crime

---

16. In holding that the felony must be viewed in the abstract we disapproved any contrary implications in People v. Pulley (1964) 225 Cal.App.2d 366, 373, 37 Cal.Rptr. 376. There it was held that a second degree felony-murder instruction was properly based on a violation of section 10851 of the Vehicle Code, automobile theft, because the theft in question led to a high speed chase and a collision which took the life of the victim. The Court of Appeal stated in that case: "By any reasonable standard, stealing and driving a stolen car and endeavoring to escape pursuing officers with the stolen car, entering an intersection against all rules of the road at 70 to 80 miles per hour and crashing with other cars lawfully proceeding therein, is highly dangerous." (225 Cal. App.2d at p. 373, 37 Cal.Rptr. at p. 380.) Our insistence in *Williams* that the felony be viewed in the abstract necessarily precludes a determination of inherent danger based upon this kind of reasoning.

of grand theft by false pretenses. (Pen.Code, §§ 484, 487.) Holding that the crime of grand theft, viewed in the abstract, was not inherently dangerous to human life, we went on to reject the contention of the prosecution that the subject felony should be characterized in light of the defendant's actual conduct as "grand theft medical fraud," assertedly an inherently dangerous offense. "To fragmentize the 'course of conduct' of defendant so that the felony-murder rule applies if any segment of that conduct may be considered dangerous to life would widen the rule beyond calculation. It would then apply not only to the commission of specific felonies, which are themselves dangerous to life, but to the perpetration of *any* felony during which defendant may have acted in such a manner as to endanger life. [Par.] The proposed approach would entail the rejection of our holding in *Williams*. That case limited the felony murder doctrine to such felonies as were themselves inherently dangerous to life. That decision eschews the prosecution's present sweeping concept because, once the Legislature's own definition is discarded, the number or nature of the contextual elements which could be incorporated into an expanded felony terminology would be limitless. We have been, and remain, unwilling to embark upon such an uncharted sea of felony murder." (64 Cal.2d at pp. 583–584, 51 Cal.Rptr. at p. 233, 414 P.2d at p. 361.)

*   *   *

The foregoing chronological review clearly shows that the prior decisions of this court concerning violation of Penal Code section 12021 as a basis for felony murder have applied a standard different from that required by our *Williams* and *Phillips* cases in that they have not undertaken to view that felony in the abstract when assessing the danger to human life inherent in its commission. Accordingly, in addressing ourselves to that task for the first time today, we decide what is in effect a question of novel impression in this court: *Viewed in the abstract*, is the possession of a concealable firearm by a person who has previously been convicted of a felony an offense inherently dangerous to human life?

We first consider two decisions of the Court of Appeal which have treated this question. In People v. Lovato (1968) 258 Cal.App.2d 290, 65 Cal.Rptr. 638, the specific issue before the court was whether the possession of a concealable firearm by an *alien* (which is also proscribed by section 12021 of the Penal Code) was an offense inherently dangerous to human life capable of supporting a second degree felony-murder instruction. The Court of Appeal, over the dissent of one of the three justices, held that it was not. Viewing the crime in the abstract as required by the *Williams-Phillips* principle, the court concluded: "It is common knowledge that several million aliens are living in this country and that the vast majority are peaceful and law-abiding. Undoubtedly, many are serving or have children serving in the armed forces. Consequently, to categorically hold that every alien who is intentionally in possession of a concealable weapon, regardless of the reason, is guilty of an offense inherently dangerous to human life, and hence is guilty of murder in the second degree if the offense results in a homicide, under every possible circumstance we can visualize, would manifestly lead to unjust and even absurd results. Moreover, to in effect state that a person's citizenship is the controlling factor as to whether a homicide was committed with malice is not only illogical but would constitute an affront to the judiciary which through the years has constantly striven to find compelling reasons rather than arbitrary distinctions before making rules which result in differing treatment of people." (258 Cal.App.2d at p. 293, 65 Cal.Rptr. at p. 641.)

It was urged upon the court, however, that in light of the line of cases holding that possession of a concealable firearm by a *felon* was inherently dangerous to life * * *, the same result should follow in cases involving aliens. In answering this contention the court, still applying the *Williams-Phillips* principle of considering the felony in the abstract, stated: "[W]e conclude that there is a clear, rational and logical distinction between the nature of the offense when committed by an ex-felon and when committed by an alien. *An ex-felon by his felony conviction has demonstrated instability and a propensity for crime. Thus, there is a core of logic in the assumption that if such a person arms himself with a concealable weapon he commits a crime* per se *dangerous to human life.* However, a person does not demonstrate instability, nor does he show a tendency toward crime, simply because he is not a citizen of this country. Consequently, although it may be reasonable for the Legislature to include aliens within the ambit of section 12021 for regulatory purposes, it would be illogical and unreasonable for a court to hold that every alien who violates the section necessarily commits a crime inherently dangerous to human life." (Italics added.)   (258 Cal.App. 2d at pp. 295–296, 65 Cal.Rptr. at p. 642.)

*   *   *

While we agree with the approach and reasoning of the *Lovato* court in assessing the danger inherent in the crime of possession of a concealable firearm by an *alien*, we believe that its dictum concerning such possession by an *ex-felon* departs from that approach and reasoning and reaches an incorrect conclusion. Thus, we cannot agree that, whereas on the one hand it would be "illogical" and "arbitrary" to conclude "that a person's citizenship is the controlling factor as to whether a homicide was committed with malice", yet on the other hand "there is a core of logic" in the conclusion that the presence or absence of a felony conviction on a person's past record should have such a controlling effect. The logical process by which this conclusion is reached fails to proceed beyond its own major premise: granting that "[a]n ex-felon by his felony conviction has demonstrated instability and a propensity for crime", one cannot logically achieve the conclusion that such a person, when he arms himself, commits a crime inherently dangerous to human life, unless it also be shown that one who so demonstrates instability and a propensity for crime is inherently disposed toward acts dangerous to human life. We do not think that this has been shown. To borrow the phrasing of the *Lovato* court, we have concluded that "to in effect state that [the presence or absence of a felony conviction on a person's past record] is the controlling factor as to whether a homicide was committed with malice is not only illogical but would constitute an affront to the judiciary which through the years has constantly striven to find compelling reasons rather than arbitrary distinctions before making rules which result in differing treatment of people."

It bears emphasis that, in determining whether a felony is inherently dangerous for purposes of the felony-murder rule we assess that felony *in the abstract*. The felony here in question is possession of a concealable firearm by one who has previously been convicted of a (i. e., another) felony. We do *not* look to the specific facts of the case before us in order to determine whether, in light of the nature of the particular felony of which defendant was previously convicted, his possession of a concealable firearm was inherently dangerous. Rather, we direct our attention to the genus of crimes known as felonies and determine whether the possession of a concealable firearm by one who has been convicted of *any crime within that genus* is an act inherently dangerous to human life which, as such, justifies the extreme consequence (i. e., imputed malice) which the felony-murder doctrine demands.

It is manifest that the range of antisocial activities which are criminally punishable as felonies in this state is very wide indeed. Some of these felonies, such as certain well-known crimes against the person of another, distinctly manifest a propensity for acts dangerous to human life on the part of the perpetrator. Others, just as distinctly fail to manifest such a propensity. Surely it cannot be said that a person who has committed a crime in this latter category, when he arms himself with a concealable weapon, presents a danger to human life so significantly more extreme than that presented by a non-felon similarly armed as to justify the imputation of malice to him if a homicide should result. Accordingly, because we can conceive of such a vast number of situations wherein it would be grossly illogical to impute malice, we must conclude that the violation of section 12021 by one previously convicted of a felony is not itself a felony *inherently* dangerous to human life which will support a second degree felony-murder instruction.

Thus, it was error in this case to give a second degree felony-murder instruction based upon defendant's violation of section 12021 of the Penal Code. * * *

Our consideration of an issue which may arise upon retrial reveals an even more fundamental reason why the felony-murder instruction was erroneous in this case.

Although the jury was given a second degree felony-murder instruction based upon section 12021 of the Penal Code, it was not given such an instruction based upon section 12020 of the same code. That section * * * provides in substance as here relevant that *any person* who possesses a sawed-off shotgun is guilty of a felony. Because a second degree felony-murder instruction based on section 12020 may be offered on retrial, we deem it incumbent to determine whether the offense proscribed by that section, viewed in the abstract, is inherently dangerous to human life. We conclude that it is not, and that therefore a violation of section 12020 may not properly support a second degree felony-murder instruction.

This court has stated that the purpose of the Legislature in enacting section 12020 was to outlaw the possession of "weapons common to the criminal's arsenal. * * *"

*   *   *

This purpose proceeds from the recognition that persons who possess the specialized instruments of violence listed in the section are ordinarily persons who intend to use them in violent and dangerous enterprises. Thus, rather than simply proscribing the *use* of such instruments, the Legislature has sought to prevent such use by proscribing their mere *possession*. In order to insure the intended prophylactic effect, the intent or propensity for violence of the possessor has been rendered irrelevant.

While we have no doubt that * * * the proscription of the mere possession of articles of this sort lies within the constitutional competency of the Legislature, we decline to hold that such a statute, which makes no distinction between the innocent "collector" and the hardened criminal, can be utilized to posit malice aforethought in a prosecution for murder. Looking at the subject felony in the abstract, as we are required to do, it appears that to permit the application of the felony-murder doctrine on the ground of violation of section 12020 would "erode [   ] the relation between criminal liability and moral culpability" beyond all recognition and would extend the operation of that doctrine "beyond any rational function that it is designed to serve." (People v. Washington, supra, 62 Cal.2d 777, 783, 44 Cal.Rptr. 442, 446, 402 P.2d 130, 134.)

Viewing the matter from the standpoint of inherent danger, we find it difficult to understand how any offense of mere passive possession can be considered to supply the element of malice in a murder prosecution. To be sure, if such possession is of an extremely reckless nature manifesting a conscious disregard for human life, malice may be imputed by means of basic murder principles. Moreover, if passive possession ripens into a felonious *act* in which danger to human life is inherent, the purpose of the felony murder rule is served by its application—for it is the deterrence of such acts by felons which the rule is designed to accomplish. However, mere possession *in itself*—ignoring the propensities and conduct of the possessor—is essentially neutral in its intentional aspect and should not serve as the basis for the imputation of malice.

*　　*　　*

The judgment is reversed.

NOTES

1. Upon what, if any, policy grounds can the approach of the California Supreme Court be defended? Does it represent only a desire to limit the felony murder rule at every available opportunity?

2. Compare the analysis in Jenkins v. State, 230 A.2d 262, 268–69 (Del.1967):

> The only rational function of the felony-murder rule is to furnish an added deterrent to the perpetration of felonies which, by their nature or by the attendant circumstances, create a foreseeable risk of death. This function is not served by application of the rule to felonies not foreseeably dangerous. The rule should not be extended beyond its rational function. Moreover, application of the rule to felonies not foreseeably dangerous would be unsound analytically because there is no logical basis for imputing malice from the intent to commit a felony not dangerous to human life.

*　*　*

> Whether the commission of a particular felony in a given instance was foreseeably dangerous is for the court and jury to decide. In that determination, both the nature of the felony and the circumstances of its commission are relevant factors. Burglary * * * may, or may not, be foreseeably dangerous to human life, depending upon whether someone may be reasonably expected to be present in the building, and upon other circumstances of the case.

---

c. DEATHS CAUSED DIRECTLY BY PERSONS OTHER THAN THE FELONS

COMMONWEALTH EX REL. SMITH v. MYERS

Supreme Court of Pennsylvania, 1970.
438 Pa. 218, 261 A.2d 550.

OPINION OF THE COURT

O'BRIEN, Justice. This is an appeal from the order of the Court of Common Pleas of Philadelphia County, denying James Smith's petition for a writ of habeas corpus. The facts upon which the convictions of appellant and his co-felons, Almeida and Hough, rest are well known to this Court and to the federal courts. In addition to vexing the courts, these cases have perplexed a generation of law students, both within and without the Commonwealth, and along with their progeny, have spawned reams of critical commentary.

Briefly, the facts of the crime are these. On January 30, 1947, Smith, along with Edward Hough and David Almeida, engaged in an armed robbery of a supermarket in the City of Philadelphia. An off-duty policeman, who happened to be in the area, was shot and killed while attempting to thwart the escape of the felons. Although the evidence as to who fired the fatal shot was conflicting in appellant's 1948 trial, the court charged the jury that it was irrelevant who fired the fatal bullet · * · *. To this part of the charge appellant took a specific exception.

The jury convicted Smith of first degree murder, with punishment fixed at life imprisonment. * * *

Appellant urges that he was denied due process by virtue of the trial court's charge that it was irrelevant who fired the fatal bullet. * * *

The common law felony-murder rule * · * has been subjected to some harsh criticism, most of it thoroughly warranted. * * *

[One] * * * commentator suggests that the rule should be modified, so that a killing committed during the perpetration of a felony would create merely a *rebuttable* presumption of intention, rather than the *conclusive* presumption now created.[8] Other opponents of the felony-murder rule point out that it is hardly an essential weapon in the Commonwealth's arsenal. Our neighboring state of Ohio has managed quite well without a felony-murder rule since abolishing it over a century ago. See Robbins v. State, 8 Ohio St. 131 (1857).

In fact, not only is the felony-murder rule non-essential, but it is very doubtful that it has the deterrent effect its proponents assert. * * *

We have gone into this lengthy discussion of the felony-murder rule not for the purpose of hereby abolishing it. That is hardly necessary in the instant case. But we do want to make clear how shaky are the basic premises on which it rests. With so weak a foundation, it behooves us not to extend it further and indeed, to restrain it within the bounds it has always known. [In Commonwealth v. Almeida, 362 Pa. 596, 68 A.2d 595 (1949), cert. denied, 339 U.S. 924, the court had upheld the conviction of another participant in the robbery. In Commonwealth v. Thomas, 382 Pa. 639, 117 A.2d 204 (1955), however, the court reversed the felony murder conviction of one felon

8. Crum, Causal Relations and the Felony-Murder Rule, 1952 Wash.U. Law Q., 191, 205.

based upon the killing of a cofelon by the victim of the crime. And, in Commonwealth v. Redline, 391 Pa. 486, 137 A.2d 472 (1958), the court reversed the felony murder conviction of a felon whose cofelon had been killed by a police officer.]   *   *   *   *Redline* rejected the proximate cause tort analogy which *Almeida* found so appealing *   *   *. [T]he uninitiated might be surprised to learn that *Redline* did not specifically overrule *Almeida*. This Court did overrule *Thomas*, holding that no conviction was possible for a *justifiable* homicide, where a policeman shot a felon, but "distinguished" *Almeida* on the ground that the homicide there, where an innocent third party was killed by a policeman, was only *excusable*. This distinction was rather remarkable in view of the cases relied upon by the Court—almost all cases in which the victim was an innocent third party rather than a felon. *   *   *

In fact, even the majority in *Redline* seemed to realize that they were seizing upon a will of the wisp in attempting to refrain from *then* overruling Almeida: "It is, of course, true that the distinction thus drawn between Almeida and the instant case on the basis of the difference in the character of the victims of the homicide is more incidental than legally significant so far as relevancy to the felony-murder rule is concerned: *   *   *. In other words, if a felon can be held for murder for a killing occurring during the course of a felony, even though the death was not inflicted by one of the felons but by someone acting in hostility to them, it should make no difference to the crime of murder who the victim of the homicide happened to be." *Redline*, 391 Pa. at page 509, 137 A.2d at page 483.

The "distinction" *Redline* half-heartedly tries to draw has not escaped criticism from the commentators. While the result reached in *Redline* and most of its reasoning have met with almost unanimous approval, the *deus ex machina* ending has been condemned. One learned journal has commented:

> "It seems, however, that Almeida cannot validly be distinguished from [Redline]. The probability that a felon will be killed seems at least as great as the probability that the victim will be an innocent bystander. Any distinction based on the fact that the killing of a felon by a policeman is sanctioned by the law and therefore justifiable, while the killing of an innocent bystander is merely excusable, seems unwarranted. No criminal sanctions now attach to either in other areas of criminal law, and any distinction here would seem anomalous. Indeed, to make the result hinge on the character of the victim is, in many instances, to make it hinge on

16. 71 Harv.L.Rev. [1565,] 1566 [(1958)];
See, to similar effect, 106 U.Pa.L.Rev.
[1176,] 1178 [(1958)].

the marksmanship of resisters. Any attempt to distinguish between the cases on the theory that the cofelon assumes the risk of being killed would also be improper since this tort doctrine has no place in the criminal law in which the wrong to be redressed is a public one—a killing with the victim's consent is nevertheless murder. It is very doubtful that public desire for vengeance should alone justify a conviction of felony murder for the death of an innocent bystander when no criminal responsibility will attach for the death of a cofelon." [16]

Redline concluded, at page 510, 137 A.2d at page 483, in this manner: "The limitation which we thus place on the decision in the Almeida case renders unnecessary any present reconsideration of the extended holding of that case. It will be time enough for action in such regard if and when a conviction for murder based on facts similar to those presented by the Almeida case (both as to the performer of the lethal act and the status of its victim) should again come before this court." The time is now. The facts are not merely similar to those of *Almeida*; they are identical, Smith and Almeida being cofelons. The case law of centuries and the force of reason, both dealt with in great detail in *Redline* and above, require us to overrule *Almeida*.

The order of the court below is reversed, an appeal is allowed *nunc pro tunc,* and a new trial is granted.

NOTES

1. How can situations like those in *Almeida, Thomas,* and *Redline* be distinguished from situations in which the felony murder rule should be applied? Can this be done in a manner consistent with the purported function of the felony murder rule? In People v. Washington, 62 Cal.2d 777, 44 Cal.Rptr. 442, 402 P.2d 130 (1965) Chief Justice Traynor argued that the sole purpose of the felony-murder rule is to deter felons from killing negligently or accidentally. He then suggested that holding a defendant guilty of murder where the act of killing was not committed by him or an accomplice acting in furtherance of their common design would extend the rule beyond the function it is designed to serve. Does this explanation stand up under analysis? For example, could it reasonably be expected that the existence of a felony-murder rule might deter felons from creating dangerous situations during the commission of a felony that might cause others to kill? For example, might other felons in Almeida's situation be expected to surrender when confronted by approaching police officers rather than begin a combined gun battle and chase? In any case, would any such expectation be less reasonable than the expectation that imposing liability upon a co-felon will somehow deter felons from killing negligently or accidentally?

2. It has been held that in some circumstances at least, actions during an armed robbery are sufficiently life-endangering to justify a finding of implied malice aforethought and make a resulting killing murder on that theory. See Taylor v. Superior Court, 3 Cal.3d 578, 91 Cal.Rptr. 275, 477 P. 2d 131 (1970).

5. VOLUNTARY MANSLAUGHTER

LANG v. STATE

Court of Special Appeals of Maryland, 1969.
6 Md.App. 128, 250 A.2d 276, certiorari denied 396 U.S. 971,
90 S.Ct. 457, 24 L.Ed.2d 438.

PER CURIAM. The appellant, John Frederick Lang, was convicted of assault with intent to murder by a jury in the Criminal Court of Baltimore, Judge Meyer M. Cardin presiding. He was sentenced to ten years under the jurisdiction of the Department of Correction.

In this appeal the following questions are properly before us:

(1) Did the lower court err in failing to instruct the jury that a homicide, if committed in the "heat of passion", is reduced from murder to manslaughter; thereby reducing the crime charged, assault with intent to murder, to assault?

* * *

The exact point of dispute is whether there was sufficient evidence adduced at trial to support an instruction on the heat of passion doctrine. * * *

The relevant elements of the heat of passion doctrine are (a) that there must be passion actually aroused in the actor, (b) that such passion must be an intensity sufficient to obscure the reason of the actor, and, (c) that such passion must be due to a legally adequate provocation. Thus, in order for instruction regarding heat of passion to be required, evidence must be introduced from which the jury could have found each of the above mentioned elements. We shall consider the elements seriatim.

Evidence was introduced which could support a finding that appellant was in passionate anger or, what is more likely, that he was in passionate terror. As we mentioned above, this element involves the appellant's subjective state of mind. One witness testified that the appellant "must have been awfully scared because he looked * * * like animals * * * he was all shakey * * * his face was sort of distorted * * * how you get when when you're real mad or something." Another witness testified that appellant "looked pretty scared * * * his face didn't seem contorted." The appellant himself testified as follows:

"Q. Why did you shoot him?

"A. I was scared. I didn't know what he was going to do.

"Q.   What were you scared of?

"A.   I was scared of him, what he was going to do. I didn't know if he had a gun or what."

This testimony might also have been sufficient to support a finding that the anger or terror was sufficiently intense to obscure the appellant's reason, again a subjective inquiry.

With respect to the element of adequate provocation, the evidence showed that immediately before the shooting the victim called the appellant "a chump" and "a chicken," dared the appellant to fight, shouted obscenities at the appellant, pointed his finger at the appellant, and shook his fist at the appellant, all of this occurring at distances variously ranging from five to thirty feet. The victim was approximately fifteen feet from the appellant when shot. During the entire incident the victim was on the lawn outside of the appellant's apartment and the appellant was inside the apartment. During the latter part of the incident the appellant was standing at his window. The window sill was approximately four feet from the ground level and under the window was a window well six to seven feet in length and three to four feet in depth, with no figure given at trial as to width.

At this point our inquiry becomes an objective one, namely, whether the above facts constitute such provocation as would drive a reasonable and ordinary man into passionate anger or terror. It is generally held that mere words, threats, menaces or gestures, however offensive and insulting, do not constitute adequate provocation. However, there is authority that sufficient provocation may consist of words accompanied by conduct indicating a present intention and ability to cause the appellant bodily harm. In the instant case we understand the provocation to be merely words and gestures. The record shows no indication that the victim had a present *intention* to cause the appellant bodily harm; he (the victim) certainly made no attempt to enter the apartment through the door, and he showed no inclination to try to climb through the window. Without entering the apartment he had no present *ability* to harm the appellant, as he was unarmed during the entire incident.

We hold, therefore, that merely shouting epithets such as "chump" and "chicken," or shouting obscene words, or shaking finger or hand at the appellant, where there is no evidence of a present intent or ability to cause the appellant bodily harm will not constitute legally sufficient provocation for purposes of requiring an instruction on heat of passion. Thus it was not error for the trial court to refuse such an instruction.

NOTES

1. Concerning the effect which the provocation must have upon the killer, consider the following passage from State v. Davis, 50 S.C. 405, 27 S.E. 905, 911–12 (1897):

It is contended that there was error in the following charge: "Now, as I said before, if the testimony in this case (and you are the sole judges of that) satisfies you that the defendant here took the life of the deceased in sudden heat and passion, and upon sufficient legal provocation, and the deceased said anything or did anything to the defendant which was calculated to highly exasperate and inflame and arouse his passion, so that he had an uncontrollable impulse, and he was so inflamed with passion that he hardly knew what he was doing, and in that heat and passion he took the life of the deceased, without malice, then you can find him guilty of manslaughter." It is objected that this charge (1) prescribed a stricter rule than that required by law as to the degree of heat and passion necessary to reduce the killing from murder to manslaughter; * * The circuit judge correctly defined "manslaughter" as the killing of any human being, without malice, in sudden heat and passion, and upon sufficient legal provocation. It is contended, however, that he was not authorized to go further, and add words indicating that the heat and passion should amount to an "uncontrollable impulse," and that passion should so inflame that "he hardly knew what he was doing." * * * In the case of State v. Hill, 4 Dev. & B. 491 relied on by appellant, Gaston, J., said: "We nowhere find that the passion which in law rebuts the imputation of malice must be so overpowering as for the time to shut out knowledge and destroy volition. All the writers concur in representing this indulgence of the law to be a condescension to the frailty of the human frame, which, during the furor brevis, renders a man deaf to the voice of reason, so that, although the act done was intentional of death, it was not the result of malignity of heart, but imputable to human infirmity." "The provocation by the deceased must be the direct and controlling cause of the passion, and it must be such as naturally and instantly to produce in the minds of persons ordinarily constituted the highest degree of exasperation, rage, anger, sudden resentment, or terror, rendering the mind incapable of cool reflection." 9 Am. & Eng.Enc.Law, p. 579. In State v. Smith, 10 Rich.Law, 347, the passion which reduces a felonious killing to manslaughter is characterized as a "temporary phrensy excited by sufficient legal provocation"; and in State v. McCants, 1 Speer, *390, Judge Wardlaw speaks of this passion as "the violent impulse of anger, outstripping the tardier operations of reason, provoked by sufficient cause." It may be concluded, therefore, that "the sudden heat and passion, upon sufficient legal provocation," which mitigates a felonious killing to manslaughter, while it need not dethrone reason entirely, or shut out knowledge and volition, must be such as would naturally disturb the sway of reason, and render the mind of an ordinary person incapable of cool reflection, and produce what, according to human experience, may be called an "uncontrollable impulse to do violence."

We do not think the charge of the judge went beyond the limits above prescribed, and it was therefore not error, in so far as his charge relates to acts which the law deems adequate to provoke such passion.

See generally, Note, Manslaughter and the Adequacy of Provocation: The Reasonableness of the Reasonable Man, 106 U.Pa.L.Rev. 1021 (1958).

2. Why, as a matter of policy, should the fact that a killing was in response to adequate provocation reduce the grade of the offense for which the defendant is liable? Reconsider the material at pages 438–39, supra, concerning the significance of deliberation and impulse in grading liability.

3. Brett, The Physiology of Provocation, [1970] Crim.L.Rev. 634 suggests that individuals vary significantly in their physiological response to stress. "Fight or flight" reactions, caused by a complex relationship between the hypothalamus (a small area at the base of the brain), hormones, and the brain, include changes in pulse rate, blood pressure, level of blood glucose, and sensory perception. If this evidence that some persons are highly vulnerable to stress and others strikingly resistant to it is credited, "it at once becomes clear that the reasonable man of provocation law is a figment of the imagination." Id. at 637. An objective standard might still be justified, Brett notices, on the possibility that an individual can learn to modify and to some extent control the degree of intensity of his "fight or flight" reactions:

> [T]hat argument must stand or fall on the proposition that learning of the convictions of others for murder will act as a stimulus to people to start learning to control their reactions. There is not the slightest evidence to suppose that this educative or deterrent effect will occur, and, I would think, every reason to suppose that it will not.

Id. at 638. If the reasonable person standard is not—or cannot be— abolished, Brett recommends the use of evidence of the accused's physiological reactions under experimentally-induced conditions of stress to establish that he is close to the sensitive end of the range of "normal" reaction to stress. But he then observes:

> [A]ny attempt to * * * allow production of evidence as to ordinary behavior emanating from psychiatrists, psychologists, and sociologists, is likely to be met with the justifiable observation that much of what is currently bandied around as established scientific fact is in truth largely speculation, lacking in any scientific foundation * * *.

Id. at 640. Would it be reasonable to modify the objective provocation standard by permitting defendants to establish that they were physiologically abnormal but to deny them the opportunity to show psychological abnormality?

4. The cases frequently speak of "mutual combat" as adequate provocation to reduce a killing from murder to manslaughter. Mutual combat arises where the victim and the defendant intend to fight and are ready to do so, and the defendant acts in the "heat of blood" engendered by the situation. It is not necessary that blows have actually been struck for mutual combat to exist, but if any blows have been struck it is not material which participant struck the first blow or that the deceased may have struck no blows at all. See Whitehead v. State, 9 Md.App. 7, 262 A.2d 316 (1970).

But see also United States v. Hardin, 443 F.2d 735, 738 n. 6 (D.C.Cir. 1970): "[M]utual combat alone is not a true alternative ground for mitigating a murder to manslaughter; it is merely one of the circumstances from which the jury could find adequate provocation." If this is accurate, under what circumstances should mutual combat constitute adequate provocation? The court in Whitehead v. State, supra, noted that in that case "the [trial] court did not find that an unfair advantage was taken by appellant at the outset of the combat or that at the commencement of the contest they did not start on equal terms." Is this relevant? controlling?

5. Defendant stabbed decedent. One witness testifies that he saw defendant on top of decedent and that defendant threatened to cut decedent's head off and "to kill this honkey." Another witness testifies that before defendant and decedent fell to the floor in the altercation, "he heard the decedent call defendant a "black son-of-a bitch" and saw him slap defendant a couple of times." Is defendant entitled to an instruction on voluntary manslaughter in a prosecution for second degree murder? See State v. Fulford, 290 Minn. 236, 187 N.W.2d 270, 274 (1971): "Such provocation would, as a matter of law, be insufficient to cause the reasonably induced 'heat of passion' reducing the crime to manslaughter." Compare the concurring opinion, describing such a dismissal of the matter as "cavalier." 187 N.W.2d at 276. In resolving the matter, is the race of the defendant relevant? The race of the decedent? The cultural background of the defendant? His political and social beliefs and experience? Should any of these matters be relevant?

Consider Howard, What Colour is the "Reasonable Man"? [1961] Crim. L.Rev. 41, describing the application of the English provocation standard in the Northern Territory of Australia in cases wherein the defendant is an aborigine. In practice, Howard observes, the reasonable person standard is modified, so that the jury is asked to determine whether an ordinary reasonable aborigine in the specific vicinity would have been adequately provoked by the situation. This, he concludes, is adequate and just. But he emphasizes that the white and aborigine populations are relatively even in size, live apart and have room to do so, and as a result it is not difficult to distinguish between the different influences at work on members of the two racial groups:

> The case is very different where members of one community voluntarily join another, perhaps altogether strange in background and customs, for some economic advantage. In this situation it is reasonable that the new comers should take their adopted country as they find it, even if, as often happens, they tend to preserve their own customs and language in a separate sub-community. The law would be over-complicated if a Jamaican who killed another Jamaican in London were entitled to an inquiry by the jury whether at the time of the killing he was more under the influence of Jamaican than of English customs.

Id. at 47. Are these conclusions correct? What, if any, relevance do they have for the issues posed by State v. Fulford? For a discussion of similar difficulties in defining the term "ordinary person" in a provocation formula in Papua and New Guina, see O'Regan, Provocation and Homicide in Papua and New Guinea, 10 West.Aust.L.Rev. 1, 8–12 (1971). See generally, Brown, The "Ordinary Man" in Provocation: Anglo-Saxon Attitudes and "Unreasonable Non-Englishmen," 13 Int. & Comp.L.Q. 203 (1964).

6. In People v. Pecora, 107 Ill.App.2d 283, 246 N.E.2d 865 (1969), appellant was charged with the murder of his ex-wife. The following evidence was offered:

(1) In a custody battle concerning the children of the marriage, the ex-wife had been "cited" for immoral conduct before the children.

(2) Defendant was a member of St. Mary's Roman Catholic Church.

(3) On the evening before the killing, the deceased told the defendant that he did not know how to make love, that she had been intimate with five men, and that she had had an abortion before she married the defendant.

(4) On the evening of the killing, defendant begged the deceased to "stop her immoral conduct and to get together with him again," but "she said that she did not want any part of it because she was having too good a time."

(5) Defendant had been diagnosed as a "schizoid personality" with a "paranoid reaction," had exhibited anger and hostility towards his ex-wife, and had been hospitalized for his emotional problems.

(6) The killing occurred after the deceased made a "flip" response to defendant's plea that she give them another chance.

(7) The deceased's body contained twenty-one stab wounds.

Which of these items should be admitted as evidence? Should the jury be instructed on voluntary manslaughter? In the case cited, all of the information was received, apparently without objection, but the trial court refused to instruct on manslaughter and this was affirmed on appeal.

---

6. INVOLUNTARY MANSLAUGHTER

---

a. NEGLIGENT OMISSION

COMMONWEALTH v. WELANSKY

Supreme Judicial Court of Massachusetts, 1944.
316 Mass. 383, 55 N.E.2d 902.

LUMMUS, Justice. On November 28, 1942, and for about nine years before that day, a corporation named New Cocoanut Grove, Inc., maintained and operated a "night club" in Boston, having an entrance at 17 Piedmont Street, for the furnishing to the public for compensation of food, drink and entertainment, consisting of orchestra and band music, singing and dancing. It employed about eighty persons. The corporation, its officers and employees, and its business, were completely dominated by the defendant Barnett Welansky, who is called in this opinion simply the defendant, since his codefendants were acquitted by the jury. He owned, and held in his own name or in the names of others, all the capital stock. He leased some of the land on which the corporate business was carried on, and owned the rest, although title was held for him by his sister. He was entitled to, and took, all the profits. Internally, the corporation was operated without regard to corporate forms, as though the business were that of the defendant as an individual. It was not shown that responsibility for the number or condition of safety exits had been delegated by the defendant to any employee or other person.

The defendant was accustomed to spend his evenings at the night club, inspecting the premises and superintending the business. On November 16, 1942, he became suddenly ill, and was carried to a hospital, where he was in bed for three weeks and remained until discharged on December 11, 1942. During his stay at the hospital, although employees visited him there, he did not concern himself with the night club, because, as he testified, he "knew it would be all right" and that "the same system * * * [he] had would continue" during his absence. There is no evidence of any act, omission or condition at the night club on November 28, 1942 (apart from the lighting of a match hereinafter described), that was not within the usual and regular practice during the time before the defendant was taken ill when he was at the night club nearly every evening. While the defendant was at the hospital, his brother James Welansky and an employee named Jacob Goldfine, who were made codefendants, assumed some of the defendant's duties at the night club, but made no change in methods. * * *

A little after ten o'clock on the evening of Saturday, November 28, 1942, the night club was well filled with a crowd of patrons. It was during the busiest season of the year. An important football game in the afternoon had attracted many visitors to Boston. Witnesses were rightly permitted to testify that the dance floor had from eighty to one hundred persons on it, and that it was "very crowded." Witnesses were rightly permitted to give their estimates, derived from their observations, of the number of patrons in various parts of the night club. Upon the evidence it could have been found that at that time there were from two hundred fifty to four hundred persons in the Melody Lounge, from four hundred to five hundred in the main dining room and the Caricature Bar, and two hundred fifty in the Cocktail Lounge. Yet it could have been found that the crowd was no larger than it had been on other Saturday evenings before the defendant was taken ill, and that there had been larger crowds at earlier times. There were about seventy tables in the dining room, each seating from two to eight persons. There was testimony that all but two were taken. Many persons were standing in various rooms. The defendant testified that the reasonable capacity of the night club, exclusive of the new Cocktail Lounge, was six hundred fifty patrons. He never saw the new Cocktail Lounge with the furniture installed, but it was planned to accommodate from one hundred to one hundred twenty-five patrons.

A bartender in the Melody Lounge noticed that an electric light bulb which was in or near the cocoanut husks of an artificial palm tree in the corner had been turned off and that the corner was dark. He directed a sixteen year old bar boy who was waiting on customers at the tables to cause the bulb to be lighted. A soldier sitting with other persons near the light told the bar boy to leave it unlighted. But the bar boy got a stool, lighted a match in order to see the bulb, turned the bulb in its socket, and thus lighted it. The bar boy blew the match out, and started to walk away. Apparently the flame of the match had ignited the palm tree and that had speedily ignited the low cloth ceiling near it, for both flamed up almost instantly. The fire spread with great rapidity across the upper part of the room, causing much heat. The crowd in the Melody Lounge rushed up the stairs, but the fire preceded them. People got on fire while on the stairway. The fire spread with great speed across the foyer and into the Caricature Bar and the main dining room, and thence into the Cocktail Lounge. Soon after the fire started the lights in the night club went out. The smoke had a peculiar odor. The crowd were panic stricken, and rushed and pushed in every direction through the night club, screaming, and overturning tables and chairs in their attempts to escape.

The door at the head of the Melody Lounge stairway was not opened until firemen broke it down from outside with an axe and found it locked by a key lock, so that the panic bar could not operate. Two dead bodies were found close to it, and a pile of bodies about seven feet from it. The door in the vestibule of the office did not become open, and was barred by the clothing rack. The revolving door soon jammed, but was burst out by the pressure of the crowd. The head waiter and another waiter tried to get open the panic doors from the main dining room to Shawmut Street, and succeeded after some difficulty. The other two doors to Shawmut Street were locked, and were opened by force from outside by firemen and others. Some patrons escaped through them, but many dead bodies were piled up inside them. A considerable number of patrons escaped through the Broadway door, but many died just inside that door. Some employees, and a great number of patrons died in the fire. Others were taken out of the building with fatal burns and injuries from smoke, and died within a few days.

* * *

The defendant, his brother James Welansky, and Jacob Goldfine, were indicted for manslaughter in sixteen counts of an indictment * * *[.] Voluntarily the Commonwealth filed specifications as to those counts, by which it specified among other things that the alleged misconduct of the defendant consisted in causing or permitting or failing reasonably to prevent defective wiring, the installation of inflammable decorations, the absence of fire doors, the absence of "proper means of egress properly maintained" and "sufficient proper" exits, and overcrowding.

The defendant was found guilty * * *[.] He was sentenced to imprisonment in the State prison upon each count for a term of not less than twelve years and not more than fifteen years, the first day of said term to be in solitary confinement and the residue at hard labor *   *   *, the sentences to run concurrently.

The Commonwealth disclaimed any contention that the defendant intentionally killed or injured the persons named in the indictments as victims. It based its case on involuntary manslaughter through wanton or reckless conduct. The judge instructed the jury correctly with respect to the nature of such conduct.

Usually wanton or reckless conduct consists of an affirmative act, like driving an automobile or discharging a firearm, in disregard of probable harmful consequences to another. But where as in the present case there is a duty of care for the safety of business visitors invited to premises which the defendant controls, wanton or reckless conduct may consist of intentional failure to take such care in disregard of the probable harmful consequences to them or of their right to care. *   *   *

To define wanton or reckless conduct so as to distinguish it clearly from negligence and gross negligence is not easy. *   *   * Sometimes the word "wilful" is prefaced to the words "wanton" and "reckless" in expressing the concept. That only blurs it. Wilful means intentional. In the phrase "wilful, wanton or reckless conduct," if "wilful" modifies "conduct" it introduces something different from wanton or reckless conduct, even though the legal result is the same. Wilfully causing harm is a wrong, but a different wrong from wantonly or recklessly causing harm. If "wilful" modifies "wanton or reckless conduct" its use is accurate. What must be intended is the conduct, not the resulting harm. *   *   * The words "wanton" and "reckless" are practically synonymous in this connection, although the word "wanton" may contain a suggestion of arrogance or insolence or heartlessness that is lacking in the word "reckless." But intentional conduct to which either word applies is followed by the same legal consequences as though both words applied.

The standard of wanton or reckless conduct is at once subjective and objective *   *   *[.] Knowing facts that would cause a reasonable man to know the danger is equivalent to knowing the danger. *   *   * The judge charged the jury correctly when he said, "To constitute wanton or reckless conduct, as distinguished from mere negligence, grave danger to others must have been apparent and the defendant must have chosen to run the risk rather than alter his conduct so as to avoid the act or omission which caused the harm. If the grave danger was in fact realized by the defendant, his subsequent voluntary act or omission which caused the harm amounts to wanton or reckless conduct, no matter whether the ordinary man would have realized the gravity of the danger or not. But even if a particular defendant is so stupid [or] so heedless *   *   * that in fact he did not realize the grave danger, he cannot escape the imputation of wanton or reckless conduct in his dangerous act or omission, if an ordinary normal man under the same circumstances would have realized the gravity of the danger. A man may be reckless within the meaning of the law although he himself thought he was careful."

The essence of wanton or reckless conduct is intentional conduct, by way either of commission or of omission where there is a duty to act, which conduct involves a high degree of likelihood that substantial harm will result to another. Wanton or reckless conduct amounts to what has been variously described as indifference to or disregard of probable consequences to that other * * * or the rights of that other. * * * But we are not prepared to give unqualified approval to a further statement found in some of our reported decisions, for example in Query v. Howe, 273 Mass. 92, 96, 172 N.E. 887, that to constitute wanton or reckless conduct, disregard of the rights of another must be as complete or utter as though such rights did not exist. If taken literally, that statement would permit a trifling regard for the rights of another to exonerate a defendant from the criminal consequences of flagrant wrongdoing.

The words "wanton" and "reckless" are thus not merely rhetorical or vituperative expressions used instead of negligent or grossly negligent. They express a difference in the degree of risk and in the voluntary taking of risk so marked, as compared with negligence, as to amount substantially and in the eyes of the law to a difference in kind. * * * For many years this court has been careful to preserve the distinction between negligence and gross negligence, on the one hand, and wanton or reckless conduct on the other. * * *

Notwithstanding language used commonly in earlier cases, and occasionally in later ones,[3] it is now clear in this Commonwealth that at common law conduct does not become criminal until it passes the borders of negligence and gross negligence and enters into the domain of wanton or reckless conduct. There is in Massachusetts at common law no such thing as "criminal negligence." * * *

If by wanton or reckless conduct bodily injury is caused to another, the person guilty of such conduct is guilty of assault and battery. * * * And since manslaughter is simply a battery that causes death * * *, if death results he is guilty of manslaughter. * * *

To convict the defendant of manslaughter, the Commonwealth was not required to prove that he caused the fire by some wanton or reckless conduct. Fire in a place of public resort is an ever present danger. It was enough to prove that death resulted from his wanton

3. In early cases what is now known as wanton or reckless conduct was variously described as wilful negligence, wanton negligence, gross negligence, and culpable negligence * * *. So in criminal cases what was necessary to make conduct criminal was often so described. The expression "criminal negligence" was often used. But it seems that what we now know as wanton or reckless conduct was in fact required. The terminology, not the law, is what has changed. * * *

In other jurisdictions a variety of similar expressions has been used in describing conduct that will create criminal liability. But in many of them the substantial equivalent of wanton or reckless conduct is required. * *

or reckless disregard of the safety of patrons in the event of fire from any cause.

* * *

Judgments affirmed.

NOTES

1. What factors are relevant in determining whether a defendant's actions justify a conviction of involuntary manslaughter? Consider United States v. Escamilla, 467 F.2d 341 (4th Cir. 1972) (en banc). Escamilla and the deceased were members of a research team on T—3, "an island of glacial ice * * * which meanders slowly about the general area of the Arctic Ocean." During the summer months, it was virtually impossible to reach the island from the outside. There was no organized law enforcement, and "discipline and order on the island depended upon the cooperation of all of the men and the effectiveness of the group leader." Escamilla caused the death of the deceased on July 16 during a dispute concerning whether another member of the party, whose drinking and resultant violent behavior had become a problem, should be given some of Escamilla's wine. Escamilla had been waving a loaded gun at the deceased, and at trial he claimed it discharged accidentally; there was evidence that the gun was defective in that it tended to discharge without having the trigger pulled. The prosecution contended that Escamilla's actions in waiving a loaded gun at the deceased constituted gross negligence for purposes of liability for manslaughter. Escamilla requested that the jury be instructed as follows:

> In determining whether or not the defendant is guilty of involuntary manslaughter, the jury must measure his conduct against all of the existing circumstances and determine therefrom whether what he did was in its nature dangerous to life or grossly negligent. Some of the circumstances you may consider in this case are the location of the alleged act, and its lack of law enforcement and medical facilities * ˣ *.

Should such an instruction have been given? Why, or why not? If the circumstances mentioned are relevant, does the offered instruction make clear how they are to be considered? Could this be made clearer? How?

2. For discussions of the English law, see Turpin, Mens Rea in Manslaughter, 1962 Cambridge L.J. 200; Walker, Mens Rea in Manslaughter, 117 New.L.J. 950 (1967). Canadian law is emphasized in O'Hearn, Criminal Negligence: An Analysis in Depth, 7 Crim.L.Q. 27 (1964), 7 Crim.L.Q. 407 (1965). The development of American manslaughter law is dealt with in Coldiron, Historical Development of Manslaughter, 38 Ky.L.J. 527 (1950).

---

b. THE "UNLAWFUL ACT" DOCTRINE

STATE v. GIBSON

Court of Special Appeals of Maryland, 1968.
4 Md.App. 236, 242 A.2d 575, affirmed 254 Md. 399, 254 A.2d 691.

MURPHY, Chief Judge. A six-count indictment was returned against appellee Gibson by the Grand Jury of Baltimore County as a result of the death on September 10, 1966 of Diane Grempler by reason of appellee's alleged illegal and improper operation of a motor vehicle. Each of the first three counts of the indictment charged that appellee "did feloniously kill and slay" the deceased as a direct result of his commission of certain statutory misdemeanors, viz., that he operated his motor vehicle in violation of the motor vehicle laws of Maryland, Maryland Code (1967 Repl.Vol.) Article 66½, and more specifically:

1. *As to the first count*—that appellee, in violation of Sections 233 and 242, did fail to stop his motor vehicle in obedience to a stop sign and grant the right of way to a vehicle traveling on a paved highway.

2. *As to the second count*—that appellee, in violation of Section 209, recklessly operated his motor vehicle upon a public highway.

3. *As to the third count*—that appellee, in violation of Section 206, operated his motor vehicle under the influence of intoxicating liquors.

The fourth count of the indictment charged that appellee "did feloniously kill and slay" the deceased as a direct result of his commission of a misdemeanor, *viz.*, that he violated the provisions of Section 19.2 of the Baltimore County Code in that he bought, consumed, and possessed an alcoholic beverage on a public highway, he then being a minor.

Each of the first four counts of the indictment expressly characterized the offenses therein charged as constituting a "common law misdemeanor—manslaughter."

The fifth count of the indictment charged that appellee, while operating a motor vehicle "unlawfully in a grossly negligent manner" caused the death of the decedent. This count of the indictment was expressly based upon Section 388 of Article 27 of the Maryland Code (1967 Repl.Vol.), which provides, in pertinent part, as follows:

> "Every person causing the death of another as the result of the driving, operation or control of an automobile, motor vehicle, motorboat, locomotive, engine, car, streetcar, train or other vehicle in a grossly negligent manner, shall be guilty of a misdemeanor to be known as 'manslaughter by automobile, motor vehicle, motorboat, locomotive, engine, car, streetcar, train or other vehicle,' and the person so convicted shall be sentenced to jail or the house of correction for not more than three years, or be fined not more than $1,000.-00 or be both fined and imprisoned.   *   *   * "

*   *   *

On June 28, 1967, Judge W. Albert Menchine in the Circuit Court for Baltimore County, granted appellee's motion to dismiss [the first four counts of the indictment] stating in a brief opinion accompanying his order that under the common law, a showing of gross negli-

gence was the main requirement for conviction of involuntary manslaughter; and that as none of the four counts alleged either an intention or purpose to harm in the operation of a motor vehicle, or the
existence of gross negligence, such counts were not legally sufficient
to charge a common law offense. The State has appealed from that
order.

The State contends that involuntary manslaughter at common law
consisted of an unintentional killing while doing some unlawful act
not amounting to a felony, nor naturally tending to cause death or
great bodily harm, or in negligently doing some act lawful in itself.
More particularly, it differentiates the two classes of involuntary
manslaughter by characterizing the first class as comprising all those
cases wherein the defendant has caused the death of another as a
direct and proximate result of doing an unlawful act not amounting
to a felony, i.e., a misdemeanor (misdemeanor-manslaughter). As to
this category of involuntary manslaughter, the State urges that the
existence of negligence is not an element of the offense; that the doing of an unlawful act, which is *malum in se* or which if *malum prohibitum*,[b] was in violation of a statute provided to prevent injury to
the person, constitutes involuntary manslaughter irrespective of the
existence of negligence. The State identifies the second distinct class
of involuntary manslaughter as comprising those cases where the
defendant, while doing a lawful act in a grossly negligent manner,
kills.

It is the State's position that the common law misdemeanor-manslaughter rule is applicable in Maryland and has not been revised,
amended or repealed by the manslaughter by automobile statute (Section 388), which it contends applies only to a case where the defendant is charged with an unintentional killing in the course of doing a
lawful act in an unlawful manner, i.e., driving a motor vehicle in a
grossly negligent manner. It is upon this premise that the State
maintains that the first four counts of the indictment properly charged
the offense of common law manslaughter in that the appellee operated his vehicle in violation of the law in the four particulars set
forth in counts one through four of the indictment; that the first
three of these are *mala in se*, but even if *mala prohibita*, they were
violations of statutes calculated to prevent injury to the person.

The appellee, on the other hand, urges that the common law
crime of involuntary manslaughter where homicide was the unintentional result of an automobile accident has been repealed by Section
388, and that all cases involving the unintentional killing of a person
by an automobile can only be prosecuted under the manslaughter by
automobile statute; and that in such prosecutions the State carries

b. These terms are commonly employed
to distinguish crimes into two classes: mala in se, which are inherently
wrong, usually involving danger to
life or limb and having criminal intent as an element; and mala prohibita; which are wrong only because
so pronounced by statute.

the burden of proving gross negligence in order to obtain a conviction.

Manslaughter is a common law offense and a felony in Maryland; it may be voluntary or involuntary, depending upon the requisite intent, and since the crime is not defined by statute, it is afforded its common law meaning in this State. * * * By Section 387 of Article 27 of the Maryland Code, manslaughter, whether voluntary or involuntary, is punishable by a term of imprisonment not exceeding ten years. The crime of manslaughter by automobile created by Section 388 is a separate statutory misdemeanor, unknown to the common law, and is punishable under the statute by a designated fine and/or imprisonment in jail or the house of correction for a term not to exceed three years.

Involuntary manslaughter at common law has been generally defined as the killing of another unintentionally and without malice (1) in doing some unlawful act not amounting to a felony, or (2) in negligently doing some act lawful in itself, or (3) by the negligent omission to perform a legal duty. * * *

It is well settled in this State that where a charge of involuntary manslaughter is predicated on negligently doing some act lawful in itself, or by negligently failing to perform a legal duty (the second and third classes of involuntary manslaughter above delineated), the negligence necessary to support a conviction must be gross or criminal, *viz.*, such as manifests a wanton or reckless disregard of human life. * * * It is equally well settled that the Legislature, in enacting Section 388, making it a misdemeanor to cause the death of another as a result of operating an automobile "in a grossly negligent manner," intended to adopt this same standard of gross negligence (a wanton or reckless disregard of human life) as the minimum requirement to support a conviction for this statutory offense. * * *

It is likewise clear that the Maryland cases have generally recognized that a charge of involuntary manslaughter at common law could in some circumstances at least be based on the doing of an unlawful act. * * * [The cases] * * * seemingly share a common thread—that where a prosecution for involuntary manslaughter is based on the commission of an unlawful act causing death, the act must itself be dangerous to life. * * *

It is against this background that we examine whether the first four counts of the indictment returned against the appellee—which are expressly bottomed upon the applicability of the so called misdemeanor-manslaughter rule (an unintended homicide committed in the course of doing an unlawful act, i.e., committing a misdemeanor)— properly charge an existing offense in this State, when considered in light of the provisions of Section 388 and of the legislative intention in enacting that statute.

We note at the outset that the manner of operating a motor vehicle is commonly regulated in detail by statute or ordinance and that it is an unlawful act in itself to drive a vehicle in violation of such laws. It is not, however, a generally accepted rule that the fact alone that the operator of an automobile was violating the motor vehicle laws when his car struck and killed a person renders him, without more, guilty of involuntary manslaughter at common law. The authorities are divided on the question, some holding, as in State v. Hupf, 9 Terry 254, 101 A.2d 355 (Del.), that where a person violates a traffic statute which proximately results in the death of another, he is guilty of involuntary manslaughter, without regard to whether the violation was *malum prohibitum* or *malum in se*, and irrespective of whether there was any proof that the motorist's conduct evidenced a wanton or reckless disregard for the lives and safety of others. Other authorities support the view as articulated in State v. Strobel, 130 Mont. 442, 304 P.2d 606, that such violations of law proximately resulting in the death of another, whether the violation was *malum in se*, or *malum prohibitum*, do not constitute involuntary manslaughter, unless the element of criminal negligence is also present. Still other authorities distinguish between unlawful acts *mala prohibita* and *mala in se*, and conclude in effect, that where the violation was merely *malum prohibitum*, no criminal homicide results, unless the violation was dangerous to life and constituted a reckless disregard for the safety of others; but that where the unlawful act underlying death was *malum in se* the violator would be guilty of involuntary manslaughter, even though the unlawful act was not calculated to cause death. * * *

While [the] cases might be construed to place Maryland among those authorities which hold that an unintentional killing committed in the course of doing some non-felonious unlawful act dangerous to life or *malum in se*, constitutes involuntary manslaughter at common law, irrespective of the existence of criminal negligence, we are persuaded that if such was ever the law of this State, it no longer has any application to those cases where the homicide results unintentionally from the operation of a motor vehicle—it being our view that such cases can only be prosecuted under Section 388.

There is no legislative history to which we may turn to ascertain the exact reach of Section 388, or of the effect of that statute upon the common law felony of involuntary manslaughter. We think it plain, however, that when Section 388 was enacted by Chapter 414 of the Acts of 1941, there then existed much confusion and little enlightenment among the authorities with respect to which of the several theories underlying application of the misdemeanor-manslaughter rule was the correct one. Quite clearly, where such unintentional homicides proximately resulted from driving an automobile in violation of laws designed to regulate and control the operation of motor vehicles in the interest of public safety there was an overlapping and blurring between and among the different theories of criminal responsibility, since in most instances such a violation constituted not only an unlawful act, but one dangerous to the lives and safety of others and such as manifested a wanton and reckless disregard of human life. We believe that the Legislature in enacting Section 388 to punish persons who cause the death of another "as the result of the driving, operation or control of an automobile   *   *   *   in a grossly negligent manner," intended to treat all unintended homicides thereby resulting in the same way, without regard to whether the homicide occurred in the course of doing a lawful or an unlawful act, or whether such act was *malum in se* or merely *malum prohibitum*. To otherwise conclude would be to attribute an intention to the Legislature to permit the prosecution of offenders either for the felony of common law manslaughter, with its ten-year penalty, or for the statutory misdemeanor of manslaughter by automobile, with its three-year penalty, even though, where the prosecution is based upon gross negligence, the proof necessary to justify a conviction in either case would be precisely the same (a wanton or reckless disregard of human life). A similarly incongruous result would follow from attributing an intention to the Legislature to permit a felony conviction and ten-year sentence upon simple proof that the accidental homicide occurred in the commission of an unlawful act (a misdemeanor), while requiring a greater degree of proof under the statute to support a conviction for a lesser grade of homicide, a misdemeanor punishable by a maximum of three years imprisonment. In construing statutes, results that are unreasonable or inconsistent with common sense should be avoided, whenever possible. We conclude, therefore, that in enacting Section 388, the Legislature intended to deal with an entire subject matter-unintended homicides resulting from the operation of a motor vehicle—and that the common law crime of involuntary manslaughter, when based on homicides so occurring, is in conflict with the statute and must yield to it to the extent of the inconsistency.   *   *   *

Order affirmed.

---

c.   KILLINGS REDUCED TO MANSLAUGHTER BY "IMPERFECT" DEFENSES

SANCHEZ v. PEOPLE

Supreme Court of Colorado, 1970.
470 P.2d 857.

LEE, Justice. Plaintiff in error, Richard Bernard Sanchez, was convicted in the District Court of Mesa County of murder in the second degree and was sentenced to the penitentiary for a term of ten to forty years. By this writ of error, he seeks reversal of the judgment of conviction, and a new trial.

Sanchez asserts three grounds for reversal. We need to consider only the one proposition—that the trial court committed prejudicial error in refusing to instruct the jury on the lesser included offense of involuntary manslaughter. From a review of the record, we have concluded that Sanchez was entitled to such an instruction. Accordingly, the judgment of conviction must be reversed and the cause remanded for a new trial.

The events out of which the murder charge arose occurred in the early morning hours of October 13, 1966. At approximately 3 a.m. Felix Martinez was found dead in his apartment across the street from the Grand Junction police station. Medical evidence showed that death was caused by a puncture type stab wound which pierced the heart, allowing massive hemorrhaging. Sanchez, who had been observed earlier in the vicinity of the apartment house where Martinez was found, was arrested at his home at approximately 4:35 a.m. He was found sleeping in bed, fully clothed, and when aroused appeared to be in a drunken condition. He was taken to the police station and fully advised of his rights. Because of his obvious condition of intoxication, questioning was discontinued and later that day he was released from custody without any charges being filed against him.

Sanchez' intoxicated condition was the result of an extended drinking spree which commenced during the early afternoon hours of the preceding day and continued sporadically into the early morning hours of October 13. He and one Lucy Vigil, Mrs. Martinez' sister, were visiting in the Martinez apartment with Mrs. Martinez, awaiting Felix who finally arrived between 1 and 2 a.m. Felix had also been drinking and was described by his wife as being drunk when he arrived at the apartment. The men resumed their drinking. Eventually Martinez and his wife became involved in a violent argument, in which blows were exchanged. Sanchez sought to intervene and presumably it was in the course of his peace-making effort that Martinez was stabbed.

The evidence was far from clear as to the course of events. Although both were present in the same room, neither Mrs. Martinez nor Lucy Vigil would admit they saw Sanchez stab Felix.

After things had presumably quieted down, Sanchez and Lucy Vigil left for their home. Mrs. Martinez testified that she observed Martinez lying on the floor. Thinking he was asleep she did not bother him; but when she saw blood on his clothing she became alarmed and notified the police. Oddly enough, the investigating officer testified that he found Martinez seated at the kitchen table in a slumped-over position. The officer, not knowing whether Martinez was still alive, put him on the floor to administer first aid and then discovered that he was dead.

Three weeks later Sanchez contacted the Grand Junction police and requested to talk concerning the Martinez death. On November 11 he gave an extensive written statement in which he admitted stabbing Martinez twice during their argument. This statement was admitted into evidence. The voluntariness of this statement is not here challenged, nor is Sanchez' waiver of his right to have an attorney present at the time it was taken. At the trial Sanchez testified in his own behalf. He repudiated the statement and denied the stabbing.

Among other things the statement contains the following questions and answers:

"Q. Is my understanding correct, then, up to the point that you stabbed him when he lunged at you, this had been mostly argument, then, between the two of you, it was verbal?

"A. Yes, and threatening, more or less, like he said, 'I will kill you, you little son-of-a-bitch, who do you think you are?' It was just stuff like that."

*   *   *

"Q. Now, Richard, is there anything else concerning what happened on this night in question that you would like to tell us or that you would like to include in this statement?

"A. Well, yes, I guess, and that is, hell, I was just afraid of getting hurt, otherwise I wouldn't have used a knife on him. I was afraid, if you got somebody to call you names and say, 'I will kill you, you little son-of-a-bitch,' or something like that—you know, you get pretty mad, and then if he was intoxicated or something, you just don't know what he might do or anything, and look what it got me."

The trial court instructed the jury on second degree murder and voluntary manslaughter only; it refused to give the instruction on involuntary manslaughter, although such was specifically requested and tendered by Sanchez.

It is well-established that a defendant in a homicide case is entitled to an instruction on lesser included offenses when there is evidence, however manifested, whether presented by the people or by the defense, to indicate the commission of the lesser offense. *   *   *

It was the defendant's theory—and there was evidence to support it—that he was threatened with harm from Martinez; that he was only acting in self-defense at the time of the stabbing; and that he did not intend to kill Martinez, but only to protect himself. In other words, if in the act of defending himself he overreacted to a belief that he was in danger from Martinez and the killing resulted from the application of excessive force, then the exercise of his right of self-defense, lawful in the first instance, became unlawful by reason of the manner in which he defended himself. Under these circumstances the killing would not be legally justified. However, the criminal culpability, assuming the evidence was believed by the jury, would be limited to involuntary manslaughter—"* * * the killing of a human being without any intent so to do; in the commission of an unlawful act or a lawful act which probably might produce such a consequence, in an unlawful manner; * * *." C.R.S.1963, 40–2–7.

Thus it was the jury's function to determine in the first instance whether Sanchez did in fact administer the fatal blow, he having repudiated the incriminating admission in his written statement. It was also within the jury's province to disbelieve his testimony of repudiation and to ascribe truth to the written statement from which the jury could conclude that his actions were within the realm of self-defense and were thus justifiable; or the jury could conclude his actions were beyond the scope of legitimate self-defense by reason of the application of excessive force; or the jury could conclude that Sanchez did in fact intentionally kill as a result of a serious provocation, but without malice; or, finally, that he killed maliciously, but without deliberation or premeditation. Under the evidence the jury was entitled to consider each and all of these alternatives. That we may concur in the belief of the trial court that the evidence is "improbable, unreasonable or slight," is of no moment, as such determination is in the exclusive province of the jury.

*   *   *

NOTES

1. See generally, Parker, A Plea of Self-Defense Resulting in Manslaughter, 3 Alberta L.Rev. 16 (1963).

2. Why is involuntary rather than voluntary manslaughter the appropriate category for those who kill under circumstances giving rise to an "imperfect" defense? W. LaFave and A. Scott, Criminal Law 584 n. 7 (1972) observe that in the cases such killings are generally described as manslaughter without any modifying adjective. They then conclude, without explanation, that voluntary manslaughter "is the proper classification." Section 608 of the Proposed Federal Criminal Code (reprinted at page 517) provides that a defendant's reckless or negligent belief that circumstances are such that his conduct would, if the circumstances were as he believed, be within one of the generally applicable defenses, "is not excuse in a prosecution for an offense for which negligence or recklessness, as the case may be, suffices to establish culpability." If this is—or were to be—the law, why should not "imperfect defense" cases be involuntary manslaughter on the theory that the culpable act consists of negligently creating circumstances which make it necessary to kill?

VIII. DEFENSES NOT DIRECTLY RELATED TO THE BASIC REQUIREMENTS FOR LIABILITY

A number of so-called "defenses" to criminal liability are really only a challenge to the prosecution's case in the sense that they amount to either questioning whether the prosecution has proved one element of the offense or offering proof that tends to show that one element did not exist. This is most common in regard to those matters such as mistake of fact which merely "disprove" the existence of the requisite state of mind required for liability. These matters were covered in Part III. B. 6. Part VI deals with those matters which generally do not involve challenging the prosecution's proof of the elements of the offense, but rather involve the establishment of facts which establish that the defendant is entitled to acquittal despite the adequacy of proof of all elements of the offense. These are the true "defenses" to criminal liability.

A. THE GENERAL PRINCIPLE OF JUSTIFICATION AND DURESS

PROPOSED FEDERAL CRIMINAL CODE (STUDY DRAFT, 1970)

§ 608. Conduct Which Avoids Greater Harm

Conduct is justified if it is necessary and appropriate to avoid harm clearly greater than the harm which might result from such conduct and the situation developed through no fault of the actor. The necessity and justifiability of such conduct may not rest upon considerations pertaining only to the morality and advisability of the penal statute defining the offense, either in its general application or with respect to its application to a particular class of cases arising thereunder.

NOTE

This statement of the doctrine of "necessity" was deleted from the final draft. Similar formulations may be found in Smith-Hurd Ill.Ann.Stat. ch. 38, § 7.13 and McKinney Consol.Laws of N.Y. (Penal) § 35.05(2).

PEOPLE v. RICHARDS

California Court of Appeal, 1969.
269 Cal.App.2d 768, 75 Cal.Rptr. 597.

SIMS, Associate Justice. Defendant has appealed from a judgment of conviction rendered on jury verdicts which found him guilty of escape from a state prison without force or violence in violation of subdivision (b) of section 4530 of the Penal Code, and sane at the time of the commission of the offense. He contends that the trial court committed prejudicial error in refusing to receive evidence, embodied in an offer of proof, on a proposed defense of coercion and duress as justification for the offense charged, and in refusing to give proffered instructions on the same issue. These points are examined and found wanting. The judgment must be affirmed.

On July 19, 1967, defendant was assigned to a farm crew as an inmate of the California Correctional Training Facility, Soledad, Monterey County. Sometime after 2:30 p. m. defendant left the work area without permission and hid in a corn field until dark. Defendant then proceeded to the main road, and caught a ride to King City. He was apprehended by the California Highway Patrol on July 20, 1967 at 2:30 a. m. at a service station in King City. Defendant was still in prison dress, and he made no attempt to resist arrest.

On his return to the prison on July 20th, defendant was admonished as to his constitutional rights and questioned by a correctional officer as to his motive for escape. Defendant stated that he left prison without permission because "he felt he was doing too much time, that he was proceeding to Los Angeles to his mother's place to engage a lawyer to see if something couldn't be done."

The prison records officer authenticated the "Summary of Sentence Data" which indicated defendant's commitment and his movement in and through the state prison system. On cross-examination the defendant brought out, over objection, that while at a conservation center camp between November 10, 1966 and March 28, 1967 he had complained that there was pressure from other inmates to engage in homosexual activity. The court sustained an objection to a question propounded to determine if the records indicated whether or not the authorities at the center had checked into the defendant's complaint. According to the summary, the complaints, coupled with a very poor camp record, resulted in defendant's retransfer to Soledad in March.

In his opening statement the attorney for the defendant stated: "Ladies and gentlemen of the jury, you heard what is called a prima facie case of escape. The law provides that in certain circumstances there are defenses to crimes * * *. The law as to the various defenses will be stated to you by the Court. I will not attempt to state it. But the defense we are raising is called duress. Coercion. And we are going to present a series of witnesses, including the defendant himself, and these witnesses and the defendant will tell you of the threats made to his life and the reason that he ran away in order to save his own life, at least in his own mind he was doing this. And this will be the nature of our defense * * *."

The training officer in charge of defendant's work detail was called as a witness for the defendant. He testified that he had worked in the prison system for approximately 20 years and was familiar with the expression used by prisoners around the prison; that "a snitch" was someone who tells on someone else; and that if one prisoner disclosed that another prisoner was forcing him to commit homosexual acts it would be considered one of the more serious, if not the most serious, form of snitching. An objection to the relevancy and materiality of the next question—"What in your experience usually happens to inmates who snitch?"—was sustained.[2]

The court, at the request of the defendant, thereupon heard argument outside the presence of the jury. In the course of this argument the defendant adverted to the provisions of subdivision Eight of section 26 of the Penal Code.[3] He represented to the court that acts of sodomy had been inflicted on the defendant, that the defendant did snitch, that threats were made upon his life, that the guards would do nothing, and that defendant had exhausted every possible remedy short of escape to avoid the threat of death. The court adhered to the view that the threat, in order to be a justification, would have to be a threat designed to directly induce the act with which the defendant was charged. In response to the court's invitation to make an offer of proof, the defendant represented that inmate Joel Blume would testify "that inmates told him to remain away from the defendant * * * because Wayne Richards was going * * * to be killed * * * so keep his distance away from him or he would be killed too." Defendant himself would testify that "he was told by Mr. Blume who confided in him that he was marked to be killed or seriously injured and that the defendant understood this was going to be imminent, immediate, or as soon as possible and he felt that he had two possibilities, one to go to the guards, something that he's tried in the past and the guards have only responded by telling him to punch

2. No review has been sought of the propriety of the court's ruling on this question, which merely initiated the discussion which followed. In any event, it would appear that the defendant's, not the officer's knowledge and experience would be the only relevant evidence on the defendant's motivation if it in fact were a proper issue.

3. Section 26 of the Penal Code provides in part: "All persons are capable of committing crimes except those belonging to the following classes: * * Eight—Persons (unless the crime be punishable with death) who committed the act or made the omission charged under threats or menaces sufficient to show that they had reasonable cause to and did believe their lives would be endangered if they refused."

someone in the mouth or to commit probably a worse crime than escape, and, number two, to remove himself from the threat; and the only other way to remove himself from the threat is to remove himself from the imprisonment, the prison itself; and for this reason the defendant took the only alternative that he saw."

The court sustained the prosecution's objection to the testimony which had been offered. Thereupon, the defendant rested without presenting any further evidence.[4]

The instructions offered by the defendant included the following subjects: the effect of threats and menace as set forth in CALJIC Instruction No. 71–F (Revised) as found in 1967 Cumulative pocket part;[5] considerations governing the determination of whether a danger should be considered as imminent and immediate, predicated on People v. Villegas (1938) 29 Cal.App.2d 658, 85 P.2d 480 (see infra);[6] and an instruction on necessity as a defense.[7] The court in fact in-

---

4. At the sanity trial * * * defendant testified that "near to just prior" to his escape he had been forced with violence to submit to homosexual acts at Soledad; that he had told on some inmates at the conservation center (who presumably had engaged in similar attacks); that he learned that word of his having done so had reached Soledad; that five inmates showed him a piece of steel like a knife and told him "* * * you told on our friends up there * * *. Before this week is over we're going to [shank (stab) you]"; that three nights later he was jumped from behind by two inmates who got him in position on a lawn and had him by the neck; that they told him he had a choice; that they said "You snitched. You're dead" but that he could avoid trouble by submitting to acts of sodomy; that on his refusal they said, "You don't have any choice" and "We'll see you before the week is over, we'll see what you're going to be or not"; that he reported his fears to a correctional lieutenant and was told to settle down and to find himself an old man to take care of him; that on the Sunday (July 16th, three days) prior to his escape on July 19th he reported his trouble to the chaplain and was advised to try to defend himself and fight his persecutors; that he did not seek further psychiatric help because consultations at the camp with a nurse, a doctor, the head counselor and a psychologist had produced only advice to grow up and fight back; that he never voluntarily submitted to

any homosexual acts or had any desire to engage in them; that he found them revolting; that he did not know how to fight and could not bring himself to fight; and that he thought the threats were serious, that he would be dead, and he just wanted to get away.

5. This instruction read: "A person is not guilty of crime when he commits an act or engages in conduct, otherwise criminal, when acting under threats and menaces under the following circumstances: 1. Where the threats and menaces are such that they would create in the mind of a reasonable person the fear that his life would be in imminent and immediate danger if he did not commit the act or engage in the conduct charged, and 2. If such person then believed that his life would be so endangered. This rule does not apply to threats, menaces, and fear of future danger to his life."

6. This instruction read: "Whether a danger should be considered an imminent and immediate danger as opposed to a future danger is a question of fact to be determined by you the jury. Whether a danger is imminent or immediate will depend on all the surrounding circumstances, including the defendant's ability to withdraw and avoid the danger."

7. This instruction read: "Necessity is a defense to criminal prosecution under certain circumstances. As a defense to escape from a penal institu-

structed the jury, "The reasons, if any, given for the alleged escape are immaterial and not to be considered by you as in any way justifying or excusing, if there was such. The only requirement for the commission of the crime of escape is that the defendant intentionally, wilfully, and unlawfully, departed from the limits of his custody." Since the defendant's offer of proof had been rejected, there was no evidence to show any legal justification, and the instructions were properly refused. They are only material insofar as they highlight the respective contentions of the parties on the question of what type of coercion, compulsion or necessity may relieve a person of responsibility for what would otherwise be a criminal act.

In the argument concerning the admission of evidence there was a failure to articulate the distinction between the compulsion or duress recognized in the code (see fns. 3, 5 and 6, supra), and the principle of necessity (fn. 7, supra) which recognizes a defense of justification because of the duress occasioned by extrinsic circumstances. This distinction has been generally recognized by text writers in the field of criminal law.

The court properly rejected the evidence insofar as it was offered to show the defendant's lack of capacity to commit the offense under provisions of Penal Code section 26 (see fn. 3, supra). The statute, since it refers to the option to refuse or accept, contemplates that the threat or menace be accompanied by a direct or implied demand or request that the actor commit the criminal act. In his case there was no offer to show that anyone demanded or requested that the defendant escape. * * *

In People v. Sanders (1927) 82 Cal.App. 778, 256 P. 251, the court approved an instruction reading as follows: " ' * * * a person who commits an act under threats or menaces sufficient to show that he

tion the defense is necessarily limited to those cases where the remedy to the situation producing the necessity lies beyond the control of the prison authorities and personnel. For example, if a prison caught fire the inmates would probably not be guilty of the crime of escape if they fled to save themselves from the conflagration. On the other hand if an inmate escaped because he felt escape necessary to save himself from treatment at the hands of the imprisoners [sic] authority then this would not be a valid defense, since by being imprisoned it is expected that an inmate should accept the policies, actions, and treatment of the imprisoning authorities as part of his punishment. Your task is to determine first, whether correction of the conditions producing the necessity was within or beyond the control of the imprisoning authorities. If correction of the conditions producing the necessity was beyond the control of the imprisoning authorities then necessity is no defense to any type of escape. If correction of the conditions producing the necessity was beyond the control of the imprisoning and [sic] authorities, as in the case of a fire out of control then necessity may be a defense to an escape accomplished without force or violence. Whether the correction of conditions giving rise to a necessity was or was not within the control of the imprisoning authorities in this is a question of fact for you the jury to determine."

had reasonable cause to believe and did believe that his life would be endangered if he refused, is incapable of committing a crime.

" 'In order for duress or fear produced by threats or menace to be a valid, legal excuse for doing anything, which otherwise would be criminal, the act must have been done under such threats or menaces as show that the life of the person threatened or menaced was in danger, or that there was reasonable cause to believe and actual belief that there was such danger. The danger must not be one of future violence, but of present and immediate violence at the time of the commission of the forbidden act. The danger of death at some future time in the absence of danger of death at the time of the commission of the offense will not excuse. A person who aids and assists in the commission of the crime, or who commits a crime, is not relieved from criminality on account of fears excited by threats or menaces unless the danger be to life, nor unless that danger be present and immediate.' " (82 Cal.App. at p. 785, 256 P. at p. 254. Accord: People v. Villegas, supra, 29 Cal.App.2d 658, 661, 85 P.2d 480, and see Annotation, Criminal Law—Defense—Coercion (1955) 40 A.L.R.2d 908.) If the statutory test of capability were deemed to be applicable to the evidence contained in the offer of proof, it still falls short of establishing that there was a present and immediate danger to defendant's life on the afternoon he secreted himself and left the confines of the prison. It may further be noted that his subsequent testimony reflected that he was given alternative courses of action. The submission to sodomy, abhorrent as it may be, falls short of loss of life. The commission of that offense, in response to the threat to his life, accompanied by requests or directions to submit, would fall within the statutory pattern.

There remains for consideration the question of whether the evidence offered by the defendant should have been received to show justification on the grounds of necessity. The principle has been phrased as follows: "An act which would otherwise be a crime may be excused if the person accused can show that it was done only in order to avoid consequences which could not otherwise be avoided, and which, if they had followed, would have inflicted upon him, or upon others whom he was bound to protect, inevitable and irreparable evil; that no more was done than was reasonably necessary for that purpose; and that the evil inflicted by it was not disproportionate to the evil avoided." (Clark & Marshall, Law of Crimes (6th Ed., Wingersky, 1958) p. 322, quoting from Stephen, Digest of the Criminal Law, art. 32. See also American Law Institute, Model Penal Code (Proposed Official Draft 1962) § 3.02.)

In People v. Whipple (1929) 100 Cal.App. 261, 279 P. 1008, the court stated, "In this state the common law is of no effect so far as the specification of what acts or conduct shall constitute a crime is

concerned   *   *   *   likewise with excuses or justifications—if no
statutory excuse or justification apply as to the commission of the
particular offense, neither the common law nor the so-called 'unwritten law' may legally supply it." The court noted "if the facts
were as stated by the defendant, he was subjected to brutal treatment
of extreme atrocity." The defendant contended that the brutal and
inhumane treatment he received made his imprisonment intolerable
and justified the escape. The court, nevertheless, upheld the action
of the trial court " * * * in instructing the jury that an excuse for
the escape of defendant, founded upon any alleged unsanitary conditions, or alleged harsh, brutal or inhumane treatment received by him
at the hands of his custodian, would constitute no defense in the law
for the commission of the offense." From the foregoing it would
appear that the principle of justification by necessity is not recognized
under the law of this state, except as it is embodied in the Penal Code.

Nevertheless in *Whipple* the court, as an alternative ground of
decision, did recognize the existence of the principle, and found that it
did not apply to the facts to which the defendant had testified. The
opinion recites, "Although authority exists to the effect that, generally speaking, absolute necessity will excuse the commission of a criminal offense [citations]; so far as the crime of escaping from a jail is
concerned, the authorities are in practical accord in holding that
ordinary adverse circumstances will not present such a condition as
will support a legal excuse for effecting an escape. * * * The
court concluded, "It is manifest that to allow a prisoner to decide
whether the conditions justify him in attempting to escape would be
destructive of the necessary discipline which must be maintained in any
well-ordered prison. * * * Generally speaking, when a man has
been lawfully convicted of a crime, and a judgment of imprisonment
has been regularly entered against him, it becomes his duty to submit
to the penalty. Unquestionably, it is the duty of the state and of its officers to accord to the prisoner such safety and humane treatment as
may be consistent with the safekeeping of the prisoner. It is, unfortunately, possible for the conditions of imprisonment to be so unwhole-
some as to seriously imperil the health and life of the prisoner by exposure to infection and disease, and unhappily it is possible for prison
guards to subject prisoners to abuses and serious physical injury unjustified by any disciplinary need. However, a prisoner who escapes
for any such reason does so at his peril."

Defendant seeks to avoid the effect of this controlling precedent
on the theory that *Whipple* recognized that the improper treatment
might constitute a justification for escape if the defendant had exhausted all other alternatives. The court did observe, " * * * the
record fails to disclose any attempt on the part of defendant to show
that, before escaping, he had, in good faith or at all, endeavored to be
relieved by lawful means from any alleged improper irregularities or

practices which he claimed were present in the matter of his confinement." Nevertheless immediately thereafter the court acknowledged, "In a remote mountain camp, far from the sheriff's office, what relief could he obtain by telling his custodian that he wanted to see the sheriff? If the defense could be admitted at all, it should not be conditioned upon the making of a plainly useless request." It is, therefore, apparent that the court's decision would not have been altered had *Whipple* shown, as the defendant alleges here, that he had reported his complaints to the authorities and had been denied relief.

In *Whipple,* and as well this case, the reviewing court was struck by the enormity of the pressure to which the defendant was subjected if his allegations were true. The court observed, " * * * it is with very great reluctance that we admit that, under practically all of the authorities, the foregoing opinion states the established law. * * * The function of the court is to declare the law as it is, and we are not authorized to usurp the place of the Legislature, which has the power to make laws, and the duty to make just laws."

The Legislature has in fact adopted many statutes regulating the treatment of prisoners. The courts of this state have extended the use of the writ of habeas corpus to protect the fundamental basic rights of prisoners. The principle of justification by necessity, if applicable, involves a determination that "the harm or evil sought to be avoided by such conduct is greater than that sought to be prevented by the law defining the offense charged." The compulsion from the harm or evil which the actor seeks to avoid, should be present and impending, as in the case of the threat or menace contemplated by the Penal Code. This is not a case where the prisoner departed from the limits of his custody while pursued by those who would take his life because he "snitched," or by those who sought by force and violence to have him submit to sodomy. Moreover, any and all alternative courses should be considered, and it must be determined that the threatened consequences could not otherwise be avoided. The evil sought to be prevented is not only the escape of the prisoner in question, but also, as noted in *Whipple,* supra, the destruction of the general discipline of the prison.

The balancing of all of these factors leads to the conclusion that the principles set forth in *Whipple* should be adhered to and applied in this case. The prisoner should be denied self-help by escape, and should be relegated to relief through established administrative channels, or, that failing, through the courts. The trial court properly rejected defendant's offer of proof and the instructions which depended upon that evidence.

The judgment is affirmed.

NOTES

1.   The same result was reached in State v. Green, 470 S.W.2d 565 (Mo. Sup.Ct.1971) (En Banc) which involved factual allegations remarkably similar to those in *Richards*. A possibly relevant distinction is that Green alleged that he had not only been subjected to multiple homosexual rape on two occasions and had unsuccessfully sought aid from prison authorities by injuring or feigning to injure himself, but that on the day of his escape he was told by five inmates of their plans to so assault him that evening. Does the alleged prevalence of coerced homosexuality in American jails and prisons (State v. Green, supra, at 569 n. 1 (dissenting opinion of Judge Seiler)) suggest the practical wisdom of the judgments in *Richards* and *Green*? In People v. Noble, 18 Mich.App. 300, 170 N.W.2d 916 (1969), Chief Judge Lesinski wrote: "Finally, defendant protests that he only fled the prison work camp in desperation to avoid homosexual attacks by other prisoners. The problem of homosexuality in the prisons is serious and perplexing, and never more so than in a case such as this where such activity is forced upon a young man against his will. However, the answer to the problem is not the judicial sanctioning of escapes. While we have no reason to doubt the sincerity of this defendant, it is easy to visualize a rash of escapes, all rationalized by unverifiable tales of sexual assault. The solution must rather come from some kind of penological reform." Comments on this problem may be found in 45 S.Cal.L.Rev. 1062 (1972) and 6 U.San.Fran.L.Rev. 430 (1972).

2.   Missouri has recognized that a homicide may be justified if necessary to prevent sodemy. State v. Robinson, 328 S.W.2d 667, 670–671 (Mo. Sup.Ct.1959). If Green had killed an inmate-assailant to prevent a forcible act of sodomy would it be a denial of due process to refuse to allow him to offer this defense? Is it consistent with due process to deny Richards and Green the opportunity to convince a jury that escape was a necessary and lesser evil than submission to further sexual assault?

3.   The principle of justification is, as is illustrated by this section, expressed in a number of well-recognized defenses. In all but one of these criminal liability is sought to be avoided because the defendant's conduct is alleged to have been a justifiable or excusable response to the conduct of another person. The exception is the defense of necessity which involves the defendant's response to the pressures of natural rather than human forces. Although seldom employed it has been involved in some of the most dramatic cases in the annals of Anglo-American jurisprudence. These are cases in which the rules of positive law and their rationales, which normally operate quite satisfactorily, seem inadequate to deal with the harsh conflict between the urge for self preservation and our commitment to the sanctity of life. A brilliant exposition of this philosophical and jurisprudential thicket is Fuller, "The Case of the Speluncean Explorers," 62 Harv.L.Rev. 616 (1949). Also of interest is Brody, "Son of the Speluncean Explorer," 55 Iowa L.Rev. 1233 (1970) and Glazebrook, "The Necessity Plea in English Criminal Law," 30 Camb.L.J. 88 (1972).

4. In April 1841 an American vessel carrying emigrants struck an ice-berg and had to be abandoned. Nine crew members and thirty-two pas-sengers got into the ship's longboat commanded by the first mate; the cap-tain and others were in another boat. Before the two boats separated the captain advised the crew members to obey the mate's orders as though they were his own. After a day a storm arose and the overladen and leaky long-boat seemed to the mate destined to sink. He directed the seamen, including one Holmes, to throw overboard all unmarried, adult, male passengers. Six-teen passengers were thus lost. The next day, the boat, still afloat, was sighted by a ship and all aboard were saved. On arrival in port Holmes was tried for manslaughter. What defenses would you offer? What result would be appropriate? United States v. Holmes, 26 F.Cas. 360 (No. 15,383) (C.C.E.D.Pa.1842).

5. In 1884 three English seamen and a cabin boy, the victims of a shipwreck, were adrift in an open boat 1,600 miles from the Cape of Good Hope. After twenty days, the last nine without food, two of the seamen over the dissent of the third killed the weakened boy. The three men fed upon the body and blood of the boy for four days until they were rescued. It was agreed that had they not so fed they would probably not have sur-vived to be rescued. On their return to England the two instigators were tried for murder. What is the proper verdict and, if it is guilty, what is the proper penalty? Regina v. Dudley & Stephens, 14 Q.B.D. 273 (1884). The facts surrounding the prosecution are to be found in Mallin, "In Warm Blood: Some Historical and Procedural Aspects of Regina v. Dudley and Stephens, 34 U.Chi.L.Rev. 387 (1967).

6. The difficulty of balancing evils where human life is placed in both trays of the scale is reduced where qualitative distinctions may be made. Thus, in almost all American anti-abortion statutes an exception was made by legislative judgment for cases in which the abortion was deemed neces-sary for the preservation of the woman's life. In prosecutions under stat-utes which did not contain such an exception the necessity plea would pre-sumably have been available as a common law defense. See, e. g., La.Rev. Stat. § 14:87 (1964) which contains no exception but had been interpreted, in conjunction with La.Rev.Stat. § 37:1285(6) (dealing with revocation of physicians' certificate), as excepting abortions done by a physician "for the relief of a woman whose life appears in peril". Rosen v. Louisiana State Board of Medical Examiners, 318 F.Supp. 1217, 1225 (D.C.E.D.La.1970).

7. If the defendant is involved in an automobile accident resulting in injuries to the driver of the other car and to himself, should the necessity of obtaining medical care for himself be a defense to a charge of failure to stop and render aid? What factors would influence your judgment? The relative severity of the injuries; the presence of negligence by one or the other drivers? What if the defendant's child was injured? Cf. Woods v. State, 121 S.W.2d 604 (Tex.Crim.App.1938). Should it be a defense to a charge of driving while intoxicated that the defendant who had no tele-phone was in search of medical aid for a severe cut suffered when he fell on his whiskey bottle? That he was taking his wife to the hospital for treatment of injuries suffered when he struck her in a drunken rage? That he was taking her because she had begun labor prematurely? Cf. Butter-field v. State, 317 S.W.2d 943 (Tex.Ct.Crim.App.1958).

8. Should necessity be permitted as a defense for defendants charged with grand larceny arising when a group of unemployed persons in the depths of the great depression seized groceries after the local public relief chairman had refused them an increase in their flour allowance? State v. Moe, 174 Wash. 303, 24 P.2d 638 (1933).

PROPOSED FEDERAL CRIMINAL CODE (1971)

§ 610. Duress

(1) Affirmative Defense. In a prosecution for any offense it is an affirmative defense that the actor engaged in the proscribed conduct because he was compelled to do so by threat of imminent death or serious bodily injury to himself or another. In a prosecution for an offense which does not constitute a felony, it is an affirmative defense that the actor engaged in the proscribed conduct because he was compelled to do so by force or threat of force. Compulsion within the meaning of this section exists only if the force, threat or circumstances are such as would render a person of reasonable firmness incapable of resisting the pressure.

(2) Defense Precluded. The defense defined in this section is not available to a person who, by voluntarily entering into a criminal enterprise, or otherwise, willfully placed himself in a situation in which it was foreseeable that he would be subjected to duress. The defense is also unavailable if he was negligent in placing himself in such a situation, whenever negligence suffices to establish culpability for the offense charged.

Comment

This section excuses from criminal liability conduct which is engaged in because of certain compelling circumstances which would have caused even a person of reasonable firmness to succumb. Present federal law recognizes the defense only where the apprehension of immediate death or serious injury is created by another person. The section affords a broader protection covering such apprehension regardless of the source of the threat or the identity of the victim. For misdemeanors, any force or threat of force which compels the conduct is sufficient to excuse it. Two factors constrict the availability of what may seem to be a very liberal excuse; the burden of proof is imposed upon the defendant and a jury finding that a person of reasonable firmness would not have been able to resist the pressure is required.

Among the alternatives are: (1) to provide that the offense should not be available in the case of certain exceptionally grave offenses, e. g., murder; and (2) to provide that compulsion should reduce the grade of the offense rather than constitute a full defense.

B. ENTRAPMENT

SHERMAN v. UNITED STATES

United States Supreme Court, 1958.
356 U.S. 369, 78 S.Ct. 819, 2 L.Ed.2d 848.

Mr. Chief Justice WARREN delivered the opinion of the Court.

The issue before us is whether petitioner's conviction should be set aside on the ground that as a matter of law the defense of entrapment was established. Petitioner was convicted under an indictment charging three sales of narcotics in violation of 21 U.S.C. § 174, 21 U.S.C.A. § 174. A previous conviction had been reversed on account of improper instructions as to the issue of entrapment. 2 Cir., 200 F.2d 880. In the second trial, as in the first, petitioner's defense was a claim of entrapment: an agent of the Federal Government induced him to take part in illegal transactions when otherwise he would not have done so.

In late August 1951, Kalchinian, a government informer, first met petitioner at a doctor's office where apparently both were being treated to be cured of narcotics addiction. Several accidental meetings followed, either at the doctor's office or at the pharmacy where both filled their prescriptions from the doctor. From mere greetings, conversation progressed to a discussion of mutual experiences and problems, including their attempts to overcome addiction to narcotics. Finally Kalchinian asked petitioner if he knew of a good source of narcotics. He asked petitioner to supply him with a source because he was not responding to treatment. From the first, petitioner tried to avoid the issue. Not until after a number of repetitions of the request, predicated on Kalchinian's presumed suffering, did petitioner finally acquiesce. Several times thereafter he obtained a quantity of narcotics which he shared with Kalchinian. Each time petitioner told Kalchinian that the total cost of narcotics he obtained was twenty-five dollars and that Kalchinian owed him fifteen dollars. The informer thus bore the cost of his share of the narcotics plus the taxi and other expenses necessary to obtain the drug. After several such sales Kalchinian informed agents of the Bureau of Narcotics that he had another seller for them. On three occasions during November 1951, government agents observed petitioner give narcotics to Kalchinian in return for money supplied by the Government.

At the trial the factual issue was whether the informer had convinced an otherwise unwilling person to commit a criminal act or whether petitioner was already predisposed to commit the act and exhibited only the natural hesitancy of one acquainted with the narcotics trade. The issue of entrapment went to the jury, and a conviction resulted. Petitioner was sentenced to imprisonment for ten years. The Court of Appeals for the Second Circuit affirmed. 240 F.2d 949. We granted certiorari. 353 U.S. 935, 77 S.Ct. 812, 1 L.Ed.2d 758.

In Sorrells v. United States, 287 U.S. 435, 53 S.Ct. 210, 77 L.Ed. 413, this Court firmly recognized the defense of entrapment in the federal courts. The intervening years have in no way detracted from the principles underlying that decision. The function of law enforcement is the prevention of crime and the apprehension of criminals. Manifestly, that function does not include the manufacturing of crime. Criminal activity is such that stealth and strategy are necessary weapons in the arsenal of the police officer. However, "A different question is presented when the criminal design originates with the officials of the government, and they implant in the mind of an innocent person the disposition to commit the alleged offense and induce its commission in order that they may prosecute." 287 U.S. at page 442, 53 S.Ct. at page 212. Then stealth and strategy become as objectionable police methods as the coerced confession and the unlawful search. Congress could not have intended that its statutes were to be enforced by tempting innocent persons into violations.

However, the fact that government agents "merely afford opportunities or facilities for the commission of the offense does not" constitute entrapment. Entrapment occurs only when the criminal conduct was "the product of the *creative* activity" of law-enforcement officials. (Emphasis supplied.) See 287 U.S. at pages 441, 451, 53 S.Ct. at pages 212, 216. To determine whether entrapment has been established, a line must be drawn between the trap for the unwary innocent and the trap for the unwary criminal. The principles by which the courts are to make this determination were outlined in Sorrells. On the one hand, at trial the accused may examine the conduct of the government agent; and on the other hand, the accused will be subjected to an "appropriate and searching inquiry into his own conduct and predisposition" as bearing on his claim of innocence. See 287 U.S. at page 451, 53 S.Ct. at page 216.

We conclude from the evidence that entrapment was established as a matter of law. In so holding, we are not choosing between conflicting witnesses, nor judging credibility. Aside from recalling Kalchinian, who was the Government's witness, the defense called no witnesses. We reach our conclusion from the undisputed testimony of the prosecution's witnesses.

It is patently clear that petitioner was induced by Kalchinian. The informer himself testified that, believing petitioner to be undergoing a cure for narcotics addiction, he nonetheless sought to persuade petitioner to obtain for him a source of narcotics. In Kalchinian's own words we are told of the accidental, yet recurring, meetings, the ensuing conversations concerning mutual experiences in regard to narcotics addiction, and then of Kalchinian's resort to sympathy. One request was not enough, for Kalchinian tells us that additional ones were necessary to overcome, first, petitioner's refusal, then his evasiveness, and then his hesitancy in order to achieve capitulation. Kalchinian not only procured a source of narcotics but apparently also induced petitioner to return to the habit. Finally, assured of a catch, Kalchinian informed the authorities so that they could close the net. The Government cannot disown Kalchinian and insist it is not responsible for his actions. Although he was not being paid, Kalchinian was an active government informer who had but recently been the instigator of at least two other prosecutions. Undoubtedly the impetus for such achievements was the fact that in 1951 Kalchinian was himself under criminal charges for illegally selling narcotics and had not yet been sentenced.[3] It makes no difference that the sales for which petitioner was convicted occurred after a series of sales. They were not independent acts subsequent to the inducement but part of a course of conduct which was the product of the inducement. In his testimony the federal agent in charge of the case admitted that he never bothered to question Kalchinian about the way he had made contact with petitioner. The Government cannot make such use of an informer and then claim disassociation through ignorance.

The Government sought to overcome the defense of entrapment by claiming that petitioner evinced a "ready complaisance" to accede to Kalchinian's request. Aside from a record of past convictions, which we discuss in the following paragraph, the Government's case is unsupported. There is no evidence that petitioner himself was in the trade. When his apartment was searched after arrest, no narcotics were found. There is no significant evidence that petitioner even made a profit on any sale to Kalchinian. The Government's characterization of petitioner's hesitancy to Kalchinian's request as the natural wariness of the criminal cannot fill the evidentiary void.

The Government's additional evidence in the second trial to show that petitioner was ready and willing to sell narcotics should the opportunity present itself was petitioner's record of two past narcotics convictions. In 1942 petitioner was convicted of illegally selling narcotics; in 1946 he was convicted of illegally possessing them. However, a nine-year-old sales conviction and a five-year-old possession conviction are insufficient to prove petitioner had a readiness to sell narcotics at the time Kalchinian approached him, par-

3. "Q. But you had made a promise, an agreement, though, to cooperate with the Federal Bureau of Narcotics before you received a suspended sentence from the court?

"A. [Kalchinian]. I had promised to cooperate in 1951.
"Q. And that was before your sentence?

"A. Yes, that was before my sentence." R. 99.

Kalchinian received a suspended sentence in 1952 after a statement by the United States Attorney to the Judge that he had been cooperative with the Government. R. 89, 98.

ticularly when we must assume from the record he was trying to overcome the narcotics habit at the time.

The case at bar illustrates an evil which the defense of entrapment is designed to overcome. The government informer entices someone attempting to avoid narcotics not only into carrying out an illegal sale but also into returning to the habit of use. Selecting the proper time, the informer then tells the government agent. The set-up is accepted by the agent without even a question as to the manner in which the informer encountered the seller. Thus the Government plays on the weaknesses of an innocent party and beguiles him into committing crimes which he otherwise would not have attempted. Law enforcement does not require methods such as this.

It has been suggested that in overturning this conviction we should reassess the doctrine of entrapment according to principles announced in the separate opinion of Mr. Justice Roberts in Sorrells v. United States, 287 U.S. 435, 453, 53 S.Ct. 210, 217, 77 L.Ed. 413. To do so would be to decide the case on grounds rejected by the majority in Sorrells and, so far as the record shows, not raised here or below by the parties before us. We do not ordinarily decide issues not presented by the parties and there is good reason not to vary that practice in this case.

At least two important issues of law enforcement and trial procedure would have to be decided without the benefit of argument by the parties, one party being the Government. Mr. Justice Roberts asserted that although the defendant could claim that the Government had induced him to commit the crime, the Government could not reply by showing that the defendant's criminal conduct was due to his own readiness and not to the persuasion of government agents. The handicap thus placed on the prosecution is obvious.[7] Furthermore, it was the position of Mr. Justice Roberts that the factual issue of entrapment—now limited to the question of what the government agents did—should be decided by the judge, not the jury. Not only was this rejected by the Court in Sorrells, but where the issue has been presented to them, the Courts of Appeals have since Sorrells unanimously concluded that unless it can be decided as a matter of law, the issue of whether a defendant has been entrapped is for the jury as part of its function of determining the guilt or innocence of the accused.

To dispose of this case on the ground suggested would entail both overruling a leading decision of this Court and brushing aside the possibility that we would be creating more problems than we would supposedly be solving.

7. In the first appeal of this case Judge Learned Hand stated: "Indeed, it would seem probable that, if there were no reply [to the claim of inducement], it would be impossible ever to secure convictions of any offences which consist of transactions that are carried on in secret." United States v. Sherman, 2 Cir., 200 F.2d 880, 882.

The judgment of the Court of Appeals is reversed and the case is remanded to the District Court with instructions to dismiss the indictment.

Reversed and remanded.

Mr. Justice FRANKFURTER, whom Mr. Justice DOUGLAS, Mr. Justice HARLAN, and Mr. Justice BRENNAN join, concurring in the result.

Although agreeing with the Court that the undisputed facts show entrapment as a matter of law, I reach this result by a route different from the Court's.

*   *   *

It is surely sheer fiction to suggest that a conviction cannot be had when a defendant has been entrapped by government officers or informers because "Congress could not have intended that its statutes were to be enforced by tempting innocent persons into violations." In these cases raising claims of entrapment, the only legislative intention that can with any show of reason be extracted from the statute is the intention to make criminal precisely the conduct in which the defendant has engaged. That conduct includes all the elements necessary to constitute criminality. Without compulsion and "knowingly," where that is requisite, the defendant has violated the statutory command. If he is to be relieved from the usual punitive consequences, it is on no account because he is innocent of the offense described. In these circumstances, conduct is not less criminal because the result of temptation, whether the tempter is a private person or a government agent or informer.

The courts refuse to convict an entrapped defendant, not because his conduct falls outside the proscription of the statute, but because, even if his guilt be admitted, the methods employed on behalf of the Government to bring about conviction cannot be countenanced. As Mr. Justice Holmes said in Olmstead v. United States, 277 U.S. 438, 470, 48 S.Ct. 564, 575, 72 L.Ed. 944 (dissenting), in another connection, "It is desirable that criminals should be detected, and to that end that all available evidence should be used. It also is desirable that the government should not itself foster and pay for other crimes, when they are the means by which the evidence is to be obtained. *   *   * [F]or my part I think it a less evil that some criminals should escape than that the government should play an ignoble part." Insofar as they are used as instrumentalites in the administration of criminal justice, the federal courts have an obligation to set their face against enforcement of the law by lawless means or means that violate rationally vindicated standards of justice, and to refuse to sustain such methods by effectuating them. They do this in the exercise of a recognized jurisdiction to formulate and apply "proper standards for the enforcement of the federal criminal law in the federal courts," McNabb v. United States, 318 U.S. 332, 341, 63 S.Ct. 608, 613, 87 L.Ed. 819, an obligation that goes beyond the conviction of the particular defendant before the court. Public confidence in the fair and honorable administration of justice, upon which ultimately depends the rule of law, is the transcending value at stake.

*   *   *

The crucial question, not easy of answer, to which the court must direct itself is whether the police conduct revealed in the particular case falls below standards, to which common feelings respond, for the proper use of governmental power. For answer it is wholly irrelevant to ask if the "intention" to commit the crime originated with the defendant or government officers, or if the criminal conduct was the product of "the creative activity" of law-enforcement officials. Yet in the present case the Court repeats and purports to apply these unrevealing tests. Of course in every case of this kind the intention that the particular crime be committed originates with the police, and without their inducement the crime would not have occurred. But it is perfectly clear from such decisions as the decoy letter cases in this Court, e. g., Grimm v. United States, 156 U.S. 604, 15 S.Ct. 470, 39 L.Ed. 550, where the police in effect simply furnished the opportunity for the commission of the crime, that this is not enough to enable the defendant to escape conviction.

The intention referred to, therefore, must be a general intention or predisposition to commit, whenever the opportunity should arise, crimes of the kind solicited, and in proof of such a predisposition evidence has often been admitted to show the defendant's reputation, criminal activities, and prior disposition. The danger of prejudice in such a situation, particularly if the issue of entrapment must be submitted to the jury and disposed of by a general verdict of guilty or innocent, is evident. The defendant must either forego the claim of entrapment or run the substantial risk that, in spite of instructions, the jury will allow a criminal record or bad reputation to weigh in its determination of guilt of the specific offense of which he stands charged. Furthermore, a test that looks to the character and predisposition of the defendant rather than the conduct of the police loses sight of the underlying reason for the defense of entrapment. No matter what the defendant's past record and present inclinations to criminality, or the depths to which he has sunk in the estimation of society, certain police conduct to ensnare him into further crime is not to be tolerated by an advanced society. And in the present case it is clear that the Court in fact reverses the conviction because of the conduct of the informer Kalchinian, and not because the Government has failed to draw a convincing picture of petitioner's past criminal conduct. Permissible police activity does not vary according to the particular defendant concerned; surely if two suspects have been solicited at the same time in the same manner, one should not go to jail simply because he has been convicted before and is said to have a criminal disposition. No more does it vary according to the suspicions, reasonable or unreasonable, of the police concerning the defendant's activities. Appeals to sympathy, friendship, the possibility of exorbitant gain, and so forth, can no more be tolerated when directed against a past offender than against an ordinary law-abiding citizen. A contrary view runs afoul of fundamental principles of equality under law, and would espouse the notion that when dealing with the criminal classes anything goes. The possibility that no matter what his past crimes and general disposition the defendant might not have committed the particular crime unless confronted with inordinate inducements, must not be ignored. Past crimes do not forever outlaw the criminal and open him to police practices, aimed at securing his repeated conviction, from which the ordinary citizen is protected. The whole ameliorative hopes of modern penology and prison administration strongly counsel against such a view.

This does not mean that the police may not act so as to detect those engaged in criminal conduct and ready and willing to commit further crimes should the occasion arise. Such indeed is their obligation. It does mean that in holding out inducements they should act in such a manner as is likely to induce to the commission of crime only these persons and not others who would normally avoid crime and through self-struggle resist ordinary temptations. This test shifts attention from the record and predisposition of the particular defendant to the conduct of the police and the likelihood, objectively considered, that it would entrap only those ready and willing to commit crime. It is as objective a test as the subject matter permits, and will give guidance in regulating police conduct that is lacking when the reasonableness of police suspicions must be judged or the criminal disposition of the defendant retrospectively appraised. It draws directly on the fundamental intuition that led in the first instance to the outlawing of "entrapment" as a prosecutorial instrument. The power of government is abused and directed to an end for which it was not constituted when employed to promote rather than detect crime and to bring about the downfall of those who left to themselves, might well have obeyed the law. Human nature is weak enough and sufficiently beset by temptations without government adding to them and generating crime.

What police conduct is to be condemned, because likely to induce those not otherwise ready and willing to commit crime, must be picked out from case to case as new situations arise involving different crimes and new methods of detection. The Sorrells case involved persistent solicitation in the face of obvious reluctance, and appeals to sentiments aroused by reminiscences of experiences as companions in arms in the World War. Particularly reprehensible in the present case was the use of repeated requests to overcome petitioner's hesitancy, coupled with appeals to sympathy based on mutual experiences with narcotics addiction. Evidence of the setting in which the inducement took place is of course highly relevant in judging its likely effect, and the court should also consider the nature of the crime involved, its secrecy and difficulty of detection, and the manner in which the particular criminal business is usually carried on.

NOTES

1. Where the origin-of-intent test enunciated by the majority in *Sherman* is employed, the defendant's predisposition becomes a crucial issue. Evidence, ordinarily inadmissible, such as the defendant's criminal record or even testimony as to alleged criminal conduct for which the defendant was never prosecuted, will be permitted on this point. For examples of judicial efforts to limit the use of such evidence see United States v. Johnston, 426 F.2d 112 (7th Cir. 1970) commented upon in 71 Columb.L.Rev. 157 (1971), and Hansford v. United States, 112 U.S.App.D.C. 359, 303 F.2d 219 (1962).

2. Should the issue of entrapment be decided by the judge or the jury? Consider the views of Chief Justice Traynor dissenting in People v. Moran, 1 Cal.3d 755, 83 Cal.Rptr. 411, 463 P.2d 763 (1970):

> [S]ubmission of the issue to the jury cannot be justified on the ground that it goes to the defendant's guilt or innocence. The crucial issue is whether the court or the jury can best achieve the purpose of the defense: the deterrence of impermissible police conduct. A jury verdict of guilty or not guilty tells the police nothing about the jury's evaluation of the police conduct. A verdict of guilty may mean that the jury did not believe the defendant's testimony that would have established entrapment. It may also mean that the jury did not believe that the conduct created a substantial risk of inducing one not ready to commit the offense into doing so. Since the defendant may assert entrapment and also deny that he committed the crime a "not guilty" verdict may also shed no light on the jury's assessment of police conduct. Moreover, even when the verdict settles the issue of entrapment in the particular case, it "cannot give significant guidance for official conduct for the future. Only the court, through the gradual evolution of explicit standards in accumulated precedents, can do this with the degree of certainty that wise administration of criminal justice demands." (Sherman v. United States, supra, 356 U.S. 369, 385, 78 S.Ct. 819, 827. (Frankfurter, J., concurring). In other areas involving police conduct, we have recognized the paramount importance of committing the assessment of such conduct to the court. Thus, the trial court, subject to appropriate appellate review, determines the admissibility of confessions and other evidence claimed to have been illegally obtained. It should also determine the issue of entrapment.

3. Informers used in law enforcement must normally be compensated in some way. Often this involves agreements not to prosecute the informer for his own criminal activity. Sometimes cash payments are made. See, e. g., United States v. Grimes, 438 F.2d 391 (6th Cir. 1971); Donnelly, "Ju-

dicial Control of Informants, Spies, Stool Pigeons and Agent Provocateurs", 60 Yale L.J. 1091 (1951); "Informers in Federal Narcotics Prosecutions," 2 Colum.J.L. & Soc.Prob. 47 (1966); and "Entrapment by Federal Officers", 33 N.Y.U.L.Rev. 1033 (1958).

———

UNITED STATES v. RUSSELL

United States Supreme Court, 1973.
411 U.S. 423, 93 S.Ct. 1637, 36 L.Ed.2d 366.

Mr. Justice REHNQUIST delivered the opinion of the Court.

Respondent Richard Russell was charged in three counts of a five count indictment returned against him and codefendants John and Patrick Connolly. After a jury trial in the District Court, in which his sole defense was entrapment, respondent was convicted on all three counts of having unlawfully manufactured and processed methamphetamine ("speed") and of having unlawfully sold and delivered that drug in violation of 21 U.S.C. §§ 331(q)(1), (2), 360a(a), (b) (Supp. V, 1964). He was sentenced to concurrent terms of two years in prison for each offense, the terms to be suspended on the condition that he spend six months in prison and be placed on probation for the following three years. On appeal the United States Court of Appeals for the Ninth Circuit, one judge dissenting, reversed the conviction solely for the reason that an undercover agent supplied an essential chemical for manufacturing the methamphetamine which formed the basis of respondent's conviction. The court concluded that as a matter of law "a defense to a criminal charge may be founded upon an intolerable degree of governmental participation in the criminal enterprise." United States v. Russell, 459 F.2d 671, 673 (CA9 1972). We granted certiorari, 409 U.S. 911 (1972), and now reverse that judgment.

There is little dispute concerning the essential facts in this case. On December 7, 1969, Joe Shapiro, an undercover agent for the Federal Bureau of Narcotics and Dangerous Drugs, went to respondent's home on Whidbey Island in the State of Washington where he met with respondent and his two codefendants, John and Patrick Connolly. Shapiro's assignment was to locate a laboratory where it was believed that methamphetamine was being manufactured illicitly. He told the respondent and the Connollys that he represented an organization in the Pacific Northwest that was interested in controlling the manufacture and distribution of methamphetamine. He then made an offer to supply the defendants with the chemical phenyl-2-propanone, an essential ingredient in the manufacture of methamphetamine, in return for one-half of the drug produced. This offer was made on the condition that Agent Shapiro be shown a sample of the drug which they were making and the laboratory where it was being produced.

During the conversation Patrick Connolly revealed that he had been making the drug since May 1969 and since then had produced three pounds of it.[2] John Connolly gave the agent a bag containing a quantity of methamphetamine that he represented as being from "the last batch that we made." Shortly thereafter, Shapiro and Patrick Connolly left respondent's house to view the laboratory which was located in the Connolly house on Whidbey Island. At the house Shapiro observed an empty bottle bearing the chemical label phenyl-2-propanone.

By prearrangement Shapiro returned to the Connolly house on December 9, 1969, to supply 100 grams of propanone and observe the chemical reaction. When he arrived he observed Patrick Connolly and the respondent cutting up pieces of aluminum foil and placing them in a large flask. There was testimony that some of the foil pieces accidentally fell on the floor and were picked up by the respondent and Shapiro and put into the flask.[3] Thereafter Patrick Connolly added all of the necessary chemicals, including the propanone brought by Shapiro, to make two batches of methamphetamine. The manufacturing process having been completed the following morning, Shapiro was given one-half of the drug and respondent kept the remainder. Shapiro offered to buy, and the respondent agreed to sell, part of the remainder for $60.

About a month later Shapiro returned to the Connolly house and met with Patrick Connolly to ask if he was still interested in their "business arrangement." Connolly replied that he was interested but that he had recently obtained two additional bottles of phenyl-2-propanone and would not be finished with them for a couple of days. He provided some additional methamphetamine to Shapiro at that time. Three days later Shapiro returned to the Connolly house with a search warrant and, among other items, seized an empty 500-gram bottle of propanone and a 100-gram bottle, not the one he had provided, that was partially filled with the chemical.

There was testimony at the trial of respondent and Patrick Connolly that phenyl-2-propanone was generally difficult to obtain. At the request of the Bureau of Narcotics and Dangerous Drugs, some chemical supply firms had voluntarily ceased selling the chemical.

At the close of the evidence, and after receiving the District Judge's standard entrapment instruction, the jury found the respondent guilty on all counts charged. On appeal the respondent conceded that the jury could have found him predisposed to commit the offenses, 459 F.2d at 672, but argued that on the facts presented there was entrapment as a matter of law. The Court of Appeals agreed, although it did not find the District Court had misconstrued or misap-

---

2. At trial Patrick Connolly admitted making this statement to Agent Shapiro but asserted that the statement was not true.

3. Agent Shapiro did not otherwise participate in the manufacture of the drug or direct any of the work.

plied the traditional standards governing the entrapment defense. Rather, the court in effect expanded the traditional notion of entrapment, which focuses on the predisposition of the defendant, to mandate dismissal of a criminal prosecution whenever the court determines that there has been "an intolerable degree of governmental participation in the criminal enterprise." In this case the court decided that the conduct of the agent in supplying a scarce ingredient essential for the manufacture of a controlled substance established that defense.

This new defense was held to rest on either of two alternative theories. One theory is based on two lower court decisions which have found entrapment, regardless of predisposition, whenever the government supplies contraband to the defendants. United States v. Bueno, 447 F.2d 903 (C.A.5 1971); United States v. Chisum, 312 F.Supp. 1307 (C.D.Cal.1970). The second theory, a nonentrapment rationale, is based on a recent Ninth Circuit decision that reversed a conviction because a government investigator was so enmeshed in the criminal activity that the prosecution of the defendants was held to be repugnant to the American criminal justice system. Greene v. United States, 454 F.2d 783 (C.A.9 1971). The court below held that these two rationales constitute the same defense, and that only the label distinguishes them. In any event, it held that "[b]oth theories are premised on fundamental concepts of due process and evince the reluctance of the judiciary to countenance 'overzealous law enforcement.'" 459 F.2d, at 674, quoting Sherman v. United States, 356 U.S. 369, 381 (1958). (Frankfurter, J., concurring).

* * *

In the instant case respondent asks us to reconsider the theory of the entrapment defense as it is set forth in the majority opinions in *Sorrells* and *Sherman*. His principal contention is that the defense should rest on constitutional grounds. He argues that the level of Shapiro's involvement in the manufacture of the methamphetamine was so high that a criminal prosecution for the drug's manufacture violates the fundamental principles of due process. The respondent contends that the same factors that led this Court to apply the exclusionary rule to illegal searches and seizures, Weeks v. United States, 232 U.S. 383 (1914); Mapp v. Ohio, 367 U.S. 643 (1961), and confessions, Miranda v. Arizona, 384 U.S. 436 (1966), should be considered here. But he would have the Court go further in deterring undesirable official conduct by requiring that any prosecution be barred absolutely because of the police involvement in criminal activity. The analogy is imperfect in any event, for the principal reason behind the adoption of the exclusionary rule was the government's "failure to observe its own laws." Mapp v. Ohio, supra, 367 U.S., at 659. Unlike the situations giving rise to the holdings in *Mapp* and *Miranda,* the government's conduct here violated no independent constitutional right of the respondent. Nor did Shapiro violate any federal statute or rule or commit any crime in infiltrating the respondent's drug enterprise.

Respondent would overcome this basic weakness in his analogy to the exclusionary rule cases by having the Court adopt a rigid constitutional rule that would preclude any prosecution when it is shown that the criminal product would not have been possible had not an undercover agent "supplied an indispensable means to the commission of the crime that could not have been obtained otherwise, through legal or illegal channels." * * *

The record discloses that although the propanone was difficult to obtain it was by no means impossible. The defendants admitted making the drug both before and after those batches made with the propanone supplied by Shapiro. Shapiro testified that he saw an empty bottle labeled phenyl-2-propanone on his first visit to the laboratory on December 7, 1969. And when the laboratory was searched pursuant to a search warrant on January 10, 1970, two additional bottles labeled phenyl-2-propanone were seized. Thus, the facts in the record amply demonstrate that the propanone used in the illicit manufacture of methamphetamine not only *could* have been obtained without the intervention of Shapiro but was in fact obtained by these defendants.

While we may some day be presented with a situation in which the conduct of law enforcement agents is so outrageous that due process principles would absolutely bar the government from invoking judicial processes to obtain a conviction, cf. Rochin v. California, 342 U.S. 165 (1952), the instant case is distinctly not of that breed. Shapiro's contribution of propanone to the criminal enterprise already in process was scarcely objectionable. The chemical is by itself a harmless substance and its possession is legal. While the government may have been seeking to make it more difficult for drug rings, such as that of which respondent was a member, to obtain the chemical, the evidence described above shows that it nonetheless was obtainable. The law enforcement conduct here stops far short of violating that "fundamental fairness, shocking to the universal sense of justice," mandated by the Due Process Clause of the Fifth Amendment. Kinsella v. United States ex rel. Singleton, 361 U.S. 234, 246 (1960).

The illicit manufacture of drugs is not a sporadic, isolated criminal incident, but a continuing, though illegal, business enterprise. In order to obtain convictions for illegally manufacturing drugs, the gathering of evidence of past unlawful conduct frequently proves to be an all but impossible task. Thus in drug-related offenses law enforcement personnel have turned to one of the only practicable means of detection: the infiltration of drug rings and a limited participation in their unlawful present practices. Such infiltration is a recognized and permissible means of apprehension; if that be so, then the supply of some item of value that the drug ring requires must, as a general rule, also be permissible. For an agent will not be taken into the confidence of the illegal entrepreneurs unless he has something of value to offer them. Law enforcement tactics such as this can hardly be said to violate "fundamental fairness" or "shocking to the universal sense of justice," *Kinsella,* supra.

Respondent also urges as an alternative to his constitutional argument, that * * * the views of Justices Roberts and Frankfurter, concurring in *Sorrells* and *Sherman,* respectively, which make the essential element of the defense turn on the type and degree of governmental conduct, be adopted as the law.

We decline to overrule these cases. *Sorrells* is a precedent of long standing that has already been once reexamined in *Sherman* and implicitly there reaffirmed. Since the defense is not of a constitutional dimension, Congress may address itself to the question and adopt any substantive definition of the defense that it may find desirable.

* * *

* * * [I]t [does not] seem particularly desirable for the law to grant complete immunity from prosecution to one who himself planned to commit a crime, and then committed it, simply because government undercover agents subjected him to inducements which might have seduced a hypothetical individual who was not so predisposed. We are content to leave the matter where it was left by the Court in *Sherman* * * *[.]

Several decisions of the United States district courts and courts of appeals have undoubtedly gone beyond this Court's opinions in *Sorrells* and *Sherman* in order to bar prosecutions because of what they thought to be for want of a better term "overzealous law enforcement." But the defense of entrapment enunciated in those opinions was not intended to give the federal judiciary a "chancellor's foot" veto over law enforcement practices of which it did not approve. The execution of the federal laws under our Constitution is confided primarily to the Executive Branch of the Government, subject to applicable constitutional and statutory limitations and to judicially fashioned rules to enforce those limitations. We think that the decision of the Court of Appeals in this case quite unnecessarily introduces an unmanageably subjective standard which is contrary to the holdings of this Court in *Sorrells* and *Sherman.*

Those cases establish that entrapment is a relatively limited defense. It is rooted not in any authority of the Judicial Branch to dismiss prosecutions for what it feels to have been "overzealous law enforcement," but instead in the notion that Congress could not have intended criminal punishment for a defendant who has committed all the elements of a prescribed offense, but who was induced to commit them by the government.

* * * It is only when the government's deception actually implants the criminal design in the mind of the defendant that the defense of entrapment comes into play.

Respondent's concession in the Court of Appeals that the jury finding as to predisposition was supported by the evidence is, therefore, fatal to his claim of entrapment. He was an active participant in an illegal drug manufacturing enterprise which began before the government agent appeared on the scene, and continued after the government agent had left the scene. He was, in the words of *Sherman*, supra, not an "unwary innocent" but an "unwary criminal." The Court of Appeals was wrong, we believe, when it sought to broaden the principle laid down in *Sorrells* and *Sherman*. Its judgment is therefore

Reversed.

[The dissenting opinion of Mr. Justice Douglas, with Mr. Justice Brennan concurring, is omitted.]

Mr. Justice STEWART, with whom Mr. Justice BRENNAN and Mr. Justice MARSHALL join, dissenting.

* * *

In my view [the] objective approach to entrapment advanced by the concurring opinions in *Sorrells* and *Sherman* is the only one truly consistent with the underlying rationale of the defense.

In the case before us, I think that the District Court erred in submitting the issue of entrapment to the jury, with instructions to acquit only if it had a reasonable doubt as to the respondent's predisposition to committing the crime. Since, under the objective test of entrapment, predisposition is irrelevant and the issue is to be decided by the trial judge, the Court of Appeals, I believe, would have been justified in reversing the conviction on this basis alone. But since the appellate court did not remand for consideration of the issue by the District Judge under an objective standard, but rather found entrapment as a matter of law and directed that the indictment be dismissed, we must reach the merits of the respondent's entrapment defense.

Since, in my view, it does not matter whether the respondent was predisposed to commit the offense of which he was convicted, the focus must be, rather, on the conduct of the undercover government agent. What the agent did here was to meet with a group of suspected producers of methamphetamine, including the respondent; to request the drug; to offer to supply the chemical phenyl-2-propanone in exchange for one-half of the methamphetamine to be manufactured therewith; and, when that offer was accepted, to provide the needed chemical ingredient, and to purchase some of the drug from the respondent.

It is undisputed that phenyl-2-propanone is an essential ingredient in the manufacture of methamphetamine; that it is not used for any other purpose; and that, while its sale is not illegal, it is difficult to obtain, because a manufacturer's license is needed to purchase it, and because many suppliers, at the request of the Federal Bureau of Narcotics and Dangerous Drugs, do not sell it at all. It is also undisputed that the methamphetamine which the respondent was prosecuted for manufacturing and selling was all produced on December 10, 1969, and that all the phenyl-2-propanone used in the manufacture of that batch of the drug was provided by the government agent. In these circumstances, the agent's undertaking to supply this ingredient to the respondent, thus making it possible for the Government to prosecute him for manufacturing an illicit drug with it, was, I think, precisely the type of governmental conduct that the entrapment defense is meant to prevent.

Although the Court of Appeals found that the phenyl-2-propanone could not have been obtained without the agent's intervention—that "there could not have been the manufacture, delivery, or sale of the illicit drug had it not been for the Government's supply of one of the essential ingredients," 459 F.2d 671, 672—the Court today rejects this finding as contradicted by the facts revealed at trial. The record, as the Court states, discloses that one of the respondent's accomplices, though not the respondent himself, had obtained phenyl-2-propanone from independent sources both before and after receiving the agent's supply, and had used it in the production of methamphetamine. This demonstrates, it is said, that the chemical was obtainable other than through the government agent; and hence the agent's furnishing it for the production of the methamphatamine involved in this prosecution did no more than afford an opportunity for its production to one ready and willing to produce it. Thus, the argument seems to be, there was no entrapment here, any more than there would have been if the agent had furnished common table salt, had that been necessary to the drug's production.

In cannot be doubted that if phenyl-2-propanone had been wholly unobtainable from other sources, the agent's undercover offer to supply it to the respondent in return for part of the illicit methamphetamine produced therewith—an offer initiated and carried out by the agent for the purpose of prosecuting the respondent for producing methamphetamine—would be precisely the type of governmental conduct that constitutes entrapment under any definition. For the agent's conduct in that situation would make possible the commission of an otherwise totally impossible crime, and, I should suppose, would thus be a textbook example of instigating the commission of a criminal offense in order to prosecute someone for committing it.

But assuming in this case that the phenyl-2-propanone was obtainable through independent sources, the fact remains that that used for the particular batch of methamphetamine involved in all three counts of the indictment with which the respondent was charged— i. e., that produced on December 10, 1969—was supplied by the Government. This essential ingredient was indisputably difficult to obtain, and yet that used in committing the offenses of which the respondent was convicted was offered to the respondent by the government agent, on the agent's own initiative, and was readily supplied

to the respondent in needed amounts. If the chemical was so easily
available elsewhere, then why did not the agent simply wait until
the respondent had himself obtained the ingredients and produced the
drug, and then buy it from him? The very fact that the agent felt
it incumbent upon him to offer to supply phenyl-2-propanone in return for the drug casts considerable doubt on the theory that the
chemical could easily have been procured without the agent's intervention, and that therefore the agent merely afforded an opportunity
for the commission of a criminal offense.

In this case, the chemical ingredient was available only to licensed persons, and the Government itself had requested suppliers not
to sell that ingredient even to people with a license. Yet the government agent readily offered and supplied that ingredient to an unlicensed person and asked him to make a certain illegal drug with it.
The Government then prosecuted that person for making the drug
produced *with the very ingredient* which its agent had so helpfully
supplied. This strikes me as the very pattern of conduct that should
be held to constitute entrapment as a matter of law.

It is the Government's duty to prevent crime, not to promote it.
Here, the Government's agent asked that the illegal drug be produced
for him, solved his quarry's practical problems with the assurance that
he could provide the one essential ingredient that was difficult to obtain, furnished that element as he had promised, and bought the finished product from the respondent—all so that the respondent could
be prosecuted for producing and selling the very drug for which the
agent had asked and for which he had provided the necessary component. Under the objective approach that I would follow, this respondent was entrapped, regardless of his predisposition or "innocence."

In the words of Mr. Justice ROBERTS:

"The applicable principle is that courts must be closed to the
trial of a crime instigated by the government's own agents.
No other issue, no comparison of equities as between the
guilty official and the guilty defendant, has any place in the
enforcement of this overruling principle of public policy."
Sorrells v. United States, supra, at 459.

I would affirm the judgment of the Court of Appeals.

NOTES

1. State Bar Committee on Revision of the Penal Code, Final Draft
Texas Penal Code (1970):

§ 8.05. Entrapment

(a) It is a defense to prosecution that a peace officer, or a
person directed by a peace officer, induced the commission of an
offense, in order to obtain evidence of the commission for prosecu-

tion, by methods creating a substantial risk that the offense would be committed by one not otherwise ready to commit it. However, there is no defense under this section if the peace officer, or person directed by him, merely afforded the actor an opportunity to commit the offense.

(b) The defense provided by this section is available even though the actor denies commission of the conduct charged to constitute the offense.

(c) On written motion of the defendant, the court shall determine as a matter of fact and law, after a hearing without the jury, whether the defendant was entrapped to commit the offense. The defendant shall file the motion with the court at least 10 days before the trial begins, or if the court sets a pretrial hearing, the defendant shall file the motion during the hearing. However, the court for good cause shown may permit filing the motion at a later time determined by the court.

(d) If the court determines the defendant was entrapped to commit the offense, it shall acquit him if the state has concluded its case, or dismiss the offense with prejudice if the state has not concluded its case. If the court determines the defendant was not entrapped, but believes reasonable minds could differ over the issue, the court shall submit the entrapment defense to the jury.

To what extent would this alter the defense of entrapment as presently employed in most jurisdictions? Compare this formulation with the following proposal made by the American Civil Liberties Union in its Report of its testimony before the Senate Subcommittee on Criminal Law and Procedures on the Final Report of the National Commission on Reform of the Federal Criminal Laws. 37–38 (March 21, 1972).

§ 702. Entrapment

(1) Defense. It is a defense that the defendant was entrapped into committing the offense.

(2) Entrapment Defined. Entrapment occurs (i) when a law enforcement agent induces the commission of an offense, using persuasion or other means likely to cause normally law abiding persons to commit the offense; or (ii) when the criminal design originates with a law enforcement agent and he implants in the mind of an innocent person the disposition to commit an offense and induce its commission in order that the government may prosecute; or (iii) when the law enforcement agent induces the criminal act without reasonable suspicion [probable cause] that the person being solicited to commit an offense or with whom an illegal transaction is initiated is engaged in or prepared to engage in such offense or transaction. Conduct merely affording a person an opportunity to commit an offense does not constitute entrapment.

(3) The defense afforded by this section may be raised under a plea of not guilty. The defendant shall be entitled to have the issue of entrapment decided by the court and to have the fact that the defense has been raised and evidence introduced in support

thereof kept from the attention of the jury. Evidence of the defendant's past criminal conduct is inadmissible on the entrapment issue.

(4) Law Enforcement Agent Defined. In this section "law enforcement agent" includes personnel of state and local law enforcement agencies as well as of the United States, and any person cooperating with such an agency.

2. To what extent can the problems of official misconduct inherent in entrapment situations be ameliorated by making such conduct a defense to prosecution? Is our national experience with the exclusionary rule with respect to searches and seizures and confessions relevant? Should the misbehaving officer be subject to direct sanctions?

3. Would an alternative solution be to change the substantive criminal law with respect to the crimes which appear to engender such activity? How much weight should this consideration be given in evaluating the present drug laws?

C. DEFENSE OF PERSONS OR PROPERTY

PROPOSED FEDERAL CRIMINAL CODE (1971)

§ 601. Justification

(1) Defense. Except as otherwise expressly provided, justification or excuse under this Chapter is a defense.

(2) Danger to Other Persons. If a person is justified or excused in using force against another, but he recklessly or negligently injures or creates a risk of injury to innocent persons, the justifications afforded by this Chapter are unavailable in a prosecution for such recklessness or negligence, as the case may be.

*   *   *

§ 603. Self-Defense

A person is justified in using force upon another person in order to defend himself against danger of imminent unlawful bodily injury, sexual assault or detention by such other person, except that:

(a) a person is not justified in using force for the purpose of resisting arrest, execution of process, or other performance of duty by a public servant under color of law, but excessive force may be resisted; and

(b) a person is not justified in using force if (i) he intentionally provokes unlawful action by another person in order to cause bodily injury or death to such other person, or (ii) he has entered into a mutual combat with another person or is the initial aggressor. A person's use of defensive force after he withdraws from an encounter and indicates to the other person that he has done so is justified if the latter nevertheless continues or menaces unlawful action.

§ 604. Defense of Others

A person is justified in using force upon another person in order to defend anyone else if (a) the person defended would be justified in defending himself, and (b) the person coming to the defense has not, by provocation or otherwise, forfeited the right of self-defense.

§ 606. Use of Force in Defense of Premises and Property

Force is justified if it is used to prevent or terminate an unlawful entry or other trespass in or upon premises, or to prevent an unlawful carrying away or damaging of property, if the person using such force first requests the person against whom such force is to be used to desist from his interference with the premises or property, except that:

(a) request is not necessary if (i) it would be useless to make the request, or (ii) it would be dangerous to make the request, or (iii) substantial damage would be done to the property sought to be protected before the request could effectively be made;

(b) the use of force is not justified to prevent or terminate a trespass if it will expose the trespasser to substantial danger of serious bodily injury.

§ 607. Limits on the Use of Force: Excessive Force; Deadly Force

(1) Excessive Force. A person is not justified in using more force than is necessary and appropriate under the circumstances.

(2) Deadly Force. Deadly force is justified in the following instances:

(a) when it is expressly authorized by a federal statute or occurs in the lawful conduct of war;

[(a) when it is authorized by a federal law or occurs in the necessary and appropriate conduct of war;]

(b) when used in lawful self-defense, or in lawful defense of others, if such force is necessary to protect the actor or anyone else against death, serious bodily injury, or the commission of a felony involving violence, except that the use of deadly force is not justified if it can be avoided, with safety to the actor and others, by retreat or other conduct involving minimal interference with the freedom of the person menaced. A person seeking to protect someone else must, before using deadly force, try to cause that person to retreat, or otherwise comply with the requirements of this provision, if safety can be obtained thereby; but (i) a public servant or an officer of a ship or aircraft justified in using force in the performance of his duties or a person justified in using force in his assistance need not desist from his efforts because of resistance or threatened resistance by or on behalf of the person against whom his action is directed, and (ii) no person is required to retreat from his dwelling, or place of work, unless he was the original aggressor or is assailed by a person who he knows also dwells or works there;

(c) when used by a person in possession or control of a dwelling or place of work, or a person who is licensed or privileged to be thereon, if such force is necessary to prevent commission of arson, burglary, robbery or a felony involving violence upon or in the dwelling or place of work or to prevent a person in flight immediately after committing a robbery or burglary from taking the fruits thereof from the dwelling or place of work, and the use of force other than deadly force for such purposes would expose anyone to substantial danger of serious bodily injury;

(d) when used by a public servant authorized to effect arrests or prevent escapes, if such force is necessary to effect an arrest or to prevent the escape from custody of a person who has committed or attempted to commit a felony involving violence, or is attempting to escape by the use of a deadly weapon, or has otherwise indicated that he is likely to endanger human life or to inflict serious bodily injury unless apprehended without delay;

(e) when used by a guard or other public servant, if such force is necessary to prevent the escape of a prisoner from a detention facility unless he knows that the prisoner is not such a person as described in paragraph (d) above. A detention facility is any place used for the confinement, pursuant to a court order, of a person (i) charged with or convicted of an offense, or (ii) charged with being or adjudicated a youth offender or juvenile delinquent, or (iii) held for extradition, or (iv) otherwise confined pursuant to court order;

(f) when used by a public servant, if such force is necessary (i) to prevent overt and forceful acts of treason, insurrection or sabotage, or (ii) to prevent murder, manslaughter, aggravated assault, arson, robbery, burglary or kidnapping in the course of a riot if the deadly force is employed following reasonable notice of intent to employ deadly force, and does not carry with it an unreasonable danger to life of nonparticipants in the riot, and is employed pursuant to a decision or order of a public servant having supervisory authority over ten or more other public servants concerned in the suppression of the riot;

(g) when used by an officer of a ship or aircraft if such force is necessary to prevent overt and forceful acts of mutiny, after the participants in such acts against whom such force is to be used have been ordered to cease and given reasonable notice of intent to employ deadly force;

(h) when used by a duly licensed physician, or a person acting at his direction, if such force is necessary in order to administer a recognized form of treatment to promote the physical or mental health of a patient and if the treatment is administered (i) in an emergency, or (ii) with the consent of the patient or, if the patient is a minor or an incompetent person, with the consent of his parent, guardian or other person entrusted with his care and supervision, or (iii) by order of a court of competent jurisdiction;

(i) when used by a person who is directed or authorized to use deadly force by a public servant or an officer of a ship or aircraft and who does not know that, if such is the case, the public servant or such officer is himself not authorized to use deadly force under the circumstances.

§ 608. Excuse

(1) Mistake. A person's conduct is excused if he believes that the factual situation is such that his conduct is necessary and appropriate for any of the purposes which would establish a justification or excuse under this Chapter, even though his belief is mistaken, except that, if his belief is negligently or recklessly held, it is not an excuse in a prosecution for an offense for which negligence or recklessness, as the case may be, suffices to establish culpability. Excuse under this subsection is a defense or affirmative defense according to which type of defense would be established had the facts been as the person believed them to be.

(2) Marginal Transgression of Limit of Justification. A person's conduct is excused if it would otherwise be justified or excused under this Chapter but is marginally hasty or excessive because he was confronted with an emergency precluding adequate appraisal or measured reaction.

§ 619. Definitions for Chapter 6

In this Chapter:

(a) "force" means physical action, threat or menace against another, and includes confinement;

(b) "deadly force" means force which a person uses with the intent of causing, or which he knows to create a substantial risk of causing, death or serious bodily injury.

Intentionally firing a firearm or hurling a destructive device
in the direction of another person or at a moving vehicle in
which another person is believed to be constitutes deadly
force. A threat to cause death or serious bodily injury, by the
production of a weapon or otherwise, so long as the actor's
intent is limited to creating an apprehension that he will use
deadly force if necessary, does not constitute deadly force;

(c) "premises" means all or any part of a building or real
property, or any structure, vehicle or watercraft used for
overnight lodging of persons, or used by persons for carrying on business therein;

(d) "dwelling" means any building or structure, though
movable or temporary, or a portion thereof, which is for the
time being a person's home or place of lodging.

---

1. DEFENSE OF SELF

STATE v. ABBOTT

Supreme Court of New Jersey, 1961.
36 N.J. 63, 174 A.2d 881.

WEINTRAUB, C. J.   Frank Abbott was convicted of atrocious
assault and battery.   The Appellate Division affirmed, 64 N.J.Super.
191, 165 A.2d 537 (1960), and we granted certification, 34 N.J. 176,
167 A.2d 676 (1961).

Abbott shared a common driveway with his neighbors, Michael
and Mary Scarano.   The Scaranos engaged a contractor to pave their
portion.   Abbott obtained some asphalt from the contractor and made
a doorstop to keep his garage door from swinging onto the Scaranos'
property.   Nicholas Scarano, who was visiting with the Scaranos, his
parents, objected to Abbott's innovation.   After some words between
them a fist fight ensued.

Although Abbott managed to land the first punch, with which he
sent Nicholas to the ground, a jury could find Nicholas was the aggressor.   At this point Michael Scarano came at Abbott with a hatchet.
Michael said the tool had just been returned to him by the contractor,
and denied he meant to use it as a weapon.   According to Abbott,
Mary Scarano followed, armed with a carving knife and large fork.
The actors gave varying versions of what happened, but the end result was that all of the Scaranos were hit by the hatchet.   Nicholas
received severe head injuries.   Abbott claimed he too suffered a laceration.

Abbott admitted he finally wrested the hatchet from Michael
but denied he wielded it at all.   Rather he insisted that the Scaranos

were injured during a common struggle for the instrument.   A jury could, however, find Abbott intentionally inflicted the blows.

Abbott was separately indicted for atrocious assault and battery upon each of the Scaranos.   There was a common trial of these indictments.   The jury acquitted Abbott of the charges relating to Michael and Mary, but found him guilty as to Nicholas.

The principal question is whether the trial court properly instructed the jury upon the issue of self-defense.   The trial court charged upon the subject of excessive force, as to which Abbott does not complain.   It charged also upon the subject of retreat, and it is here that error is alleged.   Although the jury could have found Abbott used excessive force, we cannot know whether the jury found for him on that subject and convicted because he had failed to retreat in accordance with the trial court's instruction.

As to retreat, the trial court charged upon two hypotheses.   One was that the critical events occurred upon Abbott's property.   Upon that basis, the court said Abbott could stand his ground, and, of course, of this Abbott does not complain.   The second hypothesis was that the alleged offense occurred upon the common driveway. * * * the trial court held that since all the principals were equally entitled to be on the driveway, Abbott could not claim immunity from the ordinary retreat rule.   Abbott does not question that thesis, but disputes the court's statement of the conditions under which an obligation to retreat would arise.

* * *

The subject of retreat usually arises in homicide matters.   We will first discuss it in that context, and then consider whether the principles apply to a charge of atrocious assault and battery, and if they do, whether the trial court correctly guided the jury in this difficult area.

We should make it clear that we are discussing the doctrine of retreat and not the subject of the use of excessive force.   If the force used was unnecessary in its intensity, the claim of self-defense may fall for that reason.   In the discussion which follows we assume a defendant used no more force than he believed necessary to protect himself in the circumstances as they reasonably appeared to him, and consider only whether the claim of self-defense should be denied because he could have avoided the use of that force by retreating.

The question whether one who is neither the aggressor nor a party to a mutual combat must retreat has divided the authorities. Self-defense is measured against necessity.   From that premise one could readily say there was no necessity to kill in self-defense if the use of deadly force could have been avoided by retreat.   The critics of the retreat rule do not quarrel with the theoretical validity of this conclusion, but rather condemn it as unrealistic.   The law of course should not denounce conduct as criminal when it accords with the behavior of reasonable men. Upon this level, the advocates of no-retreat say the manly thing is to hold one's ground, and hence society should not demand what smacks of cowardice. Adherents of the re-treat rule reply it is better that the assailed shall retreat than that the life of another be needlessly spent. They add that not only do right-thinking men agree, but further a rule so requiring may well induce others to adhere to that worthy standard of behavior. There is much dispute as to which view commands the support of ancient precedents, a question we think it would be profitless to explore.

* * * Our Court of Errors and Appeals deliberately adopted the retreat rule with an awareness of the contending views, * * * The Model Penal Code embraces the retreat rule while acknowledging that on numerical balance a majority of the precedents oppose it. Model Penal Code § 3.04, comment 3, at p. 24 (Tent.Draft No. 8, 1958).

We are not persuaded to depart from the principle of retreat. We think it salutary if reasonably limited. Much of the criticism goes not to its inherent validity but rather to unwarranted applications of the rule. For example, it is correctly observed that one can hard-ly retreat from a rifle shot at close range. But if the weapon were a knife, a lead of a city block might well be enough. Again, the rule cannot be stated baldly, with indifference to the excitement of the occasion. As Mr. Justice Holmes cryptically put it, "Detached reflec-tion cannot be demanded in the presence of an uplifted knife." Brown v. United States, 256 U.S. 335, 343, 41 S.Ct. 501, 502, 65 L.Ed. 961, 963 (1921). Such considerations, however, do not demand that a man should have the absolute right to stand his ground and kill in any and all situations. Rather they call for a fair and guarded statement of appropriate principles.

We believe the following principles are sound:

1. The issue of retreat arises only if the defendant resorted to a deadly force. It is deadly force which is not justifiable when an opportunity to retreat is at hand. Model Penal Code § 3.04(2) (b) (iii). As defined in § 3.12(2) a deadly force means "force which the actor uses with the purpose of causing or which he knows to create a substantial risk of causing death or serious bodily harm."

Hence, it is not the nature of the force defended against which raises the issue of retreat, but rather the nature of the force which the accused employed in his defense. If he does not resort to a deadly force, one who is assailed may hold his ground whether the attack upon him be of a deadly or some lesser character. Although it might be argued that a safe retreat should be taken if thereby the use of *any* force could be avoided, yet, as the comment in the Model Penal Code observes (at p. 23), "The logic of this position never has been accept-ed when moderate force is used in self-defense; here all agree that the actor may stand his ground and estimate necessity upon that basis."

Hence, in a case like the present one, the jury should be instructed that Abbott could hold his ground when Nicholas came at him with his fists, and also when Michael and Mary came at him with the several instruments mentioned, and that the question of retreat could arise only if Abbott intended to use a deadly force.

2. What constitutes an opportunity to retreat which will defeat the right of self-defense? As § 3.04(2) (b) (iii) of the Model Penal Code states, deadly force is not justifiable "if the actor *knows* that he can avoid the necessity of using such force *with complete safety* by retreating * * *." We emphasize "knows" and "with complete safety." One who is wrongfully attacked need not risk injury by retreating, even though he could escape with something less than serious bodily injury. It would be unreal to require nice calculations as to the amount of hurt, or to ask him to endure any at all. And the issue is not whether in retrospect it can be found the defendant could have retreated unharmed. Rather the question is whether he knew the opportunity was there, and of course in that inquiry the total circumstances including the attendant excitement must be considered. We add that upon a retrial the facts as developed in the light of this principle may be such that Abbott would be entitled to an instruction that if his version of the approach by Michael and Mary is accepted, the issue of retreat must be resolved in Abbott's favor.

3. There has been some uncertainty in the language of our cases upon the burden of proof with respect to self-defense. The decisions are treated in State v. Chiarello, N.J.Super., 174 A.2d 506 (1961) where the Appellate Division correctly said that although the burden is upon a defendant to adduce evidence to support the defense, yet if such evidence appears either in the State's case or upon the defendant's case, the issue must be left to the jury with this instruction: that the burden is upon the State to prove beyond a reasonable doubt that the defense is untrue, and hence there must be an acquittal if there is a reasonable doubt as to whether defendant did act in self-defense within the definition of that defense. Accordingly, if the issue of retreat is raised in connection with the defense of self-defense, the jury should be instructed that the burden is also the State's to prove beyond a reasonable doubt that defendant knew he could have retreated with complete safety, and that if a reasonable doubt upon that question should exist, the issue of retreat must be resolved in defendant's favor.

As we have said, the subject of retreat arises most often in homicide cases. It is equally pertinent if the charge is assault with intent to kill. Here the charge is atrocious assault and battery, a crime which involves vicious or brutal conduct. An intent to kill is not an ingredient of that offense, but an intent to do serious bodily harm would seem to be implicit. The doctrine of retreat reflects a policy with respect to the use of deadly force, and the same policy considerations equally obtain if the end result is something less than murder. The Appellate

Division held the doctrine applicable to atrocious assault and battery. The comment to Article 3 of the Model Penal Code (at p. 3) expresses the same view, saying, "If the particular force, for example, would be unjustifiable in a prosecution for homicide it should be equally unjustifiable if the victim survives and what is charged is an assault." This seems sound, and hence an instruction upon the subject is appropriate in a trial for atrocious assault and battery, but the instruction should be expressly centered about the use of deadly force.

We turn to the instruction of the trial court. It reads:

> "* * * If you find the charges involved or either of them happened on the joint or common driveway and that the defendant had an available opportunity to retreat and you also find that he was or appeared to be threatened by assault and battery with imminent danger of life or serious bodily harm, again there is no duty to retreat. On the other hand, under the latter circumstances, if you find that he did not appear to be threatened by assault and battery with imminent danger of life or great bodily harm, he had a duty to retreat and if he failed to retreat the defense of self-defense would not avail him and would not constitute a defense to these charges or any of these charges if you find that he had a duty to retreat."

It is at once apparent that the charge consists of abstract propositions, unanchored to the factual setting. It will be recalled the encounter had two phases, although one quickly followed the other. The first phase was an unarmed attack by Nicholas which Abbott met in kind; the second involved, as the jury could find, an attack or apparent attack by hatchet in the hands of Michael and by kitchen utensils allegedly wielded by Mary, both aided by Nicholas who had arisen from the initial punch. We have no way of knowing whether the jury understood Abbott was required to retreat when first assailed by Nicholas alone. The jury may well have so gathered since the instruction excluded self-defense "if you find that he [Abbott] did *not* appear to be threatened by assault and battery with imminent danger of life or great bodily harm," and of course Nicholas's attack with his fists readily fitted within those terms.

The State asks us to assume the jury understood an unarticulated premise, i.e., that the court was referring solely to the hatchet affair. If we could so assume, still under the instruction the obligation to retreat would depend upon the nature of the attack upon Abbott rather than the amount of force Abbott intended to employ. In short, there was no reference to the use of a deadly force by Abbott. And if we should read the charge in still another way, to wit, that the court was merely defining its prior reference to "an available opportunity" to retreat and hence meant that the opportunity was not "available" if retreat would have subjected Abbott to imminent danger to his life or of great bodily harm but was "available" if he could get away with a hurt of lesser character, still the charge would be incorrect. This is so because there is no obligation to retreat unless retreat can be effected "with complete safety," and indeed with knowledge that retreat can be so effected. Further, upon that interpretation, the instruction would be devoid of any statement of the facts prerequisite for consideration of the subject, i.e., an intent by the defendant to use a deadly force.

We have said enough to indicate the insufficiency of the charge. Even upon study and restudy we are not sure we can extract the thesis the trial court held. A jury which listens to a single reading of an instruction cannot be expected to debate its meaning and reach a correct view of it. A charge should be a clear, unambiguous guide related to the evidence in the case. The conviction must be reversed.

GRAY v. STATE

Supreme Court of Alaska, 1970.
463 P.2d 897.

BONEY, Justice. [The deceased, police officer Strong, had staked out a liquor store. He was in plain clothes and hiding in a stockroom. Defendant Dewey Gray and his brother Willie entered, robbed and tied the clerk who only heard the subsequent shooting. Dewey Gray testified that Strong had emerged shooting without speaking; that Willie was shot and that in fright he, Dewey, shot and was then shot himself. Although wounded, both of the Grays were able to flee.]

Appellants at trial attempted to rely on the privilege of self-defense as a justification for the admitted shooting of Officer Strong. The trial court refused to instruct the jury on the elements of self-defense and the amount of force that may be used in effecting arrest. On appeal it is appellants' contention that a person may claim self-defense when he reasonably defends himself from the use of excessive force by an arresting officer.

The overwhelming weight of authority indicates that a person subjected to an unlawful arrest may use reasonable force to defend himself. In the case of Miller v. State, 462 P.2d 421 (Alaska December 15, 1969), we modified this rule by holding that there was no right to resist a peaceful arrest, even though the arrest was unlawful. The *Miller* case did not deal, however, with the circumstances of the present case, where it has been claimed that the arrest was unlawful because Officer Strong used unprivileged force to effect the arrest. An officer in making an arrest is privileged by statute to use only that force which is necessary to restrain the arrested person. To the use of necessary force the arrested person cannot claim the privilege of self-defense. If more than necessary force is used, then the officer commits an unprivileged assault on the arrested person. To an arresting officer's unprivileged use of force, the arrested person must have the right to use reasonable force to defend himself.

However, the state contends that one who provokes "the difficulty" may not claim self-defense and that appellants provoked the difficulty by committing the armed robbery. Authority clearly supports the contention in this respect and indicates that a person who provokes a difficulty thereby forfeits his right to self-defense. This doctrine has been extended to preclude a person who commits a felony from claiming self-defense not only to the intended victim of the felony, but also as to any person intervening in an attempt either to prevent the crime or to apprehend the criminal.

This court is faced, then, with two competing principles. On the one hand is the doctrine that a person has the right to use necessary force to protect himself against an unlawful arrest involving excessive force; on the other hand is the doctrine that a person provoking a difficulty forfeits his right to self-defense. We believe that, in the particular circumstances before us now, the latter doctrine must prevail. In our recent opinion in Miller v. State, we said in part:

> The control of man's destructive and aggressive impulses is one of the great unsolved problems of our society. Our rules of law should discourage the unnecessary use of physical force between man and man. Any rule which promotes rather than inhibits violence should be re-examined. Along with increased sensitivity to the rights of the criminally accused there should be a corresponding awareness of our need to develop rules which facilitate decent and peaceful behavior by all.

Here we are again presented with a situation which calls for further development and refinement in light of the guidelines which were articulated in *Miller*. Given the exigencies of the circumstances which flowed from appellants' still incomplete armed robbery, we can perceive of no persuasive policy reasons for according appellants the privilege of self-defense. We hold, therefore, that a person who commits an armed robbery forfeits his right to claim as a defense the necessity to protect himself against the use of excessive force by either the intended victim of the robbery or by any person intervening to prevent the crime or to apprehend the criminal, absent a factual showing that at the time the violence occurred, the dangerous situation created by the armed robbery no longer existed.

Accordingly, in the instant case, even if it is conceded that there is some evidence that Officer Strong used excessive force in attempting to arrest the Gray brothers, the perilous situation created by the armed robbery continued to exist at the time the shooting occurred. The uncontradicted evidence shows that Officer Strong was killed by Dewey Gray while the Grays were in the course of perpetrating an armed robbery. This is one of the most dangerous crimes known to man.

Both Dewey and Willie Gray were still inside the robbed premises and in possession of the stolen money when surprised by Officer Strong, and the gun Dewey used in the robbery was still in his hand. It is no answer that the suddenness of Officer Strong's attempts to stop the commission of this crime prevented appellants from manifesting their intent to abandon the robbery or to surrender. Here appellants created the very situation which precluded any effective communication at the time in question.

* * *

Before a self-defense instruction will be required, two evidentiary tests must be met. First there must be some evidence that excessive force was used to effect an arrest or stop the commission of a felony. Second, there must be some evidence from which a jury could conclude that the dangerous situation created by the felony no longer existed. In the case now before us the second requirement has not been met.

To permit appellants to justify their slaying of Officer Strong by claiming self-defense on the facts of this record would be to fashion a rule of law unresponsive to society's need for protection against just such extraordinarily dangerous conduct. This would not, in our view, tend to "facilitate decent and peaceful behaviour by all." To bestow such a privilege to slay would be manifestly unsound.

NOTES

1. If Abbott had killed one of the Scaranos in the honest but unreasonable belief that deadly force was necessary in self-defense, should he be held liable for any grade of criminal homicide? Why? If you believe that self-preservation is instinctual how can punishment of Abbott under the hypothetical facts be justified?

2. Does the requirement that the defendant's belief in the necessity for his use of deadly force be *reasonable* add anything to our analysis? Can the use of deadly force be necessary if it was *unreasonable* under the circumstances as they would have appeared to a reasonable man in the defendant's situation? Apparently both the legislature and Supreme Court of Nebraska thought so. In 1969 the legislature enacted Neb.Rev.Stat. § 29–114 (1969 Cum.Supp.) which provided:

No person in this state shall be placed in legal jeopardy of any kind whatsoever for protecting, by any means necessary, himself, his family, or his real or personal property, or when coming to the aid of another who is in imminent danger of or the victim of aggravated assault, armed robbery, holdup, rape, murder, or any other heinous crime.

When substantial question of self defense in such a case shall exist, which needs legal investigation or court action for the full determination of the facts, and the defendant's actions are subsequently found justified under the intent of this section, the State of

Nebraska shall indemnify or reimburse such defendant for all loss of time, legal fees, court costs, or other expense involved in his defense.

In State v. Goodseal, 186 Neb. 359, 183 N.W.2d 258 (1971), the court, sua sponte, held that the statute was an unconstitutional attempt to delegate to those asserting the right of self-defense the power to decide the punishment of the aggressor. The court focused solely on the first paragraph of § 29–114 and relied heavily on the fact that efforts to amend the statute to make reference to "reasonable means" had been defeated. It did not refer to the second paragraph of the section, yet would not the process of determining the existence of justification there contemplated involve an evaluation of something more than the honesty of the defendant's belief in the necessity for his actions?

3. A invites B and C to his place of business. An altercation ensues between B and C. A requests B to leave. This causes a conflict between A and B which escalates to the point where A is in reasonable fear of imminent danger to his life from B. May A use deadly force even if he has a safe retreat by leaving his place of business? Commonwealth v. Johnston, 438 Pa. 485, 263 A.2d 376 (1970). If, as the *Johnston* court announces, "life is sacred," what reason can be offered for extending the "no retreat" rule to a defendant's place of business?

If our society believes that a man's home (and even, perhaps, his place of work) is a "sanctuary" from which flight is unnecessary as a precondition to the use of deadly force, should he be required to retreat into his home if that would offer safety or may he stand on his porch and use deadly force? State v. Bonano, 59 N.J. 515, 284 A.2d 345 (1971) (defendant armed with pistol need not retreat before assailant brother-in-law mounting porch steps armed with knife; "a porch or similar appurtenance" is deemed to come within the concept of being within one's dwelling house).

The *Bonano* decision reflects the special importance of the home as a place of safety. Under this view force, including deadly force, to prevent a forcible entry into a dwelling may be resorted to earlier than would otherwise be authorized under the rules pertaining to prevention of crime, defense of self or, of course, of property. Although the decisions are not entirely in agreement it seems clear that deadly force may not be employed merely to prevent trespass without more. Rather there must be a reasonable apprehension that the assailant intends to make forcible entry for the purpose of committing a felony or to inflict personal harm on the occupants. However, once entry has been made the normal standards for the rise of force, including the no-retreat rule, are employed for deciding the issue of justification. State v. Brookshire, 353 S.W.2d 681 (Mo.Sup.1962); State v. Couch, 52 N.M. 127, 193 P.2d 405 (1946).

4. Is the *Gray* court saying that an armed robber may be executed if apprehended in the course of his crime? Would it be a desirable legal principle that there can be no claim of self-defense if the killing of the defendant would have been justifiable or excusable homicide? What if the deceased was employing deadly force in the honest and reasonable but erroneous belief that the defendant was engaged in a violent felony?

5. One of the errors claimed by Abbott on appeal was the trial court's sustaining of an objection to the following portion of defense counsel's direct examination of the defendant.

"Q. How much do you weigh, Mr. Abbott? A. At the present time?

Q. At the present time. A. Just close to 200 pounds, right now.

Q. Now, on July 15, 1957 [the date of the alleged crime] do you know how much you weighed? About July 15, not necessarily on that day, say within a few pounds either way. A. About 135, 140 pounds, I guess.

Q. Why was your weight so low at that time?

Mr. Loftus: I object on the ground it is irrelevant. I don't see any relevancy to this situation.

The Court: I will sustain the objection."

174 A.2d at 887. Was the ruling of the trial judge correct? What if at the time of the altercation the defendant, as he claimed, was recovering from serious injuries and illness? To what extent, if at all, should the physical characteristics of the defendant be admissible on the issue of self-defense? His psychological characteristics? *Compare* Abbott *with* State v. Bess, 53 N.J. 10, 247 A.2d 669 (1968).

6. The court in *Abbott* approved the view that the burden of persuasion with respect to the defense of self-defense rests with the prosecution. In a minority of jurisdictions the defendant not only has the burden of producing evidence with respect to self-defense but also has the burden of persuasion, usually by a preponderance. See State v. Millett, 273 A.2d 504, 505–508 (Me.1971). Which view more fully expresses the belief that human life is the supreme value?

---

2. DEFENSE OF OTHERS

PEOPLE v. YOUNG

New York Supreme Court, Appellate Division, 1961.
12 A.D.2d 262, 210 N.Y.S.2d 358.

BREITEL, Justice. The question is whether one is criminally liable for assault in the third degree if he goes to the aid of another who he mistakenly, but reasonably, believes is being unlawfully beaten, and thereby injures one of the apparent assaulters. In truth, the seeming victim was being lawfully arrested by two police officers in plain clothes. Defendant stands convicted of such a criminal assault, for which he received a sentence of 60 days in the workhouse, the execution of such sentence being suspended.

Defendant, aged 40, regularly employed, and with a clean record except for an $8 fine in connection with a disorderly conduct charge

19 years before in Birmingham, Alabama, observed two middle-aged men beating and struggling with a youth of 18. This was at 3:40 p. m. on October 17, 1958 in front of 64 West 64th Street in Manhattan. Defendant was acquainted with none of the persons involved; but believing that the youth was being unlawfully assaulted, and this is not disputed by the other participants, defendant went to his rescue, pulling on or punching at the seeming assailants. In the ensuing affray one of the older men got his leg locked with that of defendant and when defendant fell the man's leg was broken at the kneecap. The injured man then pulled out a revolver, announced to defendant that he was a police officer, and that defendant was under arrest. It appears that the youth in question had played some part in a street incident which resulted in the two men, who were detectives in plain clothes, seeking to arrest him for disorderly conduct. The youth had resisted, and it was in the midst of this resistance that defendant came upon the scene.

At the trial the defendant testified that he had known nothing about what had happened before he came upon the scene; that he had gone to his aid because the youth was crying and trying to pull away from the middle-aged men; and that the older men had almost pulled the trousers off the youth. The only detective who testified stated, in response to a question from the court, that defendant did not know and had no way of knowing, so far as he knew, that they were police officers or that they were making an arrest.

Two things are to be kept sharply in mind in considering the problem at hand. The first is that all that is involved here is a criminal prosecution for simple assault (Penal Law, § 244), and that the court is not concerned with the incidence of civil liability in the law of torts as a result of what happened on the street. Second, there is not here involved any question of criminal responsibility for interfering with an arrest where it is known to the actor that police officers are making an arrest, but he mistakenly believes that the arrest is unlawful.

In this State there are no discoverable precedents involving mistake of fact when one intervenes on behalf of another person and the prosecution has been for assault, rather than homicide. (The absence of precedents in this state and many others may simply mean that no enforcement agency would prosecute in the situations that must have occurred.) No one would dispute, however, that a mistake of fact would provide a defense if the prosecution were for homicide. This divided approach is sometimes based on the untenable distinction that mistake of fact may negative a "specific" intent required in the degrees of homicide but is irrelevant to the general intent required in simple assault, or, on the even less likely distinction, that the only intent involved in assault is the intent to touch without consent or legal justification (omitting the qualification of unlawfulness). The last, of course, is a partial confusion of tort law with criminal law, and even then is not quite correct (Restatement, Torts, §§ 63–75).

There have been precedents elsewhere among the states. There is a split among the cases and in the jurisdictions. Most hold that the rescuer intervenes at his own peril, but others hold that he is excused if he acts under mistaken but reasonable belief that he is protecting a victim from unlawful attack. Many of the cases which hold that the actor proceeds at his peril involve situations where the actor was present throughout, or through most, or through enough of the transaction and, therefore, was in no position to claim a mistake of fact. Others arise in rough situations in which the feud or enmity generally to the peace officer is a significant factor. Almost all apply unanalytically the rubric that the right to intervene on behalf of another is no greater than the other's right to self-defense, a phrasing of ancient but questionable lineage going back to when crime and tort were not yet divided in the common law—indeed, when the right to private redress was not easily distinguishable from the sanction for the public wrong.

*   *   *

More recently in the field of criminal law the American Law Institute in drafting a model penal code has concerned itself with the question in this case. Under section 3.05 of the Model Penal Code the use of force for the protection of others is excused if the actor behaves under a mistaken belief (Model Penal Code, Tent.Draft No. 8, May 9, 1958.)

The comments by the reporters on the Model Penal Code are quite appropriate. After stating that the defense of strangers should be assimilated to the defense of oneself the following is said:

"In support of such a ruling, it may perhaps be said that the potentiality for deterring the actor from the use of force is greater where he is protecting a stranger than where he is protecting himself or a loved one, because in the former case the interest protected is of relatively less importance to him; moreover the potential incidence of mistake in estimating fault or the need for action on his part is increased where the defendant is protecting a stranger, because in such circumstances he is less likely to know which party to the quarrel is in the right. These arguments may be said to lead to the conclusion that, in order to minimize the area for error or mistake, the defendant should act at his peril when he is protecting a stranger. This emasculates the privilege of protection of much of its content, introducing a liability without fault which is indefensible in principle. The cautious potential actor who knows the law will, in the vast majority of cases, refrain from acting at all. The result may well be that an innocent person is injured without receiving assistance from bystanders. It seems far preferable, therefore, to predicate the justification upon the actor's belief, safeguarding if thought necessary against abuse of the privilege by the imposition of a requirement of proper care in evolving the belief. Here, as elsewhere, the latter problem is dealt with by the general provision in Section 3.09." (Model Penal Code, Tent.Draft No. 8, supra, at p. 32.)

Apart from history, precedents, and the language distinctions that may be found in the statutes, it stands to reason that a man should not be punished criminally for an intent crime unless he, indeed, has the intent. Where a mistake of relevant facts is involved the premises for such intent are absent. True, there are occasions in public policy and its implementation for dispensing with intent and making one responsible for one's act even without immediate or intentional fault. This is generally accomplished by statute, and generally by statute which expressly dispenses with the presence of intent. Thus, it may well be that a Legislature will determine that in order to protect the police in their activities and to make it difficult to promote false defenses one may proceed against a police officer while acting in the line of duty only at one's peril, * * *. But this is not a part of the intent crime of assault as it existed under common law or as it exists today under the statutes.

Indeed, if the analysis were otherwise, then the conductor who mistakenly ejects a passenger for not having paid his fare would be guilty of assault, which is hardly the case. So, too, a police officer who came to the assistance of a brother police officer would be guilty of assault if it should turn out that the brother police officer was engaged in making an unlawful arrest or was embarked upon an assault of his own private motivation.

It is a sterile and desolate legal system that would exact punishment for an intentional assault from one like this defendant, who acted from the most commendable motives and without excessive force. Had the facts been as he thought them, he would have been a hero and not condemned as a criminal actor. The dearth of applicable precedents—as distinguished from theoretical generalizations never, or rarely, applied—in England and in most of the states demonstrates that the benevolent intervenor has not been cast as a pariah. It is no answer to say that the policeman should be called when one sees an injustice. Even in the most populous centers, policemen are not that common or that available. Also, it ignores the peremptory response to injustice that the good man has ingrained. Again, it is to be noted, in a criminal proceeding one is concerned with the act against society, not with the wrong between individuals and the right to reparation, which is the province of tort.

Accordingly, the judgment of conviction should be reversed, on the law, and the information dismissed.

VALENTE, Justice (dissenting).

I dissent and would affirm the conviction because the intent to commit a battery was unquestionably proven; and, since there was no relationship between defendant and the person whom the police officers were arresting, defendant acted at his peril in intervening and striking the officer. Under well-established law, defendant's rights were no greater than those of the person whom he sought to protect; and since the arrest was lawful, defendant was no more privileged to assault the police officer than the person being arrested.

The conclusion that defendant was properly convicted in this case comports with sound public policy. It would be a dangerous precedent for courts to announce that plain-clothes police officers attempting lawful arrests over wrongful resistance are subject to violent interference by strangers ignorant of the facts, who may attack the officers with impunity so long as their ignorance forms a reasonable basis for a snap judgment of the situation unfavorable to the officers. Although the actions of such a defendant, who acts on appearances, may eliminate the specific intent required to convict him of a felony assault, it should not exculpate him from the act of aggressive assistance to a law breaker in the process of wrongfully resisting a proper arrest.

I do not detract from the majority's views regarding commendation of the acts of a good Samaritan, although it may be difficult in some cases to distinguish such activities from those of an officious intermeddler. But opposed to the encouragement of the "benevolent intervenor" is the conflicting and more compelling interest of protection of police officers. In a city like New York, where it becomes necessary to utilize the services of a great number of plain-clothes officers, the efficacy of their continuing struggle against crime should not be impaired by the possibility of interference by citizens who may be acting from commendable motives. It is more desirable—and evidently up to this point the Legislature has so deemed it—that in such cases the intervening citizen be held to act at his peril when he assaults a stranger, who unknown to him is a police officer legally performing his duty. In this conflict of interests, the balance preponderates in favor of the protection of the police rather than the misguided intervenor.

PEOPLE v. YOUNG

Court of Appeals of New York, 1962.
11 N.Y.2d 274, 229 N.Y.S.2d 1, 183 N.E.2d 319.

PER CURIAM. Whether one, who in good faith aggressively intervenes in a struggle between another person and a police officer in civilian dress attempting to effect the lawful arrest of the third person, may be properly convicted of assault in the third degree is a question of law of first impression here.

The opinions in the court below in the absence of precedents in this State carefully expound the opposing views found in other jurisdictions. The majority in the Appellate Division have adopted the minority rule in the other States that one who intervenes in a struggle between strangers under the mistaken but reasonable belief that he is protecting another who he assumes is being unlawfully beaten is thereby exonerated from criminal liability. The weight of authority holds with the dissenters below that one who goes to the aid of a third person does so at his own peril.

While the doctrine espoused by the majority of the court below may have support in some States, we feel that such a policy would not be conducive to an orderly society. We agree with the settled policy of law in most jurisdictions that the right of a person to defend another ordinarily should not be greater than such person's right to defend himself. Subdivision 3 of section 246 of the Penal Law, Consol.Laws, c. 40, does not apply as no offense was being committed on the person of the one resisting the lawful arrest. Whatever may be the public policy where the felony charged requires proof of a specific intent and the issue is justifiable homicide (cf. People v. Maine, 166 N.Y. 50, 59 N.E. 696), it is not relevant in a prosecution for assault in the third degree where it is only necessary to show that the defendant knowingly struck a blow.

In this case there can be no doubt that the defendant intended to assault the police officer in civilian dress. The resulting assault was forceful. Hence motive or mistake of fact is of no significance as the defendant was not charged with a crime requiring such intent or knowledge. To be guilty of third degree assault "It is sufficient that the defendant voluntarily intended to commit the unlawful act of touching" (1 Wharton's Criminal Law and Procedure [1957], § 338, p. 685). Since in these circumstances the aggression was inexcusable the defendant was properly convicted.

Accordingly, the order of the Appellate Division should be reversed and the information reinstated.

NOTE

Does the "alter ego" rule for evaluating the scope of one's right to defend another which is embraced by the Court of Appeals in *Young* abandon moral culpability as a prerequisite to criminal liability? If so, under what rationale can punishment of Young be justified? Will we have a more "orderly society" if people are discouraged from intervening to protect others from physical violence? *Compare* State v. Fair, 45 N.J. 77, 211 A.2d 359 (1965). The *Young* decision is critically examined in 63 Colum.L.Rev. 160 (1963) and 111 U.Pa.L.Rev. 506 (1963).

3. DEFENSE OF PROPERTY

RUSSELL v. STATE

Supreme Court of Alabama, 1929.
219 Ala. 567, 122 So. 683.

Robert Russell was convicted of murder in the first degree, and he appeals.

FOSTER, J. According to defendant's evidence, decedent and two others went to defendant's home to repossess a cooking stove, upon which it was claimed one of them had acquired by transfer a conditional (or lease) sale contract, from the alleged seller to defendant; that defendant informed them that if they had a writ of detinue it was perfectly all right, but otherwise not to get the stove; that they said they did not need any law, that law cost money, etc., and went on in the kitchen to take it; that defendant had no gun, but picked up a pick handle and followed them to the kitchen, and they went to the stove; that defendant told them they had to get out and leave his home, and he was not going to give up the stove without the proper means. One of them said to defendant that he must put that stick down, or he would give defendant a "stick fit," and made a motion for his hip and pointed his finger at defendant, and said, "I will shoot you in two, boy." Defendant threw down the pick handle and ran out to where his wife was in the yard, and told her to go in there and tell them to get out of there and leave his house; that defendant then went to a neighbor's next door and procured a gun (pistol) and came back home, and went to the front porch where one of the men was, and told him to stay out of his house; defendant then heard his wife and little kids crying out, and he ran back in the house, and heard her begging them to stop taking out the stove and leave; that as defendant came to the door, deceased said, "didn't we put you out once"; defendant said, "yes, you put me out once, but I am back here again"; that defendant went up to him and caught him by the right arm, and would not let him go with the stove, and told him to put the stove down and get out; that one of the party, not deceased, said "set it down, and I will put that son of a bitch out of here to stay this time," and when he said that defendant shot as the men were putting down the stove, and the bullet, after going through the warming closet, hit the companion of deceased who had made the remark, but he was not killed, and defendant shot again as deceased at the same time kicked defendant, and deceased was hit by that shot, which killed him. Defendant then ran, and went off to another mine some 12 or 15 miles away, where he was later arrested. Neither deceased nor any of his companions displayed a weapon, and if they had one it was not shown.

The testimony for the state was that no threats were made, no anger displayed; that when defendant returned with the weapon he placed it against deceased and shot and killed him without warning or provocation, after having shot and wounded his companion.

* * *

We think that charges 6, 27, and 28, refused appellant, conflict with the rules of law which we have found to be generally accepted as authoritative. The portion of the general charge attacked in brief seems correctly to assert the same principle. It is the following statements: "This defendant would not be justified under the laws of Alabama in shooting the deceased, to prevent the removal from his house of a stove or range. The law would not justify a homicide to prevent the commission of a trespass upon the doctrine of self-defense." * * *

We think the charges were properly refused, and the excerpt from the general charge now argued by appellant as being erroneous was also without error, for the reasons which we will now discuss.

It is well understood that deceased and his companions did not have the right to take possession of the stove, if, in doing so, it was necessary to commit a breach of the peace, or to use violence. Street v. Sinclair, 71 Ala. 110. It is stated in Street v. Sinclair, supra: "But he proceeds at his own peril if he commits the slightest assault, or other breach of the public peace, for, if individuals were thus allowed to redress their own private injuries, the peace of society and good order of government would cease." In another case it is said: "It is a settled principle of our law, that every one has the right to defend his person and property against unlawful violence, and may employ as much force as is necessary to prevent its invasion. Property would be of little value, if the owner was bound to stand with folded arms and suffer it taken by him who is bold and unscrupulous enough to seize it. But when it is said a man may rightfully use as much force as is necessary for the protection of his person and property, it must be recollected the principle is subject to this most important qualification, that he shall not, except in extreme cases, inflict great bodily harm, or endanger human life. State v. Morgan [25 N.C.] 3 Ired. 186 [38 Am. Dec. 714]. The preservation of human life, and of limb and member from grievous harm, is of more importance to society than the protection of property. Compensation may be made for injuries to, or the destruction of, property; but for the deprivation of life there is no recompense; and for grievous bodily harm, at most, but a poor equivalent. It is an inflexible principle of the criminal law of this State, and we believe of all the states, as it is of the common law, that for the prevention of a bare trespass upon property, not the dwelling-house, human life can not be taken, nor grievous bodily harm inflicted. If in the defense of property, not the dwelling-house, life is taken with a deadly weapon, it is murder, though the killing may be actually necessary to prevent the trespass." Simpson v. State, 59 Ala. 1, 14, 31 Am.Rep. 1; * * *

The rule at common law is that one may prevent an aggressor from entering his home, when the door is closed, even to the taking of life. But once inside peaceably, even though misbehaving, the owner cannot intentionally take his life for his refusal to leave, though he may use reasonable force to exclude him.

A felonious homicide is committed by one who inflicts death merely in opposing an unlawful endeavor to carry away his property. He has the right to resist, but not to the taking of life.

Our conclusion is that the charges refused appellant conflict with these well-established principles.

Charges 14 and 17 justify defendant in killing deceased if the latter were committing a felony in defendant's home. It is sometimes said that "the law will justify the taking of life when it is done from necessity to prevent the commission of a felony." But this rule has limitations not now material.

Decedent and his companions were attempting to repossess property under a claim of right, by virtue of a conditional sale contract. We do not think a jury would be justified in finding a felonious intent under those circumstances. That intent is a necessary element of such a felony as may be claimed against the parties on that occasion. There is no claim here that they were acting under a mere dishonest pretense of right to the stove. There was therefore no felony, and the charges were abstract, if not bad for other reasons.

The doctrine of want of necessity to retreat when defendant is attacked in his own home as embraced in some of the refused charges has no application when, as here, there does not seem to have been a just cause to believe that an attack was about to be made on defendant such as would justify him in his claim of self-defense.

Affirmed.

STATE v. DOOLEY

Supreme Court of Missouri, 1894.
121 Mo. 591, 26 S.W. 558.

GANTT, P. J. [Marshall Bennett and Constable Evans had executed a warrant for the arrest of Gus Price for the theft of two horses. They took the horses, although without warrant, from the defendants, W. H. Dooley and his son Harvey, who had hired them from Price and apparently had agreed to purchase them. Defendants pursued and recaptured the horses from Bennett and Evans at gun point accompanied with threats of death. Defendants were convicted of assault with intent to kill, without malice, and fined $100 each.]

* * *

The ninth instruction for the state told the jury that "even though they should believe that Richard T. Bennett and George C. Evans irregularly or improperly obtained possession of the horses in controversy, yet such fact would not justify defendants in retaking the same by force, nor by the use of a deadly weapon," whereas defendants, in their sixth instruction, which was refused by the court, prayed the court to instruct the jury "that if the defendants had possession of said horses, and George C. Evans, Richard Bennett, and Gus Price took said team from defendants, without defendants' authority, and drove away with said horses, and that immediately thereafter the defendants followed said parties, and demanded and took said horses away from said Bennett, Evans, and Price, and used no more force than was necessary to do so, then defendants are guilty of no crime." The propriety of the giving of the said instruction for the state, and refusal of said instruction for defendants, will determine the merits of this appeal. That the evidence sustains the claim that the defendants were in the actual possession of the horses, claiming a property or possessory right in or to them, must be, we think, conceded. Their conduct must be measured, so far as this charge is concerned, by the facts as they existed that morning, or reasonably appeared to exist. Now, Bennett and Evans had no writ or authority to take the horses. Conceding they had a warrant for Price, that did not authorize them to seize the horses in the possession of a third person. Admitting that they were without lawful authority to take the horses, but that they did so, two questions arise: First, could defendants lawfully recapture them without resorting to the process of the courts? And, secondly, how much force could they lawfully use in affecting a recapture?

The first question must be answered in the affirmative. If the jury found, as we think there was evidence from which they could so find, that the defendants were in possession of these horses, in good faith claiming said possession, and Bennett and Evans, without authority, forcibly, in their presence, took them from their driver, the defendants had the right to retake them from Bennett and Evans.

And this brings us to the second, and important, inquiry in this case: How much force might defendants exert in reclaiming the horses? The power to retake is incident to the right to defend, but it is sometimes said that the right to recapture property is more limited than its defense, when in actual possession; and, while it is allowed, the courts have been cautious in defining the right, and justly so, on account of the danger usually attending the recapture, both to the owner and the peace of the community. When one's property is taken with a felonious intent, the urgency of the recapture is vastly greater than when there is a simple conflict in the claim of title to the property. In the case of felony great force may be resorted to with propriety; but where there is, clearly, no felony, but a mere dispute as to the legal ownership, a resort to violence disproportionate to the value of the property, and where peaceful remedies would prove equal-ly efficacious, should not be sustained. * * * In State v. Morgan, 3 Ired. 186, a constable had seized the defendant's gun, which was his "arms for muster," and was privileged by law from seizure. The de-fendant drew his axe on the constable, and said "Give up the gun, or I'll split you down." After some further parley, the matter was ar-ranged, and the gun released. On an indictment for an assault with intent to kill, the question was whether the conditional threat, coupled with the act of holding the axe in a position to strike, constituted an assault with intent to kill. Judge Gaston said: "Assuming, then, that the constable had wrongfully taken the gun, and that the defendant had a right to require its return, and that exertion of force, nothing short of that which was begun on the part of the defendant, would have availed to compel its return, in our opinion, the assault is not justified. It was made with a deadly weapon, which, if used, would have probably occasioned death, and made without any previous re-sistance on the part of the officer. It was therefore an assault with intent to kill. If this intent were lawful, the assault with that in-tent was lawful. If the intent was unlawful, the assault cannot be justified. Now, when it is said that a man may rightfully use as much force as is necessary for the protection of his person or prop-erty, it should be recollected that this rule is subject to this most im-portant modification: that he shall not, except in extreme cases, en-danger human life, or great bodily harm. * * * The purpose is, indeed, rightful, but it is not one of such paramount necessity as to justify a resort to such desperate means." The case at bar is strik-ingly similar to the case of State v. Morgan, supra. In this case, as in that, the act of the defendants in presenting two deadly weapons at Bennett and Evans was apparently a most dangerous assault, ac-companied with a present purpose to do great bodily harm, or kill them; and the only declaration by which the character of the as-sault is mitigated, or attempted to be changed, is that their purpose was not unconditional, but having commenced the assault, and pro-ceeded far enough to put Evans and Bennett in extreme danger, they suspended long enough to permit them to comply unconditionally with their demands to loose the horses.

* * *

Several witnesses in this case testified that the defendant William H. Dooley had his pistol drawn, and his son Harvey, to use his own expression, "covered Bennett with his rifle" before they demanded the horses. In his testimony, defendant W. H. Dooley, when asked, if they had not given him the horses, if it was not his purpose to use his pistol, answered, "I was after those horses. If I had to use them, I would have scuffled with them awhile, first. If they had attempted to shoot, we would have drawed there, and might have got them." In other words, not only his conduct, but his own testimony, indicated that he had a settled and determined purpose to shoot Bennett and

Evans unless they complied with his demands. The pistol and rifle were both in position to shoot before the demand was made. If the defendants did effect the recapture of the horses by presenting the loaded revolver and rifle at Bennett and his party, then they exceeded the force authorized by law, and the unlawful taking of the horses by Bennett is no justification for such an assault.

* * * Had the court, in the ninth instruction for the state, only said that defendants would not be justified in retaking said horses by the use of a deadly weapon, that instruction would have been correct; but it went further, and said they would not be justified in retaking "by force." Now, we have seen that defendants were authorized to regain their lawful possession by force, provided that force did not consist of "means reasonably calculated to endanger life, or great bodily harm;" and hence the instruction, in this respect, denied defendants a right vouchsafed them by the law. The defendants' sixth instruction should have been modified so as to restrict their right to recapture to such force as was reasonably necessary to effect that purpose, provided it did not extend to the use of a deadly weapon or to an assault likely to produce death or great bodily harm. Subject to this qualification, it is a question of fact for the jury, in each case, how much force is reasonable and necessary.

* * * This eighth instruction was also erroneous in that it denies, as does the second instruction for the defendant, the right to pursue and take the property. If, as we understand these two instructions, they limit the right of defendants to retake to the immediate time and place of taking, and deny it if the horses were temporarily taken out of their sight, in the flight to Higginsville, although the pursuit was immediate, we think they restrict the right of recaption too narrowly. With these modifications, the instructions will fairly present the case to the jury on a new trial. The judgment is reversed, and the cause remanded for a new trial. All of this division concur.

NOTES

1. A, a farmer, had experienced considerable damage to his watermelon crop apparently due to local boys. He set out six spring guns, shotguns rigged to be discharged by the tripping of a wire. Danger signs were allegedly posted at each end of the watermelon patch. S neighbor's son of 14 entered the patch and was severely injured by a shotgun blast. A was convicted of shooting with intent to wound. The conviction was affirmed, the court concluding that, although A *might* be justified in using such a device to prevent the entry of a *felon* into his *dwelling,* A could not use deadly force to expel a trespasser in the absence of reasonable grounds to fear great bodily harm. State v. Childers, 133 Ohio St. 508, 14 N.E.2d 767 (1938).

An extensive review of both civil and criminal cases involving the use of mechanical devices for the protection of property may be found in Katko v. Briney, 183 N.W.2d 657 (Iowa 1971). There the court affirmed a verdict of $20,000 actual and $10,000 punitive damages for injuries caused to the trespassing plaintiff by a spring gun set by the defendant in his abandoned farmhouse.

2. Aside from situations such as the spring gun in *Childers* the defense of property will usually be raised as only one of several forms of justification: self-defense, defense of habitation, and prevention of crime.

Although the right to use force in defense of property has been the subject of rather ringing rhetoric, see State v. Lee, 258 N.C. 44, 127 S.E.2d 774 (1962), it is clear that, in general, our law values property far below life and limb.

3. How would the *Dooley* case be resolved under the proposed Federal Criminal Code? If there is a difference in result, how can it be justified?

D. RESISTANCE TO UNLAWFUL ARREST

STATE v. KOONCE

Superior Court of New Jersey, Appellate Division, 1965.
89 N.J.Super. 169, 214 A.2d 428.

CONFORD, S. J. A. D. Certain charges against the defendants arising out of an arrest of defendant Kurt Koonce ("Kurt," hereinafter) by Newark police officers for selling liquor to a minor were tried before the Municipal Court of the City of Newark. The charge against Kurt of unlawful sale to a minor was, according to the docket record, "dismissed for lack of evidence." A complaint against Kurt for assault and battery on Police Officer Costanzo resulted in a conviction and a 90-day jail term in the county penitentiary. Both Kurt and Florence Koonce ("Florence," hereinafter) were convicted on a complaint of assault and battery on Police Captain Zizza; Kurt was sentenced to time spent in jail and Florence to a $25 fine.

On appeal to the Essex County Court, and after a trial *de novo* Kurt was found guilty of the assault on Costanzo but acquitted of the charge as to Zizza. He was sentenced to a 90-day jail term. Florence was found guilty of the assault on Zizza and fined $25.

* * *

Defendants' second appellate point is that "defendants' alleged conduct, in repelling an unlawful arrest, was legally justified." Here defendants invoke the common-law rule that a citizen may use such force as may be reasonably necessary to repel or prevent an illegal arrest. They contend that since the statutory offense of selling liquor to a minor, though denominated a "misdemeanor," is punishable by imprisonment for not more than 90 days, it is in the category of common-law misdemeanor rather than felony for purposes of applying the general common-law rule that a peace officer may arrest without a warrant (there was no warrant here) for a misdemeanor only if the offense was committed in his presence.

* * *

We turn, then, to the first premise of the thesis advanced: Kurt Koonce did not violate R.S. 33:1–77, N.J.S.A., in the presence of the arresting police; therefore, his arrest for that offense was unlawful. We have little difficulty in agreeing with defendants to this extent, i. e., that assuming a violation of the statutory proscription of *sale* to a minor by some person connected with the operation of the Glitter Club on the occasion in question in the presence of the officers, the officers had insufficient basis for a determination that Kurt was the offender to justify his arrest.

* * *

We are thus finally brought to the determinative issue in the case. Is the so-called common-law rule of right of a citizen to physical resistance to an illegal arrest by a police officer to be taken to be the law of New Jersey in present-day society? We have concluded to the contrary.

While, as indicated above, there is no doubt that the common-law rule is that a citizen has the right of reasonable resistance, even to the extent of force, to an illegal arrest by a police officer, and American jurisdictions, generally, continued to adhere thereto, no New Jersey court of highest jurisdiction has expressly applied or approved that rule, to our knowledge, nor is it declared by legislative enactment, and we are therefore free to examine the question of its continued justification as a part of our non-statutory law in contemporary civilization.

* * *

In Brown v. State, 62 N.J.L. 666, 42 A. 811 (E. & A.1899), defendant was convicted of murder when he shot a plainclothes policeman in escaping after an arrest by the latter on suspicion of a felony or attempted felony. The opinion of Mr. Justice Dixon, dissenting from an affirmance, states that the issues involved the question of the lawfulness of the arrest, since failure of the State to prove such lawfulness should have caused the arrest to be "treated as any other unlawful interference with personal liberty,—as an act which may be lawfully resisted". In the course of its determination that the portions of the trial court's charge under attack contained nothing prejudicially injurious to defendant's rights, the opinion of the majority had no occasion to express agreement or disagreement with Justice Dixon's thus stated view, the charge containing nothing in derogation of defendant's supposed common-law rights in the respect noted.

Both the Uniform Arrest Act and the Model Penal Code recommend abolition of the common-law rule. Section 5 of the former provides:

"If a person has reasonable ground to believe that he is being arrested by a peace officer, it is his duty to refrain from using force or any weapon in resisting arrest regardless of whether or not there is a legal basis for the arrest."

Professor Warner, Reporter to the Interstate Commission on Crime, which formulated the Uniform Arrest Act, explained the background of the law of arrest preceding organization of regular metropolitan police forces in early 19th Century England as follows:

"[It] was developed largely during a period when most arrests were made by private citizens, when bail for felonies was usually unattainable, and when years might pass before the royal judges arrived for a jail delivery. Further, conditions in the English jails were then such that a prisoner had an excellent chance of dying of disease before trial." Warner, "The Uniform Arrest Act," 28 Va.L.Rev. 315 (1942).

See also Hall, "Legal and Social Aspects of Arrest," 49 Harv.L.Rev. 566, 578–92 (1936).

In the Warner article cited above the author goes on to discuss the rule here at issue:

"It has always been illegal to resist a lawful arrest. But [contra] if the arrest is unlawful * * *. The rule developed when long imprisonment, often without the opportunity of bail, 'goal [sic] fever,' physical torture, and other great dangers were to be apprehended from arrest, whether legal or illegal. * * *

When the law of arrest developed, resistance to an arrest by a peace officer did not involve the serious dangers it does today. Constables and watchmen were armed only with staves and swords, and the person to be apprehended might successfully hold them off with his own weapon and thus escape." (28 Va.L.Rev., at p. 330)

The new rule of the Uniform Act was justified in the same article on two grounds: first, that the fate of today's arrestee is usually a few hours in a reasonably clean place of detention rather than the probable consequences awaiting the arrestee of yore. (Id., at p. 315); second, and more important:

"Today, every [American] police officer is armed with a pistol and has orders not to desist from making an arrest though there is forceful resistance. Accordingly, successful resistance is usually possible only by shooting the officer to prevent him from shooting first." (Id., at p. 330)

Section 5 of the Uniform Arrest Act, or the equivalent thereof, is statute law in New Hampshire, Rhode Island, California and Delaware.

There is much discussion in the literature of arrest law as to the *quantum* of force which should be permitted the officer in a legal arrest and an arrestee in an unlawful arrest. See, inter alia, Moreland, "The Use of Force in Effecting or Resisting Arrest," 33 Neb.L. Rev. 408 (1954); "Justification for the Use of Force in the Criminal Law," 13 Stan.L.Rev. 566 (1961). These writings indicate a consensus that a line must be drawn beyond which the fracas resulting from an arrest may not go. The two works just cited submit that the officer's force must be tailored to the crime, i. e., that an officer may not kill to apprehend a driver whose hour has expired on the parking meter, but may use great force to subdue a murderer. Another commentator puts forth the tentative generalization that the victim of an unlawful arrest should be permitted to resist only if less than serious bodily harm will be inflicted upon the arrester. "Criminal Law: Force That May be Used to Resist an Illegal Arrest," 9 Okla.L. Rev. 60, 65 (1956).

But it seems to us that an appropriate accommodation of society's interests in securing the right of individual liberty, maintenance of law enforcement, and prevention of death or serious injury not only of the participants in an arrest fracas but of innocent third persons, precludes tolerance of any formulation which validates an arrestee's resistance of a police officer with force merely because the arrest is ultimately adjudged to have been illegal. Force begets force, and escalation into bloodshed is a frequent probability. The right or wrong of an arrest is often a matter of close debate as to which even lawyers and judges may differ. In this era of constantly expanding legal protections of the rights of the accused in criminal proceedings, one deeming himself illegally arrested can reasonably be asked to submit peaceably to arrest by a police officer, and to take recourse in his legal remedies for regaining his liberty and defending the ensuing prosecution against him. At the same time, police officers attempting in good faith, although mistakenly, to perform their duties in effecting an arrest should be relieved of the threat of physical harm at the hands of the arrestee.

*   *   *

The concept of self-help is in decline. It is antisocial in an urbanized society. It is potentially dangerous to all involved. It is no longer necessary because of the legal remedies available.

Being confident that the Supreme Court of New Jersey would approve the foregoing views, we declare it to be the law of this State that a private citizen may not use force to resist arrest by one he knows or has good reason to believe is an authorized police officer engaged in the performance of his duties, whether or not the arrest is illegal under the circumstances obtaining.

So much decided, shall these defendants as a consequence stand rightfully convicted of assault? It must be remembered that when the inculpated conduct occurred it was undoubtedly the general understanding that the common-law rule of right of resistance to an illegal arrest applied in this State * * *

In the foregoing circumstances, the judicial evocation of an altered rule of criminal law should have prospective application only. It is uniformly recognized that it would be fundamentally unjust to render criminal, by an overruling decision, conduct which was not criminal when it occurred. This would be equivalent in effect on the accused of an *ex post facto* statute.

* * *

For the foregoing reasons, the conduct of the defendants having been free from criminality when it transpired it will not be rendered criminal by our present declaration that hereafter, as more specifically stated hereinabove, it shall not be lawful to resist a police officer undertaking to effect an arrest notwithstanding the illegality of the arrest.

Judgments reversed.

STATE v. MULVIHILL

Supreme Court of New Jersey, 1970.
57 N.J. 151, 270 A.2d 277.

FRANCIS, J. Defendant Mulvihill was charged by indictment with violating N.J.S.A. 2A:90-4 in that he allegedly committed an assault and battery upon a Somerville policeman who was in uniform and acting in the performance of his duty at the time. He was convicted at a jury trial in which the court refused to allow him to defend by asserting self-defense and declined to submit that issue to the jury for determination. On appeal, the conviction was reversed and a new trial ordered. This Court granted the State's petition for certification.

The testimony reveals that Officer Dowling was operating a patrol car along a public street in Somerville, N. J. While doing so, he observed the defendant Mulvihill, a 20-year-old youth, and two other persons standing in front of a pizzeria. He noticed Mulvihill pouring something from a bottle into a paper cup held by one of the other two persons. Since there was a local ordinance prohibiting the drinking of alcoholic beverages on a public street, the officer stopped the car, got out and called to the young men to come over to him. As they did so, Mulvihill threw the paper cup on the sidewalk. Dowling asked him what was in the cup and defendant did not answer.

The testimony as to the events which immediately followed is in conflict. However, for the purpose of determining whether the legal issue of self-defense was available for jury consideration, it is necessary to consider the facts in the light most favorable to the defendant. According to Mulvihill, when he failed to disclose what he had been drinking the officer grabbed him and asked to smell his breath. He held his breath and remained silent, whereupon Dowling shook him "back and forth" by the shoulders, and said "I should arrest you, you punk." Mulvihill tried to pull away and Dowling "jerked him back around" with the result that both men fell. They arose with Dowling still holding him. When he tried to pull free, Dowling struck defendant on the side of the head with his gun lacerating his scalp. Mulvihill then fell toward Dowling and they both went down again. The officer's right hand was being held by Mulvihill who was trying to keep the gun pointing away from himself, while the officer was endeavoring to direct it at him and saying "Stop or I'll shoot." Mulvihill testified that at this time he was trying to avoid being shot. Then the gun went off, harmlessly, and with his right hand Mulvihill punched the officer in the left side of the face. It was for this blow that he was indicted. In the meantime, other officers appeared and defendant was immobilized.

On the assumption *as a matter of law* that Mulvihill had been arrested before he struck the allegedly criminal blow, the trial court informed defense counsel that no discussion of or reliance upon self-defense would be permitted in summation, nor would that issue be submitted in the charge for consideration by the jury. The action was taken because the court believed * * * it was required by State v. Koonce. That belief, of course, was incorrect.

Koonce held that "a private citizen may not use force to resist arrest by one he knows or has good reason to believe is an authorized police officer engaged in the performance of his duties, whether or not the arrest is illegal under the circumstances obtaining." 89 N.J. Super. at 184, 214 A.2d at 436. The opinion put to rest the notion that the common law rule existing in some jurisdictions, which permits a citizen to resist, even with reasonable force, an unlawful arrest by a police officer, was applicable in New Jersey. Instead, the Appellate Division adopted the above quoted contrary doctrine, and we think rightly so. Accordingly, in our State when an officer makes an arrest, legal or illegal, it is the duty of the citizen to submit and, in the event the seizure is illegal, to seek recourse in the courts for the invasion of his right of freedom.

However, as the Appellate Division said in reversing the conviction here, it went no further in *Koonce* than to hold that the citizen must submit peaceably to an apparently authorized arrest or other apparently lawful restraint by a police officer, even if it later proves to have been illegal. If the citizen resists the arrest, the officer is not only justified in but has the duty of employing such force as is reasonably necessary to overcome the resistance and accomplish the arrest. But, as the Appellate Division noted, that principle is not dispositive in all cases of an arrestee's right to claim self-defense to a charge of assault and battery on the officer. If, in effectuating the arrest or the temporary detention, the officer employs excessive and unnecessary force, the citizen may respond or counter with the use of reasonable force to protect himself, and if in so doing the officer is injured no criminal offense has been committed.

There is sound reason for a difference in the rights and duties of the citizen in the two situations. Despite his duty to submit quietly without physical resistance to an arrest made by an officer acting in the course of his duty, even though the arrest is illegal, his right to freedom from unreasonable seizure and confinement can be protected, restored and vindicated through legal processes. However, the rule permitting reasonable resistance to excessive force of the officer, whether the arrest is lawful or unlawful, is designed to protect a person's bodily integrity and health and so permits resort to self-defense. Simply stated, the law recognizes that liberty can be restored through legal processes but life or limb cannot be repaired in a courtroom. And so it holds that the reason for outlawing resistance to an unlawful arrest and requiring disputes over its legality to be resolved in the courts has no controlling application on the right to resist an officer's excessive force.

Two qualifications on the citizen's right to defend against and to repel an officer's excessive force must be noticed. He cannot use greater force in protecting himself against the officer's unlawful force than reasonably appears to be necessary. If he employs such greater force, then he becomes the aggressor and forfeits the right to claim self-defense to a charge of assault and battery on the officer. Furthermore, if he knows that if he desists from his physically defensive measures and submits to arrest the officer's unlawfully excessive force would cease, the arrestee must desist or lose his privilege of self-defense.

It has been suggested that the latter qualification is not reasonable because it would require a citizen being subjected to excessive force or attack and defending against it to make a split second determination, amounting to a gamble, as to whether if he terminates his defensive measures, he will suffer further beyond arrest. But application of the rule does not require such action as should follow opportunity for detached reflection. It merely commands that the citizen's conduct be reasonable in the light of all the circumstances apparent to him at the moment. And thus it is a counter-protective measure for the original aggressor officer. Administration of the

rule should be no more difficult than those dealing with the duty
of an assaulted person to retreat to avoid the attack or the duty not
to continue the affray after the original aggressor ceases the assault;
once the danger is past, the original victim cannot continue measures
that were originally defensive. *Cf.* State v. Abbott, 36 N.J. 63, 69–73,
174 A.2d 881 (1961).

Applying the stated principles to the present case, it is plain
that the trial court erred in eliminating self-defense from the case
as a matter of law. Two bases exist for that conclusion. The jury
could have found on the disputed facts that Dowling had informed
Mulvihill expressly, or by his course of conduct, that he was under
arrest for an ordinance violation offense. If such a finding were
made, it would follow that Dowling was justified in using such force
in overcoming Mulvihill's resistance as was reasonably necessary to
make the arrest effective. But it was open to the jury to find also
that the resistance was such that the officer, in attempting to overcome it, employed unnecessary and excessive force when he drew his
gun and struck Mulvihill in the head with it so as to cause a lacer-
ated scalp. They could have found further that this caused Mulvihill reasonably to feel and to fear that an effort was being made to
point the gun at him and to fire it. Assuming a finding of such facts
and that they preexisted the charged assault and battery on the officer, defendant was entitled to have the issue of self-defense passed
upon by the jury.

The second and more crucial basis for accepting self-defense as
a legitimate contention in the case was not considered at all at the
trial level. The court assumed as a matter of law that Mulvihill had
been arrested before the alleged assault and battery was committed.
But there was a clear factual dispute on that point. According to
defendant, Officer Dowling simply said: "I should arrest you, you
punk." Obviously that statement did not constitute an arrest nor
did it, in conjunction with the circumstances existing when the statement was made (as the jury could have found them), constitute a
temporary detainer by an officer in the pursuit of his official duty
for purposes of investigation. If Mulvihill was believed on this aspect of the case, then the fracas between the two men took on the
character of a combat between two private individuals. In such
situation he was entitled to have the jury decide whether in striking
Dowling with his fists he was defending himself against the officer's
onslaught with a gun.

Accordingly, we agree with the Appellate Division that the conviction must be reversed and the case remanded for retrial. Assuming substantially the same factual controversy on the retrial, the jury
must be called upon to decide whether Mulvihill was arrested before
the physical combat arose. Then they should be instructed that once
that issue has been decided they should consider the matter of self-
defense in accordance with the controlling principles outlined above.

As explained earlier, we have outlined the disputed facts most favorably to the defendant. That was done in order to deal with his contention that the claim of self-defense was an issue which the trial court was obliged to submit to the jury for determination. In holding that the evidence was sufficient to require such submission, we are not indicating a view that defendant's version of the facts should be accepted. The problem of credibility between defendant and the State's witnesses is a matter for resolution by the jury. Officer Dowling's account of the affair, as noted by the Appellate Division, was that he placed defendant Mulvihill under arrest for drinking on a public street. Then "[a]s he told defendant to get into the police car, the latter struck him on the left side of the face. He was knocked to the ground by the blow and immediately got up and grabbed defendant. Defendant and the officer 'tussled' and again both fell to the ground. The officer again got up from the ground and told defendant that he was going to handcuff him and put him into the police car, whereupon defendant kicked the officer in the groin and grabbed him around the waist with one hand on the officer's gun, causing both of them to fall to the sidewalk a third time. As they were on the ground, the officer and defendant struggled for the officer's gun and it discharged against the side of the adjoining building." 105 N.J.Super. at 460–461, 253 A.2d at 176. If that version of the fracas is believed by the jury, the defendant would be guilty of the offense charged against him, and accordingly the jury would not reach the question whether the officer used excessive force in overcoming defendant's resistance to his removal to police headquarters.

The judgment of the Appellate Division is affirmed and the cause remanded for new trial.

NOTES

1. The *Koonce* decision and that of the Alaska Supreme Court in Miller v. State, 462 P.2d 421 (1969), appear to be the only state judicial abrogations of the right to resist arrest. A similar movement is taking place in the Federal courts. United States v. Ferrone, 438 F.2d 381 (3rd Cir. 1971) (no right to forcibly resist execution of search warrant); United States v. Beyer, 426 F.2d 773 (2nd Cir. 1970) (no right to resist unlawful arrest); United States v. Simon, 409 F.2d 474 (7th Cir. 1969) (no right to resist lawful arrest or, as dictum, unlawful arrest). The same result has been achieved by statute in California, Delaware, Illinois, New Hampshire, New York, and Rhode Island. West's Ann.Cal.Penal Code § 834 (1970); 11 Del.Code Ann. § 1905 (1953); Smith-Hurd Ill.Ann.Stat. ch. 38, § 7–7 (1972); N.H.Rev.Stat.Ann. 594.5 (1955); McKinney Consol.Laws of N.Y. (Penal Law) § 35.27; R.I.Gen.Laws 1956, § 12–7–10.

It has been argued that eliminating self-help facilitates unlawful arrests and thus violates the Fourth Amendment's prohibition against unreasonable seizures and the due process clause of the Fourteenth Amendment. Two courts which have addressed these contentions have rejected them on the grounds that inasmuch as reasonable force in the exercise of self-help is unlikely to be effective in escaping an armed and technologically sophisticated police force these statutes do not, in fact, contribute to the deprivation of liberty. State v. Ramsdell, 109 R.I. 320, 285 A.2d 399 (1971) and People v. Curtis, 70 Cal.2d 347, 74 Cal.Rptr. 713, 450 P.2d 33 (1969).

2. One of the few pieces criticizing the trend illustrated by the preceding cases is Chevigny, The Right to Resist an Unlawful Arrest, 78 Yale L.Rev. 1128 (1969). The author argues that the premises concerning alternative resolutions, such as civil damage actions, are to a great extent illusory and, moreover, beside the point. The crucial question for Mr. Chevigny is whether a citizen who impulsively resists the arbitrary and unlawful exercise of police power should be punished. Since the Chevigny article many successful actions have been brought under the Civil Rights Act of 1871, Rev.Stat. § 1979, 42 U.S.C.A. § 1983, for damages due to unlawful arrest, imprisonment and mistreatment by police and other public officials. E. g., McDaniel v. Carroll, 457 F.2d 968 (6th Cir. 1972) (award of compensatory and punitive damages against sheriff, deputy sheriff and surety on sheriff's bond for injuries sustained by plaintiffs when shot by deputy in course of effort to arrest affirmed; amount not stated); Roberts v. Williams, 456 F.2d 819 (5th Cir. 1972) (award of $85,000 against superintendent of Mississippi county prison farm for damages resulting from accidental discharge of shotgun held by trusty guard remanded for consideration of other possible elements of damages); Jenkins v. Averett, 424 F.2d 1228 (4th Cir. 1970) (award of $448 for out-of-pocket expenses resulting from defendant police officer's shooting of plaintiff in course of chase rejected as inadequate and remanded for consideration of other elements of compensatory and punitive damages); Sexton v. Gibbs, 327 F.Supp. 134 (N.D.Tex.1970) aff'd per curiam 446 F.2d 904 (5th Cir. 1971) (awards of $500 and $250 made against two police officers for unlawful arrest and search of plaintiff's car). Nevertheless, it seems probable that the great majority of those subject to unlawful treatment by the police, particularly when it is only an unlawful arrest, are unlikely to recover lost employment or wages much less any compensation for the indignity experienced. If so, does it not seem inequitable that such persons should also be liable for criminal sanctions if they initially resisted such mistreatment?

Can the new "no sock" rule be justified by its possible effect on the conduct of the police? That is, by possibly reducing police anticipation of physical conflict might it make them less apt to interpret verbal remonstrance or passive reluctance as signals for the exercise of force on their part with its potential for escalation? If the net effect of the new rule is a reduction in physical injuries to police and public would that be a satisfactory answer to Chevigny's argument?

Given the realities of our society, is the risk of unlawful arrest experienced equally by all segments of our population? Are the possibilities for rapid and meaningful relief? Is the no-resistance rule a form of "class-legislation"?

E. PREVENTION OF CRIME

VILIBORGHI v. STATE

Supreme Court of Arizona, 1935.
45 Ariz. 275, 43 P.2d 210.

LOCKWOOD, Chief Justice. Jeff Viliborghi, hereinafter called defendant, was informed against by the county attorney of Maricopa county for the crime of murder. He was tried before a jury, which returned a verdict of manslaughter, and after judgment on the verdict had been returned, this appeal was taken.

The evidence introduced by the state in its case in chief tended to show the following facts: Deceased, one Alfredo Carrion, a Mexican boy about sixteen years old, and two companions of about the same age had attended a moving picture show the evening of the homicide. On their way home they decided to run a race, and did so, finishing the race in front of a store owned by defendant. While standing there talking together, a shot was fired from the interior of the store, and deceased fell to the ground. His companions ran home and informed deceased's parents and notified the police, thereafter returning to the store, where they found the body of deceased, the cause of death being a gunshot wound in the brain. Defendant was arrested, and while he was under arrest admitted to various witnesses that he fired the shot which killed the deceased. This, of course, under the statute, was sufficient to make a prima facie case of second-degree murder, and put upon defendant the burden of proving circumstances of mitigation, or that justified or excused the killing. Section 5050, R.C.1928.

Defendant claimed the killing to be justifiable under subdivisions 1 and 2 of section 4590, R.C.1928, which section reads in part as follows:

"4590. Justifiable homicide; bare fear as justification: Homicide is also justifiable when committed by any person: 1. When resisting any attempt to murder any person, or to commit a felony, or to do some great bodily injury upon any person; or, 2. when committed in defense of habitation, or property, against one who manifestly intends or endeavors, by violence or surprise, to commit a felony, or manifestly intends and endeavors, in a violent, riotous, or tumultuous manner, to enter the habitation of another for the purpose of offering violence to any person therein; * * *

"A bare fear of the commission of any of the offenses mentioned in subdivisions two and three hereof, is not sufficient to justify a homicide. But the circumstances must be sufficient to excite the fears of a reasonable person, and the party killing must have acted under the influence of such fears alone."

In order to sustain this defense, he offered evidence which tended to show the following facts:

Defendant had been engaged in the grocery business at the location where the killing occurred since 1925. The premises occupied by him as a store were also used for his residence, and he lived there alone. Three times between 1925 and the date of the killing his premises had been burglarized, or an attempt at burglary made, and on one occasion some unknown person had attempted to shoot him while he was in the building. The night of the killing defendant closed his store and retired about 10 p. m., but some time shortly thereafter he was awakened by hearing a noise in the front part of the building. Believing that some one was about to again rob the premises, he was afraid to turn on any light or expose himself before the windows. He arose from his bed, secured a revolver, and crept into the store part of the building to determine what the situation was, and, if it could be done safely, to go out through the front door to call for help. He continued to hear various noises around the building, and as he progressed toward the front he saw a human hand reaching in the front window and apparently trying to unhook the fastenings thereof. Believing that burglars were trying to break into the building, and that his life and property were in danger, he fired his revolver through the window and immediately heard the footfalls of persons running away. He went back to his bedroom, partially dressed, and the noises having ceased, went through the front door and turned on the electric light and saw a body lying on the sidewalk. Beside it he saw a jar of preserves and a bottle of pickles which had evidently been taken from a shelf adjacent to the broken window through which he saw the hand entering. On examining the body he discovered it was that of a sixteen year old boy. He had known the boy before, but had had no previous difficulties with him or any of his family. He thereupon notified the police and was arrested and placed in the city jail. * * *

The seventh, eighth, ninth, and tenth assignments of error discuss certain instructions given by the court, and we consider them together. As we have said, the vital issue was whether the defendant was justified in firing the fatal shot. In order for the jury to determine this it was necessary that the court should instruct them under what circumstances the law considers a homicide justifiable or excusable, and it is contended by defendant that the instructions objected to necessarily gave the jury an entirely wrong understanding of the law.

The defendant asked for the following instruction as to the law of justifiable homicide, which was given:

"You are instructed, gentlemen, that any citizen of this state has a right to defend his habitation, his home, against any unlawful or violent intrusion by another, without his consent, for a felonious purpose, and his right to defend his home is governed by the same rule which governs a man's right to defend his person. Now, if at the time the defendant Viliborghi shot and killed the deceased, the latter was attempting to, or the defendant had reasonable ground to believe that the deceased was attempting to, make an unlawful and forcible intrusion upon the habitation of the defendant against the will of the defendant, and that the defendant believed at the time that it was necessary for the protection of his home or his person against an unlawful and violent intrusion by the deceased, and you further find that the belief and fear on the part of the defendant was reasonable, viewing the same from the standpoint of a reasonable man at the time, then the defendant had a right under our law to protect his person or his home, even to the extent of taking the life of the deceased. And if you so find from the evidence in this case, you will find the defendant not guilty, or, if after considering all the evidence in this case, you have a reasonable doubt on this question, you will give the defendant the benefit of that doubt and render a verdict of not guilty."

This we think is a correct general statement of the law as applicable to the evidence in this case, and if no further instructions on the subject of justifiable homicide had been given, the jury could not have been misled. The court, however, in addition thereto, gave the following instructions at the request of the state:

"Gentlemen, if you believe from the evidence in this case beyond a reasonable doubt that the deceased, together with others, was passing the store or standing in front of the store of the defendant, and did not attempt to burglarize defendant's store, then I charge you that the defendant was not justified in taking the life of the deceased, and in that event he would be guilty of either murder or manslaughter—that is, if you believe from the evidence beyond a reasonable doubt that the defendant fired the shot which resulted in the death of the deceased."

"I instruct you, gentlemen of the jury, that the right to kill to protect one's habitation, or to prevent the commission of a felony, is based upon the law of necessity or apparent necessity; the right is limited to prevention and does not extend to punishment for an act already committed."

"I instruct you in this regard that if you find from the evidence beyond a reasonable doubt that the defendant shot the deceased for the purpose of punishment and not to prevent the commission of a felony, then I instruct you that he was not justified in shooting the deceased, unless you further find from the evidence that defendant was in actual or apparent danger of losing his life, or sustaining great bodily injury."

"I instruct you that the owner may resist an entry into his store or house but he has no right to kill unless it be necessary, or apparently necessary, to prevent a felonious stealing or destruction of his property, or to defend himself against loss of life, or great bodily harm, and if you find from the evidence in this case beyond a reasonable doubt that defendant did not shoot the deceased until after the entry or taking of the merchandise in question, if you find that deceased did enter and take the merchandise of defendant, then I instruct you that the defendant would not be justified in taking the life of the deceased, except to defend his own life, or save himself from great bodily injury."

"You are instructed, gentlemen of the jury, that the law does not give one the right to take the life of another merely to prevent the theft of property and in this respect, I charge you that if you believe from the evidence beyond a reasonable doubt that this defendant shot and killed the deceased merely to prevent the theft or loss of the canned goods, even though you find that the deceased was in the act of stealing the said canned goods, but if the defendant had no reasonable cause to believe that his life was in imminent danger, then I instruct you that you should return a verdict of guilty."

On comparing these instructions with the one given at the request of the defendant, it is obvious that they do not agree as to the law, and cannot in any reasonable manner be reconciled.

It was the contention of defendant, sustained by evidence offered in his behalf, that the deceased was, at the time the fatal shot was fired, actually engaged in a first-degree burglary, with the intent to commit petit larceny. * * * This offense of itself is merely a misdemeanor, and the killing of a thief who is engaged merely in a misdemeanor is not justifiable. It may be urged that, since under our statute the burglary is completed as soon as the felonious entry is made, the actual taking of property as a result of and immediately after the entry is not burglary, but merely petit larceny, and therefore the owner of the premises can only resist such taking in the manner allowed for the prevention of a misdemeanor. We think this is a most unreasonable limitation of the law of justifiable homicide. If this be the law, all a burglar needs to do is to complete his entry, and he may then with impunity continue his burglarious purpose without fear of being shot by the justly incensed home owner, so long as he tells the latter that he has no intention of taking more than $50 worth of property. We cannot conceive such to be the law, and hold that so far as the question of justifiable homicide is concerned, when goods are stolen during the commission of a burglary, the entire act from beginning to end is a felony, and any one who may kill the perpetrator before he has fully completed his purpose is to be tried by the rules applying to homicides committed to prevent felonies, and not those which govern misdemeanors. It therefore follows that the owner of the premises burglarized may, at any stage of a burglary, kill the burglar if it be reasonably necessary to prevent the final completion of his felonious purpose, regardless at what stage of the crime the shooting occurs. He may, even after the burglary has been completed, and the burglar is withdrawing from the scene of his crime, if the latter attempts to resist or flee from arrest, use such force as is reasonably necessary for the apprehension of the offender, even to the taking of life. And in all of such cases the question of the necessity of the killing depends upon the reasonable apprehension and belief of the defendant, and not whether such apprehension and belief was justified by the facts as they actually existed. With these tests it clearly appears that the instructions complained of were erroneous in several respects.

The first one states positively that, regardless of what the circumstances would lead the defendant, as a reasonable man, to believe, if as a matter of fact the deceased was not actually engaged in an attempt to burglarize the defendant's store, the latter would be guilty of either murder or manslaughter in killing him. It omits entirely the test of reasonable grounds for belief, and directs the jury to return their verdict on the facts as they actually existed, and not as they appeared to the reasonable apprehension of the defendant.

The second instruction is correct, for under no circumstance may one person shoot another as a punishment for a crime which has been committed.

The third instruction is somewhat ambiguous in that it might be construed to mean that, after the entry had been completed, even though the burglary is still in progress, the owner of the premises may not kill to prevent the completion of the attempted crime. This, as we have said, is not the law. This instruction alone, however, in view of the general instructions, would probably not be reversible error, for the ambiguity is hardly of such a serious nature that, taking the instructions as a whole, it would mislead the jury.

The fourth instruction, however is fatally erroneous. It states flatly that if the defendant killed the deceased to prevent the loss of the canned goods which are referred to in the evidence, even though the deceased was in the act of stealing them, he would be guilty of manslaughter. As we have stated, had the stealing been a simple misdemeanor, the instruction would have been correct, but the whole evidence shows beyond doubt that if the deceased did steal the canned goods referred to, it must have been done in the perpetration of a burglary, and the stealing was therefore part of a felony and the defendant was justified in killing the deceased if it was reasonably necessary to prevent its completion. In no possible way can this instruction be reconciled with the law, and it is obvious that it, considered with the evidence which appears in the record, was in the highest degree prejudicial, and could not be cured by a reference to the general instructions.

Because of the various errors which we have discussed, we are of the opinion that the defendant did not have that fair and impartial trial guaranteed him by the law, and the judgment of the superior court is therefore reversed, and the case remanded for a new trial.

SAULS v. HUTTO

United States District Court, E.D.La., 1969.
304 F.Supp. 124.

RUBIN, District Judge. A police officer who shot and killed a fleeing seventeen-year-old suspected of committing a felony is here sued for damages. The suit raises the question of justification for the use of deadly force in contemporary society.

On March 21, 1965, at about 10:00 p. m., two police officers, James Hutto and Frederick C. Ruppert, Jr., were operating Patrol Car 54. They drove to an ice cream parlor to investigate a complaint. While they were there, a Mustang automobile was driven recklessly past them at a high rate of speed. They jumped in the patrol car and, with Hutto driving, pursued the Mustang. Hutto turned on the blue police warning light and sounded the siren. But the driver of the Mustang continued to flee, driving through the streets of New Orleans at a high rate of speed. The defendants therefore suspected the speeding car was stolen.

There were four young men in the car. Philip Paul Bartlett, also known as Philip Sauls, was driving. According to the testimony of the three passengers, he had invited them for a ride. They also testified that Bartlett had told them the automobile belonged to his brother. In fact Bartlett had stolen the car by putting a jumper wire on the ignition circuit.

Four pistol shots were fired by Officer Ruppert at the racing car in an effort to bring it to a halt. One shot missed completely; two struck the car but did not penetrate it; and the last shot, which was fired at the car as it careened to its right around a corner on Esplanade Street, penetrated the right front door, ricocheted off the dashboard and fell spent inside the vehicle.

When the passengers heard Ruppert's shots and realized that the police were after them, one of them urged Bartlett to stop. Bartlett, however, said that the car was stolen, and that he could not afford to stop.

Bartlett lost control of the Mustang, and it crashed into a parked car. The police car also stopped, and the two policemen ran up, guns in hand. Three of the juveniles surrendered and Ruppert took them into custody. Bartlett, however, tried to escape, crouching as he ran away. Officer Hutto ran after him. He shot once at the fleeing boy, and his shot struck Bartlett in the back. Because Bartlett was bent over, the bullet went through his body at an angle, penetrated his liver, spleen, stomach and heart, and he fell dead in the street.

Shortly thereafter, Hutto said that he had not intended to kill Bartlett, but being excited, he was not entirely certain what had happened. One of the other occupants of the car was later found to be carrying a weapon. Some also had prior police records. All of them were hardened youths, and all later were convicted and sentenced for theft.

Defendants contend they had probable cause to arrest Bartlett for theft, and they are correct.

Suit is brought by the natural mother of the deceased (an illegitimate child) for damages under the Civil Rights Act, 42 U.S.C.A. § 1983, and other Louisiana law, LSA–C.C. Arts. 2315, 2316, under the doctrine of pendent jurisdiction. The police officers are no longer with the New Orleans police force and are presently unemployed. Therefore, should the plaintiff prevail, there is scant likelihood that any recovery can be effected, but the plaintiff seeks vindication for her son.

*   *   *

Officer Hutto had probable cause to arrest Bartlett for theft, a felony not involving danger to life or person, and he reasonably believed that the suspect could not be immediately apprehended without the use of deadly force. In these circumstances, was he legally justified in shooting at the deceased? There has been a spate of literature dealing with this problem,[9] and various state legislatures have recently been reconsidering their laws to reflect current attitudes on it.

At common law, any person, whether policeman or private citizen, was privileged to use *any* force necessary, albeit deadly, to apprehend a fleeing felon if he had cause to believe a felony had been committed. Deadly force, however, was never permissible to apprehend misdemeanants. To a great extent, this view was based on the fact that, at common law, felonies were punishable by death.

Louisiana has not followed the common law approach. The provisions of the Louisiana Criminal Code and Code of Criminal Procedure when read together limit the use of deadly force even by police officers to situations involving danger to life or person.

Article 220 of the Code of Criminal Procedure provides:

> "A person shall submit peaceably to a lawful arrest. The person making a lawful arrest may use reasonable force to effect the arrest and detention, and also to overcome any resistance or threatened resistance of the person being arrested or detained."

The draftsmen of the Code pointed out in the Official Comment to Article 220 that the "requirement of reasonableness would preclude

9. See, e. g., Note, "The Use of Deadly Force in the Apprehension of Fugitives from Arrest," 14 McGill L.J. 293 (1968); Tsimbinos, "The Justified Use of Deadly Force," 4 Criminal Law Bulletin 3 (1968); McDonald, "Use of Force by Police to Effect Lawful Arrest," 9 Criminal Law Quarterly 435 (1966–67); Robin, "Justifiable Homicide by Police Officers," 54 Journal of Criminal Law, Criminology, and Police Science, 225 (1963); Comment, "Justification for the Use of Force in the Criminal Law," 13 Stan.L.Rev. 566 (1961); Comment, "The Use of Deadly Force in the Protection of Property Under the Model Penal Code," 59 Col. L.Rev. 1212 (1959).

the use of clearly inappropriate force." More significant assistance in determining what is reasonable force on the part of police officers is provided by the definition of justifiable homicide in the Louisiana Criminal Code:

> "A homicide is justifiable:
>
> (1) When committed in self-defense * * *
>
> (2) When committed, for the purpose of preventing a violent or forcible felony involving danger to life or of great bodily harm, by one who reasonably believes that such an offense is about to be committed and that such action is necessary for its prevention. * * * " LSA–R.S. 14:20.

Thus, deadly force may not be used to prevent the commission of a felony involving only property, a marked departure from the common law rule.

Since it is illegal for one to use deadly force to *prevent* the commission of a felony involving only property, it is unreasonable (and inappropriate) for a policeman to use deadly force to *arrest* a man suspected of committing such a crime.

The current Regulations on Firearms of the New Orleans Police Department also limit the use of deadly force in felony cases. They provide:

> "The use of deadly force shall be restricted to the apprehension of perpetrators, who in the course of their criminal actions threaten the use of deadly force or apprehensions when officers believe that the person whose arrest is sought will cause death or serious bodily harm if his apprehension is delayed."

The use of deadly force in apprehending persons suspected of committing felonies not involving danger to life or person has never been specifically considered by Louisiana's appellate courts. However, three cases have held that deadly force may not lawfully be used to arrest a misdemeanant or prevent the commission of a misdemeanor. State v. Turner, 1938, 190 La. 198, 182 So. 325; State v. Plumlee, 1933, 177 La. 687, 149 So. 425; Graham v. Ogden, 3d La.App., 1963, 157 So.2d 365. And two of them, State v. Turner, supra, and State v. Plumlee, supra, indicate that deadly force can be used only to prevent "a great crime." Both LSA–R.S. 14:20, which does not permit the use of deadly force in crimes not involving danger to life or person and LSA–R.S. 14:67, which provides for a 10 year maximum sentence for theft, suggest that Bartlett had not committed "a great crime," and that Officer Hutto acted unlawfully in using deadly force in an attempt to apprehend him.

The Model Penal Code [16] of the American Law Institute has followed the same approach as Louisiana and does not permit the use of deadly force to make an arrest for a crime involving only property.[18] The various interests at stake have been balanced; the felon's life may be taken only if his escape would provide a threat to the life or personal safety of his fellow citizens.

Our society does not lightly forfeit human life. No longer is there a host of felonies punishable by death. Indeed, since June, 1967, no one has been executed in the United States for a criminal offense. Fifteen states have entirely eliminated the death penalty. Elsewhere capital punishment may be decreed only after due process of law has been afforded.

Hence a man's life may not be take on the spot by a police officer without substantial justification. Bartlett, a theft suspect and reckless driver, was not killed by Officer Hutto in self defense; nor was he slain to prevent a crime involving danger to life or person, or even to property, from being completed. The theft of the automobile had been completed and its reckless course through New Orleans streets was at an end. The automobile and three of its passengers were in custody. There was no longer any danger to pedestrians or other drivers, as there had been, of course, while Bartlett was driving with the police in hot pursuit. Bartlett's death was not the result of the bullets fired at the fleeing automobile. He was shot only to prevent his escape.

If Bartlett had been arrested, fairly tried, and convicted for theft, he could have been sentenced to "not more than 10 years with or without hard labor." He would have been eligible for parole after serving one-third of his sentence. If he had in addition been tried and convicted of resisting arrest, his maximum sentence on that charge would have been six months and a $500 fine.

Professor Mikell [sic] puts the question bluntly:

"It has been said, 'Why should not the man be shot down, the man who is running away with an automobile? * * *' May I ask what are we killing him for * * *. Are we killing him for stealing the automobile? If we catch

---

16. The Model Penal Code provides: "The use of deadly force is not justifiable under this Section, unless:
    (i) the arrest is for a felony * * ;
    (iv) the [police officer] believes that:
    (1) the crime for which the arrest is made involved conduct including the use or threatened use of deadly force; or
    (2) there is a substantial risk that the person to be arrested will cause death or serious bodily harm if his apprehension is delayed."

American Law Institute, Model Penal Code, Section 3.07(2) (b) (i), (iv), pp. 56–57 (1962).

18. Professor Wechsler eloquently stated the basis for the Model Penal Code's (and Louisiana's) position:
"The preservation of life has such moral and ethical standing in our culture and society, that the deliberate sacrifice of life merely for the protection of property ought not to be sanctioned by law." American Law Institute Proceedings, 1958, pp. 285–286.

him and try him we throw every protection around him. We say he cannot be tried until 12 men of the grand jury indict him, and then he cannot be convicted until 12 men of the petit jury have proved him guilty beyond a reasonable doubt, and then when we have done all that, what do we do to him? Put him before a policeman and have a policeman shoot him? Of course not. We give him three years in a penitentiary. It cannot be then that we allow the officer to kill him because he stole the automobile, because the statute provides only three years in a penitentiary for that.

* * * Is it for fleeing that we kill him? Fleeing from arrest is also a common-law offense and is punishable by a light penalty * * *. If we are not killing him for stealing the automobile and not killing him for fleeing, what are we killing him for?" Michael & Wechsler, Criminal Law and Its Administration, p. 82, n. 3 (1940).[24]

Louisiana's courts likely would take this view: a police officer is not justified in shooting at a man who is suspected of stealing an automobile in order to apprehend him. A bullet in the back is not Louisiana's penalty for fleeing to escape arrest. Deadly force may be used only when life itself is endangered or great bodily harm is threatened.

Under LSA–C.C. Art. 2315, plaintiff is entitled to recover damages from Officer Hutto for the wrongful death of her son. A hearing will be held to determine damages. Officer Ruppert did not participate in Bartlett's killing, and judgment is rendered dismissing the suit as to him.

NOTES

1. Normally, the use of deadly force to prevent crime is limited to the prevention or termination of "dangerous" or "atrocious" felonies. However, it has been held that such language extends to the prevention of statutory rape. Moore v. State, 91 Tex.Cr.R. 118, 237 S.W. 931 (1922). More representative of the premises and application of this defense is Commonwealth v. Emmons, 157 Pa.Super. 495, 43 A.2d 568 (1945), where the court held that deadly force may not be employed to prevent the apparent theft of defendant's automobile when there was no danger to her person or threatened intrusion into her home.

24. Nor is the need to deter resistance to arrest a sufficient justification for the use of deadly force. If this be society's concern, then resisting arrest itself should be made a serious felony. The limited statistical evidence available indicates that there has been no significant increase in felonies in those states that have forbidden the use of deadly force in preventing the commission of crimes not involving danger to life or person. See F.B.I. Uniform Crime Report (1961); New York City Police Department Statistical Reports, June–October, 1967, p. 1. Police Commissioner Howard Leary of New York has stated:

"It is a step forward to have a clear statement that irresponsible teenagers whose actions happen to amount to felonies against property are not for that reason alone subject to death at the hands of a police officer attempting to arrest them."

2. Should there be any distinction made between private citizens and the police with respect to the use of deadly force to prevent crime? If so, why? What distinctions should be drawn? Should the same conclusions be reached with respect to the use of such force in making an arrest? See Commonwealth v. Chermansky, 430 Pa. 170, 242 A.2d 237, 32 A.L.R.3d 1072 (1968) and Note, Justifiable Use of Deadly Force by the Police: A Statutory Survey, 12 Wm. & Mary L.Rev. 67 (1970).

3. Even with respect to crimes that normally threaten serious personal injury should the use of deadly force be conditioned on the existence of a reasonable belief in its necessity—as to the existence of such danger and the futility of lesser measures—on the particular occasion? Does the fact that capital punishment may be unconstitutional affect your decision?

4. In Pennsylvania, one employing deadly force to effect the arrest of a person whom he reasonably believes to have committed a felony will be held criminally liable if, despite his belief and the necessity for the use of such force, the person killed or injured is, in fact, innocent. Commonwealth v. Duerr, 158 Pa.Super. 484, 45 A.2d 235 (1946). Is this rule a desirable device for assuring extreme caution by the police and others in the use of deadly force?

NOTE ON OTHER DEFENSES

Certain other defenses may be mentioned in passing since they are so rarely invoked.

One such defense is that a law enforcement officer is not liable for conduct which would otherwise be an offense if the conduct was engaged in for the purpose of enforcing the law. For example, in Lilly v. West Virginia, 29 F.2d 61 (4th Cir. 1928), defendant, a Federal prohibition agent, had struck and killed a pedestrian in the course of a high speed chase of a suspected bootlegger and had been convicted of involuntary manslaughter. On appeal the defendant claimed that the trial court had erred in refusing an instruction to the effect that he should be acquitted if the jury found that at the time of the accident he was attempting in good faith to execute the laws of the United States and used reasonable care under the circumstances. Instead, the trial court directed the jury that the defendant had no right to break the local or state traffic laws. In reversing the appellate court noted that traffic ordinances could not reasonably be seen as binding public officials when speed and right of way are necessary to the performance of their public duty.

This view is apparently so common that cases charging law enforcement officers with crimes under similar circumstances are exceedingly rare. One exception is Reigan v. People, 120 Colo. 472, 210 P.2d 991 (1949) where the court affirmed the convictions (with fines of $300) of two game wardens as accessories before the fact to the crime of unlawfully trapping beaver because they had entrapped two young men into this conduct. The court quoted with approval from an earlier Colorado case: " ' * * * when, in their zeal, or under a mistaken sense of duty, detectives suggest the commission of a crime, and instigate others to take part in its commission in order to arrest them while in the act, although the purpose may be to capture old offenders, their conduct is not only reprehensible, but criminal, and ought to be rebuked, rather than encouraged, by the courts.' "

Such problems are most likely to arise in "entrapment" situations in which the officer's conduct is likely to be such that if engaged in by a private citizen would probably constitute aiding and abetting or/and conspiracy. See, e. g., Green v. United States, 454 F.2d 783 (9th Cir. 1972) where the police conduct led the court to uphold the entrapment defense while making clear that the officer was not himself liable to criminal charges. Should the "entrapper's" status as a law enforcement officer preclude his prosecution? It has been argued that if our interest is in eliminating the practice of entrapment such prosecutions rather than the exoneration of the "entrapped" would be more effective. Mikell, The Doctrine of Entrapment in the Federal Courts, 90 U.Pa.L.Rev. 245, 264–65 (1942).

Consent is another defense that is rarely offered. Its scope is explained by the following provision from the Proposed Federal Criminal Code.

PROPOSED FEDERAL CRIMINAL CODE (1971)

§ 1619.   Consent as a Defense

(1) When a Defense.   When conduct is an offense because it causes or threatens bodily injury, consent to such conduct or to the infliction of such injury by all persons injured or threatened by the conduct is a defense if:

(a) neither the injury inflicted nor the injury threatened is such as to jeopardize life or seriously impair health;

(b) the conduct and the injury are reasonably foreseeable hazards of joint participation in a lawful athletic contest or competitive sport; or

(c) the conduct and the injury are reasonably foreseeable hazards of an occupation or profession or of medical or scientific experimentation conducted by recognized methods, and the persons subjected to such conduct or injury, having been made aware of the risks involved, consent to the performance of the conduct or the infliction of the injury.

(2) Ineffective Consent.   Assent does not constitute consent, within the meaning of this section, if:

(a) it is given by a person who is legally incompetent to authorize the conduct charged to constitute the offense and such incompetence is manifest or known to the actor;

(b) it is given by a person who by reason of youth, mental disease or defect, or intoxication is manifestly unable or known by the actor to be unable to make a reasonable judgment as to the nature or harmfulness of the conduct charged to constitute the offense; or

(c) it is induced by force, duress or deception.

Comment

Often the effect of consent is specified in the definition of an offense, e. g., rape, theft. But an explicit consent provision for crimes of assault and endangerment is necessary because they are crimes of infliction of bodily injury upon others, and even intentional infliction of injury may be consented to, as in surgery. The defense provided here serves to explicate matters which would, absent the statute, probably be resolved by prosecutorial discretion.

In People v. Samuels, 250 Cal.App.2d 501, 58 Cal.Rptr. 439, cert. denied 390 U.S. 1024, 88 S.Ct. 1404, 20 L.Ed.2d 281, the defendant, a physician, claimed that he harmlessly released his sadomasochistic urges by making films in which volunteers were bound and subjected to "faked" whippings. He appealed his conviction for aggravated assault on the grounds that the trial court failed to instruct that the volunteer's consent was an absolute defense. In affirming, the appellate court held that consent was not a defense apparently because it believed that any consent to such behavior would be the product of a mental aberration and hence ineffective.

Why should a distinction be drawn between Dr. Samuels' diversion and professional football or boxing? Is it a question of how many people enjoy the activity or are entertained by it? See the comment on the *Samuels* case in 81 Harv.L.Rev. 1339 (1968).

Should the deceased's consent, or indeed request, be a defense to a charge of murder where the defendant merely placed poison within the reach of his incurably-ill wife? People v. Roberts, 211 Mich. 187, 178 N.W. 690 (1920). Does your answer depend on whether you accept the *Samuels* court's assertion that consent to possible serious injury equals impaired mental faculties and therefore cannot be deemed consent? Is your answer different if the defendant is a doctor who, at the request of his terminally-ill patient "permits" death by ending or not initiating "extraordinary" medical procedures? What if he hastens death by administering fatal amounts of sedation. See generally Myers, The Human Body and the Law 139–59 (1970) and Morris, Voluntary Euthanasia, 45 Wash.L.Rev. 239 (1970).

In some few states statutes provide that it shall be a defense to misdemeanors that the injured person, if any, has compromised his civil claim. Thus, in State v. Garoutte, 95 Ariz. 234, 388 P.2d 809 (1964), the court reluctantly affirmed the dismissal of a charge of misdemeanor manslaughter in the driving of a motor vehicle because, pursuant to such a statute in Arizona, the widow and legal representative of the deceased's minor children appeared and acknowledged financial satisfaction for the injuries sustained. The court's reluctance was due, in part, to its perception of the seeming anomaly that the defendant's ability to pay damages rather than his lack of culpability had saved him. Is the notion of compensation in lieu of punishment, embodied in such compromise statutes, repugnant to you? Where the defendant's intent was no higher than negligence isn't tort law a more desirable model for resolution of the problems caused by the defendant? Are there any differences, other than the recipient of the payment, between the approach embodied in these compromise statutes and the pattern of enforcement of "public welfare" offenses?

In primitive societies, including that of the Saxons, such payments to the victim or his family were the norm even as to conduct that we would readily designate criminal. See Wolfgang, Victim Compensation in Crimes of Personal Violence, 50 Minn.L.Rev. 223 (1965). Although we distinguish compensation from punishment, which, if any, of the appropriate goals of the criminal law are sacrificed by such schemes? (Distinguish here between programs requiring restitution or compensation by the offender and those in which the state makes payments to the victims of crime as a form of social insurance. See, e. g., Note, New York Crime Victims Compensation Board Act: Four Years Later, 7 Colum.J.L. & Soc.Prob. 25 (1971).

Finally, note should be made of the defense of domestic authority. The basic rationale of this defense is that parents are entrusted by society with the duty of training children and may, in the execution of that duty, physically punish the child with moderation. Problems may arise when the punishment results in serious injury or death as in State v. England, 220 Ore. 395, 349 P.2d 668, 89 A.L.R.2d 392 (1960), where a father was charged with involuntary manslaughter through negligence. His successful defense was based on a state statute which provided that a homicide is excusable when committed "by accident or misfortune in lawfully correcting a child or servant". The appellate court affirmed on the grounds that the reference to "accident" was intended as a defense to criminal charges based merely on negligence.

Teachers are seen in many jurisdictions as standing "in loco parentis" (in the place of the parent) with respect to corporal punishment in connection with schooling. The defense of "domestic authority" has in the past been seen available to a teacher charged with assault due to even "excessive or severe" punishment unless it was of such a nature as to produce or threaten lasting injury or was administered with express or implied malice. State v. Lutz, 65 Ohio L.Abs. 402, 113 N.E.2d 757 (C.P.1953).

F.   INSANITY AND RELATED MATTERS

The substantive criminal law has traditionally attempted to provide for some consideration of the fact that some offenders are psychologically abnormal. The integration of formal substantive criminal law and developing knowledge concerning human behavior is one of the most challenging and difficult tasks of the law.

Despite the existence of a number of theoretical frameworks for considering human behavior, the law has, especially in recent years, dealt most extensively with psychodynamic psychology. This has been true for several reasons. First, psychodynamic theory has found favor with medical doctors, and the law has generally regarded physicians as the most desirable "experts" on psychological abnormality. Thus those whose expertise is most often offered to courts have been psychodynamically oriented.

But in addition psychodynamic theory appears, on the surface at least, to be that theoretical approach most easily integrated with the substantive criminal law. Criminal law assumes the existence of "free will" in most individuals, and consequently regards most crimes as the result of a "free" (and consequently "culpable") decision to do the prohibited act. Although there has been an increasing willingness to recognize exceptions, the law is likely to continue for the foreseeable future to insist upon assuming the existence of free will in most offenders. Criminal liability has, as the material on state of mind developed, been defined partially in terms of the potential offender's conscious mental processes. In the task of integrating criminal liability and psychological abnormality, it is clear that less difficulty exists (on a theoretical level, at least) if the framework used to explain the psychological abnormality is consistent (or at least is not inconsistent) with these two fundamental tenets of substantive criminal law: the existence of "free will" and the significance of conscious thought processes upon human behavior. Judged by this criterion, psychodynamic psychology seems well suited to the task. Although much emphasis has been upon unconscious processes, psychodynamic theory (in some forms) also recognizes that conscious thought processes have some effect upon human behavior.[a] Moreover, by positing the possible existence of something ("mental illness" or "psychopathology") which exists in some but not all individuals and which may affect behavior, psychodynamic theory permits explanation of the exceptional case in terms that are not necessarily inconsistent with the existence of free will in other cases. Perhaps in part at least because of this compatibility with the assumptions

a. Dynamic psychology has been described as a completely deterministic approach which "rejects free will but replaces it with the libido." R. Caldwell, Criminology 191 (1956). This seems to be the substance of some statements by some dynamically-oriented psychologists. See, e. g., Zilboorg, Psychoanalysis and Criminology, in Encyclopedia of Criminology 402 (V. Branham & S. Kutask eds. 1949): "It is easily seen that criminal behavior is not a rational process. It has little to do with intellect * * *. Crime is deeply rooted in the instincts of man, and it is usually an act of the instinctual, impulsive life of the criminal individual." But a number of dynamically-oriented psychologists see no necessity for such a position, and postulate that in the absence of stress an individual does possess "free will" and his actions may be determined by intellectual deliberation and choice. P. Roche, The Criminal Mind 23 24 (1958). See Weiss, Determinism and Freedom in Psychoanalysis: Awareness and Responsibility, 28 Am.J. Psychoanalysis 59 (1968). This is logically consistent with the therapeutic approach of many dynamically-oriented mental health personnel. Therapy is designed, by providing insight into unconscious processes, to enable the patient to develop conscious control over his activity. Id. at 60. It is also consistent with the conclusions of many dynamic investigators who acknowledge an inability to demonstrate that personality malformation is "the cause" of all crime. See, e. g., W. Healy, Mental Conflicts and Misconduct 7–8 (1917), indicating that he was able to identify "mental conflict" as the cause of the delinquency in only about seven per cent of the cases studied.

of the criminal law, psychodynamic theory has become that theoretical approach most often involved in criminal litigation.[b]

This section, then, poses the issue of the integration of psychological abnormality (generally described in psychodynamic terms) and substantive criminal law. Emphasis is intended to be not only upon doctrine and theory, but also upon actual practice and the impact of practice upon either doctrine or theory or both. Because most of the limited empirical investigations of the impact in practice of substantive criminal law doctrine have been done in this area, it provides the best available vehicle for injecting into the consideration of what the law is and should be considerations of practical limitations imposed by the "real world" and possible undesirable "side effects" of reform in the law-in-the-books.

---

1. INTRODUCTION

---

a. THE THEORETICAL LEGAL FRAMEWORK

The "insanity" defense was offered to negate the required element of specific criminal intent by purporting to show that the defendant was not capable, because of his physical and psychological condition, of forming the necessary criminal intent. If his conduct was the product of a mental disease or defect, it was not the product of criminal intent as the law requires.

United States v. Henry, 417 F.2d
267, 270 (2nd Cir. 1969)

b. See G. Shadoan, Law and Tactics in Federal Criminal Cases 243–44 (1964):

In order to pursuade the jury, the psychiatrist must do more than merely apply psychiatric labels to the defendant's condition. * * * He must explain the data upon which his conclusions are based and the reasoning process by which he reached those conclusions.

Only those psychiatrists of the "dynamic school" are equipped by both training and orientation to discern and describe the origin and development of the defendant's particular mental illness and its effect on his personality development, mental and emotional processes and behavior

controls. Those trained in the "organic [or 'descriptive'] school," on the other hand, are concerned with mere diagnostic classification based on currently manifested symptoms rather than dynamic theories explaining the origin and development of personality or with the concepts of motivation and adaption of behavior.

* * * Unless the defendant's current symptomatology is so gross that a mere description and classification of his behavior will convince the jury of his lack of criminal responsibility, a psychiatrist of the "organic" school will not make an effective witness.

[T]he court fails to recognize that there is no need for [an insanity] defense to remove criminal liability since it has concluded that no crime is established once mental illness * * * has cast doubt on *mens rea* * * *

[T]here emerges a purpose for the "insanity defense" which * * * has remained of extremely low visibility. That purpose seems to be obscured because thinking about [the relationship between insanity and *mens rea*] has generally been blocked by our collective conscience and our religious and moral traditions. Assuming the existence of [a] relationship between "insanity" and "*mens rea,*" the defense is not to absolve of criminal responsibility "sick" persons who would otherwise be subject to criminal sanction. Rather, its real function is to authorize the state to hold those "who must be found not to possess the guilty *mens rea,*" even though the criminal law demands that no person be held criminally responsible if doubt is cast on any material element of the offense charged * * *.

[T]he insanity defense is not designed * * * to define an exception to criminal liability, but rather to define for sanction an exception from among those who would be free of liability. It is as if the insanity defense were prompted by an affirmative answer to the silently posed question, "Does *mens rea* or any essential element of an offense exclude from liability a group of persons whom the community wishes to restrain? * * * " So conceived, the problem really facing the criminal process has been how to obtain authority to sanction the "insane" who would be excluded from liability by an overall application of the general principles of the criminal law.

> J. Goldstein and Katz, Abolish the "Insanity Defense"—Why Not? 72 Yale L.J. 853, 863–65 (1963)[c]

Mentally deranged persons can be separated from the mass of mankind by scientific tests, and can be given treatment instead of being subjected to punitive sanctions. Being a defined class, their segregation from punishment does not impair the efficacy of the sanction for people generally.

> G. Williams, Criminal Law, The General Part 347 (1st ed. 1953)

[I]t has been argued that insane offenders need not be punished because insane potential offenders cannot be deterred, and the exclusion from punishment of such offenders would not impair the gen-

c. Reprinted by permission of The Yale Law Journal Company and Fred B. Rothman & Company from The Yale Law Journal, Vol. 52, p. 853.

eral deterrent function of the criminal law on noninsane potential offenders. * * * It is obvious that all offenders are nondeterrable in the sense that they were not deterred by the existing system of criminal sanctions. It is similarly obvious that all offenders could be deterred by some set of circumstances. And it is far from obvious, although it may be true, that insane offenders can be deterred only by means far more immediate in application than necessary to deter noninsane offenders. * * * [T]he * * * argument [also] focuses only on the criminal law purpose of deterrence by intellectual balancing of pleasure and pain. The creation of the senses of abhorrence and responsibility might well be impaired by such an approach. And the community's respect for the justness of the criminal law, on which its utility must rest, would almost certainly be reduced. Finally, it is not at all clear that the existence of an insanity loophole would not diminish to some degree the general deterrent effect of the criminal law.

> Livermore and Meehl, The Virtues of M'Naghten,
> 51 Minn.L.Rev. 789, 798 ,793–94, 799 (1967)

Modern penal law is founded on moral culpability. The law punishes a person for a criminal act only if he is morally responsible for it. To do otherwise would be both inhumane and unenlightened. As was said in Holloway v. United States, 80 U.S.App.D.C. 3, 5, 148 F.2d 665, 666, "Our collective conscience does not allow punishment where it cannot impose blame." It is this fundamental principle that exempts from punishment certain types of insane criminals.

> United States v. Fielding, 148
> F.Supp. 46, 49 (D.D.C.1957)
> (Holtzoff, J.)

[I]nsanity [may be] inconsistent with moral failure. A person may be morally blameless if under the circumstances it would be unreasonable to expect avoidance of the forbidden conduct. * * *

At least two difficulties arise in equating the reasonableness of expecting compliance with moral blameworthiness. First and most obvious is the absence of any standard by which to judge the reasonableness of expecting compliance. In addition, even in those cases where opinion is nearly unanimous that compliance cannot reasonably be expected, the criminal law has often imposed moral condemnation. Thus, in a nondefensive situation, one may not take another's life to save one's own even though it is known that the actor will almost certainly do so. That one acting reasonably is ignorant of the existence of a particular penal statute is no defense though one cannot be reasonably expected to comply with an unknown rule.

Livermore and Meehl, The Virtues of M'Naghten, 51 Minn.L.Rev. 789, 794 (1967)

NOTE

The subject of this section is the effect of mental illness upon a defendant's liability. This must be distinguished from the effect of mental illness upon the ability of the government to put a defendant on trial. Local law as well as the federal constitutional requirement of due process are violated if a defendant is tried while he is incompetent to stand trial by reason of mental illness or defect. Pate v. Robinson, 383 U.S. 375, 86 S.Ct. 836, 15 L.Ed.2d 815 (1966). A defendant is incompetent if, as the result of mental illness or defect, he lacks the present ability to consult with his lawyer with a reasonable degree of rational understanding or to understand the proceedings. Dusky v. United States, 362 U.S. 402, 80 S.Ct. 788, 4 L.Ed.2d 824 (1960).

If a defendant is declared incompetent and is subsequently found to have recovered to the point of competency, he may be tried and convicted of the crime; the finding of incompetency is no bar to later trial and conviction if competency is restored. Of course, at the trial the defendant may raise the defense of insanity. But the fact that he was previously incompetent has no formal impact upon whether he is also entitled to be acquitted by reason of insanity.

---

b.   INCIDENCE OF THE ISSUE

LEWIN, INCOMPETENCY TO STAND TRIAL: LEGAL AND ETHICAL ASPECTS OF AN ABUSED DOCTRINE, 1969 LAW AND THE SOCIAL ORDER

233, 234–35.

Judging from the experience of the state of Michigan, in which one of America's major criminal courts sits, the incidence of mental disease occurring in persons suspected of crime is not uncommon; indeed, it is frequently seen. The Detroit Recorder's Court, which handles over 6,000 felony cases annually, has a psychiatric clinic attached to it, and this clinic performs nearly 2,500 psychiatric examinations annually. * * * In a recent field survey of Michigan defense attorneys most active in the practice of criminal law, over 75 percent admitted having frequent contact with mentally ill defendants. Other jurisdictions report similar statistics, and the nation's mental institutions are overcrowded with mentally ill persons caught up in the criminal process.

A. MATTHEWS, MENTAL DISABILITY AND
THE CRIMINAL LAW

26–30, 32, 34 (1970).d

Frequency of Criminal Responsibility Cases

* * *

Published criminal statistics do not record responsibility cases as we have defined that term. Just as state criminal statistics do not record whether the defense was one of alibi or self-defense, they do not report if the defense was based on insanity. Similarly, a successful defense of insanity is usually counted as an "acquittal" rather than an "acquittal on the grounds of insanity."

California comes closest to counting responsibility cases according to our definition. In California the defense of insanity cannot be presented at trial unless the defendant has entered a plea of not guilty by reason of insanity at the arraignment. The entry of the insanity plea is noted on the court record and reported to the California Bureau of Criminal Statistics. * * * In 1965, of 36,643 felony dispositions, a plea of not guilty by reason of insanity was entered in 464 cases (1.3 percent of the total). Of this number, 213 pleas were withdrawn and an additional 56 cases were dismissed or placed off calendar, leaving a total of 195 cases tried in which a plea of insanity had not been withdrawn. (This figure represents 0.53 percent of the total felony dispositions in California during 1965.) Of this number, 109 defendants were acquitted and 86 convicted. How many of the 109 were acquitted "on account of insanity" is not known. Recorded admissions to Atascadero State Hospital in California show that during fiscal 1965, 66 persons were admitted after a finding of not guilty by reason of insanity; in 1966, 61 persons were admitted. These figures tend to indicate that roughly three-fifths of the total of 109 acquittals were on the grounds of insanity.

Nor is it known whether the defense of insanity was actually presented in these cases or in the 86 cases in which a conviction resulted. * * *

Unpublished data from New York, Illinois, and Michigan, consisting of recorded admissions to the maximum-security hospitals in these three states, reveal that only a handful of such admissions occur there each year. In New York, for the year ending March 31, 1963, two persons were admitted after a finding of not guilty by reason of insanity. Only seven persons in the hospital's whole inmate population were committed as the result of a finding of not guilty by reason of insanity. In Michigan, we were told that only "a few" ad-

d. Reprinted by permission of the American Bar Foundation, Chicago, Illinois.

missions occur each year. As of November 1964, only fourteen persons were at the hospital as the result of an acquittal on grounds of insanity. During the fiscal year ending June 30, 1965, no persons were admitted to the comparable hospital in Illinois. Reports for other years indicate that only a few admissions of this kind occur each year.

Officials interviewed in Miami, Chicago, New York City, San Francisco, and Detroit told us that responsibility cases were "rare," "a few," "hardly ever occur," and the like. For example, the prosecuting attorneys, defense counsel, and judges with whom we talked in Detroit could recollect only one successful defense of insanity in the preceding five years. To test the actual frequency of dispositions based on lack of criminal responsibility in Detroit, and incidentally to test the recollection of the Detroit officials, the staff undertook a review of the homicide indictments over a five-year period in the city of Detroit. The results * * * were that one person in five years, a defendant charged with second degree murder, had been found not guilty by reason of insanity at trial. We can thus conclude that official recollection of such cases is quite accurate and that the actual frequency of responsibility cases is, as reported to us, in fact rare.

The criminal courts in the District of Columbia have been the subject of several special studies * * *. It is apparent that the volume of criminal responsibility cases in the District of Columbia is higher than in the other jurisdictions studied. The number of persons acquitted on grounds of insanity in Washington, D. C., rose steadily from 1954, when there were three such cases, until 1962 when sixty-six defendants were found not guilty by reason of insanity—5.1 percent of all felony cases terminated and 13.8 percent of all felony cases tried. Since 1962 acquittals because of insanity have declined to a total of twenty-six in 1966. One peculiarity of the District of Columbia system is the frequency of acquittals on grounds of insanity in misdemeanor cases—a pattern of disposition which is virtually unknown elsewhere * * *.

To summarize: in each jurisdiction criminal responsibility cases constitute a small percentage of all cases; in Illinois, New York, Michigan, and Florida only a handful of cases occur each year; there is a somewhat higher frequency in California and a still higher frequency in the District of Columbia.[11]

11. On the basis of population size—well over eighteen million in California and about three-quarters of a million in the District of Columbia—we would expect California to have twenty-four times as many cases as the District of Columbia; in fact, if the estimated 1965 totals of insanity acquittals in felonies in California (66) and Washington, D.C. (35) are compared on this basis, the District of Columbia had nearly thirteen times as many cases as California. Put differently, given the estimated number of acquittals on grounds of insanity in California in 1965, we would expect about three such acquittals in the District of Columbia. This was the actual number of acquittals in 1954, the year Durham was decided, and since then there have always been many more than three * * *[.]

Characteristics of Responsibility Cases: "Traditional" and "Exceptional" Cases

It is sometimes stated in the literature that the defense of insanity is raised only in homicide or capital cases. This is *generally* true in the areas studied, except California and Washington, D. C., but it is not *literally* true anywhere. In Michigan, for example, where there is no capital punishment, five of the fourteen cases resulting in hospitalization were not homicide cases. In California and Washington, D. C. * * * the defense of insanity is raised in felonies other than homicide in larger number than in homicide cases. Elsewhere, however, the defense is limited largely to capital cases * * *.

What emerges is a rough distinction between "traditional" cases typified by the homicide cases observed during the field portion of this study, and "exceptional" cases typified by the cases we observed in the District of Columbia, none of which was a homicide case. The traditional cases have some common elements. Typically the charge is capital, frequently a case of homicide. Often the trial is attended by much publicity, and there is a positive identification of the accused as the perpetrator of the crime. More likely than not the crime will be a violent one and not one requiring deliberation such as murder by poisoning. Frequently there is no possible defense for the act except insanity. Finally, negotiated alternatives such as a plea of guilty are usually clearly excluded, often at the outset, because of a combination of the foregoing factors, or because negotiation is inhibited by a mandatory death penalty or the fact of attendant publicity or the viciousness of the crime. While such cases are serious, they are not necessarily the most bizarre ones. The truly bizarre case is more likely to be disposed of earlier in the proceedings, at the competency stage; for example, in New York State in 1964, 450 patients at Matteawan State Hospital had been sent there following a finding of incompetence to stand trial upon a charge of homicide, compared to a dozen patients committed there following an acquittal on grounds of insanity.

By "exceptional" cases we mean nothing more mysterious than cases in which we would not expect an insanity plea, the common elements characteristic of "traditional" cases being absent. * * *

"Exceptional" cases occur routinely in the District of Columbia, * * * but elsewhere the insanity defense is restricted largely to "traditional" cases and is in any event rarely used.

---

c. THE REQUIREMENT OF "MENTAL ILLNESS"

Although they vary in other aspects, all of the formulations of the insanity defense contain a basic requirement that the defendant have been "mentally ill" or its equivalent. Consider at this point whether this is an important or proper part of an insanity defense. Reconsider the matter in examining various alternative formulations of the defense.

T. SZASZ, THE MYTH OF MENTAL ILLNESS

15 American Psychologist 113, 114–15, 117 (1960).e

My aim * * * is to raise the question "Is there such a thing as mental illness?" and to argue that there is not. * * *

The term "mental illness" is widely used to describe something which is very different than a disease of the brain. * * *

The concept of illness, whether bodily or mental, implies deviation from some clearly defined norm. In the case of physical illness, the norm is the structural and functional integrity of the human body. Thus, although the desirability of physical health, as such, is an ethical value, what it is can be stated in anatomical and physiological terms. What is the norm deviation from which is regarded as mental illness? This question cannot be easily answered. But whatever this norm might be, we can be certain of only one thing: namely, that it must be stated in terms of psychosocial, ethical, and legal concepts. * * * [T]he widespread psychiatric opinion that only a mentally ill person would commit homicide illustrates the use of a legal concept as a norm of mental health. The norm from which deviation is measured whenever one speaks of a mental illness is a psychosocial and ethical one. * * *

[M]y aim in presenting this argument was expressly to criticise and counter a prevailing contemporary tendency to deny the moral aspects of psychiatry * * * and to substitute for them allegedly value free medical considerations. * * *

While I have argued that mental illnesses do not exist, I obviously did not imply that the social and psychological occurrences to which this label is currently being attached also do not exist. * * * They are real enough. It is the labels we give them that concerns us. * * *

NOTES

1. Consider the following attempts to define the term "mental illness" (or its equivalent) in formulations of the insanity test:

> Whenever the mental condition of a defendant is in issue, two basic questions are presented. One is whether he is afflicted with a mental illness or disease which acted to produce

the conduct with which he is charged. This is entirely a medical, psychiatric question, in which the law has only incidental interest. It is answerable only by medical experts in the application of medical standards. The other, a fundamentally different and wholly legal question, is whether the defendant is to be charged with criminal responsibility for his conduct. Medical considerations play a part—but only a part—in its answer.

State v. Crose, 88 Ariz. 389, 357 P.2d 136 (1960)

In Hawaii, emotional insanity, unassociated with a disease of the brain, as defined below, is not an excuse for a crime. In order to constitute a defense * * *, the mental derangement under which the defendant acted at the time of the commission of the alleged offense must be caused by or be the effect of a disease of the brain rendering her incompetent to discern the nature and criminality of the act done by her. Territory v. Alcosiba, 36 Haw. 231. "Mental derangement, as indicated by the term itself, denotes a disordered or unsound mind. It is interchangeable in meaning with the word 'insanity.' Many authorities have referred to insanity as a disease of the mind. However, it is now generally conceded that insanity or mental derangement is rather the result or manifestation in the mind of a disease of the brain, and by disease is meant any underdevelopment, pathological condition, lesion or malfunctioning of the brain or any morbid change or deterioration in the organic functions or structure thereof."

State v. Foster, 44 Hawaii 403, 354 P.2d 960, 972 (1960)

The statute * * * uses the term "mental disease or defect" in a generalized sense which * * * merely means a mind sufficiently disordered to cause the results indicated * * *. The term was not intended to designate any specific form or forms or medical classifications of mental disease.

State v. Garrett, 391 S.W.2d 235, 239 (Mo.1965)

We agree * * * that the law cannot "distinguish between psysiological, emotional, social and cultural sources of the impairment"—assuming, of course, requisite testimony establishing exculpation under the pertinent standard—and all such causes may be both referred to by the expert and considered by the trier of fact.

Breadth of input under the insanity defense is not to be confused with breadth of the doctrines establishing the defense. * * * [T]he latitude for salient evidence of, e. g., social and cultural factor pertinent to an abnormal condition of the mind significantly affecting capacity and controls, does not mean that such factors may be taken as establishing a separate defense for persons whose mental condition is such that blame can be imposed. We have rejected a broad "injustice" approach that would have opened the door to expositions of e. g., cultural deprivation, unrelated to any abnormal condition of the mind.

* * *

[W]e have not accepted suggestions to adopt a rule that disentangles the insanity defense from a medical model, and announces a standard for exculpating anyone whose capacity for control is insubstantial, for whatever cause or reason. There may be logic in these submissions, but we are not sufficiently certain of the nature, range, and implications of the conduct involved to attempt an all-embracing unified field theory. The applicable rule can be discerned as the cases arise in regard to other conditions—somnambulism or other automatism; blackouts due, e. g., to overdose of insulin; drug addiction. Whether these somatic conditions should be governed by a rule comparable to that herein set forth for mental disease would require, at a minimum, a judicial determination, which takes medical opinion into account, finding convincing evidence of an ascertainable condition characterized by "a broad consensus that free will does not exist."

United States v. Brawner, 471 F.2d 969 (D.C.Cir. 1972)

2.   Consider the following from Morris, Psychiatry and the Dangerous Criminal, 41 S.Cal.L.Rev. 514, 520 (1968):

It too often is overlooked that one group's exculpation from criminal responsibility confirms the inculpation of other groups. Why not permit the defense of dwelling in a Negro ghetto? Such a defense would not be morally indefensible. Adverse social and subcultural background is statistically *more* criminogenic than is psychosis; like insanity, it also severely circumscribes the freedom of choice which a non-deterministic criminal law (all present criminal law systems) attributes to accused persons. True, a defense of social adversity would politically be intolerable; but that does not vitiate the analogy for my purposes. You argue that insanity destroys, undermines, diminishes man's capacity to reject what is wrong and to adhere to what is right. So does the ghetto—more so. But surely, you reply, I would not have us punish the sick. Indeed I would, if you insist on punishing the grossly deprived. To the extent that criminal sanctions serve punitive purposes, I fail to see the difference between these two defenses. To the extent that they serve rehabilitative, treatment, and curative purposes I fail to see the need for the difference.

---

2.   FORMULATIONS OF THE INSANITY DEFENSE

---

a.   THE M'NAGHTEN RULES

DANIEL M'NAGHTEN'S CASE

House of Lords, 1843.
10 Cl. & F. 200, 8 Eng.Rep. 718.

The prisoner had been indicted for that he, on the 20th day of January 1843, * * * did kill and murder * * * Edward Drummond. The prisoner pleaded Not guilty.

Evidence having been given of the fact of the shooting of Mr. Drummond, and of his death in consequence thereof, witnesses were called on the part of the prisoner, to prove that he was not, at the time of committing the act, in a sound state of mind. The medical evidence was in substance this: That persons of otherwise sound mind, might be affected by morbid delusions: that the prisoner was in that condition: that a person so labouring under a morbid delusion, might have a moral perception of right and wrong, but that in the case of the prisoner it was a delusion which carried him away beyond the power of his own control, and left him no such perception; and that he was not capable of exercising any control over acts which had connexion with his delusion: that it was of the nature of the disease with which the prisoner was affected, to go on gradually until it had reached a climax, when it burst forth with irresistible intensity: that a man might go on for years quietly, though at the same time under its influence, but would all at once break out into the most extravagant and violent paroxysms.

* * *

Verdict, Not guilty, on the ground of insanity.

This verdict, and the question of the nature and extent of the unsoundness of mind which would excuse the commission of a felony of this sort, having been made the subject of debate in the House of Lords * * *, it was determined to take the opinion of the Judges on the law governing such cases.

Lord Chief Justice Tindal: * * *

The first question proposed by your Lordships is this: "What is the law respecting alleged crimes committed by persons afflicted with insane delusion in respect of one or more particular subjects or persons: as, for instance, where at the time of the commission of the alleged crime the accused knew he was acting contrary to law, but did the act complained of with a view, under the influence of insane delusion, of redressing or revenging some supposed grievance or injury, or of producing some supposed public benefit?"

In answer to which question, assuming that your Lordships' inquiries are confined to those persons who labour under such partial delusions only, and are not in other respects insane, we are of opinion that, notwithstanding the party accused did the act complained of with a view, under the influence of insane delusion, of redressing or revenging some supposed grievance or injury, or of producing some public benefit, he is nevertheless punishable according to the nature of the crime committed, if he knew at the time of committing such crime that he was acting contrary to law; by which expression we understand your Lordships to mean the law of the land.

Your Lordships are pleased to inquire of us, secondly, "What are the proper questions to be submitted to the jury, where a person alleged to be afflicted with insane delusion respecting one or more particular subjects or persons, is charged with the commission of a crime (murder, for example), and insanity is set up as a defence?" And, thirdly, "In what terms ought the question to be left to the jury as to the prisoner's state of mind at the time when the act was committed?" And as these two questions appear to us to be more conveniently answered together, we have to submit our opinion to be, that the jurors ought to be told in all cases that every man is to be presumed to be sane, and to possess a sufficient degree of reason to be responsible for his crimes, until the contrary be proved to their satisfaction; and that to establish a defence on the ground of insanity, it must be clearly proved that, at the time of the committing of the act, the party accused was labouring under such a defect of reason, from disease of the mind, as not to know the nature and quality of the act he was doing; or, if he did know it, that he did not know he was doing what was wrong. The mode of putting the latter part of the question to the jury on these occasions has generally been, whether the accused at the time of doing the act knew the difference between right and wrong: which mode, though rarely, if ever, leading to any mistake with the jury, is not, as we conceive, so accurate when put generally and in the abstract, as when put with reference to the party's knowledge of right and wrong in respect to the very act with which he is charged. If the question were to be put as to the knowledge of the accused solely and exclusively with reference to the law of the land, it might tend to confound the jury, by inducing them to believe that an actual knowledge of the law of the land was essential in order to lead to a conviction; whereas the law is administered upon the principle that every one must be taken conclusively to know it, without proof that he does know it. If the accused was conscious that the act was one which he ought not to do, and if that act was at the same time contrary to the law of the land, he is punishable; and the usual course therefore has been to leave the question to the jury, whether the party accused had a sufficient degree of reason to know that he was doing an act that was wrong: and this course we think is correct, accompanied with such observations and explanations as the circumstances of each particular case may require.

The fourth question which your Lordships have proposed to us is this:—"If a person under an insane delusion as to existing facts, commits an offence in consequence thereof, is he thereby excused?" To which question the answer must of course depend on the nature of the delusion: but, making the same assumption as we did before, namely, that he labours under such partial delusion only, and is not in other respects insane, we think he must be considered in the same situation as to responsibility as if the facts with respect to which the delusion exists were real. For example, if under the influence of his delusion he supposes another man to be in the act of attempting to take away his life, and he kills that man, as he supposes, in self-defence, he would be exempt from punishment. If his delusion was that the deceased had inflicted a serious injury to his character and fortune, and he killed him in revenge for such supposed injury, he would be liable to punishment.

NOTES

1.　Parsons v. State, 81 Ala. 577, 2 So. 854 (1887):

If the rule declared by the English judges be correct, it necessarily follows that the only possible instance of excusable homicide, in cases of delusional insanity, would be where the delusion, if real, would have been such as to create, in the mind of a reasonable man, a just apprehension of imminent peril to life or limb. The personal fear or timid cowardice of the insane man, although created by disease acting through a prostrated nervous organization, would not excuse undue precipitation of action on his part. Nothing would justify assailing his supposed adversary except an overt act, or demonstration on the part of the latter, such as, if the imaginary facts were real, would, under like circumstances, have justified a man perfectly sane in shooting or killing. If he dare fail to reason, on the supposed facts embodied in the delusion, as perfectly as a sane man could do on a like state of realities, he receives no mercy at the hands of the law. It exacts of him the last pound of flesh. It would follow also, under this rule, that the partially insane man, afflicted with delusions, would no more be excusable than a sane man would be, if, perchance, it was by his fault the difficulty was provoked, whether by word or deed; or if, in fine, he may have been so negligent as not to have declined combat when he could do so safely, without increasing his peril of life or limb. If this has been the law heretofore, it is time it should be so no longer. It is not only opposed to the known facts of modern medical science, but it is a hard and unjust rule to be applied to the unfortunate and providential victims of disease.

2.　Many of the objections to the M'Naghten Rules might be avoided if its terms were broadly defined and applied. In State v. Esser, 16 Wis.2d 567, 115 N.W.2d 505 (1962), the court held that expert witnesses were to be permitted to testify as to defendants' mental illness even if they could not express an opinion favorable to the defendant on whether he met the M'Naghten test. Further, the jury was not to be instructed that insanity as defined by M'Naghten was the only insanity recognized by the law. This would permit a defendant to argue that he did not "know the nature and quality" of his act because he lacked an "emotional understanding" of them, as where he intellectually realized killing was wrong but experienced an overwhelming emotional urge to kill. Should the language of the M'Naghten rules be so interpreted?

STATE v. HARKNESS

Supreme Court of Iowa, 1968.
160 N.W.2d 324.

MASON, Justice.   This is an appeal from judgment following a jury verdict convicting defendant Earl E. Harkness of second degree murder * * *.

The jury found, and there is no evidence upon the record submitted upon this appeal to dispute the fact, defendant shot and killed Dale Edgington April 18, 1966.   He was sentenced to 40 years in the penitentiary at Fort Madison.

Defendant lived in a one-room cabin upon farm ground owned by one Arthur Stevenson.   He was not employed by Stevenson, but was simply permitted to live there, from time to time picking up sticks and generally looking after the place.   (There were a farm house and other buildings in the vicinity of defendant's cabin.)

Stevenson had hired Dale Edgington (deceased) to do some bulldozing and this involved clearing the land, part of which was proximal to defendant's cabin.   Defendant complained to Stevenson that Edgington was running the bulldozer too close to his building, destroying the yard.

Doctor Truax, the psychiatrist who later examined defendant, testified defendant told him he had argued with Edgington about driving the bulldozer too close to the cabin, and asked him to keep it away.   Further, Edgington had driven so close he broke the front sidewalk and almost pushed the cabin over.

Sunday, one week prior to April 18, deceased and some of his relatives were out looking over the farm and observed someone peering out a window in the farm house.   Deceased explained it was probably "the old squatter who lived in the cabin."   They proceeded to the farm house, walked in and were confronted by defendant who ordered them from the house.

Monday morning Edgington returned, attempted to start his bulldozer but apparently decided not to because it was too wet and then left.

Defendant grabbed one of his many rifles and walked to the creek to see how much it had rained.   While there, he observed Edgington driving toward him rapidly in a pickup truck.   Edgington stopped and apparently began kidding defendant about how much it had rained. Defendant felt that he was being ridiculed and told Edgington to move away.   When Edgington did not, defendant "became very angry."

Defendant told Dr. Truax he remembered picking up his rifle, lifting it into a firing position, but did not remember moving the safety or pulling the trigger.   The next thing he remembered was being in his cabin "with the vague feeling that he had killed something."   He claimed a partial amnesia for the period of the shooting itself.

Defendant then drove to Mount Pleasant to the sheriff's office. Finding sheriff and deputy gone, he told the sheriff's wife he thought he was the man the sheriff was looking for, that he had just shot a man.

The defense relies almost wholly upon the testimony of Dr. Richard Allen Truax, a medical doctor who is presently a resident in psychiatry at the psychopathic hospital at the University of Iowa. Dr. Truax first met defendant June 8, 1966, when he was admitted to psychopathic hospital in Iowa City for purposes of evaluation.

The psychiatric evaluation is based upon the following. Data is compiled to construct a life history; then the patient is given a mental status evaluation to evaluate his intellectual function to see if there is any gross evidence of mental illness. He is observed in a series of interviews as to his emotional responses to the examiner and is given a physical examination. An electroencephalogram (a tracing or linear record of the electric currents generated by the brain) is given as well as a brain scan. Psychological and neurological tests are run. Dr. Truax personally had eight conversations with the patient over a period of approximately five weeks, each lasted 30 to 90 minutes. Finally, the patient is observed during his stay at the hospital to see what sort of person he is on the ward, partially stemming from his conversation and interrelationship with other people on the ward.

Basically, the life history is as follows. Early in life defendant engaged in farming, the junk business and later worked as a night watchman, as well as a part-time construction worker. He had a tendency to avoid people and lived by himself. His sister and brother more or less left him alone while he was working on the home farm. He preferred to work as a night watchman where he was alone, not around other people who disturbed him. After his mother died, he spent all of his free time in a shack out in the country away from people, avoiding people, seeming to question their motives and not wanting to get involved with them. Dr. Truax stated, "This aspect was part of an overall pattern permeating his life history. He learned to leave his brother alone as in doing so things would go pretty much okay. However, one time he did assault his brother with a hammer, and took an ax after a neighbor."

Defendant's brother Ival testified about the defendant's attempt to assault him with a hammer until his mother intervened and called the sheriff. Also, "as to Earl's disposition and temper, he don't bother nobody as long as nobody bothers him. When somebody bothers him, he gets pretty mad. I wouldn't know what all he would do when he gets mad."

*   *   *

Defendant was found to be in good physical health. His neurological examination revealed some early organic brain damage.

Observations of defendant's behavior at the hospital revealed the following. "He remained aloof from other people. He seemed to be suspicious of them. * * * Basically, he would tend to withdraw from activities. He would be friendly on approach, but he would withdraw from people as soon as he could. He stayed by himself."

Dr. Truax related the following from conversation had with defendant during interviews. "When he first arrived, I questioned him concerning the murder, and as he would relate the details of his encounter with the deceased, he became very angry, his face was flushed, his blood pressure went up. * * *. Mr. Harkness felt the deceased was ridiculing him and told him to move away. He didn't. Mr. Harkness said he became very angry. He does not remember exactly what the argument was about. * * * He has been consistent in his history as he has given it to me over quite a few hours of talking. This consistency, of course, is an indication that he is telling the truth."

Dr. Truax then stated the conclusions from the psychiatric evaluation and correlated them with facts already divulged in the life history. While Dr. Truax is himself not a board psychiatrist, he was at all times concerned during the evaluation under the supervision of Dr. Noyes, a board psychiatrist, and in conference with Dr. Paul Huston, director of the hospital. Also Dr. Truax testified his views represent substantially those of the medical staff at the hospital.

"Our medical findings and conclusions concerning Mr. Harkness were that we were dealing with an eccentric, suspicious, reclusive individual who easily felt other people were out to annoy him and that he would have to defend himself from them. * * *

"Our diagnosis of Mr. Harkness' condition is that he has a paranoid personality. Individuals who suffer from a paranoid personality have many of the traits of a schizoid personality coupled with an exquisite sensitivity in inter-personal relations, and with a conspicuous tendency to utilize a projection mechanism expressed by suspiciousness, envy, extreme jealousy and stubbornness. * * * When we speak of projection, this is a method where a person attributes his own thoughts and actions to sources outside of himself. For example, a man may be extremely angry, but he does not think in terms of the 'I' am angry. He thinks 'other people are angry at me, those people out there are angry at me.' This is not something that an individual can control himself, not to any significant degree. In this case, Mr. Harknesss' condition is not treatable to any significant degree. If he were to be placed in a similar situation again most likely the same thing would happen again. There is no medical treatment that will cure this paranoid personality that Mr. Harkness has.

"*   *   *   *   *   *   *   *   *   *

"We cannot say for certain whether or not Mr. Harkness was in the mental state that he was aware of the nature and consequences of his act or not.

"He has a suspicious personality. When stressed by somebody or something that would be a minor stress to somebody else, he could easily imagine that things were happening that were not happening, and then not be able to remember this episode, but we have no proof that this happened. You see, Mr. Harkness is a man that is not totally sane or totally insane. If he is stressed enough he loses control of his thought processes. * * *

"Q. Now, Dr. Truax, based on a reasonable medical certainty and concerning the mental illness or defect which you described Mr. Harkness as having did he lack substantial capacity either to appreciate the wrongfulness of his conduct or to conform his conduct to the requirements of law on April 16, 1966, at the time of the alleged crime? A. On this question I cannot honestly say if he had substantial capacity or not. * * * I could venture an opinion, but it would be an opinion only and it would not be an opinion that would be firm enough so that I think I should give it.

" * * * * * * * * * * "

Cross-examination brought the following testimony.

"Q. Do you have any proof that Earl Harkness has not been malingering, proof, you may have an opinion or belief, but proof? A. I have proof to the reasonable medical certainty of 85–90%.

"Toward law and order, basically Mr. Harkness seems to be a man who believes in law and order and tries to comply with it, and it has been because he is so stressed by being around other people that he gets away from people. He cannot handle his hostility. He can't handle closeness with them. He gets away from them rather than get in trouble. In this case he felt surrounded apparently by this man. He was in around the shack, but the man was also around there, and it was just too much for him.

" * * * * * * * * * * *

"We suspect defendant has cerebral arteriosclerosis with reasonable medical certainty based upon the findings of the psychological test in the fact that his blood pressure would rise to such tremendous levels with only a little bit of stress being placed upon him. Now, just what the results of this impediment to the flow of blood to his brain are we really can't say. Certainly there are other people that have cerebral vascular disease that don't commit murder. I do not wish to make that connection here. * * *

" * * * * * * * * * * *

"Q. Doctor, do you know what the defendant's attitude is toward shooting another human being? A. He regards killing another human being as wrong. However, although he will say this, his emotions are confused to the point where he doesn't feel toward another human being like the rest of us feel. He was able at times for instance to laugh about the situation he was in and about what he had done. His way of feeling toward other people is distorted, but yet he knows that in a legal sense it is wrong to murder somebody. He knows now as he looks back on it he shouldn't have done it.

" *　　*　　*　　*　　*　　*　　*　　*　　*

"It is possible for a person to be legally sane at the instance of a shooting and then immediately thereafter by reason of the traumatic experience of having participated in such an event to become psychotic. * * *, but a paranoid personality itself is something that is more crystalized and something that is more developed. This is something that starts out in formative years of life, and it is possible that a person after commission of a crime may develop an acute psychotic episode but a person would not develop a crystalized disorder like a paranoid personality after the commission of a crime.

" *　　*　　*, now again this history that he gives of his past life is far too complex a thing, a person can't fake a paranoid personality over a period of years. This is just too big a thing to fake. I don't think I could do it or a psychiatrist would have a hard time doing it if such a thing could be faked. * * *

" *　　*　　*　　*　　*　　*　　*　　*　　*

"Q. Would you say the defendant is possessed of anti-social impulses? A. Well, Mr. Harkness has aggressive impulses that he has difficulty controlling. This isn't a voluntary thing that he wants to do, anti-social things as far as we can determine. He does not fall under the category of a sociopathic personality, but he has these urges and impulses within which he has a hard time controlling, and at times he can disrupt into anti-social acts if he is stressed to a sufficient degree.

"Q. By the same token you are also saying that he has and does intend control of these impulses at least to a point? A. To a point. It depends on how much he is stressed. Certainly not anywhere near the point where most of us can.

" *　　*　　*　　*　　*　　*　　*　　*　　*

"Q. Doctor, would the defendant have committed an act if a policeman were looking on? A. I suspect he would have. Again this is a speculative question, but I suspect he would have.

"Q. Do you feel that if he is released he might kill again? A. Yes. If he was given weapons and allowed to be in a situation where somebody could aggravate him, it certainly could happen again.

" *　　*　　*　　*　　*　　*　　*　　*　　*

"Q. Doctor, would you agree that every human being has a breaking point? A. Well, I would say every human being has a breaking point perhaps that would be absolute under sufficiently adverse circumstances, but not to the degree that every person has a breaking point in everyday life. * * * Given enough stress most people will break. Most normal people would not break under the stress that Mr. Harkness breaks under."

Dr. Truax was then asked why the defendant turned himself in to the sheriff after he had shot Dale Edgington.

"A. Well, I presume again here you are asking me for a judgmental answer. I presume he shot the man—at the time when he had little emotional control, perhaps wasn't quite aware of what he was doing. After he stopped for a minute he looked back and could see this is a mistake. This is something that is against the law perhaps more than that if I run away people will be after me, so he decided to do the thing most people would do if they find out they have made a tragic mistake of this type."

Instruction 21 stated * * * in substance the M'Naghten rule.

It is fair to assume the jury placed great emphasis upon Dr. Truax's testimony that defendant knew generally the difference between right and wrong and regarded killing another human being as wrong in the legal sense. Although defendant claimed partial amnesia at the time of the shooting, when he realized shortly thereafter he had killed something he turned himself in to the sheriff's office, and now looking back on the incident realizes what he did was wrong. This, coupled with the doctor's inability to say with any degree of certainty that at the time of the shooting defendant did not know what he was doing or that what he was doing was wrong, certainly enabled if not compelled this jury, under the instructions given, to find defendant at the moment of the shooting knew what he was doing, that it was wrong, was sane and guilty.

NOTES

1. Could a jury which was conscientiously trying to apply the M'Naghten test to the facts of Harkness reach any result other than conviction? If not, is this desirable? Consider the following criticism of M'Naghten by Judge Bazelon in Durham v. United States, 214 F.2d 862 (D.C.Cir. 1954):

> Medico-legal writers in large number, The Report of the Royal Commission on Capital Punishment 1949–1953, and The Preliminary Report by the Committee on Forensic Psychiatry of the Group for the Advancement of Psychiatry present convincing evidence that the right-and-wrong test is "based on an entirely obsolete and misleading conception of the nature of insanity." The science of psychiatry now recognizes that a man is an integrated personality and that reason, which is only one element in that personality, is not the sole determinant of his conduct. The right-wrong test, which considers knowledge or reason alone, is therefore an inadequate guide to mental responsibility for criminal behavior. As Professor Sheldon Glueck of the Harvard Law School points out in discussing the right-wrong tests, which he calls the knowledge tests:

"It is evident that the knowledge tests unscientifically abstract out of the mental make-up but one phase or element of mental life, the cognitive, which, in this era of dynamic psychology, is beginning to be regarded as not the most important factor in conduct and its disorders. In brief, these tests proceed upon the following questionable assumptions of an outworn era in psychiatry: (1) that lack of knowledge of the 'nature or quality' of an act (assuming the meaning of such terms to be clear), or incapacity to know right from wrong, is the sole or even the most important symptom of mental disorder; (2) that such knowledge is the sole instigator and guide of conduct, or at least the most important element therein, and consequently should be the sole criterion of responsibility when insanity is involved; and (3) that the capacity of knowing right from wrong can be completely intact and functioning perfectly even though a defendant is otherwise demonstrably of disordered mind." [29]

* * *

By its misleading emphasis on the cognitive, the right-wrong test requires court and jury to rely upon what is, scientifically speaking, inadequate, and most often, invalid and irrelevant testimony in determining criminal responsibility.

The fundamental objection to the right-wrong test, however, is not that criminal irresponsibility is made to rest upon an inadequate, invalid or indeterminable symptom or manifestation, but that it is made to rest upon *any* particular symptom. In attempting to define insanity in terms of a symptom, the courts have assumed an impossible role, not merely one for which they have no special competence. As the Royal Commission emphasizes, it is dangerous "to abstract particular mental faculties, and to lay it down that unless these particular faculties are destroyed or gravely impaired, an accused person, whatever the nature of his mental disease, must be held to be criminally responsible * * *." In this field of law as in others, the fact finder should be free to consider all information advanced by relevant scientific disciplines.

2. The defendant in Harkness had a long history of what was apparently a "mental illness." But how important is this to an "insanity" defense? There is apparently a significant amount of general concern over the reliance by criminal defendants upon "temporary insanity" as a defense.

Insofar as the phrase "temporary insanity" has any legal significance, it seems to refer to those situations in which it is asserted that the defendant was "mentally ill"—or exhibited symptoms of mental illness—only at the time of the offense. In fact, the substance of the expert testimony may be that the crime itself was the only gross observable symptom of mental illness. It is clear, then, that "temporary insanity' is not a separate de-

29. Glueck, Psychiatry and the Criminal Law, 12 Mental Hygiene 575, 580 (1928), as quoted in Deutsch, The Mentally Ill in America 396 (2d ed. 1949); and see, e. g., Menninger, The Human Mind 450 (1937); Guttmacher & Weihofen, Psychiatry and the Law 403-08 (1952).

fense to liability but merely one category of situations that may arise under any formulation of the generally-applicable insanity defense. See generally Block, Temporary Insanity—First Line of Defense, 15 U.Miami L. Rev. 392 (1961), who reports that "temporary insanity" was raised in forty per cent of the capital cases tried in Florida's Eleventh Circuit in 1957. Id. at 395. Probably the main difficulty of asserting the insanity defense in a "temporary insanity" situation is the task of convincing the finder of fact that despite the absence of long-term symptoms (or any symptoms other than the offense) the defendant was in fact "mentally ill" and that the "mental illness" had the impact upon him required by the applicable criterion. There are indications that although frequently raised, the "temporary insanity" case seldom is successful. See Block, supra.

3. Professor Wechsler has noted "impressive arguments" against broadening the insanity defense by abandoning the M'Naghten test:

> The purpose of the penal law is to express a formal social condemnation of forbidden conduct, buttressed by sanctions calculated to prevent it—not alone by incapacitating and so far as possible correcting the offending individual, but also by their impact on the general imagination, i. e., through the medium of general deterrence. Considerations of equality and of effectiveness conspire to demand that sanctions which are threatened generally be applied with generality upon conviction—not that the sentence disregard differences in circumstances or in individuals but that the sentence be imposed within the framework of such formal condemnation and conviction. Responsibility criteria define a broad exception. The theory of the exception is that it is futile thus to threaten and condemn persons who through no fault of their own are wholly beyond the range of influence of threatened sanctions of this kind. So long as there is any chance that the preventive influence may operate, it is essential to maintain the threat. If it is not maintained, the influence of the entire system is diminished upon those who have the requisite capacity, albeit that they sometimes may offend.

> On this analysis, the category of the irresponsible must be defined in extreme terms. The problem is to differentiate between the wholly non-deterrable and persons who are more or less susceptible to influence by law. The category must be so extreme that to the ordinary man, burdened by passion and beset by large temptations, the exculpation of the irresponsibles bespeaks no weakness in the law. He does not identify himself and them; they are a world apart. This will be found to be the case in every instance where M'Naghten operates; with tight administration that distinguishes with care between the irresistible and unresisted impulse, it is the case under this test as well, though doubts about the possibility of such administration surely have their point. Beyond such extreme incapacities, however, the exception cannot go. This, to be sure, is not poetic justice. It is public justice, which in the interest of the common good prescribes a standard all must strive to satisfy who can, those whose nature or nurture leads them to conform with difficulty no less than those who find compliance easy. Only so can the general effort be required and maintained. If finer distinctions are in order, let them be weighed with other factors that have bearing

on the nature of the sentence and the mitigations that at that point may be made.

Wechsler, The Criteria of Criminal Responsibility, 22 U.Chi.L.Rev. 367, 374–75 (1955). How persuasive are they?

---

b. THE IRRESISTABLE IMPULSE TEST

PARSONS v. STATE

Supreme Court of Alabama, 1887.
81 Ala. 577, 2 So. 854.

Appeal from city court of Birmingham; SHARPE, Judge.

The indictment in this case charged that the defendants Nancy J. Parsons and Joe Parsons, unlawfully and with malice aforethought, killed Bennett Parsons, by shooting him with a gun. * * *

The court gave the following among other charges, at the request of the state, to which defendants duly excepted: * * * "(5) If the jury believe, from all the testimony, that the defendants at the time of the killing were in such a state of mind as to know that the act they were committing was unlawful and morally wrong, they are responsible as a sane person, if the jury believe they committed the act with which they are charged."

The defendants asked the following charges in writing, which the court refused to give, and to which rulings of the court exceptions were duly reserved: * * * "(8) If the jury believe from the evidence that the prisoners or either of them was moved to action by an insane impulse controlling their will or their judgment, then they are, or the one so affected is, not guilty of the crime charged." * * *

The jury, on their retirement, found the defendants guilty of murder in the second degree, and this appeal is prosecuted from the judgment rendered on such finding.

SOMERVILLE, J. * * * We do not hesitate to say that we reopen the discussion of this subject with no little reluctance, having long hesitated to disturb our past decisions on this branch of the law. Nothing could induce us to do so except an imperious sense of duty, which has been excited by a protracted investigation and study, impressing our minds with the conviction that the law of insanity as declared by the courts on many points, and especially the rule of criminal accountability, and the assumed tests of disease, to that extent which confers legal irresponsibility, have not kept pace with the progress of thought and discovery in the present advanced stages of medical science. * * *

It is everywhere admitted, and as to this there can be no doubt, that an idiot, lunatic, or other person of diseased mind, who is afflicted to such extent as not to know whether he is doing right or wrong, is not punishable for any act which he may do while in that state. Can the courts justly say, however, that the only test or rule of responsibility in criminal cases is the power to distinguish right from wrong, whether in the abstract, or as applied to the particular case? Or may there not be insane persons, of a diseased brain, who, while capable of perceiving the difference between right and wrong, are, as matter of fact, so far under *the duress of such disease* as to destroy *the power to choose* between right and wrong? Will the courts assume as a fact, not to be rebutted by any amount of evidence, or any new discoveries of medical science, that there is and can be no such state of mind as that described by a writer on psychological medicine as one "in which the reason has lost its empire over the passions, and the actions by which they are manifested, to such a degree that the individual can neither repress the former, nor abstain from the latter?" Dean, Med.Jur. 497.

We first consider what is *the proper legal rule of responsibility in criminal cases.* No one can deny that there must be two constituent elements of legal responsibility in the commission of every crime, and no rule can be just and reasonable which fails to recognize either of them: (1) Capacity of intellectual discrimination; and (2) freedom of will. Mr. Wharton, after recognizing this fundamental and obvious principle, observes: "If there be either incapacity to distinguish between right and wrong as to the particular act, or delusion as to the act, or inability to refrain from doing the act, there is no responsibility." 1 Whart.Crim.Law. (9th Ed.) § 33. Says Mr. Bishop, in discussing this subject: "There cannot be, and there is not, in any locality or age, a law punishing men for what they cannot avoid." 1 Bish.Crim.Law, (7th Ed.) § 383b. If therefore, it be true, as matter of fact, that the disease of insanity can, in its action on the human brain through a shattered nervous organization, or in any other mode, so affect the mind as to subvert the freedom of the will, and thereby destroy the power of the victim *to choose* between the right and wrong, although he perceive it,—by which we mean the power of volition to adhere in action to the right and abstain from the wrong,—is such a one criminally responsible for an act done under the influence of such controlling disease? We clearly think not, and such we believe to be the just, reasonable, and humane rule, towards which all the modern authorities in this country, legislation in England, and the laws of other civilized countries of the world, are gradually but surely tending   *   *   *[.]

In the present state of our law, under the rule in *McNaghten's Case,* we are confronted with this practical difficulty, which itself demonstrates the defects of the rule. The courts, in effect, charge the juries, as matter of law, that no such mental disease exists as that often testified to by medical writers, superintendents of insane hospitals, and other experts; that there can be, as matter of scientific fact, no cerebral defect, cogenital or acquired, which destroys the patient's power of self control,—his liberty of will and action,— provided only he retains a mental consciousness of right and wrong. The experts are immediately put under oath, and tell the juries just the contrary, as matter of evidence; asserting that no one of ordinary intelligence can spend an hour in the wards of an insane asylum without discovering such cases, and in fact that "the whole management of such asylums presupposes a knowledge of right and wrong on the part of their inmates." Guy & F. Forensic Med. 220. The result in practice, we repeat, is that the courts charge one way, and the jury, following an alleged higher law of humanity, find another, in harmony with the evidence.

* * *

It is no satisfactory objection to say that the rule above announced by us is of difficult application. The rule in *McNaghten's Case* * * * is equally obnoxious to a like criticism. The difficulty does not lie in the rule, but is inherent in the subject of insanity itself. The practical trouble is for the courts to determine in what particular cases the party on trial is to be transferred from the category of sane to that of insane criminals; where, in other words, the border line of punishability is adjudged to be passed. But, as has been said in reference to an every-day fact of nature, no one can say where twilight ends or begins, but there is ample distinction nevertheless between *day* and *night*. We think we can safely rely in this matter upon the intelligence of our juries, guided by the testimony of men who have practically made a study of the disease of insanity; and enlightened by a conscientious desire, on the one hand, to enforce the criminal laws of the land, and, on the other, not to deal harshly with any unfortunate victim of a diseased mind, acting without the light of reason or the power of volition.

* * *

The judgment is reversed, and the cause remanded. In the meanwhile the prisoners will be held in custody until discharged by due process of law.

STATE v. HARRISON

Supreme Court of Appeals of West Virginia, 1892.
36 W.Va. 729, 15 S.E. 982.

BRANNON, J. * * *

This "irresistible impulse" test has been only recently presented, and, while it is supported by plausible arguments, yet it is rather refined, and introduces what seems to me a useless element of distinction for a test, and is misleading to juries, and fraught with great danger to human life, so much so that even its advocates have warn-ingly said it should be very cautiously applied, and only in the clearest cases. What is this "irresistible impulse?" How shall we of the courts and juries know it? Does it exist when manifested in one single instance, as in the present case, or must it be shown to have been habitual, or at least to have evinced itself in more than a single instance * * * We have kleptomania and pyromania, which better works on medical jurisprudence tell us cannot excuse crime where there is capacity to know the character of the act. Shall we intro· duce homicidal mania, and allow him of the manslaying propensity to walk innocent through the land while yet not insane, but capable of knowing the nature and wrong of his murderous act? For myself I cannot see how a person who rationally comprehends the nature and quality of an act, and knows that it is wrong and criminal, can act through irresistible innocent impulse. Knowing the nature of the act well enough to make him otherwise liable for it under the law, can we say that he acts from irresistible impulse, and not criminal design and guilt?

NOTES

1. Is there such a phenomena as "irresistible impulse?" Consider the following views:

> [T]he American law of several states remain[s] bound by old-fash-ioned individualism. This expresse[s] itself in the seemingly logical rule of the so-called "irresistible impulse."

> There is with one exception no symptom in the whole field of psychopathology that would correspond to a really ungovernable or uncontrollable impulse. That exception is an obsessive-compulsive neurosis. Compulsions are felt by the individual as acts which he would much rather not do but which he subjectively feels impelled to do—the alternative being a most unpleasant and subjectively un-bearable anxiety. Yet compulsions play no role in criminal acts. Psychiatry is not a vague science. It can be stated definitely and flatly that compulsions are always unimportant and harmless acts. A patient may have to count the windows of a room or of a building, he may have to wipe off the doorknob with his handkerchief (for fear of germs), he may have to avoid stepping on the cracks of a pavement, he may have to leave the elevator on the twelfth floor and walk up to the thirteenth; but he never has to commit a truly compulsive criminal act. Obsessions, often associated with compul-sions, are not acts but ideas. They also come into the patient's mind against his will and judgment. They are usually of serious nature. For example, "What would happen if I use the table knife to slash my husband's throat?" "How can I help jumping out of the win-dow?" "What if I'd yell out loudly an obscene word in the theater just at that moment when all is silent just before the curtain goes up?" These obsessions, although it is almost impossible for the patient (before he is cured) to believe it, are never acted out.

In the whole literature of psychiatry and psychoanalysis there is not a single case where a violent act, homicidal or suicidal, constituted a symptom in an obsessive-compulsive neurosis. It is therefore always bad psychopathology to speak of a compulsive murder or a compulsive suicide.

The medico-legal theory of the irresistible impulse is advocated only by laymen and by psychiatrists who are scientifically not sufficiently oriented. It lends an air of scientific literalness and accuracy to a purely legal definition without any foundation in the facts of life or science. On account of this basic obscurity the rule of the so-called "irresistible impulse" is socially backward.

Fredric Wertham, M.D., The Show of Violence 13–14 (1950)

2. If those persons whose ability to control their actions was destroyed by mental illness can be identified, does the "irresistable impulse" test provide an adequate method for describing them? Consider the following comments by Judge Bazelon in Durham v. United States, 214 F.2d 862 (D.C.Cir. 1954):

The term "irresistible impulse" * * * carries the misleading implication that "diseased mental condition[s]" produce only sudden, momentary or spontaneous inclinations to commit unlawful acts.[42]

As the Royal Commission found:

"* * * In many cases * * * this is not true at all. The sufferer from [melancholia, for example] experiences a change of mood which alters the whole of his existence. He may believe, for instance, that a future of such degradation and misery awaits both him and his family that death for all is a less dreadful alternative. Even the thought that the acts he contemplates are murder and suicide pales into insignificance in contrast with what he otherwise expects. The criminal act, in such circumstances, may be the reverse of impulsive. It may be coolly and carefully prepared; yet it is still the act of a madman. This is merely an illustration; similar states of mind are likely to lie behind the criminal act when murders are committed by persons suffering from schizophrenia or paranoid psychoses due to disease of the brain."[43]

* * * We find that the "irresistible impulse" test is also inadequate in that it gives no recognition to mental illness characterized by brooding and reflection and so relegates acts caused by such illness to the application of the inadequate right-wrong test.

42. Impulse, as defined by Webster's New International Dictionary (2d ed. 1950), is:
"1. Act of impelling, or driving onward with *sudden* force; impulsion, esp., force so communicated as to produce motion *suddenly*, or *immediately* * * *.
"2. An incitement of the mind or spirit, esp. in the form of an *abrupt* and vivid suggestion, prompting some *unpremeditated* action or leading to unforeseen knowledge or insight; a *spontaneous* inclination * * *.
"3. * * * motion produced by a *sudden* or *momentary* force * *.' [Emphasis supplied.]

43. Royal Commission [on Capital Punishment 1949–53,] Report 110 * * * [(1953)] [.]

c. THE AMERICAN LAW INSTITUTE'S "CONTROL" TEST

MODEL PENAL CODE (TENT. DRAFT NO. 4, 1955)

Article 4. Responsibility

Section 4.01. Mental Disease or Defect Excluding Responsibility

(1) A person is not responsible for criminal conduct if at the time of such conduct as a result of mental disease or defect he lacks substantial capacity either to appreciate the criminality of his conduct or to conform his conduct to the requirements of law.

(2) The terms "mental disease or defect" do not include an abnormality manifested only by repeated criminal or otherwise antisocial conduct.

*   *   *

Alternative formulations of paragraph (1).

(a) A person is not responsible for criminal conduct if at the time of such conduct as a result of mental disease or defect his capacity either to appreciate the criminality of his conduct or to conform his conduct to the requirements of law is so substantially impaired that he cannot justly be held responsible.

(b) A person is not responsible for criminal conduct if at the time of such conduct as a result of mental disease or defect he lacks substantial capacity to appreciate the criminality of his conduct or is in such state that the prospect of conviction and punishment cannot constitute a significant restraining influence upon him.

Comment

*   *   *

The draft accepts the view that any effort to exclude the non-deterrables from strictly penal sanctions must take account of the impairment of volitional capacity no less than of impairment of cognition; and that this result should be achieved directly in the formulation of the test, rather than left to mitigation in the application of *M'Naghten*. It also accepts the criticism of the "irresistible impulse" formulation as inept in so far as it may be impliedly restricted to sudden, spontaneous acts as distinguished from insane propulsions that are accompanied by brooding or reflection.

Both the main formulation recommended and alternative (a) deem the proper question on this branch of the inquiry to be whether the defendant was without capacity to conform his conduct to the requirements of law. * * * The application of the principle will call, of course, for a distinction between incapacity, upon the one hand, and mere indisposition on the other. Such a distinction is inevitable in the application of a standard addressed to impairment of volition. We believe that the distinction can be made.

Alternative (b) states the issue differently. Instead of asking whether the defendant had capacity to conform his conduct to the requirements of law, it asks whether, in consequence of mental disease or defect, the threat of punishment could not exercise a significant restraining influence upon him. To some extent, of course, these are the same inquiries. To the extent that they diverge, the latter asks a narrower and harder question, involving the assessment of capacity to respond to a single influence, the threat of punishment. Both Dr. Guttmacher and Dr. Overholser considered the assessment of responsiveness to this one influence too difficult for psychiatric judgment. Hence, though the issue framed by the alternative may well be thought to state the question that is most precisely relevant for legal purposes, the Reporter and the Council deemed the inquiry impolitic upon this ground. In so far as non-deterrability is the determination that is sought, it must be reached by probing general capacity to conform to the requirements of law. The validity of this conclusion is submitted, however, to the judgment of the Institute.

4. One further problem must be faced. In addressing itself to impairment of the cognitive capacity, *M'Naghten* demands that impairment be complete: the actor must *not* know. So, too, the irresistible impulse criterion presupposes a complete impairment of capacity for self-control. The extremity of these conceptions is, we think, the point that poses largest difficulty to psychiatrists when called upon to aid in their administration. The schizophrenic, for example, is disoriented from reality; the disorientation is extreme; but it is rarely total. Most psychotics will respond to a command of someone in authority within the mental hospital; they thus have some capacity to conform to a norm. But this is very different from the question whether they have the capacity to conform to requirements that are not thus immediately symbolized by an attendant or policeman at the elbow. Nothing makes the inquiry into responsibility more unreal for the psychiatrist than limitation of the issue to some ultimate extreme of total incapacity, when clinical experience reveals only a graded scale with marks along the way. * * *

We think this difficulty can and must be met. The law must recognize that when there is no black and white it must content itself with different shades of gray. The draft, accordingly, does not demand *complete* impairment of capacity. It asks instead for *substantial* impairment. This is all, we think, that candid witnesses, called on to infer the nature of the situation at a time that they did not observe, can ever confidently say, even when they know that a disorder was extreme.

If substantial impairment of capacity is to suffice, there remains the question whether this alone should be the test or whether the criterion should state the principle that measures how substantial it must be. To identify the degree of impairment with precision is, of course, impossible both verbally and logically. The recommended formulation is content to rest upon the term "substantial" to support the weight of judgment; if capacity is greatly impaired, that presumably should be sufficient. Alternative (a) proposes to submit the issue squarely to the jury's sense of justice, asking expressly whether the capacity of the defendant "was so substantially impaired that he can not justly be held responsible." Some members of the Council deemed it unwise to present questions of justice to the jury, preferring a submission that in form, at least, confines the inquiry to fact. The proponents of the alternative contend that since the jury normally will feel that it is only just to exculpate if the disorder was extreme, that otherwise conviction is demanded, it is safer to invoke the jury's sense of justice than to rest entirely on the single word "substantial", imputing no specific measure of degree. The issue is an important one and it is submitted for consideration by the Institute.

* * *

Paragraph (2) of section 4.01 is designed to exclude from the concept of "mental disease or defect" the case of so-called "psychopathic personality." The reason for the exclusion is that, as the Royal Commission put it, psychopathy "is a statistical abnormality; that is to say, the psychopath differs from a normal person only quantitatively or in degree, not qualitatively; and the diagnosis of psychopathic personality does not carry with it any explanation of the causes of the abnormality." While it may not be feasible to formulate a definition of "disease", there is much to be said for excluding a condition that is manifested only by the behavior phenomena that must, by hypothesis, be the result of disease for irresponsibility to be established. Although British psychiatrists have agreed, on the whole, that psychopathy should not be called "disease", there is considerable difference of opinion on the point in the United States. Yet it does not seem useful to contemplate the litigation of what is essentially a matter of terminology; nor is it right to have the legal result rest upon the resolution of a dispute of this kind.

MODEL PENAL CODE (P.O.D. 1962)

Article 4.   Responsibility

Section 4.01.   Mental Disease or Defect Excluding Responsibility

(1) A person is not responsible for criminal conduct if at the time of such conduct as a result of mental disease or defect he lacks

substantial capacity either to appreciate the criminality [wrongful-ness] of his conduct or to conform his conduct to the requirements of law.

(2) As used in this Article, the terms "mental disease or de-fect" do not include an abnormality manifested only by repeated criminal or otherwise anti-social conduct.

UNITED STATES v. POLLARD

United States District Court for the Eastern District of Michigan, 1959.
171 F.Supp. 474, set aside 282 F.2d 450, mandate clarified 285 F.2d 81.

LEVIN, District Judge. The defendant, Marmion Pollard, hav-ing waived indictment, the Government instituted this prosecution on a three-count information charging him, under Section 2113(d), Title 18 U.S.C.A., with the attempted robbery of the Chene-Medbury Branch of the Bank of the Commonwealth and the 24th-Michigan Branch of the Detroit Bank & Trust Company on May 21, 1958, and the attempted robbery on June 3, 1958, of the Woodrow Wilson-Davison Branch of the Bank of the Commonwealth. These banks, members of the Federal Reserve System and insured by the Federal Deposit Insurance Corporation, are located in Detroit, Michigan.

On arraignment, the accused pleaded guilty before another judge of this Court. Subsequently, upon advice of counsel, he moved to set aside the guilty plea on the ground that he was insane at the time he committed the acts upon which the prosecution was based. The Court, with the acquiescence of the Government, permitted the defendant to withdraw his guilty plea, and a plea of not guilty was entered. The case was then assigned to me for trial.

Prior to trial, I was advised that a psychiatric report of a psy-chiatrist retained by the defendant indicated that the defendant was, at the time of the offenses, suffering from a diseased mind which produced an irresistible impulse to commit the criminal acts. Sub-sequently, a report was submitted to the Government by each of two psychiatrists who had examined the defendant at its request. These reports, which were made available to me, agreed with the conclu-sion of the defendant's psychiatrist. It then appeared to me that it would be in the interest of justice to secure a psychiatric evaluation of defendant's state of mind based upon more extensive study. I was particularly desirous of having such a study made inasmuch as the psychiatric reports submitted to me were based on interviews that did not exceed a maximum of two hours with each of the three psy-chiatrists. I, thereupon, on October 10, 1958, entered an order that the defendant be sent to the United States Medical Center at Springfield, Missouri. After a study of thirty days, the Medical Center submitted a report which was introduced in evidence. The gist of the report may be set out as follows:

> During the period under inquiry, "a dissociative state may have existed and that his [defendant's] actions may not have been consciously motivated.
>
> "It is, therefore, our opinion that during the period in question, Pollard, while intellectually capable of knowing right from wrong, may have been governed by unconscious drives which made it impossible for him to adhere to the right.
>
> " * * * We readily acknowledge our inability either to marshal sufficient objective facts or formulate a completely satisfactory theory on which to base a solid opinion as to subject's responsibility during the period in question." [1]

The defendant elected to be tried by the Court without a jury. During the trial, the following facts appeared:

The defendant is an intelligent, twenty-nine year old man. In 1949, he married and, during the next four years, three sons and a daughter were born of this marriage. He was apparently a well-adjusted, happy, family man. In 1952, he became a member of the Police Department of the City of Detroit and continued to work as a policeman until he was apprehended for the acts for which he is now being prosecuted. In April, 1956, his wife and infant daughter were brutally killed in an unprovoked attack by a drunken neighbor.

On May 21, 1958, one day before he remarried, at about 11:00 A.M., defendant entered the 24th-Michigan Branch of the Detroit Bank & Trust Company. He paused for a few moments to look over the bank and then proceeded to an enclosure in which a bank official was at work. He told the official, whom he believed to be the manager, that he wanted to open a savings account. He then walked through a swinging gate into the enclosure, sat down at the desk, pulled out a gun and pointed it at the official. He ordered the official to call a teller. When the teller arrived, the defendant handed a brown paper grocery bag to him and told him to fill it with money. While it was being filled, defendant kept the bank official covered. The teller filled the bag with money as ordered and turned it over to the defendant. Thereupon, defendant ordered the bank official to

---

1. Not only is this report, in the light most favorable to the defendant, inconclusive but in part is based upon facts which were not substantiated during the trial. The personal and social history section of the report states that after his wife's death "it was noted by his supervisors that he [defendant] became less efficient, less interested, more withdrawn and a noticeably less effective policeman". However, the police department records introduced in evidence reveal that the defendant's police work covering the period of inquiry, if anything, was more effective than his service prior to the death of his wife.

accompany him to the exit. As both the defendant and bank official approached the exit, the official suddenly wrapped his arms around the defendant, who then dropped the bag and fled from the bank and escaped.

About 4:00 P.M., on the same day, he entered the Chene-Medbury Branch of the Bank of the Commonwealth and walked to a railing behind which a bank employee was sitting. He pointed his gun at the man and told him to sit quietly. The employee, however, did not obey this order but instead raised an alarm, whereupon the defendant ran from the bank and again escaped.

After the defendant was apprehended by the Detroit Police under circumstances which I shall later relate, he admitted to agents of the Federal Bureau of Investigation that after his abortive attempts to rob the two banks, he decided to rob a third bank and actually proceeded on the same day to an unnamed bank he had selected but decided not to make the attempt when he discovered that the bank was "too wide open"—had too much window area so that the possibility of apprehension was enhanced.

On June 3, at about 3:00 P.M., the defendant entered the Woodrow Wilson-Davison Branch of the Bank of the Commonwealth and went directly to an enclosure behind which a male and female employee were sitting at desks facing each other. Defendant held his gun under a jacket which he carried over his right arm. He ordered the woman employee to come out from behind the railing. In doing so, she grasped the edge of her desk. Defendant, in the belief that she may have pushed an alarm button, decided to leave but ordered the woman to accompany him out of the bank. When they reached the street, he told her to walk ahead of him, but not to attract attention. Defendant noticed a police car approaching the bank and waited until it passed him, then ran across an empty lot to his car and again escaped.

On June 11, 1958, he attempted to hold up a grocery market. He was thwarted in the attempt when the proprietor screamed and, becoming frightened, the defendant fled. In so doing, he abandoned his automobile in back of the market where he had parked it during the holdup attempt. Routinely, this car was placed under surveillance and later when the defendant, dressed in his Detroit Police Officer's uniform, attempted to get in it, he was arrested by detectives of the Detroit Police Force.

After his apprehension, the defendant confessed to eleven other robberies, or attempted robberies.

The three psychiatrists who submitted the written reports, all qualified and respected members of their profession, testified that in their opinion the defendant, at the time he committed the criminal acts, knew the difference between right and wrong and knew that the acts he committed were wrong but was suffering from a "traumatic neurosis" or "dissociative reaction", characterized by moods of depression and severe feelings of guilt, induced by the traumatic effect of the death of his wife and child and his belief that he was responsible for their deaths because by his absence from home he left them exposed to the actions of the crazed, drunken neighbor. They further stated that he had an unconscious desire to be punished by society to expiate these guilt feelings and that the governing power of his mind was so destroyed or impaired that he was unable to resist the commission of the criminal acts. In their opinion, however, the defendant was not then, nor is he now, psychotic or committable to a mental institution.

Three of defendant's fellow police officers, called as defense witnesses, testified that during the period in which the defendant committed the criminal acts he had a tendency to be late for work; that at times he was despondent; and that he occasionally seemed to be lost in thought and did not promptly respond to questions directed to him. One of the officers testified that on one occasion, he repeatedly beat the steering wheel of the police car in which they were riding, while at the same time reiterating the name of his murdered wife. However, none of them found his conduct or moods to be of such consequence that they believed it necessary to report the defendant to a superior officer.

Defendant's present wife, who impressed me as an intelligent person, testified that on two occasions defendant suddenly, and for no reason apparent to her, lapsed into crying spells and that he talked to her once or twice about committing suicide. She also testified that during one such period of depression he pointed a gun at himself; that she became frightened and called the police; that the police came, relieved him of his gun, and took him to the precinct police station; and that after his release he appeared jovial and acted as if nothing had happened. Defendant's brother-in-law stated that the defendant had always been a very happy person but that he became noticeably despondent after the death of his wife and child and expressed a desire to commit suicide because he now no longer had a reason for living.

*   *   *

Counsel for defendant contends that since all the medical testimony was to the effect that the defendant was suffering from an irresistible impulse at the time of the commission of the offenses, this Court must accept this uncontroverted expert testimony and find him not guilty by reason of insanity.

*   *   *

I have great respect for the profession of psychiatry. Vast areas of information have been made available through its efforts. I have found much comfort in having the assistance of psychiatrists in the disposition of many cases on sentence. Yet, there are compelling reasons for not blindly following the opinions of experts on controlling issues of fact.   Expert testimony performs a valuable function in explaining complex and specialized data to the untutored lay mind.   When the experts have made available their knowledge to aid the jury or the Court in reaching a conclusion, their function is completed.   The opinions and judgments or inferences of experts, even when unanimous and uncontroverted, are not necessarily conclusive on the trier of the facts and may be disregarded when, in the light of the facts adduced, such judgments, opinions or inferences do not appear valid.   The jury, in determining the probative effect to be given to expert testimony, is not to disregard its own experience and knowledge and its collective conscience.   It follows that this is also true of the judge sitting without a jury.

The psychiatrists, as I hereinbefore related, testified that the defendant suffered from severe feelings of depression and guilt;   and that in their opinion he had an irresistible impulse to commit criminal acts, an unconscious desire to be apprehended and punished; and that he geared his behavior to the accomplishment of this end. However, his entire pattern of conduct during the period of his criminal activities militates against this conclusion.   His conscious desire not to be apprehended and punished was demonstrably greater than his unconscious desire to the contrary.   After his apprehension, despite searching interrogation for over five hours by Detroit Police Officers and by agents of the Federal Bureau of Investigation, he denied any participation in criminal conduct of any kind.   It was only after he was positively identified by bank personnel that he finally admitted that he did attempt to perpetrate the bank robberies.   I asked one of the psychiatrists to explain this apparent inconsistency. In answer to my question, he stated that although the defendant had an unconscious desire to be apprehended and punished, when the possibility of apprehension became direct and immediate, the more dominating desire for self-preservation asserted itself.   This explanation may have merit if applied to individual acts.   However, the validity of a theory that attempts to explain the behavior of a person must be determined in light of that person's entire behavioral pattern and not with reference to isolated acts which are extracted from that pattern.   The defendant's pattern of behavior of May 21, 1958, discloses that the desire for self-preservation was not fleeting and momentary but continuing, consistent and dominant.   What, then, becomes of the theory of irresistible impulse?   Looking to the events of that day, I am asked to believe, first, that the defendant, acting pursuant to an irresistible impulse, selected a bank site to rob, entered the bank to accomplish that end, purposely failed in the attempt and when the end he sought, apprehension, was in view, escaped because of the dominance, at the moment of ultimate accomplishment, of the stronger drive for self-preservation.   I must then believe that when the defendant knew he was apparently free from detection, his compulsive state reasserted itself and that he again went through the steps of planning, abortive attempt and escape. And if I acquiesce in this theory, what other psychiatric theory explains his subsequent conduct—his plan to rob a third unnamed bank and the rejection of that plan because of his subjective belief that the possibility of apprehension would be too great? If the theory remains the same, then it appears that in the latter case, the fear of apprehension and punishment tipped "the scales enough to make resistible an impulse otherwise irresistible." Guttmacher and Weihofen, Psychiatry and the Law, 413. It is a logical inference that, in reality, the other robbery attempts were made as the result of impulses that the defendant did not chose voluntarily to resist because, to him, the possibility of success outweighed the likelihood of detection which is in essence a motivation for all criminal conduct. The impulse being resistible, the defendant is accountable for his criminal conduct.

Psychiatrists admit that the line between irresistible impulse and acts which are the result of impulses not resisted is not easy to trace. Guttmacher and Weihofen, Psychiatry and the Law. To the extent that the line may be traced, the distinguishing motivation of the action, whether the act is performed to satisfy an intrinsic need or is the result of extrinsic provocation, is a determining factor. Admittedly, motivations may be mixed. However, all the facts have clearly established that defendant's criminal activity was planned to satisfy an extrinsic need by a reasoned but anti-social method. The defendant had financial problems of varying degrees of intensity throughout his life. He had financial difficulties during his first marriage. He was now embarking upon a second marriage. He was about to undertake the responsibility of supporting not only a wife and himself, but also four children, three of them the product of his first marriage. In statements given to agents of the Federal Bureau of Investigation admitting his criminal activity, he stated: "Inasmuch as I was about to marry my second wife, I decided that I would not lead the same type of financially insecure life that I led with my first wife. I needed about $5,000 in order to buy a house. My only purpose in deciding to rob a bank was to obtain $5,000 and if I obtained the money, I did not intend to continue robbing." Defendant's entire pattern of conduct was consistent with this expressed motivation.

Life does not always proceed on an even keel. Periods of depression, feelings of guilt and inadequacy are experienced by many of us. Defendant was a devoted husband and loving father. His feelings of despondency and depression induced by the brutal killing of his wife and infant daughter were not unnatural. How else the defendant should have reacted to his tragic loss I am not told. His conduct throughout this crucial period did not cause any concern among his colleagues. All stated unequivocally that in their opinion he was sane. Significant also is the fact that his present wife married him on May 22, 1958, after a year of courtship. It is a permissible inference that defendant's conduct relative to his mental condition, as related by her, did not suggest to her that the defendant was insane.

I am satisfied beyond a reasonable doubt that the defendant committed the acts for which he is now charged and that when he committed them he was legally sane.

I, therefore, adjudge the defendant guilty of the three counts of the information.

POLLARD v. UNITED STATES

United States Court of Appeals for the Sixth Circuit, 1960.
282 F.2d 450, mandate clarified 285 F.2d 81.

McALLISTER, Chief Judge. * * * It is submitted by the government that whether appellant acted as a result of an irresistible impulse was a question of fact which was determinable by the trier of the facts—in this case, by the District Court, sitting without a jury, and that it properly found appellant guilty.

Appellant's counsel contends that the government did not prove appellant guilty beyond a reasonable doubt; and, further, that there was no evidence to sustain the trial court's finding that appellant was guilty beyond a reasonable doubt.

*   *   *

It is submitted by the government that, regardless of the unanimous testimony of six expert psychiatrists and a physician, appellant, in their opinion, acted under an irresistible impulse, and in spite of the fact that there was no evidence by experts or laymen to the contrary, the trial court was entitled to exercise its independent judgment "by weighing of the case in its entirety, as opposed to being bound by what might be considered to be uncontradicted expert opinion evidence," and to find, under the evidence in this case, that, beyond a reasonable doubt, appellant did not act under an irresistible impulse.

*   *   *

[A]cts that appear rational are not to be taken by the factfinder as evidence of sanity, where all of the other evidence in the case is proof of a defendant's mental unsoundness.

*   *   *

It is true, as the government suggests, that the Report of the Neuropsychiatric Staff Conference of the Medical Center was an opinion that Pollard, during the period in question, *may* have been governed by unconscious drives which made it impossible for him to adhere to the right, and that the staff "acknowledges [its] inability either to marshall sufficient objective facts or formulate a completely satisfactory theory on which to base a solid opinion as to [Pol-lard's] responsibility during the period in question." However, the staff did conclude that "the weight of objective historical evidence available to us tends to support the conclusion of previous examiners" and that the current findings indicated that during the period of the attempted robberies "a disassociative state may have existed and that his actions may not have been consciously activated."

* * *

From all of the evidence of the lay witnesses, * * * it can-not be affirmatively concluded that Pollard was sane. Obviously, as a result of the murder of his wife and child while he was absent from his home, he was suffering from some grave disorder, and that disorder was, in the opinion of all the psychiatric and medical ex-perts, a disassociative reaction resulting in Pollard's commission of the acts charged because of an irresistible impulse.

* * *

It is emphasized by the government that Pollard was motivated to attempt the bank robberies because of his need for financial se-curity. * * *

The claimed motivation seems pointless. Pollard, during his first marriage, had been receiving the regular salary of a policeman with promotions, of approximately $450 a month. His first wife, at that time, was receiving about $300 a month as a clerk with the Michigan Unemployment Compensation Commission. Their joint in-come was almost twice what a regular policeman's salary would be. His second wife, at the time of her marriage to him, had money of her own—enough to pay her own bills, and take care of her daughter with the money which was paid for support by her former husband. She had previously held a position for six years with the Michigan Bell Telephone Company. She considered herself to be relatively comfortable financially. Between the time of Pollard's arrest on June 11, 1958, and his trial, she had, herself, paid off about $700 in bills that he had owed. Pollard's financial condition could not be considered a reasonable motivation for his attempted bank robberies. As far as income went, he was much better off than most other po-licemen and if such a financial condition could be considered a rea-sonable motivation for Pollard's attempted robberies, every other policeman in the department would have had twice the motivation to commit such crimes as Pollard had.

* * *

It is our conclusion from the record in this case that in the light of the unanimous testimony of the government's medical experts in psychiatry and appellant's expert witness, as well as the uncontra-dicted evidence of the lay witnesses, the presumption of sanity was overcome, and the government failed to sustain its burden of proving that appellant did not suffer from mental illness consequent upon the unprovoked murder of his wife and child while he was absent on police duty; and that it failed to prove that appellant did not act under irresistible impulse as a result of such mental illness.

In accordance with the foregoing, the judgment of the District Court is set aside and the case remanded for further proceedings consonant with this opinion.

SIMONS, Senior Judge (dissenting).

* * * Particularly am I unable to entertain the concept that the Appellant wished to be apprehended, while at the same time, yielding to an irresistible impulse to commit the crimes, and to escape detection and apprehension. I would sustain the conviction.

NOTE

Assuming that factors other than conscious free choice may in some cases determine behavior, does the current state of knowledge of human behavior and clinical techniques make it practical to focus in particular criminal litigation upon whether a specific past act was one of those cases? Consider the following comments:

> [I]n a case where the abnormality of mind is one which affects the accused's self-control the step between "he did not resist his impulse" and "he could not resist his impulse" is, as the evidence in this case shows, one which is incapable of scientific proof. A fortiori there is no scientific measurement of the degree of difficulty which an abnormal person finds in controlling his impulses. These problems which in the present state of medical knowledge are scientifically insoluble, the jury can only approach in a broad, common-sense way.

Regina v. Bryne, [1960] 2 Q.B. 396, 404

> There is still lacking in the psychoanalytic, psychiatric or psychologic literature a simple and comprehensible statement of the problem of individual choice, decision, volition and moral responsibility which could be applied directly to the decision-making processes of the law. * * *

> About the most we feel able to agree upon—but we think it enough for practical interprofessional cooperation—is that there is ample evidence from psychoanalysis, psychiatry and the other behavioral sciences that the more free the individual is from the internal pressures of psychopathology and the less he is burdened with the detrimental forces of adverse social, economic and cultural conditions, the more he is able to make choices and decisions, to select among alternative patterns of behavior, in a manner which appears to approximate our traditional notion of free will.

Louisell and Diamond, Law and Psychiatry: Detente, Entenete, or Concomitance, 50 Cornell L.Q. 217, 220, 221 (1965).[f]

Perhaps the earliest measure which psychiatrists utilized to assess responsibility was the degree of unreasonableness of the offender's behavior. A criminal act which seems totally alien to any goal that a rational man would pursue has traditionally been looked upon as a sign of illness. Both psychiatry and the culture as a whole are often willing to assume that the unreasonable man is a sick man and that a sick man is not responsible for his actions.

* * *

With the growth of psychoanalytic knowledge many psychiatrists have sought answers to the degree of man's responsibility in terms of the unconscious component in human behavior. They argue that if an individual behaves in an unreasonable manner because of motivations that are out of his awareness he cannot really help himself and should not be held responsible for his actions. Thus some psychoanalytic observers have argued that free will exists only to the extent that a person is aware of his motivations. According to this viewpoint, choice is available in inverse proportion to the amount of behavior or thinking which is dominated by unconscious processes.

While the author is deeply impressed with the role of the unconscious in determining behavior, he can see little value in utilizing this concept to clarify the problem of responsibility or free will. First of all, the degree to which motivation is unconscious is always relative. We have devised no means of measuring the degree to which a person is aware of his own motivations and must admit that every act carries with it a mixture of conscious and unconscious elements. We are therefore on highly tenuous grounds when we use this criterion to say that a man is responsible for one of his acts but not for another. Furthermore, the belief that out-of-awareness forces should mitigate responsibility subtly personifies the unconscious and relegates it to the role of a dangerous and unpredictable external agent. Used in this sense, it is as though the unconscious were a lurking shadow hidden somewhere in the soul of each individual, waiting only for the opportunity to commit some heinous act. This kind of thinking might lead to regrettable statements such as "It was not I who committed this offensive act but my unconscious mind." Such a notion assumes that a person's unconscious motivations are not a part of the individual in the same sense as his conscious motivations. It is in effect a denial of the existence of the person as an integrated unit.

Another way of looking at the psychoanalytic viewpoint is that an individual should not be held responsible for his actions if he is responding to internalized conflicts or misperceived oppression. While this at first glance appears to be a humanitarian notion, it could in practice grossly discriminate against the offender who is responding to more readily observable stress. Actually, the person whose criminal behavior is primarily engendered by poverty or persecution may be motivated by forces which are just as powerful and unrelenting as those which motivate the emotionally disturbed offender. Crime may be necessary for survival in either case. If the psychiatrist can be persuaded to argue that an offender should not be held responsible for behavior which is largely determined by unconscious factors, then perhaps the sociologist should be required to argue that poverty, discrimination and delinquent associations would also make the offender nonresponsible. Either approach would be compatible with a deterministic viewpoint.

S. Halleck, Psychiatry and the Dilemmas of Crime 209–11 (1967).[g]

d. THE DURHAM RULE

DURHAM v. UNITED STATES

United States Court of Appeals for the District of Columbia, 1954.
94 U.S.App.D.C. 228, 214 F.2d 862.

BAZELON, Circuit Judge. Monte Durham was convicted of housebreaking, by the District Court sitting without a jury. The only defense asserted at the trial was that Durham was of unsound mind at the time of the offense. We are now urged to reverse the conviction (1) because the trial court did not correctly apply existing rules governing the burden of proof on the defense of insanity, and (2) because existing tests of criminal responsibility are obsolete and should be superseded.

I.

Durham has a long history of imprisonment and hospitalization. In 1945, at the age of 17, he was discharged from the Navy after a psychiatric examination had shown that he suffered "from a profound personality disorder which renders him unfit for Naval service." In 1947 he pleaded guilty to violating the National Motor Theft Act and was placed on probation for one to three years. He attempted suicide, was taken to Gallinger Hospital for observation, and was transferred to St. Elizabeths Hospital, from which he was discharged after two months. In January of 1948, as a result of a conviction in the District of Columbia Municipal Court for passing bad checks, the District Court revoked his probation and he commenced service of his Motor Theft sentence. His conduct within the first few days in jail led to a lunacy inquiry in the Municipal Court where a jury found him to be of unsound mind. Upon commitment to St. Elizabeths, he was diagnosed as suffering from "psychosis with psychopathic personality." After 15 months of treatment, he was discharged in July 1949 as "recovered" and was returned to jail to serve the balance of his sentence. In June 1950 he was conditionally released. He violated the conditions by leaving the District. When he learned of a warrant for his arrest as a parole violator, he fled to the "South and Midwest obtaining money by passing a number of bad checks." After he was found and returned to the District, the Parole Board referred him to the District Court for a lunacy inquisition, wherein a jury again found him to be of unsound mind. He was readmitted to St. Elizabeths in February 1951. This time the diagnosis was "without mental disorder, psychopathic personality." He was discharged for the third time in May 1951. The housebreaking which is the subject of the present appeal took place two months later, on July 13, 1951.

According to his mother and the psychiatrist who examined him in September 1951, he suffered from hallucinations immediately after his May 1951 discharge from St. Elizabeths. Following the present indictment, in October 1951, he was adjudged of unsound mind in proceedings under § 4244 of Title 18 U.S.C.A., upon the affidavits of two psychiatrists that he suffered from "psychosis with psychopathic personality." He was committed to St. Elizabeths for the fourth time and given subshock insulin therapy. This commitment lasted 16 months—until February 1953—when he was released to the custody of the District Jail on the certificate of Dr. Silk, Acting Superintendent of St. Elizabeths, that he was "mentally competent to stand trial and * * * able to consult with counsel to properly assist in his own defense."

He was thereupon brought before the court on the charge involved here. * * *

His conviction followed the trial court's rejection of the defense of insanity in these words:

> "I don't think it has been established that the defendant was of unsound mind as of July 13, 1951, in the sense that he didn't know the difference between right and wrong or that even if he did, he was subject to an irresistible impulse by reason of the derangement of mind.

> "While, of course, the burden of proof on the issue of mental capacity to commit a crime is upon the Government, just as it is on every other issue, nevertheless, the Court finds that there is not sufficient to contradict the usual presumption of [sic] the usual inference of sanity.

* * *

We think this reflects error requiring reversal.

* * *

It has been ably argued by counsel for Durham that the exist-ing tests in the District of Columbia for determining criminal re-sponsibility, i. e., the so-called right-wrong test supplemented by the irresistible impulse test, are not satisfactory criteria for determining criminal responsibility.

[The court's discussion of the right-wrong test and the irresisti-ble impulse test appear at pages 582 and 589, supra.]

We find that as an exclusive criterion the right-wrong test is inadequate in that (a) it does not take sufficient account of psychic realities and scientific knowledge, and (b) it is based upon one symp-tom and so cannot validly be applied in all circumstances. We find that the "irresistible impulse" test is also inadequate in that it gives no recognition to mental illness characterized by brooding and reflec-tion and so relegates acts caused by such illness to the application of the inadequate right-wrong test. We conclude that a broader test should be adopted.

B. In the District of Columbia, the formulation of tests of criminal responsibility is entrusted to the courts and, in adopting a new test, we invoke our inherent power to make the change pro-spectively.

The rule we now hold must be applied on the retrial of this case and in future cases is not unlike that followed by the New Hamp-shire court since 1870. It is simply that an accused is not criminal-ly responsible if his unlawful act was the product of mental disease or mental defect.

We use "disease" in the sense of a condition which is considered capable of either improving or deteriorating. We use "defect" in the sense of a condition which is not considered capable of either improv-ing or deteriorating and which may be either congenital, or the re-sult of injury, or the residual effect of a physical or mental disease.

Whenever there is "some evidence" that the accused suffered from a diseased or defective mental condition at the time the unlaw-ful act was committed, the trial court must provide the jury with guides for determining whether the accused can be held criminally responsible. We do not, and indeed could not, formulate an instruc-tion which would be either appropriate or binding in all cases. But under the rule now announced, any instruction should in some way convey to the jury the sense and substance of the following: If you the jury believe beyond a reasonable doubt that the accused was not suffering from a diseased or defective mental condition at the time he committed the criminal act charged, you may find him guilty. If you believe he was suffering from a diseased or defective mental condition when he committed the act, but believe beyond a reasonable doubt that the act was not the product of such mental abnormality, you may find him guilty. Unless you believe beyond a reasonable doubt either that he was not suffering from a diseased or defective mental condition, or that the act was not the product of such abnormality, you must find the accused not guilty by reason of insanity. Thus your task would not be completed upon finding, if you did find, that the accused suffered from a mental disease or defect. He would still be responsible for his unlawful act if there was no causal connection between such mental abnormality and the act. These questions must be determined by you from the facts which you find to be fairly deducible from the testimony and the evidence in this case.

The questions of fact under the test we now lay down are as capable of determination by the jury as, for example, the questions juries must determine upon a claim of total disability under a policy of insurance where the state of medical knowledge concerning the disease involved, and its effects, is obscure or in conflict. In such cases, the jury is not required to depend on arbitrarily selected "symptoms, phases or manifestations" of the disease as criteria for determining the ultimate questions of fact upon which the claim depends. Similarly, upon a claim of criminal irresponsibility, the jury will not be required to rely on such symptoms as criteria for determining the ultimate question of fact upon which such claim depends. Testimony as to such "symptoms, phases or manifestations," along with other relevant evidence, will go to the jury upon the ultimate questions of fact which it alone can finally determine. Whatever the state of psychiatry, the psychiatrist will be permitted to carry out his principal court function which, as we noted in Holloway v. U. S., "is to inform the jury of the character of [the accused's] mental disease [or defect]." [52] The jury's range of inquiry will not be limited to, but may include, for example, whether an accused, who suffered from a mental disease or defect did not know the difference between right and wrong, acted under the compulsion of an irresistible impulse, or had "been deprived of or lost the power of his will * * *."

Finally, in leaving the determination of the ultimate question of fact to the jury, we permit it to perform its traditional function which, as we said in Holloway, is to apply "our inherited ideas of moral responsibility to individuals prosecuted for crime * * *.' Juries will continue to make moral judgments, still operating under the fundamental precept that "Our collective conscience does not allow punishment where it cannot impose blame." But in making such judgments, they will be guided by wider horizons of knowledge concerning mental life. The question will be simply whether the accused acted because of a mental disorder, and not whether he displayed particular symptoms which medical science has long recognized do not necessarily, or even typically, accompany even the most serious mental disorder.

The legal and moral traditions of the western world require that those who, of their own free will and with evil intent (sometimes

52. 1945, 80 U.S.App.D.C. 3, 5, 148 F.2d 665, 667.

called *mens rea*), commit acts which violate the law, shall be criminally responsible for those acts. Our traditions also require that where such acts stem from and are the product of a mental disease or defect as those terms are used herein, moral blame shall not attach, and hence there will not be criminal responsibility. The rule we state in this opinion is designed to meet these requirements.

Reversed and remanded for a new trial.

NOTES

1. The initial reaction to Durham was quite favorable. See, e. g., Douglas, The Durham Rule: A Meeting Ground for Lawyers and Psychiatrists, 41 Iowa L.Rev. 485 (1956); Sobeloff, Insanity and the Criminal Law: From McNaghten to Durham, and Beyond, 41 A.B.A.J. 793 (1955); Symposium, 22 U.Chi.L.Rev. 317 (1955). A few voices were less enthusiastic. E. g., Roche, Durham and the Problem of Communication, 29 Temple L.Q. 264 (1956). For later discussions of the development of the Durham Rule, see Krash, The Durham Rule and Judicial Administration of the Insanity Defense in the District of Columbia, 70 Yale L.J. 904 (1961); Halleck, The Insanity Defense in the District of Columbia—A Legal Lorelei, 49 Geo.L.J. 294 (1960); Watson, Durham Plus Five Years: Development of the Law of Criminal Responsibility in the District of Columbia, 116 Am.J.Psy. 289 (1959). See also Symposium, Criminal Responsibility and Insanity—The Significance of Durham v. United States for Australian Courts, 3 U.W. Australia Am.L.Rev. 309 (1955). For a more recent discussion favoring the Durham Rule over the A.L.I. formulation, see Freedman, Guttmacher and Overholser, Mental Disease or Defect Excluding Responsibility, 1961 Wash.U.L.Q. 250.

2. Consider the following analysis:

[W]hat * * * is the basic significance of the *Durham case?* It is, I suggest, that the law has recognized modern psychiatry. It has taken notice of and acted upon the discoveries of psychiatry as to the enormous range, complexity, and variety of mental disorders and their profound effect upon behavior. It has repudiated, as too narrow and confined, a rule which in reality has no relation to the body of information, experience and techniques called psychiatry. This principle—the *M'Naghten* rule—that punishment should not be imposed upon one who as a result of mental disorder did not know he was doing wrong— is laudable, but it is not psychiatry. Under *M'Naghten*, psychiatry, so to speak, has made its way by stealth. It has been grudgingly admitted, for a price. The price was that it had to wear the garb of a restricted, ethical concept to which it had dubious claim and uncertain qualifications.

Under *Durham* this is changed: clearly, emphatically, cleanly and unmistakably. Psychiatry is given a card of admission on its own merits, and because of its own competence to aid in classifying those who should be held criminally responsible and those who should be treated as psychologically or emotionally disordered. It is not admitted to the courtroom merely as a handmaid of ethics, serving on the pretext that it can provide expert opinion as to whether the defendant knew the nature and quality of his act and whether it was right or wrong.

As the Court in *Durham* said, the psychiatrist will now be permitted to carry out his function which "is to inform the jury of the character of the accused's mental disease or defect." The law which previously, at best, had bootlegged psychiatric testimony of this general character, under *Durham* invites it to play a full part.

Under *Durham*, psychiatrists are not confronted with the necessity of choosing between conscience and justice. They are not faced with the unpalatable choice of prevaricating by testifying that an extreme paranoid did not know the difference between right and wrong—in which case he would probably be found insane—or of confessing that the defendant did know the difference, in which event he might be adjudged sane. They are at liberty to testify fully and honestly as to the defendant's mental condition and its meaning and implications.

Fortas, Implications of Durham's Case, 113 Am.J. Psychiatry 577, 581 (1957).[h]

3. One problem with the Durham test which arose very early was the meaning to be given to the word "product". In Carter v. United States, 102 U.S.App.D.C. 227, 252 F.2d 608 (1957) error was claimed in that the trial court had charged:

"By this term 'product' or 'casual connection,' you are told that the criminal act must be the consequence, a growth, natural result or substantive end of a mental abnormality or unsoundness in order for the defendant to avail himself of the defense of insanity."

The Court of Appeals found this to be inadequate. It explained:

"When we say the defense of insanity requires that the act be a 'product of' a disease, we mean that the facts on the record are such that the trier of the facts is enabled to draw a reasonable inference that the accused would not have committed the act he did commit if he had not been diseased as he was. There must be a relationship between the disease and the act, and that relationship, whatever it may be in degree, must be, as we have already said, critical in its effect in respect to the act. By 'critical' we mean decisive, determinative, causal; we mean to convey the idea inherent in the phrases 'because of', 'except for', 'without which', 'but for', 'effect of', 'result of', 'causative factor'; the disease made the effective or decisive difference between doing and not doing the act. The short phrases 'product of' and 'causal connection' are not intended to be precise, as though they were chemical formulae. They mean that the facts concerning the disease and the facts concerning the act are such as to justify reasonably the conclusion that 'but for this disease the act would not have been committed.'

"To the precise logician deduction of the foregoing inferences involves a tacit assumption that if the disease had not existed the person would have been a law-abiding citizen. This latter is not necessarily factually true and can rarely, if ever, be proved, but in the ordinary conduct of these cases

h. Reprinted from The American Journal of Psychiatry, volume 113, pages 577–582, 1957. Copyright 1957, the American Psychiatric Association.

we make that tacit assumption. For ordinary purposes we make no mention of this logician's nicety."

That this was not entirely satisfactory is suggested by then Judge Burger when he complained in Frigillana v. United States, 113 U.S.App.D.C. 328, 307 F.2d 665 (1962), that the word "product" did not, in fact, have any clear meaning in medicine or law. Psychiatrists, according to Judge Burger, tend to assume a causal connection between an unlawful act and mental disturbance and that therefor the Durham rule was leading to excusing "all mentally or emotionally disturbed persons from criminal responsibility."

4. Another problem experienced with the Durham test was the meaning of "disease" and "defect", and the use by psychiatrists of conclusory labels in this regard. In McDonald v. United States, 114 U.S.App.D.C. 120, 312 F.2d 847 (1962), the court, *per curiam*, attempted to resolve this issue.

> "Our purpose now is to make it very clear that neither the court nor the jury is bound by *ad hoc* definitions or conclusions as to what experts state is a disease or defect. What psychiatrists may consider a 'mental disease or defect' for clinical purposes, where their concern is treatment, may or may not be the same as mental disease or defect for the jury's purpose in determining criminal responsibility. Consequently, for that purpose the jury should be told that a mental disease or defect includes any abnormal condition of the mind which substantially affects mental or emotional processes and substantially impairs behavior controls. Thus the jury would consider testimony concerning the development, adaptation and functioning of these processes and controls.

> "We emphasize that, since the question of whether the defendant has a disease or defect is ultimately for the triers of fact, obviously its resolution cannot be controlled by expert opinion. The jury must determine for itself, from all the testimony, lay and expert, whether the nature and degree of the disability are sufficient to establish a mental disease or defect as we have now defined those terms. What we have said, however, should in no way be construed to limit the latitude of expert testimony."

McDonald is discussed in Acheson, McDonald v. United States: The Durham Rules Redefined, 51 Geo.L.J. 580 (1963).

The success of this effort and that of *Carter* with respect to "product" is reflected in the following case.

WASHINGTON v. UNITED STATES

United States Court of Appeals for the District of Columbia, 1967.
129 U.S.App.D.C. 29, 390 F.2d 444.

BAZELON, Chief Judge. Appellant was convicted by a jury of rape, robbery, and assault with a deadly weapon. His major defense was insanity. * * *

We all agree that this court's limited role in supervising the verdict does not imply an equally limited role in supervising the evidence which is put before the jury. To the contrary, the jury's wide latitude in deciding the issue of responsibility *requires* that trial judges and appellate judges ensure that the jury base its decision on the behavioral data which are relevant to a determination of blameworthiness.

The testimony of the defense psychiatrist, Dr. Adland, was based solely on a one hour and fifteen minute interview with defendant. Dr. Adland did not administer electroencephalogram, neurological, or physical tests, and did not have the benefit of reports of the tests given at Saint Elizabeths Hospital. He requested permission to see them, but permission was denied.

Since the defendant was at Saint Elizabeths Hospital for two months, the two Government psychiatrists had an opportunity for more prolonged observation. Yet both Dr. Owens and Dr. Hamman testified that they had seen Washington for approximately the same amount of time as Dr. Adland. Of course, they did have the benefit of the testing and observations performed by others at the Hospital. As Dr. Owens explained:

> When a patient is under constant observation, the examinations that were conducted in St. Elizabeth's by the psychiatrists, laboratory studies, psychological examinations, social service, interviews with relatives, all of this was part of the basis of my opinion that I rendered and the examination which I conducted at the medical staff conference on November 16, 1965. * * * By [constant observation] I mean 24 hours a day, and reports are submitted to the physicians as to their behavior, actions or activity while on the ward.

Unfortunately, except for brief references to a Rorschach test, none of this information was presented to the jury. The Government psychiatrists claimed to have based their conclusions on these studies, but they told the jury only the conclusions without any explanation of the studies themselves, what facts the studies uncovered, and why these facts led to the conclusions.

There was other available information, as well, which the jury was not told about. When Washington was twelve or thirteen, he was committed to Cedar Knolls, the District of Columbia School for Children. Apparently the records of that institution contained a lengthy history of Washington's childhood. At first, defense counsel moved them into evidence, but later he withdrew that request, perhaps because he thought it would be tactically unwise to make the jury read such a long report. Whatever the reason, the jury was forced to make its decision without any historical background on the defendant.

The omission of significant underlying information was one defect in the testimony. Another was that the jury was often subjected to a confusing mass of abstract philosophical discussion and fruitless disputation between lawyer and witness about legal and psychiatric labels and jargon. Dr. Hamman's entire testimony on direct examination was that Washington did not have a "passive-aggressive personality," did not suffer from any "personality trait disturbance," did not have "an irresistible impulse," was "not mentally ill," and was not "abnormal from the standpoint of psychiatric illness." A substantial part of Dr. Owens' testimony was similar.

These labels and definitions were not merely uninformative. Their persistent use served to distract the jury's attention from the few underlying facts which were mentioned. For example, the fact that Washington's difficulties "in relating adequately to other people are more severe or more extreme than the average [person's]" was immersed in a dispute about whether to classify these difficulties as a "personality defect," a "personality problem," a "personality disorder," a "disease," an "illness," or simply a "type of personality."

*   *   *

We all agree that more effort is needed in future cases to ensure that the issue of responsibility is decided upon sufficient information.
*   *   *

Soon after *Durham* we found that, although the jury was being given more information, still too much emphasis was being placed upon the labels used by the psychiatrist, upon whether he concluded that the defendant did or did not have a "mental illness." *   *   * [S]o in McDonald v. United States we gave the terms "disease" and "defect" a *legal* definition independent of their medical meanings. We clearly separated the legal and moral question of culpability from the medical-clinical concept of illness. We hoped thereby to separate the roles of the psychiatrist and the jury, with the former stating medical-clinical facts and opinions and the latter making the judgments required by the legal and moral standard. Also, we hoped that the expert's conclusion, would not be so heavily weighted in the jury's minds if we made plain that the expert and the jury had different judgments to make.

Even after *McDonald*, though, we allowed the experts to state whether they thought the defendant had a mental disease or defect.

We assumed that the expert could separate the medical judgments which he was supposed to make from the legal and moral judgments which he was not supposed to make. It has become abundantly apparent that this theory has not worked out. Too often conclusory labels—both medical and legal—have substituted, albeit unwittingly, for the facts and analysis which underlie them. The transcript in this case illustrates that they may have served more to confuse the jury than to guide it. Also, testimony in terms of "mental disease or defect" seems to leave the psychiatrist too free to testify according to his judgment about the defendant's criminal responsibility.

The trial judge should limit the psychiatrists' use of medical labels—schizophrenia, neurosis, etc. It would be undesirable, as well as difficult, to eliminate completely all medical labels, since they sometimes provide a convenient and meaningful method of communication. But the trial judge should ensure that their meaning is explained to the jury and, as much as possible, that they are explained in a way which relates their meaning to the defendant.

The problem with labels, such as, "product" and "mental disease or defect," is even more difficult. Because these labels are employed in the legal test for responsibility, there is a danger that the psychiatric witness will view them as a legal-moral rather than a medical matter. There are two possible solutions. We could simply prohibit testimony in terms of "product" and "mental disease or defect." Or we could clearly instruct the expert to stick to medical judgments and leave legal-moral judgments to the jury.

A strong minority of this court has consistently advocated that psychiatrists be prohibited from testifying whether the alleged offense was the "product" of mental illness, since this is part of the ultimate issue to be decided by the jury. We now adopt that view. The term "product" has no clinical significance for psychiatrists. Thus there is no justification for permitting psychiatrists to testify on the ultimate issue. Psychiatrists should explain how defendant's disease or defect relates to his alleged offense, that is, how the development, adaptation and functioning of defendant's behavioral processes may have influenced his conduct. But psychiatrists should not speak directly in terms of "product," or even "result" or "cause."

It can be argued that psychiatrists should also be prohibited from testifying whether the defendant suffered from a "mental disease or defect," since this too is part of the ultimate issue. But unlike the term "product," the term "mental disease or defect" may have some clinical significance to the psychiatrist. Moreover, prohibition of testimony about "mental disease or defect" would not be a panacea. Other words and other concepts may similarly be transformed into labels. For example, in *McDonald* we spoke about "abnormal" conditions of the mind, about impairment of mental and emotional processes, and about control mechanisms. The transcript of this trial illustrates how easily these concepts can become slogans, hiding facts and representing nothing more than the witness's own conclusion about the defendant's criminal responsibility.

At least for now, rather than prohibit testimony on "mental disease or defect," we shall try to help the psychiatrists understand their role in court, and thus eliminate a fundamental cause of unsatisfactory expert testimony.   *   *   *

Affirmed.

NOTES

1. R. Simon, The Jury and the Defense of Insanity 203–04 (1967) studied the effect of the Durham decision upon cases processed through the District of Columbia courts from 1951 through 1961. The study reported a fifteen-fold increase in the proportion of defendants who were acquitted on grounds of insanity. But it then noted that "the increase in the percentage of NGI verdicts took place at the expense of the acquittals and not at the expense of the guilty verdicts. There was no decrease in the percentage of pleas of guilty or guilty verdicts."

2. The American Bar Foundation's study reveals that as insanity acquittals increased in the District of Columbia, the number of defendants found incompetent to stand trial decreased. A. Matthews, Mental Disability and the Criminal Law 53 (1970). This suggests that a restrictive policy in regard to insanity acquittals means that some other method will be found to prevent the conviction of mentally ill defendants. Finding them incompetent to stand trial, of course, gives this result.

A. GOLDSTEIN, THE INSANITY DEFENSE 213 (1967)[i]

Durham's principal contribution has been less as a "solution" to the insanity problem than as a dramatic demonstration that there are no solutions. By giving the reformers their head, it has made apparent that a great deal of the criticism of the insanity defense is really misplaced—that their target is really the criminal law itself or the adversary process of trial or the complexities of modern life. The consequence has been highly beneficial. A retreat is at last beginning to be sounded from what had been almost exclusive preoccupation with the words of the insanity defense.

UNITED STATES v. BRAWNER

United States Court of Appeals for the District of Columbia Circuit, 1972.
471 F.2d 969.

LEVENTHAL, Circuit Judge.   The principal issues raised on this appeal from a conviction for second degree murder and carrying a dangerous weapon relate to appellant's defense of insanity.   After the case was argued to a division of the court, the court *sua sponte* ordered rehearing en banc.   We identified our intention to reconsider the appropriate standard for the insanity defense * * *.

We have decided to adopt the ALI rule as the doctrine excluding responsibility for mental disease or defect, for application prospectively to trials begun after this date.

* * *

Need to depart from "product" formulation and undue dominance by experts

A principal reason for our decision to depart from the *Durham* rule is the undesirable characteristic, surviving even the *McDonald* modification, of undue dominance by the experts giving testimony. * * *   The objective of *Durham* is still sound—to put before the jury the information that is within the expert's domain, to aid the jury in making a broad and comprehensive judgment.   But when the instructions and appellate decisions define the "product" inquiry as the ultimate issue, it is like stopping the tides to try to halt the emergence of this term in the language of those with a central role in the trial— the lawyers who naturally seek to present testimony that will influence the jury who will be charged under the ultimate "product" standard, and the expert witnesses who have an awareness, gained from forensic psychiatry and related disciplines, of the ultimate "product" standard that dominates the proceeding.

* * *   The more we have pondered the problem the more convinced we have become that the sound solution lies not in further shaping of the *Durham* "product" approach in more refined molds, but in adopting the ALI's formulation as the linchpin of our jurisprudence.

The ALI's formulation retains the core requirement of a meaningful relationship between the mental illness and the incident charged.   The language in the ALI rule is sufficiently in the common ken that its use in the courtroom, or in preparation for trial, permits a reasonable three-way communication—between (a) the law-trained, judges and lawyers;   (b) the experts and (c) the jurymen—without insisting on a vocabulary that is either stilted or stultified, or conducive to a testimonial mystique permitting expert dominance and encroachment on the jury's function.   There is no indication in the available literature that any such untoward development has attended the reasonably widespread adoption of the ALI rule in the Federal courts and a substantial number of state courts.

*   *   *

Interest of uniformity of judicial approach and vocabulary, with room for variations and adjustments

Adoption of the ALI rule furthers uniformity of judicial approach —a feature eminently desirable, not as a mere glow of "togetherness," but as an appreciation of the need and value of judicial communication. In all likelihood, this court's approach under *Durham*, at least since *McDonald,* has differed from that of other courts in vocabulary more than substance. Uniformity of vocabulary has an important value, however, as is evidenced from the familiar experience of meanings that "get lost in translation." No one court can amass all the experience pertinent to the judicial administration of the insanity defense. It is helpful for courts to be able to learn from each other without any blockage due to jargon. It is an impressive virtue of the common law, that its distinctive reliance on judicial decisions to establish the corpus of the law furthers a multi-party conversation between men who have studied a problem in various places at various times.

*   *   *

ALI rule is contemplated as improving the process of adjudication, not as affecting number of insanity acquittals

Amicus Dempsey is concerned that a change by this court from *Durham-McDonald* to ALI will be taken as an indication that this court intends that the number and percentage of insanity acquittals be modified. That is not the intendment of the rule adopted today, nor do we have any basis for forecasting that effect.

We have no way of forecasting what will be the effect on verdicts, of juries or judges, from the reduction in influence of expert testimony on "productivity" that reflects judgments outside the domain of expertise. Whatever its effect, we are confident that the rule adopted today provides a sounder relationship in terms of the giving, comprehension and application of expert testimony. Our objective is not to steer the jury's verdict but to enhance its deliberation.

*   *   *

Broad presentation to the jury

Our adoption of the ALI rule does not depart from the doctrines this court has built up over the past twenty years to assure a broad presentation to the jury concerning the condition of defendant's mind and its consequences. Thus we adhere to our rulings admitting expert testimony of psychologists, as well as psychiatrists, and to our many decisions contemplating that expert testimony on this subject will be accompanied by presentation of the facts and premises underlying the opinions and conclusions of the experts, and that the Government and defense may present, in Judge Blackmun's words, "all possibly relevant evidence" bearing on cognition, volition and capacity.

* * *

Issue of Causality Testimony

We are urged to reverse appellant's conviction on the ground that the trial court erred in allowing Government experts to testify in terms of "causality."

The rule of Washington v. United States, 129 U.S.App.D.C. 29, 390 F.2d 444 (1967) that experts must not frame their testimony in terms of "product," was aimed at relieving a stubborn and recurring problem—that of experts using their facility with the esoteric and imprecise language of mental disease to exert an undue dominion over the jury's deliberations. The *Washington* opinion did not refer to the prior opinion in Harried v. United States, 128 U.S.App.D.C. 330, 389 F.2d 281 (1967), wherein the court stated that narrowly drawn, concrete questions addressed to the experts on the causal connection between the forbidden act and the alleged mental disease were permissible.

Since both *Washington* and *Harried* are superseded—on this point—by our change today of the ultimate rule, it would be bootless to consider to what extent *Washington* superseded *Harried*. It suffices for disposition of this case to say only: (1) Under the rule of *Harried* the questioning of Government experts on the question of the causal connection between appellant's crime and his mental disease or defect was proper. (2) Assuming, arguendo, that these questions were not consonant with *Washington* we are unable, on this record, to discern prejudice. We think the expert testimony in this case adequately and lucidly ventilated the issues, there was no use of the term "product," and we see no sign of overreaching.

The case is remanded for further consideration by the District Court in accordance with this opinion.

* * *

So ordered.

BAZELON, Chief Judge.

* * *

[T]he paramount cause of *Durham*'s failure is the cluster of practical obstacles that stand in the way of the full disclosure of information that *Durham* hoped to secure. Here too the Court's decision sheds no new light. For no matter how felicitous its phrasing, a responsibility test cannot, singlehanded, overcome these practical obstacles. Neither *Durham* nor *Brawner* lets slip our well-guarded secret that the great majority of responsibility cases concern indigents, not affluent defendants with easy access to legal and psychiatric assistance. In a long line of cases we have been asked to confront difficult questions concerning the right to an adequate psychiatric examination, the right to psychiatric assistance in the preparation of the defense, the right to counsel at various stages of the process, the role and responsibility of a government expert who testifies on behalf of an indigent defendant, the burden of proof, the right to treatment during postacquittal hospitalization, and many more. If the promise of *Durham* has not been fulfilled, the primary explanation lies in our answers, or lack of answers, to those questions. I fear that it can fairly be said of *Brawner*, just as it should be said of *Durham*, that while the generals are designing an inspiring new insignia for the standard, the battle is being lost in the trenches. In fact, our obligation to confront the practical problems now is greater than it was in 1954, if only because our efforts to implement *Durham* have brought many of these problems to first light.

[I]t is clear that *Durham* focused the jury's attention on the wrong question—on the relationship between the act and the impairment rather than on the blameworthiness of the defendant's action measured by prevailing community standards. If the ALI test is indeed an improvement, it is not because it focuses attention on the *right* question, but only because it makes the *wrong* question so obscure that jurors may abandon the effort to answer it literally.

Instead of asking the jury whether the act was caused by the impairment, our new test asks the jury to wrestle with such unfamiliar, if not incomprehensible, concepts as the capacity to appreciate the wrongfulness of one's action, and the capacity to conform one's conduct to the requirements of law. The best hope for our new test is that jurors will regularly conclude that no one—including the experts—can provide a meaningful answer to the questions posed by the ALI test. And in their search for some semblance of an intelligible standard, they may be forced to consider whether it would be just to hold the defendant responsible for his action. By that indirect approach our new test may lead juries to disregard (or at least depreciate) the conclusory testimony of the experts, and to make the "intertwining moral, legal, and medical judgments" on which the resolution of the responsibility question properly depends. The Court's own opinion hints at this approach, maintaining that "[t]here is wisdom in the view that a jury generally understands well enough that an instruction composed in flexible terms gives it sufficient latitude so that, without disregarding the instruction, it can provide that application of the instruction which harmonizes with its sense of justice. The ALI rule generally communicates that meaning."

The Court's approach may very well succeed and encourage jurors to look behind the testimony and recommendations of the experts. But * * * there is also a significant possibility that our new test will leave the power of the experts intact—or even make possible an enlargement of their influence. In my opinion, an instruction that tells the jurors candidly what their function is, is the instruction most likely to encourage the jurors to resist encroachments on that function. * * *

Our instruction to the jury should provide that a defendant is not responsible *if at the time of his unlawful conduct his mental or emotional processes or behavior controls were impaired to such an extent that he cannot justly be held responsible for his act.* This test would ask the psychiatrist a single question: what is the nature of the impairment of the defendant's mental and emotional processes and behavior controls? It would leave for the jury the question whether that impairment is sufficient to relieve the defendant of responsibility for the particular act charged.

* * *

In a distressing number of recent cases this Court has been asked to consider questions unrelated to the substantive test of responsibility, but which have, as a practical matter, far greater impact on the operation of the defense than the language of the rule. The Court's decision to abandon *Durham-McDonald* in favor of ALI-*McDonald* does nothing to obsolete these questions or the Court's responses to them. If our paramount goal is an improvement of the process of adjudication of the responsibility issue, our attention should be focused on these questions rather than on the ultimate definition of the test. Obviously, these questions cannot all be resolved by one opinion. But the Court's approach to the disposition of this case offers some indication of the manner in which these questions will be handled in the future.

1. The one consistent note in the Court's analysis of our experience under *Durham* is the objection to domination by the experts accomplished through the productivity requirement. We attempted to deal with that problem in Washington v. United States by barring conclusory, expert testimony on the issue of productivity. Virtually all of the expert witnesses at Brawner's trial agreed that he was suffering from an abnormal condition of the mind. The issue in dispute was productivity—the ultimate issue for the jury. And the transcript is riddled with conclusory, expert testimony on that issue. It is hard to imagine a case which could make a stronger appeal for enforcement of the *Washington* rule.

The Court's unwillingness to reverse Brawner's conviction on this ground makes clear that this Court and the trial courts no longer have any weapons to combat the problem of conclusory testimony and the resulting domination by experts.

2. Since 1895 the federal courts have taken the position that if the defendant introduces "some evidence" of insanity, the issue will

be submitted to the jury and the government will bear the burden of proving responsibility beyond a reasonable doubt. Davis v. United States, 160 U.S. 469, 484 (1895). Yet as the responsibility defense has developed under our case law, it has become increasingly clear that the defendant carries an overwhelming practical burden which is not acknowledged in the traditional rule. As a practical matter, the defendant often has very great difficulty obtaining adequate expert assistance to gather the information necessary for the presentation of a significant defense. If he can obtain such information, his defense will often prove vulnerable to attack unrelated to the real merit of his responsibility claim. And even if the attack is very weak the defendant will rarely be entitled to a directed verdict.

With limited access to expert psychiatric assistance, indigent defendants normally rely on the government to provide an adequate psychiatric examination at the hospital to which the defendant is committed for observation. In a large number of cases the government's experts are called to testify on behalf of the defense, and their testimony has often proved inadequate. * * *

The practical burden on the defendant is greatly enhanced by the ease with which defense testimony can often be torn to pieces on cross-examination. Where a psychiatrist testifying for the government asserts that the defendant did not suffer from any abnormal condition which could impair his mental processes or behavior controls, defense counsel must have considerable expertise in psychiatry to pick out the weak points in the analysis. Yet "very few attorneys, if any, possess the requisite expertise, and we have no automatic procedure for enabling them to consult with psychiatric experts in the preparation and conduct of the defense." United States v. Leazer, No. 24,799 (D.C.Cir. Jan. 19, 1972), slip opinion at 14 (BAZELON, C. J., concurring). Even where the defendant has obvious symptoms of mental disorder, defense counsel is frequently helpless to rebut the suggestion by government psychiatrists that the defendant is malingering. If he produces testimony from a private psychiatrist that the defendant is not a malingerer, he is almost sure to find that the government and its expert witnesses will disparage that testimony on the grounds that it was based on an insufficient period of observation. * * *

3. ABANDONMENT OF THE INSANITY DEFENSE

WEINTRAUB, CRIMINAL RESPONSIBILITY: PSYCHIATRY ALONE CANNOT DETERMINE IT

49 A.B.A.J. 1075, 1078 (1963).

[T]he little we know suggests that insanity should have nothing to do with criminal accountability. Rather we should think of a conviction as simply a determination that the individual has demonstrated his capacity for antisocial behavior, and that having been proved, we ought then to draw upon medical knowledge for such help as it may offer in deciding what should be done with the offender.

MENTAL HEALTH ACT

1959, 7 & 8 Eliz. II, ch. 72, § 60.

(1) Where a person is convicted * * * and the following conditions are satisfied, that is to say—

(a) the court is satisfied, on the written or oral evidence of two medical practitioners * * *—

(i) that the offender is suffering from mental illness, psychopathic disorder, subnormality or severe subnormality; and

(ii) that the mental disorder is of a nature or degree which warrants the detention of the patient in a hospital for medical treatment * * *; and

(b) the court is of opinion, having regard to all the circumstances including the nature of the offense and the character and antecedents of the offender, and to the other available methods of dealing with him, that the most suitable method of disposing of the case is by means of an order under this section,

the court may by order authorise his admission to and detention in such hospital as may be specified in the order * * *.

A. GOLDSTEIN, THE INSANITY DEFENSE

223–25 (1967).j

[E]liminating the insanity defense would remove from the criminal law and the public conscience the vitally important distinction between illness and evil, or would tuck it away in an administrative process. The man who wished to contest his responsibility before the public and his peers would no longer be able to do so. Instead, he would be approached entirely in social engineering terms: How has the human mechanism gone awry? What stresses does it place upon the society? How can the stresses be minimized and the mechanism put right?

[The proposal to abolish the insanity defense] * * * overlooks entirely the place of the concept of responsibility itself in keeping the mechanism in proper running order. That concept is more seriously threatened today than ever before. This is a time of anomie —of men separated from their faiths, their tribes, and their villages —and trying to achieve in a single generation what could not previously be achieved in several. Many achieve all they expect, but huge numbers do not; these vent their frustration in anger, in violence, and in theft. In an effort to patch and mend the tearing social fabric, the state is playing an increasingly paternal role, trying to help as many as possible to realize their expectations and to soothe and heal those who cannot. As this effort gains momentum, there is a very real risk it will bring with it a culture which will not make the individuals within it feel it is important to learn the discipline of moderation and conformity to communal norms.

In such a time, the insanity defense can play a part in reinforcing the sense of obligation or responsibility. Its emphasis on whether an offender is sick or bad helps to keep alive the almost forgotten drama of individual responsibility. Its weight is felt through the tremendous appeal it holds for the popular imagination, as that imagination is gripped by a dramatic trial and as the public at large identifies with the man in the dock. In this way, it becomes part of a complex of cultural forces that keep alive the moral lessons, and the myths, which are essential to the continued order of society. In short, even if we have misgivings about blaming a particular individual, because he has been shaped long ago by forces he may no longer be able to resist, the concept of "blame" may be necessary.

However much we may concentrate our attention on the individual, we rely implicitly upon the existence of a culture, and a value system, which will enable us to move the individual toward conformity or to a reasonable nonconformity. That value system, if it is to become fixed early enough, must be absorbed from parents. And it, in turn, is a reflection of the larger culture, absorbed slowly and subtly over generations, transmitted by parent to child through the child-rearing devices extant in a given society. The concept of "blame," and insanity which is its other side, is one of the ways in which the culture marks out the extremes beyond which nonconformity may not go. It is one of the complex of elements which train people so that it becomes almost intuitive not to steal or rape or kill. A society which did not set such limits would probably, in time, become a less law-abiding society. This is not to say that there is not a good deal of room for humanizing the criminal law, or the insanity defense, but only that it is essential that "blame" be retained as a spur to individual responsibility.

Finally, the heart of the distinction between conviction and acquittal by reason of insanity lies in the fact that the former represents official condemnation. Yet the acquittal is itself a sanction, bringing with it comparable stigma and the prospect of indeterminate detention. If the choice between the two sanctions is to be made in a way that will not only be acceptable to the larger community but will also serve the symbolic function we have noted, it is important that the decision be made by a democratically selected jury rather than by experts—because the public can identify with the former but not with the latter. It does not follow, however, that the decision regarding the type of facility to which a particular offender is to be sent need also be made by the jury. Once the distinction between "blame" and compassion has been made, decisions as to disposition should be made by those who are professionally qualified.

NOTES

1. Consider the following comment upon the above passage:

> I find statements like the above outrageous. Their inherent cynicism is incredible to me: The continued order of society rests upon the perpetuation of myths and popular dramas, upon rituals of blame and fictions of responsibility. We punish by blaming individuals irrespective of their blameworthiness. This is all right if it serves "as a spur to individual responsibility." I simply refuse to buy the theme, which Goldstein seems to be asserting, that a proper function of the criminal law is to provide sacrificial victims to support the mythologies of morality, responsibility, and justice. It is just such cynical disregard of the individual which has so frequently permitted the official institutions of the administration of criminal justice to become more immoral, more irresponsible, and more unjust than any single criminal would dare to be. So the law, through capital punishment, murders with impunity. The prison, supposedly a place for penitence and reform, becomes a cesspool of sadistic brutality and exploitation. And, as a psychiatrist I am sorry to admit, our hospitals for the criminally insane are only sham hospitals—prisons in disguise, where fake

treatments are provided for imaginary ailments, perverting the healing spirit of medicine into an instrument of oppression and restraint.

Goldstein says: "The concept of 'blame,' and insanity which is its other side, is * * * one of the complex of elements which train people so that it becomes almost intuitive not to steal or rape or kill." Is it not painfully obvious that such "training" by the criminal law does not work effectively? And what lessons are trained into the minds of the people by the system of criminal justice which tolerates the penal farms of Arkansas, the mean, petty corruption of the urban municipal courts, police brutality in Selma and Oakland, and the Kafka nightmare of San Quentin's death row?

The conclusions in *The Insanity Defense* reflect the moral bankruptcy of the criminal law and the penal system. The hot issue today is "crime in the streets." The backlash of racism and bigotry reflected in this slogan have great political appeal. There is every indication that powerful political forces of reaction will not hesitate to turn the criminal law into a weapon of oppression and a device for the protection of vested power interests. What is this going to teach the black man about "the discipline of moderation and conformity to communal norms"? The unhappy truth is that the criminal law can never become an effective social force either as the embodiment of public moral values or as an educator of the individual conscience. The reason it cannot perform these tasks is that the criminal law easily becomes a tool of authoritarian control, an instrument of social oppression, and in the last analysis is only an expression of the corruption and hypocrisy of our society.

Diamond, Book Review, 56 Cal.L.Rev. 920, 922–23 (1968).[k]

2. To what extent does the following provide support for the argument that the insanity defense should be abolished:

I believe there has been gross failure, on the part of leading forensic psychiatrists as well as those responsible for the criminal justice system, sufficiently to mobilize psychiatric resources for the prevention and treatment of crime. Part of the fault lies with our monomania, our *folie à collective*, about criminal responsibility and the defense of insanity which has distracted us from many important tasks, two of which * * * [are] the task of defining the dangerous offender for sentencing and treatment purposes, and the mobilization of clinical resources for the treatment of such criminals.

Morris, Psychiatry and the Dangerous Criminal, 41 S.Cal.L.Rev. 514, 515 (1968).

3. Might not some reforms of less magnitude than abolition of the insanity defense meet some or many of the objections to the defense? Consider the following proposals:

I think [the issue of criminal responsibility] could be more satisfactorily determined by the judge than by the jury. * * *
[W]hen the [American Law] Institute considered this * * *
it was felt that the constitutional guarantee of jury trial required
that the issue be submitted to the jury in a contested case since it
was in effect an issue of guilt or innocence.

Wechsler, Insanity as a Defense, A Panel Discussion, 37 F.R.D. 365, 411
(1964).

[T]he [American Law] Institute proposals [i] would try to [achieve
the advantages of taking the responsibility decision from the
jury] without the disadvantages by fostering a system under
which, when this defense was interposed, the defendant would be
examined by a court-designated psychiatrist rather than having
the issue determined only in a battle of experts. The jury would
be told that this man had been designated by the court and the expectation and hope would be that the jury would credit his disin-
terestedness proportionately. The defendant would still be permitted to offer [other proof], to call his own witnesses if he
wanted to, but as a practical matter this would happen only rarely.
If the court-appointed expert found mental disease excluding responsibility, the prosecution frequently would acquiesce in such a
finding. If his findings were the other way, the defendant would
still be able to contest it but would have a very up-hill fight to win
before the jury.

Wechsler, Insanity as a Defense, A Panel Discussion, 37 F.R.D. 365, 411
(1964).[l]

It is possible to maintain the participation of the public in the
responsibility decision through the use of the jury and still bring
the psychiatric, scientific accuracy of the twentieth century into
the courtroom. Both concepts would be served if a panel of psychiatrists would, before voir dire, in effect explain modern psychiatry
to prospective jurors. This panel would present what could be
called "instructions" to the laymen. * * * Since the panel would
not be called by either side, there could be no challenges of imma-
teriality and prejudice. One objection to such a panel might be expense. * * * Another objection would be the possibility of debate about what actually to tell the prospective jurors. Perhaps
the American Medical Association, or some similar organization,
could establish a pattern of instructions and standards for this
panel. The composition of the panel and the selection of disciplines
to be represented might also be the subject of debate * * *.

Comment, The Psychiatrist's Role in Determining Accountability For
Crimes: The Public Anxiety and An Increasing Expertise, 52 Marq.L.Rev.
380, 391 (1969).

i. See Model Penal Code §§ 4.05, 4.07 (P.O.D.1962).

l. Reprinted with permission of West Publishing Company © 1965, from 37 F.R.D. 365.

PRESIDENT'S VERSION OF REVISED FEDERAL CRIMINAL CODE (1973)

13 Criminal Law Reporter 3001, 3002.

Sec. 502. *Insanity.*

It is a defense to a prosecution under any federal statute that the defendant, as a result of mental disease or defect, lacked the state of mind required as an element of the offense charged. Mental disease or defect does not otherwise constitute a defense.

NOTES

1. Is the Nixon Administration's proposal properly designated an abolition of the insanity defense? If enacted, would it be likely to increase or to decrease the percent of criminal defendants found not guilty by reason of insanity (or simply not guilty)? Consider the comment of Professors Goldstein and Katz, reprinted at page 565, supra. Revaluate the likely effect and desirability of this proposal after examining the material dealing with "diminished capacity" and "diminished responsibility" in Section 5, infra.

2. A similar proposal was made and defended in Robinson, Consultant's Report on Criminal Responsibility—Mental Illness: Section 503, in Working Papers of the National Commission on Reform of Federal Criminal Laws 229, 247–254 (1970). This position was also urged before the United States Court of Appeals for the District of Columbia Circuit by the National District Attorneys Association. Brawner v. United States, 471 F.2d 969, 985–986 (D.C.Cir. 1972).

---

4. SOME PRACTICAL ASPECTS OF THE INSANITY DEFENSE

A. MATTHEWS, MENTAL DISABILITY AND THE CRIMINAL LAW

34, 36–43, 46–50 (1970).m

Criminal responsibility cases are rare because defendants, given the alternatives, choose not to plead insanity as a defense. The plea has drawbacks stemming both from the procedural difficulties it involves and from the consequences that follow if it is successful. This seems strange in view of the widespread belief—a belief that has colored procedural approaches to criminal responsibility in this cen-

m. Reprinted by permission of the American Bar Foundation, Chicago, Illinois.

tury—that the defense is a great benefit to the defendant, who can readily purchase psychiatric testimony and thus have an easy way out of criminal liability.

Furthermore, since the prosecution must prove the defendant guilty beyond a reasonable doubt before the defendant is obliged in any way to offer a defense, the defense may even wait until the close of the prosecution's case at trial before presenting any evidence relating to the responsibility of the accused. Such an approach by a defendant would put the prosecution at the disadvantage of being surprised and might make it difficult for the prosecution to rebut expert psychiatric evidence of the lack of criminal responsibility. Many states have enacted legislation to circumvent this tactic, some statutes requiring the defense to furnish the prosecution and the court written notice of its intention to rely on the defense of insanity and others requiring the defense of insanity to be specially pleaded at an early stage in the criminal process or be conclusively waived. * * * [F]ew trial judges will hold the defense strictly to [such requirements]. Thus, in a case in which the defense actually waits until the prosecution has finished its presentation before raising the defense of insanity, the prosecutor is in trouble. The best he can hope for is a temporary delay of the trial and it is not even clear that he can force a psychiatric examination of an unwilling defendant, even with the aid of a statute. Before the trial, also, while the prosecutor may suspect that the defendant is planning a defense of insanity, he has no effective means of discovering either what the mental condition of the defendant is in fact or what the defendant will claim it is, nor of preparing for such an eventuality.

How is it, then, that more defendants do not rely on this tactic if in a serious case in which trial may not occur for a year, or perhaps two, a defendant may have himself psychiatrically examined by experts of his own choosing and not raise the defense until the prosecution has put on its case at trial? In practice, this advantage belongs only to defendants who are well-off. The vast majority of persons charged with crime, including those who are mentally disabled, are indigent. Indigence means, as a practical matter, that the accused typically cannot hire his own psychiatric experts freely as he could if he had money, but must depend for psychiatric evidence on "impartial" experts appointed by the court. Indigence has other consequences which also adversely affect a defendant's chances of preparing and successfully presenting a defense of insanity in court (assuming that, in view of the consequences of success, he wants to do so). It is difficult for the defendant either to obtain, as a preliminary matter, expert advice on his chances for success should he raise the defense of insanity or to obtain psychiatric evidence that might be persuasive in court.

1. *Procedural Disadvantages of the Insanity Plea*

Indigence typically means, first of all, inability to make bond. This is a special disadvantage in the case of the mentally disabled. During the time he is in jail, the accused is under the eye of the prosecution; guards will be able to testify that he was "normal." Should a psychiatrist examine him, it cannot be kept secret from the prosecution. If the defendant were out on bail, he could go to the office of a private psychiatrist without the police or prosecution finding out; if not, however, the psychiatrist must visit him in jail, where records of visitors are kept. The prosecutor learning of the visit will probably assume that a defense of insanity is forthcoming. In this respect the wealthier defendant charged with a crime serious enough to be nonbailable is no better off than the indigent.

Second, the clinical conditions for psychiatric examination at a county jail leave much to be desired, so that it will be more difficult to persuade a psychiatrist to perform an examination if it must be carried out in jail than if the patient were able to come to the psychiatrist's office. It will thus be more difficult to resist an examination by doctors employed by the prosecution or by impartial experts. Finally, the accused cannot receive psychiatric treatment—which he may need badly—in the county jail. County jails do not have a psychiatric staff and private psychiatrists are unlikely to be willing to go to these jails to administer therapy. An accused who is on the borderline of mental stability may be pushed over the edge by having to stay in the county jail for months awaiting trial. The same accused out in the community and able to visit a psychiatric clinic might be able to stand trial. Even if the doctors at the clinic do not wish to testify at the trial, the fact of psychiatric treatment will be very much in the defendant's favor. If an insanity defense occurs, evidence of a treatment relationship will be brought to the attention of the jury. More importantly, however, the fact of an ongoing therapeutic relationship is a strong bargaining point for any defendant.

* * *

The defendant's bargaining position is also undermined by the fact that making the insanity plea is tantamount to a virtual confession that the defendant did the acts charged. If the state's case is less than conclusive, as it often is, a chance for acquittal is sacrificed.[20] Even where the state's evidence is strong, there is usually some doubt in the prosecutor's mind; when the state's case consists only of circumstantial evidence, even the most zealous prosecutor will have his doubts as to whether the defendant actually committed the crime charged. The plea of insanity dissipates these doubts, and

20. The bifurcated trial, of course, obviates this particular difficulty, as is well illustrated in a recent case from the District of Columbia, holding that the trial judge may order a bifurcated trial in an appropriate case: Holmes v. United States, 363 F.2d 281 (D.C. Cir. 1966).

they may be completely removed by the admission of guilt which the defendant almost invariably makes to the examining psychiatrists and which may very well be passed on to the prosecutor because the procedure for court-appointed experts makes no provisions restricting the use or distribution of information gathered by the experts during their interview with the defendant (although its use may be limited at trial). To whatever extent the prosecutor's doubts are relieved the bargaining power of the defendant is lessened, particularly if evidence in support of the insanity plea is not developed during the psychiatric examination. The defendant may be further disadvantaged in that the statutes calling for mental examination by impartial experts sometimes provide for inpatient hospitalization which may last for months. These disabilities could be removed if the defendant had access to confidential psychiatric opinion without having to plead the insanity issue as he must now do if he is indigent.

Even supposing that the defense and prosecution have both obtained experts, the defense of insanity presents additional complications for each side. Most prosecutors and defense counsel appear to be unfamiliar with psychiatry and with psychiatric testimony. Presenting such evidence requires much more extensive preparation than in the routine trial of criminal cases. Secondly, the trial of the issue will take more time in court than any other type of criminal case. In a case important enough to go to trial, both the defense and the prosecution will probably call more than one, usually several, experts, each of whom will give a rather long direct presentation and then be cross-examined at great length by opposing counsel. The testimony of other disciplines, such as psychology and social work, may be presented. Not infrequently a parade of lay witnesses may be brought to the stand to testify on the issue of the accused's sanity. Special instructions for the jury must be prepared. All of this is an investment of the lawyers' time which they are usually quite unwilling to make if some alternative course of proceeding is open to them. Many defense counsel are court-appointed and are not adequately compensated for their work, an additional reason for their desire to avoid a lengthy trial.

Operationally, the fact that an indigent defendant must depend for psychiatric evidence on "impartial experts" appointed by the court is important because the impartial expert has characteristic views about mental illness in general and in particular about the degree of mental disability that will excuse a defendant from criminal responsibility. Since nearly all criminal defendants are indigent, impartial experts are the witnesses in almost all cases, and to the extent that they agree among themselves, such agreement is in effect the accepted operational standard of criminal responsibility in that locale, for all but the occasional defendant who can retain experts of his own choosing.

In most cases the indigent defendant will have to submit himself to examination by a board of impartial experts in order to obtain any evidence at all for the defense of insanity. These impartial experts —at least in the opinion of the defense bar—are more likely to be favorable to the prosecution than to the defense. Furthermore, the issue of competency to stand trial may need to be raised in order to get a psychiatric examination. If so, the indigent defendant runs the risk of being found incompetent to stand trial in order to obtain evidence to be used for a defense of insanity. If the charge is serious enough, upon a showing most courts will appoint an independent expert chosen by the defense, but usually only one; in a contested trial, however, the number of experts may be as important as what the experts say. Hence, the popular conception of the defense of insanity, which assumes that defense counsel hire as many psychiatrists as they like, is not accurate in the case of the indigent defendant for whom "shopping around" is an economic impossibility.

*   *   *

3.   *Dispositional Consequences of the Insanity Defense*

A more subtle ground of dissatisfaction with the defense of insanity than some of its procedural disadvantages is the inflexible "either-or" characteristic of the defense viewed in terms of dispositional alternatives. It limits the discretion of the lawyers by taking control over the disposition of the case out of their hands and placing it in the hands of a judge or jury. In cases where this defense is not involved, negotiations over charge reduction and entry of guilty plea are conducted in terms pretty well assessable by both sides: the circumstances of the offense itself, and the defendant's prior record, attitude, and prospects for staying out of further trouble. The testimony relating to the insanity issue, on the other hand, is not equally subject to discovery and appraisal, and its significance is more dependent on the eventualities of the trial process. It is therefore of less help in providing either an early or a simple disposition of the charges. When the defense of insanity is raised, it is usually because the lawyers are unable to work out any other alternatives; it is, in short, a last resort.

Furthermore, aside from capital cases, the defense of insanity in New York, Chicago, and Detroit seemed to many lawyers and psychiatrists an empty undertaking since the dispositional consequences of the successful insanity plea did not look any better than those which follow upon conviction. While there is no single explanation of this aspect of the "last resort" quality of the insanity plea, the following were given to us: (1) the inevitability of indefinite commitment if the defense is successful and the defendant found "insane"; (2) the belief that psychiatric treatment at the maximum-security hospital "does not exist" or is likely to prove ineffective; (3) the reluctance of many defendants to label themselves "maniacs" or even fit candidates for mental treatment; and (4) fear that the prospects of release are dim even if the mental health of the offender improves.

The indigent defendant is particularly at a disadvantage when it comes to disposition after a successful defense of insanity, for his prospects at the maximum-security mental institution to which he will be committed are even less hopeful than those of the defendant with money. Since these hospitals, by and large, are located far away from the major cities, the relatives of poor persons will not be able to visit them—at least not very frequently. It will be more difficult for the indigent patient to obtain a promise of employment, which is the indispensable ingredient for release from psychiatric hospitals. He will not be able to employ the legal counsel and independent psychiatric testimony which are often necessary to gain release and which, more importantly, are a means of prodding the maximum-security hospital to do something with a patient who otherwise may be "lost" among hundreds of persons similarly situated. * * *

---

5. THE "PARTIAL DEFENSE" OF "DIMINISHED CAPACITY"

PEOPLE v. WELLS

Supreme Court of California, 1949.
33 Cal.2d 330, 202 P.2d 53, certiorari denied 338 U.S. 836,
70 S.Ct. 43, 94 L.Ed. 510.

SCHAUER, Justice. Wesley Robert Wells appeals from a judgment entered upon a jury verdict that he is guilty of violation of section 4500 of the Penal Code, and from an order denying his motion for new trial. Section 4500 provides that certain kinds of assault committed by life-term prisoners "with malice aforethought" are capital offenses. Defendant contends: * * * (4) The trial court erred to his prejudice by excluding evidence of medical experts offered to show that he did not act with "malice aforethought." * * * [W]e conclude that the proffered evidence should have been received but that the error in rejecting it is not prejudicial.

* * *

In every crime there must exist a union or joint operation of act and intent. In the present case there is little dispute as to the act done by defendant; the crucial factual question is whether such act was done with the intent or motive which is an essential element of the crime denounced by section 4500 of the Penal Code; i. e., "with malice aforethought".

This issue, then, necessarily involves proof of a mental state (the specific intent or motive amounting to malice aforethought) and, as pertinent and material to resolving such issue, the prosecution (as has been shown hereinabove) was properly allowed to introduce evidence of various objective manifestations by defendant from which it could be inferred that he bore such "malice aforethought" toward prison guards as a class and toward Brown in particular.[4] Defendant was likewise properly allowed to give testimony as to his state of mind which tended to show lack of "malice aforethought."[5] But defendant was not allowed to introduce proffered evidence of physicians who had observed objective manifestations by defendant from which it could be inferred that, because he was suffering from an abnormal physical and mental condition (not insanity) at the time he injured Brown, defendant acted, not with "malice aforethought," but, as he himself testified, under fear for his personal safety and in the honest belief that he was defending himself from attack by Officers Robinson and Hogan. Defendant made and the trial court refused the following offer of proof: Two days before the assault upon Guard Brown the chief medical officer of the prison, making his customary rounds, saw defendant and was impressed by defendant's apparently abnormal state; he required defendant to report to the prison hospital where he examined defendant and caused defendant to be examined by the consulting psychiatrist of the prison; both physicians concluded that defendant was suffering from a "state of tension"; i. e., a condition in which "the whole body and mind are in a state of high sensitivity to external stimuli, and the result of this state is to cause the victim or patient to react abnormally to situations and external stimuli. *One of the characteristics of this state is that the patient possesses an abnormal fear for his personal safety and that an external stimulus apparently threatening that personal safety will cause the patient to react to it more violently and more unpredictably than the same*

---

4. In addition to the above summarized evidence of other instances of misconduct, the prosecution introduced the following evidence tending to show "malice aforethought": Testimony of a prisoner (contradicted by defendant) that on the night before the assault defendant said, "I will demand that son-of-a-bitch [Brown] be in the Warden's office [at the time of the disciplinary hearing] and I will hit him with the first thing I can get my hands on"; testimony of prison officials as to defendant's conduct, as evidencing his state of mind, immediately before the disciplinary hearing (defendant said, when he was told that he should enter the hearing room, "You'll be sorry you took me first"), at the hearing (defendant "became very noisy and upset"), and immediately after he left the hearing room and before he injured Brown (defendant was weeping and "trembling all over").

5. Defendant testified as to his feelings toward prison officers in general and Brown in particular; as to his state of mind at the time he picked up and threw the cuspidor; and as to the attitude engendered when he learned (in 1946) that, after his 1944 conviction, the deputy district attorney who prosecuted that case (and the present case) recommended to the Adult Authority that it "not fix a definite term in this case. As long as you fail to do so, his maximum sentence will remain at life, and he will be subject to prosecution under the statute which makes it a capital offense for a life term prisoner to commit an assault."

stimulus applied to a normal person. In other words, that the threshold of the fear of the patient is lower to the extent where stimuli which would normally not cause fear in the patient will cause fear in the patient suffering from this state." (Italics added.) The psychiatrist, pursuant to the results of his examination, "made to the prison authorities certain recommendations for the alleviation of this condition; [before these recommendations were acted upon defendant injured Brown]; * * * also he examined the defendant after the occurrence out of which this charge arose and is prepared to testify to his then mental and physical condition."

The proffered evidence above summarized would be incompetent to establish the defense known as "self-defense" because one's rights in self-defense are limited to such acts as are either *actually* reasonably necessary or which would appear to a *reasonable* person, under the same circumstances, to be reasonably necessary. But here the evidence was not offered to prove self-defense; it was offered solely in relation to the specific mental state which was necessarily put in issue by the charge and the not guilty plea and concerning which the prosecution had already produced substantial evidence. Under the circumstances the materiality of this evidence in defendant's case is patent. If he acted only under the influence of fear of bodily harm, in the belief, honest though unreasonable, that he was defending himself from such harm by the use of a necessary amount of force, then defendant, although he would not be guiltless of crime, would not have committed that particular aggravated offense with which he is charged, for the essential element of "malice aforethought" would be lacking. In resolving this question in a close case the jury could well be materially aided by the knowledge that, in the opinion of qualified experts, the defendant's condition was such that he might readily have acted from genuine fear rather than from a desire for vengeance or from any other malicious purpose.

* * *

The issue upon which the improperly excluded evidence was offered does not, however, appear to have been a close one. In accord with the mandate of section $4\frac{1}{2}$ of article VI of the state Constitution we have examined the entire cause, including the evidence, and have concluded that the rejection of the physicians' proffered testimonies did not result in a miscarriage of justice. Able and conscientious counsel have not on behalf of defendant pointed out, nor have we discovered, any reason for the jury's having been in doubt or difficulty in resolving against defendant the question of his state of mind. It is apparent from defendant's own frank testimony[6] that

6. "Q. [Referring to the night before Brown was injured, when defendant violated a prison rule by creating a disturbance.] You made sufficient noise to awaken every one in that immediate vicinity? * * * A. I would say yes. Q. In other words, you at that time were not concerned with awaking people, although you had been making all this fuss when you had

he set up for himself and for the prison officials standards of conduct different from those recognized by the law of this state and the rules of the prison, and that, fully aware of the probable consequences, he conducted himself in accord with such standards rather than according to law. The jury determined—and it is almost impossible to imagine that either with or without the proffered, excluded testimonies they could have determined otherwise—that defendant at the time of the charged offense was acting pursuant to such just mentioned personal standards, and malice for those who breached them, rather than under the influence of honest, mistaken fear.

For the reasons above stated the judgment and order appealed from are affirmed.

NOTES

1. Assuming that evidence of psychological abnormality is admissible on the issue of state of mind, should it be permitted to disprove any state of mind? Would there be a likelihood of complete acquittals? If so, is this desirable in a jurisdiction which has a distinct "insanity" defense? How might such a situation be avoided? Might psychological abnormality be admitted only to disprove a "specific" intent? Could this be justified? Reconsider the limitations upon the use of intoxication raised at pages 178–87, supra. See also People v. Noah, 5 Cal.3d 469, 487 P.2d 1009 (1971).

2. Consider the wisdom of legislative enactment of the following statute:

Diminished Responsibility of Offender

1. Definition of Diminished Responsibility. An offender shall be regarded as being of diminished responsibility if the trier of fact finds that at the time of the offense his psychological condition was such that he should not be regarded as fully responsible for his offense.

2. Effect of Diminished Responsibility. In any case in which the trier of fact makes a finding of diminished responsibility, the sentencing judge should consider this as a mitigating factor and should impose a less severe penalty than would be imposed had there not been such a finding. In no case in which there has been a finding of diminished responsibility may the sen-

been awakened when the officer was doing his duty in counting the cells? A. I am interested in looking out for Wells' welfare. I was due to appear before the court the next morning for disciplinary action, and I wanted to be able to present some kind of a case. * * * I rattled my cup on the door, which is proper to do if wou want to speak to the guard. The guard came up and I made my request and he said he would make his report, and I told him that I must see Lieutenant Stevenson * * * I said, 'I will give him about twenty minutes. I don't want to create any disturbance to cause anybody any trouble, but I want to see him this morning, because I am going to court.' Q. In other words, you were laying down an ultimatum? A. If you want to put it that way * * * I was going to continue to make a noise until I saw Lieutenant Stevenson * * * Any time I feel I am being misused by an officer or by anyone I resent it, and I will let them know I resent it, and if they haven't given occasion to show any different use toward me, I conduct myself as a gentleman."

tence imposed exceed, in minimum or maximum term, two-thirds of the minimum and maximum that would otherwise be authorized for offense.

3. Admissibility of Evidence of Diminished Responsibility. Any evidence tending to establish that the defendant was mentally ill or otherwise psychologically abnormal at the time of an alleged offense for which he is being tried shall be admissible.

4. Burden of Proof on Responsibility. A defendant shall be presumed to be fully responsible. Where a defendant introduces evidence which raises the issue of his responsibility, however, the prosecution must prove full responsibility beyond a reasonable doubt. If the prosecution fails to carry that burden, the defendant is entitled to a finding of diminished responsibility.

5. Instruction to Jury. In any jury trial in which the evidence raises an issue of diminished responsibility, the trial jury should be instructed on the definition of diminished responsibility, on the burden of proof on that issue, and that in evaluating responsibility they should consider any evidence of the defendant's reduced capacity to conform his conduct to the requirements of law at the time of the offense as well as any evidence of his reduced capacity to understand the nature, quality, or criminality of his action. The jury should also be told that if they find that the defendant committed the crime and was not insane at the time of the crime, but that the prosecution has not proved full responsibility at the time of the crime, they should indicate on their verdict that the defendant should be regarded as being of diminished responsibility. The jury should further be instructed that if they find that the defendant was of diminished responsibility the trial judge will be required by law to impose a less severe penalty than would otherwise be the case.

6. Nonjury Trials. Where trial of a criminal case is to the court rather than the jury, the court should consider evidence of mental illness or psychological abnormality and, where appropriate, make a specific finding of diminished responsibility.

MODEL PENAL CODE

(P.O.D.1962).

Section 4.02. Evidence of Mental Disease or Defect Admissible When Relevant to Element of the Offense; [Mental Disease or Defect Impairing Capacity as Ground for Mitigation of Punishment in Capital Cases]

(1) Evidence that the defendant suffered from a mental disease or defect is admissible whenever it is relevant to prove that the defendant did or did not have a state of mind which is an element of the offense.

[(2) Whenever the jury or the Court is authorized to determine or to recommend whether or not the defendant shall be sentenced to death or imprisonment upon conviction, evidence that the capacity of the defendant to appreciate the criminality [wrongfulness] of his conduct or to conform his conduct to the requirements of law was impaired as a result of mental disease or defect is admissible in favor of sentence of imprisonment.]

STATE v. SIKORA

Supreme Court of New Jersey, 1965.
44 N.J. 453, 210 A.2d 193.

FRANCIS, J. [Defendant shot and killed Douglas Hooey in a tavern on January 15, 1962. Following a fight between the two, defendant returned to his apartment, got a gun, and returned to the tavern where he shot Hooey. At his apartment, police found a note saying, "The first bullet is for Doug and the second is for Stella Miller." Stella Miller was defendant's former girlfriend. He was tried and convicted of first degree premeditated murder.]

The error asserted in this Court as requiring reversal of the conviction had its origin in one hypothetical question put by defense counsel to Dr. Noel C. Galen, a psychiatrist produced on behalf of the defendant.

* * *

Dr. Galen specializes in psychiatry and psychoanalysis. He received his M.D. degree in 1949. In addition to postgraduate work in neurology and psychiatry, he had three years of training as a psychoanalyst. This last training, he said, dealt with psychodynamics on a very detailed and sophisticated level. It taught him that people are a product of their own life history, their own genetic patterns, and that they all react differently under the stresses of their daily lives. As a result of his study and experience, he believes that mental disturbance and disorder, as distinguished from objective disease, are merely gradients, that people range from being essentially normal, perceiving the world substantially in its normal appearance, all the way to marked distortion of the thinking mechanism, and between the two extremes is a rather jagged line which is prone to and open to many variations. * * * Mental illness or disorder in this context is a relative term as he sees it; it is a disorganization of the personality which causes a person to react in a specific way to a specific kind of stress in a way characteristic for him.

* * *

The idea seems to be that every deed, no matter how quickly executed, is never fully the result of the apparent immediate cause, and must be judged according to the probable unconscious motivations of an individual with the actor's lifelong history. Therefore, if in the opinion of the psychodynamically oriented psychiatrist, the deed, when evaluated against a background of the individual's life history, was probably produced by unconscious rather than conscious motivations, there was no *mens rea,* no criminal intent, and therefore no criminal guilt. In his view the conduct must be considered as having been conditioned by internal and external forces quite beyond the actor's control.

[At trial, defense counsel asked Dr. Galen whether, given the facts of the case, in Dr. Galen's opinion the defendant was capable of premeditating a murder. The prosecution's objection was sustained; the following represents what Dr. Galen would have testified if he had been permitted to answer.]

According to Dr. Galen, tensions had been building up in Sikora, particularly since his female friend rejected him. When he was humiliated in the tavern by the remarks about her availability for other men because she had broken with him, and then physically beaten by Hooey and his companions, the tensions mounted to the point where they represented a situation in life with which he felt unable to cope. So he began to act in an automatic way; the manner in which a person with his personality inadequacy would characteristically act. He responded to the stress in the way which inevitably would be his way of dealing with that kind of stress. He reacted automatically in the fashion of Dr. Galen's physician friend when he was cut off by another motorist. His successive actions, walking home from the tavern, reporting the assault upon him to the police, deciding against a criminal complaint, obtaining his gun from its place of concealment in the apartment, putting the extra bullets in his pocket, writing the note that the first bullet was for Doug and the second for Stella Miller, contemplating suicide, test-firing the gun, rejecting the idea of suicide, reloading the gun on the stairway of his apartment while thinking about Hooey and the beating in the tavern, walking to the tavern to "talk" to Hooey, deciding to use the alley entrance in an effort to draw Hooey out that way, and putting four bullets into Hooey after backing some distance from the tavern while warning him not to come closer and advising him he was "liable" to find out the gun would fire if he came closer, and then walking to the Miller woman's apartment still carrying the gun and searching for her, all showed strong elements of automatism. The beating administered by Hooey in the tavern precipitated the disorganization of his personality to the extent that from then on he probably "acted in at least a semi-automatic way, and probably an automatic way."

The doctor went on to say that from the defendant's course of conduct it could be seen that he was acting in an automatic way "rather than being totally aware of his environment, and the situation * * *." Although the state was not completely an automatic one there were "strong elements of automatism" present. He was not "fully conscious of his activities" and not "completely aware" of what he was doing. The stress to which he had been subjected had distorted his personality mechanism. His personality disorder, the kind of man life had made him, when subjected to that stress prevented him from "seeing reality, or premeditating or forming a rational opinion of what is going on in his life." He had been confronted with a situation and reacted with conduct which was his characteristic way of dealing with the particular kind of stress. * * *

In short the doctor opined that the circumstances to which Sikora had been subjected imposed on his personality disorder a stress that impaired or removed his ability consciously to premeditate or weigh a design to kill. The tension was so great that he could handle it only by an automatic reaction motivated by the predetermined influence of his unconscious. Plainly the doctor meant that Sikora's response was not a voluntary exercise of his free will. The stress was such as to distort his mechanisms. During the various actions Sikora took leading up to the killing, which so clearly indicate conception, deliberation and execution of a plan to kill, he was thinking but the thinking was automatic; it was simply subconscious thinking or reaction; it was not conscious thinking. The doctor said Sikora's anxieties at the time were of such a nature that conceivably, his reaction in that automatic way and the commission of the homicide, actually prevented a further disorganization of his personality. The killing, said the doctor, was "a rational murder" but "everything this man did was irrational," and engaged in when he could not conceive the design to kill. * * *

The question now presented is whether psychiatric evidence of the nature described is admissible in first degree murder cases on the issue of premeditation. Defendant argues that it should have been received at the trial on that issue.

In [State v.] Di Paolo [, 34 N.J. 279, 168 A.2d 401, cert. denied, 368 U.S. 880, 82 S.Ct. 130 (1961)] the Chief Justice said that evidence of "any defect, deficiency, trait, condition, or illness which rationally bears upon the question" whether the defendant did in fact premeditate is admissible at a first degree murder trial. But he indicated also that if such evidence was unreliable or too speculative or incompetent when tested by concepts established in law for the determination of criminal responsibility, it should not be received on the issue of guilt or innocence. That is the situation here. * * *

Criminal responsibility must be judged at the level of the conscious. If a person thinks, plans and executes the plan at that level, the criminality of his act cannot be denied, wholly or partially, because, although he did not realize it, his conscious was influenced to think, to plan and to execute the plan by unconscious influences which were the product of his genes and his lifelong environment. So in the present case, criminal guilt cannot be denied or confined to second degree murder (when the killing was a "rational murder" and the product of thought and action), because Sikora was unaware that his decisions and conduct were mechanistically directed by unconscious influences bound to result from the tensions to which he was subjected at the time. If the law were to accept such a medical doctrine as a basis for a finding of second rather than first degree murder, the legal doctrine of *mens rea* would all but disappear from the law.   Applying Dr. Galen's theory to crimes requiring specific intent to commit, such as robbery, larceny, rape, etc., it is difficult to imagine an individual who perpetrated the deed as having the mental capacity in the criminal law sense to conceive the intent to commit it. Criminal responsibility, as society now knows it, would vanish from the scene, and some other basis for dealing with the offender would have to be found. At bottom, this would appear to be the ultimate aim of the psychodynamic psychiatrists.

WEINTRAUB, C. J. (concurring).   *   *   *

It seems clear to me that the psychiatric view expounded by Dr. Galen is simply irreconcilable with the basic thesis of our criminal law, for while the law requires proof of an evil-meaning mind, this psychiatric thesis denies there is any such thing. To grant a role in our existing structure to the theme that the conscious is just the innocent puppet of a nonculpable unconscious is to make a mishmash of the criminal law, permitting—indeed requiring—each trier of the facts to choose between the automaton thesis and the law's existing concept of criminal accountability. It would be absurd to decide criminal blameworthiness upon a psychiatric thesis which can find no basis for personal blame. So long as we adhere to criminal blameworthiness, *mens rea* must be sought and decided at the level of conscious behavior.

NOTE

Consider the following from Dix, Mental Illness, Criminal Intent, and the Bifurcated Trial, 1970 Law and the Social Order 559, 567:

> To most mental health personnel, the conscious awareness and desires of an individual at any one specific time are of minimal importance in understanding his behavior. His learned or developed reactions to stress are of primary importance, and although they may affect his conscious awareness and desire as well as his behavior, this impact upon conscious awareness and desire is of minimal significance. Therefore, when called upon in court to explain the dynamics of an offender's behavior, they will tend to explain it in terms they feel are significant. Legally speaking however, the insight is relevant only insofar as it explains how the offender's conscious awareness was affected. Theoretically, an alert trial court judge could limit testimony to that logically relevant to the state of mind defined by the substantive criminal law. But as a matter of practice it is unlikely that any such restriction will be placed on the evidence.

TABLE OF CASES

The principal cases are in italic type. Cases cited or discussed are in roman type. References are to Pages.

Abbott, State v., 518
Abrams, People v., 377
Adams, People v., 385
Ali, Commonwealth v., 235
Allen, In re, 453
Almeida, Commonwealth v., 464
Anderson, People v., 440
Atencio, Commonwealth v., 206

Bender v. State, 286
Berger, People v., 256
Berrigan, United States v., 170
Beyer, United States v., 547
Binders, State v., 141
Booth v. State, 262
Bowling, State v., 288
Brawner v. United States, 625
Brawner, United States v., 573, 614
Bready, Commonwealth v., 238
Brown, People v., 320
Budd v. Madigan, 53
Bugger, State v., 119
Byrd, United States v., 134

Carter v. United States, 608
Carter, United States v., 241
Chermansky, Commonwealth v., 559
Cleaver v. United States, 302
Cobb, State v., 210
Commonwealth v. Ali, 235
Commonwealth v. Almeida, 464
Commonwealth v. Atencio, 206
Commonwealth v. Bready, 238
Commonwealth v. Chermansky, 559
Commonwealth v. Duerr, 559
Commonwealth v. Emmons, 558
Commonwealth v. Feinberg, 202, 238
Commonwealth v. Huber, 221
Commonwealth v. Koczwara, 230
Commonwealth v. Ladd, 202
Commonwealth v. Malone, 426
Commonwealth v. Pierce, 214
Commonwealth v. Redline, 465
Commonwealth v. Thomas, 464
Commonwealth v. Welansky, 472
Commonwealth ex rel. Smith v. Myers, 463
Crawford v. United States, 117
Crose, State v., 572

Curtis, People v., 548

Daniels, State v., 141
Dixon, State v., 25
Dooley, State v., 535
Dotterweich, United States v., 161
Driver v. Hinnant, 52
Duerr, Commonwealth v., 559
Dupuy v. State, 255
Durham v. United States, 582, 589, 603
Dusky v. United States, 567
Duty, People v., 227

Easter v. District of Columbia, 52
Eisenstadt v. Baird, 97
Emmons, Commonwealth v., 558
England, State v., 562
Esser, State v., 576

Fearon, State v., 53
Feinberg, Commonwealth v., 202, 238
Ferrone, United States v., 547
Fielding, United States v., 566
Fitzpatrick, People v., 25
Flippen v. State, 214
Flood, People ex rel. Conte v., 300
Folk v. State, 116
Foster, State v., 572
Foy, United States v., 225
Freed, United States v., 161
Frigillana v. United States, 609
Furman v. Georgia, 24, 84, 438

Garoutte, State v., 561
Garrett, State v., 572
Geiger, People v., 431
Gervin v. State, 277
Giaccio v. Pennsylvania, 105, 106
Gibson, State v., 477
Gladstone, State v., 217
Gray v. State, 523
Green v. United States, 561
Griswold v. Connecticut, 97

Harkness, State v., 577
Harrington, State v., 366
Harrison, State v., 587
Hatley, State v., 138
Hebert, People v., 189

Heller, People v., 358
Henry, United States v., 564
Hernandez, People v., 162, 403
Holland, United States v., 116
Horne, State v., 398
Houchin v. State, 372
Hoy, People v., 53
Huber, Commonwealth v., 221
Hunter v. State, 169

International Minerals & Chemicals Corp., United States v., 145

Jenkins v. Averett, 548
Jones v. United States, 123

Koczwara, Commonwealth v., 230
Koonce, State v., 539
Krulewitch v. United States, 323

Ladd, Commonwealth v., 202
Lambert v. California, 142, 169
Lang v. State, 467
Lauria, People v., 303
Lego v. Twomey, 10
Leland v. Oregon, 11
Lilly v. West Virginia, 560
Logan v. State, 258
Long v. State, 173
Louisville, E. & St. L. R. Co. v. Clarke, 202
Lumley, Rex v., 451
Lutz, State v., 562
Lynch, In re, 25

McClain v. State, 227
McCollum v. State, 239
McDaniel v. Carroll, 548
McDonald v. United States, 609
McGautha v. California, 436
M'Naghten's Case, 573
Malone, Commonwealth v., 426
Mercer, State v., 110
Miller v. State, 547
Miller, United States v., 22
Mills, State v., 351
Moore v. State, 558
Moretti, State v., 317
Morissette v. United States, 149
Morrin, People v., 420
Mulvihill, State v., 543
Myers, Commonwealth ex rel. Smith v., 463

Nales, State v., 257
Nielson, State v., 375
Noah, People v., 633

Orito, United States v., 97
Ott v. State, 382

Papachristou v. Jacksonville, 99, 257
Parnell v. State, 361

Parsons v. State, 576, 585
Pate v. Robinson, 567
Pembliton, Regina v., 133
People v. Abrams, 377
People v. Adams, 385
People v. Anderson, 440
People v. Berger, 256
People v. Brown, 320
People v. Curtis, 548
People v. Duty, 227
People v. Fitzpatrick, 25
People v. Geiger, 431
People v. Hebert, 189
People v. Heller, 358
People v. Hernandez, 162, 403
People v. Hoy, 53
People v. Lauria, 303
People v. Morrin, 420
People v. Noah, 633
People v. Phillips, 447
People v. Richards, 487
People v. Roberts, 561
People v. Samuels, 561
People v. Satchell, 455
People v. Scott, 206
People v. Stamp, 448
People v. Staples, 271
People v. Wells, 630
People v. Young, 527, 531
People ex rel. Conte v. Flood, 300
Phillips, People v., 447
Pierce, Commonwealth v., 214
Pinkerton v. United States, 313
Pollard v. State, 348
Pollard v. United States, 599
Pollard, United States v., 593
Portland v. Juntunen, 53
Powell v. Texas, 38, 114
Powell, United States v., 346
Prince, United States v., 215

R. v. Cockburn, 339
R. v. Jordan, 201
Ramsdell, State v., 548
Ray v. United States, 333
Redline, Commonwealth v., 465
Regina v. Pembliton, 133
Regle v. State, 293
Reigan v. People, 560
Rex v. Lumley, 451
Richards, People v., 487
Richardson v. United States, 171
Roberts v. Williams, 548
Roberts, People v., 561
Robinson v. California, 25, 38
Roe v. Wade, 98
Rogers v. State, 331
Russell v. State, 533
Russell, United States v., 505

Samuels, People v., 561
Sanchez v. People, 482
Satchell, People v., 455

Sauls v. Hutto, 554
Scott, People v., 206
Seattle v. Hill, 53
Sexton v. Gibbs, 548
Sherman v. United States, 497
Short, United States v., 162
Sikora, State v., 635
Simon, United States v., 547
Snowden, State v., 433
Speidel v. State, 161
Spillman, State v., 214
Stamp, People v., 448
Stanley v. Georgia, 97
Staples, People v., 271
State v. Abbott, 518
State v. Binders, 141
State v. Bowling, 288
State v. Bugger, 119
State v. Cobb, 210
State v. Crose, 572
State v. Daniels, 141
State v. Dixon, 25
State v. Dooley, 535
State v. England, 562
State v. Esser, 576
State v. Fearon, 53
State v. Foster, 572
State v. Garoutte, 561
State v. Garrett, 572
State v. Gibson, 477
State v. Gladstone, 217
State v. Harkness, 577
State v. Harrington, 366
State v. Harrison, 587
State v. Hatley, 138
State v. Horne, 398
State v. Koonce, 539
State v. Lutz, 562
State v. Mercer, 110
State v. Mills, 351
State v. Moretti, 317
State v. Mulvihill, 543
State v. Nales, 257
State v. Nielson, 375
State v. Ramsdell, 548
State v. Sikora, 635
State v. Snowden, 433
State v. Spillman, 214
State v. Von Voltenburg, 257
State v. Williams, 341
State v. Young, 227
Stump v. Bennett, 11

Tegethoff v. State, 206
Terry v. Ohio, 258
Thacker v. Commonwealth, 260
Thomas, Commonwealth v., 464
Trop v. Dulles, 25
12 200-Ft. Reels of Film, United States v., 98

United States v. Berrigan, 170
United States v. Beyer, 547
United States v. Brawner, 573, 614
United States v. Byrd, 134
United States v. Carter, 241
United States v. Dotterweich, 161
United States v. Ferrone, 547
United States v. Fielding, 566
United States v. Foy, 225
United States v. Freed, 161
United States v. Henry, 564
United States v. Holland, 116
United States v. International Minerals & Chemical Corp., 145
United States v. Miller, 22
United States v. Orito, 97
United States v. Pollard, 593
United States v. Powell, 346
United States v. Prince, 215
United States v. Russell, 505
United States v. Short, 162
United States v. Simon, 547
United States v. 12 200-Ft. Reels of Film, 98
United States v. Williams, 178

Vick v. State, 53
Viliborghi v. State, 549
Virgin Islands v. Williams, 335
Von Voltenburg, State v., 257

Washington v. United States, 610
Weems v. United States, 25
Welansky, Commonwealth v., 472
Wells, People v., 630
Williams, State v., 341
Williams, United States v., 178
Winship, In re, 10
Winters v. New York, 104
Wyatt v. United States, 216

Young, People v., 527, 531
Young, State v., 227

*

INDEX

ABANDONMENT
See Attempts, Renunciation or withdrawal as defense, generally; Conspiracy, Renunciation or withdrawal as defense.

ABORTION
Constitutionality of prohibiting, 97, 411.
Feticide, 420.
Impossibility as defense, 255.

ABSOLUTE LIABILITY
See Strict Liability.

ACCESSORIES
See Parties to Crime.

ACCOMPLICES
See Parties to Crime.

ACT
See also Attempts; Conspiracy.
Generally, 109.
Automatism, 110.
Burglary, 372.
Defined by definition of crime,
Assault, 377.
Burglary, 372.
Embezzlement, 341.
Extortion, 366.
False pretenses, 348.
Kidnapping, 385.
Larceny, 331, 333.
Rape, 403.
Robbery, 357.
Necessity that act be willed or voluntary, 110.
Omission, 123.
Possession, 116, 210, 213, 257.
Rationale, 114.
Status offenses, 38, 99.

AIDING AND ABETTING
See Parties to Crime.

AIDING LAW ENFORCEMENT AS DEFENSE
See Defenses.

ALCOHOL ABUSE
See also Crimes, Relationship to alcohol use; Cruel and Unusual Punishment; Intoxication.
Generally, 29.
Alcoholism as disease, 57.

ALCOHOL ABUSE—Cont'd
Constitutionality of public intoxication laws, 38.
Extent, 29.
Non-criminal control, 54.
Public intoxication, arrest, rate, 36, 97.
Public intoxication as crime, 35.
Traffic accidents, 30.
Vehicular homicide while intoxicated, 453.

ALIBI
Burden of proof, 11.

ARRESTS
See also Defenses, Resistance to unlawful arrest.
Statistical incidence, 257.

ARSON
Generally, 375.

ASPORTATION
See Act, Defined by definition of crime, Larceny.

ASSAULT
Generally, 377–385.

ATTEMPTS
See also Vagrancy.
Generally, 245.
Act required,
Dangerous proximity test, 249.
Doctrinal formulations, 249.
Indispensable element test, 250.
Preparation distinguished, 255.
Probable desistence test, 251.
Res ipsa test, 252.
Function of criminalizing, 257.
Impossibility as defense,
Generally, 271.
Factual, 255.
Legal, 261.
Mental state,
Generally, 258.
Purpose to commit crime, 260.
Recklessness, 260.
Renunciation or withdrawal as defense, generally, 248, 271.
Statutory formulations, 247, 275.

AUTOMATISM
See Act; Defenses.

BAIL
Purpose of, 6.

BURDEN OF PROOF
See also Presumptions.
Generally, 10, 257, 618.

BURGLARY
Generally, 372–375.

CAUSATION
Generally, 188.
Homicide, felony murder, 448, 453, 463.
Intervening superceding cause, 194.
Medical treatment, 201.
Russian Roulette death, 206.
Victim's conduct, 206.

CIVIL COMMITMENT
See also Insanity Defense; Mental Ill-
ness.
Alcoholics,
Generally, 54.
Actual practice, 68.

COERCION
See Defenses, Duress.

COMPETENCY
See Insanity Defense; Mental Illness.

COMPETENCY TO STAND TRIAL
Relationship to insanity defense, 567.

COMPLICITY
See Parties to Crime.

CONDONATION
See Defenses.

CONSPIRACY
Generally, 283.
Abandonment, 320, 323.
Agreement,
Generally, 286.
"Defenses" based on lack of, 293.
Evidence of agreement, 287.
Need for at least two "guilty parties",
293.
First amendment problems, 327.
History of the offense, 323, 327.
Impossibility, 317.
Liability for crimes of co-conspirators,
Generally, 313.
Mental state, 302.
Object, generally, 288.
Organized crime, 327, 329.
Overt act, 300.
"Political crimes," 327.
Prosecutorial advantages, 323.
Renunciation or withdrawal as defense,
320, 323.
Statutory formulation, 283, 329.

CONSTITUTIONAL LIMITATIONS
See also Cruel and Unusual Punish-
ment; Due Process.
First Amendment, 282, 327.
Vagueness, 99.

CONTROL OVER BEHAVIOR
See also Insanity Defense; Mental Ill
ness.
Alcoholics, 53, 57.

CORPORATE LIABILITY
See Parties to Crime.

CORRECTIONS
Generally, 8.

CRIMES
See also Abortion; Act; Attempts;
Conspiracy; Manslaughter; Mur-
der; Rape; Solicitation.
Against the person,
Assault, 377.
False imprisonment, 385.
Kidnapping, 385.
Classification in Proposed Federal Code,
26.
Habitation offense,
Arson, 375.
Burglary, 271, 372.
Possession of burglary tools, 257.
Possession of recently stolen prop
erty as evidence of guilt, 210
213.
Mala in se, and mala prohibita, 141.
Morals offenses, 411.
Property offense,
Claim of right defense, 171.
Embezzlement, 341.
Extortion, 366.
False pretenses, 347.
Larceny, 331.
Robbery, 358.
Theft, 353.
Worthless checks, 235, 348.
Relationship to alcohol use, 31.
Statistics, 411, 452.

CRIMINALIZATION
See also Civil Commitment.
Generally, 27.
Costs of, 95.
Justifications for,
See also Punishment.
Generally, 68.
Designation of public mores, 82.
Enforcement of morality, 73.
Prevention of crime, 84.
Providing treatment, 90.
Reasons for punishing distinguished,
68.
Retribution, 72.
Satisfaction of urge to punish, 79.
Social solidarity, 73.

CRIMINAL LIABILITY
Nature of, 68.

CRIMINAL NEGLIGENCE
See Manslaughter, Involuntary.

CRUEL AND UNUSUAL PUNISH-
MENT
Generally, 24.
Narcotics addiction as crime, 38.
Public intoxication laws, 38, 52.

CULPABILITY
See Mental State.

DEATH PENALTY
See Punishment, Capital.

DEFENSES
See also Attempts, Impossibility as
defense; Conspiracy, Impossi-
bility; Diminished Capacity;
Diminished Responsibility; In-
sanity Defense; Mistake.
Generally, 486.
Affirmative,
Burden of proof, 10, 257.
Definition, 10.
Aiding law enforcement, 560.
Automatism, 110.
Condonation by victim, 561.
Consent of victim, 560.
Defense of others, 515, 527.
Defense of property,
Generally, 515, 533.
Degree of force, 535, 538.
Retaking possession, 535.
Use of spring gun, 538.
Defense of self,
Duty to retreat, 518, 526.
Right of aggressor, 523.
Domestic authority, 562.
Duress, 486.
Entrapment,
Generally, 497.
Constitutional basis, 505.
Need to deny act, 513.
Supplying contraband, 505.
Justification, 486.
Nurnberg defense, 170.
Prevention of crime, 549.
Resistance to unlawful arrest, 539.

DETERRENCE
See Criminalization, Justifications for;
Punishment.

DIMINISHED CAPACITY
See also Defenses, Automatism; Diminished Responsibility; Insanity Defense.
Generally, 630.
Relevance of testimony to state of mind
requirements, 634.

DIMINISHED RESPONSIBILITY
See also Defenses, Automatism; Diminished Capacity; Insanity Defense.
Generally, 633.

DIVERSION OF OFFENDERS
See Civil Commitment; Rehabilitation.

DOMESTIC AUTHORITY AS DE-
FENSE
See Defenses.

DUE PROCESS
See also Constitutional Limitations;
Defenses; Entrapment; Insanity
Defense; Presumptions.
Burden of persuasion,
Generally, 10, 257.
Juveniles, 10.
Notice requirement, 142, 145, 149.
Presumptions, 210, 257, 426.
Prohibition against strict liability of-
fenses, 149, 161.

DURESS
See Defenses.

DURHAM RULE
See Insanity Defense, Legal criteria.

EMBEZZLEMENT
Generally, 341.

ENTERPRISE LIABILITY
See Parties to Crime.

ENTRAPMENT
See Defenses.

EUTHANASIA
See Defenses, Consent of victim.

EXPERT TESTIMONY
See Insanity Defense.

EXTORTION
Generally, 366.

FACILITATION
See Parties to Crime.

FALSE IMPRISONMENT
Generally, 385.

FALSE PRETENSES
Generally, 347.

FELONY MURDER
See Murder.

GENERAL INTENT
See Mental State.

HEAT OF PASSION
See Manslaughter, Voluntary.

HOMICIDE
See also Causation; Diminished Capacity; Diminished Responsibility; Manslaughter; Murder.
Statistical incidence, 411, 452.

IGNORANCE
See Mistake.

IMPERFECT DEFENSES
See Manslaughter.

IMPOSSIBILITY
See Attempts; Conspiracy; Rape.

INCHOATE CRIMES
See also Attempts; Conspiracy; Solicitation.
Generally, 244.

INCOMPETENCY
See Insanity Defense; Mental Illness.

INSANITY
See Mental Illness.

INSANITY DEFENSE
See also Automatism; Diminished Capacity; Diminished Responsibility; Mental Illness.
Generally, 562.
Ability to control actions, 590.
Abolition, 620.
Burden of proof, 11, 618.
Disadvantages for defendant, 625.
Expert testimony,
Availability, 619, 627.
Effect on juries, 613.
Impartial experts, 624.
Legal limits under Durham Rule, 610.
Frequency of use,
Generally, 567.
In Washington, D. C., 613.
Informal bypassing of defense, 613.
Issue for judge rather than jury, 623.
Legal criteria,
Durham Rule, 603.
Effect of change, 613.
Irresistable impulse, 585.
M'Naghten test,
Broadly interpreted, 576.
Narrowly defined, 573.
Model Penal Code, 590.
Relationship to competency to stand trial, 567.
Post-acquittal commitment, 629.
Requirement of mental illness, 570.
Temporary insanity, 584.
Traditional cases described, 570.

INTENT
See Mental State.

INTENTIONALLY
See Mental State.

INTOXICATION
See also Alcohol Abuse.
Crimes involving recklessness, 187.
Defense, generally, 178.
Drugs, 185.

IRRESISTABLE IMPULSE TEST
See Insanity Defense.

JUSTIFICATION
See Defenses.

KIDNAPPING
Generally, 385.

KNOWLEDGE
See Mental State; Mistake.

LARCENY
Generally, 331.

M'NAGHTEN RULES
See Insanity Defense.

MAGISTRATE
Role of, 6.

MALICE AFORETHOUGHT
See Murder.

MANSLAUGHTER
Imperfect defenses reducing homicide, 482.
Involuntary,
Generally, 472.
Criminal negligence, 472.
Unlawful act doctrine, 477.
Statutory formulation, 416, 417, 419.
Voluntary,
Generally, 467.
Effect of provocation, 469.
Mutual combat, 470.
Objective standard, 470.
Provocation, words as, 467.

MENS REA
See Mental State.

MENTAL ILLNESS
See also Automatism; Diminished Capacity; Diminished Responsibility; Insanity Defense.
Dynamic psychology, 562.
Relation to criminal behavior,
Durham Rules, 608, 609.
Loss of ability to control behavior, 593.
Relationship to criminal liability, 562.

MENTAL STATE
See also Attempts; Diminished Capacity; Insanity Defense; Intoxication; Manslaughter; Mistake; Murder; Strict Liability.
Generally, 128.
General intent, 133, 141.
Intention, 130, 131.

MENTAL STATE—Cont'd
Knowledge, 130, 131, 145.
Negligence, 130, 132, 139.
Notice or scienter, 142, 145.
Property crimes,
    Arson, 375.
    Embezzlement, 341.
    False pretenses, 347.
    Larceny, 331.
Purpose, see Intention, this topic.
Recklessness, 130, 132.
Specific intent, 141.
Statutory formulation, 130.
Wilfulness, 130, 133, 138.

MERCY KILLING
Generally, 560.

MISPRISION OF FELONY
See Parties to Crime.

MISTAKE
Factual,
    Generally, 162.
    Age of subject of statutory rape, 403.
    Lesser wrong theory, 133, 138.
    Requirement of reasonableness, 162.
Legal,
    Generally, 167.
    Advice of counsel, 173.
    Belief in impropriety of government
        activity, 170.
    Belief in unconstitutionality, 169.
    Ignorance of legal duty, 142, 145.
Statutory formulations, 167.

MORALS OFFENSES
Generally, 411.

MURDER
Felony murder,
    Generally, 447.
    Abolition, 453.
    Accomplice liability, 453.
    Causation, 448, 451, 453.
    Deaths caused by victim or police, 463.
    Limitation to dangerous felonies, 455.
    Possession of firearm, 455.
    Proximate cause of death, 463, 466.
    Purpose of rule, 452.
    Second degree, 447.
    Statistical incidence, 452.
Feticide, 420.
First degree, see Premeditation, this
    topic.
Mental state,
    See also Felony murder, this topic.
    Malice, intent to do harm, 431.
        Abandoned and malignant heart,
            428, 430.
        Presumption from act of killing, 420.
        Recklessness, 426, 428.
    Premeditation,
        Generally, 433, 438, 440, 446.
Statutory formulation, 415–419.
Vehicular homicide, 428, 430, 453.

MUTUAL COMBAT
See Manslaughter, Voluntary.

NECESSITY
See Defenses.

NEGLIGENCE
See Mental State.

NURNBERG DEFENSE
See Defenses.

OMISSION
See Act.

PARTIES TO CRIME
    See also Conspiracy, Liability for
        crimes of co-conspirators; Mur-
        der, Felony murder, Accom-
        plice liability.
    Generally, 207.
Accessories,
    After the fact, 207, 224, 225.
    Before the fact, 207, 221.
    Statutory definition, 209, 224.
Accomplices, statutory definition, 209.
Aider and abettor, 207, 214.
Aiding and abetting,
    Furnishing supplies or instruments,
        221.
    Mental state required,
        Generally, 216, 221, 235.
        Requirement that principal crime be
            proven, 214, 215.
Corporate liability,
    Generally, 238.
    Statutory formulation, 241.
Facilitation, statutory formulation, 210.
Misprision of felony, 225, 227.
Principals,
    Presence at unlawful act, 210, 213, 214.
    Statutory formulation, 208, 209.
Renunciation or withdrawal as defense,
    221, 224.
Statutory definitions, 208, 209.
Vicarious liability, 230, 238.

PLEA BARGAINING
Generally, 7.

POLICE
Discretion, 5.

POSSESSION
Joint, 116, 210.
Of burglary tools as evidence of intent,
    257.
Recently stolen property as evidence of
    guilt of property offense, 210, 213.

PREMEDITATION
See Murder.

PRESUMPTIONS
Generally, 11, 257, 426, 431, 440.

PREVENTION OF CRIME
See Defenses.

PRINCIPALS
See Parties to Crime.

PRINCIPLES OF LIABILITY
See also Act; Causation; Mental State.
Generally, 107.

PROBATION AND PAROLE
See Sentencing.

PROSECUTION
Plea bargaining, 7.
Role of, 6.

PROVOCATION
See Manslaughter, Voluntary.

PUNISHMENT
See also Rehabilitation; Sentencing.
Capital, 24, 436, 438, 446.
Cruel and unusual, 24, 38, 52.
Deterrence, 21, 84.
Effectiveness on drunkenness offenders, 88.
Grading, 13, 26.
Theories of, 14, 139.
Treatment distinguished, 90.

PURPOSE
See Mental State.

RAPE
Forcible, mental state required, 162.
Statutory,
Mental state required, 403.
Mistake as to age of woman, 403.
Promiscuous complainant, 410.

RECKLESSNESS
See Mental State.

REHABILITATION
See also Punishment.
Diversionary programs, 92.
Effectiveness of group therapy, 93.
Effectiveness of programs for drunkenness offenders, 65, 93.
Substitute for criminal sanctions, 61, 90.
Techniques, 90.

RENUNCIATION
See Attempts; Conspiracy; Parties to Crime.

RESISTANCE TO ARREST
See Defenses.

RETRIBUTION
See Criminalization, Justifications for.

RIGHT TO PRIVACY
Generally, 97.
Abortion, 97, 411.

RIGHT TO PRIVACY—Cont'd
Distribution of contraceptives, 97.
Possession of obscenity in home, 97.

RIGHT TO TREATMENT
See Civil Commitment.

ROBBERY
Generally, 358.

SELF–DEFENSE
See Defenses.

SENTENCING
See also Punishment.
Generally, 15.
Death, 24, 436, 438, 446.
Discretion in, 7, 22.
Extended terms,
Special dangerous offenders, 27.
Fines, 24.
Imprisonment, 26.
Indeterminate, 15.
Judicial discretion in, 7, 22.
Length of sentences, 21, 23.
Maximum and minimum sentences, 15.
Pre-sentence reports, 7.
Probation and parole, 19, 26.
Psychiatric hospitalization as alternative, 620.

SOCIAL SOLIDARITY
See Criminalization, Justifications for.

SOLICITATION
Attempt distinguished, 277.
First Amendment problems, 282.
Statutory formulation, 280, 281.

SPECIFIC INTENT
See Mental State.

SPEECH
See also Conspiracy; Solicitation.
Advocacy of criminal conduct, 282.

SPRING GUN
See Defenses, Defense of property.

STRICT LIABILITY
Actual administration, 159.
Public welfare offenses, 149, 157, 230.
Traditional offenses, 149.

SUICIDE
Relationship to alcohol use, 30.

THEFT
Generally, 353.

TREATMENT
See Rehabilitation.

VAGRANCY
Arrest rate, 257.
Purpose of criminalizing, 257.
Statutory formulations, 99.

VAGUENESS
See Constitutional Limitations.

VICARIOUS LIABILITY
See Parties to Crime.

WHARTON'S RULE
See Conspiracy, Agreement.

WILFULNESS
See Mental State.

WITHDRAWAL
See Attempts; Conspiracy; Parties to Crime.

WEST PUBLISHING CO.